The 37-mile-long Paria Canyon trailhead follows the meandering route of a narrow slot canyon for much of its length. See chapter 7. © James Kay/Adstock Photos.

The Desert Botanical Garden in Phoenix is devoted exclusively to cacti and other desert plants. See chapter 4. © John Elk III Photography.

Horseback riding in the Superstition Mountains, which, according to legend, harbor a lost gold mine. See chapter 4. © John Elk III Photography.

The Organ Pipe Cactus National Monument preserves this rare type of cactus in one of Arizona's least visited and most remote areas. See chapter 10. © Tom Bean/Getty Images.

Arizona draws countless visitors for its golfing alone. See chapter 1 for our favorite courses. © Richard Maack/Adstock Photos.

White-water rafting on the Colorado River. See chapter 6. © *Dewitt Jones/Robert Holmes Photography.*

A magnificent view of the Grand Canyon from Cape Solitude on the South Rim. See chapter 6. © *Chuck Lawsen/Adstock Photos.*

Native American crafts are ubiquitous in the Four Corners region. See chapter 7 for a primer. Top photo: Navajo rugs, like these at the famous Hubbell Trading Post, take hundreds of hours to make. © John Elk III Photography. Bottom photo: Navajo turquoise jewelry. © Dave Bartruff Photography.

Eroded soil and red color give the Vermilion Cliffs a unique appearance. See chapter 6.
© Kerrick James/Getty Images.

The desert provides the perfect environment for hot-air ballooning—cool, still air and wide-open spaces. See chapters 4, 5, and 9 for ballooning companies in Phoenix, Sedona, and Tucson. © Michael R. Stoklos/Adstock Photos.

Frommer's

Arizona

2005

by Karl Samson

Here's what the critics say about Frommer's:

"Amazingly easy to use. Very portable, very complete."
—*Booklist*

"Detailed, accurate, and easy-to-read information for all price ranges."
—*Glamour Magazine*

"Hotel information is close to encyclopedic."
—*Des Moines Sunday Register*

"Frommer's Guides have a way of giving you a real feel for a place."
—*Knight Ridder Newspapers*

WILEY

Wiley Publishing, Inc.

About the Author

Karl Samson lives in Oregon, where he spends his time juggling his obsessions with traveling, gardening, outdoor sports, and wine. Each winter, to dry out his webbed feet, he flees the soggy Northwest to update the *Frommer's Arizona* guide. Karl is also the author of *Frommer's Seattle* and *Frommer's Washington State*.

Published by:

Wiley Publishing, Inc.

111 River St.
Hoboken, NJ 07030-5774

ISBN 0-7645-7148-6

Editor: Paul Prince
Production Editor: Donna Wright
Cartographer: Elizabeth Puhl
Photo Editor: Richard Fox
Production by Wiley Indianapolis Composition Services

Front cover photo: Sonoran Desert: Rider and horse near cactus
Back cover photo: Sunset, Cathedral Rock, Oak Creek, near Sedona

For information on our other products and services or to obtain technical support, please contact our Customer Care Department within the U.S. at 800/762-2974, outside the U.S. at 317/572-3993 or fax 317/572-4002.

Wiley also publishes its books in a variety of electronic formats. Some content that appears in print may not be available in electronic formats.

Manufactured in the United States of America

5 4 3 2 1

Contents

1 The Best of Arizona   5

2 Planning Your Trip to Arizona   21

3 For International Visitors   55

List of Maps

An Invitation to the Reader

In researching this book, we discovered many wonderful places—hotels, restaurants, shops, and more. We're sure you'll find others. Please tell us about them, so we can share the information with your fellow travelers in upcoming editions. If you were disappointed with a recommendation, we'd love to know that, too. Please write to:

Frommer's Arizona 2005
Wiley Publishing, Inc. • 111 River St. • Hoboken, NJ 07030-5774

An Additional Note

Please be advised that travel information is subject to change at any time—and this is especially true of prices. We therefore suggest that you write or call ahead for confirmation when making your travel plans. The authors, editors, and publisher cannot be held responsible for the experiences of readers while traveling. Your safety is important to us, however, so we encourage you to stay alert and be aware of your surroundings. Keep a close eye on cameras, purses, and wallets, all favorite targets of thieves and pickpockets.

Other Great Guides for Your Trip:

Arizona For Dummies
Frommer's American Southwest
Frommer's National Parks of the American West
Frommer's Portable Phoenix & Scottsdale

Frommer's Star Ratings, Icons & Abbreviations

Every hotel, restaurant, and attraction listing in this guide has been ranked for quality, value, service, amenities, and special features using a **star-rating system.** In country, state, and regional guides, we also rate towns and regions to help you narrow down your choices and budget your time accordingly. Hotels and restaurants are rated on a scale of zero (recommended) to three stars (exceptional). Attractions, shopping, nightlife, towns, and regions are rated according to the following scale: zero stars (recommended), one star (highly recommended), two stars (very highly recommended), and three stars (must-see).

In addition to the star-rating system, we also use **seven feature icons** that point you to the great deals, in-the-know advice, and unique experiences that separate travelers from tourists. Throughout the book, look for:

Finds	Special finds—those places only insiders know about
Fun Fact	Fun facts—details that make travelers more informed and their trips more fun
Kids	Best bets for kids, and advice for the whole family
Moments	Special moments—those experiences that memories are made of
Overrated	Places or experiences not worth your time or money
Tips	Insider tips—great ways to save time and money
Value	Great values—where to get the best deals

The following **abbreviations** are used for credit cards:

AE	American Express	DISC	Discover	V	Visa
DC	Diners Club	MC	MasterCard		

Frommers.com

Now that you have the guidebook to a great trip, visit our website at **www.frommers.com** for travel information on more than 3,000 destinations. With features updated regularly, we give you instant access to the most current trip-planning information available. At Frommers.com, you'll also find the best prices on airfares, accommodations, and car rentals—and you can even book travel online through our travel booking partners. At Frommers.com, you'll also find the following:

- Online updates to our most popular guidebooks
- Vacation sweepstakes and contest giveaways
- Newsletter highlighting the hottest travel trends
- Online travel message boards with featured travel discussions

What's New in Arizona

Every year I scour the state of Arizona to track down what's new and noteworthy. There are always great new hotels and restaurants to be discovered, new tour companies that have started up, new museums that have opened. Occasionally there are even new parks or other natural areas that have opened to the public. Inevitably, I also discover that a few old favorite restaurants, shops, and such have gone out of business. Worse still, I sometimes find that places I once liked no longer make the grade and have to be taken out of this guide. Following are some of my discoveries for this edition of *Frommer's Arizona*.

GENERAL The population of Arizona can be divided into city slickers and cowboys. Now if you'd like to switch horses from the former to the latter, then you need to spend some time at the **Arizona Cowboy College,** Lorill Equestrian Center, 30208 N. 152nd St., Scottsdale (© **888/330-8070;** www.cowboycollege.com), where they'll teach you not only how to ride a horse but how to saddle it. They might even let you in on how to make a horse drink after you lead it to water. See chapter 2 for more information.

PHOENIX, SCOTTSDALE & THE VALLEY OF THE SUN Urban hipsters rejoice! You have someplace to see and be seen in downtown Scottsdale. The new **James Hotel,** 7353 E. Indian School Rd., Scottsdale (© **866/50-JAMES;** www.jameshotels.com), may not be the W, but it sure is close. The bar, the restaurant, the pool, the plasma TVs—it's all good.

At **Carefree Resort & Villas,** 37220 Mule Train Rd., Carefree (© **800/949-1994;** www.carefreeresort.com), you can stay in a spacious new villa for about the same as what you would pay for an average room at some of the bigger name resorts in Scottsdale and Phoenix.

If you absolutely must keep up with your workout schedule even while you're on vacation, check out the new **Scottsdale Resort & Athletic Club,** 8235 E. Indian Bend Rd., Scottsdale (© **877/343-0033;** www.scottsdale resortandathleticclub.com). As a hotel guest, you get access to all the athletic club's facilities.

I've found lots of great Phoenix and Scottsdale restaurants to add to this book this year. For vibrant Nuevo Latino flavors, check out Scottsdale's **Deseo,** Westin Kierland Resort, 6902 E. Greenway Pkwy., Scottsdale (© **480/624-1000**). For wood-oven pizza in a cozy neighborhood restaurant setting, eat at **Grazie,** 6952 E. Main St., Scottsdale (© **480/663-9797**), in Old Town Scottsdale.

Up in the outer limits of north Scottsdale, you'll find some of the Valley's most creative cuisine at **Mosaic,** 10600 E. Jomax Rd., Scottsdale (© **480/563-9600;** www.mosaic-restaurant.com). In the same area, you can go to the opposite extreme and get a burger and a beer at **Greasewood Flat,** 27500 N. Alma School Rd., Scottsdale (© **480/585-7277**), an open-air joint the likes of which you can probably find only in Arizona. Greasewood Flat is affiliated with the adjacent **Reata Pass,** 27500 N. Alma School Pkwy., Scottsdale (© **480/ 585-7277**), an old-time steakhouse in a building that was once a stagecoach stop.

In central Phoenix, don't miss the great breads and sandwiches at **Pane Bianco,** 4404 N. Central Ave., Phoenix (© **602/234-2100**). South of downtown, you can combine a farm experience with gourmet food at **Quiessence,** 6106 S. 32nd St., Phoenix (© 602/276-0601), which is set at the back of a pecan grove.

Cowboys and Indians get equal time at a couple of unusual new museums in the Phoenix area. In downtown Phoenix you'll find the **Wells Fargo History Museum,** 100 W. Washington St. (© 602/378-1852; www.wellsfargohistory.com), which has not only an authentic stagecoach but also some great Western art and even some gold nuggets on display. South of Phoenix, on the Gila River Indian Reservation, you can learn about the Pima and Maricopa tribes at the **Huhugam Heritage Center,** 4759 N. Maricopa Rd., Chandler (© **520/ 796-3500;** www.huhugam.com). This museum isn't very large, but it is in a complex that is an architectural work of art. If you've always wanted to pet a tarantula, don't miss Glendale's **Katydid Museum,** 5060 W. Bethany Home Rd. (© **623/931-8718;** www. insectmuseum.com).

Spa goers take note, the **Spa at Camelback Inn,** 5402 E. Lincoln Dr., Scottsdale (© **800/922-2635** or 480/ 596-7040; www.camelbackspa.com), has had a complete makeover and looks absolutely marvelous.

See chapter 4 for more information.

CENTRAL ARIZONA   No visit to central Arizona is complete without a stop in the town of Jerome. This hillside mining town turned art community is now home to a good restaurant with a very odd sense of humor. **The**

Asylum, 200 Hill St. (© **928/639-3197**), is a restaurant located in a former hospital building turned hotel. Not only does the Asylum have good food and a fun atmosphere, but there are glorious views from the veranda.

Scottsdale is not the only place in Arizona to get a hip new W-style hotel. The new **Amara Creekside Resort,** 310 N. Hwy. 89A (© **866/ 455-6610;** www.amararesort.com), boasts not only the hippest rooms and interior decor in Sedona, but also claims an envious setting between the shops of uptown Sedona and the banks of tree-shaded Oak Creek.

Be sure to save your calorie quota for Sedona and just hope that you can walk off some of your meals on the area's superb hiking trails. **Cucina Rústica,** 7000 Hwy. 179, Village of Oak Creek (© **928/284-3010**), is a new restaurant from the owners of the ever popular Dahl & DiLuca in west Sedona. Great food and a great interior decor make this a real jewel. **El Portal Sedona,** 95 Portal Lane (© **800/313-0017;** www.innsedona. com), is my favorite B&B in the state, so I was delighted to find out that they also now serve superb dinners on Friday and Saturday evenings, and you don't have to be a guest at the inn to get in on these great meals.

Talk about your short run. The **Sedona Cultural Park,** which took years to build, is already out of business. Double-check the location of any event you run across that claims to take place at this former outdoor performance venue.

See chapter 5 for more information.

THE GRAND CANYON & NORTHERN ARIZONA   Don't leave Flagstaff without having a meal, or at least a glass of wine and some appetizers, at the new **Kokopelli Winery Bistro,** 6 E. Aspen St., Suite 110 (© **928/226-WINE**). The wines are from Arizona and are inexpensive and approachable. Much of the food is made with the same wines.

Think singing waiters and waitresses are a thing of the past? Think again. At **Black Bart's Steakhouse,** 2760 E. Butler Ave. (© **928/779-3142**), you get a good old-fashioned family floor show with your steak.

See chapter 6 for more information.

THE FOUR CORNERS REGION Up on the Arizona–New Mexico state line, the waters of **Lake Powell** have dropped close to 120 feet below the lake's full level. The dropping water level is due to many years of drought. Don't worry, though. There's still plenty of water in the lake and houseboating is just as popular as ever. However, if you've been dreaming of visiting **Rainbow Bridge,** be aware that you will now have to walk something like 1½ miles from the boat landing to reach the natural bridge.

See chapter 7 for more information.

TUCSON Fresh from major makeover, the **Doubletree Hotel at Reid Park,** 445 S. Alvernon Way, Tucson, AZ 85711 (© **800/222-TREE;** www.dtreidpark.com), is looking great. The same is true for and the **Radisson Suites Tucson,** 6555 E. Speedway Blvd. (© **800/333-3333;** www. radisson.com), although its room rates have since skyrocketed. If you're looking for a superb B&B surrounded by the desert, check out **La Zarzuela** © **888/848-8225;** www.zarzuela-az. com), which is located west of the city and not too far from Saguaro National Monument.

I am addicted to the carne seca burritos at El Charro Café, so I was elated to find out that you can now get carne seca at the new **Charro Grill,** 1765 E. River Rd. (© **520/615-1922**), a fast-service foothills spin-off of El Charro. There's more good Southwestern fare to be had at **HiFalutin Rapid Fire Western Grill,** 6780 N. Oracle Rd. (© **520/297-0518**), which is also in

the city's northern foothills area. **Cuvée World Bistro,** 3352 E. Speedway Blvd. (© **520/881-7577**), is my new favorite central Tucson restaurant. The food is great and the atmosphere is deliciously romantic. If you're of the mind to spend a small fortune on sushi the likes of which has never been seen in this neck of the desert, have a meal at **Yama,** 5425 N. Kolb Rd., #115 (© **520/615-1031**). Ummm, pizza! Want the best in town? Of course you do. Check out the new **Zona 78,** 78 W. River Rd. (© **520/ 888-7878**).

Sad news for fans of fine dining— the venerable **Tack Room,** long Tucson's premier special-occasion restaurant, is no longer open to the public. The last I heard, it was doing special events only.

See chapter 9 for more information.

SOUTHERN ARIZONA The closure of scenic drives by the Border Patrol has severely reduced the amount of **Organ Pipe Cactus National Monument** (© 520/387-6849; www.nps.gov/orpi) that is open to the public. You can now see so little of this rugged natural area that it is hardly worth the long drive to get there.

In the Santa Cruz Valley, south of Tucson, things seem to be booming. Two aging resorts have gotten major face-lifts in the past year. Both the **Tubac Golf Resort,** 1 Otero Rd., Tubac (© **800/848-7893;** www. tubacgolfresort.com), and the **Rio Rico Resort & Country Club,** 1069 Camino Caralampi, Rio Rico (© 800/288-4746; www.rioricoresort. com), are looking great these days. In fact they're both looking so good, it's difficult to pick a favorite.

See chapter 10 for more information.

WESTERN ARIZONA This seems to have been the year for the opening of hip hotels all across Arizona. Even Lake Havasu City, home of the very unhip London Bridge, has gotten into the act with the opening of the very attractive **Agave Inn,** 1420 McCulloch Blvd N. (© **866/854-2833;** www.agaveinn.com), which is located at the foot of the London Bridge and adjacent to the new **Javelina Cantina,** 1420 McCulloch Blvd. (© **928/855-8226**), a fun Mexican restaurant with a view of, you guessed it, the London Bridge.

Down in Yuma, in the southwest corner of the state, you can now catch art exhibits at one of the prettiest little art centers anywhere in the state. The **Yuma Art Center,** 254 S. Main St. (© **928/373-5214**), is a first-class exhibition space that would be right at home in Scottsdale's art-gallery district. Right next door to the art center is the newly renovated and reopened **Historic Yuma Theatre,** 254 S. Main St. (© **928/373-5214**), which stages a wide variety of music performances and live theater. Just a few miles west of Yuma, you can visit the **Official Center of the World** (© **760/572-0100**), which is located in Felicity, California. You can also see eye to eye with a dromedary or two at the **Saihati Camel Farm** (© **928/627-7511**).

See chapter 11 for more information.

1

The Best of Arizona

Planning a trip to a state as large and diverse as Arizona involves a lot of decision making (other than which golf clubs to take), so in this chapter we've tried to give you some direction. Below we've chosen what we feel is the very best the state has to offer—the places and experiences you won't want to miss. Although sights and activities listed here are written up in more detail elsewhere in this book, this chapter should help get you started planning your trip.

1 The Best Places to Commune with Cactus

- **Desert Botanical Garden** (Phoenix): There's no better place in the state to learn about the plants of Arizona's Sonoran Desert and the many other deserts of the world. Displays at this Phoenix botanical garden explain plant adaptations and how indigenous tribes once used many of this region's wild plants. See p. 116.

- **Boyce Thompson Arboretum** (east of Phoenix): Located just outside the town of Superior, this was the nation's first botanical garden established in a desert environment. It's set in a small canyon framed by cliffs and has desert plantings from all over the world—a fascinating place for an educational stroll in the desert. See p. 155.

- **Arizona–Sonora Desert Museum** (Tucson): The name is misleading—this is actually more a zoo and botanical garden than a museum. Naturalistic settings house dozens of species of desert animals, including a number of critters you wouldn't want to meet in the wild (rattlesnakes, tarantulas, scorpions, black widows, and Gila monsters). See p. 356.

- **Saguaro National Park** (Tucson): Lying both east and west of Tucson, this park preserves "forests" of saguaro cacti and is the very essence of the desert as so many people imagine it. You can hike it, bike it, or drive it. See p. 360.

- **Tohono Chul Park** (Tucson): Although this park is not all that large, it packs a lot of desert scenery into its modest space. Impressive plantings of cacti are the star attractions, but there are also good wildflower displays in the spring. See p. 368.

- **Organ Pipe Cactus National Monument** (west of Tucson): The organ pipe cactus is a smaller, multi-trunked relative of the giant saguaro and lives only along the Mexican border about 100 miles west of Tucson. This remote national monument has hiking trails and a couple of scenic drives. See section 1 in chapter 10.

2 The Best Active Vacations

- **Rafting the Grand Canyon:** Whether you go for 3 days or 2 weeks, nothing comes even remotely close to matching the

Arizona

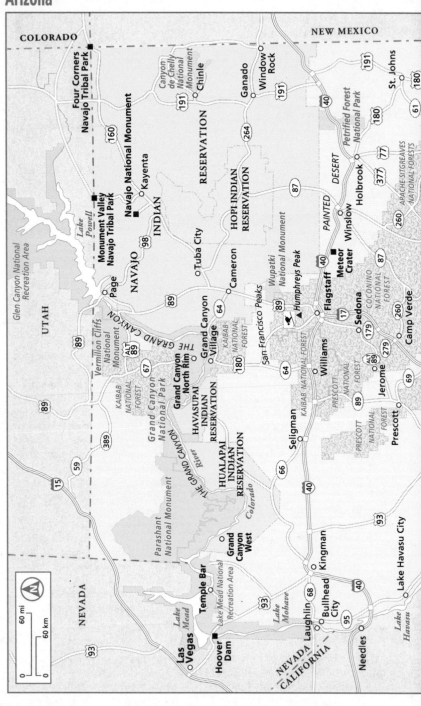

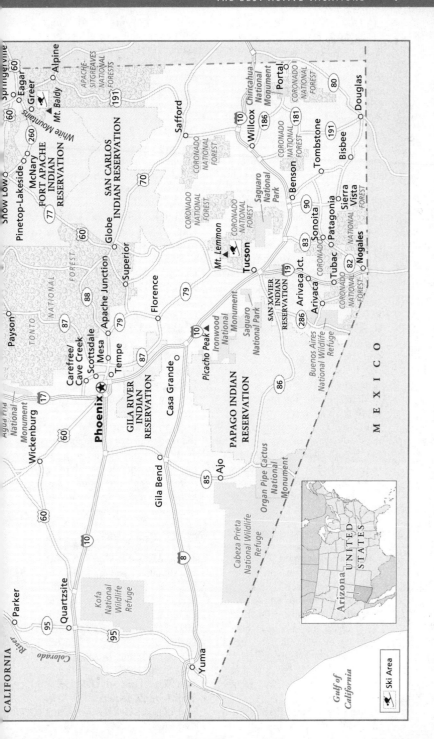

excitement of a raft trip through the Grand Canyon. Sure, the river is crowded with groups in the summer, but the grandeur of the canyon is more than enough to make up for it. See p. 240.

- **Hiking into the Grand Canyon or Havasu Canyon:** Not for the unfit or the faint of heart, a hike down into the Grand Canyon or Havasu Canyon is a journey through millions of years set in stone. This trip takes plenty of advance planning and requires some very strenuous hiking. With both a campground and a lodge at the bottom of each canyon, you can choose to make this trip with either a fully loaded backpack or just a light daypack. See p. 234 and 254.

- **Riding the Range at a Guest Ranch:** Yes, there are still cowboys in Arizona. They ride ranges all over the state, and so can you if you book a stay at one of the many guest ranches (once known as dude ranches). You might even get to drive some cattle down the trail. After a long or short day in the saddle, you can soak in a hot tub, go for a swim, or play a game of tennis before chowing down. See p. 163, 341, and 427.

- **Staying at a Golf or Tennis Resort:** If horseback riding and cowboy cookouts aren't your thing, how about as much golf or tennis as you can play? The Phoenix/Scottsdale area has the nation's greatest concentration of resorts, and Sedona and Tucson add many more options to the mix. There's something very satisfying about swinging a racquet or club with the state's spectacular scenery in the background, and the climate means you can do it practically year-round. See chapters 4, 5, and 9.

- **Mountain Biking in Sedona:** Forget Moab—too many other hard-core mountain bikers. Among the red rocks of Sedona, you can pedal through awesome scenery on some of the most memorable single-track trails in the Southwest. There's even plenty of slickrock for that Canyonlands experience. See p. 191.

- **Bird-Watching in Southeastern Arizona:** As an avid bird-watcher, I know that this isn't the most active of sports, but a birder can get in a bit of walking when it's necessary (like, maybe to get to the nesting tree of an elegant trogon). The southeast corner of the state is one of the best birding regions in the entire country. See section 6, "The Best Bird-Watching Spots," of this chapter.

3 The Best Day Hikes & Nature Walks

- **Camelback Mountain** (Phoenix): For many Phoenicians, the trail to the top of Camelback Mountain is a ritual, a Phoenix institution. Sure, there are those who make this a casual but strenuous hike, but many more turn it into a serious workout by jogging to the top and back down. I prefer a more leisurely approach so I can enjoy the views. See p. 124.

- **Picacho Peak State Park** (south of Casa Grande): The hike up this central Arizona landmark is short but strenuous, and from the top there are superb views out over the desert. The best time of year to make the hike is in spring, when the peak comes alive with wildflowers. Picacho Peak is between Casa Grande and Tucson just off I-10. See p. 156.

- **The West Fork of Oak Creek Trail** (outside Sedona): The West Fork of Oak Creek is a tiny stream that meanders for miles in a narrow steep-walled canyon. This is classic canyon country, and the hardest part of a hike here is having to turn back without seeing what's around the next bend up ahead. See p. 186.

- **The South Kaibab Trail** (Grand Canyon South Rim): Forget the popular Bright Angel Trail, which, near its start, is a human highway. The South Kaibab Trail offers better views to day hikers and is the preferred downhill route for anyone heading to Phantom Ranch for the night. This is a strenuous hike even if you go only a mile or so down the trail. Remember, the trip back is all uphill. See p. 235.

- **The White House Ruins Trail** (Canyon de Chelly National Monument): There's only one Canyon de Chelly hike that the general public can do without a Navajo guide, and that's the 2.5-mile trail to White House Ruins, a small site once inhabited by Ancestral Puebloans (formerly called Anasazi). The trail leads from the canyon rim across bare sandstone, through a tunnel, and down to the floor of the canyon. See p. 284.

- **Betatakin** (Navajo National Monument): Betatakin is one of the most impressive cliff dwellings in the Southwest, and while most people just marvel at it from a

distance, it's possible to take a ranger-led 5-mile hike to the ruins. After hiking through the remote Tsegi Canyon, you'll likely have a better understanding of the Ancestral Puebloan people who once lived here. See p. 288.

- **Antelope Canyon** (Page): More a slow walk of reverence than a hike, this trail lets you see the amazing beauty that can be created when water and rock battle each other in the Southwest. The trail leads through a picture-perfect sandstone slot canyon, which in places is only a few feet wide. See p. 295.

- **The Seven Falls Trail** (Tucson): There is something irresistible about waterfalls in the desert, and on this trail you get more than enough falls to satisfy any craving to cool off on a hot desert day. This trail is in Sabino Canyon Recreation Area in northeast Tucson. See p. 376.

- **The Heart of Rocks Trail** (Cochise County): While the big national parks and monuments in northern Arizona get all the publicity, Chiricahua National Monument, down in the southeast corner of the state, quietly lays claim to some of the most spectacular scenery in Arizona. On this trail, you'll hike through a wonderland of rocks. See p. 424.

4 The Best Scenic Drives

- **The Apache Trail** (east of Phoenix): Much of this winding road, which passes just north of the Superstition Mountains, is unpaved and follows a rugged route once ridden by Apaches. Here you'll find some of the most remote country in the Phoenix area, with far-reaching desert vistas and lots to see and do along the way. See section 12 in chapter 4.

- **Oak Creek Canyon** (Sedona): Slicing down from the pine country outside Flagstaff to the red rocks of Sedona, Oak Creek Canyon is a cool oasis. From the scenic overlook at the top of the canyon to the swimming holes and hiking trails at the bottom, this canyon road provides a rapid change in climate and landscape. See section 5 in chapter 5.

- **Canyon de Chelly National Monument** (Chinle): This fascinating complex of canyons on the Navajo Indian Reservation has only limited public access because it is still home to numerous Navajo families. However, there are roads that parallel the north and south rims of the canyon providing lots of scenic overlooks. See section 5 in chapter 7.
- **Monument Valley Navajo Tribal Park** (north of Kayenta): This valley of sandstone buttes and mesas is one of the most photographed spots in America and is familiar to people all over the world from the countless movies, TV shows, and commercials that have been shot here. A 17-mile dirt road winds through the park, giving visitors close-up views of such landmarks as Elephant Butte, the Mittens, and Totem Pole. See section 7 in chapter 7.
- **Mount Lemmon** (Tucson): Sure, the views of Tucson from the city's northern foothills are great, but the vistas from Mount Lemmon are even better. This mountain rises up from the desert like an island rising from the sea. Along the way, the road up the mountain climbs from cactus country to cool pine forests. Although a forest fire on Mount Lemmon in June 2003 left much of the mountain blackened, the views of the desert remain. See p. 376.

5 The Best Golf Courses

- **The Boulders South Course** (Carefree, near Phoenix; ℂ 480/488-9009): If you've ever seen a photo of someone teeing off beside a massive balancing rock and longed to play that same hole, then you've dreamed about playing the Boulders South Course. Jay Morrish's desert-style design plays around and through the jumble of massive boulders for which the resort is named. See p. 131.
- **The Gold Course at Wigwam Golf and Country Club** (Litchfield Park, near Phoenix; ℂ 800/909-4224): If you're a traditionalist who eschews those cactus- and rattlesnake-filled desert target courses, you'll want to be sure to reserve a tee time on the Wigwam Resort's Gold Course. This 7,100-yard resort course has long been an Arizona legend. See p. 131.
- **Gold Canyon Golf Resort** (Apache Junction, near Phoenix; ℂ 800/827-5281): Located east of Phoenix, Gold Canyon offers superb golf at the foot of the Superstition Mountains. The 2nd, 3rd, and 4th holes on the Dinosaur Mountain Course are truly memorable. They play across the foot of Dinosaur Mountain and are rated among the top holes in the state. See p. 132.
- **Troon North Golf Club** (Scottsdale; ℂ 888/TROON-US): Designed by Tom Weiskopf and Jay Morrish, this semiprivate desert-style course is named for the famous Scottish links that overlook the Firth of Forth and the Firth of Clyde—but that's where the similarities end. Troon North has two 18-hole courses, but the original, known as the Monument Course, is still the favorite. See p. 132.
- **The Tournament Players Club (TPC) of Scottsdale** (Scottsdale; ℂ 888/400-4001): If you've always dreamed of playing where the pros play, then schedule a visit to the Fairmont Scottsdale Princess, which is affiliated with

the TPC. Book a tee time on the resort's Stadium Course and you can play on the course that hosts the PGA Tour's Phoenix Open. See p. 132.

- **Sedona Golf Resort** (Sedona; © 877/733-9885): It's easy to think that all of Arizona's best courses are in the Phoenix and Tucson areas, but it just isn't so. Up in the red-rock country, at the mouth of Oak Creek Canyon, lies the Sedona Golf Resort, a traditional course with terrific red-rock views. See p. 191.
- **Lake Powell National Golf Course** (Page; © 928/645-2023): With fairways that wrap around the base of the red-sandstone bluff atop which sits the town of Page, this is one of the most scenic golf courses in the state. Walls of eroded sandstone come right down to the greens, and one tee box is up on top of the bluff. See p. 298.
- **Ventana Canyon Golf and Racquet Club** (Tucson; © 520/577-4015): Two Tom Fazio–designed courses, the Canyon Course and

the Mountain Course, are shared by two of the city's finest resorts. Both desert-style courses play through some of the most stunning scenery anywhere in the state. If we had to choose between the two, we'd go for the Canyon Course. See p. 375.

- **Omni Tucson National Golf Resort and Spa** (Tucson; © 520/575-7540): With its wide expanses of grass, this traditional course, site of the PGA Tour's Tucson Open, is both challenging and forgiving. The 18th hole of the combined Orange and Gold courses is considered one of the toughest finishing holes on the tour. See p. 375.
- **Emerald Canyon Golf Course** (Parker; © 928/667-3366): Canyons, cliffs, and ravines are the hazards you'll be avoiding on this very interesting municipal course way out on the banks of the Colorado River. While it may not be the best in the state, it plays through some astounding scenery and is a good value. See p. 441.

6 The Best Bird-Watching Spots

- **Madera Canyon:** The mountain canyons of southern Arizona attract an amazing variety of bird life, from species common in the lowland deserts to those that prefer thick forest settings. Madera is a good place to experience this variety. See p. 374.
- **Buenos Aires National Wildlife Refuge:** Gray hawks and masked bobwhite quails are among the refuge's rarer birds, but a wetland (cienaga), lake, and stream attract plenty of others. See section 2 in chapter 10.
- **Patagonia:** With a year-round stream and a Nature Conservancy preserve on the edge of town,

Patagonia is one of the best spots in the state for sighting various flycatcher species. See section 4 in chapter 10.

- **Ramsey Canyon Preserve:** Nearly 200 species of birds, including 14 species of hummingbirds, frequent this canyon, making it one of the top birding spots in the country. See p. 410.
- **San Pedro Riparian National Conservation Area:** Water is a scarce commodity in the desert, so it isn't surprising that the San Pedro River attracts a lot of animal life, including more than 300 bird species. This is a life-list bonanza spot. See p. 411.

- **Cave Creek Canyon:** Although there are other rare birds to be seen in this remote canyon, most people come in hopes of spotting the elegant trogon, which reaches the northernmost limit of its range here. See p. 425.

- **Cochise Lakes** (Willcox Ponds): Wading birds in the middle of the desert? You'll find them at the Willcox sewage-treatment ponds south of town. Avocets, sandhill cranes, and a variety of waterfowl all frequent these shallow bodies of water. See p. 425.

7 The Best Offbeat Travel Experiences

- **Taking a Vortex Tour in Sedona:** Crystals and pyramids are nothing compared to the power of the Sedona vortexes, which just happen to be in the middle of some very beautiful scenery. Organized tours shuttle believers from one vortex to the next. If you offer it, they will come. See p. 184.

- **Gazing at the Stars:** Insomniacs and stargazers will find plenty to keep them sleepless in the desert as they peer at the stars through telescopes at Lowell Observatory in Flagstaff or Kitt Peak National Observatory near Tucson. In the town of Benson, you can even stay at a B&B that doubles as an astronomical observatory. See p. 400.

- **Sleeping in a Wigwam:** Back in the heyday of Route 66, the Wigwam Motel in Holbrook lured passing motorists with its unusual architecture: concrete wigwam-shaped cabins. Today, this little motel is still a must for anyone on a Route 66 pilgrimage. See p. 279.

- **Touring Walpi Village:** Of the Hopi villages that stand atop the mesas of northeastern Arizona, only Walpi, one of the oldest, offers guided tours. Hopi guides share information on the history of the village and the Hopi culture. See p. 269.

8 The Best Family Experiences

- **Wild West Restaurants:** No family should visit Arizona without spending an evening at a "genuine" cowboy steakhouse. With false-fronted buildings, country bands, gunslingers, and gimmicks (one place cuts off your necktie, another has a slide from the bar to the dining room), these eateries are all entertainment and loads of fun. See p. 114 and 355.

- **The Grand Canyon Railway:** Not only is this train excursion a fun way to get to the Grand Canyon, but it also lets you avoid the parking problems and congestion that can prove so wearisome. Shootouts and train robberies are to be expected in this corner of the Wild West. See p. 238.

- **Arizona–Sonora Desert Museum** (Tucson): This is actually a zoo featuring the animals of the Sonoran Desert. There are rooms full of snakes, a prairie-dog town, bighorn sheep, mountain lions, and an aviary full of hummingbirds. Kids and adults love this place. See p. 356.

- **Shootouts at the O.K. Corral:** Tombstone may be "the town too tough to die," but poor Ike Clanton and his buddies the McLaury boys have to die over and over again at the frequent reenactments of the famous gunfight. See p. 415.

9 The Best Family Vacations

- **Saddling Up on a Dude Ranch:** Ride off into the sunset with your family at one of Arizona's many dude ranches (now called guest ranches). Most ranches have lots of special programs for kids. See p. 163, 341, and 427.
- **Floating on a Houseboat:** Renting a floating vacation home on lakes Powell, Mead, or Mohave is a summer tradition for many Arizona families. With a houseboat, you aren't tied to one spot and can cruise from one scenic beach to the next. See p. 299 and 434.
- **Lounging by the Pool:** While most Arizona resorts are geared primarily toward adults, there are a handful in Phoenix and Tucson that have extensive pool complexes. The kids can play in the sand, shoot down a water slide, or even float down an artificial river in an inner tube. See "The Best Swimming Pools," below.
- **Having a Grand Vacation:** You can spend the better part of a week exploring Grand Canyon National Park. There are trails to hike, mules to ride down into the canyon (if your kids are old enough), air tours by plane or helicopter, rafting trips both wild and tame, and even a train to ride to and from the canyon. See chapter 6.

10 The Best Museums

- **Heard Museum** (Phoenix): This is one of the nation's premier museums devoted to Native American cultures. In addition to historical exhibits, a huge kachina collection, and an excellent museum store, there are annual exhibits of contemporary Native American art as well as dance performances and demonstrations of traditional skills. See p. 116
- **Phoenix Art Museum** (Phoenix): This large art museum has acres of wall space and houses an outstanding collection of contemporary art as well as a fascinating exhibit of miniature rooms. See p. 120.
- **Scottsdale Museum of Contemporary Art** (Scottsdale): This is the Phoenix area's newest museum and is noteworthy as much for its bold contemporary architecture as for its wide variety of exhibits. Unlike the majority of area art galleries, this museum eschews cowboy art. See p. 120.
- **Museum of Northern Arizona** (Flagstaff): The geology, ethnography, and archaeology of this region are all explored in fascinating detail at this Flagstaff museum. Throughout the year, excellent special exhibits and festivals focus on the region's different tribes. See p. 210.
- **University of Arizona Museum of Art** (Tucson): This collection ranges from the Renaissance to the present, with a set of 15th-century Spanish religious panels the focus of the collection. Georgia O'Keeffe and Pablo Picasso are among the artists whose works are on display here. See p. 363.
- **Amerind Foundation Museum** (west of Willcox): Although located in the remote southeastern corner of the state, this museum and research center houses a superb collection of Native American artifacts. Displays focus on tribes of the Southwest, but other tribes are also represented. See p. 423.

11 The Best Places to Discover the Old West

- **Rodeos:** Any rodeo, and this state has plenty, will give you a glimpse of the Old West, but the rodeos in Prescott and Payson both claim to be the oldest in the country. Whether you head for the one in Prescott or the one in Payson, you'll see plenty of bronco busting, bull riding, and beer drinking. See p. 166 and 303.

- **Guest Ranches:** The Old West lives on at guest ranches all over the state, where rugged wranglers lead city slickers on horseback rides through desert scrub and mountain meadows. Campfires, cookouts, and cattle are all part of the experience. See p. 163, 341, and 427.

- **Monument Valley** (north of Kayenta): John Ford made it the hallmark of his Western movies, and today the starkly beautiful and fantastically shaped buttes and mesas of this valley are the quintessential Western landscape. You'll recognize it the moment you see it. See section 7 in chapter 7.

- **Old Tucson Studios** (Tucson): Although many of the original movie sets burned in a 1995 fire, this combination back lot and amusement park provides visitors with a glimpse of the most familiar Old West—the Hollywood West. Sure, the shootouts and cancan revues are silly, but it's all in good fun, and everyone gets a thrill out of seeing the occasional film crew in action. See p. 362.

- **Tombstone:** This is the real Old West—Tombstone is a real town, unlike Old Tucson. However, "the town too tough to die" was reincarnated long ago as a major tourist attraction with gunslingers in the streets, stagecoach rides, and shootouts at the O.K. Corral. See section 6 in chapter 10.

12 The Best Places to See Indian Ruins

- **Tonto National Monument** (east of Phoenix): Located east of Phoenix on the Apache Trail, this park has one of Arizona's few easily accessible cliff dwellings that still allow visitors to walk around inside the ruins; you don't have to just observe from a distance. See p. 155.

- **Besh-Ba-Gowah Archaeological Park** (Globe): These reconstructed ruins have been set up to look the way they might have appeared 700 years ago, providing a bit more cultural context than what you'll find at other ruins in the state. See p. 155.

- **Casa Grande Ruins National Monument** (west of Florence): Unlike most of Arizona's other ruins, which are constructed primarily of stone, this large and unusual structure is built of packed desert soil. Inscrutable and perplexing, Casa Grande seems to rise from nowhere. See p. 156.

- **Montezuma Castle National Monument** (north of Camp Verde): Located just off I-17, this is the most easily accessible cliff dwelling in Arizona, although it cannot be entered. Nearby Montezuma Well also has some small ruins. See p. 177.

- **Wupatki National Monument** (north of Flagstaff): Not nearly as well-known as the region's Ancestral Puebloan cliff dwellings, these ruins are set on a wide plain. A ball court similar to those found in Central America hints at cultural ties with the Aztecs. See p. 213.

- **Canyon de Chelly National Monument:** Small cliff dwellings up and down the length of Canyon de Chelly can be seen from overlooks, while a trip into the canyon itself offers a chance to see some of these ruins up close. See section 5 in chapter 7.
- **Navajo National Monument** (west of Kayenta): Both Keet Seel and Betatakin are some of the finest examples of Ancestral Puebloan cliff dwellings in the state. Although the ruins are at the end of long hikes, their size and state of preservation make these well worth the effort you'll expend to see them. See section 6 in chapter 7.

13 The Best Luxury Hotels & Resorts

- **Hyatt Regency Scottsdale Resort at Gainey Ranch** (Scottsdale; © 800/55-HYATT): Contemporary desert architecture, dramatic landscaping, a water playground with its own beach, a staff that's always at the ready to assist you, several good restaurants, and even gondola rides—it all adds up to a lot of fun at one of the most smoothly run resorts in Arizona. See p. 81.
- **Camelback Inn, A JW Marriott Resort & Spa** (Scottsdale; © 800/24-CAMEL): The Camelback Inn opened in 1936 and today is one of the few Scottsdale resorts that manage to retain an Old Arizona atmosphere while at the same time offering the most modern amenities. A recently renovated full-service spa caters to those who crave pampering, while two golf courses provide plenty of challenging fairways and greens. See p. 80.
- **The Phoenician** (Scottsdale; © 800/888-8234): This Xanadu of the resort world is brimming with marble, crystal, and works of art, and with staff seemingly around every corner, the hotel offers its guests impeccable service. Mary Elaine's, the resort's premier dining room, is one of the finest restaurants in the city, and the views are hard to beat. See p. 81.
- **The Boulders Resort and Golden Door Spa** (Carefree; © 800/553-1717): Taking its name from the massive blocks of eroded granite scattered about the grounds, the Boulders is among the most exclusive and expensive resorts in the state. Pueblo architecture fits seamlessly with the landscape, and the golf course is the most breathtaking in Arizona. See p. 86.
- **The Fairmont Scottsdale Princess** (Scottsdale; © 800/441-1414): The Moorish styling and numerous fountains and waterfalls of this Scottsdale resort create a setting made for romance. A beautiful spa, challenging golf course, and two superb restaurants—one serving Spanish cuisine and one serving gourmet Mexican fare—top it off. See p. 87.
- **Four Seasons Resort Scottsdale at Troon North** (Scottsdale; © 888/207-9696): Located in north Scottsdale not far from the Boulders, this is the most luxurious resort in Arizona. The setting is dramatic, the accommodations are spacious, and the next-door neighbor is one of Arizona's top golf courses. See p. 86.
- **Arizona Biltmore Resort & Spa** (Phoenix; © 800/950-0086): Combining discreet service and the architectural styling of Frank

Lloyd Wright, the Biltmore has long been one of the most prestigious resorts in the state. This is a thoroughly old-money sort of place, though it continues to keep pace with the times. See p. 88.

- **Royal Palms Resort and Spa** (Phoenix; ✆ 800/672-6011): With its Mediterranean styling and towering palm trees, this place seems far removed from the glitz that prevails at most area resorts. The Royal Palms is a classic, perfect for romantic getaways, and the 14 designer showcase rooms are among the most dramatic in the valley. See p. 90.

- **Enchantment Resort** (Sedona; ✆ 800/826-4180): A dramatic setting in a red-rock canyon makes this the most unforgettably situated resort in the state. If you want to feel as though you're vacationing in the desert, this place fits the bill. Guest rooms are constructed in a pueblo architectural style, and the spa is one of the finest in the state. See p. 194.

- **Loews Ventana Canyon Resort** (Tucson; ✆ 800/234-5117): With the Santa Catalina Mountains rising up in the backyard and an almost-natural waterfall only steps away from the lobby, this is Tucson's most dramatic resort. Contemporary styling throughout makes constant reference to the desert setting. See p. 335.

14 The Best Family Resorts

- **Holiday Inn SunSpree Resort** (Scottsdale; ✆ 800/852-5205): If you happen to have a child who is crazy about trains, then this resort, adjacent to the McCormick-Stillman Railroad Park (which has trains to ride, model-railroad exhibits, and a merry-go-round), is the place to stay. The resort itself has big lawns and free meals for kids under 12. See p. 85.

- **Hyatt Regency Resort at Gainey Ranch** (Scottsdale; ✆ 800/55-HYATT): With a 10-pool, 2½-acre water playground complete with sand beach, waterfalls, children's programs, and even a "Lost Dutchman Mine" where children can dig for buried treasure, this place is a kid's dream come true. See p. 81.

- **Pointe Hilton Squaw Peak Resort** (Phoenix; ✆ 800/876-4683): A water slide, tubing river, and waterfall make the water park here one of the most family oriented at any resort in the valley. Throw in a miniature-golf course, a video-game room, and a children's program, and you can be sure your kids will be begging to come back. See p. 91.

- **Pointe South Mountain Resort** (Phoenix; ✆ 877/800-4888): Let's see . . . water slides that drop nearly 70 feet straight down, a wave pool, a water play area for the youngest ones, a tubing river, horseback riding, even spa treatments for teens. Can you say fun for the whole family? See p. 93.

- **Loews Ventana Canyon Resort** (Tucson; ✆ 800/234-5117): With a playground, kids' club, croquet court, and its own waterfall, this resort has plenty to keep the kids busy. There's also a hiking trail that starts from the edge of the property, and Sabino Canyon Recreation Area is nearby. See p. 335.

- **Westin La Paloma** (Tucson; ✆ 800/WESTIN-1): Kids get their own lounge and game room, and there's a great water slide in the pool area. In summer and during holiday periods, there are special programs for the kids so parents can have a little free time. See p. 336.

15 The Best Hotels for Old Arizona Character

- **Hermosa Inn** (Phoenix; ✆ **800/ 241-1210**): The main building here dates from 1930 and was once the home of Western artist Lon Megargee. Today, the old adobe house is surrounded by beautiful gardens, and has become a tranquil boutique hotel with luxurious Southwestern-style rooms and a great restaurant. See p. 89.

- **El Tovar Hotel** (Grand Canyon Village; ✆ **888/297-2757**): This classic log-and-stone mountain lodge stands in Grand Canyon Village only feet from the South Rim of the Grand Canyon. Although the lobby is small, it's decorated with the requisite trophy animal heads and has a stone fireplace. See p. 242.

- **Grand Canyon Lodge** (Grand Canyon North Rim; ✆ **888/ 297-2757**): This, the Grand Canyon's other grand lodge, sits right on the North Rim of the canyon. Rooms are primarily in cabins, which aren't quite as impressive as the main building, but guests tend to spend a lot of time sitting on the lodge's two viewing terraces or in the sunroom. See p. 251.

- **La Posada** (Winslow; ✆ **928/ 289-4366**): Designed by Mary Elizabeth Jane Colter, who also designed many of the buildings on the South Rim of the Grand Canyon, La Posada opened in 1930 and was the last of the great railroad hotels. Today, the hotel is once again one of the finest hotels in the West and is undergoing a thorough restoration to its former glory. See p. 267.

- **Arizona Inn** (Tucson; ✆ **800/ 933-1093**): With its pink-stucco walls and colorful, fragrant gardens, this small Tucson resort dates from Arizona's earliest days as a vacation destination and epitomizes slower times, when guests came for the entire winter, not just a quick weekend getaway. See p. 330.

16 The Best Bed & Breakfasts

- **Rocamadour Bed & Breakfast for (Rock) Lovers** (Prescott; ✆ **888/771-1933**): Set amid the rounded boulders of the Granite Dells just north of Prescott, this inn combines a spectacular setting with French antiques and very luxurious accommodations. You won't find a more memorable setting anywhere in the state. See p. 170.

- **Hacienda de la Mariposa** (Verde Valley; ✆ **888/520-9095**): Set on the banks of Beaver Creek near Montezuma Castle National Monument, this inn was built in the Santa Fe style and blends beautifully with its surroundings. See p. 179.

- **Briar Patch Inn** (Sedona; ✆ **888/ 809-3030**): This collection of luxurious cottages is located in tree-shaded Oak Creek Canyon, a few miles north of Sedona. Few experiences are more restorative than breakfast on the shady banks of the creek. See p. 196.

- **El Portal Sedona** (Sedona; ✆ **800/313-0017**): Built of hand-cast adobe blocks and incorporating huge wooden beams salvaged from a railroad trestle, this inn is a work of art both inside and out. The mix of arts-and-crafts and Santa Fe styling conjures up haciendas of old. See p. 194.

- **Adobe Village Graham Inn** (Sedona; ✆ **800/228-1425**):

With its little "village" of luxury suites, this B&B is among the most elegant in the state. Everything is calculated to pamper and put you in the mood for a romantic getaway. Forget about Sedona's red rocks; these rooms are reason enough for a visit to the area. See p. 195.

- **The Inn at 410** (Flagstaff; ✆ **800/774-2008**): This restored 1907 bungalow offers a convenient location in downtown Flagstaff, pleasant surroundings, comfortable rooms, and delicious breakfasts. Rooms all feature different, distinctive themes. See p. 214.

- **Red Setter Inn & Cottage** (Greer; ✆ **888/994-7337**): This large, modern log home in the quaint mountain village of Greer is one of Arizona's most enjoyable and romantic B&Bs. It's set on the banks of the Little Colorado River in the shade of tall ponderosa pine trees. See p. 312.

- **The Royal Elizabeth** (Tucson; ✆ **877/670-9022**): Located in downtown Tucson just a block from the Temple of Music and Art, this territorial-style historic home is filled with beautiful Victorian antiques and architectural details. Guest rooms have lots of touches not often seen in historic B&Bs, including "vintage" phones, TVs, fridges, and safes. See p. 332.

- **La Zarzuela** (Tucson; ✆ **520/884-4824**): Perched high on a hill west on the west side of Tucson, this luxurious B&B boasts great views, colorful decor, and loads of outdoor spaces in which to relax in the warmth of the desert. See p. 338.

- **Across the Creek at Aravaipa Farms** (Winkelman; ✆ **520/357-6901**): If you're looking for the quintessential desert B&B experience, this is it, though it isn't exactly for everyone. To reach this inn, you have to drive *through* Aravaipa Creek (or have the innkeeper shuttle you across). Exploring the nearby wilderness area is the main activity in this remote area. See p. 339.

- **Cochise Stronghold B&B** (Cochise County; ✆ **877/426-4141**): Surrounded by the national forest and mountainsides strewn with giant boulders, this is another of the state's remote inns. The passive-solar building was built from straw bales and is not only energy-efficient but also quite beautiful. See p. 426.

17 The Best Swimming Pools

- **Hyatt Regency Scottsdale at Gainey Ranch** (Scottsdale; ✆ **800/55-HYATT**): This Scottsdale resort boasts a 10-pool, 2½-acre water playground complete with sand beach, waterfalls, sports pool, lap pool, adult pool, three-story water slide, giant whirlpool, and lots of waterfalls. See p. 81.

- **The Phoenician** (Scottsdale; ✆ **800/888-8234**): This resort's seven-pool system is as impressive as the Hyatt's, but has a much more sophisticated air. Waterfalls, a water slide, play pools, a lap pool, and the crown jewel—a mother-of-pearl pool (actually opalescent tile)—add up to plenty of aquatic fun. See p. 81.

- **Pointe Hilton Squaw Peak Resort** (Phoenix; ✆ **800/876-4683**): There's not just a pool here, there's a River Ranch, with an artificial tubing river, a water slide, and a waterfall pouring into the large, free-form main pool. See p. 91.

- **Pointe Hilton Tapatio Cliffs Resort** (Phoenix; ✆ **800/876-4683**): The Falls, a slightly more adult-oriented pool complex than that at sister property Pointe Hilton Squaw Peak Resort, includes two lagoon pools, a 40-foot waterfall, a 138-foot water slide, and rental cabanas. See p. 92.

- **Pointe South Mountain Resort** (Phoenix; ✆ 877/800-4888): The Oasis water park here leaves all the other area resort pools high and dry. There's a wave pool, a tubing river, and two terrifyingly steep water slides. It's enough to make summer in the desert seem almost bearable. See p. 93.
- **The Wyndham Buttes Resort** (Tempe; ✆ 800/WYNDHAM):

A lush stream cascading over desert rocks seems to feed this free-form pool, a desert-oasis fantasy world you won't want to leave. A narrow canal connects the two halves of the pool, and tucked in among the rocks are several whirlpools. See p. 94.

- **Westin La Paloma** (Tucson; ✆ 800/WESTIN-1): With a 177-foot-long water slide and enough poolside lounge chairs to put a cruise ship to shame, the pool at this Tucson foothills resort is a fabulous place to while away an afternoon. There's an adults-only pool, too. See p. 336.

18 The Best Places to Savor Southwest Flavors

- **Roaring Fork** (Scottsdale; ✆ 480/947-0795): Roaring Fork's chef, Robert McGrath, has long been one of the most creative chefs in the Phoenix area. The atmosphere is lively, and everything from the bread basket and bar snacks to the entrees and desserts shows an attention to detail. See p. 101.
- **Sam's Cafe** (Phoenix; ✆ 602/954-7100 and 602/252-3545): The flavors of the Southwest don't have to cost a fortune, and these restaurants are proof. Okay, so the food won't be as unforgettable as that at Roaring Fork, but you'll still get a good idea of what Southwestern cooking is all about. See p. 111.
- **Fry Bread House** (Phoenix; ✆ 602/351-2345): Unless you've traveled in the Southwest before, you probably have never had a fry-bread taco, but this stick-to-your-ribs dish is a staple on Indian reservations through Arizona. The fry-bread tacos here are the best in the state. See p. 111.
- **Blue Adobe Grille** (Mesa; ✆ 480/962-1000): This nondescript

restaurant in an otherwise forgettable area of Mesa serves some of the best Southwestern fare in the state. Not only are the meals flavorful (without being too spicy), but prices are great, too. There's even a good wine list! See p. 113.
- **The Heartline Cafe** (Sedona; ✆ 928/282-0785): Combining the zesty flavors of the Southwest with the best of the rest of the world, Sedona's Heartline Cafe frequently comes up with winners that are guaranteed to please jaded palates. See p. 202.
- **The Turquoise Room** (Winslow; ✆ 928/289-2888): Located in the restored La Posada historic hotel, this restaurant conjures up the days when the wealthy still traveled by railroad. Rarely will you find such excellent meals in such an off-the-beaten-path locale. See p. 268.
- **Janos/J Bar** (Tucson; ✆ 520/615-6100): Serving a combination of regional and Southwestern dishes, Janos has for many years been one of Tucson's premier restaurants. It's located just outside the front door of the Westin La Paloma

resort and is as formal a place as you'll find in this city. J Bar is Janos's less formal bar and grill. See p. 350 and 352.

- **Café Poca Cosa** (Tucson; © **520/622-6400**): Forget the gloppy melted cheese and flavorless red sauces. This place treats south-of-the-border ingredients with the respect they deserve. This is Mexican food the likes of which you'll never find at your local Mexican joint. See p. 342.
- **Café Terra Cotta** (Tucson; © **520/577-8100**): Café Terra Cotta was one of Arizona's pioneers in the realm of Southwestern cuisine and continues to serve creative and reasonably priced meals at its beautiful, art-filled restaurant in the Tucson foothills. See p. 352.

2

Planning Your Trip to Arizona

Whether you're headed to Arizona to raft the Grand Canyon or to golf in Scottsdale, you'll find all the advance-planning answers you need in this chapter—everything from when to go to how to get there.

1 The Regions in Brief

Phoenix, Scottsdale & the Valley of the Sun This region encompasses the sprawling metropolitan Phoenix area, which covers more than 400 square miles and includes more than 20 cities and communities surrounded by several distinct mountain ranges. It's the economic and population center of the state, and is Arizona's main winter and spring vacation destination. It is here that you'll find the greatest concentrations of resorts and golf courses. It is also where you'll find the worst traffic congestion and highest resort rates.

Central Arizona This region lies between Phoenix and the high country of northern Arizona and includes the red-rock country around the town of Sedona, which is one of the state's most popular tourist destinations. The rugged scenery around Sedona played many a role in old Western movies and has long attracted artists. Today, Sedona abounds in art galleries, recreational opportunities, and excellent lodging choices. Also within this region are historic Prescott, the former territorial capital of Arizona, and the old mining town of Jerome, which now become something of an artists' community. Several ancient Indian ruins and petroglyph sites can be found here as well.

The Grand Canyon & Northern Arizona Home to the Grand Canyon,

one of the natural wonders of the world, northern Arizona is a vast and sparsely populated region comprised primarily of public lands and Indian reservations. Because Grand Canyon National Park attracts millions of visitors each year, the city of Flagstaff and towns of Williams and Tusayan abound in accommodations and restaurants catering to canyon-bound travelers. North of the Grand Canyon and bordering on southern Utah lies the Arizona Strip, which is the most remote and untraveled region of the state. The Grand Canyon acts as a natural boundary between this region and the rest of the state, and the lack of paved roads and towns keeps away all but the most dedicated explorers. The inaccessible Parashant National Monument lies at the western end of the Arizona Strip.

The Four Corners The point where Arizona, Utah, Colorado, and New Mexico come together is the only place in the United States where four states share a common boundary. The region is also almost entirely composed of Hopi and Navajo reservation land. This region of spectacular canyons and towering mesas and buttes includes Canyon de Chelly, the Painted Desert, the Petrified Forest, and Monument Valley.

Eastern Arizona's High Country This area, which comprises the

Mogollon Rim region and the White Mountains, is a summertime escape valve for residents of the lowland desert areas, and as such abounds with mountain cabins and summer homes. Most of this high country is covered with ponderosa pine forests, laced with trout streams, and dotted with fishing lakes. Although this region comes into its own in summer, it also sees some winter visitation because it has the best ski area in the state: the Sunrise Park Resort ski area, on the White Mountain Apache Indian Reservation. Because the area lacks national parks, monuments, or other major geographical attractions, it is not really much of a destination for out-of-state visitors.

Tucson   Located a bit more than 100 miles south of Phoenix, Tucson is Arizona's second-most populous metropolitan area and is home to numerous resorts and golf courses. The main attractions include Saguaro National Park and the Arizona–Sonora Desert Museum. With mountain ranges rising in all directions, this city seems more in touch with its natural surroundings than Phoenix, though traffic congestion and sprawl also plague Tucson. If you prefer Boston to New York, San Francisco to Los Angeles, or Portland to Seattle, you'll want to vacation in Tucson rather than in Phoenix.

Southern Arizona   Southern Arizona is a region of great contrasts, from desert lowlands to mountain "islands" to vast grassy plains. Mile-high elevations also account for southeastern Arizona having one of the most temperate climates in the world. The mild climate has attracted lots of retirees, and it also brings in rare birds (and birders) and helps support a small wine industry. The western part of southern Arizona is one of the least-visited corners of the state, in part because much of this area is a U.S. Air Force bombing range. You will, however, find Organ Pipe Cactus National Monument out this way (wedged between the vast Cabeza Prieta National Wildlife Refuge and the Papago Indian Reservation). Tucson is at the northern edge of this region (and is not so temperate), but otherwise there are few towns of any size. However, there are a couple of interesting historic towns—Bisbee and Tubac—that have become artists' communities.

Western Arizona   Although Arizona is a landlocked state, its western region is bordered by hundreds of miles of lakeshore that were created by the damming of the Colorado River. Consequently, the area has come to be known as Arizona's West Coast. Despite the fact that the low-lying lands of this region are among the hottest places in the state during the summer (and the warmest in winter), Arizona's West Coast is a popular summer destination with budget-conscious desert denizens. College students and families come almost exclusively for the water-skiing, fishing, and other watersports.

2 Visitor Information

For statewide travel information, contact the **Arizona Office of Tourism,** 1110 W. Washington St., Suite 155, Phoenix, AZ 85007 (© **866/275-5816** or 602/364-3700; www.arizona guide.com). Nearly every city and town in Arizona has either a tourism office or a chamber of commerce that can also provide information. See the individual chapters for details on how to contact these sources.

Destination: Arizona—Red Alert Checklist

- Did you make golf or spa reservations?
- If you're planning on dining at any of the top-end restaurants in Phoenix or Tucson, have you made reservations?
- Have you made theater or day-tour reservations?
- If you purchased traveler's checks, have you recorded the check numbers, and stored the documentation separately from the checks?
- Did you pack your camera, an extra set of camera batteries, and enough film?
- Did you bring ID cards that could entitle you to discounts—such as AAA and AARP cards, and student IDs?
- Do you have the PINs for your credit cards?
- If you have an e-ticket, do you have documentation?
- Did you leave a copy of your itinerary with someone at home?

3 Money

What will a vacation in Arizona cost? That depends on your comfort needs. If you drive an RV or carry a tent, you can get by very inexpensively and find a place to stay almost anywhere in the state. If you don't mind staying in motels that date from the Great Depression and can sleep on a sagging mattress, you can stay for less money in Arizona than almost anyplace else in the United States (under $30 a night for a double). On the other hand, you can easily spend several hundred dollars a day on a room at one of the state's world-class resorts. If you're looking to stay in clean, modern motels at interstate highway off-ramps, expect to pay $45 to $65 a night for a double room in most places.

ATMS

The easiest and best way to get cash away from home is from an ATM (automated teller machine). The **Cirrus** (© **800/424-7787;** www.mastercard.com) and **PLUS** (© **800/843-7587;** www.visa.com) networks span the globe; look at the back of your bank card to see which network you're on, then call or check online for ATM locations at your destination. Be sure

you know your personal identification number (PIN) before you leave home and be sure to find out your daily withdrawal limit before you depart. Also keep in mind that many banks impose a fee every time a card is used at a different bank's ATM, and that the fee can be higher for international transactions (up to $5 or more) than for domestic ones (where they're rarely more than $1.50). On top of this, the bank from which you withdraw cash may charge its own fee. To compare banks' ATM fees within the U.S., use www.bankrate.com. For international withdrawal fees, ask your bank.

You can also get cash advances on your credit card at an ATM. Keep in mind that credit card companies try to protect themselves from theft by limiting the funds someone can withdraw outside their home country, so call your credit card company before you leave home.

TRAVELER'S CHECKS

Traveler's checks are something of an anachronism from the days before the ATM made cash accessible at any time. Traveler's checks used to be the only sound alternative to traveling with dangerously large amounts of cash. They were as reliable as currency, but, unlike cash, could be replaced if lost or stolen.

These days, traveler's checks are less necessary because most cities have 24-hour ATMs that allow you to withdraw small amounts of cash as needed. However, keep in mind that you will likely be charged an ATM withdrawal fee if the bank is not your own, so if you're withdrawing money every day, you might be better off with traveler's checks—provided that you don't mind showing identification every time you want to cash one.

You can get traveler's checks at almost any bank. **American Express** offers denominations of $20, $50, $100, and $500. You'll pay a service charge ranging from 1% to 4%. You can also get American Express traveler's checks over the phone by calling ℂ **800/221-7282** or online at www.americanexpress.com; Amex gold and platinum cardholders who use this number are exempt from the 1% fee.

Visa offers traveler's checks at Citibank locations nationwide, as well as at several other banks. The service charge ranges between 1.5% and 2%;

checks come in denominations of $20, $50, $100, $500, and $1,000. Call ℂ **800/732-1322** for information. AAA members can obtain checks without a fee at most AAA offices. **MasterCard** also offers traveler's checks. Call ℂ **800/223-9920** for a location near you.

If you choose to carry traveler's checks, be sure to keep a record of their serial numbers separate from your checks in the event that they are stolen or lost. You'll get a refund faster if you know the numbers.

CREDIT CARDS

Credit cards are a safe way to carry money, they provide a convenient record of all your expenses, and they generally offer good exchange rates. You can also withdraw cash advances from your credit cards at banks or ATMs, provided you know your PIN. If you've forgotten yours, or didn't even know you had one, call the number on the back of your credit card and ask the bank to send it to you. It usually takes 5 to 7 business days, though some banks will provide the number over the phone if you tell them your mother's maiden name or some other personal information.

4 When to Go

Arizona is a year-round destination, although people head to different parts of the state at different times of the year. In Phoenix, Tucson, and other parts of the desert, the high season runs from October to mid-May, with the highest hotel rates in effect from January to April. At the Grand Canyon, summer is the busy season.

The all-around best times to visit are spring and autumn, when temperatures are cool in the mountains and warm in the desert, but without extremes (although you shouldn't be surprised to get a bit of snow as late as

Memorial Day in the mountains, and thunderstorms in the desert Aug–Sept). Late spring and early autumn (specifically May and Sept) are also good times to save money—low summer rates are still in effect at the desert resorts—and to see the Grand Canyon when it's not its most crowded. In spring, you might also catch great wildflower displays, which begin in midspring and extend until May, when the tops of saguaro cacti become covered with waxy white blooms.

If for some reason you happen to be visiting the desert in July or August, be prepared for sudden thunderstorms. These storms often cause flash floods that make many roads briefly impassable. Signs warning motorists not to enter low areas when flooded are meant to be taken very seriously.

Also, don't even think about venturing into narrow slot canyons, such as Antelope Canyon near Page or the West Fork of Oak Creek Canyon, if there's any chance of a storm anywhere in the region. Rain falling miles away can send flash floods roaring down narrow canyons with no warning. In 1997, several hikers died when they were caught in a flash flood in Antelope Canyon.

One more thing to keep in mind: Sedona is just high enough that it actually gets cold in the winter—sometimes it even snows. So if you're looking for sunshine and time by the pool, book your Sedona vacation for a time other than the winter.

CLIMATE

The first thing you should know is that the desert can be cold as well as hot. Although winter is the prime tourist season in Phoenix and Tucson, night temperatures can be below freezing and days can sometimes be too cold for sunning or swimming. Although there can be several days in a row of cool, cloudy, and even rainy weather in January and February, on the whole, winters in Arizona are positively delightful.

In the winter, sun seekers flock to the deserts, where temperatures average in the high 60s by day. In the summer, when desert temperatures top 110°F (43°C), the mountains of eastern and northern Arizona are pleasantly warm, with daytime averages in the low 80s. Yuma is one of the desert communities where winter temperatures are the highest in the state, while Prescott and Sierra Vista, in the 4,000- to 6,000-foot elevation range, claim temperate climates that are just about ideal.

Phoenix's Average Temperatures & Days of Rain

	Jan	Feb	Mar	Apr	May	June	July	Aug	Sept	Oct	Nov	Dec
Avg. High (°F)	65	69	75	84	93	102	105	102	98	88	75	66
Avg. High (°C)	18	21	24	29	34	39	41	39	37	31	24	19
Avg. Low (°F)	38	41	45	52	60	68	78	76	69	57	45	39
Avg. Low (°C)	3	5	7	11	16	20	26	24	21	14	7	4
Days of Rain	4	4	3	2	1	1	4	5	3	3	2	4

Flagstaff's Average Temperatures & Days of Rain

	Jan	Feb	Mar	Apr	May	June	July	Aug	Sept	Oct	Nov	Dec
Avg. High (°F)	41	44	48	57	67	76	81	78	74	63	51	43
Avg. High (°C)	5	7	9	19	19	24	27	26	23	17	11	6
Avg. Low (°F)	14	17	20	27	34	40	50	49	41	31	22	16
Avg. Low (°C)	-10	-8	-7	-3	1	4	10	9	5	-1	-6	-9
Days of Rain	7	6	8	6	3	3	12	11	6	5	5	6

ARIZONA CALENDAR OF EVENTS

January

Tostitos Fiesta Bowl Football Classic, Sun Devil Stadium, Tempe. This college bowl game usually sells out nearly a year in advance. Call ✆ **800/635-5748** or 480/350-0900, or go to www.tostitos fiestabowl.com. January 1, 2005.

Wings over Willcox, Willcox. Birding tours, workshops, and, of course, watching the thousands of sandhill cranes that gather in the Sulphur Springs Valley near Willcox. Call ✆ **800/200-2272,** or got to www.wingsoverwillcox.com. Third weekend in January.

Barrett-Jackson Collector Car Auction, Scottsdale. More than 800 immaculately restored classic cars are auctioned off in an event attended by more than 185,000 people. Call ✆ **480/421-6694,** or go to www.barrett-jackson.com. January 27 to 30, 2005.

Phoenix Open Golf Tournament, Scottsdale. Prestigious PGA golf tournament at the Tournament Players Club. Call ✆ **602/870-4431,** or go to www.phoenixopen.com. January 31 to February 6, 2005.

Parada del Sol Parade and Rodeo, Scottsdale. The state's longest horse-drawn parade, plus a street dance and rodeo. Call ✆ **480/990-3179,** or go to www.scottsdale jaycees.com. Late January to early February.

February

World Championship Hoop Dance Contest, Phoenix. Native American dancers from around the nation take part in this colorful competition held at the Heard Museum. Call ✆ **602/251-0255,** or go to www.heard.org. February 5 to 6, 2005.

Tubac Festival of the Arts, Tubac. Exhibits by North American artists and craftspeople. Call ✆ **520/398-2704,** or go to www.tubacaz.com/festival.asp. Early to mid-February.

Tucson Gem and Mineral Show, Tucson. This huge show at the Tucson Convention Center offers seminars, museum displays from around the world, and hundreds of dealers selling just about any kind of rock you can imagine. Call ✆ **520/322-5773.** Mid-February.

Arizona Renaissance Festival, Apache Junction. This 16th-century English country fair features costumed participants and tournament jousting. Call ✆ **520/463-2700,** or go to www.renfestinfo.com. Weekends from early February to late March.

O'odham Tash, Casa Grande. One of the largest annual Native American festivals in the country, attracting dozens of tribes that participate in rodeos, arts-and-crafts exhibits, and dance performances. Call ✆ **520/836-4723.** Mid-February.

Scottsdale Arabian Horse Show, Scottsdale's Westworld. A celebration of the Arabian horse. Call ✆ **480/515-1500,** or go to www.scottsdaleshow.com. Mid- to late February.

Chrysler Classic of Tucson, Tucson. A major stop on the golf tour, held at the Omni Tucson National Golf Resort and Spa. Call ✆ **800/882-7660** or 520/571-0400, or go to www. pgatour.com. February 20 to 27, 2005.

La Fiesta de los Vaqueros, Tucson. Cowboy festival and rodeo at the Tucson Rodeo Grounds, including the Tucson Rodeo Parade, one of the world's largest nonmotorized parades. Call ✆ **800/964-5662** or 520/741-2233, or go to www.tucsonrodeo.com. February 20 and 24 to 27, 2005.

Franklin Templeton Tennis Classic, Scottsdale. Top names in men's professional tennis, including the likes of Andre Agassi and Pete Sampras, compete in this tournament at the Fairmont Scottsdale Princess resort. Call ✆ **480/922-0222,** or go to www.scottsdaletennis.com. February 21 to 27, 2005.

Flagstaff Winterfest, Flagstaff. Snowshoeing and cross-country ski tours, sleigh rides, music, and family snow games. Call ✆ **800/ 842-7293** or 928/774-4505. Month of February.

March

Heard Museum Guild Indian Fair, Phoenix. Indian cultural and dance presentations and one of the greatest selections of Native American crafts in the Southwest make this a fascinating festival. Go early to avoid the crowds. Call ✆ **602/252-8848,** or go to www. heard.org. First weekend in March.

Sedona International Film Festival, Sedona. View various new indie features, documentaries, and animated films before they (it is hoped) get picked up for wider distribution. Call ✆ **928/282-1177,** or go to www.sedonafilmfestival. com. First weekend in March.

Chandler Ostrich Festival, Chandler. Give the carnival a miss and head straight for the ostrich races. Although brief, these unusual races are something you've got to see at least once in your lifetime. Call ✆ **480/963-4571,** or go to www. ostrichfestival.com. Mid-March.

Scottsdale Arts Festival, Scottsdale Mall. This visual and performing-arts festival includes concerts, an art show, and children's events. Call ✆ **480/994-ARTS,** or go to www. scottsdalearts.org. Second weekend in March.

National Festival of the West, Scottsdale. A celebration of all things cowboy, from Western movies to music. There's a chuck-wagon cook-off, a mountain-man rendezvous, even horseback shooting contests. Call ✆ **602/996-4387,** or go to www.festivalofthe west.com. Mid-March.

Wa:k Pow Wow, Tucson. Tohono O'odham celebration at Mission San Xavier del Bac, featuring many Southwestern Native American groups. Call ✆ **520/294-5727.** Second weekend in March.

Yaqui Easter Lenten Ceremony, Tucson. Religious ceremonies at Old Pasqua Village blending Christian and Yaqui Native American beliefs. Call ✆ **520/791-4609.** Week before Easter.

Territorial Days, Tombstone. Tombstone's birthday celebration. Call ✆ **888/457-3929,** or go to www.tombstone.org. Mid-March.

Thunderbird Balloon & Air Classic, Phoenix metro area. More than 150 hot-air balloons fill the Arizona sky. Call ✆ **888/435-9746,** or go to www.thunderbirdballoonandair classic.com. Late March.

Welcome Back Buzzards, Superior. A flock of turkey vultures (buzzards) arrives annually at the Boyce Thompson Arboretum to roost in the eucalyptus trees, and this festival celebrates their arrival. Call ✆ **520/689-2811.** Late March.

April

Tucson International Mariachi Conference. Mariachi bands from all over the world come to compete before standing-room-only crowds. Call ✆ **520/838-3908,** or go to www.tucsonmariachi.org. Mid- to late April.

May

Cinco de Mayo, Phoenix and other cities. Celebration of the Mexican victory over the French in a famous 1862 battle, complete with food, music, and dancing. Call ✆ **602/ 279-4669** for details on the festivities in Phoenix. Around May 5.

Waila Festival, Tucson. A festival celebrating the social dances of the Tohono O'odham nation, featuring "chicken scratch" music—a kind of polka—and native foods. Call ✆ **520/806-9004.** Early to mid-May.

Wyatt Earp Days, Tombstone. Gunfight reenactments in memory of the shootout at the O.K. Corral. Call © **888/457-3929,** 520/457-3291, or go to www.tombstone.org. Late May.

Phippen Museum Fine Art Show and Sale, Prescott. This is the premier Western-art sale. Call © **928/778-1385,** or go to www.phippen artmuseum.org. Memorial Day weekend.

June

Prescott Frontier Days, Prescott. This is one of the state's two rodeos that claim to be the nation's oldest. Call © **800/358-1888** or 928/445-4320, or go to www.worlds oldestrodeo.com. Early July.

July

Annual Hopi Marketplace, Flagstaff. Exhibition and sale at the Museum of Northern Arizona, including cultural events. Call © **928/774-5213.** Early July.

Sidewalk Egg-frying Challenge, Oatman. In the ghost town of Oatman, located near one of the hottest places on earth, contestants use their own devices such as mirrors to fry an egg in 15 minutes. Call © **928/768-6222.** July 4th at high noon.

Independence Day. For information on fireworks displays in Phoenix, call © **602/534-FEST;** for Tucson, phone © **520/624-1817.** For other areas, contact the local chamber of commerce. July 4th.

August

Annual Navajo Marketplace, Flagstaff. Exhibition and sale at the Museum of Northern Arizona, including cultural events. Call © **928/774-5213.** First weekend in August.

Southwest Wings Birding Festival, Bisbee. Spotting hummingbirds and looking for owls and bats keep participants busy. Includes lectures and field trips throughout southeastern Arizona and Sonora, Mexico. Call © **800/946-4777** or 520/432-5421, or go to www.sw wings.org. Early August.

World's Oldest Continuous Rodeo, Payson. The second of Arizona's rodeos claiming to be the country's oldest. Call © **800/672-9766** or 928/474-4515. Mid-August.

Arizona Cowboy Poets' Gathering, Prescott. Not just traditional and contemporary poetry, but also storytelling that focuses on the cowboy lifestyle. Call © **877/928-4253** or 928/445-3122, or go to www.sharlot.org. Third weekend in August.

September

Navajo Nation Fair, Window Rock. A very large fair featuring traditional music and dancing, a fry bread contest, and more. Call © **928/871-6647,** or go to www.navajonationfair.com. Early September.

Grand Canyon Music Festival, Grand Canyon Village. For more than 20 years, this festival has been bringing classical music to the South Rim of the Grand Canyon. Call © **800/997-8285** or 928/638-9215, or go to www.grandcanyon musicfest.org. Mid-September.

Jazz on the Rocks, Sedona. Jazz festival held amid the red rocks of Sedona. Call © **928/282-1985,** or go to www.sedonajazz.com. Late September.

October

Sedona Arts Festival, Sedona. One of the better arts festivals in the state. Call © **928/204-9456.** Mid-October.

Arizona State Fair, Phoenix. Rodeos, top-name entertainment, and ethnic food. Call ☎ **602/252-6771,** or go to www.azstatefair.com. Mid- to late October.

Helldorado Days, Tombstone. Fashion show of 1880s, tribal dancers, and street entertainment. Call ☎ **888/457-3929** or 520/457-3291, or go to www.tombstone.org. Third weekend in October.

Cowboy Artists of America Annual Sale & Exhibition, Phoenix. The Phoenix Art Museum hosts the most prestigious and best-known Western-art show in the region. Call ☎ **602/257-1222,** or go to www.phxart.org. Late October to mid-November.

December

Luminaria Nights, Tucson. A glowing display of holiday lights at the Tucson Botanical Gardens. Call ☎ **520/326-9686.** First weekend in December.

Festival of Lights, Sedona. Thousands of luminarias are lit at dusk at the Tlaquepaque Arts and Crafts Village. Call ☎ **928/282-4838,** or go to www.tlaq.com. Mid-December.

Pueblo Grande Museum Indian Market, Phoenix. Largest market of its kind in the state, featuring more than 500 Native American artisans. Call ☎ **877/706-4408** or 602/495-0901, or go to www.pueblogrande.com. Second full weekend in December.

Fiesta Bowl Parade, Phoenix area. Huge, nationally televised parade, featuring floats and marching bands. Call ☎ **800/635-5748** or 480/350-0900, or got to www.tostitosfiestabowl.com. Late December.

5 Insurance

Check your existing insurance policies and credit card coverage before you buy travel insurance. You may already be covered for lost luggage, canceled tickets, or medical expenses. The cost of travel insurance varies widely, depending on the cost and length of your trip, your age, health, and the type of trip you're taking.

TRIP-CANCELLATION INSURANCE Trip-cancellation insurance helps you get your money back if you have to back out of a trip, if you have to go home early, or if your travel supplier goes bankrupt. Allowed reasons for cancellation can range from sickness to natural disasters to the State Department declaring your destination unsafe for travel. (Insurers usually won't cover vague fears, though, as many travelers discovered who tried to cancel their trips in Oct 2001 because they were wary of flying.) In this unstable world, trip-cancellation insurance is a good buy if you're

getting tickets well in advance—who knows what the state of the world, or of your airline, will be in 9 months? Insurance policy details vary, so read the fine print and especially make sure that your airline or cruise line is on the list of carriers covered in case of bankruptcy. For information, contact one of the following insurers: **Access America** (☎ 866/807-3982; www.accessamerica.com); **Travel Guard International** (☎ 800/826-4919; www.travelguard.com); **Travel Insured International** (☎ 800/243-3174; www.travelinsured.com); and **Travelex Insurance Services** (☎ 888/457-4602; www.travelex-insurance.com).

MEDICAL INSURANCE Most health insurance policies cover you if you get sick away from home, but check, particularly if you're insured by an HMO. If you require additional medical insurance, try **MEDEX International** (☎ 800/527-0218 or 410/453-6300; www.medexassist.com);

Travel Assistance International (© **800/821-2828;** www.travel assistance.com; or **Worldwide Assistance Services** (© **800/777-8710** or 202/331-1609; www.worldwide assistance.com).

LOST-LUGGAGE INSURANCE

On domestic flights, checked baggage is covered up to $2,500 per ticketed passenger. On international flights (including U.S. portions of international trips), baggage is limited to $9.07 per pound, up to approximately $640 per checked bag. If you plan to check items more valuable than the standard liability, see if your valuables are covered by your homeowner's policy, get baggage insurance as part of your comprehensive travel-insurance package, or buy Travel Guard's "Property Protect" product. Don't buy insurance at the airport, as it's usually overpriced. Be sure to take any valuables or irreplaceable items with you in your carry-on luggage, as many valuables (including books, money, and electronics) aren't covered by airline policies.

If your luggage is lost, immediately file a lost-luggage claim at the airport, detailing the luggage contents. For most airlines, you must report delayed, damaged, or lost baggage within 4 hours of arrival. The airlines are required to deliver luggage, once found, directly to your house or destination free of charge.

6 Health & Safety

STAYING HEALTHY

If you've never been to the desert before, be sure to prepare yourself for this harsh environment. No matter what time of year it is, the desert sun is strong and bright. Use sunscreen when outdoors—particularly if you're up in the mountains, where the altitude makes sunburn more likely. The bright sun also makes sunglasses a necessity.

Even if you don't feel hot in the desert, the dry air steals moisture from your body, so drink plenty of fluids. You may want to use a body lotion as well; skin dries out quickly in the desert.

It's not only the sun that makes the desert a harsh environment. There are poisonous creatures out here, too, but with a little common sense and some precautions you can avoid them. Rattlesnakes are very common, but your chances of meeting one are slight—they tend not to come out in the heat of the day. However, never stick your hand into holes among the rocks in the desert, and look to see where you're going to step before putting your foot down.

Arizona is also home to a large poisonous lizard called the Gila monster. These black-and-orange lizards are far less common than rattlesnakes, and your chances of meeting one are very slight.

Although the tarantula has developed a nasty reputation, the tiny black widow is more likely to cause illness. Scorpions are another danger of the desert. Be extra careful when turning over rocks or logs that might harbor either black widows or scorpions.

If you plan to do any camping or backcountry travel in the Four Corners region, which is where the Navajo and Hopi Indian reservations are located, you should be aware of hantavirus. This virus is spread by mice and is often fatal. Symptoms include fatigue, fever, and muscle aches; should you come down with any such symptoms within 1 to 5 weeks of traveling through the Four Corners area, see a doctor and mention that you have been in an area where hantavirus is known to occur.

If you're worried about getting sick away from home, consider purchasing medical travel insurance. (In most cases, your existing health plan will provide the coverage you need.) See the section on insurance, above, for more information.

If you suffer from a chronic illness, consult your doctor before your departure. For conditions such as epilepsy, diabetes, or heart problems, wear a **Medic Alert Identification Tag** (© **888/633-4298** or 209/668-3333; www.medicalert.org), which will immediately alert doctors to your condition and give them access to your records through a 24-hour hot line.

If you do get sick, consider asking your hotel concierge to recommend a local doctor—even his or her own.

You can also try the emergency room at a local hospital; many have walk-in clinics for emergency cases that are not life-threatening. You may not get immediate attention, but you won't pay the high price of an emergency-room visit (usually a minimum of $300 just for signing your name).

THE SAFE TRAVELER

When driving long distances, always carry plenty of drinking water, and if you're heading off onto dirt roads, extra water for your car's radiator as well. When hiking or walking in the desert, keep an eye out for rattlesnakes; these poisonous snakes are not normally aggressive unless provoked, so give them a wide berth.

7 Specialized Travel Resources

TRAVELERS WITH DISABILITIES

Most disabilities shouldn't stop anyone from traveling. There are more options and resources out there than ever before.

The U.S. National Park Service offers a **Golden Access Passport** that gives free lifetime entrance to all properties administered by the National Park Service—national parks, monuments, historic sites, recreation areas, and national wildlife refuges—for persons who are blind or permanently disabled, regardless of age. You may pick up a Golden Access Passport at any NPS entrance fee area by showing proof of medically determined disability and eligibility for receiving benefits under federal law. Besides free entry, the Golden Access Passport also offers a 50% discount on federal fees charged for using such facilities as campgrounds and boat launches, as well as on tours. For more information, go to www.nps.gov/fees_passes. htm or call © **888/467-2757.**

Many travel agencies offer customized tours and itineraries for travelers with disabilities. **Flying Wheels**

Travel (© **507/451-5005;** www.flyingwheelstravel.com) offers escorted tours and cruises that emphasize sports and private tours in minivans with lifts. **Accessible Journeys** (© **800/846-4537** or 610/521-0339; www.disabilitytravel.com) caters specifically to slow walkers and wheelchair travelers and their families and friends. **Wilderness Inquiry** (© **800/ 728-0719** or 612/676-9400; www. wildernessinquiry.org) offers trips to the Grand Canyon for persons of all abilities.

Organizations that offer assistance to travelers with disabilities include the **MossRehab Hospital** (© **800/ CALL-MOSS;** www.mossresource net.org), which provides a library of accessible-travel resources online; the **Society for Accessible Travel and Hospitality** (© **212/447-7284;** www.sath.org; annual membership fees: $45 adults, $30 seniors and students), which offers a wealth of travel resources for all types of disabilities and informed recommendations on destinations, access guides, travel agents, tour operators, vehicle rentals, and companion services; and the

American Foundation for the Blind (© 800/232-5463; www.afb.org), which provides information on traveling with Seeing Eye dogs.

For more information specifically targeted to travelers with disabilities, the community website **iCan** (www.icanonline.net/channels/travel/index.cfm) has destination guides and several regular columns on accessible travel. Also check out the quarterly magazine *Emerging Horizons* ($15 per year, $20 outside the U.S.; www.emerginghorizons.com); and *Open World Magazine* ($13 per year, $21 outside the U.S.), published by the Society for Accessible Travel and Hospitality (see above). **Mobility International USA** (© 541/343-1284; www.miusa.org) publishes *A World of Options,* a book of resources covering everything from biking trips to scuba outfitters.

GAY & LESBIAN TRAVELERS

As elsewhere in the country, the major cities in Arizona (Phoenix and Tucson) are large enough to support businesses and organizations catering specifically to the gay and lesbian communities. On the Web, check out **www.azgays.com**, which has links to gay and lesbian organizations all over the state. Also try **www.visitgayarizona.com**. To get in touch with the Phoenix gay community, contact the **1n10** (© 602/234-2752; www.1n10.org). At the community center and at gay bars around Phoenix, you can pick up various gay-oriented local publications.

Wingspan, 300 E. Sixth St., Tucson (© 520/624-1779; www.wingspanaz.org), is southern Arizona's lesbian, gay, bisexual, and transgender community center. *Tucson Observer* (www.tucsonobserver.com) is a local Tucson gay newspaper available at both Wingspan and **Antigone Bookstore,** 411 N. Fourth Ave. (© 520/792-3715).

Out and About (© 415/834-6411; www.outandabout.com) offers guidebooks and a newsletter packed with solid information on the global gay and lesbian scene.

SENIORS

Mention the fact that you're a senior when you first make your travel reservations—most major airlines offer discounts for seniors. Carry photo ID to avail yourself of senior discounts at attractions, at accommodations, and on public transportation.

Members of **AARP,** 601 E St. NW, Washington, DC 20049 (© 888/687-2277; www.aarp.org), get discounts on many lodgings, airfares, car rentals, and attractions throughout Arizona. Anyone age 50 or older can join.

The U.S. National Park Service offers a **Golden Age Passport** that gives seniors 62 and older lifetime entrance to most national parks and monuments for a one-time processing fee of $10. It must be purchased in person at any NPS facility that charges an entrance fee. Besides free entry, a Golden Age Passport also offers a 50% discount on federal fees for parking, camping, boat launching, tours, and other activities. For more information, go to www.nps.gov/fees_passes.htm or call © 888/GO-PARKS.

Many reliable agencies and organizations target the 50-plus market. **Elderhostel** (© 877/426-8056; www.elderhostel.org) arranges study programs for those ages 55 and over (and a spouse or companion of any age). Most U.S. courses last 5 to 7 days, and many include airfare, accommodations in university dormitories or modest inns, meals, and tuition.

Recommended publications offering travel resources and discounts for seniors include: the quarterly magazine *Travel 50 & Beyond* (www.travel50andbeyond.com); *Travel*

Unlimited: Uncommon Adventures for the Mature Traveler (Avalon); and *Unbelievably Good Deals and Great Adventures That You Absolutely Can't Get Unless You're Over 50* (McGraw-Hill).

FAMILIES

In summer, families flock to the Grand Canyon, often on a road trip that also takes in the canyon country of southern Utah. Remember, distances are great out here. Don't expect to find someplace to eat whenever the kids are hungry; pack food before heading out on a long drive. Also bring plenty to entertain the kids as you drive for hours through uninteresting scenery.

Be sure to check out "The Best Family Experiences," "The Best Family Vacations," and "The Best Family Resorts" sections in chapter 1. If you are planning to visit Phoenix or Tucson, see "Family-Friendly Hotels" (p. 333) and "Family-Friendly Restaurants" (p. 109 and 353), as well as "Especially for Kids" sections (p. 128 and 368) under "Seeing the Sights."

You can find good family-oriented vacation advice on the Internet from sites such as **Family Travel Network** (www.familytravelnetwork.com) and **Family Travel Files** (www.thefamily travelfiles.com). The latter offers an online magazine and a directory of off-the-beaten-path tours and tour operators for families.

Frommer's Family Vacations in the National Parks (Wiley Publishing, Inc.) has tips for enjoying your trip to Grand Canyon National Park. *How to Take Great Trips with Your Kids* (The Harvard Common Press) is full of good general advice that can apply to travel anywhere.

8 Planning Your Trip Online

SURFING FOR AIRFARES

The "big three" online travel agencies, **Expedia.com, Travelocity,** and **Orbitz,** sell most of the air tickets bought on the Internet. (Canadian travelers should try expedia.ca and Travelocity.ca; U.K. residents can go to expedia.co.uk.) Each has different business deals with the airlines and may offer different fares on the same flights, so it's wise to shop around. Expedia and Travelocity will also send you **e-mail notification** when a cheap fare becomes available to your favorite destination.

Also remember to check **airline websites,** especially those for low-fare carriers such as Southwest, whose fares are often misreported or simply missing from travel agency websites. Even with major airlines, you can often shave a few bucks from a fare by booking directly through the airline and avoiding a travel agency's transaction fee. But you'll get these discounts only by **booking online:** Most airlines now offer online-only fares that even their phone agents know nothing about. For the websites of airlines that fly to and from your destination, see "Getting There," below.

Great **last-minute deals** are available through free weekly e-mail services provided directly by the airlines. Most of these are announced on Tuesday or Wednesday and must be purchased online. Most are valid only for travel that weekend, but some (such as Southwest's) can be booked weeks or months in advance. Sign up for weekly e-mail alerts at airline websites, or check mega-sites that compile comprehensive lists of last-minute specials, such as **Smarter Living** (www.smarterliving.com). For last-minute trips, **Site59** (www.site59.com) in the U.S. and **Lastminute** (www.lastminute.com) in Europe often have better deals than the major-label sites.

If you're willing to give up some control over your flight details, use an **opaque fare service** like **Priceline** (www.priceline.com; www.priceline. co.uk for Europeans) or **Hotwire** (www.hotwire.com). Both offer rock-bottom prices in exchange for travel on a "mystery airline" at a mysterious time of day, often with a mysterious change of planes enroute. The mystery airlines are all major, well-known carriers—and the possibility of being sent from Philadelphia to Chicago via Tampa is remote; the airlines' routing computers have gotten a lot better than they used to be. But your chances of getting a 6am or 11pm flight are pretty high. Hotwire tells you flight prices before you buy; Priceline usually has better deals than Hotwire, but you have to play their "name your price" game. If you're new at this, the helpful folks at **BiddingForTravel** (www.biddingfortravel.com) do a good job of demystifying Priceline's system. Priceline and Hotwire are great for flights within North America and between the U.S. and Europe.

For much more about airfares and savvy air-travel tips and advice, pick up a copy of *Frommer's Fly Safe, Fly Smart* (Wiley Publishing, Inc.).

SURFING FOR HOTELS

Shopping online for hotels is fairly easy in the U.S., although many smaller hotels and B&Bs don't show up on websites at all. Of the "big three" sites, **Expedia** may be the best choice, thanks to its long list of special deals. **Travelocity** runs a close second. Hotel specialist sites **hotels.com** and **hoteldiscounts.com** are also reliable. An excellent free program, **TravelAxe** (www.travelaxe.net), can help you search multiple hotel sites at once.

Priceline and Hotwire are even better for hotels than for airfares; with both, you're allowed to pick the neighborhood and quality level of your hotel before offering up your money. Priceline's hotel product is better at getting five-star lodging for three-star prices than at finding anything at the bottom of the scale. *Note:* Hotwire overrates its hotels by one star—what Hotwire calls a four-star is a three-star anywhere else.

SURFING FOR RENTAL CARS

For booking rental cars online, the best deals are usually found at rental-car company websites, although all the major online travel agencies also offer rental-car reservations services.

Frommers.com: The Complete Travel Resource

For an excellent travel-planning resource, we highly recommend Frommers.com (www.frommers.com). We're a little biased, of course, but we guarantee that you'll find the travel tips, reviews, monthly vacation giveaways, and online-booking capabilities indispensable. Among the special features are our popular **Message Boards,** where Frommer's readers post queries and share advice (sometimes we authors even show up to answer questions); **Frommers.com Newsletter,** for the latest travel bargains and insider travel secrets; and **Frommer's Destinations Section,** where you'll get expert travel tips, hotel and dining recommendations, and advice on the sights to see for more than 3,000 destinations around the globe. When your research is done, the **Online Reservations System** (www.frommers.com/book_a_trip) takes you to Frommer's preferred online partners for booking your vacation at affordable prices.

Priceline and Hotwire work well for rental cars, too; the only "mystery" is which major rental company you get, and for most travelers the difference between Hertz, Avis, and Budget is negligible.

9 The 21st-Century Traveler

INTERNET ACCESS AWAY FROM HOME

Travelers have any number of ways to check their e-mail and access the Internet on the road. Of course, using your own laptop—or even a PDA (personal digital assistant) or electronic organizer with a modem—gives you the most flexibility. But even if you don't have a computer, you can still access your e-mail and even your office computer from cybercafes.

WITHOUT YOUR OWN COMPUTER

It's hard nowadays to find a city that *doesn't* have a few cybercafes. Although there's no definitive directory for cybercafes—these are independent businesses, after all—three places to start looking are at **www.cybercaptive. com** and **www.cybercafe.com**.

Aside from formal cybercafes, most **public libraries** across the country offer Internet access free or for a small charge. **Hotels** that cater to business travelers often have **in-room dataports** and **business centers,** but the charges can be exorbitant. Also, most **youth hostels** have at least one computer with access to the Internet.

To retrieve your e-mail, ask your **Internet Service Provider (ISP)** if it has a Web-based interface tied to your existing e-mail account. If your ISP doesn't have such an interface, you can use the free **mail2web** service (www. mail2web.com) to view (but not reply to) your home e-mail. For more flexibility, you may want to open a free, Web-based e-mail account with **Yahoo! Mail** (mail.yahoo.com). (Microsoft's Hotmail is another popular option, but Hotmail has severe spam problems.) Your home ISP may be able to forward your e-mail to the Web-based account automatically.

WITH YOUR OWN COMPUTER

Major ISPs have **local access numbers** around the world, allowing you to go online by simply placing a local call. Check your ISP's website or call its toll-free number and ask how you can use your current account away from home, and how much it will cost.

If you're traveling outside the reach of your ISP, the **iPass** network has dial-up numbers in most of the world's countries. You'll have to sign up with an iPass provider, who will then tell you how to set up your computer for your destinations. For a list of iPass providers, go to www.ipass. com and click on "individuals." One solid provider is **i2roam** (© **866/ 811-6209** or 920/233-5863; www. i2roam.com).

Wherever you go, bring a **connection kit** of the right power and phone adapters, a spare phone cord, and a spare Ethernet network cable.

Most business-class hotels offer dataports for laptop modems, and many hotels now also offer high-speed Internet access using an Ethernet network cable. You'll have to bring your own cables either way, so **call your hotel in advance** to find out what the options are.

Many business-class hotels in the U.S. also offer a form of computer-free Web browsing through the room TV set.

If you have an 802.11b/**wi-fi** card for your computer, several commercial companies have made wireless service available in airports, hotel lobbies, and coffee shops, primarily in the U.S.

Online Traveler's Toolbox

Veteran travelers usually carry some essential items to make their trips easier. Following is a selection of online tools to bookmark and use.

- **Visa ATM Locator** (www.visa.com), for locations of Plus ATMs worldwide, or MasterCard ATM Locator (www.mastercard.com), for locations of Cirrus ATMs worldwide.
- **The Weather Underground** (www.wunderground.com) and **Weather.com** (www.weather.com) provide weather forecasts.
- **Mapquest** (www.mapquest.com). This is the best of the mapping sites and lets you choose a specific address or destination, and in seconds, it will return a map and detailed directions.

T-Mobile Hotspot (www.t-mobile. com/hotspot) serves up wireless connections at Starbucks coffee shops nationwide. **Boingo** (www.boingo. com) and **Wayport** (www.wayport. com) have set up networks in airports and high-class hotel lobbies. Best of all, you don't need to be staying at the Four Seasons to use the hotel's network; just set yourself up on a nice couch in the lobby.

USING A CELLPHONE ACROSS THE U.S.

Just because your cellphone works at home doesn't mean it'll work elsewhere in the country. It's a good bet that your phone will work in major cities, but take a look at your wireless company's coverage map on its website before heading out— T-Mobile, Sprint, and Nextel are particularly weak in rural areas. If you need to stay in touch at a destination where you know your phone won't work, **rent** a phone that does from **InTouch USA** (© **800/872-7626;** www.intouchglobal.com) or a rental-car location, but be aware that you'll pay $1 a minute or more for airtime.

10 Getting There

BY PLANE

Arizona is served by many airlines flying to both Phoenix and Tucson from cities around the United States. Phoenix is the more centrally located of the two airports and is closer to the Grand Canyon. However, if you're planning on exploring the southern part of the state or are going to visit both Phoenix and Tucson, we recommend flying into Tucson, which is a smaller airport and charges slightly lower taxes on its car rentals. If a trip to the Grand Canyon is your only reason for visiting Arizona, consider flying into Las Vegas, which sometimes has lower airfares and better car-rental rates.

Phoenix and Tucson are both served by the following major airlines:

Alaska Airlines © 800/252-7522; www.alaskaair.com

America West © 800/235-9292; www.americawest.com

American © 800/433-7300; www.aa.com

Continental © 800/523-3273; www.continental.com

Delta © 800/221-1212; www.delta.com

Frontier © 800/432-1359; www.flyfrontier.com

Northwest/KLM © 800/225-2525; www.nwa.com
Southwest © 800/435-9792; www.southwest.com
United © 800/864-8331; www.ual.com

The following airlines serve Phoenix but not Tucson:

Air Canada © 888/247-2262; www.aircanada.ca
British Airways © 800/247-9297; www.britishairways.com
US Airways © 800/428-4322; www.usairways.com

The following airline serves Tucson but not Phoenix:

Horizon © 800/547-9308; www.horizonair.com

GETTING THROUGH THE AIRPORT

With the federalization of airport security, security procedures at U.S. airports are more stable and consistent than ever. Generally, you'll be fine if you arrive at the airport **1 hour** before a domestic flight and **2 hours** before an international flight; if you show up late, tell an airline employee and she'll probably whisk you to the front of the line.

Bring a **current government-issued photo ID** such as a driver's license or passport, and if you've got an e-ticket, print out the **official confirmation page;** you'll need to show your confirmation at the security checkpoint, and your ID at the ticket counter or the gate. (Children under 18 do not need photo IDs for domestic flights, but the adults checking in with them do.)

Security lines have gotten shorter than they were a couple of years ago, but some doozies remain. If you have trouble standing for long periods of time, tell an airline employee; the airline will provide a wheelchair. Speed up security by **not wearing metal objects** such as big belt buckles or clanky earrings. If you've got metallic

body parts, a note from your doctor can prevent a long chat with the security screeners. Keep in mind that only **ticketed passengers** are allowed past security, except for individuals escorting disabled passengers or children.

Federalization has stabilized the regulations for **what you can carry on** and **what you can't.** The general rule is that sharp things are out, nail clippers are okay, and food and beverages must be passed through the X-ray machine. Bring food in your carry-on rather than checking it, as explosive-detection machines used on checked luggage have been known to mistake food (especially chocolate) for bombs. Travelers in the U.S. are allowed one carry-on bag, plus a "personal item" such as a purse, briefcase, or laptop bag. Carry-on hoarders can stuff all sorts of things into a laptop bag; as long as it has a laptop in it, it's still considered a personal item. The Transportation Security Administration (TSA) has issued a list of restricted items; check its website (www.tsa.gov/public/index.jsp) for details.

In 2003 the TSA phased out **gate check-in** at all U.S. airports. Passengers with e-tickets and without checked bags can still beat the ticket-counter lines by using **electronic kiosks** or even **online check-in.** Ask your airline which alternatives are available, and if you're using a kiosk, bring the credit card you used to book the ticket. If you're checking bags, you will still be able to use most airlines' kiosks; again call your airline for up-to-date information. **Curbside check-in** is also a good way to avoid lines, although a few airlines still ban curbside check-in entirely; call before you go.

The TSA also recommends that you **do not lock your checked luggage** so screeners can search it by hand if necessary. The agency says to use plastic "zip ties" instead, which can be bought at hardware stores and can be easily cut off.

FLYING FOR LESS: TIPS FOR GETTING THE BEST AIRFARE

Passengers sharing the same airplane cabin rarely pay the same fare. Travelers who need to purchase tickets at the last minute, change their itinerary at a moment's notice, or fly one-way often get stuck paying the premium rate. Here are some ways to keep your airfare costs down.

- Passengers who can book their ticket **long in advance,** who can **stay over Saturday night,** or who **fly midweek** or **at less-trafficked hours** will pay a fraction of the full fare. If your schedule is flexible, say so, and ask if you can secure a cheaper fare by changing your flight plans.
- You can also save on airfares by keeping an eye out in local newspapers for **promotional specials** or **fare wars,** when airlines lower prices on their most popular routes. You rarely see fare wars offered for peak travel times, but if you can travel in the off-months, you may snag a bargain.
- Search **the Internet** for cheap fares (see "Planning Your Trip Online," earlier in this chapter).
- **Consolidators,** also known as bucket shops, are great sources for international tickets, although they usually can't beat the Internet on fares within North America. Start by looking in Sunday newspaper travel sections; U.S. travelers should focus on the *New York Times, Los Angeles Times,* and *Miami Herald.* For less-developed destinations, small travel agents who cater to immigrant communities in large cities often have the best deals. *Beware:* Bucket-shop tickets are usually nonrefundable or rigged with stiff cancellation penalties, often as high as 50% to 75% of the ticket price, and some put you on charter airlines with

questionable safety records. Several reliable consolidators are worldwide and available on the Net. **FlyCheap** (© 800/FLY-CHEAP; www.flycheap.com) has especially good access to fares for sunny destinations. **Air Tickets Direct** (© 800/778-3447; www. airticketsdirect.com) is based in Montreal and leverages the currently weak Canadian dollar for low fares.

- Join **frequent-flier clubs.** Accrue enough miles and you'll be rewarded with free flights and elite status. It's free, and you'll get the best choice of seats, faster response to phone inquiries, and prompter service if your luggage is stolen, your flight is canceled or delayed, or if you want to change your seat. You don't need to fly to build frequent-flier miles—**frequent-flier credit cards** can provide thousands of miles for doing your everyday shopping.
- For many more tips about air travel, including a rundown of the major frequent-flier credit cards, pick up a copy of *Frommer's Fly Safe, Fly Smart* (Wiley Publishing, Inc.).

BY CAR

The distance to Phoenix from Los Angeles is approximately 369 miles; from San Francisco, 778 miles; from Las Vegas, 287 miles; from Albuquerque, 455 miles; from Santa Fe, 516 miles; and from Salt Lake City, 660 miles.

If you're planning to drive through northern Arizona anytime in the winter, bring chains.

BY TRAIN

Amtrak (© 800/872-7245; www. amtrak.com) provides service aboard the *Southwest Chief* between Flagstaff (for the Grand Canyon) and Los Angeles, Albuquerque, Kansas City, and Chicago. The *Sunset Limited* connects Tucson with Orlando, New Orleans, Houston, San Antonio, El Paso, and Los Angeles. At press time, the fare from Los Angeles to Flagstaff was as low as $50 one-way and $100 round-trip. There is no rail service to Phoenix, but Amtrak *will* sell you a ticket and then put you on a bus from either Tucson or Flagstaff to Phoenix. Earlier bookings secure lower fares.

11 Escorted Tours, Package Deals & Special-Interest Vacations

Before you start your search for the lowest airfare, you may want to consider booking your flight as part of an escorted tour or a package tour. What you lose in adventure, you'll gain in time and money saved when you book accommodations, and maybe even food and entertainment, along with your flight.

PACKAGE TOURS FOR INDEPENDENT TRAVELERS

Package tours are not the same thing as escorted tours. With a package tour, you travel independently but pay a group rate. Packages usually include airfare, a choice of hotels, and car rentals. In many cases, a package that includes airfare, hotel, and transportation to and from the airport will cost you less than just the hotel alone would have, had you booked it yourself. That's because packages are sold in bulk to tour operators—who resell them to the public at a cost that drastically undercuts standard rates.

One good source of package deals is the airlines themselves. Most major airlines offer air/land packages, including **American Airlines Vacations** (© 800/321-2121; www.aavacations.com), **Continental Airlines Vacations** (© 800/301-3800; www.covacations.com), **Delta Vacations** (© 800/654-6559; www.deltavacations.com), **United Vacations** (© 888/854-3899; www.unitedvacations.com), and **US Airways Vacations** (© 800/422-3861; www.usairwaysvacations.com).

Several big **online travel agencies**—Expedia, Travelocity, Orbitz, and Site59—also do a brisk business in packages. If you're unsure about the pedigree of a smaller packager, check with the Better Business Bureau in the city where the company is based, or go online at www.bbb.org. If a packager won't tell you where it's based, don't fly with them. Packages are also advertised in the travel section of your local Sunday newspaper. Or check ads in national travel magazines such as *Arthur Frommer's Budget Travel Magazine, Travel & Leisure, National Geographic Traveler,* and *Condé Nast Traveler.*

ESCORTED TOURS

Escorted tours are structured group tours, with a group leader or guide. The price usually includes everything from airfare to hotels, meals, tours, admission costs, and local transportation.

Gray Line of Phoenix (© 800/732-0327 or 602/495-9100; www.graylinearizona.com) offers Arizona excursions lasting from 2 to 5 days. Tours include the Grand Canyon by way of Sedona and Oak Creek Canyon.

Maupintour (© 800/255-4266; http://maupintour.com), one of the largest tour operators in the world, offers an Arizona itinerary that covers the Grand Canyon, the Four Corners region, Phoenix, and Scottsdale.

SPECIAL-INTEREST VACATIONS

If you'd like to turn a trip to the Grand Canyon into an educational experience, contact the **Grand Canyon Field Institute,** P.O. Box 399, Grand

Canyon, AZ 86023 (© **866/471-4435;** www.grandcanyon.org/field institute), which offers a variety of programs from early spring to late fall. Examples include day hikes, photography and painting classes, backpacking trips for women, llama treks, archaeology trips, and plenty of guided hikes and backpacking trips with a natural-history or ecological slant.

Canyon Calling Tours, 200 Carol Canyon Dr., Sedona, AZ 86336 (© **800/664-8922;** www.canyon calling.com), offers week-long women-only tours that visit Canyon de Chelly, Lake Powell, the Grand Canyon, and Havasu Canyon. The cost is $1,695 per person.

Learning Expeditions, a program run by the **Arizona State Museum,** occasionally offers scholar-led archaeological tours, including a trip to Navajo and Hopi country. For information, contact the marketing department at the **Arizona State Museum,** P.O. Box 210026, Tucson, AZ 85721-0026 (© **520/626-8381;** www.statemuseum.arizona.edu). The **Museum of Northern Arizona,** 3101 N. Fort Valley Rd., Flagstaff, AZ 86001 (© **928/774-5211,** ext. 220; www.musnaz.org), offers educational backpacking, river-rafting, and van tours primarily in the Colorado Plateau in northern Arizona in a program called Ventures. Trips range from several days to more than a week.

If you have an interest in the Native American cultures of Arizona, contact **Crossing Worlds Journeys & Retreats,** P.O. Box 623, Sedona, AZ 86339 (© **800/350-2693** or 928/203-0024; www.crossingworlds. com), which offers tours throughout the Four Corners region, visiting the Hopi mesas as well as backcountry ruins on the Navajo Reservation.

The **Nature Conservancy,** 333 E. Virginia Ave., Suite 216, Phoenix, AZ 85004 (© **602/712-0048;** http:// nature.org), has seven Arizona preserves that are open to the public for hiking, bird-watching, and nature study and to which it operates educational field trips of 1 to 4 days.

If you enjoy the wilderness and want to get more involved in its preservation, consider a Sierra Club service trip. These trips are for the purpose of building, restoring, and maintaining hiking trails in wilderness areas. Contact the **Sierra Club Outings Department,** 85 Second St., 2nd Floor, San Francisco, CA 94105 (© **415/977-5522;** www.sierraclub. org). The Sierra Club also offers hiking, camping, and other adventure trips to various destinations in Arizona.

You can also join a work crew organized by the **Arizona Trail Association,** P.O. Box 36736, Phoenix, AZ 85067-6736 (© **602/252-4794;** www.aztrail.org). These crews spend 1 to 2 days building and maintaining various portions of the Arizona Trail, which will eventually stretch from the Utah state line to the Mexico border.

Another sort of service trip is offered by the National Park Service. It accepts volunteers to pick up garbage left by thoughtless visitors to Glen Canyon National Recreation Area. In exchange for picking up trash, you'll get to spend 5 days on a houseboat called the Trash Tracker, cruising through the gorgeous canyonlands of Lake Powell. Volunteers must be at least 18 years old, in good physical condition, and must provide their own food, sleeping bag, and transportation to the marina. For information, contact **Glen Canyon National Recreation Area,** P.O. Box 1507, Page, AZ 86040-1507 (© **928/608-6200**).

If you'd like to add a jaunt into Mexico to your Arizona trip, contact **Ajo Stage Line,** 1041 Solano St., Ajo,

AZ 85321 (© **800/942-1981** or 520/ 387-6467; www.rockypointonline. com/ajostage.htm). Owner Will Nelson leads tours to historic Spanish missions in Mexico, to El Pinacate (a remote desert wilderness on the Mexican border), and to the Gulf of California at Rocky Point, Mexico, as well as to Casas Grandes, the pottery center. Prices range from $60 to $395.

Finally, if you're interested in architecture or the ecology of urban design, you may want to help out on the continued construction of **Arcosanti,** the slow realization of Paolo Soleri's dream of a city that merges architecture and ecology. Located 70 miles north of Phoenix, Arcosanti offers 5-week learning-by-doing workshops ($1,175 per person). Contact Arcosanti, Attn: Workshop Coordinator, H.C. 74, Box 4136, Mayer, AZ 86333 (© **928/ 632-7135;** www.arcosanti.org).

In addition to these specialty-tour companies, you'll find outdoor-oriented tour companies mentioned below in "The Active Vacation Planner."

12 The Active Vacation Planner

Because Arizona is home to the Grand Canyon—the most widely known white-water-rafting spot in the world—the state is known for active, adventure-oriented vacations. For others, Arizona is synonymous with winter golf and tennis. Whichever category of active vacationer you fall into, you'll find information below to help you plan your trip.

BICYCLING With its wide range of climates, Arizona offers good biking somewhere in the state every month of the year. In winter, there's good road biking around Phoenix and Tucson, while from spring to fall, the southeastern corner of the state offers good routes. In summer, the White Mountains (in the eastern part of the state) and Kaibab National Forest (between Flagstaff and Grand Canyon National Park) offer good mountain biking. There's also excellent mountain biking at several Phoenix parks, and Tucson is one of the most bicycle-friendly cities in the country.

Backroads, 801 Cedar St., Berkeley, CA 94710-1800 (© **800/ 462-2848** or 510/527-1555; www. backroads.com), offers a 6-day, camping multisport trip through southern Utah and the Grand Canyon for around $1,300. **Western Spirit Cycling,** 478 Mill Creek Dr., Moab, UT 84532 (© **800/845-2453** or 435/259-8732; www.westernspirit. com), offers a number of interesting mountain-bike tours, including trips to both the North and South rims of the Grand Canyon and through the desert south of Tucson. Each trip is 5 days in duration and costs $895 to $925.

For information on mountain-bike tours and recommended rides in Phoenix and Tucson, see "Outdoor Pursuits" in chapters 4 and 9. You'll also find recommended rides in the Sedona and Prescott sections of chapter 5. If you plan to do much mountain-biking around the state, pick up a copy of *Fat Tire Tales and Trails,* by Cosmic Ray. This little book of rides is both fun to read and fun to use; it's available in bike shops around the state.

BIRD-WATCHING Arizona is a birder's bonanza. Down in the southeastern corner of the state, many species found primarily south of the border reach the northern limits of their territories. Combine this with several mountains that rise like islands from the desert and provide an appropriate habitat for hundreds of species, and you have some of the best bird-watching in the country.

Birding hot spots include Ramsey Canyon Preserve (known for its many species of hummingbirds), Cave Creek Canyon (nesting site for elegant trogons), Patagonia–Sonoita Creek Sanctuary (home to 22 species of fly-catchers, kingbirds, and phoebes, as well as Montezuma quails), Madera Canyon (another "mountain island" that attracts many of the same species seen at Ramsey Canyon and Sonoita Creek), Buenos Aires National Wildlife Refuge (home to masked bobwhite quails and gray hawks), and the sewage ponds outside the town of Willcox (known for avocets and sand-hill cranes). For further information on these birding spots, see chapter 10. To find out which birds have been spotted lately, call the **Tucson Audubon Society's Bird Report** (© **520/798-1005**).

Serious birders who want to be sure of adding lots of rare birds to their life lists may want to visit southeastern Arizona on a guided tour. These are available through **High Lonesome Ecotours,** 570 S. Little Bear Trail, Sierra Vista, AZ 85635 (© **800/ 743-2668;** www.hilonesome.com), which charges about $1,450 per person for an 8-day trip.

CANOEING/KAYAKING   Okay, so maybe these sports don't jump to mind when you think of the desert, but there are indeed rivers and lakes here (and they happen to be some of the best places to see wildlife). By far the most memorable place for a flat-water kayak tour is Lake Powell. **Wilderness Inquiry,** 808 14th Ave. SE, Minneapolis, MN 55414-1516 (© **800/728-0719** or 612/676-9400; www.wildernessinquiry.org), offers several 6-day trips on the lake each spring and fall. The cost is $795. **Arizona Canoe & Kayak Outfitters,** 107 E. Broadway Rd., Tempe, AZ 85282 (© **480/755-1924;** www. arizonakayak.com), offers various

canoeing and kayaking courses and tours.

There are also a couple of companies that rent canoes and offer trips on the Colorado River south of Lake Mead. See chapter 11 for details.

FISHING   The fishing scene in Arizona is as diverse as the landscape. Large and small lakes around the state offer excellent fishing for warm-water game fish such as largemouth, small-mouth, and striped bass. Good trout fishing can be found up on the Mogollon Rim and in the White Mountains there, as well as in the Grand Canyon and the more easily accessible sections of the free-running Colorado River between Glen Canyon Dam and Lees Ferry. In fact, this latter area is among the country's most fabled stretches of trout water.

Fishing licenses for nonresidents are available for 1 day, 5 days, 4 months, and 1 year. Various special stamps and licenses may also apply. Nonresident fees range from $13 for a 1-day license (valid for trout) to $52 for a 1-year license ($50 additional for a trout stamp). Keep in mind that if you're heading for an Indian reservation, you'll have to get a special permit for that reservation. For information, contact the **Arizona Game and Fish Department,** 2221 W. Greenway Rd., Phoenix, AZ 85023-4399 (© **866/ 462-0433** or 602/942-3000; www. azgfd.com).

GOLF   For many of Arizona's winter visitors, golf is the main attraction. The state's hundreds of golf courses range from easy public courses to PGA championship links that have challenged the best.

In Phoenix and Tucson, greens fees, like room rates, are seasonal. In the popular winter months, fees at resort courses range from about $90 to $250 for 18 holes, although this usually includes a mandatory golf-cart rental.

In summer, fees often drop to less than half this amount. Almost all resorts offer special golf packages as well.

For information on some of the state's top courses, see "Hot Links," below. For more information on golfing in Arizona, contact the **Arizona Golf Association,** 7226 N. 16th St., Suite 200, Phoenix, AZ 85020 (© **800/458-8484** in Arizona, or 602/ 944-3035; www.azgolf.org), which publishes a directory listing all the courses in the state. You can also access the directory online. In addition, you can pick up the *Official Arizona Golf Guide & Directory* at visitor bureaus, golf courses, and many hotels and resorts.

HIKING/BACKPACKING Arizona offers some of the most fascinating and challenging hiking in the country. All across the state's lowland deserts, there are parks and other public lands laced with trails that lead past saguaro cacti, to the tops of desert peaks, and deep into rugged canyons. The state also has vast forests that contain wilderness areas and many more miles of hiking trails. In northern Arizona, there are good day hikes in Grand Canyon National Park, in the San Francisco Peaks north of Flagstaff, near Page and Lake Powell, and in Navajo National Monument. In the Phoenix area, popular day hikes include the trails up Camelback Mountain and Piestewa (Squaw) Peak and the many trails in South Mountain Park. In the Tucson area, there are good hikes on Mount Lemmon and in Saguaro National Park, Sabino Canyon, and Catalina State Park. In the southern part of the state, there are good day hikes in Chiricahua National Monument, Coronado National Forest, the Nature Conservancy's Ramsey Canyon Preserve and Patagonia–Sonoita Creek Sanctuary, Cochise Stronghold, and Organ Pipe Cactus National Monument.

The state's two most unforgettable overnight backpack trips are the hike down to Phantom Ranch at the bottom of the Grand Canyon and the hike into Havasu Canyon, a side canyon of the Grand Canyon. Another popular backpacking trip is through Paria Canyon, beginning in Utah and ending in Arizona at Lees Ferry. There are also overnight opportunities in the San Francisco Peaks north of Flagstaff and in the White Mountains of eastern Arizona.

Guided backpacking trips of different durations and difficulty levels are offered by the **Grand Canyon Field Institute,** P.O. Box 399, Grand Canyon, AZ 86023 (© **866/471-4435;** www.grandcanyon.org/field institute), and **Discovery Treks,** 6890 Sunrise Dr., Suite 120-108, Tucson, AZ 85750 (© **888/256-8731** or 520/ 360-1418; www.discoverytreks.com).

Backroads, 801 Cedar St., Berkeley, CA 94710-1800 (© **800/462-2848** or 510/527-1555; www.backroads. com), better known for its bike trips, also offers a 6-day hiking/biking trip to Grand Canyon, Bryce Canyon, and Zion national parks for around $1,300.

HORSEBACK RIDING/WESTERN ADVENTURES All over Arizona there are stables where you can saddle up for short rides. Among the more scenic spots for riding are the Grand Canyon, Monument Valley Navajo Tribal Park, Canyon de Chelly National Monument, the red-rock country around Sedona, Phoenix's South Mountain Park, the foot of the Superstition Mountains east of Phoenix, and the foot of the Santa Catalina Mountains outside Tucson. See the individual chapters that follow for listings of riding stables; see below for information on overnight guided horseback rides.

Hot Links

You don't have to be a hotshot golfer to get all heated up over the prospect of a few rounds of golf in Arizona. Combine near-perfect golf weather most of the year with great views and some unique challenges, and you've got all the makings of a great game. Phoenix and Tucson are well-known as winter golf destinations, but the state also offers golf throughout the year at higher-altitude courses in such places as Prescott, Flagstaff, and the White Mountains.

State water-conservation legislation limits the acreage that Arizona golf courses can irrigate, which has given the state some of the most distinctive and difficult courses in the country. These desert or "target" courses are characterized by minimal fairways surrounded by natural desert landscapes. You might find yourself teeing off over the tops of cacti or searching for your ball amid boulders and mesquite. If your ball comes to rest in the desert, you can play the ball where it lies or, with a one-stroke penalty, drop it within two club lengths of the nearest point of grass (but no nearer the hole).

Keep in mind that resort courses and daily-fee public courses are not cheap. For most of the year, greens fees, which include cart rentals, range from around $100 to $200 or more. Municipal courses usually have greens fees of less than $40 for 18 holes, with cart rentals costing extra (usually about $20).

It might not seem so initially, but summer is really a good time to visit many of Arizona's golf resorts. No, they don't have air-conditioned golf carts or indoor courses, but in summer, greens fees can be less than half what they are in winter. How does $37 for a round on the famous Gold Course at the Wigwam Golf and Country Club sound?

The Phoenix metropolitan area has the greatest concentration of golf courses in the state. Whether you're looking to play one of the area's challenging top-rated resort courses or an economical-but-fun municipal course, you'll find plenty of choices.

For spectacular scenery at a resort course, it's just plain impossible to beat **The Boulders** (© **800/553-1717** or 480/488-9009), located north of Scottsdale in the town of Carefree. Elevated tee boxes beside giant balanced boulders are enough to distract anyone's concentration. Way over on the east side of the valley in Apache Junction, the **Gold Canyon Golf Resort** (© **800/827-5281** or 480/982-9449) has what have been rated as three of the best holes in the state: the 2nd, 3rd, and 4th holes on the Dinosaur Mountain course. Jumping over to Litchfield Park, on the far west side of the valley, you'll find the **Wigwam Golf and Country Club** (© **800/909-4224** or 623/935-3811) and its three 18-hole courses; the Gold Course here is legendary. The **Phoenician** (© **800/ 888-8234** or 480/423-2449) is another noteworthy resort course in the

Among the most popular guided adventures in Arizona are the mule rides down into the Grand Canyon. These trips vary in length from 1 to 2 days; for reservations and more information, call **Grand Canyon National** area. It has a mix of traditional and desert-style holes. The semiprivate **Troon North Golf Club** (© **888/TROON-US** or 480/585-5300), a course that seems only barely carved out of raw desert, garners the most local accolades (and charges some of the highest greens fees in the state). If you want to swing where the pros do, beg, borrow, or steal a tee time on the Stadium Course at the **Tournament Players Club (TPC) of Scottsdale** (© **888/400-4001** or 480/585-4334). The area's favorite municipal course is the **Papago Golf Course** (© **602/275-8428**), which has a killer 17th hole.

In recent years, Tucson has been giving the Valley of the Sun plenty of competition when it comes to great golf. Among the city's resort courses, the Mountain Course at the **Ventana Canyon Golf and Racquet Club** (© **520/577-4015**) is legendary, especially the spectacular 107-yard, par-3 hole 3. Likewise, the 8th hole on the Sunrise Course at **El Conquistador Country Club** (© **520/544-1800**) is among the most memorable par-3 holes in the area. If you want to play where the pros do, reserve a tee time at the **Omni Tucson National Golf Resort and Spa** (© **520/575-7540**), home of the Tucson Open. **Randolph North** (© **520/791-4161**), Tucson's best municipal course, is the site of the city's annual LPGA tournament. The **Silverbell Municipal Course** (© **520/791-5235**) boasts a bear of a par-5 17th hole, and at **Fred Enke Municipal Course** (© **520/791-2539**), you'll find the city's only desert-style golf course.

Courses worth trying in other parts of the state include the 18-hole course at **Rancho de los Caballeros** (© **928/684-2704**), a luxury guest ranch outside Wickenburg. *Golf Digest* has rated this course one of Arizona's top 10. For concentration-taxing scenery, few courses compare with the **Sedona Golf Resort** (© **928/284-9355**), which has good views of the red rocks; try to get a sunrise or twilight tee time. Way up in the Four Corners region, in the town of Page, you'll find the 27-hole **Lake Powell National Golf Course** (© **928/645-2023**), which is one of the most spectacular in the state. The fairways here wrap around the base of the red-sandstone bluff atop which sits the town of Page. South of Tucson, the recently renovated **Tubac Golf Resort** (© **800/848-7893** or 520/398-2211) has cows grazing along its fairways for a classic wild west feel. Along the Colorado River, there are a couple of memorable courses. Lake Havasu City's **London Bridge Golf Club** (© **928/855-2719**) offers a view of, you guessed it, the London Bridge. For more dramatic views, check out the **Emerald Canyon Golf Course** (© **928/667-3366**), a municipal course in Parker that plays up and down small canyons and offers the sort of scenery usually associated only with the most expensive desert resort courses.

Park Lodges/Xanterra Parks & Resorts (© **888/297-2757,** 303/297-2757, or, for last-minute reservations 928/638-2631; www.grandcanyon lodges.com). Be advised, however, that you'll need to make mule-ride reservations many months in advance. If at the last minute (1 or 2 days before you want to ride) you decide you want to go on a mule trip into the Grand Canyon, contact Grand Canyon National Park Lodges at its last-minute reservations phone number (see above) or stop by the **Bright Angel Transportation Desk,** in Grand Canyon Village, on the chance there might be space available.

It's also possible to do overnight horseback rides in various locations around the state. For information, contact **Richardson's D-Spur Ranch,** Peralta Rd. (P.O. Box 4587), Apache Junction, AZ 85278 (② **866/ 913-7787,** 602/810-7029, or 480/ 983-0833; www.dspurranch.com), which does overnight horseback trips to the Superstition Mountains; or **Arizona Trail Tours,** 320 Stable Lane, Rio Rico, AZ 85648 (② **800/477- 0615** or 520/281-4122; www.aztrail tours.com), which offers trips through the backcountry of southern Arizona.

Want to kick it up a notch? How about attending the **Arizona Cowboy College,** Lorill Equestrian Center, 30208 N. 152nd St., Scottsdale, AZ 85262 (② **888/330-8070** or 480/ 471-3151; www.cowboycollege.com), where you can literally learn the ropes and the brands and how to say, "Git along little dogie" like you really mean it. This is no city slicker's staged roundup; this is the real thing. You actually learn how to be a real cowboy. Six-day programs cost $1,500.

HOT-AIR BALLOONING For much of the year, the desert has the perfect environment for hot-air bal-looning—cool, still air and wide-open spaces. Consequently, there are dozens of ballooning companies operating across the state. Most are in Phoenix and Tucson, but several others operate near Sedona, which is by far the most picturesque spot in the state for a bal-loon ride. See the individual chapters for specific information.

HOUSEBOATING With the Col-orado River turned into a string of long lakes, houseboat vacations are a natural in Arizona. Although this doesn't have to be an active vacation, fishing, hiking, and swimming are usually part of a houseboat stay. Rentals are available on Lake Powell, Lake Mead, and Lake Mohave. The canyon scenery of Lake Powell makes it the hands-down best spot for a houseboat vacation—reserve well in advance for a summer trip. No prior experience (or license) is necessary, and plenty of hands-on instruction is provided before you leave the marina. See chapters 7 and 11 for more infor-mation on houseboat rentals.

SKIING Although Arizona is better known as a desert state, it does have plenty of mountains and even a few ski areas. The two biggest and best ski areas are **Arizona Snowbowl** (② **928/779-1951;** www.arizona snowbowl.com), outside Flagstaff, and **Sunrise Park Resort** (② **800/772- 7669** or 928/735-7669; www.sunrise skipark.com), on the Apache Reserva-tion outside the town of McNary in the White Mountains. Snowbowl is more popular because of the ease of the drive from Phoenix and the prox-imity to good lodging and dining options in Flagstaff. Although Snow-bowl has more vertical feet of skiing, Sunrise is our favorite Arizona ski area because it offers almost twice as many runs. Both ski areas offer rentals and lessons.

When it's a good snow year, Tucso-nans head up to **Mount Lemmon Ski Valley** (② **520/576-1321,** or 520/ 576-1400 for snow reports), the southernmost ski area in the United States. Snows here aren't as reliable as they are farther north. Because snow is so unreliable here, be sure to call first to make sure the ski area is operating.

During snow-blessed winters, cross-country skiers can find plenty of snow-covered forest roads outside Flagstaff (there's also cross-country skiing at Arizona Snowbowl), at Sunrise Park outside the town of McNary, at the South Rim of the Grand Canyon, in the White Mountains around Greer and Alpine, outside Payson on the Mogollon Rim, and on Mount Lemmon outside Flagstaff.

TENNIS After golf, tennis is the most popular winter sport in the desert, and resorts all over Arizona have tennis courts. Many resorts require you to wear traditional tennis attire and don't include court time in the room rates. No courts anywhere in the state can match the views you'll have from those at Enchantment Resort, outside Sedona. Just don't let the scenery distract you from your game. Other noteworthy tennis-oriented resorts include, in the Phoenix/Scottsdale area, the Phoenician, Copperwynd Country Club & Inn, the Fairmont Scottsdale Princess, the Pointe South Mountain Resort, and the Pointe Hilton Tapatio Cliffs Resort; and, in Tucson, the Lodge at Ventana Canyon, the Sheraton El Conquistador Resort & Country Club, the Westin La Paloma, the Westward Look Resort, and the Omni Tucson National Golf Resort & Spa.

WHITE-WATER RAFTING The desert doesn't support a lot of roaring rivers, but with the white water in the Grand Canyon you don't need too many other choices. Rafting the Grand Canyon is the dream of nearly every white-water enthusiast—if it's one of your dreams, plan well ahead. Companies and trips are limited, and they tend to fill up early. For a discussion and list of companies that run trips down the canyon, see chapter 6.

For 1-day rafting trips on the Colorado below the Grand Canyon, contact **Hualapai River Runners** (© **888/255-9550** or 928/769-2419; www.grandcanyonresort.com). For a half- or full-day float on the Colorado above the Grand Canyon, contact **Wilderness River Adventures** (© **800/528-6154** or 928/645-3279; www.lakepowell.com), which runs trips between Glen Canyon Dam and Lees Ferry.

Rafting trips are also available on the upper Salt River east of Phoenix. **Wilderness Aware Rafting** (© **800/ 231-7238;** www.inaraft.com), **Canyon Rio Rafting** (© **800/272-3353;** www.canyonrio.com), and **Mild to Wild Rafting** (© **800/567-6745;** www.mild2wildrafting.com) all run trips of varying lengths down this river (conditions permitting).

13 Getting Around

BY CAR

Because Phoenix and Tucson are major resort destinations, both have dozens of car-rental agencies. Prices at agencies elsewhere in the state tend to be higher, so if at all possible, try to rent your car in Phoenix or Tucson. However, because of high taxes at both airports, consider renting at a location outside the airport. If you stay at a hotel that offers a free airport shuttle, you can check in and then have an off-airport rental-car location pick you up and drive you to its office.

However, if you have to pay for a shuttle or taxi to either your hotel or the off-airport rental-car office, you may wipe out any savings you'd realize by renting away from the airport. Be sure to weigh all the costs carefully.

Major rental-car companies with offices in Arizona include:

Advantage © 800/777-5500; www.arac.com

Alamo © 800/462-5266; www.alamo.com

Avis © 800/831-2847; www.avis.com

Budget Ⓒ   800/527-0700;
www.budget.com
Dollar Ⓒ 800/800-4000; www.
dollar.com
Enterprise Ⓒ 800/736-8222;
www.enterprise.com
Hertz Ⓒ 800/654-3131; www.
hertz.com
National Ⓒ 800/227-7368;
www.nationalcar.com
Thrifty Ⓒ 800/847-4389; www.
thrifty.com

Rates for rental cars vary considerably between companies and with the model you want to rent, the dates you rent, and your pickup and drop-off points. If you call the same company three times and ask about renting the same model car, you may get three different quotes, depending on current availability of vehicles. It pays to start shopping early and ask lots of questions. At press time, Dollar was charging $210 per week ($317 including taxes and surcharges) in Phoenix for a compact car with unlimited mileage.

If you're a member of a frequent-flier program, check to see which rental-car companies participate in your program. Also, when making a reservation, be sure to mention any discount you might be eligible for, such as corporate, military, or AAA. Beware of coupons offering discounts on rental-car rates—they often discount the highest rates only. It's always cheaper to rent by the week, so even if you don't need a car for 7 days, you might find that it's still more economical than renting for only 4 days.

Taxes on car rentals vary between around 12% and 50% and are always at the high end at both the Phoenix and Tucson airports. You can save around 10% by renting your car at an office outside the airport. Be sure to ask about the tax and the loss-damage waiver (LDW) if you want to know what your total rental cost will be before making a reservation.

In Arizona, a right turn on a red light is permitted after a complete stop. Seat belts are required for the driver and for all passengers. Children 4 and under, or who weigh 40 pounds or less, must be in a child's car seat. General speed limits are 25 to 35 mph in towns and cities, 15 mph in school zones, and 55 mph on two-lane highways. On rural interstate highways, the speed limit ranges from 65 to 75 mph.

Always be sure to keep your gas tank topped off. In many parts of Arizona, it's not unusual to drive 60 miles without seeing a gas station. *Note:* A breakdown in the desert can be more than just an inconvenience—it can be dangerous. Always carry drinking water with you while driving through the desert, and if you plan to head off on back roads, carry extra water for the car's radiator as well.

Your best bet for a road map will be whatever you can pick up at a convenience store once you arrive. If you're a member of AAA, you can get a free map of the state that will be of some use. Other maps are available from tourist information offices in Phoenix and Tucson.

BY PLANE

Arizona is a big state (the sixth largest), so if your time is short, you might want to consider flying between cities. **America West** (Ⓒ 800/235-9292; www.americawest.com) serves the cities of Phoenix, Tucson, Flagstaff, Kingman, Prescott, Lake Havasu City, and Yuma. **Scenic Airlines** (Ⓒ 800/634-6801; www.scenic.com) and **Air Vegas** (Ⓒ 800/255-7474; www.airvegas.com) fly between Las Vegas and the Grand Canyon.

BY TRAIN

The train is not really a viable way of getting around much of Arizona because there is no north–south

Amtrak service between Grand Canyon/Flagstaff and Phoenix or between Tucson and Phoenix. However, Amtrak will sell you a ticket to Phoenix, which includes a shuttle-bus ride from Flagstaff or Tucson. You can, however, get to the town of Williams, 30 miles west of Flagstaff, on Amtrak, and in Williams transfer to the Grand Canyon Railway excursion train, which runs to Grand Canyon Village at the South Rim of the Grand Canyon (see chapter 6 for details). Be aware, however, that the Williams stop is on the outskirts of town; you'll have to arrange in advance to be picked up.

14 Tips on Accommodations

When making hotel reservations for late spring or early fall, be sure to ask when hotel rates drop for the summer or go up for the fall, so you can schedule your trip for right after the rates go down (or just before they go back up). Many resorts also have a short discounted season just before Christmas (just think, you can do your holiday shopping in Arizona).

Remember, if you don't absolutely need all the amenities of a big resort, there are dozens of chain-motel options in the Phoenix and Tucson areas. Alternatively, you can get a bit more for your money if you head to such smaller towns as Wickenburg, Bullhead City, Lake Havasu City, and Yuma. If you must stay in the Phoenix or Tucson area, head for the suburbs. The farther you drive from the resort areas, the more you can save.

If you like to stay at B&Bs, there are a few helpful resources you should know about. **Mi Casa Su Casa** (✆ **800/456-0682** or 480/990-0682; www.azres.com) can book you into hundreds of homes across the state, as can **Arizona Trails Bed & Breakfast Reservation Service** (✆ **888/799-4284** or 480/837-4284; www.arizona trails.com), which also books tour and hotel reservations. For a list of some of the best B&Bs in the state, contact the **Arizona Association of Bed & Breakfast Inns** (✆ **800/284-2589**; www.arizona-bed-breakfast.com).

TIPS FOR SAVING ON YOUR HOTEL ROOM

The **rack rate** is the maximum rate that a hotel charges for a room. It's the rate you'd get if you walked in off the street and asked for a room for the night. Hardly anybody pays these prices, however, and there are many ways around them.

- **Don't be afraid to bargain.** Most rack rates include commissions of 10% to 25% for travel agents, which some hotels may be willing to reduce if you make your own reservations and haggle a bit. Always ask whether a room less expensive than the first one quoted is available, or whether any special rates apply to you. You may qualify for corporate, student, military, senior, or other discounts. Be sure to mention membership in AAA, AARP, frequent-flier programs, or trade unions, which may entitle you to special deals as well. Find out the hotel's policy on children—do kids stay free in the room or is there a special rate?
- **Rely on a qualified professional.** Certain hotels give travel agents discounts in exchange for steering business their way, so if you're shy about bargaining, an agent may be better equipped to negotiate discounts for you.
- **Dial direct.** When booking a room in a chain hotel, compare the rates offered by the hotel's

local line with that of the toll-free number. Also check with an agent and online. A hotel makes nothing on a room that stays empty, so the local hotel reservations desk may be willing to offer a special rate unavailable elsewhere.

• **Remember the law of supply and demand.** Resort hotels are most crowded and therefore most expensive on weekends, so discounts are usually available for midweek stays. Business hotels in downtown locations are busiest during the week, so you can expect big discounts over the weekend. Avoid high-season stays whenever you can: Planning your vacation just a week before or after official peak season can mean substantial savings.

• **Avoid excess charges.** Ask whether your hotel charges for parking. Find out about surcharges imposed on local and long-distance calls—many hotels charge a fee just for dialing out on the phone in your room. Finally, ask about local taxes and service charges (common at guest ranches and high-end resorts), which could increase the cost of a room by 25% or more.

• **Consider a suite.** If you're traveling with your family or another couple, you can pack more people into a suite (which usually comes with a sofa bed), and thereby reduce your per-person rate. Remember that some places charge for extra guests.

15 Suggested Itineraries

Vacationing in Arizona almost always means doing a lot of driving, and consequently, planning out a realistic itinerary is crucial to having an enjoyable trip.

The most important thing to remember is not to bite off more than you can chew. This state is so large and varied, and has such a diversity of climates, that it is best explored in two or more trips. Below are a couple of itineraries that take the state's seasonal differences into account.

ARIZONA IN THE WINTER

Arizona in the winter means golf and desert explorations. Sure, you can go to the Grand Canyon (and even avoid the crowds), but it will be very cold, and snow often makes the area's roads impassable.

Day 1   Arrive in Phoenix, check into your hotel, and head straight for the pool—after all, lounging in the sun is one of the main reasons to be here. If you've got lots of energy, hike up Camelback Mountain or Squaw Peak

for a superb view of the valley. Head to Scottsdale for dinner.

Day 2   Play a round of golf or some tennis in the morning, or, if you're more interested in culture, visit the Heard Museum and the Phoenix Art Museum. In the afternoon, get in a swim and then visit the Desert Botanical Garden around sunset.

Day 3   Phoenix is a huge metropolitan area. To see what the desert is really like, drive the Apache Trail east of the city. This drive will take all day, so get an early start.

Day 4   Head up to Sedona to marvel at the red-rock scenery. Do a Jeep tour or rent a mountain bike and get out amid the red rocks. Be sure to take in the sunset from one of the area's great sunset spots.

Day 5   Go to Boynton Canyon for a hike in the most beautiful red-rock canyons in the area. If the weather is good, you could even make a quick trip up to the Grand Canyon, but start early. In the late afternoon, go to

Crescent Moon Recreation Site to catch the sunset on Cathedral Rock.

Day 6   Head back to Phoenix by way of Jerome, a former mining town that is now an artists' community. Peruse the galleries, visit the state park, and tour the ghost town and mine on the edge of town. If you have time, schedule a ride on the Verde Canyon Railroad. Stay in Phoenix for the night.

Day 7   Relax by the pool, do some shopping in Old Town Scottsdale, or get in another round of golf.

ARIZONA IN THE SUMMER

Summer is the time to visit the Grand Canyon and the Arizona high country. When it's 110°F (43°C) down in Phoenix, it's likely to be around 80°F (27°C) on the rim of the Grand Canyon. Summer is also the time to visit the national monuments of the Four Corners region.

Day 1   Arrive in Phoenix, preferably after dark, and drive north to Flagstaff. (Alternatively, you can fly in to Flagstaff.) Spend the night in Flagstaff. If you arrive early in the day, visit the Museum of Northern Arizona.

Day 2   Head north to the Grand Canyon and spend your first day here taking in the rim views near the park's east entrance. Shoot lots of pictures. Take a short hike down into the canyon.

Day 3   Explore the Hermit Road, perhaps hiking along the rim or taking the Hermit Trail down into the canyon a few miles.

Day 4   Hike or ride a mule down into the canyon and spend the night at Phantom Ranch or the nearby campground.

Day 5   Hike or ride your mule back up from the bottom of the canyon. Celebrate your adventure with dinner at El Tovar.

Day 6   Explore some more along Desert View Drive. Head back to Flagstaff, taking a detour to Wupatki National Monument to visit the monument's Indian ruins.

Day 7   Head back to Phoenix by way of Oak Creek Canyon and the Sedona red-rock country. Be sure to go for a swim at Slick Rock State Park.

16 Recommended Reading

HISTORY   Marshall Trimble's *Roadside History of Arizona* (Mountain Press Publishing, 2004) is an ideal book to take along on a driving tour of the state. It goes road by road and discusses events that happened in the area. If you're interested in learning more about the infamous shootout at the O.K. Corral, read Paula Mitchell Marks's *And Die in the West: The Story of the O.K. Corral Gunfight* (University of Oklahoma Press, 1996). This is a very objective, non-Hollywood look at the most glorified and glamorized shootout in Western history.

THE GRAND CANYON & THE COLORADO RIVER   John Wesley Powell's diary produced the first published account (1869) of traveling through the Grand Canyon. Today, his writings still provide a fascinating glimpse into the canyon. *The Exploration of the Colorado River and Its Canyons* (Penguin, 2003), with an introduction by Wallace Stegner, is a recent republishing of Powell's writings. Stegner, with Bernard Devoto, writes about Powell in his *Beyond the Hundredth Meridian: John Wesley Powell and the Second Opening of the West* (Penguin, 1992).

For an interesting account of the recent human history of the canyon, read Stephen J. Pyne's *How the Canyon Became Grand* (Penguin, 1999), which focuses on the explorers, writers, and artists who have contributed to our current concept of the canyon. *The Man Who Walked through Time* (Vintage, 1989), by Colin Fletcher, is a narrative of one man's hike through the rugged inner canyon. In *Down the River* (Plume Books, 1991), Western environmentalist Edward Abbey chronicles many of his trips down the Colorado and other Southwest rivers. Among the essays here are descriptions of Glen Canyon before Lake Powell was created. *Grand Canyon: True Stories of Life Below the Rim (Travelers' Tales Guides)* (Travelers' Tales Guides, 1999) provides a wide range of perspectives on the Grand Canyon experience, with essays by Edward Abbey, Colin Fletcher, Barry Lopez, and many others.

Water rights and human impact on the deserts of the Southwest have raised many controversies in the 20th century, none more heated than those centering on the Colorado River. *Cadillac Desert: The American West and Its Disappearing Water* (Penguin, 2003), by Marc Reisner, focuses on the West's insatiable need for water. *A River No More: The Colorado River and the West* (University of California Press, 1996), by Philip L. Fradkin, addresses the fate of the Colorado River.

NATURAL HISTORY & THE OUTDOORS Anyone the least bit curious about the plants and animals of the Sonoran Desert should be sure to acquire *A Natural History of the Sonoran Desert* (University of Arizona Press, 2000). Cacti, wildflowers, tarantulas, roadrunners—they're all here and described in very readable detail. You'll likely get much more out of a trip to the desert with this book at your side. Halka Chronic's *Roadside Geology of Arizona* (Mountain Press Publishing, 2003) is another handy book to keep in the car. If you're a hiker, you'll find Scott S. Warren's *Arizona (100 Classic Hikes)* (The

Mountaineers, 2000) an invaluable traveling companion.

FICTION Tony Hillerman is perhaps the best-known contemporary author whose books rely on Arizona settings. Hillerman's murder mysteries are almost all set on the Navajo Reservation in the Four Corners area and include many references to actual locations that can be seen by visitors. Among Hillerman's Navajo mysteries are *The Sinister Pig, The Wailing Wind, Hunting Badger, The First Eagle, Sacred Clowns, Coyote Waits, Thief of Time, The Blessing Way,* and *The Ghostway.*

Author J. A. Jance sets her murder mysteries in southeast Arizona's Cochise County, where she grew up. The protagonist of the series is Sheriff Joanna Brady. Titles include *Devil's Claw, Skeleton Canyon, Dead to Rights, Rattlesnake Crossing, Outlaw Mountain,* and *Tombstone Courage.*

Barbara Kingsolver, a biologist and social activist, has set several of her novels either partly or entirely in Arizona. *The Bean Trees, Pigs in Heaven,* and *Animal Dreams* are peopled by Anglo, Indian, and Hispanic characters, allowing for quirky, humorous narratives with social and political overtones that provide insights into Arizona's cultural mélange. Kingsolver's nonfiction works include *High Tide in Tucson* (HarperPerennial, 2003) and *Holding the Line: Women in the Great Arizona Mine Strike of 1983* (Cornell University Press, 1997). The former is a collection of essays, many of which focus on the author's life in Tucson, while the latter is an account of a copper-mine strike.

Edward Abbey's *The Monkey Wrench Gang* (Perennial Classics, 2000) and *Hayduke Lives!* (Back Bay Books, 1991) are tales of an unlikely gang of ecoterrorists determined to preserve the wildernesses of the Southwest, including parts of northern Arizona.

Zane Grey spent many years living in north-central Arizona and based many of his Western novels on life in this region of the state. Among his books are *Riders of the Purple Sage, The Vanishing American, Call of the Canyon, The Arizona Clan,* and *To the Last Man.*

TRAVEL   If you're particularly interested in Native American art and

crafts, you may want to search out a copy of *Trading Post Guidebook* (Northland Publishing, 1995), by Patrick Eddington and Susan Makov. It's an invaluable guide to trading posts, artists' studios, galleries, and museums in the Four Corners region.

FAST FACTS: Arizona

American Express There are offices or representatives in Phoenix and Scottsdale. For information, call ℂ **800/528-4800.**

Area Codes The area code in Phoenix is 602. In Scottsdale, Tempe, Mesa, and the east valley, it's 480. In Glendale and the west valley, it's 623. The area code for Tucson and southeastern Arizona is 520. The rest of the state is area code 928.

ATM Networks ATMs in Arizona generally use the following systems: Star, Cirrus, PLUS, American Express, MasterCard, and Visa.

Business Hours The following are general hours; specific establishments' hours may vary. Banks are open Monday through Friday from 9am to 5pm (some also Sat 9am–noon). Stores are open Monday through Saturday from 10am to 6pm and Sunday from noon to 5pm (malls usually stay open until 9pm Mon–Sat). Bars generally open around 11am, but are legally allowed to be open Monday through Saturday from 6am to 1am and Sunday from 10am to 1am.

Camera/Film Because the sun is almost always shining in Arizona, you can use a slower film—that is, one with a lower ASA number. This will give you sharper pictures. If your camera accepts different filters, and especially if you plan to travel in the higher altitudes of the northern part of the state, you'd do well to invest in a polarizer, which reduces contrast, deepens colors, and eliminates glare. Also, be sure to protect your camera and film from heat. Never leave your camera or film in a car parked in the sun: Temperatures inside the car can climb to more than 130°F (54°C), which is hot enough to damage sensitive film.

Car Rentals See "Getting Around," earlier in this chapter.

Climate See "When to Go," earlier in this chapter.

Driving Rules See "Getting Around," earlier in this chapter.

Embassies & Consulates See chapter 3.

Emergencies In most places in Arizona, call ℂ **911** to report a fire, call the police, or get an ambulance. A few small towns have not adopted this emergency phone number, so if 911 doesn't work, dial 0 (zero) for the operator and state the type of emergency.

Information See "Visitor Information," earlier in this chapter, and individual destination chapters and sections for local information offices.

Internet Access Although you will find the occasional cybercafe around Arizona (particularly in the vicinity of universities), they are not at all common. Your best bet, other than using access provided by your hotel or resort, is to head to the nearest public library or copy shop, such as Kinko's.

Legal Aid If you're in need of legal aid, first look in the local White Pages telephone directory under Legal Aid. You may also want to contact the Traveler's Aid Society.

Liquor Laws The legal age for buying or consuming alcoholic beverages is 21. You cannot purchase any alcoholic drinks from 1 to 6am Monday through Saturday and from 1 to 10am on Sunday. Beer, wine, and hard liquor are all sold in both grocery stores and convenience stores.

Pets If you plan to travel with a pet, it's always best to inform the hotel when making reservations. At Grand Canyon Village, there's a kennel where you can board your pet while you hike down into the canyon.

Police In most places in Arizona, phone ⓒ **911** for emergencies. A few small towns have not adopted this emergency phone number, so if 911 doesn't work, dial 0 (zero) for the operator and state your reason for calling.

Safety See "Insurance," and "Health & Safety," earlier in this chapter.

Taxes There's a state sales tax of 5.6% (local communities levy additional taxes), car-rental taxes and surcharges ranging from around 12% to 50%, and hotel taxes from around 6% to 17%.

Time Zone Arizona is in the mountain time zone. However, the state does not observe daylight saving time, so time differences between Arizona and the rest of the country vary with the time of year. From the last Sunday in October until the first Sunday in April, Arizona is 1 hour later than the West Coast and 2 hours earlier than the East Coast. The rest of the year, Arizona is on the same time as the West Coast and is 3 hours earlier than the East Coast. There is an exception, however—the Navajo Reservation observes daylight saving time. However, the Hopi Reservation, which is completely surrounded by the Navajo Reservation, does not.

Weather For information, call ⓒ **800/555-8355** and say "weather."

For International Visitors

Cowboys, Indians, cacti, and the Grand Canyon. Arizona and the American West are well-known and well-loved in many countries. Arizona images are familiar from Western novels, movies, television shows, and advertisements. And, of course, the Grand Canyon is one of the wonders of the world. However, despite this being the Wild West, you are likely to encounter typically American situations in Arizona, and this chapter should help you prepare for your trip.

1 Preparing for Your Trip

ENTRY REQUIREMENTS

Immigration law is a hot political issue in the United States these days, and the following requirements may have changed somewhat by the time you plan your trip. Check at any U.S. embassy or consulate for current information and requirements. You can also go to the **U.S. State Department** website at **www.travel.state.gov**.

VISAS The U.S. State Department has a **Visa Waiver Program** allowing citizens of certain countries to enter the United States without a visa for stays of up to 90 days. At press time, these countries included Andorra, Australia, Austria, Belgium, Brunei, Denmark, Finland, France, Germany, Iceland, Ireland, Italy, Japan, Liechtenstein, Luxembourg, Monaco, the Netherlands, New Zealand, Norway, Portugal, San Marino, Singapore, Slovenia, Spain, Sweden, Switzerland, and the United Kingdom. Citizens of these countries need only a valid machine-readable passport and a round-trip air or cruise ticket in their possession upon arrival. If they first enter the United States, they may also visit Mexico, Canada, Bermuda, and/or the Caribbean islands and return to the United States without a visa. Canadian citizens may enter the

United States without a visa; they need only proof of residence.

Citizens of all other countries must have (1) a valid passport that expires at least 6 months later than the scheduled end of their visit to the United States, and (2) a nonimmigrant (visitors) visa, which can be obtained from any U.S. consulate. A $100 visa application fee is charged.

To get a visa, the traveler must submit a completed application form (either in person or by mail) with a 2-inch-square photo, and must demonstrate binding ties to a residence abroad. Visa processing can take up to 30 days or more, so be sure to apply far in advance of your planned visit. If you cannot go in person, contact the nearest U.S. embassy or consulate for directions on applying by mail. Your travel agent or airline office may also be able to supply you with visa applications and instructions. The U.S. consulate or embassy that issues your visa determines whether you will receive a multiple- or single-entry visa and any restrictions on the length of your stay.

British subjects can get up-to-date passport and visa information by contacting the **U.S. Embassy London,** 24 Grosvenor Square, London, W1A

1AE (**℃ 09068/200-290** or 09055/444-546).

Irish citizens can obtain up-to-date visa information through the **Embassy of the United States Dublin,** 42 Elgin Rd., Ballsbridge, Dublin 4, Ireland (**℃ 1580/47-8472**) or by checking the "Consular Services" section of the website at http://dublin.usembassy.gov.

Australian citizens can obtain up-to-date visa information by contacting the **U.S. Embassy Canberra,** Moonah Place, Yarralumla, ACT 2600 (**℃ 1902/941-641** or 1800/687-844) or by checking the U.S. Diplomatic Mission's website at http://usembassy-australia.state.gov/consular.

Citizens of **New Zealand** can obtain up-to-date visa information by contacting the **U.S. Embassy in New Zealand,** 29 Fitzherbert Terrace, Thorndon, Wellington (**℃ 0900/878-472**), or get the information directly from the "Services to New Zealanders" section of the website at http://usembassy.org.nz.

MEDICAL REQUIREMENTS

Unless you're arriving from an area known to be suffering from an epidemic (particularly cholera or yellow fever), inoculations or vaccinations are not required for entry into the United States. If you have a medical condition that requires syringe-administered medications, carry a valid signed prescription from your physician—the Transportation Security Administration (TSA) no longer allows airline passengers to pack syringes in their carry-on baggage without documented proof of medical need. If you have a disease that requires treatment with narcotics, you should also carry documented proof with you—smuggling narcotics aboard a plane is a serious offense that carries severe penalties in the U.S.

For **HIV-positive visitors,** requirements for entering the United States are somewhat vague and change frequently. According to the latest publication of *HIV and Immigrants: A Manual for AIDS Service Providers,* the Immigration and Naturalization Service (INS) doesn't require a medical exam for entry into the United States, but INS officials may stop individuals because they look sick or because they are carrying AIDS/HIV medicine.

If an HIV-positive noncitizen applies for a nonimmigrant visa, the question on the application regarding communicable diseases is tricky no matter which way it's answered. If the applicant checks "no," INS may deny the visa on the grounds that the applicant committed fraud. If the applicant checks "yes" or if INS suspects the person is HIV-positive, it will deny the visa unless the applicant asks for a special waiver for visitors. This waiver is for people visiting the United States for a short time, to attend a conference, for instance, to visit close relatives, or to receive medical treatment. It can be a confusing situation. For up-to-the-minute information, contact the Department of Health and Human Service's **AIDSinfo** (**℃ 800/448-0440** or 301/519-0459; www.aidsinfo.nih.gov) or the **Gay Men's Health Crisis** (**℃ 800/243-7692** or 212/807-6655; www.gmhc.org).

DRIVER'S LICENSES Foreign driver's licenses are usually recognized in the United States, although you may want to get an international driver's license if your home license is not written in English.

PASSPORT INFORMATION

Safeguard your passport in an inconspicuous, inaccessible place like a money belt. Make a copy of the critical pages, including the passport number, and store it in a safe place, separate from the passport itself. If you lose your passport, visit the nearest consulate of your native country as soon as possible for a replacement.

Passport applications are downloadable from most of the websites listed below.

FOR RESIDENTS OF CANADA

You can pick up a passport application at one of 29 regional passport offices or at any Canada Post outlet. Canadian children who travel must have their own passport. However, if you hold a valid Canadian passport issued before December 11, 2001, that bears the name of your child, the passport remains valid for you and your child until it expires. Passports cost C$85 for those 16 years and older (valid 5 years), C$35 children 3 to 15 (valid 5 years), and C$20, children under 3 (valid 3 years). Applications, which must be accompanied by two identical passport-size photographs and proof of Canadian citizenship, are available at travel agencies throughout Canada or from the central **Passport Office,** Department of Foreign Affairs and International Trade, Ottawa, ON K1A 0G3 (© **800/567-6868;** www. dfait-maeci.gc.ca/passport).

FOR RESIDENTS OF THE UNITED KINGDOM

To pick up an application for a standard 10-year passport (5-year passport for children under 16), visit the nearest Passport Office, major post office, or travel agency. You can also contact the **United Kingdom Passport Service** at © **0870/521-0410** or visit its website at www.passport.gov.uk. Passports are £42 for adults and £25 for children under 16; £70 for adults and £60 for children if you apply in person at a Passport Office.

FOR RESIDENTS OF IRELAND

You can apply for a 10-year passport, costing €75, at the **Passport Office,** Setanta Centre, Molesworth St., Dublin 2 (© **01/671-1633** or 890/426-888; www.irlgov.ie/iveagh). Those

under age 18 and over 65 may be issued either a 3-year or 10-year passport. You can also apply at 1A South Mall, Cork (© **021/494-4700** or 890/426-900) or over the counter at most main post offices.

FOR RESIDENTS OF AUSTRALIA

You can pick up an application from your local post office or any branch of Passports Australia, but you must schedule an interview at the passport office to present your application materials. Call the **Australian Passport Information Service** at © **131-232,** or visit the government website at www.passports.gov.au. Passports are A$148 to A$222 for adults and A$74 to A$111 for children under 18.

FOR RESIDENTS OF NEW ZEALAND

You can pick up a passport application at any New Zealand Passports Office or download it from its website. Contact the **Passports Office** at © **0800/225-050** in New Zealand or 04/474-8100, or log on to www.passports.govt.nz. Passports are NZ$71 for adults and NZ$36 for children under 16.

CUSTOMS REQUIREMENTS
WHAT YOU CAN BRING IN

Every visitor over 21 years of age may bring in, free of duty, the following: (1) 1 liter of beer, wine, or hard liquor; (2) 200 cigarettes, 50 cigars (but not from Cuba; an additional 100 cigars may be brought in under your gift exemption), or 4.4 pounds (2kg) of smoking tobacco; and (3) $100 worth of gifts. These exemptions are offered to travelers who spend at least 72 hours in the United States and who have not claimed them within the preceding 6 months. Meat (with the exception of some canned meat products) is prohibited, as are most fruits, vegetables, and plants (including seeds, tropical plants, and the like). Foreign tourists may bring in or take out up to $10,000 in U.S. or foreign currency with no formalities; larger sums must be declared to U.S. Customs on entering or leaving, which includes filing form Customs Form 4790. For specific information regarding U.S. Customs, call your nearest U.S. embassy or consulate, or contact the **U.S. Customs & Border Protection** office at © **877/CUSTOMS,** 202/354-1000, or www.customs.gov/xp/cgov/travel.

WHAT YOU CAN TAKE HOME

U.K. citizens 18 and over returning from a non-E.U. country have a customs allowance of: 200 cigarettes, 50 cigars, or 250 grams of smoking tobacco, plus 2 liters of still table wine, plus 1 liter of spirits or strong liqueurs (over 22% volume) or 2 liters of fortified wine, sparkling wine, or other liqueurs. Also allowed are 60cc (ml) of perfume; 250cc (ml) of toilet water; and £145 worth of all other goods, including gifts and souvenirs. For more information, contact HM Customs & Excise at © **0845/010-9000** (from outside the U.K., 020/8929-0152), or consult their website at www.hmce.gov.uk.

For a clear summary of **Canadian** rules, request the booklet *I Declare,* issued by the **Canada Border Services Agency** (© **800/461-9999** in Canada, or 204/983-3500; www.cbsa-asfc.gc.ca). Canada allows its citizens a C$750 exemption, and lets them bring back duty-free 200 cigarettes, 50 cigars, and 200 grams of tobacco, plus 1.14 liters of liquor, 1.5 liters of wine, or 24 355ml cans of beer. In addition, you're allowed to mail gifts to Canada valued at less than C$60 a day, provided they're unsolicited and don't contain alcohol or tobacco (write on the package "Unsolicited gift, under $60 value"). *Note:* The $750 exemption can only be used once a year and only after an absence of 7 days.

The duty-free allowance in **Australia** is A$400 or, for those under 18, A$200. Citizens age 18 and over can bring in 250 cigarettes or 250 grams of loose tobacco, and 1,125 milliliters of alcohol. If you're returning with valuables you already own, such as foreign-made cameras, proof of purchase may be required. A helpful brochure available from Australian consulates or customs offices is *Know Before You Go.* For more information, call the **Australian Customs Service** at © **1300/363-263,** or log on to www.customs.gov.au.

The duty-free allowance for **New Zealand** is NZ$700. Citizens over 17 can bring in 200 cigarettes, 50 cigars, or 250 grams of tobacco (or a mixture of all three if their combined weight doesn't exceed 250g); plus 4.5 liters of wine or beer, or 1.125 liters of liquor. New Zealand currency does not carry import or export restrictions. Fill out a certificate of export, listing the valuables you are taking out of the country; that way, you can bring them back without paying duty. For more information, contact **New Zealand Customs,** The Customhouse, 17–21 Whitmore St., Box 2218, Wellington (© **0800/428-786** or 04/473-6099; www.customs.govt.nz).

INSURANCE

Although it's not required of travelers, health insurance is highly recommended. Unlike many European countries, the United States does not usually offer free or low-cost medical care to its citizens or visitors. Doctors and hospitals are expensive, and in most cases require advance payment or proof of coverage before they render their services. Other policies can cover everything from the loss or theft of your baggage to trip cancellation to the guarantee of bail in case you're arrested. Good policies also cover the costs of an accident, repatriation, or death. See the "Insurance" and "Health & Safety" sections in chapter

2 for more information. In Europe, packages such as **Europ Assistance** are sold by automobile clubs and travel agencies at attractive rates. **Worldwide Assistance Services** (℡ 800/777-8710; www.worldwideassistance.com) is the agent for Europ Assistance in the United States.

Although lack of health insurance may prevent you from being admitted to a hospital in nonemergencies, don't worry about being left on a street corner to die: The American way is to fix you now and bill you later.

INSURANCE FOR BRITISH TRAVELERS

Most big travel agents offer their own insurance and will probably try to sell you their package when you book a holiday. Think before you sign. **Britain's Consumers' Association** recommends that you insist on seeing the policy and reading the fine print before buying travel insurance. **The Association of British Insurers** (℡ 020/7600-3333; www.abi.org.uk) gives advice by phone and publishes *Holiday Insurance and Motoring Abroad,* a free guide to policy provisions and prices. You might also shop around for better deals: Try **Columbus Direct** (℡ 0845/330-8518; www.columbusdirect.net).

INSURANCE FOR CANADIAN TRAVELERS

Canadians should check with their provincial health plan offices or call **Health Canada** (℡ 613/957-2991; www.hc-sc.gc.ca) to find out the extent of their coverage and what documentation and receipts they must take home in case they are treated in the United States.

MONEY

CURRENCY The U.S. monetary system is very simple: The most common **bills** are the $1 (colloquially, a "buck"), $5, $10, and $20 denominations. There are also $2 bills (seldom encountered), $50 bills, and $100 bills (the last two are usually not welcome as payment for small purchases). All the paper money was recently redesigned, making the famous faces adorning them disproportionately large. The old-style bills are still legal tender.

There are seven denominations of coins: 1¢ (1 cent, or a penny); 5¢ (5 cents, or a nickel); 10¢ (10 cents, or a dime); 25¢ (25 cents, or a quarter); 50¢ (50 cents, or a half dollar); the gold "Sacagawea" coin worth $1; and, prized by collectors, the rare, older silver dollar.

Note: The "foreign-exchange bureaus" so common in Europe are rare even at airports in the United States, and nonexistent outside major cities. It's best not to change foreign money (or traveler's checks denominated in a currency other than U.S. dollars) at a small-town bank, or even a branch in a big city; in fact, leave any currency other than U.S. dollars at home—it may prove a greater nuisance to you than it's worth.

TRAVELER'S CHECKS Though traveler's checks are widely accepted, make sure that they're denominated in U.S. dollars, as foreign-currency checks are often difficult to exchange. The three traveler's checks that are most widely recognized—and least likely to be denied—are **Visa, American Express,** and **Thomas Cook.** Be sure to record the numbers of the checks, and keep that information in a separate place in case the checks get lost or stolen. Most businesses are pretty good about taking traveler's checks, but you're better off cashing them in at a bank (in small amounts, of course) and paying in cash. Remember: You'll need identification, such as a driver's license or passport, to use a traveler's check.

CREDIT CARDS & ATMs Credit cards are the most widely used form of payment in the United States. Among

> **Tips In Case of Emergency**
>
> Be sure to keep a copy of all your travel papers separate from your wallet or purse, and leave a copy with someone at home should you need it faxed in an emergency.

the most commonly accepted are **Visa** (www.visa.com), which is BarclayCard in Britain; **MasterCard** (www.mastercard.com), which is BarclayCard in Britain and EuroCard in Europe; **American Express** (www.americanexpress.com), **Diners Club** (www.dinersclub.com), and **Discover** (www.discovercard.com). You must have a credit or charge card to rent a car. There are, however, a handful of stores, restaurants, guest ranches, and B&Bs that do not take credit cards. Most businesses display a sticker near their entrance to let you know which cards they accept. (*Note:* Businesses may require a minimum purchase, usually around $10, to use a credit card.) Check the websites listed above to find an ATM or location where you can get a cash advance on your credit card.

It is strongly recommended that you bring at least one major credit card. Hotels, car-rental companies, and airlines usually require a credit card imprint as a deposit against expenses, and in an emergency a credit card can be priceless.

You'll find **automated teller machines (ATMs)** are easily found in U.S. cities. Some ATMs allow you to draw U.S. currency against your bank and credit cards. Check with your bank before leaving home, and remember that you need your personal identification number (PIN) to do so. Most ATMs accept Visa, MasterCard, and American Express, as well as ATM cards from other U.S. banks. Expect to be charged up to $2 per transaction, however. One way around these fees is to ask for cash back at grocery stores, which generally accept ATM cards and don't charge

usage fees. Of course, you'll have to purchase something first.

SAFETY
GENERAL   SUGGESTIONS
Although tourist areas are generally safe, U.S. urban areas tend to be less safe than those in Europe. You should always stay alert. This is particularly true of large American cities. If you're in doubt about which neighborhoods are safe, don't hesitate to make inquiries with the hotel's front desk staff or the local tourist office.

Avoid deserted areas, especially at night, and don't go into public parks after dark unless there's a concert or similar occasion that will attract a crowd.

Avoid carrying valuables with you on the street, and keep expensive cameras or electronic equipment bagged up or covered when not in use. If you're using a map, try to consult it inconspicuously—or better yet, study it before you leave your room. Hold onto your pocketbook, and place your billfold in an inside pocket. In theaters, restaurants, and other public places, keep your possessions in sight.

Always lock your room door—don't assume that once you're inside the hotel you are automatically safe and no longer need to be aware of your surroundings. Hotels are open to the public, and in a large hotel, security may not be able to screen everyone who enters.

DRIVING SAFETY Driving safety is important too, and carjacking is not unprecedented. Question your rental agency about personal safety and ask for a traveler-safety brochure when you pick up your car. Obtain written directions—or a map with the route clearly marked—from the agency showing how to get to your destination. (Many agencies now offer the option of renting a cellphone for the duration of your car rental; check with the rental agent when you pick up the car. Otherwise, contact **InTouch USA** at ✆ **800/872-7626** or www.intouch usa.com for short-term cellphone rental.) And, if possible, arrive and depart during daylight hours.

If you drive off a highway and end up in a neighborhood that looks unsafe, leave the area as quickly as possible. If you have an accident, even on the highway, stay in your car with the doors locked until you assess the situation or until the police arrive. If you're bumped from behind on the street or are involved in a minor accident with no injuries, and the situation appears to be suspicious, motion to the other driver to follow you. Go directly to the nearest police station, well-lit service station, or 24-hour store.

Park in well-lit and well-traveled areas whenever possible. Always keep your car doors locked, whether the vehicle is attended or unattended. Never leave any packages or valuables in sight. If someone attempts to rob you or steal your car, don't try to resist the thief/carjacker. Report the incident to the police department immediately by calling ✆ **911.**

2 Getting to the U.S.

Arizona has two main airports— Phoenix Sky Harbor Airport in the center of the state and Tucson International Airport in the southern part of the state. If you are heading directly to the Grand Canyon, you should also consider flying in to the Las Vegas's McCarran International Airport (www.mccarran.com), which often has cheaper flights and (better car rental rates). However, this latter airport is not convenient if you are heading to any other part of Arizona.

Airlines with direct or connecting service from London to Phoenix (along with their phone numbers in Great Britain) include **Air Canada** (✆ 0871/220-1111; www.aircanada. ca), **American** (✆ 207/365-0777 in London, or 8457/789-789 outside London; www.aa.com), **British Airways** (✆ 0870/850-9850; www. britishairways.com), **Continental** (✆ 0129/377-6464; www.continental. com), **Delta** (✆ 0800/414-767; www.delta.com), **Northwest/KLM** (✆ 08705/074-074; www.nwa.com), **United** (✆ 0845/8-444-777; www. ual.com), and **US Airways** (✆ 0845/ 600-3300; www.usairways.com).

American, Continental, Delta, Northwest, and United fly into Tucson.

From Canadian cities, there are flights to Phoenix on **Air Canada** (✆ 888/247-2262; www.aircanada.ca), as well as many of the major U.S. carriers. However, Air Canada does not have direct flights to Tucson. For low airfares, check **America West** (800/235-9292; www.americawest. com) and **Alaska Airlines** (✆ 800/ 252-7522; www.alaskaair.com) first.

From New Zealand and Australia, there are flights to Los Angeles on **Qantas** (✆ 13 13 13 in Australia; www.qantas.com.au) and **Air New Zealand** (✆ 0800/737-000 in Auckland; www.airnewzealand.co.nz). Continue on to Phoenix or Tucson on a U.S. carrier.

If you're heading to the Grand Canyon, it's easier to take a flight from Los Angeles to Las Vegas.

AIRLINE DISCOUNTS Travelers from overseas can take advantage of the APEX (Advance Purchase Excursion) fares offered by all major U.S. and European carriers. For more money-saving airline advice, see "Getting There," in chapter 2.

IMMIGRATION & CUSTOMS CLEARANCE Visitors arriving by air, no matter what the port of entry, should cultivate patience before setting foot on U.S. soil. Getting through immigration control can take as long as 2 hours on some days, especially summer weekends. This is especially true now that security has been beefed up at U.S. airports due to the September 11, 2001, terrorist attacks.

3 Getting Around the U.S.

For specific information on traveling to and around Arizona, see "Getting There" and "Getting Around," in chapter 2.

BY PLANE Some large airlines (for example, United and Delta) offer travelers on their transatlantic or transpacific flights special discount tickets under the name **Visit USA,** allowing mostly one-way travel from one U.S. destination to another at very low prices. These discount tickets are not on sale in the United States and must be purchased abroad in conjunction with your international ticket. This system is the best, easiest, and fastest way to see the United States at low cost. Get information well in advance from your travel agent or the office of the airline concerned because the conditions attached to these discount tickets can be changed without advance notice.

BY CAR The United States is a car culture through and through. Driving is the most convenient and comfortable way to travel here. The interstate highway system connects cities and towns all over the country, and in addition to these high-speed, limited-access roadways, there's an extensive network of federal, state, and local highways and roads. Driving will give you a lot of flexibility in making, and altering, your itinerary and in allowing you to see off-the-beaten-path destinations that cannot be reached easily by public transportation. You'll also have easy access to inexpensive motels at interstate highway off-ramps.

BY TRAIN International visitors can buy a **USA Railpass,** good for 15 or 30 days of unlimited travel on **Amtrak** (© 800/872-7245; www.amtrak.com). These passes are available through many foreign travel agents. (With a foreign passport, you can also buy passes at staffed Amtrak offices in the United States, including locations in San Francisco, Los Angeles, Chicago, New York, Miami, Boston, and Washington, D.C.) Reservations are generally required and should be made for each part of your trip as early as possible. Amtrak also offers an **Air/Rail Travel Plan** that allows you to travel by both train and plane; for information, call © 877/937-7245.

BY BUS Although bus travel is often the most economical form of transit for short hops between U.S. cities, it can also be slow and uncomfortable—certainly not an option for everyone (particularly in situations where Amtrak, which is far more luxurious, offers similar rates). **Greyhound/Trailways** (© 800/229-9424 or 214/849-8100; www.greyhound.com), the sole nationwide bus line, offers an unlimited-travel **Ameripass/Discovery Pass** for 7 days at $229, 15 days at $339, 30 days at $459, and 60 days at $619. Passes must be purchased at a Greyhound terminal or online at www.greyhound.com. Special rates are available for seniors and students.

FAST FACTS: **For the International Traveler**

Automobile Organizations Auto clubs can supply maps, suggested routes, guidebooks, accident and bail-bond insurance, and emergency road service. **AAA** is the major auto club in the United States. If you belong to an auto club in your home country, inquire about AAA reciprocity before you leave. You may be able to join AAA even if you're not a member of a reciprocal club; to inquire, call AAA at ✆ **800/222-4357.** AAA is actually an organization of regional auto clubs; so look under "AAA Automobile Club" in the White Pages of the telephone directory. AAA's nationwide emergency road service telephone number is ✆ **800/AAA-HELP.**

Business Hours See "Fast Facts: Arizona," in chapter 2.

Currency See "Money," above.

Currency Exchange You'll find currency-exchange services in major international airports. There's a **Travelex** office (✆ 800/287-7362 or 602/275-8768; www.travelex.com) at Sky Harbor Airport (Terminal 4) in Phoenix, but not at Tucson International Airport. In Phoenix, **Bank of America,** 201 E. Washington St. (✆ 888/279-3264 or 602/523-2371), will exchange money, as will some of the bank's other branches. You can also change money at the **American Express** office in Biltmore Fashion Park, 2508 E. Camelback Rd. (✆ 602/468-1199). Also ask at your hotel desk; some hotels might be able to change major currencies for you. Elsewhere, it can be very difficult to change money.

Drinking Laws The legal age for purchase and consumption of alcoholic beverages is 21; proof of age is required and often requested at bars, nightclubs, and restaurants, so it's always a good idea to bring ID when you go out. Beer and wine can often be purchased in supermarkets, but liquor laws vary from state to state. In Arizona, liquor is sold at supermarkets.

Do not carry open containers of alcohol in your car or any public area that isn't zoned for alcohol consumption. The police can, and probably will, fine you on the spot. And nothing will ruin your trip faster than getting a citation for DUI ("driving under the influence"), so don't even think about driving while intoxicated.

Electricity The United States uses 110–120 volts AC (60 cycles), compared with 220–240 volts AC (50 cycles) in most of Europe, Australia, and New Zealand. If your small appliances use 220–240 volts, you'll need a 110-volt transformer and a plug adapter with two flat parallel pins to operate them here.

Embassies & Consulates All embassies are located in Washington, D.C. Some consulates are located in major U.S. cities, and most nations have a mission to the United Nations in New York City. If your country isn't listed below, call directory information in Washington, D.C. (✆ 202/555-1212), for the number of your national embassy.

The embassy of **Australia** is at 1601 Massachusetts Ave. NW, Washington, DC 20036-2273 (✆ 202/797-3000; www.austemb.org). The nearest is at Century Plaza Towers, 2049 Century Park E., 19th Floor, Los Angeles, CA 90067 (✆ 310/229-4800).

The embassy of **Canada** is at 501 Pennsylvania Ave. NW, Washington, DC 20001 (© **202/682-1740**; www.canadianembassy.org). The nearest consulate is at 550 S. Hope St., 9th Floor, Los Angeles, CA 90071-2627 (© **213/346-2700**).

The embassy of **Ireland** is at 2234 Massachusetts Ave. NW, Washington, DC 20008 (© **202/462-3939**; www.irelandemb.org). The nearest consulate is at 100 Pine St., 33rd Floor, San Francisco, CA 94111 (© **415/392-4214**).

The embassy of **New Zealand** is at 37 Observatory Circle NW, Washington, DC 20008 (© **202/328-4800**; www.nzemb.org). The nearest consulate is at 12400 Wilshire Blvd., Suite 1150, Los Angeles, CA 90025 (© **310/207-1605**).

The embassy of the **United Kingdom** is at 3100 Massachusetts Ave. NW, Washington, DC 20008 (© **202/588-7800**; www.britainusa.com). The nearest consulate is at 11766 Wilshire Blvd., Suite 1200, Los Angeles, CA 90025-6538 (© **310/481-0031**).

Emergencies Dial © **911** to report a fire, call the police, or get an ambulance. This is a free call (no coins are required at public telephones).

If you encounter serious problems, contact **Traveler's Aid Society International** (© **202/546-1127**; www.travelersaid.org) to help direct you to a local branch. This nationwide, nonprofit, social-service organization geared to helping travelers in difficult straits offers services that might include reuniting families separated while traveling, providing food and/or shelter to people stranded without cash, or even emotional counseling.

Gasoline (Petrol) Petrol is known as gasoline (or simply "gas") in the United States, and petrol stations are known as both gas stations and service stations. Gasoline costs less here than it does in Europe, and taxes are already included in the printed price. One U.S. gallon equals 3.8 liters or .85 imperial gallons.

Holidays Banks, government offices, post offices, and many stores, restaurants, and museums are closed on the following legal national holidays: January 1 (New Year's Day), the third Monday in January (Martin Luther King Day), the third Monday in February (Presidents' Day, Washington's Birthday), the last Monday in May (Memorial Day), July 4th (Independence Day), the first Monday in September (Labor Day), the second Monday in October (Columbus Day), November 11 (Veterans' Day/Armistice Day), the fourth Thursday in November (Thanksgiving Day), and December 25 (Christmas). Also, the Tuesday following the first Monday in November is Election Day and is a federal government holiday in presidential election years (held every 4 years).

Legal Aid If you are "pulled over" for a minor infraction (such as speeding), never attempt to pay the fine directly to a police officer; this could be construed as attempted bribery, a much more serious crime. Pay fines by mail, or directly into the hands of the clerk of the court. If accused of a more serious offense, say and do nothing before consulting a lawyer. Here the burden is on the state to prove a person's guilt beyond a reasonable doubt, and everyone has the right to remain silent, whether he or she is suspected of a crime or actually arrested. Once arrested, a person can make one telephone call to a party of his or her choice. Call your embassy or consulate.

Mail Mailboxes are blue with a red-and-white stripe and carry the inscription U.S. MAIL. Outside of major urban areas, such mailboxes can be difficult to locate. Look in front of supermarkets and at other large shopping centers. If your mail is addressed to a U.S. destination, don't forget to add the five- or nine-digit postal code (or zip code) after the two-letter abbreviation of the state to which the mail is addressed.

Domestic postage rates are 23¢ for a postcard and 37¢ for a letter. International mail rates vary. For example, a 1-ounce first-class letter to Europe or Asia costs 80¢ (60¢ to Canada and Mexico); a first-class postcard to Europe or Asia costs 70¢ (50¢ to Canada and Mexico).

Taxes The United States has no value-added tax (VAT) or other indirect tax at the national level. Every state, county, and city has the right to levy its own local tax on all purchases. Taxes are already included in the price of certain services, such as public transportation, cab fares, telephone calls, and gasoline.

In Arizona, the state sales tax is 5.6%, but communities can add local sales tax on top of this. Expect to pay around 28% tax on car rentals at the Tucson airport and around 50% in taxes and surcharges at the Phoenix airport (around 10% less if you rent outside the airports). Hotel room taxes range from around 6% to 17%.

Telephone & Fax The telephone system in the United States is run by private corporations, so rates, especially for long-distance service and operator-assisted calls, can vary widely. Generally, hotel surcharges on long-distance and local calls are astronomical, so you're usually better off using a **public pay telephone,** which you'll find clearly marked in most public buildings and private establishments as well as on the street. Grocery stores, convenience stores, and gas stations almost always have them. Many supermarkets and convenience stores also sell **prepaid calling cards** in denominations up to $50; these cards can be the least expensive way to call home. Many public phones at airports now accept American Express, MasterCard, and Visa. **Local calls** made from public pay phones in most locales cost either 35¢ or 50¢. Pay phones do not accept pennies, and few take anything larger than a quarter.

Most long-distance and international calls can be dialed directly from any phone. **For calls within the United States and to Canada,** dial 1 followed by the area code and the seven-digit number. **For other international calls,** dial 011 followed by the country code, city code, and telephone number you are calling.

Calls to area codes **800, 888, 877,** and **866** are toll-free. However, calls to numbers in area codes **700** and **900** (chat lines, bulletin boards, "dating" services, and so on) can be very expensive—usually 95¢ to $3 or more per minute.

For **reversed-charge** or **collect calls,** and for **person-to-person calls,** dial 0 (zero, not the letter *O*) followed by the area code and number you want; an operator will then come on the line, and you should specify that you are calling collect, or person-to-person, or both. If your operator-assisted call is international, ask for the overseas operator.

For **local directory assistance** ("information"), dial 411; for long-distance information, dial 1, then the appropriate area code and 555-1212.

Most hotels have **fax machines** available for guest use (be sure to ask about the charge to use it). A less expensive way to send and receive faxes may be at chain stores such as Kinko's or The UPS Store (look in the Yellow Pages under "Packing Services").

There are two kinds of telephone directories in the United States. The **White Pages** lists private households and business subscribers in alphabetical order. The inside front cover lists emergency numbers for police, fire, ambulance, the Coast Guard, poison-control center, crime-victims hot line, and so on. The first few pages tell you how to make long-distance and international calls, complete with country codes and area codes. Government numbers are usually printed on blue paper within the White Pages. Printed on yellow paper, the **Yellow Pages** lists local services, businesses, industries, and houses of worship according to category, with an index at the front or back. The Yellow Pages includes maps, postal zip codes, and public transportation routes.

Time The United States is divided into six time zones. From east to west, they are Eastern Standard Time (EST), Central Standard Time (CST), Mountain Standard Time (MST), Pacific Standard Time (PST), Alaska Standard Time (AST), and Hawaii Standard Time (HST). Always keep the changing time zones in mind if you are traveling (or even telephoning) long distances in the United States. For example, noon in New York City (EST) is 11am in Chicago (CST), 10am in Phoenix (MST), 9am in Los Angeles (PST), 8am in Anchorage (AST), and 7am in Honolulu (HST).

Arizona is in the Mountain Time zone, but it does *not* observe daylight saving time. Consequently, from the first Sunday in April until the last Sunday in October, there is no time difference between Arizona and California and other states on the West Coast. There is an exception, however—the Navajo Reservation observes daylight saving time. However, the Hopi Reservation does not.

Tipping Tipping is thoroughly ingrained in the American way of life. Here are some rules of thumb:

In hotels, tip **bellhops** at least $1 per bag ($2–$3 if you have a lot of luggage) and tip the **chamber staff** $1 to $2 per day (more if you've left a disaster area to clean up, or if you're traveling with kids and/or pets). Tip the **doorman** or **concierge** only if he or she has provided you with some specific service (for example, calling a cab for you or obtaining difficult-to-get theater tickets). Tip the **valet-parking attendant** $1 every time you get your car.

In restaurants, bars, and nightclubs, tip **service staff** 15% to 20% of the check, tip **bartenders** 10% to 15%, tip **checkroom attendants** $1 per garment, and tip **valet-parking attendants** $1 per vehicle. Tipping is not expected in cafeterias and fast-food restaurants.

Tip **cab drivers** 15% of the fare.

As for other service personnel, tip **skycaps** (luggage carriers) at airports at least $1 per bag ($2–$3 if you have a lot of luggage) and tip **hairdressers** and **barbers** 15% to 20%.

Toilets You won't find public toilets on the streets in most U.S. cities, but they can be found in hotel lobbies, bars, restaurants, museums, department stores, shopping malls, railway and bus stations, and service stations. Large hotels and fast-food restaurants are probably the best bet for good, clean facilities. Note, however, that restaurants and bars in heavily visited areas may reserve their restrooms for customers. Some establishments display a notice indicating this. You can ignore this sign or buy a cup of coffee or a soft drink, which will qualify you as a customer.

4

Phoenix, Scottsdale & the Valley of the Sun

Forget the stately cacti and cowboys riding off into the sunset; think Los Angeles without the Pacific. While the nation has carefully nurtured its image of Phoenix as a desert cow town, this city in the Sonoran Desert has rocketed into the 21st century and become the sixth-largest city in the country. Sprawling across 400 square miles of what once was cactus and creosote bushes, the greater Phoenix metropolitan area, also known as the Valley of the Sun (or, more commonly, just the Valley), is now a major metropolitan area replete with dozens of resort hotels, fabulous restaurants, excellent museums, hundreds of golf courses, world-class shopping, four pro sports teams, and a red-hot nightlife scene.

Sure, it also has traffic jams and smog, but at the end of the day, it can usually also claim to have had beautiful sunny weather. Sunshine and blue skies, day after day after day have made this one of the most popular winter destinations in the country. When Chicago weather forecasts call for snow and subzero temperatures you can have a hard time getting a tee time on a Phoenix area golf course. Phoenicians may get the summertime blues when temperatures hit the triple digits, but

from September to May, the climate here can verge on perfect—warm enough in the daytime for lounging by the pool, cool enough at night to require a jacket.

With green lawns, orange groves, swimming pools, and palm trees, it's easy to forget that Phoenix is in the middle of the desert. Water channeled in from distant reservoirs has allowed this city to flourish like a desert oasis. However, if you find yourself wondering where the desert is, you need only lift your eyes to one of the many mountains that rise up from amid the urban sprawl. South Mountain, Camelback Mountain, Mummy Mountain, Piestewa Peak, Papago Buttes, Pinnacle Peak—these rugged, rocky summits have been preserved in their natural state, and it is to these cactus-covered uplands that the city's citizens retreat when they've had enough asphalt and air-conditioning. From almost anywhere in the Valley, you're never more than 15- or 20-minute drive from some natural area where you can commune with the cactus while gazing out across a bustling, modern city.

Best of all, at the end of the day, you can retreat to a comfortable bed at one of the country's top resorts.

1 Orientation

ARRIVING

BY PLANE   Centrally located 3 miles east of downtown Phoenix, **Sky Harbor International Airport** (© **602/273-3300;** www.phxskyharbor.com) has three terminals, with a free 24-hour shuttle bus offering frequent service between them. For lost and found, call © **602/273-3307.**

Tips **A Name Change**

In early 2003, the official name of Phoenix's Squaw Peak was changed to Piestewa Peak (pronounced Pie-*ess*-too-uh) to honor Pfc. Lori Ann Piestewa, a member of the Hopi tribe and the first female soldier to be killed in the Iraq War. The peak in north Phoenix has long been a popular hiking destination. If you hear people referring to both Squaw Peak and Piestewa Peak, it's one and the same place. Ditto for Squaw Peak Parkway and Squaw Peak Drive. In early 2004, Republican state legislators announced their intentions to get the name changed back to Squaw Peak!

There are two entrances to the airport. The west entrance can be accessed from either the Piestewa Parkway (Ariz. 51) or 24th Street, while the east entrance can be accessed from the Hohokam Expressway (Ariz. 143), which is an extension of 44th Street. If you're headed to downtown Phoenix, leave by way of the 24th Street exit and continue west on Washington Street. If you're headed to Scottsdale, take the 44th Street exit, go north on Ariz. 143 and then east on Ariz. 202 to U.S. 101 north. For Tempe or Mesa, take the 44th Street exit, go north on Ariz. 143, and then head east on Ariz. 202.

SuperShuttle (© **800/BLUE-VAN** or 602/244-9000; www.supershuttle.com) offers 24-hour door-to-door van service between Sky Harbor Airport and resorts, hotels, and homes throughout the valley. Per-person fares average $6 to $10 to the downtown and Tempe area, $16 to downtown Scottsdale, and $30 to north Scottsdale.

Taxis can be found outside all three terminals and cost only slightly more than shuttle vans. You can also call **Discount Cab** (© **602/200-2000**) or **Allstate Cab** (© **602/275-8888**). A taxi from the airport to downtown Phoenix will cost around $10; to Scottsdale, between $15 and $30.

Valley Metro (© **602/253-5000;** www.valleymetro.org) provides public bus service throughout the valley, with the Red Line operating between the airport and downtown Phoenix, Tempe, and Mesa. The Red Line runs daily starting between 3 and 5am and continues operating until after midnight. The ride from the airport to downtown takes about 20 minutes and costs $1.25. There is no direct bus to Scottsdale, so you would first need to go to Tempe and then transfer to a northbound bus. You can pick up a copy of the *Bus Book,* a guide and route map for the Valley Metro bus system, at Central Station, at the corner of Central Avenue and Van Buren Street.

BY CAR   Phoenix is connected to Los Angeles and Tucson by I-10 and to Flagstaff via I-17. If you're headed to Scottsdale, the easiest route is to take the Red Mountain Freeway (Ariz. 202) east to U.S. 101 north. U.S. 101 loops all the way around the east, north, and west sides of the valley. The Superstition Freeway (U.S. 60) leads to Tempe, Mesa, and Chandler.

BY TRAIN   There is no passenger rail service to Phoenix. However, **Amtrak** (© **800/872-7245;** www.amtrak.com) will sell you a ticket to Phoenix, though you'll have to take a shuttle bus from either Flagstaff or Tucson. The scheduling is so horrible on these routes that you would have to be a total masochist to opt for Amtrak service to Phoenix.

VISITOR INFORMATION

You'll find **tourist information desks** in the baggage-claim areas of all three terminals at Sky Harbor Airport. The city's main visitor center is the **Greater Phoenix Convention & Visitors Bureau,** 50 N. Second St. (© **877/225-5749** or 602/254-6500; www.visitphoenix.com), on the corner of Adams Street in downtown Phoenix. There's also a small visitor information center at the Biltmore Fashion Park shopping center, at Camelback Road and 24th Street (© **602/254-6500**).

The **Visitor Information Line** (© **602/252-5588**) has recorded information about current events in Phoenix and is updated weekly.

If you're staying in Scottsdale, you may want to drop by the **Scottsdale Convention & Visitors Bureau Visitor Center,** Galleria Corporate Center, 4343 N. Scottsdale Rd., Suite 170 (© **800/782-1117** or 480/421-1004; www.scottsdale cvb.com).

CITY LAYOUT

MAIN ARTERIES & STREETS   Over the past decade, the Phoenix area has seen the construction of numerous new freeways, and it is now possible to drive from the airport to Scottsdale by freeway. U.S. Loop 101 forms a loop around the east, north, and west sides of the valley, providing freeway access to Scottsdale from I-17 on the north side of Phoenix and from U.S. 60 in Tempe.

I-17 (Black Canyon Fwy.), which connects Phoenix with Flagstaff, is the city's main north–south freeway. This freeway curves to the east just south of downtown (where it is renamed the **Maricopa Fwy.** and merges with I-10). **I-10,** which connects Phoenix with Los Angeles and Tucson, is called the **Papago Freeway** on the west side of the valley and as it passes north of downtown; as it curves around to pass to the west and south of the airport, it merges with I-17 and is renamed the Maricopa Freeway. At Tempe, this freeway curves around to the south and heads out of the valley.

North of the airport, **Ariz. 202 (Red Mountain Fwy.)** heads east from I-10 and passes along the north side of Tempe, providing access to downtown Tempe, Arizona State University, Mesa, and Scottsdale (via U.S. Loop 101). On the east side of the airport, **Ariz. 143 (Hohokam Expwy)** connects Ariz. 202 with I-10.

At the interchange of I-10 and Ariz. 202, northwest of Sky Harbor Airport, **Ariz. 51 (Piestewa Pkwy.)** heads north through the center of Phoenix to the U.S. Loop 101 and is the best north–south route in the city.

South of the airport off I-10, **U.S. 60 (Superstition Fwy.)** heads east to Tempe, Chandler, Mesa, and Gilbert. **U.S. Loop 101** leads north from U.S. 60 (and Ariz. 202) through Scottsdale and across the north side of Phoenix to connect with I-17. U.S. 60 and U.S. 101 provide the best route from the airport to the Scottsdale resorts. On the east side of the valley, U.S. 101 is called the Pima Freeway.

Secondary highways in the valley include the **Beeline Highway (Ariz. 87),** which starts at the east end of Ariz. 202 (Red Mountain Fwy.) in Mesa and leads to Payson, and **Grand Avenue (U.S. 60),** which starts downtown and leads west to Sun City and Wickenburg.

Phoenix and the surrounding cities of Mesa, Tempe, Scottsdale, and Chandler, and even those cities farther out in the valley, are laid out in a grid pattern with major avenues and roads about every mile. For traveling east to west across Phoenix, your best choices (other than the above-mentioned freeways) are

Camelback Road, Indian School Road, and McDowell Road. For traveling north and south, 44th Street, 24th Street, and Central Avenue are good choices. Hayden Road is a north–south alternative to Scottsdale Road, which gets jammed at rush hours.

FINDING AN ADDRESS   Central Avenue, which runs north to south through downtown Phoenix, is the starting point for all east and west street numbering. **Washington Street** is the starting point for north and south numbering. North-to-south numbered *streets* are to be found on the east side of the city, while north-to-south numbered *avenues* will be found on the west. For the most part, street numbers advance by 100 with each block. Odd-numbered addresses are on the south and east sides of streets, while even-numbered addresses are on north and west sides of streets.

For example, if you're looking for 4454 East Camelback Rd., you'll find it 44 blocks east of Central Avenue between 44th and 45th streets on the north side of the street. If you're looking for 2905 North 35th Ave., you'll find it 35 blocks west of Central Avenue and 29 blocks north of Washington Street on the east side of the street. Just for general reference, Camelback marks the 5000 block north. Also, whenever getting directions, ask for the cross street closest to where you're going. Street numbers can be hard to spot when you're driving past at 45 mph.

STREET MAPS   The street maps handed out by rental-car companies may be good for general navigation around the city, but they are almost useless for finding a particular address if it is not on a major arterial, so as soon as you can, stop at a minimart and buy a Phoenix map. Unfortunately, you'll probably also have to buy a separate Scottsdale map. Alternatively, if you are a member of AAA, you can get a good Phoenix map before you leave home. You can also get a simple map at the airport tourist information desks or at the downtown visitor center.

NEIGHBORHOODS IN BRIEF

Because of urban sprawl, Phoenix has yielded its importance to an area known as the Valley of the Sun (or just "The Valley"), an area encompassing Phoenix and its metropolitan area of more than 20 cities. Consequently, as outlying cities have taken on regional importance, neighborhoods per se have lost much of their significance. Think of the valley's many cities as automobile-oriented neighborhoods. That said, there are some actual neighborhoods worth noting.

Downtown Phoenix Roughly bordered by Thomas Road on the north, Buckeye Road on the south, 19th Avenue on the west, and Seventh Street on the east, downtown is primarily a business, financial, and government district, where both the city hall and state capitol are located. Downtown Phoenix is also the valley's prime sports, entertainment, and museum district. The Arizona Diamondbacks play big-league baseball in the **Bank One Ballpark (BOB),** while the Phoenix Suns shoot hoops at the **America West Arena.** Of course, there are also lots of sports bars in the area. There are three major performing-arts venues—the historic **Orpheum Theatre, Symphony Hall,** and the **Herberger Theater Center.** Downtown museums include the **Phoenix Museum of History** and the **Arizona Science Center,** both located in Heritage and Science Park. Other area attractions include **Heritage Square** (historic homes), the **Arizona Capitol Museum,** and the **Arizona Mining & Mineral Museum.** On the

Phoenix, Scottsdale & the Valley of the Sun

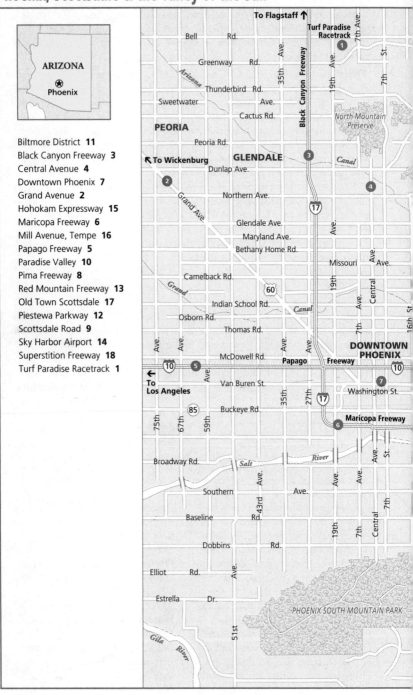

Biltmore District **11**
Black Canyon Freeway **3**
Central Avenue **4**
Downtown Phoenix **7**
Grand Avenue **2**
Hohokam Expressway **15**
Maricopa Freeway **6**
Mill Avenue, Tempe **16**
Papago Freeway **5**
Paradise Valley **10**
Pima Freeway **8**
Red Mountain Freeway **13**
Old Town Scottsdale **17**
Piestewa Parkway **12**
Scottsdale Road **9**
Sky Harbor Airport **14**
Superstition Freeway **18**
Turf Paradise Racetrack **1**

ARIZONA
★ Phoenix

To Flagstaff ↑
Bell Rd.
Turf Paradise Racetrack **1**
Greenway Rd.
Arizona
Thunderbird Rd.
Sweetwater Ave.
Cactus Rd.
North Mountain Preserve
PEORIA
Peoria Rd.
← To Wickenburg **GLENDALE** **3** Canal
Dunlap Ave.
2
Northern Ave.
Grand Ave.
17
Glendale Ave.
Maryland Ave.
Bethany Home Rd.
Missouri Ave.
Camelback Rd.
Grand
60
Indian School Rd.
Canal
Osborn Rd.
Thomas Rd.
DOWNTOWN PHOENIX
McDowell Rd. **Papago Freeway**
10 **5**
7
To Los Angeles
Van Buren St.
Washington St.
85
Buckeye Rd.
17
75th 67th 59th
35th 27th
Maricopa Freeway
6
Broadway Rd.
Salt River
Southern Ave.
43rd
Baseline Rd.
19th 7th Central
Dobbins Rd.
Elliot Rd.
Estrella Dr.
PHOENIX SOUTH MOUNTAIN PARK
51st
Gila River

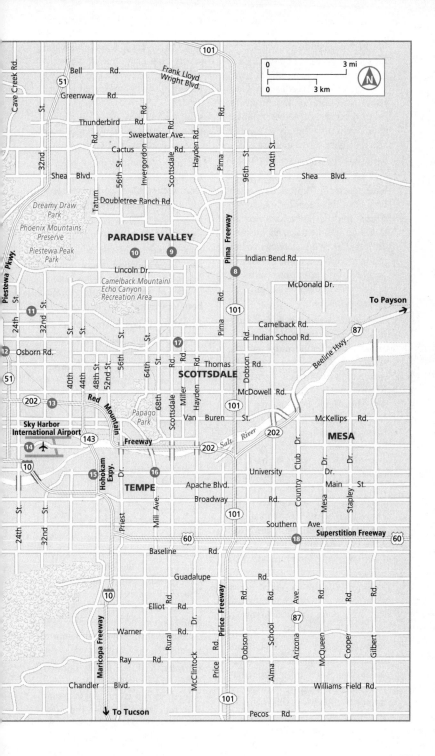

northern edge of downtown are the **Heard Museum,** the **Phoenix Central Library** (an architectural gem), and the **Phoenix Art Museum.** Currently, the core of downtown is being referred to as Copper Square in an attempt by the city to give the area a neighborhood identity.

Biltmore District The Biltmore District, also known as the **Camelback Corridor,** centers on Camelback Road between 24th and 44th streets and is Phoenix's upscale shopping, residential, and business district. The area is characterized by modern office buildings and is anchored by the Arizona Biltmore Hotel and Biltmore Fashion Park shopping mall.

Scottsdale A separate city of more than 200,000 people, Scottsdale extends from Tempe in the south to Carefree in the north, a distance of more than 20 miles. Scottsdale Road between Indian School Road and Shea Boulevard has long been known as **Resort Row** and is home to more than a dozen major resorts. However, as Scottsdale has sprawled ever northward, so, too, have the resorts, and now north Scottsdale has become the center of the resort, shopping, and restaurant scene. Downtown Scottsdale—which consists of Old Town, the Main Street Arts and Antiques District, the Marshall Way Contemporary Arts District, and the Fifth Avenue Shops—is filled with tourist shops, galleries, boutiques, Native American crafts stores, and restaurants.

Tempe Tempe is the home of Arizona State University and has lots of nightclubs and bars as well as all the other trappings of a university town. **Mill Avenue,** which has dozens of interesting shops along a stretch of about 4 blocks, is the center of activity both day and night. This is one of the few areas in the

valley where locals actually walk the streets and hang out at sidewalk cafes (Old Town Scottsdale often has people on its streets, but few are locals).

Paradise Valley If Scottsdale is Phoenix's Beverly Hills, then Paradise Valley is its Bel-Air. The most exclusive community in the valley is almost entirely residential, but you won't see too many of the more lavish homes because they're set on large tracts of land.

Mesa This eastern suburb of Phoenix is the valley's main high-tech area. Large shopping malls, numerous inexpensive chain motels, and a couple of small museums attract both locals and visitors to Mesa.

Chandler Lying to the south of Tempe, this city has been booming over the past few years. New restaurants have opened, the old downtown has gotten something of a face-lift, and there's a big new mall. This area is of interest primarily to east valley residents.

Glendale Located northwest of downtown Phoenix, Glendale has numerous historic buildings in its downtown. With its dozens of antiques and collectibles stores, it has become the antiques capital of the valley. The city also has several small museums, including the Bead Museum and Historic Saguaro Ranch. With the opening of the new Glendale Arena, home of the Phoenix Coyotes hockey team, this city has begun to exercise a newfound importance in the valley. Still to come is the new football stadium for the Arizona Cardinals.

Carefree & Cave Creek Located about 20 miles north of Old Scottsdale, these two communities represent the Old West and the New West. Carefree is a planned community and home to the prestigious

Boulders resort and Santa Fe–style El Pedregal shopping center. Neighboring Cave Creek, on the other hand, plays up its Western heritage in its architecture and preponderance of saloons, steakhouses, and shops selling Western crafts and other gifts.

2 Getting Around

BY CAR

Phoenix and the surrounding cities that together make up the Valley of the Sun sprawl across more than 400 square miles, so if you want to make the best use of your time, it's essential to have a car. Outside downtown Phoenix, there's almost always plenty of free parking wherever you go (although finding a parking space can be time consuming in Old Scottsdale and at some of the more popular malls and shopping plazas). If you want to feel like a local, opt for the ubiquitous valet parking wherever possible (just be sure to keep plenty of small bills on hand for tipping the parking attendants).

Because Phoenix is a major tourist destination, good car-rental rates are often available. However, taxes and surcharges on rentals at Sky Harbor Airport now run 50% or more, which pretty much negates any deal you might get on your rate. Expect to pay around $200 per week ($300 with taxes) for a compact car in the high season. See chapter 2 for general tips on car rentals.

All major rental-car companies have rental desks at Sky Harbor Airport, although none have pick up and drop off right in the airport. Be sure to leave time in your schedule for taking a shuttle bus to and from the airport to the rental-car lot. There are also plenty of other locations in Phoenix and Scottsdale. Rental-car companies at the airport include the following: **Advantage** (℃ 800/ 777-5500 or 602/244-0450); **Alamo** (℃ 800/462-5266 or 602/244-0897), **Avis** (℃ 800/831-2847 or 602/273-3222), **Budget** (℃ 800/527-0700), **Dollar** (℃ 800/800-4000), **Enterprise** (℃ 800/736-8222 or 602/225-0588), **Hertz** (℃ 800/654-3131 or 602/267-8822), **National** (℃ 800/227-7368 or 602/ 275-4771), and **Thrifty** (℃ 800/847-4389 or 602/244-0311).

If you'd like a bit more style while you cruise from resort to golf course to nightclub, call **Rent-a-Vette,** 1215 N. Scottsdale Rd., Scottsdale (℃ **888/308-5995** or 480/941-3001), which charges $229 to $299 per day for a Corvette. It also rents Porsche Boxters, Mustang GTs, Jaguars XK-8s, Plymouth Prowlers, and Dodge Vipers.

If a Jeep doesn't offer enough excitement and wind in your hair, how about a motorcycle? **Street Eagle of Scottsdale,** 15001 N. Hayden Rd., Scottsdale (℃ **866/730-3200** or 480/905-3200; www.streeteagle.com) rents Harley-Davidson, BMW, and Suzuki motorcycles for $99 to $149 per day. You must have a valid motorcycle driver's license. In Arizona you don't have to wear a helmet, so you really can ride with the wind in your hair.

BY PUBLIC TRANSPORTATION

Unfortunately, **Valley Metro** (℃ **602/253-5000;** www.valleymetro.maricopa.gov), the Phoenix public bus system, is not very useful to tourists. It's primarily meant to be used by commuters. However, if you decide you want to take the bus, pick up a copy of the *Bus Book* at one of the tourist information desks in the airport (where it's sometimes available), at Central Station at the corner of Central Avenue and Van Buren Street, or at any Frys supermarket. Local bus fare is $1.25; express bus fare is $1.75. A 10-ride ticket book, an all-day pass, and a monthly pass are also available.

Of slightly more value to visitors is the free **Downtown Area Shuttle (DASH),** which provides bus service within the downtown area Monday through Friday from 6:30am to 5:30pm. These buses serve regular stops every 6 to 18 minutes; they're primarily for downtown workers, but attractions along the route include the state capitol and Heritage Square. In Tempe, **Free Local Area Shuttle (FLASH)** buses provide a similar service on a loop around Arizona State University. The route includes Mill Avenue and Sun Devil Stadium. For information on both DASH and FLASH, call ℂ **602/253-5000.**

In Scottsdale, you can ride the **Scottsdale Trolley** (ℂ **480/421-1004;** www.valleymetro.org) shuttle buses between Scottsdale Fashion Square, the Fifth Avenue shops, the Main Street Arts and Antiques district, and the Old Town district. These buses operate between mid-November and the end of May and run Monday through Saturday from 11am to 6pm (until 9pm on Thurs).

BY TAXI

Because distances in Phoenix are so great, the price of an average taxi ride can be quite high. However, if you don't have your own wheels and the bus isn't running because it's late at night or the weekend, you won't have any choice but to call a cab. **Yellow Cab** (ℂ **602/252-5252**) charges $2.50 for the first mile and $1.50 per mile thereafter. **Scottsdale Cab** (ℂ **480/994-1616**) charges $2 per mile, with a $5 minimum.

FAST FACTS: Phoenix

American Express There's an American Express office in Biltmore Fashion Park, 2508 E. Camelback Rd. (ℂ **602/468-1199**), open Monday through Saturday from 10am to 6pm.

Babysitters If your hotel can't recommend or provide a sitter, contact the **Granny Company** (ℂ **602/956-4040**).

Car Rentals See "Getting Around," above.

Dentist Call the Dental Referral Service (ℂ **800/511-8663**).

Doctor Call the Maricopa County Medical Society (ℂ **602/252-2844**) for doctor referrals.

Emergencies For police, fire, or medical emergency, phone ℂ **911.**

Eyeglass Repair The **Nationwide Vision Center** (www.nationwidevision. com) has nearly 30 locations around the valley, including 7904 E. Chaparral Rd., Scottsdale (ℂ **480/874-2543**); 3202 E. Greenway, Paradise Valley (ℂ **602/788-8413**); 4615 E. Thomas Rd., Phoenix (ℂ **602/952-8667**); and 933 E. University Dr., Tempe (ℂ **480/966-4992**).

Hospitals The **Banner Good Samaritan Regional Medical Center,** 1111 E. McDowell Rd., Phoenix (ℂ **602/239-2000**), is one of the largest hospitals in the valley.

Hot Lines The **Visitor Information Line** (ℂ **602/252-5588**) has recorded tourist information on Phoenix and the Valley of the Sun.

Information See "Visitor Information," earlier in this chapter.

Internet Access If your hotel doesn't provide Internet access, your next best bet is to visit one of the **Kinko's** in the area. There are locations in downtown Phoenix at 201 E. Washington St., Suite 101 (ℂ **602/252-4055**);

off the Camelback Corridor at 3801 N. Central Ave. (✆ **602/241-9440**); and in Scottsdale just off Indian School Road at 4150 N. Drinkwater Blvd. (✆ **480/946-0500**).

Lost Property If you lose something at the airport, call ✆ **602/273-3307**; on a bus, call ✆ **602/253-5000**.

Newspapers & Magazines The *Arizona Republic* is Phoenix's daily newspaper. The Thursday edition has a special section ("The Rep") with schedules of the upcoming week's movie, music, and cultural performances. *New Times* is a free weekly journal with comprehensive listings of cultural events, films, and rock club and concert schedules. The best place to find *New Times* is at corner newspaper boxes in downtown Phoenix, Scottsdale, or Tempe.

Pharmacies Call ✆ **800/WALGREENS** for the Walgreens pharmacy that's nearest you; some are open 24 hours a day.

Police For police emergencies, phone ✆ **911**.

Post Office The Phoenix Downtown Station, 522 N. Central Ave. (✆ **602/253-9648**), is open Monday through Friday from 9am to 5pm. In Scottsdale, the Scottsdale Hopi Station, 8790 E. Via de Ventura (✆ **480/998-9356**), is open Monday through Friday from 8am to 5pm and on Saturday from 9am to 1pm.

Safety Don't leave valuables in view in your car, especially when parking in downtown Phoenix. Put anything of value in the trunk or, if you're driving a hatchback or station wagon, under the seat. Take extra precautions after dark in the south central Phoenix area and downtown. Violent acts of road rage are all too common in Phoenix, so it's a good idea to be polite when driving. Aggressive drivers should be given plenty of room.

Taxes State sales tax is 5.6% (plus variable local taxes). Hotel room taxes vary considerably by city but are mostly between 10% and 11%. It's in renting a car that you really get pounded. The total taxes and surcharges when renting a car at Sky Harbor Airport add up to around 50%! You can save around 10% (the airport concession fee recoupment charge) by renting your car at an office outside the airport.

Taxis See "Getting Around," above.

Weather For weather information, call ✆ **800/555-8355** and say "weather."

3 Where to Stay

Because the Phoenix area has long been popular as a winter refuge from cold and snow, it now has the greatest concentration of resorts in the continental United States. However, even with all the hotel rooms here, sunshine and spring training combine to make it hard to find a room on short notice between February and April. If you're planning to visit during these months, make your reservations as far in advance as possible. Also keep in mind that in winter, the Phoenix metro area has some of the highest rates in the country.

Most resorts offer a variety of weekend, golf, and tennis packages, as well as off-season discounts and corporate rates (which you can often get just by asking). We've given only the official "rack rates," or walk-in rates, below, but it

Phoenix, Scottsdale & the Valley of the Sun Accommodations

Arizona Biltmore Resort & Spa **12**
Best Western Airport Inn **41**
Best Western Bell Hotel **1**
Best Western Inn Suites
  Hotel Phoenix **5**
Camelback Inn, A JW Marriott
  Resort & Spa **15**
Days Inn Scottsdale Resort
  at Fashion Square Mall **28**
Days Inn–Tempe **36**
Doubletree Paradise Valley
  Resort **24**
Embassy Suites Biltmore **11**
Embassy Suites Phoenix North **2**
Embassy Suites Phoenix/
  Scottsdale **17**
The Fairmont Scottsdale Princess **18**
Fiesta Inn Resort **38**
Hermosa Inn **14**
Holiday Inn SunSpree Resort **20**
Hotel San Carlos **8**
Hyatt Regency Scottsdale
  Resort at Gainey Ranch **16**
James Hotel **32**
Maricopa Manor **6**
Motel 6–Mesa **35**
Motel 6–Scottsdale **27**
Motel 6–Sweetwater **3**
The Phoenician **26**
Pointe Hilton Squaw Peak Resort **13**
Pointe Hilton Tapatio Cliffs Resort **4**
Pointe South Mountain Resort **40**
Ramada Limited Scottsdale **31**
Renaissance Scottsdale Resort **22**
The Ritz-Carlton Phoenix **10**
Rodeway Inn–Airport East **37**
Rodeway Inn–Phoenix/Scottsdale **30**
Royal Palms Resort and Spa **25**
Sanctuary on Camelback
  Mountain **23**
Scottsdale Resort & Athletic Club **21**
Sierra Suites **9**
The Sunburst Resort **29**
Super 8–Phoenix Metro/Central **7**
Super 8–Tempe/Scottsdale **34**
Tempe Mission Palms Hotel **33**
Westin Kierland Resort & Spa **19**
The Wyndham Buttes Resort **39**

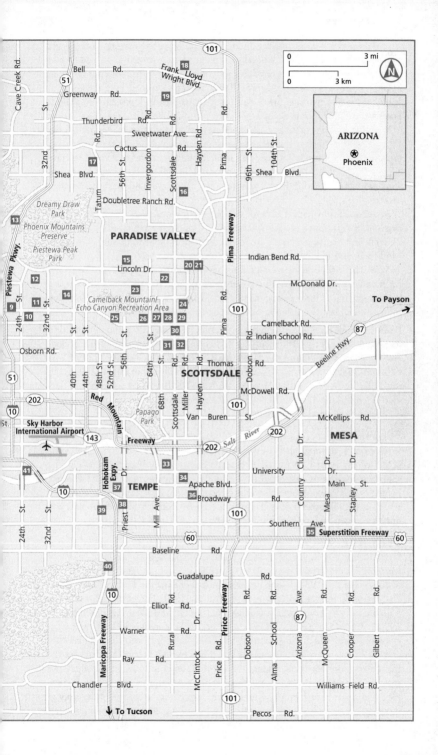

always pays to ask about special discounts or packages. Sometimes you can get a lower rate just by asking. If a hotel isn't full and isn't expected to be, you should be able to get a lower rate. Don't forget your AAA or AARP discounts if you belong to one of these organizations. Remember that business hotels downtown and near the airport often lower their rates on weekends. Don't forget to check hotel websites for special deals.

If you're looking to save even more money, consider traveling during the shoulder seasons of late spring and late summer. Temperatures are not at their midsummer peak nor are room rates at their midwinter highs. If you'll be traveling with children, always ask whether your child will be able to stay for free in your room, and whether there's a limit to the number of children who can stay for free.

Request a room with a view of the mountains whenever possible. You can overlook a swimming pool anywhere, but some of the main selling points of Phoenix and Scottsdale hotels are the views of Mummy Mountain, Camelback Mountain, and Piestewa Peak.

With the exception of valet-parking services and parking garages at downtown convention hotels, parking is free at almost all Phoenix hotels. If there is a parking charge, I have noted it. You'll find that all hotels have nonsmoking rooms and all but the cheapest have wheelchair-accessible rooms.

BED & BREAKFASTS   While most people dreaming of a Phoenix vacation have visions of luxury resorts dancing in their heads, there are also plenty of bed-and-breakfast inns around the valley. **Mi Casa Su Casa** (✆ **800/456-0682** or 480/990-0682; www.azres.com) can book you into dozens of different homes in the Valley of the Sun, as can **Arizona Trails Bed & Breakfast Reservation Service** (✆ **888/799-4284** or 480/837-4284; www.arizonatrails.com), which also books tour and hotel reservations.

SCOTTSDALE

With a dozen or more resorts lined up along Scottsdale Road, Scottsdale is the center of the valley's resort scene. Because Scottsdale is also the valley's prime shopping and dining district, this is the most convenient place to stay if you're here to eat and shop. However, traffic in Scottsdale is bad, the landscape at most resorts is flat (compared with the hillside settings in north Scottsdale), and you don't get much feel for being in the desert.

VERY EXPENSIVE

Camelback Inn, A JW Marriott Resort & Spa ✮✮✮   Set at the foot of Mummy Mountain and overlooking Camelback Mountain, the Camelback Inn, which opened in 1936, is one of the grande dames of the Phoenix hotel scene and abounds in traditional Southwestern character. Forget the glitz of The Phoenician; this place gives you old-school luxury with 21st-century enhancements. Within the past few years, the resort has undergone $50 million worth of renovations, which have brought the Camelback Inn into the 21st century and added lots of great amenities. Although the two 18-hole golf courses are the main attractions for many guests, the spa is among the finest in the state, and recently completed an $8-million renovation. There's also an extensive pool complex that appeals to families. Guest rooms, which are spread over the sloping grounds, are decorated with Southwestern furnishings and art, and all have balconies or patios. Some rooms even have their own private pools. This is an old-money sort of place that seamlessly melds tradition with modern amenities.

5402 E. Lincoln Dr., Scottsdale, AZ 85253. © 800/24-CAMEL or 480/948-1700. Fax 480/951-8469. www.camel backinn.com. 453 units. Jan to early June $279–$429 double, $639–$2,075 suite; early June to early Sept $189 double, $235–$1,550 suite; early Sept to Dec $339 double, $485–$1,550 suite. Children under 18 stay free in parent's room. AE, DC, DISC, MC, V. Small pets accepted. **Amenities:** 5 restaurants (American, Mexican, healthy); cafe; lounge; 3 pools; 2 outstanding 18-hole golf courses; pitch-and-putt green; 6 tennis courts; basketball and volleyball courts; exercise room; recently renovated and expanded full-service spa; 3 Jacuzzis; bike rentals; children's programs and playground; concierge; car-rental desk; business center; salon; room service; massage; babysitting; guest laundry and laundry service; dry cleaning. *In room:* A/C, TV, dataport, high-speed Internet access, minibar, coffeemaker, hair dryer, iron, safe, wi-fi.

Hyatt Regency Scottsdale Resort at Gainey Ranch ★★★ *Kids*   From the colonnades of palm trees to the lobby walls that slide away, this luxurious resort is designed to impress and year after year continues to be my favorite Scottsdale resort. It's relatively close in, has interesting architecture, and beautiful grounds. What's not to love? A 2½-acre water playground serves as the resort's focal point, and the extravagant complex of 10 interconnecting swimming pools includes a water slide, a sand beach, a water-volleyball pool, waterfalls, and a huge whirlpool spa. The grounds are planted with hundreds of palm trees that frame the gorgeous views of the distant McDowell Mountains; closer at hand, original works of art have been placed throughout the resort. Guest rooms are luxurious and are designed to reflect the desert location. The Golden Swan restaurant has an unusual sunken waterside gazebo, while Ristorante Sandolo features singing servers and after-dinner gondola rides. The resort's Native American and Environmental Learning Center provides a glimpse into Native American culture and the ecology of the Sonoran Desert. With its children's programs and "Lost Dutchman Mine," where kids can dig for buried treasure, this is a super choice for families.

7500 E. Doubletree Ranch Rd., Scottsdale, AZ 85258. © 800/55-HYATT or 480/991-3388. Fax 480/483-5550. www.scottsdale.hyatt.com. 500 units. Jan to late May $280–$490 double, from $390 suite and casita; late May to early Sept $170–$275 double, from $250 suite and casita; early Sept to Dec $280–$550 double, from $390 suite and casita. Children under 18 stay free in parent's room. AE, DC, DISC, MC, V. **Amenities:** 4 restaurants (New American, Southwestern, Italian); snack bar; 2 lounges; coffee bar; juice bar; 10 pools; 27-hole golf course (with lots of water hazards); 8 tennis courts; health club and spa; 3 Jacuzzis; bike rentals; children's programs; concierge; car-rental desk; business center; 24-hr. room service; massage; babysitting; laundry service; dry cleaning; concierge-level rooms. *In room:* A/C, TV, dataport, high-speed Internet access, minibar, hair dryer, iron, safe.

The Phoenician ★★★ *Kids*   Situated on 250 acres at the foot of Camelback Mountain, this palatial resort consistently ranks among the finest resorts in the world. If you must stay at the very best, this is it. However, the character here is international, not Arizonan, so if you're looking for a sense of place, this isn't the resort for you. Polished marble and sparkling crystal abound in the lobby, but the view of the valley through a long wall of glass is what commands most guests' attention. Service here is second to none. The pool complex, which includes a water slide for the kids, is one of the finest in the state, and the resort's Centre for Well Being offers all the spa pampering anyone could ever need. There are also 27 challenging holes of golf. Mary Elaine's (p. 107) is Phoenix's ultimate special-occasion restaurant. Guest rooms are as elaborate as the public areas and have large patios and sunken tubs for two. However, as luxurious as the rooms are, it's questionable whether they warrant the price tag.

6000 E. Camelback Rd., Scottsdale, AZ 85251. © 800/888-8234 or 480/941-8200. Fax 480/947-4311. www.thephoenician.com. 654 units. Jan–May $625 double, from $1,550 suite; June to mid-Sept $295 double, from $995 suite; mid-Sept to Dec $525 double, from $1,450 suite. Children under 12 stay free in parent's room. AE, DC, DISC, MC, V. Valet parking $26. Pets under 25 lb. accepted. **Amenities:** 3 restaurants (French, Southwestern, Italian); 4 snack bars/cafes; lounge; 9 pools; 27-hole golf course; putting green; 12 tennis courts;

health club and spa; Jacuzzi; lawn games; bike rentals; children's programs; concierge; car-rental desk; business center; shopping arcade; salon; 24-hour room service; massage; babysitting; laundry service; dry cleaning; executive-level rooms. *In room:* A/C, TV, dataport, high-speed Internet access, minibar, hair dryer, iron, safe.

Renaissance Scottsdale Resort ★★ (Value)

If I were coming to Scottsdale for a romantic getaway, I would stay here. Located adjacent to the upscale Borgata shopping center (which is designed to resemble the Tuscan hill town of San Gimignano), this is a casual yet luxurious boutique resort that feels like an isolated hideaway. Forget the hustle and bustle of other area resorts. Set amid shady lawns, the Renaissance Scottsdale Resort consists of spacious suites designed for those who need plenty of room and comfort. More than 100 of the suites have their own private hot tubs on private patios (very romantic), and all units are done in Southwestern style. Several excellent restaurants are within walking distance, which makes this a good choice for gourmands who don't want to spend their vacation fighting rush-hour traffic on Scottsdale Road.

6160 N. Scottsdale Rd., Scottsdale, AZ 85253. (C) **800/HOTELS-1** or 480/991-1414. Fax 480/951-3350. http://renaissancehotels.com/phxsr. 171 units. Jan–May $229–$289 double, $269–$349 suite; June to early Sept $89 double, $109–$129 suite; early Sept to Dec $199 double, $249–$309 suite. Children stay free in parent's room. AE, DC, DISC, MC, V. Pets under 25 lb. accepted ($50 deposit). **Amenities:** Restaurant (Mediterranean); lounge; poolside snack bar; 2 pools; putting green; 4 tennis courts; access to nearby health club; 2 Jacuzzis; bike rentals; concierge; business center; shopping arcade; 24-hr. room service; massage; babysitting; laundry service; dry cleaning; croquet court. *In room:* A/C, TV, dataport, minibar, coffeemaker, hair dryer, iron, safe.

Sanctuary on Camelback Mountain ★★★

The James may be the hippest hotel in Scottsdale these days, but this place did the W Hotel/Philippe Starck thing first, and I still like the contemporary rooms here better than those at the James. This is also one of the valley's most visually breathtaking spa resorts. Located high on the northern flanks of Camelback Mountain, the lushly landscaped property has great views across the valley, especially from the restaurant and lounge. The extremely spacious guest rooms are divided between the more conservative deluxe casitas and the boldly contemporary spa casitas. With their dyed-cement floors, kidney-shaped daybeds, and streamline-moderne cabinetry, these latter units are absolutely stunning. Bathrooms are huge and some have private outdoor soaking tubs. The spa, which is open only to resort guests and spa members, is one of the prettiest in the valley.

5700 E. McDonald Dr., Paradise Valley, AZ 85253. (C) **800/245-2051** or 480/948-2100. Fax 480/483-7314. www.sanctuaryaz.com. 98 units. Late Dec to early May $395–$595 double; early May to early June and early Sept to mid-Dec $295–$495 double; early June to early Sept and mid-Dec $155–$335 double. Children under 18 stay free in parent's room. AE, DC, DISC, MC, V. Pets accepted. **Amenities:** 2 restaurants (New American, spa cuisine); lounge; 4 pools; 5 tennis courts; fitness center; full-service spa; Jacuzzi; concierge; business center; room service; massage; babysitting; laundry service; dry cleaning. *In room:* A/C, TV, dataport, high-speed Internet access, minibar, coffeemaker, hair dryer, iron.

The Sunburst Resort ★★ (Value)

An exceptional location in the heart of the Scottsdale shopping district, a dramatic Southwestern styling (the focal point of the lobby is a massive sandstone fireplace), and a small but well-designed pool area are the main reasons I like this little resort. Set in a lushly planted courtyard are a small lagoon-style pool, complete with sand beach and short water slide, and a second pool with flame-topped columnar waterfalls. An artificial stream and faux sandstone ruins all add up to a fun desert fantasy landscape (although not on the grand scale to be found at some area resorts). The guest rooms have all been recently renovated, and while they don't have the Southwestern flavor they once did, they are still quite comfortable. A new little spa is a definite plus here; though small, it has a great feel.

4925 N. Scottsdale Rd., Scottsdale, AZ 85251. (800/528-7867 or 480/945-7666. Fax 480/946-4056. www.sunburstresort.com. 204 units. Jan to late May $209 double, $399 suite; late May to early Sept $99 double, $199 suite; early Sept to Dec $189 double, $349 suite. AE, DC, DISC, MC, V. Children under 18 stay free in parent's room. **Amenities:** Restaurant (Southwestern/New American); lounge; snack bar; 2 pools; exercise room; access to nearby health club; full-service spa; Jacuzzi; summer children's programs; concierge; business center; room service; massage; babysitting; laundry service; dry cleaning. *In room:* A/C, TV, dataport, minibar, coffeemaker, hair dryer, iron, safe, wi-fi.

Westin Kierland Resort & Spa ★★★ *Kids*   Painted the color of the Arizona's red rock canyons, this new resort is located just off Scottsdale Road and adjacent to the Kierland Commons "urban village" shopping center. Throughout the resort you'll find interpretive plaques, artworks by Arizona artists, and historic photos that provide loads of insights into Arizona history and natural history. The convenient location and distinct sense of place make this my favorite of the Phoenix area's new crop of megaresorts. Guest rooms all have balconies or patios, and although the bathrooms aren't all that large, this minor inconvenience is compensated for by Westin's Heavenly Beds, which are incredibly comfortable, pillow-top beds. Excellent Nuevo Latino cuisine is served at Deseo, and there's a great cowboy-style bar as well. The spa specializes in skin treatments and has a wide variety of fitness equipment, a 24-hour lap pool, and a restaurant. Then there's the main pool area, which includes a long tubing river, a water slide, a beach area, and another large pool.

6902 E. Greenway Pkwy., Scottsdale, AZ 85254. (800/WESTIN-1 or 480/624-1000. Fax 480/624-1001. www.westin.com/kierlandresort. 735 units. Jan to early May $279–$529 double; early May to early June $189–$369 double; early June to mid-Sept $109–$269 double; mid-Sept to Dec $189–$489 double. Children under 18 stay free in parent's room. AE, DC, DISC, MC, V. Pets accepted. **Amenities:** 5 restaurants (Nuevo Latino, American); poolside snack bar; espresso bar/ice-cream parlor; 2 lounges; 3 pools; 3 9-hole golf courses; 2 tennis courts; health club; full-service spa with 20 treatment rooms; 4 Jacuzzis; game room; children's programs; concierge; business center; 24-hr. room service; massage; laundry service; dry cleaning; concierge-level rooms. *In room:* A/C, TV, dataport, minibar, coffeemaker, hair dryer, iron, safe, wi-fi.

EXPENSIVE

Doubletree Paradise Valley Resort ★★ *Value*   With its low-rise design and textured-block construction, this resort gives a bow to the pioneering architectural style of Frank Lloyd Wright, and thus stands out from comparable resorts in the area. Built around several courtyards containing swimming pools, bubbling fountains, and gardens with desert landscaping, the property has much the look and feel of the nearby Hyatt Regency Scottsdale (although on a less grandiose scale and at more bearable room rates). Mature palm trees lend a sort of Moorish feel to the grounds and cast fanciful shadows in the gardens. Accommodations have a very contemporary feel, with lots of blond wood and, in some cases, high ceilings that make the rooms feel particularly spacious. With its distinctive styling and convenient location, this is an excellent close-in choice.

5401 N. Scottsdale Rd., Scottsdale, AZ 85250. (877/445-6677 or 480/947-5400. Fax 480/481-0209. www.paradisevalley.doubletree.com. 378 units. Jan–Mar $149–$249 double, from $249 suite; Apr and Sept–Dec $99–$169 double, from $199 suite; May–Aug $65–$119 double, from $159 suite. Children under 18 stay free in parent's room. AE, DC, DISC, MC, V. Pets accepted ($75 non-refundable deposit). **Amenities:** 2 restaurants (Southwestern, American); lounge; snack bar; 2 outdoor pools; putting green; 2 tennis courts; 2 racquetball courts; exercise room; 2 Jacuzzis; saunas; bike rentals; children's programs; concierge; car-rental desk; business center; room service; massage; babysitting; laundry service; dry cleaning; concierge-level rooms. *In room:* A/C, TV, dataport, high-speed Internet access, minibar, coffeemaker, hair dryer, iron.

Embassy Suites Phoenix/Scottsdale ★   With its stylish, contemporary interior decor, this is one of the area's few hotels that will appeal to hip, young, travelers. Of course, this place doesn't have nearly the buzz of the new James Hotel in Old Town Scottsdale, it does provide plenty of space in its suites and great views of nearby mountains. As soon as you see the dyed concrete floor and unusual wall sculpture in the lobby, you'll know that this is not your standard business hotel. However, it might be difficult to take your eyes off the views across Stonecreek Golf Course to Camelback Mountain, Mummy Mountain, and Piestewa Peak, and those views just get better the higher up you go (be sure to ask for a room on the south side of an upper floor). Keep in mind that this is an all-suite property; the two-room accommodations are very spacious and come complete with galley kitchens.

4415 E. Paradise Village Pkwy. S., Phoenix, AZ 85032. ℂ **800/EMBASSY** or 602/765-5800. Fax 602/765-5890. www.embassysuitesaz.com. 270 units. Jan–Apr $189–$219 double; May $169–$189 double; June to mid-Sept $89 double; late Sept to Dec $179–$209 double. Rates include full breakfast and a cocktail reception. Children under 18 stay free in parent's room. AE, DC, DISC, MC, V. **Amenities:** Restaurant (American); lounge; small outdoor pool; exercise room; access to nearby health club; Jacuzzi; concierge; car-rental desk; business center; 24-hr. room service; laundry service; dry cleaning. *In room:* A/C, 2 TVs, dataport, high-speed Internet access, kitchenette, fridge, coffeemaker, hair dryer, iron, safe.

James Hotel ⊰⊱   Move over W; here comes James. Until this past year, Scottsdale had a surprising dearth of hip hotels. Hipsters and fashionistas had nowhere to stay when they came to town to check out Scottsdale's hot nightlife scene. All that changed with the opening of the James, the first of a hotel chain that hopes to compete with the ultrahip W chain. In the lobby, James Bond movies are projected on the walls, and trendy types gather at the bar (just practice saying "shaken not stirred"). The exterior of the hotel is all sharp angles and bright walls of color. Guest rooms are the absolute opposite—monochromatic save for a few strategically placed splashes of color. The minimalist 1950s retro style, and the huge plasma TVs and CD players make it perfectly clear that this place is designed for hip young travelers. Be sure to check out the minibar, where you'll find Odwalla bars, soy chips, all the makings for martinis, and even condoms. The hotel's Fiamma Trattoria is just about the hottest place in town these days, but, although the food is good, the service can be horrible.

7353 E. Indian School Rd., Scottsdale, AZ 85251. ℂ **866/50-JAMES,** 888/500-8080, or 480/308-1100. Fax 480/308-1200. www.jameshotels.com. 200 units. Jan to mid-Apr $175–$285 double; late Apr to May and Sept–Dec $145–$215 double; June–Aug $95–$165 double. AE, DC, DISC, MC, V. Pets accepted. **Amenities:** Restaurant (Italian); lounge; 2 outdoor pools; large, well-equipped exercise room; Jacuzzi; concierge; business center; room service; massage and spa services; laundry service; dry cleaning. *In room:* A/C, TV, dataport, high-speed Internet access, minibar, coffeemaker, hair dryer, iron, safe, wi-fi.

Scottsdale Resort & Athletic Club ⊰⊱⊰⊱   Fitness fanatics rejoice; this club's for you. If you can't stand the thought of giving up your workout just because you're on vacation, book a stay at this little boutique hotel just off busy Scottsdale Road and adjacent to the Silverado Golf Course. With standard rooms and huge 1- and 2-bedroom "villas," this place is plenty comfortable, but the main reason I like this hotel is because it's affiliated with the Scottsdale Athletic Club, a large workout facility that emphasizes its tennis program. The basic rooms are a real steal for Scottsdale, and while the villas/suites are quite a bit more expensive, they are gigantic and have fireplaces, DVD players, full kitchens, and washers and dryers. On top of all this, you get a view of Camelback Mountain.

8235 E. Indian Bend Rd., Scottsdale, AZ 85250. ℂ **877/343-0033.** Fax 480/344-0650. www.scottsdaleresort andathleticclub.com. 28 units. Jan–Apr $199 double, $299–$459 suite; May–Sept $109 double, $179–$249 suite; Oct–Dec $129 double, $199–$299 suite. AE, DC, DISC, MC, V. **Amenities:** Restaurant (International); 3 pools; 11 tennis courts; health club; full-service spa; Jacuzzi; sauna; room service; dry cleaning. *In room:* A/C, TV/DVD, dataport, high-speed Internet access, fridge, coffeemaker, hair dryer, iron, wi-fi.

MODERATE

Days Inn Scottsdale Resort at Fashion Square Mall *(Value)*   This is one of the last close-in, economical hotels in the Old Town Scottsdale area, and its location adjacent to the Scottsdale Fashion Square mall makes this a great choice for shopoholics. This may be just an aging chain motel, but green lawns, tall palm trees, and a convenient location all make it recommendable.

4710 N. Scottsdale Rd., Scottsdale, AZ 85251. ℂ **800/DAYS-INN** or 480/947-5411. Fax 480/946-1324. www. scottsdaledaysinn.com. 167 units. Jan–Mar $99–$189 double; Apr–Dec $59–$189 double. Rates include continental breakfast. Children under 18 stay free in parent's room. AE, DC, DISC, MC, V. **Amenities:** Poolside bar; small outdoor pool; putting green; tennis court; Jacuzzi; car-rental desk; courtesy shopping shuttle; coin-op laundry; dry cleaning service. *In room:* A/C, TV, dataport, fridge, coffeemaker, hair dryer, iron.

Holiday Inn SunSpree Resort *(★★)* *(Kids)*   This place is not nearly as luxurious or as stylish as the nearby Doubletree or Sunburst, but families will appreciate the resort's kid-friendly character. Long one of the valley's best resort deals, the SunSpree has been upgrading over the past few years—and its rates seem to be creeping up. Still, compared with other area options, it is relatively economical. Situated on 16 acres amid wide expanses of lawn, the SunSpree is adjacent to the McCormick-Stillman Railroad Park, which is a total kid-magnet. Adults can golf at the adjacent Scottsdale Silverado Golf Club, while nongolfers can avail themselves of many other recreational options. Guest rooms have a plush feel that belies the reasonable rates. Ask for a room with a mountain view or a lakeside unit with patio.

7601 E. Indian Bend Rd., Scottsdale, AZ 85250. ℂ **800/852-5205** or 480/991-2400. Fax 480/998-2261. www.sunspreeresorts.com/scottsdale-rst. 200 units. Jan to early Apr $129–$169 double; mid-Sept to Dec and early Apr to late May $90–$129 double; late May to early Sept $59–$89 double. Children 12 and under stay free in parent's room. AE, DC, DISC, MC, V. **Amenities:** Restaurant (New American); lounge; outdoor pool; volleyball court; lawn games; exercise room; Jacuzzi; bike rentals; summer children's programs; room service; coin-op laundry; dry cleaning. *In room:* A/C, TV, dataport, fridge, coffeemaker, hair dryer, iron, safe, free local calls.

INEXPENSIVE

Despite the high-priced real estate, Scottsdale does have a few relatively inexpensive chain motels, although during the winter season, prices are higher than you'd expect. The rates given here are for the high season. **Motel 6–Scottsdale,** 6848 E. Camelback Rd. (ℂ **480/946-2280**), offers doubles for $66 to $72. **Rodeway Inn–Phoenix/Scottsdale,** 7110 E. Indian School Rd. (ℂ **480/946-3456**), has rates of $59 to $169 double.

Ramada Limited Scottsdale *(Value)*   For convenience and price, this motel can't be beat (at least not in Scottsdale). Located at the west end of the Fifth Avenue shopping district, the Ramada Limited is within walking distance of some of the best shopping and dining in Scottsdale. The three-story building is arranged around a central courtyard, where you'll find the small pool. Guest rooms are large and have been fairly recently renovated.

6935 Fifth Ave., Scottsdale, AZ 85251. ℂ **800/528-7396** or 480/994-9461. Fax 480/947-1695. www.ramada scottsdale.com. 92 units. Jan–Mar $75–$129 double; Apr and Oct–Dec $69–$89 double; May–Sept $50–$60 double. Rates include continental breakfast. Children 18 and under stay free in parent's room. AE, DC, DISC, MC, V. Pets accepted. **Amenities:** Small outdoor pool; exercise room; coin-op laundry; laundry service. *In room:* A/C, TV, dataport, fridge, coffeemaker, hair dryer, iron, free local calls.

NORTH SCOTTSDALE, CAREFREE & CAVE CREEK

North Scottsdale is the brave new world for Valley of the Sun resorts. Situated at least a 30-minute drive from downtown Scottsdale, this area may be too far out of the mainstream for many visitors. However, if you're willing to stay this far north of all the action, what you'll get is the newest resorts, the most spectacular hillside settings, and the best golf courses.

VERY EXPENSIVE

The Boulders Resort and Golden Door Spa ✹✹✹   Set amid a jumble of giant boulders 45 minutes north of Scottsdale, this was the first luxury golf resort to open in the rugged foothills of the north Valley. Back when Boulders opened it was the only game in town, but now, with competition from the nearby Four Seasons, it isn't as unique as it once was. Still, the adobe buildings that blend unobtrusively into the desert and the two acclaimed golf courses still capture the essence of the upscale desert lifestyle. If you can tear yourself away from the fairways, you can relax around the pool, play tennis, take advantage of the resort's Golden Door Spa, or even try your hand at rock climbing. The lobby is in a Santa Fe–style building with tree-trunk pillars and a flagstone floor, and the guest rooms continue the pueblo styling with stucco walls, beehive fireplaces, and beamed ceilings. For the best views, ask for one of the second-floor units. Bathrooms are large and luxuriously appointed, with tubs for two and separate showers. In addition to the upscale on-site restaurants, there are several other dining options at the adjacent El Pedregal Festival Marketplace.

34631 N. Tom Darlington Dr. (P.O. Box 2090), Carefree, AZ 85377. ✆ **800/553-1717,** 800/WYNDHAM, or 480/488-9009. Fax 480/488-4118. www.wyndhamluxury.com. 215 units. Late Dec to late Apr $625 double, from $799 villa; late Apr to early Sept $225 double, from $435 villa; early Sept to early Dec $500 double, from $799 villa; early Dec to mid-Dec $250 double, from $435 villa (for all rates there is an additional $29–$33 nightly service charge). AE, DC, DISC, MC, V. Pets accepted ($100). **Amenities:** 8 restaurants (Regional American, Southwestern, Mexican, spa cuisine, bakery/deli); lounge; 4 pools; 2 18-hole golf courses; 8 tennis courts; exercise room; full-service spa; 3 Jacuzzis; bike rentals; children's programs; concierge; business center; pro shop; shopping arcade; salon; room service; massage; babysitting; laundry service; dry cleaning. In room: A/C, TV, dataport, minibar, coffeemaker, hair dryer, iron, safe.

Copperwynd Resort and Club ✹✹ (Value   Although it's a ways from Old Town Scottsdale, this boutique hotel, high on a ridge overlooking the town of Fountain Hills, is one of the most luxurious resorts in the area. The hotel is surrounded by a rugged desert landscape, which is one of the reasons I like this place so much: You know you're in the desert when you stay here. The resort has a fabulous tennis facility and an impressive health club and small spa, and although there's no golf course on the premises, there is one adjacent. The views are among the finest in the valley, and the Jacuzzi tucked into a rocky hillside is as romantic as they come. All guest rooms have great views and feature a sort of European deluxe decor. Balconies provide plenty of room for taking in the vista. There's an excellent restaurant on the premises, so the distance from town isn't as significant as it might otherwise be.

13225 N. Eagle Ridge Dr., Fountain Hills, AZ 85268. ✆ **877/707-7760** or 480/333-1900. www.copperwynd. com. 40 units. Late Dec to late Apr $249–$425 double, $1,000–$1,600 villa; late Apr to mid-May and late Sept to late Dec $179–$249 double, $800–$1,000 villa; late May to late Sept $129–$189 double, $400–$500 villa. AE, DC, DISC, MC, V. **Amenities:** 2 restaurants (New American, American); lounge; juice bar; 2 pools; 9 tennis courts; health club and full-service spa; 3 Jacuzzis; saunas; bike rentals; children's programs; game room; concierge; pro shop; room service; massage; babysitting; laundry service; dry cleaning. In room: A/C, TV, dataport, high-speed Internet access, fridge, coffeemaker, hair dryer, iron, safe, free local calls, wi-fi.

Four Seasons Resort Scottsdale at Troon North ✹✹✹   Located in the foothills of north Scottsdale adjacent to and with privileges at the Troon North golf course (one of the state's most highly acclaimed courses), Four Seasons has knocked the nearby Boulders resort from its pinnacle. This super-luxurious resort may not feel as expansive as Boulders, but in every other aspect it is superior. With casita accommodations scattered across a boulder-strewn hillside, Four Seasons can certainly boast one of the most dramatic settings in the valley, and with a hiking trail to the nearby Pinnacle Peak Park, the resort is a good choice for anyone who wants to explore the desert on foot. Likewise, the guest rooms and suites are among the most lavish you'll find in Arizona. If you can afford it, opt for one with a private plunge pool and an outdoor shower—a luxury usually found only in tropical resorts. With three restaurants on the premises, it's easy to forget how far out of the Scottsdale mainstream this resort is.

10600 E. Crescent Moon Dr., Scottsdale, AZ 85262. ✆ **888/207-9696** or 480/515-5700. Fax 480/515-5599. www.fourseasons.com. 210 units. Jan to mid-May $445–$625 double; $695–$4,000 suite; mid-May to early Sept $155–$225 double, $395–$2,000 suite; early Sept to Dec $425–$575 double, $695–$4,000 suite. Children under 18 stay free in parent's room. AE, DC, DISC, MC, V. Pets accepted. **Amenities:** 3 restaurants (Italian, steakhouse, Mexican); lounge; large 2-level pool; 2 18-hole golf courses; 4 tennis courts; large exercise room; spa; Jacuzzi; bike rentals; children's programs; concierge; car-rental desk; business center; 24-hr. room service; massage; babysitting; guest laundry; laundry service; dry cleaning. *In room:* A/C, TV/VCR, dataport, high-speed Internet access, minibar, coffeemaker, hair dryer, iron, safe.

EXPENSIVE

Carefree Resort & Villas ⚸   Although this place is nowhere near as luxurious as the nearby Boulders resort, it isn't nearly as expensive either. Basically, this place aims to compete with the older resorts down in Scottsdale. The difference here is that you're out of the Scottsdale traffic and you're close to the unspoiled desert that lies to the north of Carefree. And with Cave Creek just down the road, you've got plenty of western character close at hand. Horseback riding, hiking, and mountain biking are all nearby, too. While the rooms around the main pool show their age, the big new villa suites are some of the nicest and most spacious rooms in the valley. These rooms overlook the nearby mountains and adjacent golf course.

37220 Mule Train Rd., Carefree, AZ 85377. ✆ **800/949-1994** or 480/488-5300. Fax 480/595-3719. www.carefree-resort.com. 360 units. Jan to early Apr $229–$259 double; $279–$329 suite or villa; early Apr to late May $169–$189 double, $219–$249 suite or villa; late May to mid-Sept $99–$119 double, $149–$179 suite or villa; mid-Sept to Dec $179–$199 double, $229–$259 suite or villa. Children under 18 stay free in parent's room. AE, DC, DISC, MC, V. Pets accepted ($45 fee). **Amenities:** 2 restaurants (eclectic, American); 2 lounges; 3 pools; 5 tennis courts; exercise room; full-service spa; 2 Jacuzzis; bike rentals; car-rental desk; business center; room service; massage; laundry service; dry cleaning. *In room:* A/C, TV, dataport, high-speed Internet access, coffeemaker, hair dryer, iron, free local calls.

The Fairmont Scottsdale Princess ⚸⚸⚸   Can you say guilty pleasure. I know this place, with its Moorish-palace styling, doesn't belong in Phoenix, but I still love it. It feels as if you're vacationing in Spain. With its royal palms, tiled fountains, and waterfalls, the Princess offers an exotic atmosphere unmatched by any other valley resort. It's also home to the Phoenix Open golf tournament and the city's top tennis tournament, which means the two golf courses here are superb and the courts are top-notch. There's also the Willow Stream spa and a water playground complete with two water slides. This resort, located a 20-minute drive north of Old Town Scottsdale, will delight anyone in search of a romantic hideaway, while families will enjoy both the water playground and the pond where kids can go fishing. The decor of the guest rooms is elegant Southwestern, and the spacious bathrooms have double vanities and separate showers and tubs. All units have private balconies. The Marquesa serves superb Spanish cuisine, while upscale Mexican food and mariachis are the specialties at La Hacienda. (See "Where to Dine," later in this chapter.)

7575 E. Princess Dr., Scottsdale, AZ 85255. ℂ **800/441-1414** or 480/585-4848. Fax 480/585-0086. www.fairmont.com. 650 units. $159–$589 double, $319–$3,800 suite. Children under 12 stay free in parent's room. AE, DC, DISC, MC, V. Pets accepted. **Amenities:** 4 restaurants (Spanish, Mexican, steakhouse, American); 3 lounges; 4 pools; 2 18-hole golf courses; 7 tennis courts; exercise room; full-service spa; Jacuzzi; concierge; car-rental desk; business center; golf and tennis pro shops; shopping arcade; salon; 24-hr. room service; massage; babysitting; laundry service; dry cleaning. *In room:* A/C, TV, dataport, minibar, coffeemaker, hair dryer, iron, safe.

MODERATE

Cave Creek Tumbleweed Motel ☆   Located in the heart of rowdy Cave Creek, the valley's wildest and most western community, this little motel is nothing fancy, but it still seems to stay packed for much of the year. Be sure to book early. Although the guest rooms have a bit of western character, the popularity of this place is due in large part to the fun atmosphere of surrounding saloons and cowboy steakhouses. Although it's at least a 30-minute drive from here to Phoenix, the desert is a whole lot closer here than it is to Phoenix and Scottsdale's budget motels.

6333 E. Cave Creek Rd., Cave Creek, AZ 85327. ℂ **480/488-3668**. www.tumbleweedhotel.com. 24 units. $99–$159 double. Children under 18 stay free in parent's room. AE, MC, V. Pets accepted ($75 refundable deposit). **Amenities:** Outdoor pool. *In room:* A/C, TV, coffeemaker.

CENTRAL PHOENIX & THE CAMELBACK CORRIDOR

This area is the heart of the upscale Phoenix shopping and restaurant scene and is home to the Arizona Biltmore, one of the most prestigious resorts in the city. Old money and new money rub shoulders along the avenues here, and valet parking is de rigueur. Located roughly midway between Old Scottsdale and downtown Phoenix, this area is a good bet for those intending to split their time between the downtown Phoenix cultural and sports district and the world-class shopping and dining in Scottsdale. The area has only one golf resort, but boasts a couple of smaller boutique hotels with loads of Arizona character.

VERY EXPENSIVE

Arizona Biltmore Resort & Spa ☆☆☆   For decades this has been the favored Phoenix address of celebrities, politicians, and old money, and the distinctive cast-cement blocks inspired by a Frank Lloyd Wright design make this a unique architectural gem. It's the historic character and timeless elegance that really set this place apart. Let the beautiful people and the new money have The Phoenician; I'll take the Biltmore. The wide lawns, colorful flower gardens, and views of Piestewa Peak make outdoor lounging here an absolute joy (just bring me a gin and tonic over at the croquet court). While the two golf courses and expansive spa are the main draws for many guests, the children's activities center also makes this a popular choice for families. Of the several different styles of accommodations, the "resort rooms" are quite comfortable and come with balconies or patios. Those rooms in the Arizona Wing are also good choices. The villa suites are the most spacious and luxurious of all. Afternoon tea, a Phoenix institution, is served in the lobby.

2400 E. Missouri Ave., Phoenix, AZ 85016. ℂ **800/950-0086** or 602/955-6600. Fax 602/381-7600. www.arizonabiltmore.com. 738 units. Jan to mid-May $395–$600 double, from $685 suite; late May to early Sept $195–$275 double, from $325 suite; early Sept to Dec $340–$550 double, from $605 suite. Rates do not include a $15 daily service fee. Children under 18 stay free in parent's room. AE, DC, DISC, MC, V. Pets under 20 lb. accepted in cottage rooms ($250 deposit, $50 nonrefundable). **Amenities:** 5 restaurants (New American, Southwestern, American); lounge; 8 pools (1 with a water slide and 1 with rental cabanas); 2 18-hole golf courses plus 18-hole putting course; 7 tennis courts; lawn games; health club and full-service spa; 2 Jacuzzis; saunas; bike rentals; children's programs; concierge; car-rental desk; courtesy shopping shuttle; business center; room service; massage; laundry service; dry cleaning; executive-level rooms. *In room:* A/C, TV, dataport, high-speed Internet access, minibar, hair dryer, iron, safe.

Embassy Suites Biltmore 🌟🌟   Located across the parking lot from the Biltmore Fashion Park (Phoenix's most upscale shopping center), this hotel makes a great base if you want to be within walking distance of half a dozen good restaurants. The enormous atrium is filled with interesting tile work and other artistic Southwestern touches, as well as tropical greenery, waterfalls, and ponds filled with koi (colorful Japanese carp). The hotel's atrium also houses the breakfast area and a romantic lounge with huge banquettes shaded by palm trees. Unfortunately, the rooms, all suites, are dated and a bit of a letdown, but they're certainly large. All in all, this hotel is a good value, especially when you consider that rates include both breakfast and afternoon drinks.

2630 E. Camelback Rd., Phoenix, AZ 85016. ℭ **800/EMBASSY** or 602/955-3992. Fax 602/955-6479. www. phoenixbiltmore.embassysuites.com. 232 units. Jan to late Mar $209–$289 double; Apr to late May $169–$219 double; June to early Sept $89–$159 double; mid-Sept to Dec $179–$259 double. Rates include full breakfast and afternoon drinks. Children under 18 stay free in parent's room. AE, DC, DISC, MC, V. Valet parking $8. Pets accepted ($25). **Amenities:** Restaurant (steakhouse); lounge; outdoor pool; exercise room; access to nearby health club; Jacuzzi; children's programs; concierge; courtesy car; business center; room service; massage; babysitting; coin-op laundry; laundry service; dry cleaning; executive-level rooms. *In room:* A/C, TV, dataport, fridge, coffeemaker, hair dryer, iron, wi-fi.

Hermosa Inn 🌟🌟 *Finds*   This luxurious boutique hotel, once a guest ranch, is now one of the few hotels in the Phoenix area to offer a bit of Old Arizona atmosphere, and every time I arrive here, I breathe a great big sigh of relief. This place is all about Southwest style and getting a little peace and quiet. Originally built in 1930 as the home of cowboy artist Lon Megargee, the inn is situated on more than 6 acres of neatly landscaped gardens in an upscale residential neighborhood. I love it that this place is luxurious, yet feels completely removed from the hustle and bustle of Scottsdale's big, touristy resorts. The only other place with this sort of tranquil feel is the nearby Royal Palms, which has more of a service-oriented resort feel. Rooms vary from cozy to spacious and are individually decorated in tastefully contemporary Western decor. The largest suites, which have more Southwestern flavor than just about any other rooms in the area, incorporate a mixture of contemporary and antique furnishings. The dining room, located in the original adobe home, serves excellent food in a rustic, upscale setting (see Lon's, in "Where to Dine," later in this chapter).

5532 N. Palo Cristi Rd., Paradise Valley, AZ 85253. ℭ **800/241-1210** or 602/955-8614. Fax 602/955-8299. www.hermosainn.com. 35 units. Early Jan to Apr $290–$340 double, $490–$690 suite; May 1 to late May $190–$240 double, $390–$590 suite; late May to mid-Sept $110–$160 double, $310–$510 suite; mid-Sept to early Jan $250–$300 double, $450–$650 suite. Rates include continental breakfast. Children under 18 stay free in parent's room. AE, DC, DISC, MC, V. Take 32nd St. north from Camelback Rd., turn right on Stanford Rd., and turn left on N. Palo Cristi Rd. From Lincoln Dr., turn south on N. Palo Christi Rd. (east of 32nd St.). Pets accepted ($50 fee). **Amenities:** Restaurant (New American/Southwestern); lounge; outdoor pool; tennis court; access to nearby health club; 2 Jacuzzis; concierge; business center; room service; massage; babysitting; laundry service; dry cleaning. *In room:* A/C, TV, dataport, high-speed Internet access, minibar, coffeemaker, hair dryer, iron, safe.

The Ritz-Carlton Phoenix 🌟🌟 *Overrated*   Located directly across the street from the Biltmore Fashion Park shopping center in the heart of the Camelback Corridor business and shopping district, the Ritz-Carlton is the city's finest non-resort hotel and is known for providing impeccable service. The public areas are filled with European antiques, which, however, feel completely out of place in Phoenix. With so little regional character, this really isn't the sort of place where I would choose to stay if I wanted to come home from my vacation with a sense of having been to Arizona. Still the hotel is utterly sophisticated and regularly ranks among the top hotels in the world. In the guest rooms, you'll find reproductions of antique furniture and marble bathrooms with ornate fixtures. An elegant lobby lounge serves afternoon tea as well as cocktails, while a clublike lounge offers fine cigars and premium spirits. At press time, the hotel was planning to renovate all of its rooms, which should make this an even more luxurious option.

2401 E. Camelback Rd., Phoenix, AZ 85016. ⓒ 800/241-3333 or 602/468-0700. Fax 602/553-0685. www.ritz carlton.com/hotels/phoenix. 281 units. $159–$325 double, $419–$2,500 suite. Children under 18 stay free in parent's room. AE, DC, DISC, MC, V. Valet parking $22. **Amenities:** Restaurant (French bistro); 2 lounges; pool; exercise room; access to nearby health club; saunas; concierge; business center; 24-hr. room service; massage; babysitting; laundry service; dry cleaning; executive-level rooms. In room: A/C, TV, dataport, high-speed Internet access, minibar, hair dryer, iron, safe.

Royal Palms Resort and Spa ★★   This place is so romantic and beautiful that the moment you set foot in the first cloistered garden, you just might imagine you hear a flamenco guitarist playing. Located midway between Old Town Scottsdale and Biltmore Fashion Park, the Royal Palms was constructed more than 50 years ago by Cunard Steamship executive Delos Cooke. Done in Spanish mission style, the boutique hotel is still filled with European antiques that once belonged to Cooke. Surrounding the building, and giving the property the tranquil feel of a Mediterranean monastery, are lush walled gardens where antique water fountains splash. The most memorable guest rooms are the deluxe casitas, each with a distinctive decor ranging from opulent contemporary to classic European. These rooms also have private back patios and front patios that can be enclosed by heavy curtains. The antiques-filled dining room, T. Cook's, is one of the city's most romantic restaurants (see "Where to Dine," later in this chapter). An adjacent bar/lounge conjures up a Spanish villa setting. The Alvadora spa provides yet another level of luxury to this already superb boutique resort. While the Scottsdale Princess does the Moorish palace on a resort scale, this gorgeous little hideaway has the feel of a Spanish villa that was transported to the Arizona desert.

5200 E. Camelback Rd., Phoenix, AZ 85018. ⓒ 800/672-6011 or 602/840-3610. Fax 602/840-6927. www.royalpalmsresortandspa.com. 117 units. Jan–May $375 double, $415–$3,000 suite; June to mid-Sept $179 double, $199–$2,000 suite; mid-Sept to Dec $375 double, $405–$3,000 suite. Rates do not include daily service fee of $19. AE, DC, DISC, MC, V. **Amenities:** Restaurant (Mediterranean); snack bar; lounge; outdoor pool with cabanas; exercise room; access to nearby health club; full-service spa; Jacuzzi; concierge; business center; 24-hr. room service; massage; laundry service; dry cleaning. In room: A/C, TV, dataport, minibar, coffeemaker, hair dryer, iron, safe.

EXPENSIVE

Maricopa Manor   Centrally located between downtown Phoenix and Scottsdale, the Maricopa is just a block off busy Camelback Road, and has long been Phoenix's best B&B. Over the past couple of years, new owners have been giving the inn a much-needed makeover and have been adding lots of Arts and Crafts details. The inn's main building, designed to resemble a Spanish manor house, was built in 1928, and the orange trees, palms, and large yard all lend an Old Phoenix atmosphere. All guest rooms are large, comfortable suites. One suite has a sunroom and kitchen, while another has two separate sleeping areas. There are tables in the garden where you can eat your breakfast, which is delivered to your door.

15 W. Pasadena Ave., Phoenix, AZ 85013. ℂ **800/292-6403** or 602/274-6302. Fax 602/266-3904. www.
maricopamanor.com. 7 units. Jan–Mar $139–$199 double; Apr and Nov–Dec $129–$179 double; May and
Oct $109–$139 double; June–Sept $99–$109 double. Rates include continental breakfast. Children under 12
stay free in parent's room. AE, DC, DISC, MC, V. Pets accepted. **Amenities:** Outdoor pool; access to nearby
health club; Jacuzzi. *In room:* A/C, TV/VCR/DVD, dataport, fridge, coffeemaker, hair dryer, iron, wi-fi.

MODERATE

Sierra Suites ⭐   Billing itself as a temporary residence and offering discounts
for stays of 5 days or more, this hotel consists of studio-style apartments located
just north of Camelback Road and not far from Biltmore Fashion Park. Although
designed primarily for corporate business travelers on temporary assignment in
the area, this lodging makes a good choice for families as well. All units have full
kitchens, big closets and bathrooms, and separate sitting areas.

5235 N. 16th St., Phoenix, AZ 85016. ℂ **800/4-SIERRA** or 602/265-6800. Fax 602/265-1114. www.sierra
suites.com. 113 units. $69–$179 double. Children 18 and under stay free in parent's room. AE, DC, DISC, MC,
V. Pets accepted ($100 fee). **Amenities:** Small outdoor pool; exercise room; Jacuzzi; coin-op laundry; dry
cleaning. *In room:* A/C, TV, dataport, high-speed Internet access, kitchen, coffeemaker, hair dryer, iron.

NORTH PHOENIX

Some of the valley's best scenery is to be found in north Phoenix, where several
small mountains have been protected as parks and preserves; the two Pointe
Hilton resorts claim great locations close to these parks. However, the valley's
best shopping and dining, as well as most major attractions, are all at least a 30-
minute drive away (through generally unattractive parts of the city).

VERY EXPENSIVE

JW Marriott Desert Ridge Resort & Spa ⭐⭐⭐   With 950 rooms, this is
the largest resort in the state and stays crowded with conference groups, which
can leave vacation travelers feeling a bit overlooked. Still, if you just want to
spend some time in the sun drinking margaritas by the pool and not venturing
out to explore the city, this place is great. It has been designed to make sure guests
want for nothing and has such a wide range of restaurants (including a Roy's from
Hawaii and a Starbucks), that you can spend several days here without leaving the
property and not feel as though you're missing anything. There are also 4 acres of
water features and pools (including a tubing "river") and a large spa with its own
lap pool. At the resort's grand entrance, desert landscaping and rows of palm trees
give the resort a sense of place, and the roll-up walls of the multilevel lobby let
plenty of balmy desert air in during the cooler months. Guest rooms have balconies and hints of Mediterranean styling and are designed primarily for business
travelers. Be sure to ask for a room with a view to the south; these rooms look out
to several of Phoenix's mountain preserves. Personally, I think this place is just
way too big, but I've heard you can get some great rates on Priceline.com.

5350 E. Marriott Blvd., Phoenix, AZ 85054. ℂ **800/835-6206** or 480/293-5000. Fax 480/293-3600. www.jw
desertridgeresort.com. 950 units. Jan to early Apr $369–$429 double; early Apr to early June $289–$369 double; early June to early Sept $149–$179 double; early Sept to Dec $299–$339 double; $549–$1,458 suite
year-round. Children stay free in parent's room. AE, DC, DISC, MC, V. **Amenities:** 5 restaurants (Southwestern, Hawaiian fusion, Italian, steakhouse, healthy); 2 snack bars/cafes; 3 lounges; 5 pools; 2 18-hole golf
courses; 8 tennis courts; health club; full-service spa; 2 Jacuzzis; children's programs; concierge; car-rental
desk; business center; 24-hr. room service; massage; babysitting; coin-op laundry; laundry service; dry cleaning. *In room:* A/C, TV, dataport, high-speed Internet access, minibar, coffeemaker, hair dryer, iron, safe.

EXPENSIVE

Pointe Hilton Squaw Peak Resort ⭐⭐⭐ *Kids*   Located at the foot of
Piestewa Peak (formerly Squaw Peak), this lushly landscaped resort makes a big

splash with its Hole-in-the-Wall River Ranch, a 9-acre aquatic playground that features a tubing "river," water slide, waterfall, sports pool, and lagoon pool. An 18-hole putting course and game room also help make it a great family vacation spot. The resort is done in the Spanish villa style, and most of the guest rooms are large suites outfitted with a mix of contemporary and Spanish colonial–style furnishings. The resort has enough restaurants and snack bars to keep you content here for a good long stay. For a family vacation, this place is hard to beat. However, I prefer the nearby Pointe Hilton Tapatio Cliffs Resort for its much more dramatic hillside setting and location adjacent to the hiking trails of the North Mountain Recreation Area.

7677 N. 16th St., Phoenix, AZ 85020-9832. ℂ 800/876-4683 or 602/997-2626. Fax 602/997-2391. www.pointe hilton.com. 563 units. Jan to mid-Apr $189–$299 double, $1.300 grande suite; mid-Apr to late May and mid-Sept to Dec $109–$249 double, $1,300 grande suite; late May to Sept $89–$129 double, $1,300 grande suite. Rates do not include daily resort fee of $9. Children under 18 stay free in parent's room. AE, DC, DISC, MC, V. **Amenities:** 3 restaurants (American, Southwestern); 2 snack bars; 5 lounges; 8 pools; 18-hole golf course (4 miles away by shuttle); 4 tennis courts; health club (extra charge) and small spa; 6 Jacuzzis; saunas; bike rentals; children's programs; concierge; car-rental desk; business center; room service; massage; babysitting; laundry service; coin-op laundry; dry cleaning. *In room:* A/C, TV, dataport, high-speed Internet access, minibar, coffeemaker, hair dryer, iron.

Pointe Hilton Tapatio Cliffs Resort ★★★   If you love to lounge by the pool, then this resort is a great choice. The Falls, a 3-acre water playground, includes two lagoon pools, a 138-foot water slide, 40-foot cascades, a whirlpool tucked into an artificial grotto, and rental cabanas for that extra dash of luxury. If you're a hiker (as I am), you'll want to make this your first choice in the area. The trails of the North Mountain Recreation Area begin on the edge of the property, and from here you can hike for miles through the desert. The resort also has a golf course, though it is a short drive away. All rooms are spacious suites with Southwest-inspired furnishings; corner units are particularly bright. Situated on the shoulder of North Mountain, this resort has walkways and steep roads (get your heart and brakes checked); at the very top of the property is Different Pointe of View, a pricey restaurant with one of the finest views in the city (see "Where to Dine," later in this chapter). This resort is slightly more adult-oriented than the nearby Pointe Hilton Squaw Peak Resort, but is very similar.

11111 N. Seventh St., Phoenix, AZ 85020. ℂ 800/876-4683 or 602/866-7500. Fax 602/993-0276. www.pointehilton.com. 585 units. Jan to mid-Apr $189–$299 double, $1,300 grande suite; mid-Apr to late May and mid-Sept to Dec $109–$249 double, $1,300 grande suite; late May to early Sept $89–$129 double, $1,300 grande suite. Rates do not include $9 daily resort fee. Children under 18 stay free in parent's room. AE, DC, DISC, MC, V. **Amenities:** 3 restaurants (Mediterranean, American, Mexican); 2 poolside cafes; 5 lounges; 7 pools; golf course; 2 tennis courts; fitness center (extra charge); small full-service spa; 8 Jacuzzis; sauna; steam room; bike rentals; seasonal children's programs; concierge; car-rental desk; free shuttle between Pointe Hilton properties; business center; room service; massage; babysitting; laundry service; dry cleaning. *In room:* A/C, TV, dataport, high-speed Internet access, minibar, coffeemaker, hair dryer, iron.

MODERATE/INEXPENSIVE

Among the better moderately priced chain motels in north Phoenix are the **Best Western Inn Suites Hotel Phoenix,** 1615 E. Northern Ave., at 16th Street (ℂ **800/752-2204** or 602/997-6285), charging high-season rates of $79 to $119 double; and the **Best Western Bell Hotel,** 17211 N. Black Canyon Hwy. (ℂ **877/263-1290** or 602/993-8300), charging $89 to $109 double.

Among the better budget chain motels are the **Motel 6–Sweetwater,** 2735 W. Sweetwater Ave. (ℂ **602/942-5030**), charging $50 to $56 double; and **Super 8–Phoenix Metro/Central,** 4021 N. 27th Ave. (ℂ **602/248-8880**), charging $46 to $51.

Embassy Suites Phoenix North ★★ *Value*   This resortlike hotel in north Phoenix is right off I-17, a 30- to 45-minute drive from the rest of the valley's resorts (and good restaurants)—but if you happen to have relatives in Sun City or are planning a trip north to Sedona or the Grand Canyon, it's a good choice. The lobby of the mission-style hotel has the feel of a Spanish church interior, but instead of a cloister off the lobby, there's a garden courtyard with a huge pool and lots of palm trees. The guest rooms are all suites, although furnishings are fairly basic and bathrooms small.

2577 W. Greenway Rd., Phoenix, AZ 85023. © 800/EMBASSY or 602/375-1777. Fax 602/993-5693. www. embassy-suites.com. 314 units. $99–$149 double. Children under 18 stay free in parent's room. Rates include full breakfast. AE, DC, DISC, MC, V. Pets accepted ($50 fee). **Amenities:** Restaurant; lounge; snack bar; complimentary cocktail reception; large pool and children's pool; tennis court; exercise room; Jacuzzi; car-rental desk; room service; laundry service; coin-op laundry; dry cleaning. *In room:* A/C, TV, dataport, fridge, coffeemaker, hair dryer, iron.

DOWNTOWN, SOUTH PHOENIX & THE AIRPORT AREA

Unless you're a sports fan or are in town for a convention, there's not much to recommend in downtown Phoenix. You can walk to the Bank One Ballpark and America West Arena, but this 9-to-5 area can feel like a modern ghost town at night.

VERY EXPENSIVE

Pointe South Mountain Resort ★★★ *Kids*   Oh to be a kid again! If I were a 12-year-old, I would insist, no, demand, that my parents bring me to this resort. Then I would spend all day every day of my vacation playing in the pool. Located on the south side of the valley, this sprawling resort abuts the 17,000-acre South Mountain Park, and is one of the best choices in the valley for families. The resort's Oasis water park (complete with a wave pool, a tubing "river," a twisty water slide, and two free-fall-style water slides that are the tallest at any resort in the state), is a huge hit with kids. With stables right at the resort, you and the kids can also ride into the sunset on South Mountain. There are even spa programs for girls and kids' golf and tennis programs. Adult golfers will enjoy the resort's course, which has an island green on the 18th hole. The guest rooms, all suites, feature contemporary Southwestern furnishings and lots of space. There's a wide range of restaurant choices, including Rustler's Rooste, a cowboy steakhouse that serves rattlesnake appetizers (see "Where to Dine," below).

7777 S. Pointe Pkwy., Phoenix, AZ 85044. © 877/800-4888 or 602/438-9000. Fax 602/431-6535. www.pointes outhmtn.com. 640 units. Early Jan to Apr $309 double; May $269 double; June to early Sept $169 double; early Sept to Dec $299 double. Rates do not include $16 daily resort fee. Children 12 and under stay free in parent's room. AE, DC, DISC, MC, V. **Amenities:** 6 restaurants (steakhouse, Mexican, Southwestern, International); 3 lounges; 11 outdoor pools (including 6-acre water park); 18-hole golf course; 5 tennis courts; basketball and volleyball courts; racquetball court; health club; full-service spa; 3 Jacuzzis; children's programs; concierge; car-rental desk; business center; pro shop; room service; massage; babysitting; coin-op laundry; laundry service; dry cleaning; executive-level rooms; horseback riding. *In room:* A/C, TV, dataport, high-speed Internet access, minibar, coffeemaker, hair dryer, iron.

Sheraton Wild Horse Pass Resort ★★★   Named for the wild horses that still roam the desert hereabouts, this resort is located a 20-minute drive south of Phoenix Sky Harbor International Airport on the Gila River Indian Reservation. The location is unique in the valley in that guest rooms look out across miles of undeveloped desert, which gives this resort a remote feel. Throw in horseback riding, a full-service spa featuring desert-inspired treatments, a golf course, a nature trail along a 2½-mile-long re-creation of the Gila River, and a pool with a water slide, and you'll find plenty to keep you busy here. The resort is owned by the Maricopa and Pima tribes, who go out of their way to share their culture with resort guests. There is even a cultural concierge on staff. Guest rooms have great beds, small patios, and large bathrooms with separate tubs and showers. The menu in Kai, the main dining room, focuses on the indigenous flavors of the Southwest. The only drawback here is that the resort is a long way from the action in Scottsdale. Plan to stay put for a few days.

5594 W. Wild Horse Bass Blvd. (P.O. Box 94000), Phoenix, AZ 85070-4000. © 866/837-4156 or 602/225-0100. Fax 602/225-0300. www.wildhorsepassresort.com. 500 units. Early Jan to late May $259–$389 double, $640–$950 suite; late May to mid-Sept $110–$245 double, $600–$950 suite; mid-Sept to early Jan $259–$389 double, $600–$950 suite. Children stay free in parent's room. AE, DC, DISC, MC, V. Pets accepted. **Amenities:** 5 restaurants (Southwestern, American); snack bar; 2 lounges; 4 outdoor pools; 2 18-hole golf courses; 2 tennis courts; health club; full-service spa; 2 Jacuzzis; horseback riding; children's programs; concierge; car-rental desk; business center; shopping arcade; 24-hr. room service; massage; babysitting; laundry service; dry cleaning; casino. *In room:* A/C, TV, dataport, high-speed Internet access, minibar, coffeemaker, hair dryer, iron, safe.

EXPENSIVE

The Wyndham Buttes Resort ⭐⭐   Located only 3 miles from Sky Harbor Airport, this resort makes the most of its craggy hilltop location, and although some people complain that the freeway in the foreground ruins the view, the rocky setting and desert landscaping leave no doubt you're in the Southwest. The only other resorts in the area with as much of a desert feel are Boulders and Four Seasons, both of which are quite a bit more expensive than this resort. From the cactus garden, stream, waterfall, and fishpond *inside* the lobby to the circular restaurant and free-form swimming pools, every inch of this resort is calculated to take your breath away. The pools (complete with waterfalls) and four whirlpools (one of which is the most romantic in the valley) are the best reasons to stay here. Guest rooms are stylishly elegant. The city-view rooms are a bit larger than the hillside-view rooms, but second-floor hillside-view rooms have patios. Unfortunately for fans of long soaks, most bathrooms have only three-quarter-size tubs. The Top of the Rock restaurant snags the best view around, and sunset dinners are memorable.

2000 Westcourt Way, Tempe, AZ 85282. © 800/WYNDHAM or 602/225-9000. Fax 602/438-8622. www. wyndhambuttes.com. 353 units. Jan to mid-Apr $189–$299 double, from $475 suite; mid-Apr to mid-May $159–$199 double, from $475 suite; mid-May to early Sept $89–$129 double, from $375 suite; mid-Sept to Dec $159–$269 double, from $475 suite. Children under 16 stay free in parent's room. AE, DC, DISC, MC, V. Pets accepted ($25 fee). **Amenities:** 3 restaurants (New American/Southwestern, American, bar and grill); 3 lounges; 2 pools; 4 tennis courts; volleyball courts; exercise room; access to nearby health club; spa services; 3 Jacuzzis; sauna; bike rentals; concierge; business center; room service; massage; dry cleaning; executive-level rooms. *In room:* A/C, TV, dataport, high-speed Internet access, coffeemaker, hair dryer, iron.

MODERATE/INEXPENSIVE

Chain options in the airport area include the **Best Western Airport Inn,** 2425 S. 24th St. (© **602/273-7251**), charging $89 to $129 double; and **Rodeway Inn–Airport East,** 1550 S. 52nd St. (© **480/967-3000**), charging $70 to $110 double. All rates are for high season.

Hotel San Carlos ⭐   If you don't mind staying in downtown Phoenix with the convention crowds, you'll get good value at this historic hotel. Built in 1928 and listed on the National Register of Historic Places, the San Carlos provides that touch of elegance and charm missing from other downtown choices. Unfortunately, bedrooms are rather small by today's standards, and the decor needs updating. If you're up for a splurge, check out the suites, which are named for celebrities that stayed here in the hotel's heyday.

202 N. Central Ave., Phoenix, AZ 85004. ℂ 866/253-4121 or 602/253-4121. Fax 602/253-6668. www.hotel sancarlos.com. 133 units. Jan–Apr $146–$166 double, $227 suite; May–Aug $99–$110 double, $140 suite; Sept–Dec $113–$133 double, $195 suite. Children under 18 stay free in parent's room. Rates include continental breakfast. AE, DC, DISC, MC, V. Parking $5. **Amenities:** 3 restaurants (steakhouse, Irish pub, cafe); rooftop pool; concierge; laundry service; dry cleaning. *In room:* A/C, TV, dataport, coffeemaker, iron.

TEMPE, MESA & THE EAST VALLEY

For the most part, south Phoenix is one of the poorest parts of the city. However, it does have a couple of exceptional resorts, and Phoenix South Mountain Park is one of the best places in the city to experience the desert. Tempe, which lies just a few miles east of the airport, is home to Arizona State University, and consequently supports a lively nightlife scene. Along Tempe's Mill Avenue, you'll find one of the only neighborhoods in the valley where locals actually get out of their cars and walk the streets. Tempe is also convenient to Papago Park, which is home to the Phoenix Zoo, the Desert Botanical Garden, the Arizona Historical Society Museum, a municipal golf course, and hiking and mountain-biking trails.

EXPENSIVE

Fiesta Inn Resort ⭐ *Value*   Reasonable rates, green lawns, palm- and eucalyptus-shaded grounds, and a location close to the airport, ASU, and Tempe's Mill Avenue make this older, casual resort one of the best deals in the valley. Okay, so it doesn't have the desert character of The Wyndham Buttes Resort across the freeway, and it isn't as stylish as the resorts in Scottsdale, but you can't argue with the rates. The large guest rooms, although a bit dark, have an appealing retro mission styling. You may not feel like you're in the desert when you stay here (due to the lawns and shade trees), but you'll certainly get a lot more for your money than at other area hotels in this price range.

2100 S. Priest Dr., Tempe, AZ 85282. ℂ 800/528-6481 or 480/967-1441. Fax 480/967-0224. www.fiestainn resort.com. 270 units. Jan to late Apr $175 double; late Apr to May $135 double; June–Sept $89 double; Oct–Dec $149 double. Children under 12 stay free in parent's room. AE, DISC, MC, V. Pets accepted ($50 deposit). **Amenities:** 2 restaurants (American/Southwestern); lounge; pool; 3 tennis courts; exercise room; Jacuzzi; bike rentals; concierge; car-rental desk; courtesy airport shuttle; business center; room service; laundry service; dry cleaning. *In room:* A/C, TV, dataport, high-speed Internet access, fridge, coffeemaker, hair dryer, iron, free local calls.

Gold Canyon Golf Resort ⭐⭐ *Value*   Unless you're an avid golfer, this place is going to seem way too far out of the city. However, if you just want to play golf, then this older resort at the foot of the Superstition Mountains is a great choice. Located way out on the east side of the valley near Apache Junction (at least a 30- to 45-min. drive from the airport), Gold Canyon is a favorite of devoted golfers who come to play some of the most scenic holes in the state. Although nongolfers will appreciate the scenery, the small pool and the lack of an exercise room make it clear that golfers, not swimmers, take the fore here. The spacious guest rooms are housed in blindingly white pueblo-inspired buildings; some have fireplaces, while others have whirlpools. The deluxe golf-course rooms are definitely worth the higher rates. The limited dining options here and in the immediate vicinity are a drawback, but if golf is your game and you've just got to play the Dinosaur Mountain course, then the lack of menu variety shouldn't matter too much.

6100 S. Kings Ranch Rd., Gold Canyon, AZ 85218. ℂ 800/624-6445 or 480/982-9090. Fax 480/983-9554. www.gcgr.com. 91 units. Jan–Mar $135–$185 double; Apr–Sept $89–$139 double; Sept–Dec $115–$165 double. Children under 18 stay free in parent's room. AE, DC, DISC, MC, V. Pets accepted ($75 fee). **Amenities:** 2 restaurants (American); lounge; pool; 2 highly regarded 18-hole golf courses; small spa; Jacuzzi; bike rentals; concierge; business center; room service; laundry service; dry cleaning. *In room:* A/C, TV, dataport, minibar, coffeemaker, hair dryer, iron.

Tempe Mission Palms Hotel ★★ I've always like this hotel simply for its great location right on Mill Avenue in downtown Tempe. However, this past year, the hotel revamped all its rooms with bold colors and modern geometric patterns. They're a bit wild but totally gorgeous—perfect for Mill Avenue. Sure this is more a business hotel (ergonomic desk chairs), but with a rooftop pool, tennis court, the Mill Avenue nightlife scene right outside the front door, this is a great choice for young, active travelers who want to be right in the action. Come in the spring and you won't want to leave the courtyard, which is scented by the flowers of citrus trees.

60 E. Fifth St., Tempe, AZ 85281. © 800/547-8705 or 480/894-1400. Fax 480/968-7677. www.mission palms.com. 303 units. Jan–Apr $179–$199 double, $329 suite; May–June $129–$169 double, $269 suite; July–Aug $99–$129 double, $219 suite; Sept–Dec $149–$199 double, $299 suite. Rates do not include $6 daily hospitality fee. Children under 18 stay free in parent's room. AE, DC, DISC, MC, V. Pets accepted ($100 deposit, $25 nonrefundable). **Amenities:** Restaurant (Southwestern); 2 lounges; outdoor pool; tennis court; exercise room; access to nearby health club; 2 Jacuzzis; concierge; courtesy airport shuttle; business center; room service; laundry service; dry cleaning. In room: A/C, TV, dataport, coffeemaker, hair dryer, iron, wi-fi.

MODERATE/INEXPENSIVE

Apache Boulevard in Tempe becomes Main Street in Mesa, and along this stretch of road there are numerous old motels charging some of the lowest rates in the valley. However, these motels are very hit-or-miss. If you're used to staying at nonchain motels, you might want to cruise this strip and check out a few places. Otherwise, try the chain motels mentioned below (which tend to charge $20–$40 more per night than nonchain motels).

Chain options in the Tempe area include the **Days Inn–Tempe,** 1221 E. Apache Blvd. (© **480/968-7793**), charging $50 to $119 double; and **Super 8–Tempe/Scottsdale,** 1020 E. Apache Blvd. (© **480/967-8891**), charging $65 to $105 double.

Chain options in the Mesa area include the **Motel 6–Mesa,** 336 W. Hampton Ave. (© **480/844-8899**), charging $52 to $56 double; and **Super 8–Mesa,** 6733 E. Main St. (© **480/981-6181**), charging $63 to $71 double.

WEST VALLEY

The Wigwam Resort ★★ Located 20 minutes west of downtown Phoenix and more than twice as far from Scottsdale, this property opened its doors to the public in 1929 and remains one of the nation's premier golf resorts. It's a classic, with old-school gentility, but when the money all headed to Scottsdale, this place was left feeling like an island amid the affordable housing of the west Valley. As at the Arizona Biltmore and the Camelback Inn, this is an old-money sort of place, and the traditional-style golf courses are the main reason most people choose this resort, which, although elegant, is set amid flat lands that lack the stunning desert scenery of the Scottsdale area. Most of the guest rooms are in Santa Fe–style buildings, surrounded by green lawns and colorful gardens, and all of the spacious units feature contemporary Southwestern furniture. Some units have fireplaces, but the rooms to request are those along the golf course. The Wigwam has a very traditional feel about it. In 2003, the resort underwent an extensive renovation that gave this gracefully aging golf resort a fresh new look.

300 Wigwam Blvd., Litchfield Park, AZ 85340. © **800/327-0396** or 623/935-3811. Fax 623/935-3737. www.wigwamresort.com. 331 units. Early Jan to mid-May $365–$425 double, from $455 suite; late May to early Sept $199–$239 double, from $259 suite; mid-Sept to Dec $309–$359 double, from $385 suite. Rates do not include $12 daily resort fee. Children under 18 stay free in parent's room. AE, DC, DISC, MC, V. Pets accepted ($50 deposit, $25 nonrefundable). **Amenities:** 3 restaurants (Southwestern, American); 2 lounges; 2 pools; 3 18-hole golf courses; 9 tennis courts; croquet court; health club; spa services; 2 Jacuzzis; bikes; children's programs; concierge; car-rental desk; 24-hr. room service; massage; babysitting; laundry service; dry cleaning; executive-level rooms. In room: A/C, TV, dataport, minibar, coffeemaker, hair dryer, iron, safe.

4 Where to Dine

The Valley of the Sun boasts hundreds of excellent restaurants, with most of the best dining options concentrated in the Scottsdale Road and Biltmore Corridor areas. If you want to splurge on only one expensive meal while you're here, consider a resort restaurant that offers a view of the city lights. Other meals not to be missed are the cowboy dinners served amid Wild West decor at such places as Pinnacle Peak Patio and Rustler's Rooste.

Phoenix also has plenty of big and familiar chains. At the **Hard Rock Cafe,** 3 S. Second St. (© **602/261-7625**), you can toss down a burger and buy that all-important T-shirt to prove you were here. There's a **California Pizza Kitchen,** 2400 E. Camelback Rd. (© **602/553-8382**), in Phoenix's Biltmore Fashion Park, and another branch in Scottsdale at 10100 N. Scottsdale Rd., 1 block south of Shea Boulevard (© **480/596-8300**).

The big chain steakhouses are also duking it out here. You'll find two **Ruth's Chris** steakhouses: in the Biltmore district at 2201 E. Camelback Rd. (© **602/ 957-9600**), and in the Scottsdale Seville shopping plaza, 7001 N. Scottsdale Rd. (© **480/991-5988**). **Morton's** steakhouses are located in the Biltmore district in the Shops at the Esplanade, 2501 E. Camelback Rd. (© **602/955-9577**), and in north Scottsdale at 15233 N. Kierland Blvd. (© **480/951-4440**).

If you'd rather be in Hawaii, you can always eat at one of the **Roy's** here in town; they're at the Scottsdale Seville shopping center, 7001 N. Scottsdale Rd. (© **480/905-1155**) and the JW Marriott Desert Ridge Resort & Spa, 5350 E. Marriott Dr., Scottsdale (© **480/419-7697**).

Good places to go trolling for a place to eat include the trendy Biltmore Fashion Park shopping center, at Camelback Road and 24th Street (© **602/254-6500**), and Old Town Scottsdale. At the former, you'll find the chain restaurant California Pizza Kitchen (mentioned above) as well as nearly a dozen other excellent restaurants. In downtown Scottsdale, within an area of roughly 4 square blocks, you'll find about a dozen good restaurants. A few of my favorites in both places are listed in the following pages.

Phoenix is a sprawling city, and it can be a real pain to have to drive around in search of a good lunch spot. If you happen to be visiting the Phoenix Art Museum, the Heard Museum, or the Desert Botanical Garden anytime around lunch, stay put for your noon meal. All three of these attractions have cafes serving decent, if limited, menus.

SCOTTSDALE
EXPENSIVE

Bloom 🌟🌟 *Value* NEW AMERICAN   Located in the upscale Shops at Gainey Village, Bloom is affiliated with two of my favorite Tucson restaurants—Wildflower and Bistro Zin—and you'll see a bit of both establishments here. This place is big and always buzzing with energy. The minimalist decor emphasizes flowers, an elegant wine bar serves a wide range of flights (tasting assortments), and the bistro-style menu has lots of great dishes in a wide range of prices. Opt for one of the salads, such as fresh artichoke hearts with shaved Parmesan and white-truffle drizzle; there are also enough interesting appetizers that a dinner of small plates would be extremely satisfying. Among the entrees, the roast duck with whipped potatoes and drunken cherry sauce is excellent.

8877 N. Scottsdale Rd. © 480/922-5666. www.tasteofbloom.com. Reservations recommended. Main courses $8–$12 lunch, $13–$24 dinner. AE, DC, DISC, MC, V. Mon–Thurs 11am–3pm and 5–9:30pm; Fri–Sat 11am–3pm and 5–10:30pm; Sun 5–9pm.

Phoenix, Scottsdale & the Valley of the Sun Dining

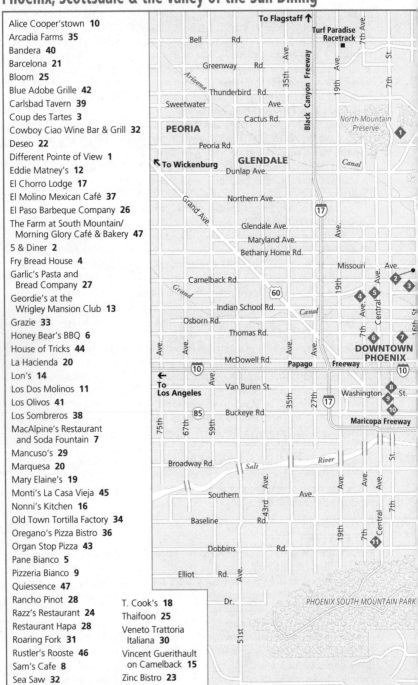

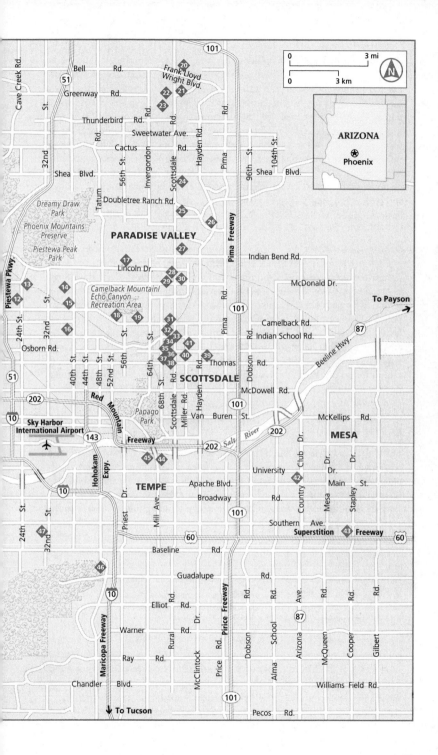

Cowboy Ciao Wine Bar & Grill ⚜ SOUTHWESTERN/FUSION   Delicious food with a global influence and a fun, trendy atmosphere outfitted in "cowboy chic" make this a great place for a memorable meal. Located in fashionable downtown Scottsdale, it attracts a diverse crowd. Not-to-be-missed dishes include the exotic mushroom pan-fry and the TM soup. Keep an eye out for the porcini-crusted rib-eye steak, which sometimes shows up as a nightly special and is another good choice for mushroom fans. Cowboy Ciao is also notable for its wine list and bar, where customers can order a flight of wines. When it comes time for dessert, don't miss the warm bread pudding with cherries, cranberries, and pine nuts, or, if you're feeling adventurous, opt for the Mexican chocolate pot de crème with chipotle cream. Unfortunately, service here can be uneven.

7133 E. Stetson Dr. (at Sixth Ave.). ✆ **480/WINE-111.** www.cowboyciao.com. Reservations recommended. Main courses $9–$25 lunch, $16–$33 dinner. AE, DC, DISC, MC, V. Tues–Thurs 11:30am–2:30pm and 5–10pm; Fri–Sat 11:30am–2:30pm and 5–11pm; Sun–Mon 5–10pm.

Deseo ⚜⚜⚜ NUEVO LATINO   If your taste buds have fallen asleep from one too many uninspired meals, bring them to Deseo and wake them up. Jaded palates and sleepy taste buds will thank you profusely when you introduce them to the vibrant flavors on this restaurant's seviche menu. Don't even bother trying to decide between Ecuadorian seviche (shrimp, roasted tomatoes, avocado slices, popcorn, and corn nuts), Thai seviche (tuna and calamari infused with coconut water, basil, chiles, and lime), and scallop seviche (spicy lemon-saffron sauce, crispy lemon rings, cilantro, and coriander oil). Just order the trio of seviches. Better yet, order two trios and call it dinner. Wash everything down with a minty mojito for an unforgettable meal. Hot appetizers? Entrees? You can't go wrong, but the mahimahi is particularly memorable. Even the bread basket, with Peruvian cheese rolls and paper-thin fried plantain slices, is an absolute delight.

Westin Kierland Resort, 6902 E. Greenway Pkwy. ✆ **480/624-1000.** Main courses $26–$38. AE, DC, DISC, MC, V. Mon–Sat 6–10pm.

El Chorro Lodge ⚜ CONTINENTAL   Built in 1934 as a school for girls and converted to a lodge and restaurant 3 years later, El Chorro is a valley landmark and one of the area's last old traditional establishments. Even if the interior is a little dowdy, at nighttime the lights twinkle on the saguaro cactus and the restaurant takes on a timeless tranquillity. The adobe building houses several dining rooms, but the patio is the place to be, either in the daytime or on a chilly night when there's a fire crackling in the patio fireplace. Both old-timers and families like the traditional decor and menu, which features such classics as chateaubriand and rack of lamb. In addition to the favorites, there are several low-fat and low-salt dishes, as well as seafood options. Save room for the legendary sticky buns.

5550 E. Lincoln Dr. ✆ **480/948-5170.** www.elchorro.com. Reservations recommended. Main courses $9–$62 dinner. AE, DC, DISC, MC, V. Mon–Thurs 11am–2pm and 5:30–10pm; Fri 11am–2pm and 5:30–11pm; Sat 5:30–11pm; Sun 9am–2pm and 5:30–10pm.

Mancuso's ⚜⚜ NORTHERN ITALIAN/CONTINENTAL   With its ramparts, towers, stone walls, and narrow alleyways, the Borgata shopping plaza is modeled after the Tuscan village of San Gimignano, so it seems only fitting that Mancuso's would affect the look of a castle banquet hall. A cathedral ceiling, arched windows, and huge roof beams set the stage for the gourmet cuisine; a pianist playing soft jazz sets the mood. If you lack the means to start your meal with the beluga caviar, perhaps carpaccio *di manzo*—sliced raw beef with mustard sauce and capers—will do. Veal is a specialty (with osso buco a long-time favorite), but it's always difficult just to get past the pasta offerings. Fish and daily seafood specials round out the menu. The professional service will have you feeling like royalty by the time you finish your dessert. Who needs a trip to Tuscany when you have Mancuso's?

At the Borgata, 6166 N. Scottsdale Rd. ℂ **480/948-9988.** www.mancusosrestaurant.com. Reservations recommended. Main courses $16–$30. AE, DC, DISC, MC, V. Sun–Thurs 5–10pm; Fri–Sat 5–10:30.

Rancho Pinot ★★ NEW AMERICAN   Rancho Pinot, hidden at the back of a nondescript shopping center adjacent to the upscale Borgata shopping plaza, combines a homey cowboy-chic decor with nonthreatening contemporary American cuisine, and has long been a favorite with Scottsdale and Phoenix residents. Look elsewhere if you're craving wildly creative flavor combinations, but if you like simple, well-prepared food, Rancho Pinot may be the place. My favorite starter is the grilled squid salad with preserved lemon; for an entree, you can always count on the handmade pasta or Nonni's chicken, braised with white wine, mushrooms, and herbs. There's a short but well-chosen list of beers and wines by the glass. The staff is friendly and tends to treat you as though you're a regular, even if it's your first visit.

6208 N. Scottsdale Rd. (southwest corner of Scottsdale Rd. and Lincoln Dr.). ℂ **480/367-8030.** Reservations recommended. Main courses $18–$29. AE, DC, DISC, MC, V. Tues–Sun 5:30–10pm. Summer hours subject to change.

Razz's Restaurant ★★ SOUTHWEST/ECLECTIC   Chef/owner Razz Kamnitzer has long been one of the most creative chefs in Scottsdale, so it may seem a bit unusual to find his superb restaurant in a nondescript old shopping center. However, step through the door and you'll immediately be immersed in the conviviality that characterizes this locals' favorite. For the full-on experience, take a seat at the chef's island counter where you can order a chef's sampler dinner of as many or as few courses ($10–$13 per course) as you want. Razz makes the choices and you sit back and enjoy. You might wind up with spicy Indonesian noodles, Portuguese-style clams, or duck cakes with nopalito cactus sauce.

10315 N. Scottsdale Rd. ℂ **480/905-1308.** www.razzsrestaurant.com. Reservations recommended. Main courses $20–$28. AE, DC, DISC, MC, V. Tues–Thurs 5–9pm; Fri–Sat 5–10pm.

Restaurant Hapa ★★ PAN-ASIAN   Even this far from the Pacific, pan-Asian cuisine can cause a stir, and if you've got deep pockets and a taste for unusual fusion fare, don't leave town without scheduling a meal here. Before your appetizer even arrives, you might snack on herb flat bread with a soy dipping sauce or an *amuse bouch* (complimentary bite) of coconut curry with pine nuts. We're particularly partial to the strong flavor combinations that can be found on the appetizer list. The mussels in Thai coconut broth are unforgettable. Also keep an eye out for miso-marinated fish entrees. I once had sea bass prepared this way here, and it was the best piece of fish I'd ever tasted. The atmosphere is casual yet sophisticated, and attracts a lot of restaurant-industry folks from around the valley.

6204 N. Scottsdale Rd. (southwest corner of Scottsdale Rd. and Lincoln Dr.). ℂ **480/998-8220.** www.restaurant hapa.com. Reservations recommended. Main courses $25–$36. AE, DC, MC, V. Mon–Sat 5:30–10pm.

Roaring Fork ★★ SOUTHWESTERN   This restaurant is the creation of chef Robert McGrath, who was once the chef at The Phoenician's Windows on the Green, and the food here is among the most creative Southwestern fare you'll find in the valley. The bread basket alone, filled with herb-infused rolls and corn muffins accompanied by honey-chile butter, is enough to make you weep with joy. Be sure you try the sugar-and-chile-cured duck breast with green-chile macaroni, a house specialty. If you can't get a table, dine in the saloon or the saloon patio, where you'll see bowls of interesting munchies such as spicy jerky. Don't miss the huckleberry margaritas. Happy hour (Mon–Sat 4–7pm) is a good time for an early meal from the saloon menu.

4800 N. Scottsdale Rd. (in the Finova Building at the corner of Goldwater Blvd.). (C) **480/947-0795.** www.roaringfork.com. Reservations highly recommended. Main courses $16–$29. AE, DISC, MC, V. Mon–Sat 5–10pm; Sun 4:30–9pm.

Sea Saw ★★ JAPANESE   *Food & Wine* magazine recently named Chef Nobuo Fukuda one of the 10 best chefs in the U.S., but you'd never guess that this tiny unpretentious place is home to such a celebrated chef. At his hole-in-the-wall restaurant in Old Town Scottsdale, Fukuda is letting his creativity blossom. The menu lists only 20 dishes (10 warm and 10 cool). Not one of these dishes can really be considered sushi, so don't look for California rolls here. Instead, consider the seared tuna *tataki* or warm white fish carpaccio. Because the restaurant is affiliated with the adjacent Cowboy Ciao and Kazamierz World Wine Bar, there is an overwhelmingly long wine list that includes lots of premium sakes as well as all the reds and whites you would expect.

7133 E. Stetson Dr. (C) **480/481-WINE.** www.seasaw.net. Reservations not accepted. All plates $10–$16; tasting menu $100. MC, V. Sun–Thurs 5:30–10pm; Fri–Sat 5:30–11pm.

MODERATE

Arcadia Farms ★ NEW AMERICAN   Long a favorite of the Scottsdale ladies-who-lunch crowd, this Old Town restaurant features a romantic setting and well-prepared contemporary fare. Arcadia Farms is committed to healthy food and sustainable agricultural practices, and only organic lettuces and herbs are used in the dishes served here. Try the raspberry goat cheese salad with jicama and candied pecans—it's delicious. The warm mushroom, spinach, and goat cheese tart is another winner. Try to get a seat on the shady patio. This restaurant also operates cafes at the Desert Botanical Garden, the Heard Museum, and the Phoenix Art Museum.

7014 E. First Ave. (C) **480/941-5665.** www.arcadiafarmscafe.com. Reservations recommended. Main courses $10–$13. MC, V. Daily 11am–3pm.

Bandera ★ (Value) AMERICAN   Once you've gotten a whiff of the wood-roasted chickens turning on the rotisseries in Bandera's back-of-the-building, open-air stone oven, you'll know exactly what to order when you finally get seated at this perennially popular spot in Old Town. What an aroma! The succulent spit-roasted chicken is the meal to have here, and make sure you get it with some of Bandera's great mashed potatoes. Sure, you could order prime rib or clams, but you'd be a fool if you did. Stick with the chicken or maybe the barbecued ribs, and you won't go wrong.

3821 N. Scottsdale Rd. (C) **480/994-3524.** Reservations not accepted. Main courses $13–$26. AE, DC, MC, V. Sun–Thurs 4:30–10pm; Fri–Sat 4–11pm.

Barcelona ★★ MEDITERRANEAN/NEW AMERICAN   Supper clubs are all the rage in the Valley of the Sun these days, and this is the biggest and boldest of them all. The building appears to have been lifted straight out of the restaurant's namesake Spanish city, and is illuminated by giant torches. There are three bar areas, including one outdoors (for smokers), and several dining areas.

The menu doesn't break any new ground, but it does have surprisingly low prices for such a gorgeous setting. The main dining room faces the bandstand and converts into a dance floor late in the evening; music is primarily jazz, R&B, and Top 40. This is definitely a see-and-be-seen sort of place, with a brisk beautiful-people bar scene late at night. There's usually a good happy hour here Monday through Friday from 4 to 7pm.

There's a second Barcelona in Chandler at 900 N. 54th St. (© **480/785-9004**).

15440 Greenway-Hayden Loop. © **480/603-0370**. www.barcelonadining.com. Reservations highly recommended. Main courses $12–$32. AE, DC, DISC, MC, V. Mon–Wed 11:30am–2pm and 4–10pm; Thurs–Fri 11:30am–2pm and 4–11pm; Sat 4–11pm.

Carlsbad Tavern 🐾 NEW MEXICAN   Carlsbad Tavern blends the fiery tastes of New Mexican cuisine with a hip and humorous bat-theme atmosphere (a reference to Carlsbad Caverns). The menu lists traditional New Mexican dishes such as *carne adovada* (pork simmered in a fiery red-chile sauce), as well as nouvelle Southwestern specialties such as grilled chicken, andouille sausage, black beans, and pine nuts tossed with pasta in a spicy peppercorn-cream sauce. Cool off your taste buds with a prickly-pear margarita. A lagoon makes this place feel like a beach bar, while the patio fireplace is cozy on a cold night.

3313 N. Hayden Rd. (south of Osborn). © **480/970-8164**. www.carlsbadtavern.com. Reservations recommended for dinner. Main courses $7.25–$20. AE, DISC, MC, V. Mon–Sat 11am–1am; Sun 1pm–1am (limited menu daily 10 or 11pm–1am).

Thaifoon 🐾🐾 THAI   This may not exactly be traditional Thai food, but it sure is good. Thaifoon merges a hip upscale setting with flavorful Thai cuisine at economical prices. In fact, the food here is so good, you'll likely find yourself coming back repeatedly to try more dishes. The Thai-style coconut-mushroom soup here may not be traditional, but it's the best I've ever had. The many shrimp dishes are all packed with lively flavors. Don't miss the great tropical cocktails.

At The Shops at Gainey Village, 8777 N. Scottsdale Rd. © **480/998-0011**. www.thaifoon.com. Call ahead to be put on waiting list. Main courses $6–$17. AE, DISC, MC, V. Daily 11am–10pm.

Old Town Tortilla Factory 🐾 MEXICAN   Moderately priced Mexican restaurants abound in Phoenix and Scottsdale, but this is one of the most enjoyable. Located in an old house surrounded by attractive patios and citrus trees that bloom in winter and spring, this place stays busy both for its creative Mexican fare and for its lively bar scene (more than 80 premium tequilas are available). As you enter the restaurant grounds, you might see someone making the tortillas of the day. These tortillas come in a dozen different flavors, and will arrive at your table accompanied by chile-flavored butter. The rich tortilla soup and the tequila-lime salad make good starters. For an entree, try the pork chops crusted with ancho chile powder and raspberry sauce.

6910 E. Main St. © **480/945-4567**. www.oldtowntortillafactory.com. Reservations accepted only for parties of 6 or more. Main courses $10–$31. AE, DC, DISC, MC, V. Sun–Thurs 5–10pm; Fri–Sat 5–11pm.

Veneto Trattoria Italiana 🐾 VENETIAN ITALIAN   This pleasantly low-key bistro, specializing in the cuisine of Venice, serves simple and satisfying "peasant food," including traditional pork-and-garlic sausages served with grilled polenta and braised savoy cabbage. *Baccala mantecato* (creamy fish mousse on grilled polenta, made with dried salt cod soaked overnight in milk) may sound unusual, but it's absolutely heavenly. Other good bets include the salad of thinly sliced smoked beef, shaved Parmesan, and arugula. For a finale, the *semifreddo con frutta secca,* a partially frozen meringue with dry fruits in a pool of raspberry sauce, has an intoxicating texture. There's a welcoming bistro ambience inside and outdoor seating on the patio (where you almost forget you're in a shopping center).

6137 N. Scottsdale Rd., in Hilton Village. ℂ **480/948-9928.** www.venetotrattoria.com. Reservations recommended. Main courses $8–$18 lunch, $13–$22.75 dinner. AE, DC, DISC, MC, V. Mon–Sat 11:30am–2:30pm and 5–10pm.

Zinc Bistro ★★ *Finds* FRENCH   It may seem incongruous to find the perfect French bistro in sunny Scottsdale, and in a modern shopping center at that, but here it is. This place is a perfect reproduction of the sort of bistro you may have loved on your last trip to Paris. Everything is authentic, from the zinc bar to the sidewalk cafe seating to the hooks under the bar for ladies' purses. And of course there's the waitstaff in their long white aprons. Try the cassoulet with duck confit, the omelet piled high with shoestring potatoes, or anything that comes with the fabulous bistro fries.

15034 N. Scottsdale Rd. ℂ **480/603-0922.** Reservations accepted only for parties of 6 or more. Main courses $8–$15 lunch, $8–$28 dinner. AE, DC, DISC, MC, V. Sun–Thurs 11am–10pm (late-night menu until midnight).

INEXPENSIVE

El Molino Mexican Café ★ *Finds* MEXICAN   Located a bit out of the Old Town Scottsdale mainstream, this little Mexican joint is little more than a fast-food place, but it serves the best chimichangas in town. If you're among the few people in this country still not familiar with what a chimichanga is, it's a deep-fried burrito. That said, the chimis here have crispy, light shells and are packed full of tasty fillings. Try a chimi with machaca (shredded and spiced beef) or the green chili meat and we're sure you'll become a convert. If fried food just doesn't do it for you, opt for a couple of green corn tamales, which are an Arizona specialty.

3554 N. Goldwater Blvd. ℂ **480/946-4494.** Reservations not accepted. Main courses. $2.60–$9.50. MC, V. Mon–Sat 9am–8pm.

El Paso Barbeque Company ★ BARBECUE   This is Scottsdale-style barbecue, with an upscale cowboy decor. If you're in the mood for raucous good times, this place is worth the trip for some lip-smacking barbecue, which runs the gamut from ribs to smoked chicken to more uptown dishes such as barbecued salmon and prime rib. The pulled pork with a smoky sauce and fresh coleslaw is scrumptious. There's also a wide variety of sandwiches, which makes this a good lunch spot or place to get carryout.

8220 N. Hayden Rd. ℂ **480/998-2626.** www.elpasobarbeque.com. Reservations accepted for parties of 12 or more. Main courses $7.50–$22. AE, DC, DISC, MC, V. Sun–Thurs 11am–10pm; Fri–Sat 11am–11pm.

Garlic's Pasta and Bread Company AMERICAN/ITALIAN   This little lunch spot is tucked into the back of the same shopping center that houses the more upscale Roy's, and although you could conceivably grab an early dinner here, this is first and foremost a great spot for a quick lunch if you happen to be cruising Scottsdale Road at midday. Creative sandwiches are the big attraction, but there are also pasta salads, soups, and even brick-oven pizzas.

At the Scottsdale Seville shopping center, 7001 N. Scottsdale Rd. ℂ **480/368-9699.** Reservations not accepted. Main courses $5.50–$8. AE, MC, V. Mon–Fri 9:30am–6pm; Sat 9:30am–5:30pm.

Grazie ★ *Finds* PIZZA   This little neighborhood pizzeria and wine bar over on the quiet west end of Main Street is the absolute antithesis of nearby Oregano's— sophisticated and full of contemporary art. Forget about the tourist scene; this place is a neighborhood hangout. Come here for dinner if you're looking for someplace to sip Italian wines and share a couple of designer pizzas from the wood-fired oven. Start your meal with the carpaccio *bresaol,* which is served with arugula and Parmigiano-Reggiano cheese, and a lemon vinaigrette or the Emiliana salad, made with arugula, baby greens, Parmigiano-Reggiano, red onions, red bell peppers, and pine nuts. The pizzas here have paper-thin crusts, so don't worry about filling up before it's time to order tiramisu.

6952 E. Main St. © 480/663-9797. Reservations recommended Fri–Sat nights. Main courses $8–$14. AE, MC, V. Daily 5–10pm.

Los Olivos ★ MEXICAN Los Olivos is a Scottsdale institution, one of the last restaurants in Old Town that dates to the days when cowboys tied up their horses on Main Street. Although the food is just standard Mexican fare, the building is a fascinating work of folk-art construction. The entrance is a bit like a cement cave, with strange figures rising up from the roof. Amazingly, this throwback to slower times is only steps away from the new Scottsdale Museum of Contemporary Art. The tortillas are made fresh on the premises. On Friday and Saturday nights, there's Latin dancing from 9pm until 1am.

There's another Los Olivos up in north Scottsdale, at 15544 N. Pima Rd. (© **480/596-9787**).

7328 Second St. © 480/946-2256. www.losolivosrestaurant.com. Reservations recommended. Main courses $5.50–$14. AE, DISC, MC, V. Sun–Thurs 11am–10pm; Fri–Sat 11am–11pm.

Los Sombreros ★ *Finds* MEXICAN Although this casual Mexican restaurant is in an attractive old house, it doesn't look all that special from the outside. However, chef Jeffrey Smedstad is a graduate of the Scottsdale Culinary Institute and brings surprising creativity to the Mexican dishes served here. Start with the chunky homemade guacamole, which is some of the best in the city. Be sure to order the *puerco en chipotle,* succulent, slow-roasted pork in tomatillo chipotle sauce. Finish it all off with the flan, which will spoil you for any other flan anywhere else. For a real treat, get it with almond-flavored tequila.

2534 N. Scottsdale Rd. (at McKellips Rd.), Tempe. © 480/994-1799. Main courses $12–$15. Reservations not accepted. AE, DC, DISC, MC, V. Sun and Tues–Thurs 4:30–9pm; Fri–Sat 4:30–10pm.

Oregano's Pizza Bistro PIZZA/PASTA With very reasonable prices and a location convenient to the many shops and galleries of downtown Scottsdale, this sprawling pizza joint (two buildings and the courtyard/parking lot between) is a big hit with the area's young crowd. Both the thin-crust pizzas—topped with the likes of cilantro pesto and shredded chicken—and the Chicago stuffed pizzas are all the good things pizza should be. The menu also offers artichoke lasagna, barbecued chicken wings, salads, and even a pizza cookie for dessert. Because this is such a popular spot, expect a wait at dinner.

Other locations are in Phoenix at 1008 E. Camelback Rd. (© **602/241-0707**), in Tempe at 523 W. University Dr. (© **480/858-0501**), and in north Scottsdale at 7215 E Shea. Blvd. (© **480/348-0500**).

3622 N. Scottsdale Rd. (south of Indian School Rd.). © 480/970-1860. www.oreganos.com. Reservations not accepted. Main courses $6–$20. AE, DC, DISC, MC, V. Mon–Thurs 11am–9pm; Fri–Sat 11am–10pm; Sun noon–9pm.

NORTH SCOTTSDALE, CAREFREE & CAVE CREEK
VERY EXPENSIVE

Marquesa ★★★ MEDITERRANEAN The Marquesa, with an ambience reminiscent of an 18th-century Spanish villa, is as romantic a restaurant as you'll find in the valley. The menu is a contemporary interpretation of Mediterranean cuisine, and though the prices are high, I can think of few better places for a special dinner. The offerings change with the seasons, but expect them to be ripe with exotic ingredients imported from around the world, and count on almost every dish being an intensive labor of love. Paella Valenciana, the signature dish, includes such ingredients as lobster, escargot, shrimp, and cockles, and should not be missed. The Sunday "market-style" brunch is one of the best in the valley.

At the Fairmont Scottsdale Princess, 7575 E. Princess Dr. (about 12 miles north of downtown Scottsdale). ☎ 480/585-4848. Reservations recommended. Main courses $32–$44; prix-fixe menu $80; brunch $49. AE, DC, DISC, MC, V. Wed–Sat 6–10pm; Sun 10am–2:30pm. Closed mid-June to mid-Sept.

EXPENSIVE

La Hacienda ★★ GOURMET MEXICAN   As you may guess from the price range below, this is not your average taco joint. La Hacienda serves gourmet Mexican cuisine in an upscale, glamorous-but-rustic setting reminiscent of an early 1900s hacienda (stone tiled floor, Mexican glassware and crockery, a beehive fireplace). Be sure to start with the *antojitos* (appetizers) platter, which might include pork flautas (a rolled-up fried tortilla), baked shrimp, crabmeat enchiladas, and a blue-corn quesadilla made with squash blossoms, wild mushrooms, and goat cheese. We like the chicken glazed with a tequila-pomegranate sauce and the quail stuffed with duck, dried fruits, and cheese. However, the rack of lamb crusted with pumpkin seeds has long been a local favorite. There's even Mexican spa cuisine here, and live music lends a party atmosphere.

At the Fairmont Scottsdale Princess, 7575 E. Princess Dr. (about 12 miles north of downtown Scottsdale). ☎ 480/585-4848. Reservations recommended. Main courses $22–$35. AE, DC, DISC, MC, V. Thurs–Tues 5:30–10pm.

Michael's ★★ NEW AMERICAN/INTERNATIONAL   Located in the Citadel shopping/business plaza in north Scottsdale, this restaurant was once a remote culinary outpost. But as Scottsdale's upscale suburbs have marched ever northward, the city has bulldozed its way to Michael's doorstep. The setting is simple yet elegant, which allows the drama of food presentation to take the fore. To start things off, do not miss the "silver spoons" hors d'oeuvres—tablespoons each containing three or four ingredients that burst with flavor. From there, it's on to such main courses as rosemary-scented lamb chop eggplant, goat-cheese lasagna, and tomato confit. If you can't afford a full dinner or just don't feel like a big meal, head upstairs to the bar, where there's great bar food to accompany your drinks.

8700 E. Pinnacle Peak Rd., N. Scottsdale. ☎ 480/515-2575. www.michaelsrestaurant.com. Reservations recommended. Main courses $8–$16 lunch, $21–$29 dinner, prix-fixe menu $65 ($100–$110 with wine). AE, DC, DISC, MC, V. Mon–Fri 11am–2pm and 6–9pm; Sat 6–9pm; Sun 10am–2pm (brunch) and 6–9pm.

Mosaic ★★★ *Finds* NEW AMERICAN   The Pinnacle Peak area of north Scottsdale has seen a proliferation of high-end restaurants in recent years, and this just may be the best of a very good bunch. Okay, so dinner here is going to set you back quite a bit, but the food is superb, and if you come before the sun goes down, you can soak up some of the best desert views in the valley. Chef/owner Deborah Knight is one of the best new chefs in the valley and likes to show off her culinary creativity with a menu that changes regularly and is always provocative and daring. How about bacon-wrapped kangaroo tenderloin or snapping turtle soup to start things out? For an entree, you might order a rosemary-and-sage grilled ostrich filet or wild boar chops with a sauce made from dried strawberries and roses. You get the picture; this is a foodie's nirvana.

10600 E. Jomax Rd., N. Scottsdale. ℂ 480/563-9600. www.mosaic-restaurant.com. Main courses $24–$38. Reservations recommended. AE, DC, DISC, MC, V. Tues–Sun 5:30–9 or 10pm.

MODERATE

The Original Crazy Ed's Satisfied Frog Saloon & Restaurant *Finds*

AMERICAN/BARBECUE   Cave Creek is the Phoenix area's favorite cowtown hangout and is filled with Wild West–theme saloons and restaurants. Crazy Ed's—affiliated with the Black Mountain Brewing Company, which produces Cave Creek Chili Beer—is my favorite. You'll find Crazy Ed's in Frontier Town, a tourist-trap cow town, but don't let the location put you off. This place is just plain fun, with big covered porches and sawdust on the floor. Although the restaurant offers dishes "from the pond" and "from the chicken coop," you should stick to steaks and barbecue.

At Frontier Town, 6245 E. Cave Creek Rd., Cave Creek. ℂ 480/488-3317. www.satisfiedfrog.com. Reservations recommended on weekends. Main courses $7–$18 lunch, $12–$24 dinner. AE, DISC, MC, V. Sun–Thurs 11am–10pm; Fri–Sat 11am–11pm.

INEXPENSIVE

Greasewood Flat ★ *Finds* AMERICAN   Burgers and beer are the mainstays

at this rustic open-air restaurant in the Pinnacle Peak area of north Scottsdale, but the limited menu has only managed to make this place immensely popular. Located down a potholed gravel road behind Reata Pass steakhouse, Greasewood Flat is another desert party spot where families, motorcycle clubs, cyclists, and horseback riders all rub shoulders. Place your order at the window and grab a seat at one of the picnic tables. While you wait for you meal, you can also peruse all the old farm equipment that is scattered around the grounds. This place is the antithesis of north Scottsdale posh, and that's exactly why we love. Only in Arizona could you find a place like this.

27500 N. Alma School Rd. ℂ 480/585-7277. Reservations not accepted. Main courses $3.50–$6.50. No credit cards. Daily 11am–1am.

CENTRAL PHOENIX & THE CAMELBACK CORRIDOR
VERY EXPENSIVE

Mary Elaine's ★★★ FRENCH   There quite simply is no place else in Arizona to compare with Mary Elaine's, and if you happen to be in town for a major wedding anniversary or milestone birthday, this is the place to celebrate. At least once in your life you have to splurge the sort of dining experience provided at Mary Elaine's. Situated atop the posh Phoenician resort, this elegant restaurant is the pinnacle of Arizona dining not only for its haute cuisine, but also for its award-winning wine list (and master sommelier), exemplary service, and superb table settings (Austrian crystal, French silver, and Wedgwood china). Chef Bradford Thompson has worked both with famed New York restaurateur Daniel Boulud and Phoenix's own Vincent Guerithault. Thompson's menu focuses on classic French cuisine with an emphasis on impeccably fresh ingredients, and foie gras, truffles, lobster, and Beluga caviar all make frequent appearances. Menus change seasonally, and there are also themed tasting menus. Try to make a reservation that allows you to take in the sunset.

At The Phoenician, 6000 E. Camelback Rd. ℂ 480/423-2530. Reservations highly recommended. Jackets required for men. Main courses $50; 3-course dinner $87 (plus $45 for matched wines); 6-course tasting menu $120 (plus $75 for matched wines). AE, DC, DISC, MC, V. Tues–Thurs 6–10pm; Fri–Sat 6–11pm.

EXPENSIVE

Coup des Tartes *Finds* COUNTRY FRENCH   Chain restaurants, theme restaurants, restaurants that are all style and little substance: Sometimes in Phoenix it seems impossible to find a genuinely homey little hole in the wall that serves good food. Don't despair; Coup des Tartes is just what you've been looking for. With barely a dozen tables and no liquor license (bring your own wine; $8 corkage fee), it's about as removed from the standard Phoenix glitz as you can get without boarding a plane and leaving town. Start your meal with pâté de campagne or brie brûlée, covered with caramelized apples. The entree menu changes regularly, but the Moroccan lamb shank with couscous is so good that it is always on the menu. The filet mignon, with the sauce of the moment, is another good choice. Of course, for dessert, you absolutely must have a tarte.

4626 N. 16th St. (1 block south of Camelback Rd.). © 602/212-1082. Reservations recommended. Main courses $13–$33. AE, MC, V. Tues–Sat 5:30–10pm.

Eddie Matney's ★★ NEW AMERICAN   Eddie Matney has been on the Phoenix restaurant scene for many years now, and continues to keep local diners happy with his mix of creativity and comfort. This upscale bistro is in a glass office tower at Camelback Road's most upscale corner, which means it's a popular power-lunch and business-dinner spot, but it also works well for a romantic evening out. The menu ranges far and wide for inspiration and features everything from Eddie's famous meatloaf to grilled ahi tuna. If you're not up for a splurge, avail yourself of the half-price happy-hour appetizers in the bar, Monday through Thursday from 4 to 11pm and Friday and Saturday from 4pm to midnight.

2398 E. Camelback Rd. © 602/957-3214. www.eddiematneys.com. Reservations recommended. Main courses $9–$15 lunch, $13–$29 dinner. AE, DC, DISC, MC, V. Mon–Thurs 11:30am–2:30pm and 5–10pm; Fri 11:30am–2:30pm and 5–10:30pm; Sat 5–10:30pm; Sun 5–10pm.

Lon's ★★ AMERICAN REGIONAL   Located in an old adobe hacienda built by cowboy artist Lon Megargee and surrounded by colorful gardens, this restaurant is one of the most Arizonan places in the Phoenix area, and the patio, with its views of Camelback Mountain, is so tranquil that you'll likely want to start shopping for a house in the neighborhood. At midday this place is popular with both retirees and the power-lunch set, while at dinner it bustles with a wide mix of people. Dinner entrees are reliable, though not quite as imaginative as the appetizers (I like to skip the entrees and just make a meal of appetizers). The bar is cozy and romantic.

At the Hermosa Inn, 5532 N. Palo Cristi Rd. © 602/955-7878. www.lons.com. Reservations recommended. Main courses $10–$15 lunch, $19–$34 dinner. AE, DC, DISC, MC, V. Mon–Fri 11:30am–2pm and 6–10pm; Sat 6–10pm; Sun 10am–2pm (brunch) and 6–10pm.

T. Cook's ★★★ MEDITERRANEAN   Ready to pop the question? On your honeymoon? Celebrating an anniversary? This is the place for you. There just isn't a more romantic restaurant in the valley. Located within the walls of the Mediterranean-inspired Royal Palms Resort & Spa, it's surrounded by decades-old gardens and even has palm trees growing right through the roof of the dining room. The focal point of the open kitchen is a wood-fired oven that turns out a fabulous spit-roasted chicken as well as an impressive platter of paella. T. Cook's continues to make big impressions right through to the dessert course.

At the Royal Palms Resort and Spa, 5200 E. Camelback Rd. © 602/808-0766. www.royalpalmshotel.com. Reservations highly recommended. Main courses $11–$16 lunch, $24–$30 dinner. AE, DC, DISC, MC, V. Mon–Sat 6–10am, 11am–2pm, and 5:30–10pm; Sun 10am–2pm (brunch) and 5–10:30pm.

Kids Family-Friendly Restaurants

Organ Stop Pizza (p. 113)   A mighty Wurlitzer organ, with all the bells and whistles, entertains families while they chow down on pizza at long, communal tables. Nobody cares if the kids run around, and there are enough theatrics to keep them interested even if they can't relate to the music.

Pinnacle Peak Patio (p. 114)   Way out in north Scottsdale, this Wild West steakhouse comes complete with cowboys, shootouts, hayrides, and live music nightly.

Rustler's Rooste (p. 114)   Similar to Pinnacle Peak but closer to downtown Phoenix and Tempe, Rustler's Rooste has a slide from the lounge to the main dining room, a big patio, and live cowboy bands nightly. See if you can get your kids to try the rattlesnake appetizer—it tastes like chicken.

Vincent Guerithault on Camelback ☆☆ SOUTHWESTERN   Vincent's has long been one of the Phoenix bastions of Southwestern cuisine. However, the menu lately seems to have shifted its emphasis off the Southwest and back to classic European dishes. Although you could order a lobster salad or grilled salmon with braised leeks and black-truffle butter, if you're from outside the region, you should stick to the Southwestern dishes. Don't miss the duck tamale or the tequila soufflé, and for an entree (if you're feeling adventurous), the veal sweetbreads with blue corn meal have long been a favorite here. The clientele tends to be older, well-off Phoenicians who have been eating here for years. For a more casual dining experience, don't miss Vincent's Market Bistro, which is to one side of the main restaurant and serves plenty of great food. There's also a weekly farmers' market here (call for details).

3930 E. Camelback Rd. ☎ **602/224-0225.** www.vincentsoncamelback.com. Reservations highly recommended. Main courses $9.50–$14 lunch, $26–$32 dinner. AE, DC, DISC, MC, V. Main dining room: Mon–Fri 11:30am–2pm and 5–10pm, Sat 4:30–10:30pm, Sun 5–10pm; Market Bistro: Mon–Fri 7am–6pm, Sat 9am–3pm, Sun 8am–3pm. Closed Sun–Mon June–Sept.

MODERATE

Nonni's Kitchen ☆☆ MEDITERRANEAN   This casual neighborhood restaurant is affiliated with the ever-popular Rancho Pinot in Scottsdale, which means you can be sure the food will be great. Located in the Arcadia neighborhood south of Camelback Road, Nonni's is well worth searching out. The decor is minimalist Southwestern modern, and the small bar area is popular with residents of the neighborhood. Preparations are simple and emphasize fresh (often organic) ingredients. Don't miss the succulent Nonni's Sunday chicken served with toasted polenta. There's a long list of wines by the glass, and right next door you'll find Postino, a great wine bar.

4410 N. 40th St. ☎ **602/977-1800.** Reservations recommended. Main courses $16–$22. AE, DC, MC, V. Tues–Sun 5:30–10pm.

INEXPENSIVE

5 & Diner AMERICAN   If it's 2am and you just have to have a big burger and a side of fries after a night of dancing, head for the 24-hour 5 & Diner. You can't miss it—it's the classic streamliner diner that looks as though it just materialized from New Jersey.

Other locations are in Paradise Valley at 12802 N. Tatum Blvd. (© **602/ 996-0033**), and in Scottsdale at Scottsdale Pavilions, 9069 E. Indian Bend Rd. (© **480/949-1957**).

5220 N. 16th St. © **602/264-5220**. www.5anddiner.com. Sandwiches/plates $5–$13. AE, MC, V. Daily 24 hr.

Pane Bianco ⭐ *(Finds)* BAKERY/SANDWICHES   Chris Bianco, owner of downtown's immensely popular Pizzeria Bianco, has another winner on his hands with this casual counter-service bakery and sandwich shop not far from the Heard Museum. The menu consists of only four sandwiches and a couple of salads, but all the breads are baked on the premises in a wood-fired oven. The housemade mozzarella is exquisitely fresh and is served both as a caprese salad with tomatoes and basil and in a focaccia sandwich with the same ingredients. And that focaccia—the best in Phoenix.

4404 N. Central Ave. © **602/234-2100**. Main courses $8. AE, DISC, MC, V. Tues–Sat 11am–3pm.

DOWNTOWN, SOUTH PHOENIX & THE AIRPORT AREA
EXPENSIVE

Quiessence ⭐⭐ *(Finds)* NEW AMERICAN   I love this place for the simple fact that it is as far from a typical Phoenix/Scottsdale dining experience as you can get without going to the airport and getting on a plane. Set at the back of a shady pecan grove not far from South Mountain Park, Quiessence is surrounded by organic vegetable gardens. It is those gardens, and the freshness of the ingredients they provide that makes the food here so wonderful, but it is the delightfully rural setting that makes Quiessence truly special. Come for lunch before going for a hike in the park (or bring a change of clothes and come for dinner after a hike). The herbed chicken here is so good, it goes way beyond overcoming chicken's stigma of being meat that's actually good for you. Don't pass it up if it's on the menu. Oh, and by the way, the desserts are outrageously good!

6106 S. 32nd St. © **602/276-0601**. Reservations recommended. Main courses $12–$17 lunch, $19–$27 dinner. AE, MC, V. Tues–Fri 11am–2pm and 5–10pm.

MODERATE

Alice Cooper'stown ⭐ BARBECUE   Owned by Alice Cooper himself, this sports-and-rock theme restaurant/bar is downtown's premier eat-o-tainment center. Sixteen video screens (usually showing sporting events) are the centerpiece of the restaurant, but there's also an abundance of memorabilia, including guitars once used by the likes of Fleetwood Mac and Eric Clapton. The waitstaff

---

Forbidden City in the Desert

So you're driving along the Loop 202 freeway near Sky Harbor Airport and this strange mirage materializes. You think you're seeing a mall-sized complex of classical Chinese buildings. Don't worry, it's not a hallucination—it's the **COFCO Chinese Cultural Center**, 668 N. 44th St. (© **602/275-8578**; www. phxchinatown.com). This fascinating complex includes several Chinese restaurants, Asian art galleries and antiques stores, and an Asian supermarket. There's also a Chinese garden with numerous traditional viewing pavilions.

even wears Alice Cooper makeup. Barbecue is served in various permutations, including a huge barbecue sandwich. If you were a fan, this place is a hit; if you weren't, it's a miss.

101 E. Jackson St. ⓒ 602/253-7337. www.alicecooperstown.com. Reservations not accepted. Sandwiches/barbecue $8–$18. AE, DC, MC, V. Sun–Thurs 11am–10pm; Fri–Sat 11am–11pm.

Sam's Cafe ★★ (Value) SOUTHWESTERN Sam's Cafe, one of only a handful of decent downtown restaurants, offers food that's every bit as imaginative, but not nearly as expensive, as that served at other (often overrated) Southwestern restaurants in Phoenix. Breadsticks with picante-flavored cream cheese, grilled vegetable tacos, and angel-hair pasta in a spicy jalapeño sauce with shrimp and mushrooms all have a nice balance of flavors. The downtown Sam's has a large patio that overlooks a fountain and palm garden; it stays packed with the lunchtime, after-work, and convention crowds.

There's another Sam's in Biltmore Fashion Park, 2566 E. Camelback Rd. (ⓒ **602/954-7100**).

At the Arizona Center, 455 N. Third St. ⓒ 602/252-3545. www.sams-cafe.com. Reservations recommended. Main courses $7–$18. AE, DISC, MC, V. Daily 11am–10pm.

INEXPENSIVE

The Farm at South Mountain/Morning Glory Café & Bakery ★ (Finds)
SANDWICHES/SALADS If being in the desert has you dreaming of shady trees and green grass, you'll enjoy this little oasis reminiscent of a New England orchard. A rustic outbuilding has been converted to a stand-in-line lunch restaurant where you can order a focaccia sandwich or a delicious pecan turkey Waldorf salad. Breakfast means baked goods such as muffins and scones. The grassy lawn is ideal for a picnic. At the back of the farm, you'll find the breakfast cafe, and on Saturdays from 9am to 1pm, there is a farmers' market here.

6106 S. 32nd St. ⓒ 602/276-6360. Sandwiches and salads $8.95. MC, V. Sept–June Tues–Sun 8am–3pm (if weather is inclement, call to be sure it's open). Closed June through mid-Sept. Take Exit 151A off I-10 and go south on 32nd St.

Fry Bread House (Finds) NATIVE AMERICAN Fry bread is just what it sounds like—fried bread—and it's a mainstay on Indian reservations throughout the West. Although you can eat these thick, chewy slabs of fried bread plain, salted, or with honey, they also serve as the wrappers for Indian tacos, which are made with meat, beans, and lettuce. If you've already visited the Four Corners region of Arizona, then you've probably had an Indian taco. Forget all those others you've had—the Indian tacos here are the best in the state. Try one with green chili. If you still have room for dessert, do not miss the fry bread with chocolate and butter.

4140 N. Seventh Ave. ⓒ 602/351-2345. Main courses $2.60–$6.40. DISC, MC, V. Mon–Thurs 10am–7pm; Fri–Sat 10am–8pm.

Honey Bear's BBQ (Finds) BARBECUE With a menu that's limited to pork, beef, and chicken barbecue, pork ribs, and hot links, it's almost impossible to go wrong no matter what you order at this casual, fast-food-style joint near the Heard Museum and Phoenix Art Museum. Follow it all up with sweet-potato pie.

There's another location at 5012 E. Van Buren St. (ⓒ **602/273-9148**).

2824 N. Central Ave. ⓒ 602/279-7911. Sandwiches and dinners $3.80–$14. AE, MC, V. Daily 10am–9:30pm.

Los Dos Molinos ★ MEXICAN   I hope you travel with a fire extinguisher. You're gonna need it if you eat at this legendary hot spot in south Phoenix. The food here is New Mexican style, which means everything, with the exception of the margaritas, is incendiary. Actually there are a few dishes for the timid, but people who don't like their food fiery know enough to stay away from this place. So popular is the food here that there's even a Los Dos Molinos in New York. Here in the Phoenix area, there's another at 260 S. Alma School Rd., Mesa (© **480/969-7475**).

8646 S. Central Ave. © **602/243-9113.** Reservations not accepted. Main courses $4–$13. AE, DC, DISC, MC, V. Tues–Fri 11am–2:30pm and 5–9pm; Sat 11am–9pm.

MacAlpine's Restaurant and Soda Fountain *Finds* AMERICAN   This is the oldest operating soda fountain in the Southwest, and it hasn't changed much since its opening in 1928. Wooden booths and worn countertops show the patina of time. Big burgers and sandwiches make up the lunch offerings, and should be washed down with a lemon phosphate, chocolate malted, or egg cream. There are Friday and Saturday night swing dances here, so bring your dancing shoes and brush up on your Lindy.

2303 N. Seventh St. © **602/262-5545.** Sandwiches/specials $4–$7. AE, MC, V. Mon–Fri 11am–2pm; Sat 11am–3pm.

Pizzeria Bianco ★ PIZZA   Even though this historic brick building is located in the heart of downtown Phoenix, the atmosphere is so cozy it feels like your neighborhood local, and the wood-burning oven turns out deliciously rustic pizzas. One of my favorites is made with red onion, Parmesan, rosemary, and crushed pistachios. Don't miss the fresh mozzarella, either: Pizzeria Bianco makes its own, and it can be ordered as an appetizer or on a pizza.

At Heritage Square, 623 E. Adams St. © **602/258-8300.** Reservations accepted only for parties of 6 or more. Pizzas $9–$13. AE, MC, V. Tues–Sat 5–10pm; Sun 5–9pm.

TEMPE & MESA
MODERATE

House of Tricks ★★ NEW AMERICAN   Despite the name, you'll find far more treats here than tricks. Housed in a pair of old Craftsman bungalows surrounded by a garden of shady trees, this restaurant has a completely different feel from modern Mill Avenue, Tempe's main drag, which is only 2 blocks away. This is where Arizona State University students take their parents when they come to visit, but it's also a nice spot for a romantic evening and a good place to try innovative cuisine without blowing your vacation budget. The garlic-inspired Caesar salad and the house-smoked salmon with avocado, capers, and lemon cream are good bets for starters. Among the entrees, the seared ahi tuna is a good bet. The grape-arbor-covered patio, where there's also a shady bar, is by far the more pleasant place to sit.

114 E. Seventh St., Tempe. © **480/968-1114.** www.houseoftricks.com. Reservations recommended. Main courses $6–$11 lunch, $17–$20 dinner. AE, DC, DISC, MC, V. Mon–Sat 11am–10pm.

Monti's La Casa Vieja ★ AMERICAN   If you're tired of the glitz and glamour of the Valley of the Sun and are looking for Old Arizona, head to Monti's La Casa Vieja. The adobe building was constructed in 1873 (*casa vieja* means "old house" in Spanish) on the site of the Salt River ferry, which operated in the days when the river flowed year-round and Tempe was nothing more than a ferry crossing. Today, local families who have been in Phoenix for generations know Monti's well, and rely on the restaurant for solid meals and low prices—you can get a filet mignon for as little as $10. The dark dining rooms are filled with memorabilia of the Old West.

1 W. Rio Salado Pkwy. (at Mill Ave.), Tempe. © 480/967-7594. www.montis.com. Reservations recommended for dinner. Main courses $8–$30. AE, DC, DISC, MC, V. Sun–Thurs 11am–10pm; Fri–Sat 11am–11pm.

INEXPENSIVE

Blue Adobe Grille 🐾🐾 *Finds* MEXICAN   Wedged between a Taco Bell and an aging bowling alley, this restaurant looks like just the sort of place you should drive right past. Don't! Despite appearances, this New Mexican–style restaurant serves deliciously creative southwestern fare at very economical prices. To get an idea of what the food here is all about, order the Santa Fe plate with tenderloin relleno, a shrimp enchilada, and carne *adovada*. Of course, there are great margaritas, but there's also a surprisingly good wine list. This place is a hangout for Chicago Cubs fans and makes a good dinner stop on the way back from driving the Apache Trail.

144 N. Country Club Dr., Mesa. © 480/962-1000. blueadobegrille.com. Reservations recommended Fri–Sat. Main courses $8–$22. AE, DC, DISC, MC, V. Sun–Thurs 11am–9pm; Fri–Sat 11am–10pm.

Organ Stop Pizza 🐾 *Kids* PIZZA   The pizza here may not be the best in town, but the mighty Wurlitzer theater organ, the largest in the world, sure is memorable. The massive instrument, which contains more than 5,500 pipes, has four turbine blowers to provide the wind to create the sound, and with 40-foot ceilings in the restaurant, the acoustics are great. As you marvel at the skill of the organist, who performs songs ranging from the latest pop tunes to *The Phantom of the Opera*, you can enjoy simple pizzas, pastas, or snack foods such as nachos or onion rings.

1149 E. Southern Ave. (at Stapley Dr.), Mesa. © 480/813-5700. www.organstoppizza.com. Pizzas and pastas $4.70–$16. No credit cards. Thanksgiving to mid-Apr Sun–Thurs 4–9pm, Fri–Sat 4–10pm; mid-Apr to Thanksgiving Sun–Thurs 5–9pm, Fri–Sat 5–10pm.

DINING WITH A VIEW

Different Pointe of View 🐾🐾 CLASSIC FRENCH/REGIONAL AMERICAN   If you're staying anywhere on the north side of Phoenix or Scottsdale and crave a dining room with a view, then put the SUV in low and drive to the top of the hill at the Pointe Hilton Tapatio Cliffs Resort. Built into a mountaintop, this restaurant takes in dramatic, sweeping vistas of the city, mountains, and desert through its curving walls of glass. Come early, and you can enjoy northerly views from the lounge before heading into the south-facing dining room. The menu veers toward French haute cuisine and American fine dining. Despite the excellent food, award-winning wine list, and live jazz Wednesday through Saturday, the view steals the show.

At the Pointe Hilton Tapatio Cliffs Resort, 11111 N. Seventh St. © 602/866-6350. www.differentpointeof view.com. Reservations highly recommended. Main courses $26–$48. AE, DC, DISC, MC, V. Sun–Thurs 6–9:30pm; Fri–Sat 6–10pm (lounge open later). Closed Sun–Mon in summer.

Geordie's at the Wrigley Mansion Club 🐾🐾 CONTINENTAL   Located on a hilltop adjacent to the Arizona Biltmore resort, this sprawling mansion was built between 1929 and 1931 by chewing gum magnate William Wrigley, Jr., for his wife, Ada. Today the mansion operates as a private club (annual dues are $10 and are given to charity). The views are splendid and the meals are memorable. If it's on the menu, be sure to start with the parsnip-and-mushroom bisque; you won't be able to resist wiping up the last drops of soup with some of the delicious breads from the bread basket. If you can, save room for the crème brûlée, which is served in an edible chocolate-lined phyllo cup. Before or after lunch, you can take a guided tour of the mansion.

2501 E. Telawa Trail. © **602/955-4079** or 602/553-7387. www.wrigleymansionclub.com. Reservations recommended. Main courses $8–$16 lunch, $14–$32 dinner; Sun brunch $33. AE, DC, DISC, MC, V. Tues 11am–2pm; Wed–Fri 11am–2pm and 6–10pm; Sat 6–10pm; Sun 10am–2:30pm.

COWBOY STEAKHOUSES

Cowboy steakhouses are family restaurants that generally provide big portions of grilled steaks and barbecued ribs, outdoor and "saloon" dining, live country music, and various other sorts of entertainment. See p. 126 for details.

Pinnacle Peak Patio Steakhouse & Microbrewery 🌟 *Kids* STEAKHOUSE Once located miles out in the desert, this "Hollywood Western" steakhouse is now surrounded by some of the valley's poshest suburbs. Despite the million-dollar homes, this joint still knows how to keep the Wild West alive. Although you can indulge in mesquite-broiled steaks with all the traditional trimmings, a meal here is more an event than just an opportunity to put on the feed bag. The real draw is all the entertainment—gunfights, cowboy bands, two-stepping, and cookouts. Also of interest are the museum-like displays of interesting collections including can openers, police badges, and license plates. Businessmen, beware! Wear a tie into this place, and you'll have it cut off and hung from the rafters.

10426 E. Jomax Rd., Scottsdale. © **480/585-1599**. www.pppatio.com. Reservations accepted only for parties of 8 or more. Main courses $6.50–$25; children's menu $2.50–$6.50. AE, DC, DISC, MC, V. Mon–Thurs 4–10pm; Fri–Sat 4–11pm; Sun noon–10pm. Take 101 to exit 36 (Pima Rd./Princess Dr.). Go north on Pima Rd., east on Happy Valley Rd., north on Alma School Pkwy., and watch for the sign on the left.

Reata Pass 🌟 STEAK Of all the cowboy steakhouses in the Phoenix area, this is by far the most authentic. Part of the large restaurant is even housed in an old stagecoach stop, and the building incorporates an adobe building that dates back to 1862. With live music, a huge patio set with picnic tables, and happy hours both early and late, this place is a nonstop party. In the warmer months, have your 28-day aged Angus beef steak out under the stars or the clear blue Sonoran desert sky. In business since the 1950s, this totally casual and thoroughly rustic roadhouse is a local's favorite, a place to see what Phoenix was like before it began to sprawl.

27500 N. Alma School Pkwy. © **480/585-7277**. Reservations recommended. Main courses $7–$28. AE, DISC, MC, V. Mon–Thurs 11am–10:30pm; Fri 11am–11pm; Sat 7am–11pm; Sun 7am–10:30pm.

Rustler's Rooste 🌟 *Kids* STEAKHOUSE This location, in the middle of a sprawling golf resort, doesn't exactly seem like cowboy country. However, up at the top of the hill, you'll find a fun Western-theme restaurant where you can start your meal by scooting down a big slide from the bar to the main dining room. While the view north across Phoenix is entertainment enough for most people, there are also cowboy bands playing for those who like to kick up their heels. If you've ever been bitten by a snake, you can exact your revenge here by ordering the rattlesnake appetizer. Follow that (if you've got the appetite of a hardworking cowpoke) with the enormous cowboy "stuff" platter consisting of, among other things, steak kebabs, barbecued ribs, cowboy beans, fried shrimp, barbecued chicken, and skewered swordfish.

At the Pointe South Mountain Resort, 7777 S. Pointe Hwy., Phoenix. © **602/431-6474**. www.rustlersrooste. com. Reservations not accepted, but there's a call-ahead waiting list. Main courses $13–$32. AE, DC, DISC, MC, V. Daily 5–10pm.

ESPRESSO BARS, BAKERIES & ICE CREAM PARLORS

Perhaps it's the heat or the sunshine, but espresso is not the ubiquitous drink here in Phoenix that it is in many other parts of the country. However, there are still plenty of places to get a good latte or cappuccino. In Scottsdale, try **The Village Coffee Roastery,** 8120 N. Hayden Rd., Suite E-104 (© **480/905-0881**), which roasts its own beans, or **The Coffee Bean & Tea Leaf,** in the Shops at Gainey Village, 8877 N. Scottsdale Rd. (© **480/315-9335**). If you find yourself craving a decadent dessert in Scottsdale, head to the **Author's Café,** 4014 N. Goldwater Blvd. no. 104 (© **480/481-3998**), at the west end of Main Street. The cases here are filled with towering cakes and divinely decadent pastries; come early in the week for the best and freshest selection. This cafe also has live music on Friday and Saturday nights.

Along the Camelback Corridor, there's **Hava Java,** 3166 E. Camelback Rd. (© **602/954-9080**), in the Safeway Shopping Center. Not far from the Heard Museum, there's **Lux,** 4404 N. Central Ave. (© **602/266-6469**), which serves the best espresso in Phoenix, which isn't surprising when you learn that the owners started out in Seattle. This is also the hippest espresso bar in town, and right next door there's a great little bakery run by the owners of Pizzeria Bianco.

If ever there were a place where ice cream is a necessity, it is Arizona. In the desert heat, ice cream is a survival food, a means to cool off when the temperatures soar. When the heat gets to be too much for you, head to some of these great chill-out spots. Scottsdale's **Sugar Bowl,** 4005 N. Scottsdale Rd. (© **480/946-0051**), in the heart of Old Town, is a long-time locals favorite that has been immortalized in "Family Circus" cartoons. If you find yourself dying from the heat as you motor through central Phoenix on a toasty afternoon, there's no better antidote than **Mary Coyle,** 5521 N. Seventh Ave. (© **602/265-0405**), which makes its own ice cream and has been in business for more than 50 years. However, the absolute cream of the crop is The Phoenician resort's **Café & Ice Cream Parlour,** 6000 E. Camelback Rd. (© **480/941-8200**). Not only can you cool off with house-made ice cream, but the pastries here are positively divine. To top it all off, you get to hang out at this posh resort for as long as you can make your ice cream last.

BREAKFAST, BRUNCH & QUICK BITES

Most of Phoenix's best Sunday brunches are to be had at restaurants in major hotels and resorts. Among the finest are those served at **Marquesa** (at the Scottsdale Princess), **T. Cook's** (at the Royal Palms Resort and Spa, p. 90), the **Golden Swan** (at the Hyatt Regency Scottsdale, p. 81), **Wright's** (at the Arizona Biltmore Resort & Spa, p. 88), the **Terrace Dining Room** (at The Phoenician, p. 81), and **Top of the Rock** (at The Wyndham Buttes Resort, p. 94). However, for a unique experience, make a brunch reservation at **Geordie's at the Wrigley Mansion** (see above), 2501 E. Telawa Trail (© **602/955-4079**), a historic mansion now owned by Geordie Hormel (of the Spam-making family). Don't worry, the food is great.

The **Desert Botanical Garden,** 1201 N. Galvin Pkwy., in Papago Park (© **480/941-1225;** www.dbg.org), serves brunch with its Music in the Garden concerts held on Sunday from September to March. Tickets are $16 and include admission to the gardens, but meals cost extra.

If your idea of the perfect breakfast is a buttery croissant and a good cup of coffee, try **La Madeleine,** 3102 E. Camelback Rd. (© **602/952-0349;** www. lamadeleine.com), *the* place for a leisurely French breakfast amid antique farm implements. Other branches are at Fashion Square Mall, 7014 E. Camelback Rd., Scottsdale (© 480/945-1663), and at 10625 N. Tatum Blvd. at Shea Blvd. in Paradise Valley (© 480/483-0730).

For smoothies, muffins, and healthy things, try **Wild Oats Natural Marketplace,** which has stores at 3933 E. Camelback Rd. at 40th Street (© 602/954-0584), and in Scottsdale at 7129 E. Shea Blvd. at Scottsdale Road (© 480/905-1441).

5 Seeing the Sights

THE DESERT & ITS NATIVE CULTURES

Deer Valley Rock Art Center ⭐   Located in the Hedgepeth Hills in the northwest corner of the Valley of the Sun, the Deer Valley Rock Art Center preserves an amazing concentration of Native American petroglyphs, some of which date back 5,000 years. Although these petroglyphs may not at first seem as impressive as those at more famous sites, the sheer numbers make this a fascinating spot. The drawings, which range from simple spirals to much more complex renderings of herds of deer, are on volcanic boulders along a quarter-mile trail. An interpretive center provides background information on this site and on rock art in general. From October through April, there are guided tours Saturdays at 10am and Tuesdays and Thursdays at 1pm. From May through September, there are tours on Saturdays at 7:30am.

3711 W. Deer Valley Rd. © 623/582-8007. www.asu.edu/clas/anthropology/dvrac. Admission $5 adults, $3 seniors and students, $2 children 6–12. Oct–Apr Tues–Sat 9am–5pm, Sun noon–5pm; May–Sept Tues–Fri 8am–2pm, Sat 7am–5pm, Sun noon–5pm. Closed major holidays. Take the Loop 101 highway west to 27th Avenue, go north to Deer Valley Rd. and go west 2 ½ miles to just past 35th Ave.

Desert Botanical Garden ⭐⭐⭐   Located in Papago Park adjacent to the Phoenix Zoo and devoted exclusively to cacti and other desert plants, this botanic garden displays more than 20,000 plants from all over the world. The Plants and People of the Sonoran Desert Trail is the state's best introduction to ethnobotany (human use of plants) in the Southwest. Along the trail are interactive displays that demonstrate how Native Americans once used wild and cultivated plants. You can make a yucca-fiber brush and practice grinding corn and mesquite beans. At the Center for Desert Living, there are demonstration gardens and an energy- and water-conservation research house. On the Harriet K. Maxwell Desert Wildflower Trail, you'll find an ever-changing palette of colorful wildflowers throughout much of the year. If you come late in the day, you can stay until after dark and see night-blooming flowers and dramatically lit cacti. A cafe on the grounds serves good food and makes a great lunch spot. In spring and fall, there are also concerts in the garden. In early December, during *Las Noches de las Luminarias,* the gardens are lit at night by luminarias (candles inside small bags).

At Papago Park, 1201 N. Galvin Pkwy. © 480/941-1225. www.dbg.org. Admission $9 adults, $8 seniors, $5 students 13–18, $4 children 3–12. Oct–Apr daily 8am–8pm; May–Sept daily 7am–8pm. Closed July 4th and Christmas. Bus: 3.

Heard Museum ⭐⭐⭐   The Heard Museum is one of the nation's finest museums dealing exclusively with Native American cultures and is an ideal introduction to the indigenous peoples of Arizona. The extensive exhibit **Native Peoples of the Southwest** examines the culture of each of the major tribes of the region and includes a Navajo hogan, an Apache wickiup, and a Hopi corn-grinding display. In the Katsina Doll Gallery, you'll get an idea of the number of different kachina spirits that populate the Hopi and Zuni religions, while the Crossroads Gallery offers a fascinating look at contemporary Native American art. On many weekends, there are performances by singers and dancers, and throughout the week, artists demonstrate their work. Guided tours are offered daily. The annual **Indian Fair and Market,** held on the first weekend in March, includes traditional dances along with arts and crafts.

The museum also operates **Heard Museum North,** at El Pedregal Festival Marketplace, 34505 N. Scottsdale Rd., in Carefree. This gallery features changing exhibits and is open Monday through Saturday from 10am to 5:30pm and Sunday from noon to 5pm. Admission is $3 for adults and is free for children 12 and under.

2301 N. Central Ave. ℭ **602/252-8848.** www.heard.org. Admission $7 adults, $6 seniors, $3 children 4–12. Daily 9:30am–5pm. Closed major holidays. Bus: Blue (B), Red (R), or O.

Huhugam Heritage Center ⚑ Although this architectural gem adjacent to the Sheraton Wild Horse Pass Resort was not fully open when I visited, it did have a small exhibit on ancient Native American trading trails through the desert. However, the main reason to visit this new facility operated by the Pima and Maricopa tribes is not only to learn about these tribe's culture, but to admire the fascinating architecture and ethnobotanical garden. The center complex is built within a huge berm that was designed to resemble a giant pot buried in the ground.

4759 N. Maricopa Rd., Chandler. ℭ **520/796-3500.** www.huhugam.com. Admission $5 adults, $3 seniors, $2 children 6–12. Sat 10am–4pm.

Pueblo Grande Museum and Archaeological Park Located near Sky Harbor Airport and downtown Phoenix, the Pueblo Grande Museum and Archaeological Park houses the ruins of an ancient Hohokam village that was one of several villages along the Salt River between A.D. 300 and 1400. Sometime around 1450, this and other villages were mysteriously abandoned. Some speculate that drought and a buildup of salts from irrigation water reduced the fertility of the soil and forced the people to seek more fertile lands. The small museum displays many of the artifacts that have been dug up on the site. Although these exhibits are actually more interesting than the ruins themselves, there are also some reconstructed and furnished Hohokam-style houses that give a good idea of how the Hohokam lived. The museum sponsors interesting workshops (some just for kids), demonstrations, and tours (including petroglyph hikes). The **Pueblo Grande Museum Indian Market,** held in mid-December at Steele Indian School Park, which is on the northeast corner of Indian School Road and Central Avenue, is the largest of its kind in the state and features more than 500 Native American artisans.

4619 E. Washington St. (between 44th and 48th sts.). ℭ **877/706-4408** or 602/495-0901. www.pueblo grande.com. Admission $2 adults, $1.50 seniors, $1 children 6–17; free on Sun. Mon–Sat 9am–4:45pm; Sun 1–4:45pm. Closed major holidays. Bus: 1.

ART MUSEUMS

Arizona State University Art Museum at Nelson Fine Arts Center ⚑ Although it isn't very large, this museum is memorable for its innovative architecture and excellent temporary exhibitions. With its purplish-gray stucco facade and pyramidal shape, the stark, angular building conjures up images of sunsets on desert mountains. The entrance is down a flight of stairs that leads to a cool underground garden area. Inside are galleries for crafts, prints, contemporary art, and Latin American art, along with outdoor sculpture courts and a gift shop. The collection of American art includes works by Georgia O'Keeffe, Edward Hopper,

Phoenix, Scottsdale & the Valley of the Sun Attractions

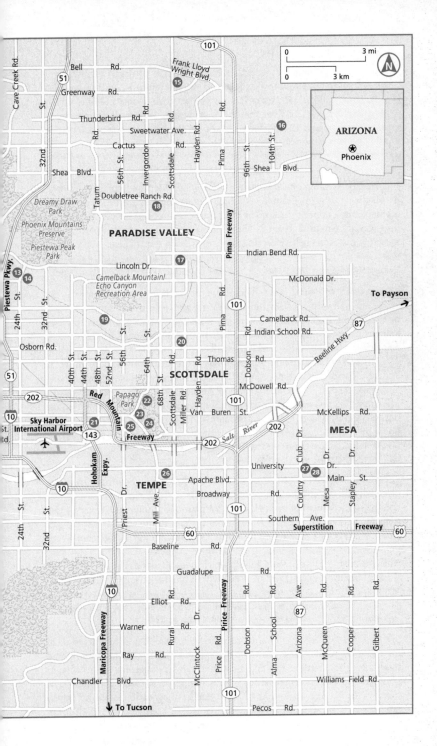

Scottsdale, Arizona area map

0 3 mi
0 3 km

N

ARIZONA

⊛ Phoenix

To Payson →

Cave Creek Rd.

Bell Rd.

51

Greenway Rd.

32nd St.

Frank Lloyd Wright Blvd.

15

Thunderbird Rd.

Rd.

16

Sweetwater Ave.

104th St.

Cactus Rd.

56th St.

Invergordon

Scottsdale

Hayden Rd.

Pima

96th St.

Shea Blvd.

Shea Blvd.

Tatum

Dreamy Draw Park

Doubletree Ranch Rd.

18

Phoenix Mountains Preserve

Piestewa Peak Park

PARADISE VALLEY

Pima Freeway

Indian Bend Rd.

Piestewa Pkwy.

Lincoln Dr.

17

McDonald Dr.

13

14

Camelback Mountain/ Echo Canyon Recreation Area

101

24th St.

32nd St.

Camelback Rd.

87

Osborn Rd.

19

48th St.

52nd St.

56th St.

64th St.

Scottsdale Rd.

Indian School Rd.

Beeline Hwy.

20

Thomas Rd.

Dobson Rd.

51

40th St.

44th St.

SCOTTSDALE

Hayden Rd.

Miller Rd.

McDowell Rd.

McKellips Rd.

202

Red Mountain

Papago Park

22

68th St.

Van Buren St.

101

MESA

10

Sky Harbor International Airport

21

23

25 24

Freeway

Salt River

202

Country Club Dr.

Dr.

Dr.

143

202

University

27 28

Main St.

Mesa

Stapley

Hohokam Expy.

26

Apache Blvd.

Rd.

10

TEMPE

Priest Dr.

Mill Ave.

Broadway

101

24th St.

32nd St.

Southern Ave.

Superstition Freeway

60

60

Baseline Rd.

Guadalupe Rd.

Maricopa Freeway

10

Elliot Rd.

Rural Rd.

Price Rd.

Price Freeway

Dobson Rd.

School Rd.

Arizona Ave.

McQueen Rd.

Cooper Rd.

Gilbert Rd.

Warner Rd.

87

Ray Rd.

McClintock Dr.

Alma

Chandler Blvd.

Williams Field Rd.

10

↓ **To Tucson**

101

Pecos Rd.

Moments Love Story

Take a walk around the Scottsdale Mall, a refuge of green lawns and shade trees in downtown Scottsdale, and you just might fall in love, make that on *Love*. Robert Indiana's famous pop art *Love* image, the one with the skewed letter "O," yes the one that became a postage stamp, has been installed as a 12-foot-tall sculpture on the lawn outside the Scottsdale Center for the Arts.

and Frederic Remington. Definitely a must for both art and architecture fans. Across the street is the Ceramics Research Center and Gallery, which showcases the university's extensive collection of fine art ceramics and is open Wednesday through Saturday from 10am to 5pm. This latter center is another place not to miss. You just won't believe the amazing creativity on display here.

10th St. and Mill Ave., Tempe. ✆ 480/965-2787. http://asuartmuseum.asu.edu. Free admission. Tues 10am–9pm (10am–5pm in summer); Wed–Sat 10am–5pm. Closed major holidays. Bus: Red (R), 1, 66, or 72.

Phoenix Art Museum ✯✯   This is one of the largest art museums in the Southwest, and within its labyrinth of halls and galleries is a respectable collection that spans the major artistic movements from the Renaissance to the present. Exhibits cover decorative arts, historic fashions, Spanish-colonial furnishings and religious art, and, of course, works by members of the Cowboy Artists of America. The collection of modern and contemporary art is particularly good, with works by Diego Rivera, Frida Kahlo, Pablo Picasso, Alexander Calder, Henry Moore, Georgia O'Keeffe, Henri Rousseau, and Auguste Rodin. The popular Thorne Miniature Collection consists of tiny rooms on a scale of 1 inch to 1 foot. Because this museum is so large, it frequently mounts traveling blockbuster exhibits.

1625 N. Central Ave. (at McDowell Rd.). ✆ 602/257-1222. www.phxart.org. Admission $9 adults, $7 seniors and students, $3 children 6–17; free on Thurs. Tues–Wed and Fri–Sun 10am–5pm; Thurs 10am–9pm. Closed major holidays. Bus: Blue (B), Red (R), or 0.

Scottsdale Museum of Contemporary Art ✯✯   Scottsdale may be obsessed with art featuring lonesome cowboys and solemn Indians, but this boldly designed museum makes it clear that patrons of contemporary art are also welcome here. Cutting-edge art, from the abstract to the absurd, fills the galleries, with exhibits rotating every few months. In addition to the main building, there are several galleries in the adjacent Scottsdale Center for the Arts, which also has a pair of Dale Chihuly art-glass installations. The museum shop is full of beautiful items, most of which will fit in your suitcase.

7374 E. Second St., Scottsdale. ✆ 480/994-ARTS. www.smoca.org. Admission $7 adults, $5 students, free for children 15 and under; free on Thurs. Tues–Wed and Fri–Sat 10am–5pm; Thurs 10am–8pm; Sun noon–5pm. Bus: 41, 50, or 72. Also accessible via Scottsdale Trolley shuttle bus.

Shemer Art Center ✯   This art center may be small, but it mounts some of the more interesting little shows in the valley. Exhibits change monthly and showcase Arizona artists. You might catch an exhibit of ceramic art, jewelry, or photography. The art center, which is housed in a 1920s Santa Fe mission–style home in the Arcadia neighborhood, also offers a variety of art classes. It's easy to miss as you're speeding along Camelback Road, so keep your eyes peeled. On Monday evenings, there are sometimes classical music concerts.

5005 E. Camelback Rd. ✆ 602/262-4727. http://phoenix.gov/PARKS/shemer.html. Free admission. Mon and Wed–Fri 10am–5pm; Tues 10am–9pm; Sat 9am–1pm. Bus: 50.

HISTORY MUSEUMS & HISTORIC LANDMARKS

Arizona Capitol Museum ✦   In the years before Arizona became a state, the territorial capital moved from Prescott to Tucson, then back to Prescott, before finally settling in Phoenix. In 1898, a stately territorial capitol building was erected (with a copper roof to remind the local citizenry of the importance of that metal in the Arizona economy). Atop this copper roof was placed the statue *Winged Victory*, which still graces the old capitol building today. This building no longer serves as the actual state capitol, but has been restored to the way it appeared in 1912, the year Arizona became a state. Among the rooms on view are the senate and house chambers, as well as the governor's office. Excellent exhibits provide interesting perspectives on early Arizona events and lifestyles. There are free guided tours at 10am and 2pm.

1700 W. Washington St. 📞 602/542-4675. www.lib.az.us/museum. Free admission. Mon–Fri 8am–5pm. Closed state holidays. Bus: 1 or DASH downtown shuttle.

Arizona Historical Society Museum in Papago Park ✦   This museum, at the headquarters of the Arizona Historical Society, focuses its well-designed exhibits on the history of central Arizona. Temporary exhibits on the lives and works of the people who helped shape this region are always highlights of a visit. An interesting permanent exhibit features life-size statues of everyday people from Arizona's past (a Mexican miner, a Chinese laborer, and so on). Quotes relate their individual stories, while props reveal what items they might have traveled with during their days in the desert.

1300 N. College Ave. (just off Curry Rd.), Tempe. 📞 480/929-0292. www.tempe.gov/ahs. Admission $5 adults, $4 seniors and students, free for children under 12. Tues–Sat 10am–4pm; Sun noon–4pm. Bus: 66.

Historic Heritage Square   Although the city of Phoenix was founded as recently as 1870, much of its history has been obliterated. However, if you have an appreciation for old homes and want a glimpse of how Phoenix once looked, stroll around this collection of some of the city's few remaining 19th-century houses, which stand here on the original town site. All of the buildings are listed on the National Register of Historic Places, and most display Victorian architectural styles popular at the end of the 19th century. Today, the buildings house museums, restaurants, and gift shops. The Eastlake Victorian Rosson House, furnished with period antiques, is open for tours. The Stevens House features the Arizona Doll and Toy Museum. The Forest's Carriage House has a gift shop and ticket window for the Rosson House tours. The Teeter House now serves as a Victorian tearoom (with cocktails and live jazz in the evening); the old Baird Machine Shop contains Pizzeria Bianco; and the Thomas House is home to Bar Bianco.

115 N. Sixth St., at Monroe. 📞 602/262-5029. www.rossonhousemuseum.org. Rosson House tours $4 adults, $3 seniors and students, $1 children 6–12. Hours vary for each building; call for information. Bus: Red (R), 0, 1, or DASH downtown shuttle.

Historic Sahuaro Ranch   Phoenix and neighboring valley communities started out as farming communities, but today there's little sign of this early agricultural heritage. This historic ranch in Glendale is one noteworthy exception. With its tall date palms, resident peacocks, and restored farmhouse, Sahuaro Ranch is a great introduction to what life was like here in the late 19th and early 20th centuries. The old fruit-packing shed now serves as a gallery hosting temporary exhibits; tours of the main house are offered.

9802 N. 59th Ave. (at Mountain View Rd.), Glendale. 📞 623/930-4200. www.sahuaroranch.org. Admission $3, free for children 12 and under. Wed–Fri 10am–2pm; Sat 10am–4pm; Sun noon–4pm. Closed June–Sept and major holidays. Bus: 59.

Phoenix Museum of History ⭐ Located adjacent to Heritage Square in downtown Phoenix, this state-of-the-art museum is one of the anchors of the city's downtown revitalization plan. It presents an interesting look at the history of a city that, to the casual visitor, might not seem to *have* any history. Interactive exhibits make this place much more interesting than your average local history museum. One unusual exhibit explores how "lungers" (tuberculosis sufferers) inadvertently helped originate the tourism industry in Arizona. There's also an exhibit on ostrich ranching.

105 N. Fifth St. ✆ 602/253-2734. www.pmoh.org. Admission $5 adults, $3.50 seniors and students, $2.50 children 7–12, free for children 6 and under. Tues–Sat 10am–5pm. Closed major holidays. Bus: Red (R), 0, 1, or DASH downtown shuttle.

Wells Fargo History Museum ⭐ *Finds* Yes, this museum is small, and yes, it's run by the Wells Fargo Bank, but the collection of artifacts here goes a long way toward conjuring up the Wild West so familiar from Hollywood movies. Not only is there an original Wells Fargo stagecoach on display, but there are also gold nuggets to ogle, old photos from the *real* Wild West, and plenty of artifacts and memorabilia from the days of stagecoach travel. There are also original paintings by N. C. Wyeth and bronze sculptures by Frederic Remington and Charles Russell.

100 W. Washington St. ✆ 602/378-1852. www.wellsfargohistory.com. Free admission. Mon–Fri 9am–5pm. Bus: Red (R), 0, 1, or DASH downtown shuttle.

SCIENCE & INDUSTRY MUSEUMS

Arizona Science Center ⭐ *Kids* So, the kids weren't impressed with the botanical garden of the Native American artifacts at the Heard Museum. Bring 'em here. They can spend the afternoon pushing buttons, turning knobs, and otherwise interacting with all kinds of cool science exhibits. In the end, they might even learn something in spite of all the fun they had. The science center also includes a planetarium and a large-screen theater, both of which carry additional charges.

600 E. Washington St. ✆ 602/716-2000. www.azscience.org. Admission $9 adults, $7 seniors and children 3–12. Planetarium and film combination tickets also available. Daily 10am–5pm. Closed Thanksgiving and Christmas. Bus: Red (R), 0, 1, or DASH downtown shuttle.

Mesa Southwest Museum ⭐⭐ *Kids* This is one of the best museums in the valley, and its wide variety of exhibits appeals to people with a range of interests. For the kids, there are animated dinosaurs on an indoor "cliff" with a roaring waterfall, plus plenty of dinosaur skeletons. Also of interest are an exhibit on movies that have been filmed in the state, a display on Arizona mammoth kill sites, some old jail cells, and a walk-through mine mock-up with exhibits on the Lost Dutchman Mine. There's also a mock-up of a pre-Columbian temple and an artificial cave filled with beautiful mineral specimens.

53 N. MacDonald St. (at First St.), Mesa. ✆ 480/644-2230. www.ci.mesa.az.us/swmuseum/default.asp. Admission $6 adults, $5 seniors and students, $3 children 3–12. Tues–Sat 10am–5pm; Sun 1–5pm. Closed major holidays. Bus: Red (R).

A MUSEUM MISCELLANY: PLANES, FLAMES & MORE

Arizona Mining & Mineral Museum Arizonans have been romancing the stones for more than a century at colorfully named mines, such as the Copper Queen, Sleeping Beauty, and Lucky Boy. Out of such mines have come countless tons of copper, silver, and gold, as well as beautiful minerals with tongue-twisting names. Chalcanthite, chalcoaluminate, and chrysocolla are just some of the richly colored minerals on display at this small downtown museum. Rather than playing up the historical or profit-making side of the industry, exhibits focus on the amazing variety of Arizona minerals. Displays have a dated feel, but the beauty of the minerals makes this an interesting stop.

1502 W. Washington St. ☎ **602/255-3791.** www.admmr.state.az.us. Admission $2 adults. Mon–Fri 8am–5pm; Sat 11am–4pm. Closed state holidays. Bus: 1 or DASH downtown shuttle.

The Bead Museum   You'll see beads and body adornments from around the world at this interesting little museum in the Glendale antiques district. Beads both ancient and modern are on display, and exhibits often focus on such subjects as beaded bags, prayer beads, or natural beads.

5754 W. Glenn Dr., Glendale. ☎ **623/931-2727.** www.beadmuseumaz.org. Admission $4 adults, $2 children. Mon–Sat 10am–5pm (Thurs until 8pm); Sun 11am–4pm. Bus: 24.

Hall of Flame Firefighting Museum 🌟 *Kids*   The world's largest firefighting museum houses a fascinating collection of vintage firetrucks. The displays date from a 1725 English hand pumper to several classic engines from the 20th century. All are beautifully restored and, of course, fire-engine red (mostly). In all, there are more than 90 vehicles on display.

At Papago Park, 6101 E. Van Buren St. ☎ **602/275-3473.** www.hallofflame.org. Admission $5.50 adults, $4 seniors, $3 students 6–17, $1.50 children 3–5, free for children under 3. Mon–Sat 9am–5pm; Sun noon–4pm. Closed New Year's Day, Thanksgiving, and Christmas. Bus: 3.

ARCHITECTURAL HIGHLIGHTS

Arizona Biltmore   This resort hotel, although not designed by Frank Lloyd Wright, shows the famed architect's hand in its distinctive cast-cement blocks. It also displays sculptures, furniture, and stained glass designed by Wright. The best way to soak up the ambience of this exclusive resort (if you aren't staying here) is over dinner, a cocktail, or tea. To learn more about the building, however, reserve ahead for a tour, given Tuesday, Thursday, and Saturday at 2:30pm.

2400 E. Missouri Ave. ☎ **602/955-6600.** Tours $10 (free for resort guests).

Burton Barr Library   This library is among the most daring pieces of public architecture in the city, and no fan of futuristic art or science fiction should miss it. The five-story cube is partially clad in enough ribbed copper sheeting to produce roughly 17,500,000 pennies. The building's design makes use of the desert's plentiful sunshine to provide light for reading, but also incorporates computer-controlled louvers and shade sails to reduce heat and glare.

1221 N. Central Ave. ☎ **602/262-4636.** www.phoenixpubliclibrary.org. Free admission. Mon–Thurs 10am–9pm; Fri–Sat 10am–6pm; Sun noon–6pm. Bus: Red (R), Blue (B), or 0.

(*Finds* **Out of This World Rocks**

On October 9, 1992, a meteorite slammed into a car in Peekskill, New York. It was a nightmare come to life for the car's owner, but a dream come true for the tabloids. Here was a reminder of just how dangerous out-of-this-world rocks can be. You can see a piece of the Peekskill meteorite, and dozens of other otherworldly rocks at Arizona State University's **Center for Meteorite Studies,** Bateman Physical Sciences Center, Palm Walk and University Drive (☎ **480/965-6511;** http://meteorites.asu.edu) on the ASU campus. The center, which is just a single small room, is open Monday through Friday from 9am to 5pm, and admission is free.

Frommer's Favorite Phoenix Experiences

Hiking Up Camelback Mountain or Piestewa Peak. Hiking the trails up these two mountains is a favorite activity among the city's more active residents. Both trails are steep climbs, but the views from up top are superb. Bring water and start early in the morning if it's going to be a hot day.

Strolling Through the Desert Botanical Garden After Dark. This cactus-filled garden is beautiful any time of day, but is particularly enjoyable after dark, when the crowds are gone and hidden lights illuminate the cacti.

Hanging Out Midday at the Oasis. Phoenix and Scottsdale have plenty of great pools, but the Oasis water park at the Pointe South Mountain Resort is the biggest and the best. Not only are there terrifyingly steep water slides, but there's a wave pool also.

Taking the Scottsdale Art Walk. Thursday evenings from October to May, both dilettantes and connoisseurs turn out to visit the nearly 60 galleries in downtown Scottsdale, many of which have artists on hand and provide complimentary refreshments.

Attending a Spring-Training Baseball Game. Get a head start on all your fellow baseball fans by going to a spring-training game while you're in Phoenix. Just be sure to book your hotel well in advance; these games are the biggest thing going in the valley each spring.

Mountain Biking in South Mountain or Papago Park. The trails of these two desert parks are ideal for mountain biking, and whether you're a novice making your first foray onto the dirt or a budding downhill racer, you'll find miles of riding that are just your speed.

Spending the Day at a Spa. When it comes to stress relief, there's nothing like a massage or an herbal wrap. The chance to lie back and do nothing at all is something few of us take the time for anymore. And, for the price of a single 1-hour treatment, you can usually spend the whole day at a spa.

Cosanti   This complex of cast-concrete structures served as a prototype and learning project for architect Paolo Soleri's much grander Arcosanti project, currently under construction north of Phoenix (see "En Route to Northern Arizona," later in this chapter). It's here at Cosanti that Soleri's famous bells are cast, and most weekday mornings you can see the foundry in action. Visit between 9:30 and 12:30 for the best chance of seeing bronze bells being poured.

6433 E. Doubletree Ranch Rd., Paradise Valley. © 800/752-3187 or 480/948-6145. www.cosanti.com. Suggested donation $1. Mon–Sat 9am–5pm; Sun 11am–5pm. Closed major holidays. Drive 1 mile west of Scottsdale Rd. on Doubletree Ranch Rd.

Mystery Castle ✦ (*Finds*)   Built for a daughter who longed for a castle more permanent than those built in sand at the beach, Mystery Castle is a wondrous work of folk-art architecture. Boyce Luther Gulley, who had come to Arizona in hopes of curing his tuberculosis, constructed the castle during the 1930s and

Hunt's Tomb: The Great Pyramid of Phoenix

If you're driving through Papago Park, perhaps on your way to the Desert Botanical Garden, and see a shimmering white pyramid on a hilltop, you might at first imagine that you're having a heat-induced hallucination. Not so. The pyramid is real. However, it was *not* built by wandering Aztecs or ancient Egyptians. It is the tomb of Governor George W. P. Hunt, who was the first, second, third, sixth, seventh, eighth and 10th governor of Arizona! No other governor in any state has served so many terms in office as Hunt, who was born in 1859 and died in 1934. The tomb is accessible from a parking area near the zoo.

early 1940s using stones from the property. The resulting 18-room fantasy has 13 fireplaces, parapets, and many other unusual touches. Tours are usually led by Mary Lou Gulley, the daughter for whom the castle was built.

800 E. Mineral Rd. (C) **602/268-1581.** Admission $5 adults, $2 children 5–15. Thurs–Sun 11am–4pm. Closed July–Sept. Take Central Ave. south to Mineral Rd. (2 miles south of Baseline Rd.) and turn east.

Taliesin West ★★★   Frank Lloyd Wright fell in love with the Arizona desert and, in 1937, built Taliesin West as a winter camp that served as his home, office, and school. Today, the buildings of Taliesin West are the headquarters of the Frank Lloyd Wright Foundation and School of Architecture.

Tours explain the campus buildings and include a general introduction to Wright and his theories of architecture. Wright believed in using local materials in his designs, and this is much in evidence at Taliesin West, where local stone was used for building foundations. With its open-walled buildings and patio areas, Taliesin West also showcases Wright's ability to integrate indoor and outdoor spaces.

Expanded Insight Tours ($16–$22), behind-the-scenes tours ($45), guided desert walks ($20), apprentice shelter tours ($30), and night hikes ($25) are also available at certain times of year. Call ahead for schedule information.

In downtown Scottsdale, you'll find Wright Downtown, 7079 E. Fifth Ave. (© **480/990-7710**), a shop that sells reproductions of Wright designs and also has lots of books about the architect.

12621 Frank Lloyd Wright Blvd. (at Cactus/114th St.), Scottsdale. (C) **480/860-8810** for information or 480/860-2700, ext. 494 or 495, for reservations. www.franklloydwright.org. Basic tours: Nov–Apr $18 adults, $15 seniors and students, $5 children 4–12; May–Oct $13 adults, $10 students and seniors, $4.50 children 4–12. Nov–Apr daily 9am–4:15pm; May–Oct daily 9am–4pm. Closed Tues–Wed July–Aug, Easter, Thanksgiving, Christmas, New Year's Day, and occasional special events. From Scottsdale Rd., go east on Shea Blvd. to 114th St., then north 1 mile to the entrance road.

Wrigley Mansion   Situated on a hilltop adjacent to the Arizona Biltmore, this elegant mansion was built by chewing-gum magnate William Wrigley, Jr., between 1929 and 1931 as a present for his wife, Ada. Designed with Italianate styling, the many levels and red-tile roofs make it seem like an entire village. The mansion is now a National Historic Landmark, with the interior restored to its original elegance. Although this is currently a private club, membership is only $10 and basically gives you dining privileges (see p. 113 for information on dining here at Geordie's).

2501 E. Telawa Trail. (C) **602/955-4079.** www.wrigleymansionclub.com. Tours $11; Tues–Fri 10am and 2pm. Call for restaurant hours and reservations.

WILD WEST THEME TOWNS

Despite a population running to the millions, Phoenix and Scottsdale still occasionally like to present themselves as grown-up Wild West cow towns. But since there are more Ford Mustangs than wild mustangs around these parts, you'll have to get out of town way before sundown if you want a taste of the Old West. Scattered around the valley are a handful of Hollywood-style cow towns that are basically just tourist traps, but, hey, if you've got the kids along, you owe it to them to visit at least one of these places.

Cave Creek, founded as a gold-mining camp in the 1870s, is the last of the valley towns that still has some semblance of Wild West character, but this is rapidly fading as area real-estate prices skyrocket and Scottsdale's population center moves ever northward. Still, you'll see several steakhouses, saloons, and shops selling Western and Native American crafts and antiques. The main family attraction is a place called **Frontier Town,** which is right on Cave Creek Road in the center of town. It's a sort of mock cow town that is home to the Black Mountain Brewing Company, which brews Cave Creek Chili Beer. You can try this fiery beer at **The Original Crazy Ed's Satisfied Frog Saloon & Restaurant** (p. 107), located here in Frontier Town. To learn more about the history of this area, stop in at the **Cave Creek Museum,** at Skyline Drive and Basin Road (© **480/488-2764**). It's open from October to May, Tuesday through Sunday from 1 to 4:30pm; admission is $3 for adults and $2 for seniors and students.

Goldfield Ghost Town (Kids)   Over on the east side of the valley, just 4 miles northeast of Apache Junction, you'll find a reconstructed 1890s gold-mining town. Although it's a bit of a tourist trap—gift shops, an ice-cream parlor, and the like—it's also home to the **Superstition Mountain Museum** (© **480/983-4888**), which has interesting exhibits on the history of the area. Of particular note is the exhibit on the Lost Dutchman gold mine, perhaps the most famous mine in the country despite the fact that its location is unknown. Goldfield Mine Tours provides guided tours of the gold mine beneath the town. The Superstition Scenic Narrow Gauge Railroad circles the town, and the **Goldfield Livery** (© **480/982-0133**) offers horseback riding and carriage rides. If you're here at lunchtime, you can get a meal at the steakhouse/saloon.

Ariz. 88, 4 miles northeast of Apache Junction. © 480/983-0333. www.goldfieldghosttown.com. Museum admission $4 adults, $3 seniors, $2 children 6–17; train rides $4 adults, $3.50 seniors, $2 children 5–12; mine tours $6 adults, $5 seniors, $3 children 6–12; horseback rides $25 for 1 hr., $45 for 2 hr. Town open daily 10am–5pm; museum, tour, and ride hours vary. Closed Christmas.

(*Finds* **Don't Bug Me!**

Want to hold a tarantula in your hand? Pet a giant millipede? Then head out to Glendale and the **Katydid Insect Museum,** 5060 W. Bethany Home Rd., #7 (© **623/931-8718**; www.insectmuseum.com). This tiny strip-mall museum is affiliated with an exterminating company, but it has an astonishing collection of live and mounted bugs. Best of all (or is it worst of all?), this is a hands-on place. The museum is open Monday through Friday from 11am to 4pm, and admission is $4 adults, $3 seniors, $2 children ages 7 to 11, and $1 children ages 3 to 6.

Carefree Living

Carefree, a planned community established in the 1950s and popular with retirees, is much more subdued than its neighbor Cave Creek, which effects a sort of Wild West character. Ho Hum Road and Easy Street are just two local street names that reflect the sedate nature of Carefree, which is home to the exclusive **Boulders**. This resort boasts a spectacular setting, a Golden Door Spa, and a couple of excellent restaurants. On Easy Street, in what passes for Carefree's downtown, you'll find one of the world's largest sundials. The dial is 90 feet across, and the gnomon (the part that casts the shadow) is 35 feet tall. From the gnomon hangs a colored glass star, and in the middle of the dial is a pool of water and a fountain. Also downtown is a sort of reproduction Spanish-village shopping area, and just south of town, adjacent to the Boulders, is the upscale **El Pedregal Festival Marketplace** shopping center, with interesting boutiques, galleries, and a few restaurants.

PARKS & ZOOS

Perhaps the most unusual park in the Phoenix metro area centers on **Tempe Town Lake** (© 480/350-8625; www.tempe.gov/rio), which was created in 1999 by damming the Salt River with inflatable dams. Tempe's 2-mile-long lake offers boat rentals and tours, and lining the north and south shores are bike paths and parks. The best lake access is at Tempe Town Beach, at the foot of the Mill Avenue Bridge. Here you can rent kayaks and other small boats, and even take a brief boat tour with **Rio Lago Cruise** (© 480/517-4050). Boat tours, offered Saturday and Sunday at 1, 3, and 5pm, cost $6 for adults, $5 for seniors and children 6 to 12, and $4 for children 5 and under. Tempe Town Lake is the focus of a grand development plan known as the Rio Salado Project, which will eventually include a hotel and other commercial facilities.

Among the city's most popular parks are its natural areas and preserves. These include Phoenix South Mountain Park, Papago Park, Phoenix Mountains Preserve (site of Piestewa Peak), North Mountain Preserve, North Mountain Recreation Area, and Camelback Mountain–Echo Canyon Recreation Area. For more information on these parks, see "Hiking," "Bicycling," and "Horseback Riding" under "Outdoor Pursuits," below.

Not far from downtown Phoenix is the **Steele Indian School Park,** at Third Street and Indian School Road (© 602/495-0739). This park, as its name implies, was once an Indian school. Several of the old buildings are still standing, but it's the many new fountains, gardens, and interpretive displays that make this such a fascinating place. A stop here can easily be combined with a visit to the nearby Heard Museum.

Phoenix Zoo ★ *Kids*   Forget about polar bears and other cold-climate creatures; this zoo focuses its attention primarily on animals that come from climates similar to that of the Phoenix area (although the rainforest exhibit is a definite exception). Most impressive of the displays are the African savanna and the baboon colony. The Southwestern exhibits are also of interest, as are the giant Galápagos tortoises. All animals are kept in naturalistic enclosures, and what

Now *That's* a Fountain

Arizona loves its water features. Reservoirs, canals, pools, fountains. They're everywhere in the desert. You'd never think that water is in short supply around these parts. One of the strangest water features is the Fountain Hills fountain less than 20 miles northeast of Scottsdale. This fountain, for which the town is named, is the tallest fountain in the world. Using 600 horse-power pumps it shoots water 560 feet into the air! The fountain operates daily from 9am to 9pm every hour on the hour for 15 to 30 minutes. To find the fountain, take Shea Boulevard east from Scottsdale Road or U.S. 101.

with all the palm trees and tropical vegetation, the zoo sometimes manages to make you forget that this really is the desert.

At Papago Park, 455 N. Galvin Pkwy. ℂ 602/273-1341. www.phoenixzoo.org. Admission Sept–May $12 adults, $9 seniors, $5 children 3–12; June–Aug $9 adults, $7 seniors, $5 children 3–12. Sept–May daily 9am–5pm; June–Aug daily 7am–8pm. Closed Christmas. Bus: 3.

ESPECIALLY FOR KIDS

In addition to the following suggestions, kids are likely to enjoy the Arizona Science Center, the Mesa Southwest Museum, the Hall of Flame Firefighting Museum, and the Phoenix Zoo—all described in detail above.

Arizona Doll & Toy Museum   This small museum is located in the historic Stevens House on Heritage Square in downtown Phoenix. The miniature classroom peopled by doll students is a favorite exhibit. With dolls dating from the 19th century, this is a definite must for doll collectors.

At Heritage Square, 602 E. Adams St. ℂ 602/253-9337. Admission $3 adults, $1 children. Tues–Sat 10am–4pm; Sun noon–4pm. Closed Aug. Bus: Red (R), 0, 1, or DASH downtown shuttle.

Arizona Museum for Youth   Using both traditional displays and participatory activities, this museum allows children to explore the fine arts and their own creativity. It's housed in a refurbished grocery store, which for past exhibits has been transformed into a zoo, a ranch, and a foreign country. Exhibits are geared mainly to toddlers through 12-year-olds, but all ages can work together to experience the activities.

35 N. Robson St. (between Main and First sts.), Mesa. ℂ 480/644-2467. www.arizonamuseumforyouth.com. Admission $3.50, free for children under 2. Fall–spring Tues–Fri 1–5pm, Sat–Sun 9am–5pm; summer Tues–Sun 9am–5pm. Closed New Year's Day, Thanksgiving, and Christmas. Bus: Red (R).

Castles & Coasters   Located adjacent to Metrocenter, one of Arizona's largest shopping malls, this small amusement park boasts an impressive double-loop roller coaster, plenty of tamer rides, four 18-hole miniature-golf courses, and a huge pavilion full of video games.

9445 N. Metro Pkwy. E. ℂ 602/997-7575. www.castlesncoasters.com. Ride and game prices vary; all-day passes $12–$23. Open daily (hours change seasonally; call ahead). Bus: Red (R) or 27.

CrackerJax Family Fun & Sports Park   Two miniature-golf courses are the main attraction here, but you'll also find a driving range, a professional putting course for grown-up golfers, batting cages, go-cart tracks, a bumper-boat lagoon, and a video-game arcade.

16001 N. Scottsdale Rd. (¼ mile south of Bell Rd.), Scottsdale. ℂ 480/998-2800. www.crackerjax.com. Activity prices vary; multiple-activity passes $12–$17 adults, $11–$17 children. Open daily (hours change seasonally; call ahead). Bus: 72.

McCormick-Stillman Railroad Park   If you or your kids happen to like trains, you won't want to miss this park. On the grounds are restored cars and engines, two old railway depots, model railroad layouts operated by a local club, and, best of all, a ½-scale model railroad that takes visitors around the park. There's also a 1929 carousel and a general store.

7301 E. Indian Bend Rd. (at Scottsdale Rd.), Scottsdale. ℂ 480/312-2312. www.therailroadpark.com. Train and carousel rides $1; museum admission $1 adults, free for children 12 and under. Hours vary with the season; call for schedule. Bus: 72.

6 Organized Tours & Excursions

The Valley of the Sun is a sprawling, often congested place, and if you're unfamiliar with the area, you may be surprised at how great the distances are. If map reading and urban navigation are not your strong points, consider taking a guided tour. There are numerous companies offering tours of both the Valley of the Sun and the rest of Arizona. However, tours of the valley tend to include only brief stops at highlights.

BUS TOURS   **Gray Line of Phoenix** (ℂ **800/732-0327** or 602/495-9100; www.graylinearizona.com) is one of the largest tour companies in the valley. It offers a 4-hour tour of Phoenix and the Valley of the Sun for $40; reservations are necessary. The tour points out such local landmarks as the state capitol, Heritage Square, Arizona State University, and Old Town Scottsdale.

GLIDER RIDES   The thermals that form above the mountains in the Phoenix area make this an ideal place for sailplane (glider) soaring. On the south side of the valley in Maricopa, **Arizona Soaring** (ℂ **520/568-2318**; www.azsoaring.com) offers sailplane rides as well as instruction. A basic 20-minute flight is $86; for $115 to $150, you can take an aerobatic flight with loops, rolls, and inverted flying. To reach the airstrip, take I-10 east to Exit 162A, go 15 miles, turn west on Ariz. 238, and continue 6½ miles. On the north side of the valley, there's **Turf Soaring School,** 8700 W. Carefree Hwy., Peoria (ℂ **602/439-3621**; www.turfsoaring.com), which charges $95 for a basic flight and $135 for an aerobatic flight. This outfitter also offers flights for two people ($160–$210), although your combined weight can't exceed 300 pounds. Reservations are a good idea at either place.

HOT-AIR BALLOON RIDES   The still morning air of the Valley of the Sun is perfect for hot-air ballooning, and because of the stiff competition, prices are among the lowest in the country—between $125 and $150 per person for a 1- to 1½-hour ride. Companies to try include **Over the Rainbow** (ℂ **602/225-5666;** www.letsgoballooning.com), **Zephyr Balloon/A Aerozona Adventure**

⸜Tips Top Gun

Ever wanted to be a fighter pilot? Well, at **Fighter Combat International** (ℂ **866/FLY-HARD;** www.fightercombat.com) you can find out if you've got the right stuff. This company, which operates out of the Williams Gateway Airport in Mesa, offers a variety of adventure aerobatic flights, including mock dogfights. Best of all, you get to fly the plane up to 75% of the time and learn how to do loops, rolls, spins, and other aerobatic moves. Flights start at $295; for the full Top Gun experience, you'll have to shell out $945.

(© **888/991-4260** or 480/991-4260; www.azballoon.com), and **Adventures Out West** (© **800/755-0935** or 602/996-6100; www.adventuresoutwest.com).

JEEP TOURS   After spending a few days in Scottsdale, you'll likely start wondering where the desert is. Well, it's out there, and the easiest way to explore it is to book a Jeep tour. Most hotels and resorts have particular companies they work with, so start by asking your concierge. Alternatively, you can contact one of the following companies. Most will pick you up at your hotel, take you off through the desert, and maybe even let you try panning for gold or shooting a six-gun. Rates are around $75 to $85 for a 4-hour tour. Companies include **Arizona Desert Mountain Jeep Tours** (© **800/567-3619** or 480/860-1777; www.azdesertmountain.com) and **Arizona Bound Tours** (© **480/994-0580;** www.arizonabound.com).

If you want to really impress your friends when you get home, you'll need to try something a little different. How about a Hummer tour? Sure, a Hummer is nothing but a Jeep on steroids, but these military-issue off-road vehicles still turn heads. Contact **Desert Storm Hummer Tours** (© **866/374-8637** or 480/922-0020; www.dshummer.com), which charges $95 for a 4-hour tour, or **Stellar Adventures** (© **877/878-3552** or 602/402-0584; www.stellaradventures.com), which charges $120 for a basic 4-hour tour and $155 for its extreme tour. Desert Storm Hummer Tours also offers night tours ($125) that let you spot wildlife with night-vision equipment.

SCENIC FLIGHTS   If you're short on time but want to at least see the Grand Canyon, book an air tour in a small plane. **Westwind Tours** (© **888/869-0866** or 480/991-5557; www.westwindaviation.com) charges $280 to $654 for its Grand Canyon tours and $390 to $445 for its Monument Valley tours. This company flies out of the Deer Valley Airport in the northwest part of the valley.

7 Outdoor Pursuits

BICYCLING   Although the Valley of the Sun is a sprawling place, it's mostly flat and has numerous paved bike paths, which makes bicycling a breeze as long as it isn't windy or, in the summer, too hot. In Scottsdale, **Arizona Outback Adventures,** 7607 E. McDowell Rd. (© **866/455-1601** or 480/945-2881; www.azoutbackadventures.com) rents cruisers for $25 per day and mountain bikes for $35 to $65 per day. Mountain-biking trail maps are also available. This company also does half-day guided mountain-bike rides.

Among the best mountain-biking spots in the city are Papago Park (at Van Buren St. and Galvin Pkwy.), Phoenix South Mountain Park (use the entrance off Baseline Rd. on 48th St.), and North Mountain Preserve (off Seventh St. between Dunlap Ave. and Thunderbird Rd.). With its rolling topography and wide dirt trails, Papago Park is the best place for novice mountain-bikers to get in some desert riding (and the scenery here is great). For hard-core pedalers, Phoenix South Mountain Park is the place to go. The National Trail is the ultimate death-defying ride here, but there are lots of trails for intermediate riders, including the Desert Classic Trail and the short loop trails just north of the parking area at the 48th Street entrance. North Mountain is another good place for intermediate riders.

There's also plenty of good mountain biking up in the Cave Creek area, where you can rent a bike for $35 a day at **Bikes Out West in Cave Creek,** 6149 Cave Creek Rd. (© **480/488-5261**). This shop also offers guided mountain-bike tours for $75 per person. If you'd like a guide for some of the best biking in the desert, contact **Desert Biking Adventures** (© **888/249-BIKE** or 602/320-4602; www.desertbikingadventures.com), which leads 2-, 3-, and 4-hour tours (and specializes in downhill rides). Prices range from $70 to $97.

If you'd rather confine your cycling to a paved surface, there's no better route than Scottsdale's **Indian Bend Wash greenbelt,** a paved path that extends for more than 10 miles along Hayden Road (from north of Shea Blvd. to Tempe). The Indian Bend Wash pathway can be accessed at many points along Hayden Road. At the south end, the path connects to paved paths on the shores of Tempe Town Lake and provides easy access to Tempe's Mill Avenue shopping district.

GOLF With nearly 200 courses in the Valley of the Sun, golf is just about the most popular sport in Phoenix and one of the main reasons people flock here in winter. Sunshine, spectacular views, and the company of coyotes, quails, and doves make playing a round of golf here a truly memorable experience.

Despite the number of courses, it can still be difficult to get a tee time on any of the more popular courses (especially during the months of Feb, Mar, and Apr). If you're staying at a resort with a course, be sure to make your tee-time reservations at the same time you make your room reservations. If you aren't staying at a resort, you might still be able to play a round on a resort course if you can get a last-minute tee time. Try one of the tee-time reservations services below.

The only thing harder than getting a winter or spring tee time in the valley is facing the bill at the end of your 18 holes. Greens fees at most public and resort courses range from $90 to $170, with the top courses often charging $200 to $250 or more. Municipal courses, on the other hand, charge under $40. You can save money on many courses by opting for twilight play, which usually begins between 1 and 3pm.

You can get more information on Valley of the Sun golf courses from the **Greater Phoenix Convention & Visitors Bureau,** 50 N. Second St. (© **877/225-5749** or 602/254-6500; www.visitphoenix.com).

It's a good idea to make reservations well in advance. You can avoid the hassle of booking tee times yourself by contacting **Golf Xpress** (© **888/679-8246** or 602/404-GOLF; www.azgolfxpress.com), which can make reservations farther in advance than you could if you called the golf course directly, and can sometimes get you lower greens fees as well. This company also makes hotel reservations, rents golf clubs, and provides other assistance to golfers visiting the valley. For last-minute reservations, call **Stand-by Golf** (© **800/655-5345;** www.discountteetimes.com).

The many resort courses are the favored fairways of valley visitors. For spectacular scenery, the two Jay Morrish–designed 18-hole courses at the **Boulders** ★★, North Scottsdale Road and Carefree Highway, Carefree (© **800/553-1717** or 480/488-9009), just can't be beat. Given the option, play the South Course, and watch out as you approach the tee box on the 7th hole—it's a real heart-stopper. Tee times for nonresort guests are very limited in winter and spring (try making reservations a month in advance if you aren't staying at the resort). You'll pay $240 to $250 for a round. In summer, you can play for $75 to $95 (just be sure you get the earliest possible tee time and bring plenty of water).

Jumping over to Litchfield Park, on the far west side of the valley, there's the **Wigwam Golf and Country Club** ★, 300 Wigwam Blvd. (© **800/909-4224** or 623/935-3811), which has, count 'em, three championship 18-hole courses. The Gold Course is legendary, but even the Blue and Red courses are worth playing. These are traditional courses for purists who want vast expanses of green rather than cactus and boulders. In high season, greens fees are $133 for any of the three courses and $43 in summer. Reservations for nonguests can be made no more than 7 days in advance.

Way over on the east side of the valley at the foot of the Superstition Mountains is the **Gold Canyon Golf Resort** ☆, 6100 S. Kings Ranch Rd., Gold Canyon (© **800/827-5281** or 480/982-9449; www.gcgr.com), which has been rated the best public course in the state and has three of the state's best holes— the 2nd, 3rd, and 4th on the visually breathtaking, desert-style Dinosaur Mountain course. Greens fees on this course range from $145 to $175 in winter and from $60 to $70 in summer. The Sidewinder course is more traditional and less dramatic, but much more economical. Greens fees are $85 to $100 in winter and $40 to $50 in summer. Reserve a week in advance. It's well worth the drive.

If you want a traditional course that has been played by presidents and celebrities alike, try to get a tee time at one of the two 18-hole courses at the **Arizona Biltmore Country Club,** 24th Street and Missouri Avenue (© **602/955-9655**). The courses here are more relaxing than challenging, good to play if you're not yet up to par. Greens fees are $93 to $165 in winter and spring, $34 to $48 in summer. Reservations can be made up to a month in advance. There's also a championship 18-hole putting course.

Of the two courses at the **Camelback Golf Club,** 7847 N. Mockingbird Lane (© **800/24-CAMEL** or 480/596-7050), the Resort Course underwent a $16-million redesign a few years ago and has new water features and bunkers. The Club Course is a links-style course with great mountain views and lots of water hazards. Resort Course greens fees are $140 to $165 in winter and $50 to $60 in summer; Club Course fees are $100 to $125 in winter and $40 to $50 in summer. Reservations can be made up to 60 days in advance.

Set at the base of Camelback Mountain, the **Phoenician Golf Club,** 6000 E. Camelback Rd. (© **800/888-8234** or 480/423-2449; www.thephoenician.com), at the valley's most glamorous resort, has 27 holes that mix traditional and desert styles. Greens fees for nonresort guests are $110 to $180 in winter and spring, $60 to $90 in summer, and can be made up to 60 days in advance.

Of the valley's many daily-fee courses, it's the two 18-hole courses at **Troon North Golf Club** ☆☆☆, 10320 E. Dynamite Blvd., Scottsdale (© **888/TROON-US** or 480/585-5300; www.troongolf.com), seemingly just barely carved out of raw desert, that garner the most local accolades. This is the finest example of a desert course that you'll find anywhere in the state, and with five tee boxes on each hole, golfers of all levels will be thoroughly challenged. Greens fees are $240 to $275 in winter and spring, $75 to $90 in summer. Reservations are taken up to 30 days in advance.

If you want to swing where the pros do, beg, borrow, or steal a tee time on the Tom Weiskopf and Jay Morrish–designed Stadium Course at the **Tournament Players Club (TPC) of Scottsdale** ☆☆, 17020 N. Hayden Rd. (© **888/400-4001** or 480/585-4334; www.playatpc.com), which hosts the Phoenix Open. The 18th hole has standing room for 40,000 spectators, but hopefully there won't be that many around the day you double bogey on this hole. The TPC's second 18, the Desert Course, is actually a municipal course, thanks to an agreement with the landowner, the Bureau of Land Management. Stadium course fees top out at $218 in winter and spring, $88 in summer. Desert Course fees are $59 in winter and spring and $43 in summer.

The **Kierland Golf Club,** 15636 Clubgate Dr., Scottsdale (© **888/ TROON-US** or 480/922-9283; www.troongolf.com), which was designed by Scott Miller and consists of three 9-hole courses that can be played in combination, is another much-talked-about local daily-fee course. It's affiliated with the Westin Kierland Resort. Greens fees are $140 to $170 in winter, $65 to $75 in summer. Book up to 30 days in advance.

The Pete Dye–designed **ASU-Karsten Golf Course,** 1125 E. Rio Salado Pkwy., Tempe (© **480/921-8070;** www.asukarsten.com), part of Arizona State University, is also highly praised and a very challenging training ground for top collegiate golfers. Greens fees are $75 to $89 in winter and $25 to $35 in summer. Phone reservations are taken up to 14 days in advance; online reservations are taken up to 30 days in advance.

If you're looking for good value in traditional or links-style courses, try the Legacy Golf Resort, Stonecreek Golf Club, or Ocotillo Golf Resort. The **Legacy Golf Resort,** 6808 S. 32nd St. (© **888/828-FORE** or 602/305-5550; www.legacy golfresort.com), which was the site of the 2000 LPGA tournament, is a fairly forgiving course on the south side of the valley. Greens fees are $99 to $129 in winter and $29 to $69 in summer.

Stonecreek Golf Club, 4435 E. Paradise Village Pkwy. (© **602/953-9110;** www.americagolf.com), conveniently located in Paradise Valley close to Old Scottsdale, is named for the artificial stream that meanders through the course. Greens fees are $59 to $95 in winter.

Ocotillo Golf Club, 3751 S. Clubhouse Dr., Chandler (© **888/624-8899** or 480/917-6660), in the southeast part of the valley, has three 9-hole courses centered around 95 acres of man-made lakes, and that means a lot of challenge. Greens fees are $155 in winter and $30 to $45 in summer.

If you want to take a crack at a desert-style course or two but don't want to take out a second mortgage, try Dove Valley Ranch Golf Club, Rancho Mañana Golf Club, or We-Ko-Pa Golf Club. **Dove Valley Ranch Golf Club,** 33244 N. Black Mountain Pkwy., Cave Creek (© **480/488-0009;** www.dovevalley ranch.com), designed by Robert Trent Jones, Jr., was voted Arizona's best new public course when it opened in 1998. It's something of a merger of desert and traditional styles. Greens fees are $135 in winter.

Rancho Mañana Golf Club, 5734 E. Rancho Mañana Blvd., Cave Creek (© **480/488-0398;** www.ranchomanana.com), on the north side of the valley near the Boulders, makes a good introduction to desert-style courses, as it's not as challenging as some other options in the area. Greens fees are $115 to $135 in winter.

We-Ko-Pa Golf Club, 18200 East Toh Vee Circle, Fountain Hills (© **480/ 836-9000;** www.wekopa.com), is located off the Beeline Highway (Ariz. 87) on the Fort McDowell Yavapai Nation in the northeast corner of the valley, and gets rave reviews from area golfers. The course name is Yavapai for "Four Peaks," which is the mountain range you'll be marveling at as you play. The desert crowds the fairways here, so make sure you keep your ball on the grass. Greens fees are $180 in winter and $65 in summer. Reservations are taken up to 90 days in advance.

Of the municipal courses in Phoenix, **Papago Golf Course,** 5595 E. Moreland St. (© **602/275-8428**), at the foot of the red sandstone Papago Buttes, offers fine views and a killer 17th hole. This is such a great course that it's used for Phoenix Open qualifying. **Encanto Golf Course,** 2605 N. 15th Ave. (© **602/ 253-3963**), is the third-oldest course in Arizona and, with its wide fairways and lack of hazards, is very forgiving. **Cave Creek Golf Course,** 15202 N. 19th Ave. (© **602/866-8076**), in north Phoenix, is another good, economical choice. In winter, greens fees at these three municipal courses are $19 to $35 to walk and $25 to $41 with a golf cart. For details on these courses, go to www.ci.phoenix. az.us/SPORTS/golf.html.

HIKING   Several mountains around Phoenix, including Camelback Mountain and Piestewa Peak, have been set aside as parks and nature preserves, and these natural areas are among the city's most popular hiking spots. The city's largest nature preserve, **South Mountain Park/Preserve** (© **602/495-0222**), covers 16,000 acres and is said to be the largest city park in the world. This park contains miles of hiking, mountain-biking, and horseback-riding trails, and the views of Phoenix (whether from along the National Trail or from the parking lot at the Buena Vista Lookout) are spectacular, especially at sunset. To reach the park's main entrance, drive south on Central Avenue, which leads right into the park. Once inside the park, turn left on Summit Road and follow it to the Buena Vista Lookout, which provides a great view of the city and is the trail head for the National Trail. If you hike east on this trail for 2 miles, you'll come to an unusual little tunnel that makes a good turnaround point.

   Another good place to get in some relatively easy and convenient hiking is at **Papago Park** (© **602/262-4837**), home to the Desert Botanical Garden, the Phoenix Zoo, and the fascinating Hole in the Rock (a red-rock butte with a large natural opening in it). There are both paved and dirt trails within the park; the most popular hikes are around the Papago Buttes (park on W. Park Dr.) and up onto the rocks at Hole in the Rock (park past the zoo at the information center).

   Perhaps the most popular hike in the city is the trail to the top of **Camelback Mountain,** in **Echo Canyon Recreation Area** (© **602/256-3220**), near the boundary between Phoenix and Scottsdale. This is the highest mountain in Phoenix, and the 1.25-mile Summit Trail to the top gains 1,200 feet and is very steep, yet on any given day there will be ironmen and ironwomen nonchalantly jogging up and down to stay fit. At times, it almost feels like a health-club singles scene. The views are the finest in the city. To reach the trail head, drive up 44th Street until it becomes McDonald Drive, turn right on East Echo Canyon Drive, and continue up the hill until the road ends at a parking lot, which is often full. Don't attempt this one in the heat of the day, and bring at least a quart of water.

   At the east end of Camelback Mountain is the Cholla Trail, which, at 1.75 miles in length, isn't as steep as the Summit Trail (at least not until you get close to the summit, where the route gets steep, rocky, and quite difficult). The only parking for this trail is along Invergordon Road at Chaparral Road, just north of Camelback Road (along the east boundary of The Phoenician resort). Be sure to park in a legal parking space and watch the hours that parking is allowed. There's a good turnaround point about 1.5 miles up the trail, and great views down onto the fairways of the golf course at The Phoenician.

   Piestewa Peak, in the **Phoenix Mountains Preserve** (© **602/262-7901**), offers another aerobic workout of a hike and has views almost as spectacular as those from Camelback Mountain. The round-trip to the summit is 2.5 miles. Piestewa Peak is reached from Piestewa Peak Drive (formerly Squaw Peak Dr.) off Lincoln Drive between 22nd and 23rd streets.

Of all the popular mountain trails in the Phoenix area, the trail through **Pinnacle Peak Park,** 26802 N. 102nd Way (© **480/312-0990;** www.scottsdaleaz. gov/parks/pinnacle), in north Scottsdale is my favorite. The trail through the park is a 3.5-mile round-trip hike and is immensely popular with the local fitness crowd. Forget about stopping to smell the desert penstemon. If you don't keep up the pace, someone's liable to knock you off the trail into a prickly pear. If you can find a parking space (arrive before 9am on weekends) and can ignore the crowds, you'll be treated to views of rugged desert mountains (and posh desert suburbs). There are guided hikes Wednesday through Sunday at 10am. To find the park from central Scottsdale, go north on Pima Road, east on Happy Valley Road, north on Alma School Parkway, and turn left at the sign for Pinnacle Peak Patio restaurant.

For much less vigorous hiking (without the crowds), try **North Mountain Park** (© **602/262-7901**), in North Mountain Preserve. This natural area, located on either side of Seventh Street between Dunlap Avenue and Thunderbird Road, has more flat hiking than Camelback Mountain or Piestewa Peak.

HORSEBACK RIDING   Even in the urban confines of the Phoenix metro area, people like to play at being cowboys. Keep in mind that most stables require or prefer reservations. Because any guided ride is going to lead you through interesting desert scenery, your best bet is to pick a stable close to where you're staying.

On the south side of the city, try **Ponderosa Stables,** 10215 S. Central Ave. (© **602/268-1261**), or **South Mountain Stables,** 10005 S. Central Ave. (© **602/ 276-8131**), both of which lead rides into South Mountain Park and charge between $23 for a 1-hour ride $60 for a 4-hour ride. These stables also offer fun dinner rides ($29) to the T-Bone Steakhouse, where you buy your own dinner before riding back under the stars. If you have time for only one horseback ride while you're in Phoenix, make it this latter ride.

If you're staying in the Scottsdale area, your best bet is **MacDonald's Ranch,** 26540 N. Scottsdale Rd. (© **480/585-0239;** www.macdonaldsranch.com), which charges $30 for a 1-hour ride and $50 for a 2-hour ride.

On the north side of the valley, **Cave Creek Outfitters,** off Dynamite Boulevard on 144th Street (© **888/921-0040** or 480/471-4635), offers 2-hour rides for $60.

On the east side of the valley, on the southern slopes of the Superstitions, you'll find the **Richardson's D-Spur Ranch,** Peralta Road, Apache Junction (© **866/913-7787,** 602/810-7029, or 480/983-0833; www.dspurranch.com), which charges $26 for a 1-hour ride, $50 for a 2-hour ride, and $190 per person for an overnight trip.

TENNIS   Most major hotels in the area have tennis courts, and there are several tennis resorts around the valley. If you're staying someplace without a court, try the **Scottsdale Ranch Park,** 10400 E. Via Linda, Scottsdale (© **480/ 312-7774**). Court fees range from $3 to $6 for 1½ hours.

WATER PARKS   At **Waterworld Safari Water Park,** 4243 W. Pinnacle Peak Rd. (© **623/581-8446;** www.golfland.com), you can free-fall down the Kilimanjaro speed slide or catch a gnarly wave in the wave pool. **Mesa Golfland-Sunsplash,** 155 W. Hampton Ave., Mesa (© **480/834-8319;** www.golfland.com), has a wave pool and a tunnel called the Black Hole. **Big Surf,** 1500 N. McClintock Rd. (© **480/947-2477;** www.golfland.com), has a wave pool, a speed slide, and more.

All three of these parks charge $20 for adults, $16.25 for children 3 to 11, $1 for children 2 and under. Waterworld Safari Water Park and Mesa Golfland-Sunsplash are open from around Memorial Day weekend to Labor Day weekend, Monday through Thursday from 10am to 8pm, Friday and Saturday from 10am to 9pm, and Sunday from 11am to 7pm. Big Surf is open from around Memorial Day to Labor Day, Monday through Saturday from 10am to 6pm and Sunday from 11am to 7pm.

WHITE-WATER RAFTING & TUBING   The desert may not seem like the place for white-water rafting, but up in the mountains to the northeast of Phoenix, the **Upper Salt River** still flows wild and free and offers some exciting rafting. Most years from about late February to late May, snowmelt from the White Mountains turns the Salt into a river filled with exciting Class III and IV rapids (sometimes, however, there just isn't enough water). Companies operating full-day, overnight, and multi-day rafting trips on the Upper Salt River (conditions permitting) include **Wilderness Aware Rafting** (© 800/231-7238; www.inaraft.com), **Canyon Rio Rafting** (© 800/272-3353; www.canyonrio.com), and **Mild to Wild Rafting** (© 800/567-6745; www.mild2wildrafting.com). Prices range from $90 to $115 for a day trip.

Tamer river trips can be had from **Salt River Recreation** (© 480/984-3305; www.saltrivertubing.com), which has its headquarters 20 miles northeast of Phoenix on Power Road at the intersection of Usery Pass Road in Tonto National Forest. For $12, the company will rent you a large inner tube and shuttle you by bus upriver for the float down. The inner-tubing season runs from mid-May to September.

8 Spectator Sports

Phoenix is nuts for pro sports and is one of the few cities in the country with teams for all four of the major sports (baseball, basketball, football, and hockey). Add to this baseball's spring training, professional women's basketball, two major golf tournaments, tennis tournaments, the annual Fiesta Bowl college football classic, and ASU football, basketball, and baseball, and you have enough action to keep even the most rabid sports fans happy. The all-around best month to visit is March, when you could feasibly catch baseball's spring training, the Suns, the Coyotes, and ASU basketball and baseball, as well as the Safeway International LPGA Tournament.

Call **Ticketmaster** (© 480/784-4444; www.ticketmaster.com) for tickets to most of the events below. For sold-out events, try **Tickets Unlimited** (© 800/289-8497 or 602/840-2340; www.ticketsunlimitedinc.com) or **Ticket Exchange** (© 800/800-9811 or 602/254-4444).

AUTO RACING   At the **Phoenix International Raceway,** 7602 S. 115th Ave. at Baseline Road, Avondale (© 602/252-2227; www.phoenixinternational raceway.com), there's NASCAR and IndyCar racing on the world's fastest 1-mile oval. Tickets range from $10 to $45.

BASEBALL   Back in 2001, the **Arizona Diamondbacks** (© 888/777-4664 or 602/514-8400; www.azdiamondbacks.com) surprised most of the nation by beating the New York Yankees in the last inning of the last game of the World Series. Such an edge-of-the-seat upset makes for rabidly loyal fans for this team, which plays in downtown Phoenix at the state-of-the-art Bank One Ballpark (BOB). The ballpark's retractable roof allows for comfortable play during the blistering summers, and makes this one of the only enclosed baseball stadiums with natural grass. Tickets to ball games are available through the Bank One Ballpark ticket office and cost between $10 and $95. The best seats are in sections J and Q.

For decades, baseball's spring training season has been immensely popular, especially with fans from northern teams, and don't think that the Cactus League's preseason exhibition games are any less popular just because the Diamondbacks are World Series winners and play all summer. **Spring-training games** may rank second only to golf in popularity with winter visitors to the valley. Nine major league baseball teams have spring-training camps around the valley during March and April, and exhibition games are scheduled at seven different stadiums. Tickets cost $4 to $24. Get a schedule from a visitor center, check the *Arizona Republic* while you're in town, or go to www.cactus-league.com. Games often sell out, especially on weekends, so be sure to order tickets in advance. The spring-training schedule for 2005 should be out by December 2004.

Teams training in the valley include the **Anaheim Angels,** Tempe Diablo Stadium, 2200 W. Alameda Dr. (48th St. and Broadway Rd.), Tempe (© 602/438-9300 or 480/784-4444 for tickets; www.angelsbaseball.com); the **Chicago Cubs,** HoHoKam Park, 1235 N. Center St., Mesa (© 800/905-3315 for tickets or 480/964-4467; www.cubspringtraining.com); the **Kansas City Royals,** Surprise Recreation Campus, 15850 N. Bullard Ave., Surprise (© 623/594-5600 or 480/784-4444 for tickets; www.kansascityroyals.com); the **Milwaukee Brewers,** Maryvale Baseball Park, 3600 N. 51st Ave., Phoenix (© 800/933-7890 for tickets or 623/245-5500; www.milwaukeebrewers.com); the **Oakland Athletics,** Phoenix Municipal Stadium, 5999 E. Van Buren St., Phoenix (© 602/392-0217 or 480/784-4444 for tickets; www.oaklandathletics.com); the **San Diego Padres,** Peoria Sports Complex, 16101 N. 83rd Ave., Peoria (© 623/878-4337 or 480/784-4444 for tickets; www.padres.com); the **San Francisco Giants,** Scottsdale Stadium, 7408 E. Osborn Rd., Scottsdale (© 800/905-3315 for tickets or 480/990-7972; www.sfgiants.com); the **Seattle Mariners,** Peoria Sports Complex, 16101 N. 83rd Ave., Peoria (© 623/878-4337 or 480/784-4444 for tickets; www.seattlemariners.com); and the **Texas Rangers,** Surprise Recreation Campus, 15850 N. Bullard Ave., Surprise (© 623/594-5600 or 480/784-4444 for tickets; www.texasrangers.com).

BASKETBALL The NBA's **Phoenix Suns** play at the America West Arena, 201 E. Jefferson St. (© **800/4-NBA-TIX** or 602/379-SUNS; www.suns.com). Tickets cost $13 to $95. Suns tickets are hard to come by; if you haven't planned ahead, try contacting the box office the day before or the day of a game to see if tickets have been returned. Otherwise, you'll have to try a ticket agency and pay a premium.

Phoenix also has a WNBA team, the **Phoenix Mercury** (© **602/252-9622** or 602/514-8333; www.wnba.com/mercury), which plays at the America West Arena between late May and mid-August. Tickets cost $11 to $103.

FOOTBALL The **Arizona Cardinals** (© **800/999-1402,** 602/379-0102, or 623/266-5000; www.azcardinals.com) are in the process of building a new stadium in the west valley city of Glendale. However, until the new stadium is completed in 2006, the Cardinals will continue to play at Arizona State University's Sun Devil Stadium. Tickets cost $30 to $150 and go on sale around late June or early July.

While the Cardinals get to use Sun Devil Stadium, this field really belongs to Arizona State University's **Sun Devils** (© 480/965-2381). Tickets range from $20 to $30. The stadium is home to the Fiesta Bowl Football Classic.

GOLF TOURNAMENTS   It's not surprising that, with nearly 200 golf courses and ideal golfing weather throughout the fall, winter, and spring, the Valley of the Sun hosts three major PGA tournaments each year. Tickets for all three are available through Ticketmaster outlets (see above).

January's **Phoenix Open Golf Tournament** (© 602/870-4431; www.phoenixopen.com) is the largest. Held at the Tournament Players Club (TPC) of Scottsdale, it attracts more spectators than any other golf tournament in the world (more than 500,000 each year). The 18th hole has standing room for 40,000. Tickets start at $25.

Each March, the **Safeway International LPGA Tournament** (© 877/983-3300 or 602/495-4653; www.safewaygolf.com), held at the Superstition Mountain Golf & Country Club, 3976 S. Ponderosa Dr., lures nearly 100 of the top women golfers from around the world. Daily tickets are $15; weekly tickets are $50.

HOCKEY   Ice hockey in the desert? It may not make sense, but even Phoenicians are crazy about ice hockey (maybe it's all those northern transplants). In fact, the NHL's **Phoenix Coyotes** (© 480/563-PUCK; www.phoenix coyotes.com) have a state-of-the-art new arena in Glendale (northwest of downtown Phoenix). Tickets cost $15 to $225.

HORSE/GREYHOUND RACING   **Turf Paradise,** 1501 W. Bell Rd. (© 602/942-1101; www.turfparadise.com), is Phoenix's horse-racing track. The season runs from late September to mid-May. Admission ranges from $2 to $5.

The **Phoenix Greyhound Park,** 3801 E. Washington St. (© 602/273-7181; www.phoenixgreyhoundpark.com), is a fully enclosed, air-conditioned facility offering seating in various grandstands, lounges, and restaurants. There's racing throughout the year; tickets are free to $3.

RODEOS, POLO & HORSE SHOWS   Cowboys, cowgirls, and other horsey types will find plenty of the four-legged critters going through their paces most weeks at **Westworld Equestrian Center,** 16601 N. Pima Rd., Scottsdale (© 480/312-6802; www.scottsdaleaz.gov/westworld). With its hundreds of stables, numerous equestrian arenas, and a polo field, this complex provides an amazing variety of entertainment and sporting events. There are rodeos, polo matches, horse shows, horseback rides, and horseback-riding instruction.

TENNIS TOURNAMENTS   Each February, top international men's tennis players compete at the **Franklin Templeton Tennis Classic** (© 480/922-0222; www.scottsdaletennis.com), at the Fairmont Scottsdale Princess, 7575 E. Princess Dr., Scottsdale. Tickets run from $14 to $72 (tickets to later rounds are more expensive) and are available through Ticketmaster outlets (see above).

9 Day Spas

Ever since the first "lungers" showed up in the Phoenix area hoping to cure their tuberculosis, the desert has been a magnet for those looking to get healthy. In the first half of the 20th century, health spas were all the rage in Phoenix, and with the health-and-fitness trend continuing to gather steam, it comes as no surprise that spas are now once again immensely popular in the Valley of the Sun.

In the past few years, several of the area's top resorts have added new full-service spas or expanded existing ones to cater to guests' increasing requests for services such as massages, body wraps, mud masks, and salt glows.

If you can't or don't want to spend the money to stay at a top resort and avail yourself of the spa, you may still be able to indulge. Most resorts open their spas to the public, and for the cost of a body treatment or massage, you can spend the day at the spa, taking classes, working out in an exercise room, lounging by the pool, and otherwise living the life of the rich and famous. Barring this indulgence, you can slip into one of the valley's many day spas and take a stress-reduction break the way other people take a latte break.

If you want truly spectacular surroundings and bragging rights, head north to the **Golden Door Spa at the Boulders,** 34631 N. Tom Darlington Dr., Carefree (© **800/553-1717** or 480/595-3500; www.goldendoorspas.com). Although this spa has the most name recognition of any spa in the valley, it is, unfortunately, not the most impressive. However, at 33,000 square feet and with 24 treatment spaces, it is certainly large. The turquoise wrap, the spa's signature treatment, is a real desert experience. Most 50-minute treatments cost around $110 to $135. Packages are $270 to $1,400.

Willow Stream–The Spa at Fairmont, 7575 E. Princess Dr. (© **800/441-1414** or 480/585-4848; www.fairmont.com), is my favorite valley spa. Designed to conjure up images of the journey to Havasu Canyon, it includes a rooftop swimming pool and a large hot tub in a grotto below the pool. Because this is one of the largest spas in the valley, you'll stand a better chance of getting last-minute reservations here. Most 60-minute treatments cost $129 to $139. Packages range from $199 to $669; there are also several package options for couples.

The **Spa at Gainey Village,** 7477 E. Doubletree Ranch Rd., Scottsdale (© **480/609-6980;** www.thespaatgaineyvillage.com), is a state-of-the-art spa and health club near the Hyatt Regency Scottsdale. Although the health club, which is popular with the Scottsdale Mercedes set, seems to be the main draw, the spa offers a wide range of specialized treatments, including massage in a hydrotherapy tub, couples massages (complete with champagne and fruit), and just about anything else you can think of. With any 1-hour treatment (average price $95), you can use the extensive exercise facilities or take a class. Packages range from $95 to $365.

Located high on the flanks of Mummy Mountain, the **Spa at Camelback Inn,** 5402 E. Lincoln Dr., Scottsdale (© **800/922-2635** or 480/596-7040; www.camelbackspa.com), has long been one of the valley's premiere spas. In order to keep up with all the new spas in the valley, this luxurious place recently underwent an $8-million renovation that completely transformed the space. Needless to say, this is still one of the best and most conveniently located spas in the valley. For the cost of a single 1-hour treatment—between $115 and $135— you can use all the facilities. Among the treatments available are a para-joba body moisturizer that will leave your skin feeling like silk. Packages run from $175 to $310.

The **Centre for Well Being,** at The Phoenician, 6000 E. Camelback Rd., Scottsdale (© **800/843-2392** or 480/423-2452; www.thephoenician.com), is one of the valley's most prestigious spas. For as little as $130, you can get a 50-minute spa treatment (anything from a botanical hydrating wrap to Turkish body scrub) and then spend the day using the many facilities. Packages range from $270 to $555.

The historic setting and convenient location of the **Arizona Biltmore Spa,** 2400 E. Missouri Ave. (℗ **602/381-7632;** www.arizonabiltmore.com), make this facility an excellent choice if you're spending time along the Camelback Corridor. The spa menu includes dozens of different treatments, including massages with lavender and a cactus flower body wrap. If you have just one 50-minute treatment (priced between $115 and $155), you can use all of the spa's facilities for the rest of the day. Packages cost $290 to $590.

The **Mist Spa,** 7171 N. Scottsdale Rd., Scottsdale (℗ **877/MIST-SPA** or 480/905-2882; www.themistspa.com), has a Japanese design, complete with Japanese-style massage rooms and a tranquil rock garden in a central courtyard. Treatments, which include the likes of collagen facials, Dead Sea mud wraps, and green-tea detoxifying wraps, cost around $155 for an 80-minute session. Massages run $105 for 50 minutes. Packages range from $155 to $450. For the cost of a single 1-hour spa treatment, you can use the spa for the entire day.

10 Shopping

For the most part, shopping in the valley means malls. They're everywhere, and they're air-conditioned, which, we're sure you'll agree, makes shopping in the desert far more enjoyable when it's 110°F (43°C) outside.

Scottsdale and the Biltmore District of Phoenix (along Camelback Rd.) are the valley's main upscale shopping areas, with several high-end centers and malls. The various distinct shopping districts of downtown Scottsdale are among the few outdoor shopping areas in the valley and are home to hundreds of boutiques, galleries, jewelry stores, Native American crafts stores, and souvenir shops. The Western atmosphere of Old Town Scottsdale is partly real and partly a figment of the local merchants' imaginations, but nevertheless it's the most popular tourist shopping area in the valley. With dozens of galleries in the Main Street Arts and Antiques District and the nearby Marshall Way Contemporary Arts District, it also happens to be the heart of the valley's art market.

For locals, Scottsdale's shopping scene has been moving steadily northward, and in the past couple of years two new shopping centers—Kierland Commons and the Shops at Gainey Village—have been basking in the limelight. Both of these shopping centers are on North Scottsdale Road.

Shopping hours are usually Monday through Saturday from 10am to 6pm and Sunday from noon to 5pm; malls usually stay open until 9pm Monday through Saturday.

ANTIQUES & COLLECTIBLES

With more than 80 antiques shops and specialty stores, downtown Glendale (northwest of downtown Phoenix) is the valley's main antiques district. You'll find the greatest concentration of antiques stores just off Grand Avenue between 56th and 59th avenues. Five times a year, the **Phoenix Fairgrounds Antique Market** (℗ **623/587-7488** or 602/717-7337; www.azantiqueshow.com), Arizona's largest collectors' show, is held at the Arizona State Fairgrounds, 19th Avenue and McDowell Road. Shows are usually in January, February, May, September, and November.

Antique Trove   If you love browsing through packed antiques malls searching for your favorite collectibles, then this should be your first stop in the valley. It's one of the biggest antiques malls in the area, and within a block are two other big antiques malls. 2020 N. Scottsdale Rd., Scottsdale. ℗ **480/947-6074.**

Arizona West Galleries   Nowhere else in Scottsdale will you find such an amazing collection of cowboy collectibles and Western antiques. There are antique saddles and chaps, old rifles and six-shooters, sheriffs' badges, spurs, and the like. 7149 E. Main St., Scottsdale. *C* **480/994-3752.**

Bishop Gallery for Art & Antiques   This cramped shop is wonderfully eclectic, featuring everything from Asian antiques to unusual original art. Definitely worth a browse. 7164 Main St., Scottsdale. *C* **480/949-9062.**

ART

In the Southwest, only Santa Fe is a more important art market than Scottsdale, and along the streets of Scottsdale's Main Street Arts and Antiques District and the Marshall Way Contemporary Arts District, you'll see dozens of galleries selling everything from monumental bronzes to contemporary art created from found objects. On Main Street, you'll find primarily cowboy art, both traditional and contemporary, while on North Marshall Way, you'll discover much more imaginative and daring contemporary art.

In addition to the galleries listed here, you'll usually find a huge tent full of art along Scottsdale Road in north Scottsdale. The annual **Celebration of Fine Art** (*C* **480/443-7695;** www.celebrateart.com) takes place each year between mid-January and late March. Not only will you get to see the work of 100 artists, but on any given day, you'll also find dozens of the artists at work on the premises. Admission is $7 for adults and $6 for seniors. Call or check the website for this year's location and hours of operation.

Art One   This gallery specializes in works by art students and other area cutting-edge artists. The works here can be surprisingly good, and prices are very reasonable. 4120 N. Marshall Way, Scottsdale. *C* **480/946-5076.** www.artonegalleryinc.com.

Chiaroscuro   With two other galleries in Santa Fe, this is one of the Southwest's premier contemporary art galleries. 7160 Main St., Scottsdale. *C* **480/429-0711.** www.chiaroscurosantafe.com.

gallerymateria   Representing emerging artists from the Americas, Asia, and Europe, this fascinating gallery focuses on contemporary fine crafts, including furniture, ceramics, and jewelry. 4222 N. Marshall Way, Scottsdale. *C* **480/949-1262.** www.gallerymateria.com.

Hollywood Cowboy   If you believe that nothing says *cowboy* like an old Western movie, then be sure to check out the movie posters at this Cave Creek poster gallery. Old B Westerns are the specialty. 6070 Cave Creek Rd., Cave Creek. *C* **480/949-5646.**

Lisa Sette Gallery   If you aren't a fan of cowboy or Native American art, don't despair. Instead, drop by this gallery, which represents international and local artists working in a wide mix of media. 4142 N. Marshall Way, Scottsdale. *C* **480/ 990-7342.** www.lisasettegallery.com.

Meyer Gallery   This gallery is notable for its selection of Old West, landscape, and mood paintings by living Impressionists. Most interesting are the original paintings for the covers of Western pulp-fiction novels. 7173 E. Main St., Scottsdale. *C* **877/947-6372** or **480/947-6372.** www.meyergalleries.com.

Raymond E. Johnson's Overland Gallery of Fine Art   Traditional Western and Russian Impressionist paintings form the backbone of this gallery's fine collection. These are museum-quality works (prices sometimes approach $100,000) and definitely worth a look. However, this gallery also shows the angular Southwest landscapes of Ed Mell. 7155 Main St., Scottsdale. © 800/920-0220 or 480/947-1934. www.overlandgallery.com.

Riva Yares Gallery This is one of Scottsdale's largest and most respected contemporary art galleries and has a second location in Santa Fe. You may not have room in your car for the monumental sculptures sold here, but I'm sure they'll deliver one for you. If you're lucky, you might stumble on a show by George Segal, Milton Avery, or Fritz Scholder. 3625 Bishop Lane, Scottsdale. © 480/947-3251. www.rivayares.com.

Roberts Gallery The feathered masks and sculptures of Virgil Walker are the highlights here, and if you have an appreciation for fine detail work, you'll likely be fascinated by these pieces. Walker's annual show is held on Thanksgiving weekend. El Pedregal Festival Marketplace, 34505 N. Scottsdale Rd., Carefree. © 480/488-1088.

Wilde Meyer Gallery Brightly colored and playful are the norm at this gallery, which represents Linda Carter-Holman, a Southwestern favorite who does cowgirl-inspired paintings. There's also a Wilde Meyer gallery at 8777 N. Scottsdale Rd. (© 480/488-3200). 4142 N. Marshall Way, Scottsdale. © 480/945-2323.

BOOKS

Major chain bookstores in the area include **Borders,** at 2402 E. Camelback Rd., Phoenix (© 602/957-6660), 699 S. Mill Ave., Tempe (© 480/921-8659), and 4555 E. Cactus Rd., Phoenix (© 602/953-9699); and **Barnes & Noble,** at 10235 N. Metro Parkway E., Phoenix (© 602/678-0088), 4847 E. Ray Rd., Phoenix (© 480/940-7136), and 10500 N. 90th St., Scottsdale (© 480/391-0048).

The Poisoned Pen The store name and the police-style outline of a body on the floor should give you a clue as to what sort of bookstore this is. If you still haven't figured out that it specializes in mysteries, then maybe you should stick to other genres. 4014 N. Goldwater Blvd., Suite 101, Scottsdale. © 888/560-9919 or 480/947-2974. www.poisonedpen.com.

FASHION

In addition to the options mentioned below, there are lots of great shops in malls all over the city. Favorite destinations for upscale fashions include Biltmore Fashion Park, the Borgata of Scottsdale, El Pedregal Festival Marketplace, and Scottsdale Fashion Square. See "Malls & Shopping Centers," below, for details.

For cowboy and cowgirl attire, see "Western Wear," below.

Carole Dolighan The hand-painted, handwoven dresses, skirts, and blouses here abound in rich colors. Each is unique. At the Borgata, 6166 N. Scottsdale Rd., Scottsdale. © 480/922-0616.

Objects This eclectic shop carries hand-painted, wearable art both casual and dressy, along with unique artist-made jewelry, contemporary furnishings, and all kinds of delightful and unusual things. 8787 N. Scottsdale Rd., Scottsdale. © 480/994-4720. www.objectsgallery.com.

Uh Oh Uh Oh carries simple, tasteful, and oh-so-elegant (as well as Scottsdale hip) fashions, footwear, jewelry, and accessories. There's another store at La Mirada shopping center, 8900 E. Pinnacle Peak Rd., Scottsdale (© 480/515-0203). At Kierland Commons, 15210 N. Scottsdale Rd., Scottsdale. © 480/991-1618. www.uhohclothing.com.

GIFTS & SOUVENIRS

Arizona Highways If you've ever seen a copy of *Arizona Highways* magazine, you'll know what to expect from this gift shop in Old Towns Scottsdale—coffee-table books filled with gorgeous photos of Arizona, books about Arizona, local salsas, and all sorts of other Arizona-inspired gifts. 7235 E. First Ave. © 480/945-7261.

Bischoff's Shades of the West This is a one-stop shop for all things Southwestern. From T-shirts to regional foodstuffs, this sprawling store has it all. It carries good selections of candles, Mexican crafts, and wrought-iron cabinet hardware that can give your kitchen a Western look. 7247 Main St., Scottsdale. © 480/945-3289. www.shadesofthewest.com.

Sphinx Date Ranch Dates—either you love 'em or you hate 'em. No other fruit is as closely associated with the desert as these super-sweet little palm fruits. At this little shop just south of Old Town Scottsdale, you can buy all kinds of dates and date products. 3039 N. Scottsdale Rd., Scottsdale. © 800/482-3283 or 480/941-2261. www.sphinxdateranch.com.

GOLF

In Celebration of Golf Sort of a supermarket for golfers (with a touch of Disneyland thrown in), this amazing store sells everything from clubs and shoes to golf art and golf antiques. There are even unique golf cars on display in case you want to take to the greens in a custom car. A golf simulation room allows you to test out new clubs. An old club-maker's workbench, complete with talking mannequin, makes a visit to this shop educational as well as fun. Also at Kierland Commons, 15220 N. Scottsdale Rd. (© **480/948-1766**). At Scottsdale Seville, 7001 N. Scottsdale Rd., Suite 172, Scottsdale. © 800/310-9459 or 480/951-4444. www.celebrategolf.com.

JEWELRY

Cornelis Hollander Although this shop is much smaller and not nearly as dramatic as that of the nearby Jewelry by Gauthier store, the designs are just as cutting edge. Whether you're looking for classic chic or trendy modern designs, you'll find plenty to interest you here. There's a second store in north Scottsdale at 32607 N. Scottsdale Rd. (© **480/575-5583**). 4151 N. Marshall Way, Scottsdale. © 480/423-5000. www.cornelishollander.com.

Jewelry by Gauthier This elegant store sells the designs of the phenomenally talented Scott Gauthier. The stylishly modern pieces use precious stones and are miniature works of art. 4211 N. Marshall Way, Scottsdale. © 888/411-3232 or 480/941-1707. www.jewelrybygauthier.com.

Molina Boutique If you can spend as much on a necklace as you can on a Mercedes, then this is *the* place to shop for your baubles. Although you don't need an appointment, it's highly recommended. You'll then get personalized service as you peruse the Tiffany exclusives and high-end European jewelry. 3134 E. Camelback Rd. © 800/257-2695 or 602/955-2055. www.molinafinejewelers.com.

MALLS & SHOPPING CENTERS

Biltmore Fashion Park This open-air shopping plaza with garden courtyards is *the* place to be if shopping is your obsession. Storefronts bear the names of exclusive boutiques such as Gucci and Cartier. Saks Fifth Avenue and Macy's are the two anchors. There are also more than a dozen moderately priced restaurants here. 2502 E. Camelback Rd. (at 24th St.). ℂ 602/955-8400. www.shopbiltmore.com.

The Borgata of Scottsdale   Designed to resemble a medieval Italian village complete with turrets, stone walls, and ramparts, the Borgata is far and away the most architecturally interesting mall in the valley. It contains about 50 upscale boutiques, galleries, and restaurants. On Friday afternoons, there's live jazz. 6166 N. Scottsdale Rd. ℂ 480/998-1822. www.borgata.com.

El Pedregal Festival Marketplace   Located adjacent to the Boulders resort 30 minutes north of Old Scottsdale, El Pedregal is the most self-consciously Southwestern shopping center in the valley, and it's worth the long drive out just to see the neo–Santa Fe architecture. The shops offer high-end merchandise, fashions, and art. The Heard Museum also has a branch here. 34505 N. Scottsdale Rd., Carefree. ℂ 480/488-1072. www.elpedregal.com.

Kierland Commons   The urban-village concept of a shopping center—narrow streets, sidewalks, and residences mixed in with retail space—has been taking off all over the country. Here in Scottsdale, urban village has taken on Texas-size proportions, but despite the grand scale of this shopping center, it still has a great feel. You'll find Tommy Bahama, Ann Taylor Loft, Crate & Barrel, and even a few shops you may never have heard of before. 15210 N. Scottsdale Rd. ℂ 480/348-1577. www.kierlandcommons.com.

Scottsdale Fashion Square   Scottsdale has long been the valley's shopping mecca, and for years this huge mall has been the reason why. It now houses five major department stores—Nordstrom, Dillard's, Neiman Marcus, Macy's, and Robinsons-May—and smaller stores such as Eddie Bauer, J. Crew, and Louis Vuitton. E. Camelback and Scottsdale roads, Scottsdale. ℂ 480/990-7800. www.westcor.com.

The Shops at Gainey Village   This upscale shopping center is much smaller than Kierland Commons farther up Scottsdale Road, but is no less impressive, especially after dark when lights illuminate the tall palm trees. In addition to several women's clothing stores, there are a couple of great restaurants. N. Scottsdale and Doubletree Ranch roads. ℂ 480/998-1822.

NATIVE AMERICAN ARTS, CRAFTS & JEWELRY

Bischoff's at the Park   This museum-like store and gallery is affiliated with another Bischoff's right across the street (see "Gifts & Souvenirs," above). However, this outpost carries higher-end jewelry, Western-style home furnishings and clothing, ceramics, sculptures, books and music with a regional theme, and contemporary paintings. 3925 N. Brown Ave., Scottsdale. ℂ 480/946-6155. www.shadesof thewest.com.

Faust Gallery   Old Native American baskets and pottery, as well as old and new Navajo rugs, are the specialties at this interesting shop. It also sells Native

---

Finds **To Die for Chocolates**

Forget Godiva. If you really want to taste what a chocolate confection can achieve in the right hands, visit **Chocolates by Bernard Callebaut,** Kierland Commons, 15211 N. Kierland Blvd., Scottsdale ((ℂ **480/315-1002**). These chocolates are filled with flavored cream and other luscious delights. Just remember to eat them before the desert heat melts them.

American and Southwestern art, including ceramics, paintings, bronzes, and unusual sculptures. 7103 E. Main St., Scottsdale. ℂ 480/946-6345. www.faustgallery.com.

Gilbert Ortega Museum Gallery   You'll find Gilbert Ortega shops all over the valley, but this is the biggest and best. As the name implies, there are museum displays throughout the store. Jewelry is the main attraction, but there are also baskets, sculptures, pottery, rugs, paintings, and kachinas. 3925 N. Scottsdale Rd. ℂ 480/990-1808.

Heard Museum Gift Shop   The Heard Museum (see "Seeing the Sights," earlier in this chapter) has an astonishing collection of well-crafted and very expensive Native American jewelry, art, and crafts of all kinds. This is the best place in the valley to shop for Native American arts and crafts; you can be absolutely assured of the quality. Because the store doesn't have to charge sales tax, you'll save a bit of money. At the Heard Museum, 2301 N. Central Ave. ℂ 800/252-8344 or 602/252-8344. www.heard.org.

John C. Hill Antique Indian Art   While shops selling Native American art and artifacts abound in Scottsdale, few offer the high quality available in this tiny shop. Not only does the store have one of the finest selections of Navajo rugs in the valley, including quite a few older rugs, but there are also kachinas, superb Navajo and Zuni silver-and-turquoise jewelry, baskets, and pottery. 6962 E. First Ave., Scottsdale. ℂ 480/946-2910.

Old Territorial Shop   This is the oldest Indian arts-and-crafts store on Main Street and offers good values on jewelry, concha belts, kachinas, fetishes, pottery, and Navajo rugs. 7077 W. Main St., Scottsdale. ℂ 480/945-5432. www.oldterritorialshop.com.

River Trading Post   If you are a collector of Native American art or artifacts, don't miss this amazing shop. Not only are there high-quality Navajo rugs, but there are also museum-quality pieces of ancient Southwestern pottery. 7140 E. First Ave. ℂ 480/444-0001. www.rivertradingpost.com.

OUTLET MALLS & DISCOUNT SHOPPING

Arizona Mills   This huge mall in Tempe is on the cutting edge when it comes to shop-o-tainment. You'll find lots of name-brand outlets, a video arcade, a multiplex theater, and an IMAX theater. 5000 Arizona Mills Circle, Tempe. ℂ 480/491-9700. www.arizonamills.com. From I-10, take the Baseline Rd. east exit. From U.S. 60, exit Priest Dr. south.

My Sister's Closet   This is where the crème de la crème of Scottsdale's used clothing comes to be resold. You'll find such labels as Armani, Donna Karan, and Calvin Klein. Prices are pretty reasonable, too. Also at Town & Country shopping plaza, 2033 E. Camelback Road, Phoenix (ℂ 602/954-6080) and Desert Village, 23435 N. Pima Rd., Suite 171 (ℂ 480/419-6242). At Lincoln Village, 6204 N. Scottsdale Rd. (near Trader Joe's), Scottsdale. ℂ 480/443-4575. www.mysisters closet.com.

WESTERN WEAR

Az-Tex Hat Company   If you're looking to bring home a cowboy hat, this is a good place to get it. The small shop in Old Scottsdale offers custom shaping and fitting of both felt and woven hats. There's also a store at 15044 N. Cave Creek Rd., Phoenix (ℂ 602/971-9090). 3903 N. Scottsdale Rd., Scottsdale. ℂ 800/972-2116 or 480/481-9900. www.aztexhats.com.

Out West If the revival of 1950s cowboy fashions and interior decor has hit your nostalgia button, then you'll want to high-tail it up to this eclectic shop. All things Western are available, and the fashions are both beautiful and fun (although fancy and pricey). 7003 E. Cave Creek Rd., Cave Creek. ℰ 480/488-0180.

Saba's Western Stores Since 1927, this store has been outfitting Scottsdale's cowboys and cowgirls, visiting dude ranchers, and anyone else who wants to adopt the look of the Wild West. Call for other locations around Phoenix. 7254 Main St., Scottsdale. ℰ 480/949-7404. www.sabaswesternwear.com.

Sheplers Western Wear Although it isn't the largest Western-wear store in the valley, Sheplers is still sort of a department store of cowboy duds. If you can't find it here, it just ain't available in these parts. Other locations include 8999 E. Indian Bend Rd., Scottsdale (ℰ 480/948-1933); and 2643 E. Broadway Rd., Mesa (ℰ 480/827-8244). 9201 N. 29th Ave. ℰ 602/870-8085. www.sheplers.com.

Stockman's Cowboy & Southwestern Wear This is one of the oldest Western-wear businesses in the valley, although the store is now housed in a modern shopping plaza. You'll find swirly skirts, denim jackets, suede coats, and flashy cowboy shirts. Prices are reasonable and quality is high. 23587 N. Scottsdale Rd. (at Pinnacle Peak Rd.), Scottsdale. ℰ 480/585-6142.

11 Phoenix & Scottsdale After Dark

If you're looking for nightlife in the Valley of the Sun, you won't have to look hard, but you may have to drive quite a ways. Although much of the nightlife scene is centered on Old Scottsdale, Tempe's Mill Avenue, and downtown Phoenix, you'll find things going on all over.

The weekly *Phoenix New Times* tends to have the most comprehensive listings for clubs and concert halls. *The Rep Entertainment Guide,* in the Thursday edition of the *Arizona Republic,* also lists upcoming events and performances. *Get Out,* published by the *Tribune,* is another tabloid-format arts-and-entertainment publication that is available free around Scottsdale, Phoenix, and Tempe. Other publications to check for abbreviated listings are *Valley Guide Quarterly, Key to the Valley, Where Phoenix/Scottsdale,* and *Quick Guide Arizona,* all of which are free and can usually be found at hotels and resorts.

Tickets to many concerts, theater performances, and sporting events are available through **Ticketmaster** (ℰ 480/784-4444; www.ticketmaster.com), which has outlets at Wherehouse Records, Tower Records, Robinsons-May department stores, and Fry's Marketplace stores.

THE CLUB & MUSIC SCENE

Even if it were not in the middle of the desert, the Scottsdale club scene would be red hot. Packed into a couple of dozen blocks surrounding Old Town Scottsdale, near the corner of Camelback and Scottsdale roads, there are dozens of trendy dance clubs and chic bars. This is where the wealthy fashionistas (and the wannabes) come to party. The crowd is young, affluent, and beautiful. With all the beautiful people cruising around in Porsches and limousines, it's easy to think you're in L.A. Current red-hot nightspots include **Mist** and **Axis/Radius,** but there are always new places opening up in the neighborhood. Cruise along **Stetson Drive,** which is divided into two sections (east and west of Scottsdale Rd.) to find the latest hot spots.

While Scottsdale is the nexus of nightclubbing for the fashion conscious, the valley also has plenty of other clubs and bars for those who don't own Prada products. Other nightlife districts include Tempe's Mill Avenue and downtown Phoenix. This latter area comes into its own after basketball and baseball games and concerts at the America West Arena.

Mill Avenue in Tempe is a good place to wander around until you hear your favorite type of music. The bars and clubs here are mostly within walking distance of one another. Because Tempe is a college town, the crowd tends to be young and rowdy.

Downtown Phoenix is home to Symphony Hall, the Herberger Theater Center, and several sports bars. However, much of the action revolves around games and concerts at the America West Arena and Bank One Ballpark (BOB).

As we're sure you know if you're a denizen of any urban nightlife scene, clubs come and go. To find out what's hot, get a copy of the *New Times*. Many dance clubs in the Phoenix area are open only on weekends, so be sure to check what night the doors will be open. Bars and clubs are allowed to serve alcohol until 1am.

COMEDY & CABARET

The Tempe Improv   With the best of the national comedy circuit harassing the crowds and rattling off one-liners, the Improv is the valley's most popular comedy club. Dinner is served and reservations are advised. 930 E. University Dr., Tempe. © 480/921-9877. www.improvclubs.com. Cover $12–$20, plus 2-item minimum.

COUNTRY

Handlebar-J   We're not saying that this Scottsdale landmark is a genuine cowboy bar, but cowpokes do make this one of their stops when they come in from the ranch. You'll hear live git-down two-steppin' nightly; free dance lessons are given Wednesdays, Thursdays, and Sundays. 7116 E. Becker Lane, Scottsdale. © 480/948-0110. www.handlebarj.com. No cover to $4.

Rusty Spur Saloon   A small, rowdy, drinkin' and dancin' place frequented by tourists, this bar is a lot of fun, with peanut shells all over the floor, dollar bills stapled to the walls, and the occasional live act in the afternoon or evening. 7245 E. Main St., Old Scottsdale. © 480/425-7787. www.rustyspursaloon.com.

DANCE CLUBS & DISCOS

Axis/Radius   If you're looking to do a bit of celebrity-spotting, Axis is one of the best places in town to keep your eye out. Currently one of Scottsdale's hottest dance clubs and liveliest singles scenes, this two-story glass box is a boldly contemporary space with an awesome sound system. 7340 E. Indian Plaza (2 blocks east of Scottsdale Rd. and 1 block south of Camelback Rd.), Scottsdale. © 480/970-1112. Cover $7–$10.

Barcelona   It's big, it's beautiful, and it's busy. This is Scottsdale's premier supper club, and Thursday through Saturday nights, after the dinner crowd gives up its tables, Barcelona becomes one of the city's top dance spots. The crowd ranges primarily from 30s to 50s. 15440 Greenway-Hayden Loop. © 480/603-0370. www.barcelonadining.com. No cover to $10.

Buzz   In Scottsdale, folks like to think big. The resorts are big, the houses are big, the cars are big, the restaurants are big, and the nightclubs are big. Buzz is no exception and claims the largest dance floor in the valley and a monstrous sound-and-light system. Clientele is primarily of the barely legal persuasion. 10345 N. Scottsdale Rd. (at Shea Blvd.). © 480/991-3866. No cover to $10.

Club Rio   Popular primarily with students from ASU, which is just across the Tempe Town Lake, this club has a dance floor big enough for football practice. Music is primarily Top 40, alternative, and retro, and there are also plenty of live shows. 430 N. Scottsdale Rd., Tempe. ✆ **480/894-0533**. www.clubrio.com. Cover $7–$10.

Jetz Americana   Under the same management as the ever popular Axis/Radius, this restaurant/nightclub is currently one of the hottest spots in Scottsdale for the well dressed and the well-off. 10050 N. Scottsdale Rd. ✆ **480/948-2606**. No cover to $7.

MacAlpine's Restaurant and Soda Fountain   This is definitely not your typical dance club. By day, this 1928 soda fountain and diner is the city's most authentic place to get a root-beer float, but on Friday and Saturday nights, DJs spin classic swing tunes. There are dance lessons before the music starts at 8pm. The higher cover charge includes a buffet dinner and dance lessons. 2303 N. Seventh St. ✆ **602/262-5545**. Cover $8–$18.

Myst   Housed in the space that once held the immensely popular Sanctuary club, Myst appeals to the same perfectly dressed crowd that Sanctuary did before. The decor has changed a little, but it still *the* place to see and be seen in Scottsdale. 7340 E. Shoeman Lane, Scottsdale. ✆ **480/970-5000**. Cover $10.

Pepin   Fridays and Saturdays, a DJ plays Latin dance music from 9:30pm on at this small Spanish restaurant located in the Scottsdale Mall. Thursday through Saturday evenings, there are also live flamenco performances. 7363 Scottsdale Mall, Scottsdale. ✆ **480/990-9026**. Cover $7.

ROCK, BLUES & JAZZ
Char's Has the Blues   You wouldn't think to look at this little cottage, but it really does have those mean-and-dirty, low-down blues. All of the best blues brothers and sisters from around the city and around the country make the scene here. 4631 N. Seventh Ave., 4 blocks south of Camelback Rd. ✆ **602/230-0205**. www.chars hastheblues.com. Cover $1–$10.

A League of Our Own   The dinner club/jazz club is a concept that has taken off in a big way here in the valley, and this out-of-the-way spot is at the forefront. Wednesday through Saturday, there's live jazz by some of the best local musicians. At Uptown Plaza, Central Ave. and Camelback Rd. ✆ **602/265-2354**. www.league supperclub.com. No cover to $5.

The Rhythm Room   This blues club, long the valley's most popular, books quite a few national acts as well as the best of the local scene, and has a dance floor if you want to move to the beat. 1019 E. Indian School Rd. ✆ **602/265-4842**. www.rhythmroom.com. Cover $3–$20.

Sugar Daddy's   So you're used to cheap drinks and appetizers at happy hour, but how about live music? This place has rock and blues bands for happy hour on Fridays starting at 4pm, on Saturdays starting at 2pm, and for Sunday brunch; and it features live music most nights at 9pm. There's a huge patio as well. The crowd tends to be college age or slightly older. 3102 N. Scottsdale Rd. ✆ **877/570-0479** or 480/970-6556. www.sugardaddysaz.com. No cover to $2.

THE BAR, LOUNGE & PUB SCENE
AZ88   Located across the park from the Scottsdale Center for the Arts, this sophisticated bar/restaurant has a cool ambience that's just right for a cocktail before or after a performance. There's also a great patio area. 7353 Scottsdale Mall, Scottsdale. ✆ **480/994-5576**.

Bar Bianco 👤   Located downtown on Heritage Square, this little wine bar is in a restored historic home and is affiliated with Pizzeria Bianco, the tiny and ever-popular designer pizza place right next door. With candles burning in every room, this is a very romantic place for a drink. 609 E. Adams St. ℂ 602/528-3699.

Dos Gringos   When you don't fee like getting dressed up to go out on the town, this is a great choice. With its open-air bar, Dos Gringos is patterned after Mexican beach bars and can be loads of fun on a Saturday night. 4209 N. Craftsman Court, Scottsdale. ℂ 480/423-3800. www.dosgringosaz.com.

Durant's   In business for decades, Durant's has long been downtown Phoenix's favorite after-work watering hole with the old guard and has caught on with the young martini-drinking crowd as well. Through wine coolers, light beers, and microbrews, Durant's remained true to the martini and other classic cocktails. 2611 N. Central Ave. ℂ 602/264-5967. www.durantsfinefoods.com.

Four Peaks Brewing Company   Consistently voted the best brewpub in Phoenix, this Tempe establishment, housed in a former creamery, brews good beers and serves decent pub grub. A favorite of ASU students. There's a second brewpub in north Scottsdale at the corner of Hayden Road and Frank Lloyd Wright Boulevard (ℂ **480/991-1795**). 1340 E. Eighth St., Tempe. ℂ 480/303-9967. www.fourpeaks.com.

Hyatt Regency Scottsdale Lobby Bar 👤👤   The open-air lounge just below the main lobby of this posh Scottsdale resort sets a romantic stage for nightly live music (often flamenco or Caribbean steel drum music). Wood fires burn in patio fire pits, and the terraced gardens offer plenty of dark spots for a bit of romance. Be sure to try the house's fruit-infused vodkas. 7500 E. Doubletree Ranch Rd., Scottsdale. ℂ 480/991-3388.

Rula Bula 👤   The middle of the desert may seem like an odd place for an Irish pub, but Rula Bula has such an authentic feel that it's easy to imagine that it's damp and dreary outside. 401 S. Mill Ave., Tempe. ℂ 480/929-9500. www.rulabula.com.

Six 👤   There are those who frequent this posh bar just to see the look on newcomers' faces when they see the high-tech unisex bathrooms—the glass is transparent until you go inside! Currently Friday nights are retro night. 7310 E. Stetson Dr., Scottsdale. ℂ 480/663-6620.

T. Cook's 👤👤   If you aren't planning on having dinner at this opulent Mediterranean restaurant, at least stop by for a cocktail in the bar. With its mix of Spanish-colonial and 1950s tropical furnishings, this is as romantic a lounge as you'll find anywhere in the valley. You can also snuggle with your sweetie out on the patio by the fireplace. At the Royal Palms Resort & Spa, 5200 E. Camelback Rd. ℂ 602/808-0766.

WINE BARS

Cave Creek Coffee Co. & Wine Purveyors   Located way up north in the cow town of Cave Creek, this hip coffeehouse doubles as a lively wine bar. When I'm up in the Carefree/Cave Creek area, this is my favorite hangout. 6033 E. Cave Creek Rd., Cave Creek. ℂ 480/488-0603. www.cavecreekcoffee.com.

Kazimierz World Wine Bar 👤   Sort of a spacious speakeasy crossed with a wine cellar, this unmarked place, associated with the nearby Cowboy Ciao restaurant, offers the same wide selection of wines available at the restaurant. There's live jazz and dozens of wines by the glass. 7137 E. Stetson Dr., Scottsdale. ℂ 480/946-3004. www.kazbar.net.

Postino ★★ This immensely popular wine bar is located in the heart of the Arcadia neighborhood south of Camelback Road. Casual yet stylish, the bar has garage-style doors that roll up to expose the restaurant to the outdoors. Choose from a great selection of wines by the glass and a limited menu of European-inspired appetizers. 3939 E. Campbell Ave. (✆) 602/852-3939.

COCKTAILS WITH A VIEW
The Valley of the Sun has more than its fair share of spectacular views. Unfortunately, most of them are from expensive restaurants. All these restaurants have lounges, though, where for the price of a drink (and perhaps valet parking) you can sit back and ogle a crimson sunset and the purple mountains' majesty. Among the best choices are **Different Pointe of View,** at the Pointe Hilton Tapatio Cliffs Resort; **Rustler's Rooste,** at the Pointe South Mountain Resort; and **Top of the Rock,** at The Wyndham Buttes Resort.

The Squaw Peak Bar Can't afford the lifestyles of the rich and famous? Try just pulling up a comfortable chair and faking it for a while. For the cost of a couple of drinks, you can sink into a seat here at the Biltmore's main lounge and watch the sunset test its color palette on Piestewa Peak (formerly Squaw Peak). Alternatively, you can slide into a seat near the piano and let the waves of mellow jazz wash over you. At the Arizona Biltmore Resort & Spa, 2400 E. Missouri Ave. (✆) 602/955-6600.

Thirsty Camel Whether you've already made your millions or are still working your way up the corporate ladder, you owe it to yourself to spend a little time in the lap of luxury. You may never drink in more ostentatious surroundings than here at Charles Keating's Xanadu. The view is one of the best in the city. At The Phoenician, 6000 E. Camelback Rd. (✆) 480/941-8200.

SPORTS BARS
Alice Cooper'stown Sports and rock mix it up at this downtown restaurant/bar run by, you guessed it, Alice Cooper. The Bank One Ballpark is only a block away. See p. 136 for more information. 101 E. Jackson St. (✆) 602/253-7337. www.alicecooperstown.com. Most nights no cover; special shows up to $25.

Majerle's Sports Grill If you're a Phoenix Suns fan, you won't want to miss this sports bar located only a couple of blocks from the America West Arena, where the Suns play. Suns memorabilia covers the walls. 24 N. Second St. (✆) 602/253-0118. www.majerles.com.

McDuffy's With 70 TVs and two dozen beers on tap, this is a favorite of Sun Devils fans. 230 W. Fifth St. (a block off Mill Ave.), Tempe. (✆) 480/966-5600. www.mcduffys.com.

GAY & LESBIAN BARS & CLUBS
Ain't Nobody's Bizness Located in a small shopping plaza, this is the city's most popular lesbian bar, with pool tables and a smoke-free lounge. On weekends, the dance floor is usually packed. 3031 E. Indian School Rd. (✆) 602/224-9977. www.aintnobodysbizness-az.com.

Amsterdam This downtown Phoenix bar may not look like much from the outside, but through the doors, you'll find a classy spot that's known across the valley for its great martinis. Mondays feature martini specials and there's usually a female impersonator one night of the week. Other nights, there's live music or DJ dance music. 718 N. Central Ave. (✆) 602/258-6122. www.amsterdambar.com.

THE PERFORMING ARTS

Although downtown Phoenix claims the valley's greatest concentration of performance halls, including Symphony Hall, the Orpheum Theatre, and the Herberger Theater Center, there are major performing-arts venues scattered across the valley. No matter where you happen to be staying, you're likely to find performances being held somewhere nearby.

Calling these many valley venues home are such major companies as the Phoenix Symphony, Scottsdale Symphony Orchestra, Arizona Opera Company, Ballet Arizona, Center Dance Ensemble, Actors Theatre of Phoenix, and Arizona Theatre Company. Adding to the performances held by these companies are the wide variety of touring companies that make stops here throughout the year.

While you'll find box-office phone numbers listed below, you can also purchase most performing-arts tickets through **Ticketmaster** (© **480/784-4444;** www.ticketmaster.com). For sold-out shows, check with your hotel concierge, or try **Tickets Unlimited** (© **800/289-8497** or 602/840-2340; www.ticketsun limitedinc.com).

MAJOR PERFORMING-ARTS CENTERS

Phoenix's premier performance venue is **Symphony Hall,** 225 E. Adams St. (© **602/262-7272**), home to the Phoenix Symphony and the Arizona Opera Company. It also hosts touring Broadway shows and various other concerts and theatrical productions.

The **Orpheum Theatre,** 203 W. Adams St. (© **602/262-7272**), is the most elegant hall in the valley. The historic Spanish-colonial baroque theater was built in 1929, and at the time was considered the most luxurious theater west of the Mississippi. Today, its ornately carved sandstone facade stands in striking contrast to the glass-and-steel City Hall building, with which the theater shares a common wall.

Although it isn't the largest performance venue in town, the **Celebrity Theatre,** 440 N. 32nd St. (© **602/267-1600;** www.celebritytheatre.com), seems to be booking lots of great acts these days. With its revolving stage and no seat farther than 75 feet from the performers, this is a great place to catch the likes of James Brown, The Temptations, or Wynonna.

The **Dodge Theatre,** 400 W. Washington St. (© **602/379-2888;** www.dodge theatre.com), is another of Phoenix's major downtown performance halls and seats from 2,000 to 5,000 people. It books many top names in entertainment as well as Broadway shows and international touring companies.

The Frank Lloyd Wright–designed **ASU's Gammage Auditorium,** Mill Avenue and Apache Boulevard, Tempe (© **480/965-3434;** www.asugammage. com), on the Arizona State University campus, is at once massive and graceful. This 3,000-seat hall hosts everything from barbershop quartets to touring Broadway shows.

The **Scottsdale Center for the Arts,** 7380 E. Second St., Scottsdale (© **480/ 994-ARTS;** www.scottsdaleperformingarts.org), hosts a variety of performances and series, ranging from alternative dance to classical music. This center seems to get the best of the touring performers who come through the valley.

In Scottsdale, near the Borgata shopping center, you'll find ASU's **Kerr Cultural Center,** 6110 N. Scottsdale Rd. (© **480/596-2660;** www.asukerr.com), a tiny venue in a historic home. It offers up an eclectic season that includes music from around the world.

OUTDOOR VENUES & SERIES

Given the weather, it should come as no surprise that Phoenicians like to attend performances under the sun and stars.

The city's top outdoor venue is the **Cricket Pavilion,** a half-mile north of I-10 between 79th and 83rd avenues (© **602/254-7200;** http://cricket-pavilion.com). This 20,000-seat amphitheater is open year-round and hosts everything from Broadway musicals to rock concerts.

The **Mesa Amphitheater,** at University Drive and Center Road, Mesa (© **480/644-2560**), is a much smaller amphitheater that holds a wide variety of concerts in spring and summer, and occasionally other times of year as well.

Throughout the year, the **Scottsdale Center for the Arts,** 7380 E. Second St., Scottsdale (© **480/994-ARTS;** www.scottsdaleperformingarts.org), stages outdoor performances in the adjacent Scottsdale Amphitheater on the Scottsdale Civic Center Mall. The Sunday A'fair series runs from October to April, with free concerts from noon to 4:30pm on selected Sundays of each month. Performances range from acoustic blues to zydeco.

Two perennial favorites of valley residents take place in particularly attractive surroundings. The Music in the Garden concerts at the **Desert Botanical Garden,** 1201 N. Galvin Pkwy., in Papago Park (© **480/941-1225;** www.dbg.org), are held on Sundays between September and March. The season always includes an eclectic array of musical styles. Tickets are $16 and include admission to the gardens. Sunday brunch is served for an additional charge. There are also Friday night jazz concerts. Up on the north side of the valley, just outside Carefree, **El Pedregal Festival Marketplace,** 34505 N. Scottsdale Rd., Scottsdale (© **480/488-1072;** www.elpedregal.com) stages jazz, blues, and rock concerts on Thursday evenings from mid-April through mid-July. Tickets are $10 to $15. Other times of year, there is free live music on weekends from noon to 3pm.

Outdoor concerts are also held at various parks and plazas around the valley during the warmer months. Check local papers for listings.

CLASSICAL MUSIC, OPERA & DANCE

The **Phoenix Symphony** (© **800/776-9080** or 602/495-1999; www.phoenixsymphony.org), the Southwest's leading symphony orchestra, performs at Symphony Hall (tickets mostly run $20–$53), while the **Scottsdale Symphony Orchestra** (© **480/945-8071;** www.scotsymph.org) performs at the Scottsdale Center for the Arts (tickets go for $17–$20).

Opera buffs may want to see what the **Arizona Opera Company** (© **602/266-7464;** www.azopera.com) has scheduled. This company stages up to five operas, both familiar and more obscure, and splits its time between Phoenix and Tucson. Tickets cost $25 to $115. Performances are held at Symphony Hall.

Ballet Arizona (© **888/3-BALLET** or 602/381-1096; www.balletaz.org) will be performing at the Orpheum this year and stages both classical and contemporary ballets; tickets run $12 to $102. The **Center Dance Ensemble**

(*Moments* **Literary Lunch Break**

At downtown Phoenix's **Herberger Theater Center,** 222 E. Monroe St. (© **602/254-7399**), lunch break means the actors hit the stage while the audience grabs sandwiches. Between March and August, 30- to 45-minute plays are staged at noon on Tuesdays, Wednesdays, and Thursdays. Tickets are only $5, as are sandwiches.

(© 602/252-8497; www.centerdance.com), the city's contemporary dance company, stages several productions a year at the Herberger Theater Center. Tickets cost $20. Between September and April, **Southwest Arts & Entertainment** (© 602/482-6410) brings acclaimed dance companies and music acts from around the world to Phoenix, with performances staged primarily at the Orpheum. Tickets range from $18 to $45.

THEATER

With nearly a dozen professional companies and the same number of nonprofessional companies taking to the boards throughout the year, there is always some play being staged somewhere in the valley.

The **Herberger Theater Center,** 222 E. Monroe St. (© **602/254-7399;** www. herbergertheater.org), which is located downtown and vaguely resembles a Spanish colonial church, is the city's main venue for live theater. Its two Broadway-style theaters together host hundreds of performances each year, including productions by the **Actors Theatre of Phoenix (ATP)** and the **Arizona Theatre Company (ATC).** ATP (© 602/253-6701; www.atphx.org) tends to stage smaller, lesser-known off-Broadway-type works, with musicals, dramas, and comedies equally represented; tickets go for $20 to $44. The annual production of *A Christmas Carol* is always a big hit. ATC (© **602/256-6995;** www.aztheatre co.org) is the state theater company of Arizona and splits its performances between Phoenix and Tucson. Founded in 1967, it's the major force on the Arizona thespian scene. Productions range from world premieres to recent Tony award–winners to classics. Tickets run $20 to $51.

The **Phoenix Theatre,** 100 E. McDowell Rd. (© **602/254-2151;** www. phoenixtheatre.net), has been around for almost 80 years and stages a wide variety of productions; tickets are $25 to $32. If your interest lies in Broadway plays, see what **Broadway in Arizona** (© **480/965-3434;** www.broadwayacrossamer-ica.com/tempe) has scheduled. The series, focusing mostly on comedies and musicals, is held at the Gammage Auditorium in Tempe; tickets cost roughly $20 to $75. The **Theater League** (© **602/952-2881** or 602/262-7272; www. theaterleague.com) is another series that brings in Broadway musicals. Performances are held in the Orpheum Theatre, and tickets range from $33 to $43.

Scottsdale's small **Stagebrush Theatre,** 7020 E. Second St. (© **480/990-7405**), is a community theater that features tried-and-true comedies and musicals, with the occasional drama thrown in. Tickets are $18 to $20. The **Arizona Jewish Theatre Co.** (© 602/264-0402; www.azjewishtheatre.org), which stages plays by Jewish playwrights and with Jewish themes, performs at Playhouse on the Park, in the Viad Corporate Center, 1850 N. Central Ave. (at Palm Lane). Tickets range from $25 to $29.

CASINOS

Casino Arizona at Salt River   This is actually two separate operations that together comprise the most conveniently located casino in the area. They're both just off U.S. 101 on the east side of Scottsdale and offer plenty of slot machines, cards, and other games of chance. Of course, they've got a free shuttle, too. U.S. 101 and Indian Bend Rd., and U.S. 101 and McKellips Rd. © **480/850-7777.** www.casinoaz.com.

Fort McDowell Casino   Located about 45 minutes northeast of Scottsdale, this Indian casino is the oldest in the state, offering slot machines, poker, keno, bingo, and free shuttles from hotels around the valley. On Fort McDowell Rd. off Ariz. 87, 2 miles northeast of Shea Blvd., Fountain Hills. © **800/THE-FORT.** www.fortmcdowellcasino.com.

12 A Side Trip from Phoenix: The Apache Trail ⟨★⟨★

There isn't a whole lot of desert or history left in Phoenix, but only an hour's drive to the east you'll find quite a bit of both. The **Apache Trail,** a narrow, winding, partially gravel road that snakes its way around the north side of the Superstition Mountains, offers some of the most scenic desert driving in central Arizona. Along the way are ghost towns and legends, saguaros and century plants, ancient ruins and artificial lakes. You could easily spend a couple days traveling this route, though most people make it a day trip. Pick and choose the stops that appeal to you, and be sure to get an early start.

If you'd rather leave the driving to someone else, consider **Apache Trail Jeep Tours** (✆ 480/982-7661; www.apachetrailtours.com), which offers guided half-day and full-day tours of along the Apache Trail. This company also offers off-road adventures in the Superstition Mountains and Four Peaks area. Tours range in price from $70 to $165.

To start this drive, head east on U.S. 60 to the town of Apache Junction, and then go north on Ariz. 88. About 4 miles out of town, you'll come to **Goldfield Ghost Town,** a reconstructed gold-mining town (see "Wild West Theme Towns" under "Seeing the Sights," earlier in this chapter). Leave yourself plenty of time if you plan to stop here.

Not far from Goldfield is **Lost Dutchman State Park** (✆ 480/982-4485), where you can hike into the rugged Superstition Mountains and see what the region's gold seekers were up against. Springtime wildflower displays here can be absolutely gorgeous. Park admission is $6 per vehicle; a campground charges $12 per site.

Continuing northeast, you'll reach **Canyon Lake,** set in a deep canyon flanked by colorful cliffs and rugged rock formations. It's the first of three reservoirs you'll pass on this drive. The three lakes provide much of Phoenix's drinking water, without which the city would never have been able to grow as large as it is today. Here at Canyon Lake, you can go for a swim at the Acacia Picnic Area or the nearby Boulder Picnic Area, which is in a pretty side cove. You can also take a cruise on the *Dolly* **steamboat** (✆ 480/827-9144; www.dolly steamboat.com). A 90-minute jaunt on this reproduction paddle wheeler costs $15 for adults and $8.50 for children 6 to 12. Lunch and dinner cruises are also available, and there's a lakeside restaurant at the boat landing. But if you're at all hungry, try to hold out for nearby **Tortilla Flat** (✆ 480/984-1776; www.tortilla flataz.com), an old stagecoach stop with a restaurant, saloon, and general store. Don't miss the prickly-pear ice cream and frozen yogurt (guaranteed spineless).

A few miles past Tortilla Flat, the pavement ends and the truly spectacular desert scenery begins. Among the rocky ridges, arroyos, and canyons of this stretch of road, you'll see saguaro cacti and century plants (a type of agave that dies after sending up its flower stalk, which can reach heights of 15 ft.). Next you'll come to **Apache Lake,** which is not nearly as spectacular a setting as Canyon Lake, though it does have the **Apache Lake Marina and Resort** (✆ 928/467-2511; www.apachelake.com), with a motel, restaurant, general store, and campground. If you're inclined to turn this drive into an overnight trip, this would be a good place to spend the night. Room rates are $75 to $90; boat rentals are available.

Shortly before reaching pavement again, you'll see **Theodore Roosevelt Dam.** This dam, built in 1911, forms Roosevelt Lake and is the largest masonry dam in the world. However, a face-lift a few years ago hid the original masonry construction; it now looks much like any other concrete dam in the state.

Continuing on Ariz. 88, you'll next come to **Tonto National Monument** ⚑ (© **928/467-2241;** www.nps.gov/tont), which preserves some of the southernmost cliff dwellings in Arizona. These pueblos were occupied between about 1300 and 1450 by the Salado people and are some of the few remaining traces of this tribe, which once cultivated lands now flooded by Roosevelt Lake. The lower ruins are a half-mile up a steep trail from the visitor center, while getting to the upper ruins requires a 3-mile round-trip hike. The lower ruins are open daily year-round; the upper ruins are open November through April on guided tours. Tour reservations are required (reserve at least 2 weeks in advance). The park is open daily from 8am to 5pm (you must begin the lower ruin trail by 4pm); admission is $3.

Keep going on Ariz. 88 to the copper-mining town of **Globe.** Although you can't see the mines themselves, the tailings (remains of rock removed from the copper ore) can be seen piled high all around the town. Be sure to visit **Besh-Ba-Gowah Archaeological Park** ⚑ (© **928/425-0320**), on the eastern outskirts of town. This Salado Indian pueblo site has been partially reconstructed, and several rooms are set up to reflect the way they might have looked when they were first occupied about 700 years ago. For this reason, they're among the most fascinating ruins in the state. The grounds are open daily from 9am to 6pm but the museum closes at 5pm; admission is $3 for adults, $2 for seniors, and free for children 12 and under. To get here, head out of Globe on South Broad Street to Jesse Hayes Road.

From Globe, head west on U.S. 60. Three miles west of Superior, you'll come to **Boyce Thompson Arboretum** ⚑⚑, 37615 U.S. 60 (© **520/689-2811;** http://arboretum.ag.arizona.edu), dedicated to researching and propagating desert plants. This was the nation's first botanical garden established in the desert, and is set in two small but rugged canyons. From the impressive cactus gardens, you can gaze up at sun-baked cliffs before ducking into a forest of eucalyptus trees along the stream that runs through the arboretum. As you hike the miles of nature trails, watch for the two bizarre boojum trees. The arboretum is open daily from 8am to 5pm; admission is $6 for adults and $3 for children 5 to 12.

If after a long day on the road you're looking for a place to eat, stop in at **Gold Canyon Golf Resort,** 6100 S. Kings Ranch Rd., Gold Canyon (© **480/982-9090**), which has a good formal dining room and a more casual bar and grill.

13 En Route to Tucson

Driving southeast from Phoenix for about 60 miles will bring you to the Florence and Casa Grande area, where you can learn about Indian cultures both past and present and view the greatest concentration of historic adobe buildings in Arizona. To reach Florence, drive south on I-10 to Exit 185 (Ariz. 387) and head east. If you're continuing south toward Tucson from Florence, I suggest taking the scenic **Pinal Pioneer Parkway** (Ariz. 79), which was the old highway between Phoenix and Tucson before the interstate was built. Along the way, you'll see signs identifying desert plants and a memorial to silent-film star Tom Mix, who died in a car crash here in 1940.

WHAT TO SEE & DO IN FLORENCE

Florence, which is home to a large state prison, may at first glance seem to have little to recommend it, but closer inspection turns up nearly 140 buildings on the National Register of Historic Places. The majority of these buildings were constructed of adobe and originally built in the Sonoran style, a style influenced by

Spanish architectural ideas. Most buildings were altered over the years and now display aspects of various architectural styles popular during territorial days in Arizona. The current county courthouse, built in 1891, displays one of the oddest mixes of styles. The annual **Florence Historic Tour,** which takes place on the second Saturday in February, includes 16 historic buildings. Tickets are $10 for adults and $5 for children. To find out more about the tour and the town's many historic buildings, stop in at the **Greater Florence Chamber of Commerce Visitor Center,** 291 N. Bailey St. (© **800/437-9433** or 520/868-9433; www.florence az.org), in a historic 1891 bakery in the center of town.

McFarland State Historic Park   This historic park consists of the former Pinal County Courthouse, which was built in 1878. Inside the old adobe building, you'll see some rooms that re-create the days when this was the courthouse and others that are furnished as they were when this was a hospital. Exhibits focus on local lynchings and Florence's World War II POW camp.

Main and Ruggles sts. © **520/868-5216.** www.pr.state.az.us. Admission $3 adults, $1 children 7–13. Thurs–Mon 8am–5pm. Closed Christmas.

Pinal County Historical Museum   Before touring the town, stop in at this small museum to orient yourself and learn more about the history of the area. You can blame the presence of the prison for the macabre exhibit of hanging nooses and a gas-chamber chair. There's also a collection of Tom Mix memorabilia.

715 S. Main St. © **520/868-4382.** Admission by donation. Tues–Sat 11am–4pm; Sun noon–4pm. Closed mid-July to Aug.

ATTRACTIONS ALONG THE WAY

There are a couple of **factory-outlet shopping malls** in the town of Casa Grande, at exits 194 and 198 off I-10. They are only a short distance out of your way to the south if you're headed back to Phoenix.

Casa Grande Ruins National Monument ★★   Located outside the town of Coolidge not far from Florence, this national monument preserves one of the most unusual Indian ruins in the state. In Spanish, *Casa Grande* means "Big House," and that's exactly what you'll find. In this instance, the big house is the ruin of an earth-walled structure built 650 years ago by the Hohokam people. It is speculated that the building was once some sort of astronomical observatory, but this is not known for certain. Whatever the original purpose of the building, today it provides a glimpse of a style of ancient architecture rarely seen. Instead of using adobe bricks or stones, the people who built this structure used layers of hard-packed soil, which have survived the ravages of the weather and still stand in silent testament to the Hohokam's long-ago architectural endeavors. The Hohokam began farming the valleys of the Gila and Salt rivers about 1,500 years ago, and eventually built an extensive network of irrigation canals for watering their fields. By the middle of the 15th century, the Hohokam had abandoned both their canals and their villages and disappeared without a trace.

1100 Ruins Dr. (Ariz. 87, 1 mile north of Coolidge). © **520/723-3172.** www.nps.gov/cagr. Admission $3. Daily 8am–5pm. Closed Christmas.

Picacho Peak State Park ★★   Alternatively, if you're heading to Tucson by way of I-10, and it isn't too hot outside, consider a stop at this state park, 35 miles northwest of Tucson at Exit 219. Picacho Peak, a wizard's cap of rock rising 1,500 feet above the desert, is a visual landmark for miles around. Hiking trails lead around the lower slopes of the peak and up to the summit; these trails are especially popular in spring, when the wildflowers bloom (the park is known as one of the best places in Arizona to see wildflowers). In addition to its natural beauty, Picacho Peak was the site of the only Civil War battle to take place in the state. Each March, Civil War reenactments are staged here. Campsites in the park cost $12 to $22.

Exit 219 off I-10. ℭ **520/466-3183.** www.pr.state.az.us. Admission $6 per car. Daily 8am–10pm.

14 En Route to Northern Arizona

If your idea of a great afternoon is searching out deals at factory-outlet stores, then you'll be in heaven at the **Outlets at Anthem,** 4250 W. Anthem Way (ℭ **888/482-5834** or 623/465-9500; www.outletsanthem.com). Among the offerings are Ann Taylor, Geoffrey Beene, Polo Ralph Lauren, and Levi's. Take Exit 229 (Anthem Way) off I-17.

Some 13 miles farther north is the town of Rock Springs, which is barely a wide spot in the road and is easily missed by drivers roaring up and down I-17. However, if you're a fan of pies, then do *not* miss Exit 242. Here you'll find the **Rock Springs Cafe** (ℭ **623/374-5794**), in business since 1920. Although this aging, nondescript building looks like the sort of place that would best be avoided, the packed parking lot says different. Why so popular? It's not the "hogs in heat" barbecue or the Bradshaw Mountain oysters. No, what keeps this place packed are Penny's pies, the most famous in Arizona. Every year, this places sells tens of thousands of pies. If one slice isn't enough, order a whole pie to go.

If you appreciate innovative architecture, don't miss the Cordes Junction exit (Exit 262) off I-17. Here you'll find **Arcosanti** (ℭ **928/632-7135;** www.arcosanti.org), Italian architect Paolo Soleri's vision of the future—a "city" that merges architecture and ecology. Soleri, who came to Arizona to study with Frank Lloyd Wright at Taliesin West, envisions a compact, energy-efficient city that disturbs the natural landscape as little as possible—and that's just what's rising out of the desert here at Arcosanti. The organic design built of cast concrete will fascinate both students of architecture and those with only a passing interest in the discipline. Arcosanti has been built primarily with the help of students and volunteers who live here for various lengths of time. To help finance the construction, Soleri designs and sells wind bells cast in bronze or made of ceramic. These distinctive bells are available at the gift shop. Arcosanti is open daily from 9am to 5pm, and tours are held hourly between 10am and 4pm ($8 suggested donation). If you'd like to stay overnight, there are basic accommodations ($25–$75 double) available by reservation (ℭ **928/632-6217**). You'll also find a cafe on the premises.

In 2000, some 71,000 acres of land east of I-17 between Black Canyon City and Cordes Junction were designated the **Agua Fria National Monument,** which is administered by the Bureau of Land Management, Phoenix Field Office, 21605 N. Seventh Ave., Phoenix (ℭ **623/580-5500;** www.az.blm.gov/aguafria/pmesa.htm). The monument was created to protect the region's numerous prehistoric Native American ruin sites, which date from between A.D. 1250 and 1450 (at least 450 prehistoric sites are known to exist in this area). There is very limited access to the monument, and there are no facilities for visitors. If you'd like to assist with the mapping and recording of archaeological sites here, contact **Archaeological Adventures** (ℭ **623/465-1981;** www.archaeologicadventures.com), which charges $169 per person for a day of documenting unexplored prehistoric sites in the area.

5

Central Arizona

Let's say you're planning a trip to Arizona. You're going to fly into Phoenix, rent a car, and head north to the Grand Canyon. Glancing at a map of the state, you might easily imagine that there's nothing to see or do between Phoenix and the Grand Canyon. This is the desert, right? Miles of desolate wasteland, that sort of thing. Wrong!

Between Phoenix and the Grand Canyon lies one of the most beautiful landscapes on earth, the red-rock country of Sedona. But don't get the idea that Sedona is some sort of wilderness waiting to be discovered. Decades ago, Hollywood came to Sedona to shoot Westerns; then came the artists and the retirees and the New Agers. Now it seems Hollywood is back, but this time the stars are building huge homes in the hills. There's even talk of Sedona becoming the next Aspen, albeit without a ski slope (although there is a ski area not too far away on the other side of Flagstaff).

Central Arizona isn't just red rock and retirees, though. It also has the former territorial capital of Prescott, historic sites, ancient Indian ruins, an old mining town turned artists' community, even a few good old-fashioned dude ranches out Wickenburg way. There are, of course, thousands of acres of cactus-studded desert, but there are also high mountains, cool pine forests, and a fertile river valley, appropriately named the Verde (Green) Valley. And north of Sedona's red rocks is Oak Creek Canyon, a tree-shaded cleft in the rocks with one of the state's most scenic stretches of highway running through it.

If you should fall in love with this country, don't be too surprised. People have been drawn to the region for hundreds of years. The Hohokam people farmed the fertile Verde Valley as long ago as A.D. 600, followed by the Sinagua. Although the early tribes had disappeared by the time the first white settlers arrived in the 1860s, Apache and Yavapai tribes did inhabit the area. It was to protect settlers from these hostile tribes that the U.S. Army established Fort Verde here in 1871.

When Arizona became a U.S. territory in 1863, Prescott was chosen as its capital, due to its central location. Although the town would eventually lose that title to Tucson and then to Phoenix, it was the most important city in Arizona for part of the late 19th century. Wealthy merchants and legislators rapidly transformed this pioneer outpost into a beautiful town filled with stately Victorian homes surrounding an imposing county courthouse.

Settlers were lured to this region not only by fertile land but also by the mineral wealth that lay hidden in the ground. Miners founded a number of communities in central Arizona, among them Jerome. When the mines shut down, Jerome was almost completely abandoned, but now artists and craftspeople have moved in to reclaim and revitalize the old mining town.

In the middle of the 20th century, it was sunshine and a chance to ride the range that lured people to central Arizona, and many of those visitors headed to Wickenburg. Once called the dude-ranch capital of the world, Wickenburg still clings to its Western roots and has restored much of its downtown to its 1880s appearance. It is here you'll find most of the region's few remaining dude ranches, which now call themselves "guest ranches."

1 Wickenburg

53 miles NW of Phoenix; 61 miles S of Prescott; 128 miles SE of Kingman

Once known as the dude-ranch capital of the world, the town of Wickenburg, located in the desert northwest of Phoenix, attracted celebrities and families from all over the country. Those were the days when the West had only just stopped being wild, and spending the winter in Arizona was an adventure, not just a chance to escape winter weather. Today, although the area has only a handful of dude (or guest) ranches still in business, Wickenburg clings to its Wild West image. The dude ranches that remain range from rustic to luxurious, but a chance to ride the range is still the area's main attraction.

Wickenburg lies at the northern edge of the Sonoran Desert on the banks of the Hassayampa River, one of the last free-flowing rivers in the Arizona desert. The town was founded in 1863 by Prussian gold prospector Henry Wickenburg, who discovered what would eventually become the most profitable gold and silver mine in Arizona: the Vulture Mine. The mine closed in 1942 and is now operated as a tourist attraction.

When the dude ranches flourished back in the 1920s and 1930s, Wickenburg realized that visitors wanted a taste of the Wild West, so the town gave the tenderfoots what they wanted—trail rides, hayrides, cookouts, the works. Wickenburg has even preserved one of its downtown streets much as it may have looked in 1900. If you've come to Arizona searching for the West the way it used to be, Wickenburg is a good place to look. Just don't expect staged shootouts in the streets—this ain't Tombstone.

ESSENTIALS

GETTING THERE   From Phoenix, take U.S. 60. From Prescott, take Ariz. 89. If you're coming from the west, take U.S. 60 from I-10. U.S. 93 comes down from I-40 in northwestern Arizona.

VISITOR INFORMATION   Contact the **Wickenburg Chamber of Commerce,** 216 N. Frontier St. (© **800/942-5242** or 928/684-0977; www.outwickenburgway.com). Their visitor center is open Monday through Friday from 9am to 5pm, Saturday from 9am to 2pm, and Sunday from 10am to 3pm.

SPECIAL EVENTS   **Gold Rush Days,** held on the second full weekend in February, is the biggest festival of the year in Wickenburg and has been for more than 55 years. Events include gold panning, a rodeo, and shootouts in the streets. On the second full weekend in November, the **Bluegrass Festival** features contests for fiddle and banjo. On the first weekend in December, Wickenburg holds its annual **Cowboy Poetry Gathering,** with lots of poetry and music.

EXPLORING THE AREA
A WALK AROUND TOWN

While Wickenburg's main attractions remain the guest ranches outside of town, a walk around downtown also provides a glimpse of the Old West. Most of the buildings here were built between 1890 and the 1920s (although a few are older), and although not all of them look their age, there is just enough Western character to make a stroll worthwhile (if it's not too hot).

Tips **Wickenburg After Dark**

These days, stargazing and telling stories around the campfire aren't the only things to do after dark. The **Del E. Webb Center for the Performing Arts,** 1090 S. Vulture Mine Rd. (*Ⓒ* **928/684-6624**), now brings a wide range of cultural performances to a town that once knew only horse operas.

The old **Santa Fe train station** is now the Wickenburg Chamber of Commerce, where you can pick up a map that tells a bit about the history of the buildings. The brick **post office,** almost across the street from the train station, once had a ride-up window providing service to people on horseback. **Frontier Street** is preserved as it looked in the early 1900s. The covered sidewalks and false fronts are characteristic of frontier architecture; the false fronts often disguised older adobe buildings that were considered "uncivilized" by settlers from back east. The oldest building in town is the **Etter General Store,** adjacent to the Homestead Restaurant. The adobe-walled store was built in 1864 and has long since been disguised with a false wooden front.

Two of the town's most unusual attractions aren't buildings at all. The **Jail Tree,** behind the Circle K convenience store at the corner of Wickenburg Way and Tegner Street, is an old mesquite tree that served as the local hoosegow. Outlaws were simply chained to the tree. Their families would often come to visit and have a picnic in the shade of the tree. The second, equally curious, town attraction is the **Wishing Well,** which stands beside the bridge over the Hassayampa. Legend has it that anyone who drinks from the Hassayampa River will never tell the truth again. How it became a wishing well is unclear.

You'll also find several decent art galleries around town. The **Helen Voehl Gallery,** 172 N. Washington St. (*Ⓒ* **928/684-5088**), across the railroad tracks from the chamber of commerce, has colorful and whimsical art and crafts ranging from baskets made of old lariats to hand-painted clothing. The **Gold Nugget Art Gallery,** 274 E. Wickenburg Way (*Ⓒ* **928/684-5849;** www.goldnuggetart gallery.com), is in the oldest building in town (built in 1863) and features the works of more than 30 regional artists.

MUSEUMS & MINES

Desert Caballeros Western Museum ★★ Wickenburg thrives on its Western heritage, and inside this museum you'll find an outstanding collection of Western art depicting life on the range, including works by Albert Bierstadt, Charles Russell, Thomas Moran, Frederick Remington, Maynard Dixon, and other members of the Cowboy Artists of America. The Hays "Spirit of the Cowboy" collection is an impressive display of historical cowboy gear that alone makes this museum worth a stop.

21 N. Frontier St. *Ⓒ* 928/684-2272. www.westernmuseum.org. Admission $6 adults, $4.50 seniors, $1 children 6–16. Mon–Sat 10am–5pm; Sun noon–4pm. Closed New Year's Day, Easter, July 4th, Thanksgiving, and Christmas.

Robson's Arizona Mining World Boasting the world's largest collection of antique mining equipment, this private museum is a must for anyone fascinated by Arizona's rich mining history. Located on the site of an old mining camp and with the feel of a ghost town, this museum consists of 26 buildings filled with antiques and displays. In addition to touring the museum, you can pan for gold

Central Arizona

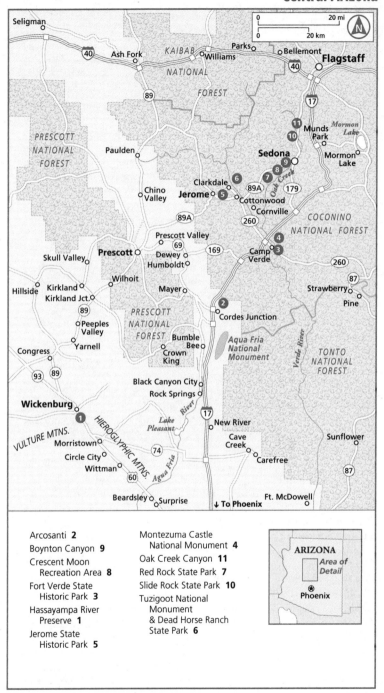

Arcosanti **2**
Boynton Canyon **9**
Crescent Moon
    Recreation Area **8**
Fort Verde State
    Historic Park **3**
Hassayampa River
    Preserve **1**
Jerome State
    Historic Park **5**

Montezuma Castle
    National Monument **4**
Oak Creek Canyon **11**
Red Rock State Park **7**
Slide Rock State Park **10**
Tuzigoot National
    Monument
    & Dead Horse Ranch
    State Park **6**

ARIZONA
Area of
Detail
Phoenix

or hike through the desert to see Native American petroglyphs. Also here on the property, you'll find Litsch's Bed & Breakfast (charging $85–$105 double; no credit cards accepted) and a restaurant.

Ariz. 71, 28 miles west of Wickenburg. © 928/685-2609. www.robsonsminingworld.com. Admission $5 adults, $4.50 seniors, free for children under 10. Oct–Apr Mon–Fri 10am–4pm, Sat–Sun 9am–5pm. Closed May–Sept. Head west out of Wickenburg on U.S. 60 and, after 24 miles, turn north on Ariz. 71.

The Vulture Mine *Kids*   Lying at the base of Vulture Peak (the most visible landmark in the Wickenburg area), the Vulture Mine was first staked by Henry Wickenburg in 1863, fueling the small gold rush that helped populate this section of the Arizona desert. Today, the Vulture Mine has the feel of a ghost town, and though you can't go down into the old mine itself, you can wander around among the aboveground shacks and mine structures on a self-guided tour or, by prior arrangement, a guided tour. Mildly interesting for those who appreciate old mines, and fun for kids.

Vulture Mine Rd. © 602/859-2743. Admission $7 adults, $6 seniors, $5 children 6–12. Fri–Sun 8am–4pm. Closed Aug. Take U.S. 60 west out of town, turn left on Vulture Mine Rd., and drive 12 miles south.

A BIRDER'S PARADISE

Hassayampa River Preserve ★   At one time the Arizona desert was laced with rivers that flowed for most, if not all, of the year. In the past 100 years, however, these rivers, and the riparian habitats they once supported, have disappeared at an alarming rate due to the damming of rivers and the lowering water tables caused by wells. Riparian areas support trees and plants that require more water than is usually available in the desert, and this lush growth provides food and shelter for hundreds of species of birds, mammals, and reptiles. Today, the riparian cottonwood-willow forests of the desert Southwest are considered the country's most endangered forest type.

The Nature Conservancy, a nonprofit organization dedicated to purchasing and preserving threatened habitats, owns and manages the Hassayampa River Preserve, which is now one of the state's most important bird-watching sites (more than 230 species of birds have been spotted here). Nature trails lead along the river beneath cottonwoods and willows and past the spring-fed Palm Lake. On-site are a visitor center and bookshop. Free naturalist-guided walks are offered on the last Saturday of the month at 8:30am (reservations required).

49614 U.S. 60 (3 miles southeast of Wickenburg on U.S. 60). © 928/684-2772. www.nature.org. Suggested donation $5 (free for Nature Conservancy members). Mid-Sept to mid-May Wed–Sun 8am–5pm; mid-May to mid-Sept Fri–Sun 8am–5pm. Closed major holidays.

OUTDOOR PURSUITS

If you're staying at a guest ranch, you'll likely get in plenty of time on horseback. But even if you aren't doing the dude-ranch thing, you can do a bit of riding with **Trails West** (© **928/684-2600**), which charges $20 for a 1-hour ride and $35 for a 2-hour ride. Make reservations a day in advance.

If you're in the area for more than a day or just can't spend another minute in the saddle, you can get out on a Jeep tour and explore the desert backcountry, visit Vulture Peak, see some petroglyphs, or check out old mines. Call **B.C. Jeep Tours** (© **928/684-7901** or 928/684-4982), which charges $50. However, if you've got time for only one Jeep tour on your Arizona vacation, make it in Sedona.

Los Caballeros Golf Club, 1551 S. Vulture Mine Rd. (© **928/684-2704**), has been rated one of the best courses in the state. Greens fees are about $120 in peak season and $30 in summer.

Hikers have a couple of interesting options. Southwest of town at the end of Vulture Mine Road (off U.S. 60), you can climb **Vulture Peak,** a steep climb best done in the cooler months. The views from up top (or even just the saddle near the top) are well worth the effort.

WHERE TO STAY
GUEST RANCHES

Flying E Ranch *Kids*   This is a working cattle ranch with 20,000 high, wide, and handsome acres for you and the cattle to roam. Family owned since 1952, the Flying E attracts plenty of repeat business, with families finding it a particularly appealing and down-home kind of place. The main lodge features a spacious lounge where guests like to gather by the fireplace. Accommodations vary in size, but all have Western-style furnishings and either twin or king-size beds. Three family-style meals are served in the wood-paneled dining room, but there's no bar, so you'll need to bring your own liquor. Also available are breakfast cookouts, lunch rides, and evening chuck-wagon dinners.

2801 W. Wickenburg Way, Wickenburg, AZ 85390. © 888/684-2650 or 928/684-2690. Fax 928/684-5304. www.flyingeranch.com. 17 units. $250–$315 double. Rates include all meals. 2- to 4-night minimum stay. MC, V. Closed May–Oct. Drive 4 miles west of town on U.S. 60. **Amenities:** Dining room; outdoor pool; tennis court; exercise room; Jacuzzi; sauna; massage; horseback riding (extra $30–$40 per person per day); horseshoes; lawn games; hayrides; guest rodeos. *In room:* A/C, TV, fridge.

Kay El Bar Guest Ranch   This is the smallest and oldest of the Wickenburg guest ranches, and its adobe buildings, built between 1914 and 1925, are listed on the National Register of Historic Places. The well-maintained ranch is quintessentially Wild West in style (old telegraph poles have been used as exposed cross beams in the ceiling of the main lodge). The setting, on the bank of the (usually dry) Hassayampa River, lends the ranch a surprisingly lush feel compared with the arid surrounding landscape. While the cottage and the Casa Grande room are the most spacious, the smaller rooms in the adobe main lodge have original Monterey-style furnishings and other classic 1950s dude-ranch decor. The ranch has only 60 acres, but it abuts thousands of acres of public lands where guests can ride or hike. The tile floor and beehive fireplace in the dining room provide an authentic Southwestern feel. Meals often feature mesquite-grilled meats and seafood.

Rincon Rd., off U.S. 93 (P.O. Box 2480), Wickenburg, AZ 85358. © 800/684-7583 or 928/684-7593. Fax 928/684-4497. www.kayelbar.com. 11 units. $325 double; $700 cottage for 4. Rates do not include 15% service charge. Rates include all meals and horseback riding. 2- to 4-night minimum stay. Children 3 and under stay free in parent's room. MC, V. Closed May to mid-Oct. **Amenities:** Dining room; lounge; small outdoor pool; Jacuzzi; horseback riding; massage. *In room:* Hair dryer, no phone.

Rancho de los Caballeros   Located on 20,000 acres 2 miles west of Wickenburg, Rancho de los Caballeros is part of an exclusive country club–resort community and as such feels more like an exclusive resort than a guest ranch. However, the main lodge itself, with its flagstone floor, copper fireplace, and colorfully painted furniture, has a very Southwestern feel. Peace and quiet are the keynotes of a visit here, and most guests focus on golf (the golf course is one of the best in the state) and horseback riding. In addition, the ranch offers skeet and trap shooting, Jeep tours, hot-air balloon rides, and guided nature walks. Bedrooms are filled with handcrafted furnishings, exposed-beam ceilings, Indian rugs, and, in some, tile floors and fireplaces. While breakfast and lunch are quite casual, dinner is more formal, with proper attire required. After dinner, you can catch a little cowboy music in the ranch's saloon.

1551 S. Vulture Mine Rd. (off U.S. 60 west of town), Wickenburg, AZ 85390. ℭ **800/684-5030** or 928/684-5484. Fax 928/684-9565. www.SunC.com. 79 units. Late Oct to Jan and early May $370–$424 double, $460 suite; Feb–Apr $426–$496 double, $558 suite. Rates do not include 15% gratuity charge. Rates include all meals. Riding and golf packages available. Children under 5 stay free in parent's room. No credit cards. Closed mid-May to mid-Oct. **Amenities:** Dining room; lounge; small outdoor pool; 18-hole golf course; 4 tennis courts; exercise room; bike rentals; children's programs; concierge; business center; massage; babysitting; laundry service; horseback riding ($35–$55 per ride). *In room:* A/C, TV, dataport, hair dryer, iron.

OTHER ACCOMMODATIONS

Best Western Rancho Grande   Located in the heart of downtown Wickenburg, this place was built in Spanish colonial style, with tile roofs, stucco walls, arched colonnades, and tile murals. There's a wide range of room types—the more you pay, the bigger things get (larger room, larger bathroom). The property is within walking distance of good restaurants and the town's historic sites.

293 E. Wickenburg Way, Wickenburg, AZ 85390. ℭ **800/854-7235** or 928/684-5445. Fax 928/684-7380. www.bwranchogrande.com. 80 units. Oct–Apr $73–$121 double; May–Sept $69–$107 double. Rates include continental breakfast. AE, DC, DISC, MC, V. Pets accepted. **Amenities:** Outdoor pool; tennis court; Jacuzzi; children's playground; business center; dry cleaning. *In room:* A/C, TV, dataport, fridge, coffeemaker, hair dryer, iron.

WHERE TO DINE

Get a quick salad, sandwich, or coffee right in the center of downtown at the friendly **Pony Espresso Café,** 233 E. Wickenburg Way (ℭ **928/684-0208**).

House Berlin GERMAN/CONTINENTAL   Wickenburg may seem like an unusual place for an authentic German restaurant, but that's exactly what you'll find right downtown. The place is small and casual and serves a mix of German and other Continental dishes. Local favorites include the Wiener schnitzel and sauerbraten.

169 E. Wickenburg Way. ℭ **928/684-5044**. Main courses $6.50–$12 lunch, $11–$16 dinner. MC, V. Tues 5–9pm; Wed–Sun 11:30am–2pm and 5–9pm.

Rancho de los Caballeros ★★ CONTINENTAL/SOUTHWESTERN Wickenburg's most exclusive guest ranch opens its restaurant to the public. The menu, which changes daily, includes plenty of classic Continental dishes as well as some contemporary Southwestern fare. You might start with tortilla soup or creamy Sonoran chowder, and then move on to a center cut pork chop, slow-smoked over apple wood and then charbroiled. Dessert options may include crème brûlée or a homemade *cajeta* caramel sundae. Men are required to wear a sports jacket or Western vest, and women must also dress appropriately.

1551 S. Vulture Mine Rd. ℭ **928/684-5484**. Reservations required. Jackets required for men. Lunch $14–$16; complete dinner $29. No credit cards. Mon–Sat 12:30–1:30pm and 6:30–8:30pm; Sun noon–2pm and 6:30–8:30pm. Closed mid-May to mid-Oct.

EN ROUTE TO PRESCOTT

Between Wickenburg and Prescott, Ariz. 89 climbs out of the desert at the town of **Yarnell,** which lies at the top of a steep stretch of road. The landscape around Yarnell is a jumble of weather-worn granite boulders that give the town a unique appearance. Several little crafts and antiques shops here are worth a stop, but the town's main claim to fame is the **Shrine of St. Joseph of the Mountains,** which is known for its carved stone stations of the cross. Watch for the sign to the shrine as you drive through town.

2 Prescott

100 miles N of Phoenix; 60 miles SW of Sedona; 87 miles SW of Flagstaff

Prescott, the former territorial capital, is an Arizona anomaly; it doesn't seem like Arizona at all. With its stately courthouse on a tree-shaded square, its well-preserved historic downtown business district, and its old Victorian homes, Prescott wears the air of the quintessential American small town, the sort of place where the Broadway show *The Music Man* might have been staged. Prescott has just about everything a small town should have: an 1890s saloon (The Palace), an old cattlemen's hotel (Hassayampa Inn), a burger shop (Kendall's), a brewpub (Prescott Brewing Company), and a European-style cafe (Café St. Michael). Add to this several small museums, a couple of other historic hotels, the strange and beautiful landscape of the Granite Dells, and the nearby Prescott National Forest, and you have a town that appeals to visitors with a diverse range of interests.

The town's pioneer history dates from 1863, when the Walker party discovered gold in the mountains of central Arizona. Soon miners were flocking to the area to seek their own fortunes. A year later, Arizona became a U.S. territory, and the new town of Prescott, located right in the center of Arizona, was made the territorial capital. Prescott lost its statewide influence when the capital moved to Phoenix, but because of the importance of ranching and mining in central Arizona, Prescott continued to be a major regional town. Today, Prescott has become an upscale retirement community, as much for its historic heritage as for its mild year-round climate. In summer, Prescott is also a popular weekend getaway for Phoenicians, since it is usually 20° cooler here than it is in Phoenix.

ESSENTIALS

GETTING THERE   Prescott is at the junction of Ariz. 89, Ariz. 89A, and Ariz. 69. If you're coming from Phoenix, take the Cordes Junction exit (Exit 262) from I-17. From Flagstaff, the most direct route is I-17 to Ariz. 169 to Ariz. 69. From Sedona, just take Ariz. 89A all the way.

America West (© 800/235-9292) offers regularly scheduled flights between Prescott's Ernest A. Love Airport, on U.S. 89, and Phoenix's Sky Harbor Airport. **Shuttle "U"** (© 800/304-6114 or 928/442-1000; www.shuttleu.com) provides service to Prescott from Sky Harbor Airport for $26 one-way, $47 round-trip.

VISITOR INFORMATION   The **Prescott Chamber of Commerce** is at 117 W. Goodwin St. (© 800/266-7534 or 928/445-2000; www.prescott.org). The visitor center is open Monday through Friday from 9am to 5pm and Saturday and Sunday from 10am to 2pm.

ORIENTATION   Ariz. 89 comes into Prescott on the northeast side of town, where it joins with Ariz. 69 coming in from the east. Five miles north of town, Ariz. 89A from Sedona also merges with Ariz. 89. The main street into town is **Gurley Street,** which forms the north side of Courthouse Plaza. **Montezuma Street,** also known as Whiskey Row, forms the west side of the plaza. If you continue south on Montezuma Street, you'll be on Ariz. 89 heading toward Wickenburg.

GETTING AROUND   For car rentals, call **Enterprise** (© 800/RENT-A-CAR or 928/778-6506), or **Hertz** (© 800/654-3131 or 928/776-1399).

SPECIAL EVENTS   The **World's Oldest Rodeo** is Prescott's biggest annual event and is held in early July. In June, there's also **Territorial Days,** which includes special art exhibits, performances, tournaments, races, and lots of food and free entertainment. In mid-July, the Sharlot Hall Museum hosts the **Prescott Indian Art Market,** and on the third weekend in August, the **Arizona Cowboy Poets Gathering** takes place here as well. In December, the city is decked out with lights, and there are numerous holiday events.

EXPLORING THE TOWN

A walk around **Courthouse Plaza** should be your introduction to Prescott. The stately old courthouse in the middle of the tree-shaded plaza sets the tone for the whole town. The building, far too large for a small regional town such as this, dates from the days when Prescott was the capital of the Arizona territory. Under the big shade trees, you'll find several bronze statues of cowboys and soldiers.

Surrounding the courthouse and extending north for a block is Prescott's **historic business district.** Stroll around admiring the brick buildings, and you'll realize that Prescott was once a very important place. Duck into an old saloon or the lobby of one of the historic hotels, and you'll understand that the town was also part of the Wild West.

To learn more about the history of Prescott, contact **Melissa Ruffner** at **Prescott Historical Tours** (© 928/445-4567). Ms. Ruffner does her tours in Victorian costume and passes out copies of her book on the territorial history of Arizona. Tours cost $40 per couple.

Phippen Museum ⚐   If you're a fan of classic Western art, you won't want to miss this small museum. Located on a hill a few miles north of town, the Phippen exhibits works by both established Western artists and newcomers and is named after the first president of the prestigious Cowboy Artists of America organization. Also on display are artifacts and photos that help place the artwork in the context of the region's history. More than 100 Arizona artists are represented in the museum store. The **Phippen Museum Western Art Show & Sale** is held each year on Memorial Day weekend.

4701 U.S. 89 N. © 928/778-1385. www.phippenartmuseum.org. Admission $5 adults, $4 seniors, free for children under 12. Mon–Sat 10am–4pm; Sun 1–4pm. Closed Mon Jan–Memorial Day.

Sharlot Hall Museum ⚐   In 1882, at the age of 12, Sharlot Hall traveled to the Arizona territory with her parents. As an adult, she began collecting artifacts from Arizona's pioneer days, and from 1909 to 1911, she was the territorial historian. In 1928, she opened this museum in Prescott's Old Governor's Mansion, a log home built in 1864. In addition to the mansion, which is furnished much as it might have been when it was built, there are several other interesting buildings that can be toured. The Frémont House was built in 1875 for the fifth territorial governor. Its traditional wood-frame construction shows how quickly Prescott grew from a remote logging and mining camp into a civilized little town. The 1877 Bashford House reflects the Victorian architecture that was popular throughout the country around the send of the 19th century. The Sharlot Hall Building houses exhibits on Native American cultures and territorial Arizona. The museum's rose garden honors famous women of Arizona. Every year in early summer, artisans, craftspeople, and costumed exhibitors participate in the **Folk Arts Fair.**

At press time, the museum was preparing to open the **Fort Whipple Museum** north of town on U.S. 89 on the grounds of what is now a Veterans

Administration hospital. The museum will focus on the history of this fort, which was active from 1863 to 1922 and has many stately officers' homes.

415 W. Gurley St. ℂ **928/445-3122**. www.sharlot.org. Suggested donation $5 adults, $10 families. May–Sept Mon–Sat 10am–5pm, Sun 1–5pm; Oct–Apr Mon–Sat 10am–4pm. Closed New Year's Day, Thanksgiving, and Christmas.

The Smoki Museum   This interesting little museum, which houses a collection of Native American artifacts in a historic stone building, is named for the fictitious Smoki tribe. The tribe was dreamed up in 1921 by a group of non-Indians who wanted to inject some new life into Prescott's July 4th celebrations. Despite its phony origins, the museum contains genuine artifacts and basketry from many different tribes, mainly Southwestern. The museum also sponsors interesting lectures on Native American topics.

147 N. Arizona St. ℂ **928/445-1230**. www.smokimuseum.org. Admission $4 adults, $3 seniors, $2 students. Apr–Dec Mon–Sat 10am–4pm, Sun 1–4pm; Jan–Mar Fri–Sat and Mon 10am–4pm, Sun 1–4pm.

OUTDOOR PURSUITS

Prescott is situated on the edge of a wide expanse of high plains with the pine forests of **Prescott National Forest** at its back. There are hiking and mountain-biking trails, several lakes, and campgrounds within the national forest. My favorite hiking and biking areas are Thumb Butte (west of town) and the Granite Mountain Wilderness (northwest of town).

Thumb Butte, a rocky outcropping that towers over the forest just west of town, is Prescott's most readily recognizable natural landmark. A 1.2-mile trail leads nearly to the top of this butte, and from the saddle near the summit, there's a panoramic vista of the entire region. The trail itself is very steep, but paved much of the way. The summit of the butte is a popular rock-climbing spot. An alternative return trail makes a loop hike possible. To reach the trail head, drive west out of town on Gurley Street, which becomes Thumb Butte Road. Follow the road until you see the National Forest signs, after which there's a parking lot, picnic area, and trail head. Parking costs $2.

The Granite Basin Recreation Area provides access to the **Granite Mountain Wilderness.** Trails lead beneath the cliffs of Granite Mountain, where you might spot peregrine falcons. For the best views, hike 1.5 miles to Blair Pass and then on up the Granite Mountain trail as far as you feel like going. To reach this area, take Gurley Street west from downtown, turn right on Grove Avenue, and follow it around to Iron Springs Road, which will take you northwest out of town to the signed road for the Granite Basin Recreation Area (less than 8 miles from downtown).

Both of the above areas also offer mountain-biking trails. Although the scenery isn't as spectacular as in the Sedona area, the trails are great. You can rent a bike and get maps and specific trail recommendations at **Ironclad Bicycles,** 710 White Spar Rd. (ℂ **928/776-1755**), which charges $20 to $50 per day for mountain bikes.

For maps and information on these and other hikes and bike rides in the area, stop by the **Bradshaw Ranger Station,** 344 S. Cortez St. (ℂ **928/443-8000;** www.fs.fed.us/r3/prescott).

North of town 5 miles on Ariz. 89 is an unusual and scenic area known as the **Granite Dells.** Jumbled hills of rounded granite suddenly jut up from the landscape, creating a maze of huge boulders and smooth rock. In the middle of this dramatic landscape lies **Watson Lake,** the waters of which push their way in among the boulders to create one of the prettiest lakes in the state. On the highway side of the lake, you'll find Watson Lake Park (© 928/776-4336), which has picnic tables and great views. Weekends and holidays throughout the year (weather permitting), you can rent **canoes and kayaks** at the lake. Reservations aren't accepted, but you can call **Prescott Outdoors** (© 928/925-1410; www.prescottoutdoors.com), to make sure they'll be at the lake with their boats.

For hiking in the Watson Lake, I recommend heading to the **Peavine Trail.** To find the trail head, turn east onto Prescott Lake Parkway, which is between Prescott and the Granite Dells, and then turn left onto Sun Dog Ranch Road. This rails-to-trails path extends for several miles through the middle of the Granite Dells and is the best way to fully appreciate the Dells (you'll be away from both people and the highway). Although this is fascinating, easy hike, it also makes a great, equally easy, mountain-bike ride. Also accessible from this same trail head is the **Watson Woods Riparian Preserve,** which has some short trails through the wetlands and riparian zone along Granite Creek. For information, contact **Prescott Parks & Recreation** (© 928/777-1122).

A couple of miles west of Watson Lake, you can hike in the recently opened **Willow Creek Park,** 3181 Willow Creek Rd. (© 928/445-1734), where several miles of trails lead through grasslands and groves of huge cottonwood trees adjacent to Willow Lake. The trails eventually lead to the edge of the Granite Dells. There's great bird-watching in the trees in this park, and there are even great blue heron and cormorant rookeries.

If you want to explore the area on horseback, try **Granite Mountain Stables** (© 928/771-9551), which offers guided trail rides in the Prescott National Forest. A 1-hour ride is $35.

Reasonably priced golf is available at the **Antelope Hills Golf Course,** 1 Perkins Dr. (© 928/776-7888). Greens fees range from $29 to $55.

SHOPPING

Downtown Prescott is filled with antiques stores, especially along North Cortez Street. In the Hotel St. Michael's shopping arcade, check out **Hotel Trading,** 110 S. Montezuma St. (© 928/778-7276), which carries some genuine Native American artifacts at reasonable prices. Owner Ernie Lister also makes silver jewelry in the style of 19th-century Navajo jewelry. On this same block are both the **Arts Prescott Cooperative Gallery,** 134 S. Montezuma St. (© 928/776-7717; www.artsprescott.com), a cooperative of local artists, and Van Gogh's Ear, 156B S. Montezuma St. (© 928/776-1080), which was founded by a splinter group from the co-op and actually has higher-quality art and crafts. Also on this block, you'll find the **Newman Gallery,** 106-A S. Montezuma St. (© 928/442-9167; www.davenewmanstudio.com), which features the colorful Western-inspired pop-culture imagery of artist Dave Newman. The **Sheryl Leonard Galleries,** 110 S. Montezuma St. (© 928/445-4225; www.sherylleonard.com), tucked into the back of the Hotel St. Michael's shopping arcade, is another contemporary art gallery worth searching out.

WHERE TO STAY
EXPENSIVE

Hassayampa Inn ✦   Built as a luxury hotel in 1927, the Hassayampa Inn, which is listed on the National Register of Historic Places, evokes the time when Prescott was the bustling territorial capital. In the lobby, exposed ceiling beams, wrought-iron chandeliers, and arched doorways all reflect the place's Southwestern heritage. Although guest rooms here tend to be very small, each guest room is unique and features either original furnishings or antiques, and all were renovated a few years ago. One room is said to be haunted, and any hotel employee will be happy to tell you the story of the ill-fated honeymooners whose ghosts are said to reside here.

122 E. Gurley St., Prescott, AZ 86301. © **800/322-1927** or 928/778-9434. Fax 928/445-8590. www.hassa yampainn.com. 67 units. $99–$189 double; $159–$249 suite. Rates include full breakfast. Children 12 and under stay free in parent's room. AE, DC, DISC, MC, V. **Amenities:** Restaurant; lounge; exercise room; room service; laundry service; dry cleaning. *In room:* A/C, TV, dataport, hair dryer, iron.

Prescott Resort, Conference Center, and Casino 🎿 This is Prescott's only full-service resort hotel, and the location, high on a hill overlooking the city and the surrounding valley and mountains, gives this resort the best views of any lodging in Prescott. If you like Western art, you'll love this place; the walls of public areas near the lobby are covered with paintings of cowboys, Indians, and horses. Guest rooms are spacious and comfortable, and each has its own balcony. If you're looking for comfortable, predictable accommodations at a modern hotel, this is your best bet in Prescott.

1500 Hwy. 69, Prescott, AZ 86301. © **800/967-4637** or 928/776-1666. Fax 928/776-8544. www.prescott resort.com. 160 units. $125–$145 double; $145–$165 suite. AE, DC, DISC, MC, V. **Amenities:** Restaurant (American); lounge; indoor pool; 2 tennis courts; racquetball court; health club; Jacuzzi; sauna; game room; business center; room service; laundry service; dry cleaning. *In room:* A/C, TV, dataport, fridge, coffeemaker, hair dryer, iron.

MODERATE

Hotel Vendome 🎿 Not quite as luxurious as the Hassayampa, yet not as basic as the St. Michael, the Vendome offers a good middle-price choice for those who want to stay in a historic hotel. Built in 1917 as a lodging house, the restored brick building is only 2 blocks from the action of Whiskey Row, but far enough away that you can get a good night's sleep. Guest rooms are outfitted with new furnishings, but some of the bathrooms still contain original claw-foot tubs. Naturally, this hotel, like several others in town, has its own resident ghost.

230 S. Cortez St., Prescott, AZ 86303. © **888/468-3583** or 928/776-0900. Fax 928/771-0395. www.vendome hotel.com. 21 units. $79–$119 double; $119–$159 2-bedroom unit. Rates include continental breakfast. Children under 12 stay free in parent's room. AE, DISC, MC, V. **Amenities:** Lounge; access to nearby health club. *In room:* A/C, TV, dataport, hair dryer, iron, free local calls.

Log Cabin Bed & Breakfast 🎿 This modern log house is located among the massive boulders of the Granite Dells, and although the inn is right on the highway, it is set back a bit from the road. While the exterior of this inn says log cabin, the interior is more classic country style. One guest room has white wicker furniture, while another has a brass bed. Two of the rooms have claw-foot tubs, and these are my favorites. My favorite room is the Cozy Fireside room, which has a claw-foot tub, a gas fireplace, and a skylight over the windows. One room has a TV and VCR.

3155 N. Hwy. 89, Prescott, AZ 86301. © **888/778-0442** or 928/778-0442. Fax 928/445-0000. www.prescott logcabin.com. 4 units. $109–$159 double. AE, DISC, MC, V. **Amenities:** Jacuzzi. *In room:* A/C, no phone.

Rocamadour Bed & Breakfast for (Rock) Lovers ⭐⭐   The Granite Dells, just north of Prescott, is the area's most fantastic feature. Should you wish to stay amid these jumbled boulders, there's no better choice than Rocamadour. Mike and Twila Coffey honed their innkeeping skills as owners of a 40-room château in France, and antique furnishings from that château can now be found throughout this inn. The most elegant pieces are in the Chambre Trucy, which also boasts an amazing underlit whirlpool tub. One cottage is built into the boulders and has a large whirlpool tub on its deck. The unique setting, engaging innkeepers, and thoughtful details everywhere you turn make this one of the state's must-stay inns.

3386 N. Hwy. 89, Prescott, AZ 86301. © 888/771-1933 or 928/771-1933. 3 units. $139–$149 double; $189 suite. AE, DC, DISC, MC, V. Rates include full breakfast. *In room:* A/C, TV/VCR.

INEXPENSIVE

Hotel St. Michael *Value*   Located right on Whiskey Row, this restored hotel, complete with resident ghost and the oldest elevator in Prescott, offers a historic setting at budget prices (don't expect the best of mattresses or most stylish furnishings). All rooms are different; some have bathtubs but no showers. The casual Café St. Michael, where breakfast is served, overlooks Courthouse Plaza.

205 W. Gurley St., Prescott, AZ 86301. © 800/678-3757 or 928/776-1999. Fax 928/776-7318. www. stmichaelhotel.com. 72 units. $59–$89 double; $99–$109 suite. Rates include continental breakfast. AE, DISC, MC, V. **Amenities:** Cafe; shopping arcade. *In room:* A/C, TV.

WHERE TO DINE

Savor a mocha and pastry while watching the world go by at the **Café St. Michael,** 205 W. Gurley St. (© **928/778-2500**), at the historic Hotel St. Michael (see "Where to Stay," above). With its pressed-tin ceiling, brick walls, and battered wood floor, this place has the feel of an old saloon. Grab picnic fare at **New Frontiers Natural Foods,** 1112 W. Iron Springs Rd. (© **928/445-7370**). For delicious baked goods, including savory turnovers, stop in at the **Pangaea Bakery,** 220 W. Goodwin St., Suite 1 (© **928/778-2953**), which is located half a block off Whiskey Row. The bakery is open Monday through Saturday from 7am to 2pm.

MODERATE

Murphy's ⭐ AMERICAN   Murphy's, housed in an 1890 mercantile building that is on the National Register of Historic Places, has long been one of Prescott's favorite special-occasion restaurants. Sparkling leaded-glass doors usher diners into a high-ceilinged room with fans revolving slowly overhead. Many of the shop's original shelves can still be seen in the lounge area, and the restaurant does a good job of creating a historic ambience. The best bets on the menu are the mesquite-broiled meats, but the fish specials can also be good. You can save a bit of money by dining early and ordering one of the sunset dinners.

201 N. Cortez St. (a block from Courthouse Plaza). © **928/445-4044**. www.murphysrestaurants.com. Reservations recommended. Main courses $7–$14 lunch, $14–$29 dinner. AE, DISC, MC, V. Sun–Thurs 11am–10pm; Fri–Sat 11am–11pm.

129½ ⭐ NEW AMERICAN   Prescott, a classic small-town-America sort of place, may seem an odd location for a classic New York–style jazz club, but this restaurant has it down. It may not be in a basement and it isn't smoky, but everything else has just the right feel. Best of all, the restaurant also has great food. Steaks are the specialty and can be had with an assortment of delicious sauces, such as pinot and green peppercorn, rosemary cream, shiitake and portobello mushroom, and bayou blend. However, my personal favorite dish is the "mile-high" beef tenderloin sandwich, which you can get with your choice of the sauces above (I like the pinot-and-green-peppercorn sauce).

129½ N. Cortez St. ℭ 928/443-9292. Reservations recommended. Main courses $10–$22. AE, DISC, MC, V. Tues–Sat 5–9:30pm.

The Palace *(Finds)* SOUTHWESTERN/STEAKHOUSE/SEAFOOD   The Palace is the oldest saloon in Arizona (in business for more than 120 years), and in 1996 was beautifully renovated and returned to the way it might have looked at the start of the 20th century. While the front of the Palace is centered around the old bar, most of the cavernous space is dedicated to a bustling dining room. The generous steaks are your best bet here. While other self-styled cowboy steakhouses are just tourist traps, this place is the genuine article. If you bump into someone carrying a shotgun, don't panic! It's probably just the owner, who likes to dress the part of a Wild West saloonkeeper. Dinner shows are held every other Monday. There's live music Friday and Saturday nights, and on Sunday afternoons, there's a honky-tonk piano player.

120 S. Montezuma St. ℭ 928/541-1996. www.historicpalace.com. Reservations suggested on weekends. Main courses $6–$9 lunch, $13–$25 dinner. AE, DISC, MC, V. Sun–Thurs 11am–3pm and 4:30–9:30pm; Fri–Sat 11am–3pm and 4:30–10:30pm.

The Rose Restaurant *(★★)* CONTINENTAL   This is Prescott's best restaurant and is a must for anyone staying in town. Chef Linda Rose brings a distinctive creative flair to her cooking and year after year continues to satisfy locals and visitors alike. Although the manicotti is a not-to-be-missed house specialty, the veal dishes can also be outstanding, and the pasta with scallops and Italian sausage is a curious combination of flavors that works well. Lately I've heard rave reviews for the osso buco, which shows up as a special from time to time. The wine list includes plenty of reasonably priced wines.

234 S. Cortez St. ℭ 928/777-8308. Reservations recommended. Main courses $16–$33. AE, DC, DISC, MC, V. Wed–Sun 5–9pm.

INEXPENSIVE

Kendall's Famous Burgers & Ice Cream BURGERS   Ask anyone in town where to get the best burger in Prescott, and you'll be sent to Kendall's on Courthouse Plaza. This bright and noisy luncheonette serves juicy burgers with a choice of more than a dozen condiments.

113 S. Cortez St. ℭ 928/778-3658. Burgers $4–$6.50. DISC, MC, V. Mon–Sat 11am–8pm; Sun 11am–6pm.

Prescott Brewing Company AMERICAN/PUB FARE   Popular primarily with a younger crowd, this brewpub keeps a good selection of its own beers on tap, but is just as popular for its cheap and filling meals. Fajitas are a specialty, along with such pub standards as fish and chips, bangers and mash, and not-so-standard spent-grain beer-dough pizzas and vegetarian dishes. The Caesar salad with chipotle dressing packs a wallop.

130 W. Gurley St. ℭ 928/771-2795. www.prescottbrewingcompany.com. Main courses $6.50–$18. AE, DISC, MC, V. Sun–Thurs 11am–10pm; Fri–Sat 11am–11pm (pub stays open 2 hr. after kitchen closes).

PRESCOTT AFTER DARK

Back in the days when Prescott was the territorial capital and a booming mining town, it supported dozens of rowdy saloons, most of which were concentrated along Montezuma Street on the west side of Courthouse Plaza. This section of town was known as **Whiskey Row,** and legend has it there was a tunnel from the courthouse to one of the saloons so lawmakers wouldn't have to be seen ducking into the saloons during regular business hours. On July 14, 1900, a fire consumed most of Whiskey Row. However, concerned cowboys and miners managed to drag the tremendously heavy bar of the Palace saloon across the street before it was damaged.

Today, Whiskey Row is no longer the sort of place where respectable women shouldn't be seen, although it does still have a few noisy saloons with genuine Wild West flavor. Most of them feature live country music on weekends and are the dark, dank sorts of places that provide solace to a cowboy after a long day's work. However, within a few blocks of Whiskey Row, you can hear country, folk, jazz, and rock at a surprisingly diverse assortment of bars, restaurants, and clubs. In fact, Prescott has one of the densest concentrations of live-music clubs in the state.

If, however, you'd rather see what this street's saloons looked like back in the old days, drop by the **Palace,** 120 S. Montezuma St. (© **928/541-1996**), which still has a classic bar up front. Just push through the swinging doors and say howdy to the fellow with the six-guns or shotgun; he's the owner. These days, the Palace is more of a restaurant than a saloon, but there's live music on the weekends. A couple of times a month, there are also dinner theater performances. Call to find out if anything is happening while you're in town.

If you want to drink where the ranchers drink and not where the hired hands carouse, head upstairs to the **Jersey Lilly Saloon,** 116 S. Montezuma St. (© **928/541-7854**), which attracts a more well-heeled clientele than the street-level saloons. On weekends, there is live music in a wide range of styles. This is my personal favorite place to party in Prescott. If you're looking for someplace a little lower key and it's a Friday or Saturday night, head down below street level on this same block to the **Vine to Wine Cellar,** 110 S. Montezuma St. (© **928/443-8932;** www.vinetowinecellar.com), which is located in the basement of St. Michael's Alley. This wine bar/wine shop books some eclectic folk music acts.

Just around the corner from the Palace is the **Prescott Brewing Company,** 130 W. Gurley St. (© **928/771-2795**), which is today's answer to the saloons of yore, brewing and serving its own tasty microbrews. Good pub fare is also served.

The **Prescott Fine Arts Association,** 208 N. Marina St. (© **928/445-3286;** www.pfaa.net), sponsors plays, music performances, children's theater, and art exhibits. The association's main building, a former church built in 1899, is on the National Register of Historic Places. The **Yavapai College Performance Hall,** 1100 E. Sheldon St. (© **928/776-2033**), also stages a wide range of shows. Also check the schedule at the Sharlot Hall Museum's open-air **Blue Rose History Theater** (© **928/445-3122**).

EN ROUTE TO OR FROM PHOENIX

If you crave a taste of the country life, stop by **Young's Farm** (© **928/632-7272;** www.youngsfarminc.com), a country store at the intersection of Ariz. 69 and 169 between I-17 and Prescott. Located in the middle of the desert, this farm stand sells a wide variety of produce as well as gourmet and unusual foods. You might find any of a number of various seasonal festivals going on here.

3 Jerome

35 miles NE of Prescott; 28 miles W of Sedona; 130 miles N of Phoenix

Few towns anywhere in Arizona make more of an impression on visitors than Jerome, a historic mining town that clings to the slopes of Cleopatra Hill high on Mingus Mountain. The town is divided into two sections that are separated by an elevation change of 1,500 vertical feet, with the upper part of town 2,000 feet above the Verde Valley. On a clear day, the view from Jerome is stupendous—it's possible to see for more than 50 miles, with the red rocks of Sedona, the Mogollon Rim, and the San Francisco Peaks visible in the distance. Add to the unforgettable views the abundance of interesting shops and galleries and the winding narrow streets, and you have a town that should not be missed.

Jerome had its start as a copper-mining town, but it was never easy to mine the ore here. For many years, the mountain's ore was mined using an 88-mile-long network of underground railroads. However, in 1918, a fire broke out in the mine tunnels, and mining companies were forced to abandon the tunnels in favor of open-pit mining.

Between 1883 and 1953, Jerome experienced an economic roller-coaster ride as the price of copper rose and fell. In the early 1950s, when it was no longer profitable to mine the copper ore of Cleopatra Hill, the last mining company shut down its operations, and almost everyone left town. By the early 1960s, Jerome looked as though it were on its way to becoming just another ghost town—but then artists who had discovered the phenomenal views and dirt-cheap rents began moving in, and slowly the would-be ghost town developed a reputation as an artists' community. Soon tourists began visiting to see and buy the artwork that was being created in Jerome, and old storefronts turned into galleries.

Jerome is now far from a ghost town, and on summer weekends the streets are packed with visitors browsing the galleries and crafts shops. The same remote and rugged setting that once made it difficult and expensive to mine copper has now become one of the town's main attractions. Because Jerome is built on a steep slope, streets through town switch back from one level of houses to the next, with narrow alleys and stairways connecting the different levels of town. All these winding streets, alleys, and stairways are lined with old brick and wood-frame buildings that cling precariously to the side of the mountain. The entire town has been designated a National Historic Landmark, and today, residences, studios, shops, and galleries stand side by side looking (externally, anyway) much as they did when Jerome was an active mining town.

ESSENTIALS

GETTING THERE Jerome is on Ariz. 89A roughly halfway between Sedona and Prescott. Coming from Phoenix, take Ariz. 260 from Camp Verde.

VISITOR INFORMATION Contact the **Jerome Chamber of Commerce** (© **928/634-2900;** www.jeromechamber.com) for information.

EXPLORING THE TOWN

Wandering the streets, soaking up the atmosphere, and shopping are the main pastimes in Jerome. Before you launch yourself on a shopping tour, you can learn about the town's past at the **Jerome State Historic Park,** off Ariz. 89A on Douglas Road in the lower section of town (© **928/634-5381**). Located in a mansion built in 1916 as a home for mine owner "Rawhide Jimmy" Douglas

---

Fun Fact **Jail Brakes?**

One unforeseen hazard of open-pit mining next to a town built on a 30-degree slope was the effect dynamiting would have on the town. Mine explosions would rock Jerome's world and eventually buildings in town began sliding downhill. Even the town jail broke loose. Without jail brakes to stop it, the jail slid 225 feet downhill (now that's a jailbreak).

and as a hotel for visiting mining executives, the Jerome State Historic Park contains exhibits on mining as well as a few of the mansion's original furnishings. Set on a hill above Douglas's Little Daisy Mine, the mansion overlooks Jerome and, dizzyingly far below, the Verde Valley. Constructed of adobe bricks made on the site, the mansion once contained a wine cellar, billiards room, marble shower, steam heat, and central vacuum system. The library has been restored as a period room. Admission is $4 for adults, $1 for children 7 to 13. It's open daily (except Christmas) from 8am to 5pm.

To learn more about Jerome's history, stop in at the **Jerome Historical Society's Mine Museum,** 200 Main St. (© 928/634-5477), which has some small and old-fashioned displays on mining. It's open daily from 9am to 4:30pm; admission is $2 for adults, $1 for seniors, and free for children 12 and under. For that classic mining-town tourist-trap experience, follow the signs up the hill from downtown Jerome to the **Gold King Mine** (© 928/634-0053; www.gold kingmine.net), where you can see lots of old, rusting mining equipment and maybe even catch a demonstration. The mine is open 9am to 5pm daily.

To get a wider perspective on both the mining history and Native American history of this area, try a four-wheel-drive tour with **Time Expeditions & Soul Journeys** (© 928/634-3497; www.arizonahealingtours.com/timexhome.html), operated by Clay Miller (who also works as a guide on the nearby Verde Canyon Railroad and is a fount of information on this region). Clay also offers hiking explorations.

Most visitors come to Jerome for the shops, which offer an eclectic blend of contemporary art, chic jewelry, one-of-a-kind handmade fashions, unusual imports and gifts, and the inevitable tacky souvenirs and ice cream (alas, no place stays undiscovered for long anymore; at least there's no McDonald's). To see what local artists are creating, stop in at the **Jerome Artists Cooperative,** 502 N. Main St. (© 928/639-4276; www.jeromeartistscoop.com), on the west side of the street where Hull Avenue and Main Street fork as you come up the hill into town. The **Raku Gallery,** 250 Hull Ave. (© 928/639-0239; www. rakugallery.com), has gallery space on two floors and walls of glass across the back, with views of the red rocks of Sedona in the distance. The **Jerome Gallery,** 240 Hull Ave. (© 928/634-7033), has good-quality ceramics, jewelry, and home furnishings. **Sky Fire,** 140 Main St. (© 928/634-8081), features an interesting collection of Southwestern and ethnic gifts and furnishings. On this same block, you'll also find **Nellie Bly,** 136 Main St. (© 928/634-0255; www.nbscopes.com), with a room full of handmade kaleidoscopes (ask to see the ones in the back room). Also don't miss the eclectic offerings of the **House of Joy,** 416 Hull Ave. (© 928/634-5339).

WHERE TO STAY

Connor Hotel of Jerome   Housed in a recently renovated historic hotel, this is the most up-to-date lodging in Jerome. Some rooms are quite spacious, with large windows to let in lots of light; views of the valley, however, are limited. Although a few of the rooms are located directly above the hotel's popular bar, which can be quite noisy on weekends, most rooms are plenty quiet enough to provide a good night's rest. Better yet, come on a weekday when the Harley-Davidson poseur crowd from the Scottsdale area isn't thundering through the streets on their hogs.

164 Main St. (P.O. Box 1177), Jerome, AZ 86331. © 800/523-3554 or 928/634-5006. www.connorhotel.com. 10 units. $90–$115 double. Children under 12 stay free in parent's room. AE, MC, V. Pets accepted. **Amenities:** Bar; limited room service; massage; babysitting. *In room:* TV, dataport, fridge, coffeemaker, hair dryer.

Ghost City Inn   With its long verandas on both floors, this restored old house is hard to miss as you drive into town from Clarkdale. It manages to capture the spirit of Jerome, with a mix of Victorian and Southwestern decor. Most bedrooms have great views across the Verde Valley (and these are definitely worth requesting). Two units feature antique brass beds, while a third has a high bed that you have to use a footstool to climb into. The rooms are on the small side, so if space is a priority, opt for the suite.

541 N. Main St. (P.O. Box T), Jerome, AZ 86331. ② **888/63-GHOST** or 928/63-GHOST. www.ghostcityinn.com. 6 units, 2 with shared bathrooms. $90–$110 double; $135 suite. Rates include full breakfast. AE, DISC, MC, V. Pets accepted ($20 nonrefundable deposit). No children under 14. **Amenities:** Jacuzzi. *In room:* TV/VCR, no phone.

The Inn at Jerome   This inn is located above a restaurant on Main Street and has similar styling to the Ghost City Inn. However, only two of the rooms here have views across the valley. One unit has a rustic log bed so high that you have to climb up into it; the other rooms' options, including a wrought-iron bed and a spool bed, are equally attractive. All units come with terry robes, ceiling fans, and evaporative coolers (almost as good as air-conditioning).

309 Main St. (P.O. Box 901), Jerome, AZ 86331. ② **800/634-5094** or 928/634-5094. www.innatjerome.com. 8 units, 6 with shared bathrooms. $55–$85 double. Rates include full breakfast. Children under 18 stay free in parent's room. AE, DISC, MC, V. **Amenities:** Restaurant. *In room:* TV, no phone.

The Surgeon's House ⭐   Built in 1917 as the home of Jerome's resident surgeon, this Mediterranean-style building has a jaw-dropping view of the Verde Valley and is surrounded by beautiful gardens. All units are suites, but the old chauffeur's quarters, located in a separate cottage across the gardens, is the one to request. This unconventionally designed room has a wall of glass opposite the bed (so you can take in the view from under the covers), an old tub in one corner, and a wall of glass blocks around the toilet. The rooms in the main house are much more traditional, filled with antiques that conjure up Jerome's heyday.

101 Hill St. (P.O. Box 998), Jerome, AZ 86331. ② **800/639-1452** or 928/639-1452. www.surgeonshouse.com. 4 units. $100–$150 suite. Rates include full breakfast. DISC, MC, V. Pets accepted ($25 per night). **Amenities:** Massage. *In room:* A/C.

WHERE TO DINE

For fresh microbrewed beers, check out the **Jerome Brewery,** 111 Main St. (② **928/639-8477**), which also serves pizzas and other simple Italian dishes. Ghost towns just aren't what they used to be. Jerome now even has a cybercafe, **Reynard–A Cyber Café,** 115 Jerome Ave. (② **928/634-3230;** www.cafe-reynard.com), which is down below street level and serves a variety of snacks and coffee drinks. It's open Thursday through Monday from 7am to 3pm. Also, don't miss the **Jerome Winery,** 403 Clark St. (② **928/639-9067**), which is located above the park in the center of town and makes a wide variety of wines from grapes grown in the Willcox area of southern Arizona. Have some appetizers, sip some wine, and soak up the views of the Verde Valley far below.

The Asylum ⭐ *Finds* ECLECTIC   As the name would imply, this restaurant (inside a former hospital building high above downtown Jerome) is a bit out of the ordinary. The bedpan full of candy at the front desk and the odd little notes in the menu will also make it absolutely clear that this place doesn't take much, other than good food, seriously. I like the distinctly Southwestern dishes, including the prickly-pear barbecued pork tenderloin with tomatillo salsa, and an unusual butternut-squash soup made with a cinnamon-lime cream sauce. Cocktails all get wacky loony-bin names, and there's also a superb wine list.

200 Hill St. ✆ **928/639-3197**. Main courses $7–$13 lunch, $18–$26 dinner. Reservations recommended. AE, DISC, MC, V. Daily 11am–3pm and 5–9pm.

Flatiron Café BREAKFAST/LIGHT MEALS   The tiny Flatiron Café is a simple breakfast-and-lunch spot in, you guessed it, Jerome's version of a flatiron building. The limited menu includes the likes of lox and bagels, a breakfast quesadilla, black-bean hummus, smoked-salmon quesadillas, fresh juices, and espresso drinks. It looks as though you could hardly squeeze in here, but there's more seating across the street. Definitely not your usual ghost-town lunch counter.

416 Main St. (at Hull Ave.). ✆ **928/634-2733**. Most items $6.50–$8. No credit cards. Fri–Wed 8:30am–3pm.

4 The Verde Valley

Camp Verde: 20 miles E of Jerome; 30 miles S of Sedona; 95 miles N of Phoenix

Named by early Spanish explorers who were impressed by the sight of such a verdant valley in an otherwise brown desert landscape, the Verde Valley has long been a magnet for both wildlife and people. Today, the valley is one of Arizona's richest agricultural and ranching regions and is quickly gaining popularity with retirees. Cottonwood and Clarkdale are old copper-smelting towns, while Camp Verde was an army post back in the days of the Indian Wars. All three towns have some interesting historical buildings, but it is the valley's two national monuments—Tuzigoot and Montezuma Castle—that are the main attractions.

Long before the first European explorers entered the Verde Valley, the Sinagua people were living by the river and irrigating their fields with its waters. Sinagua ruins can still be seen at Tuzigoot and Montezuma Castle. By the time the first pioneers began settling in this region, the Sinaguas had long since disappeared, but Apaches had claimed the valley as part of their territory. Hundreds of years of Verde Valley history and prehistory can be viewed at sites such as Fort Verde State Park and the national monuments. This valley is also the site of the most scenic railroad excursion in the state.

ESSENTIALS

GETTING THERE   Camp Verde is just off I-17 at the junction with Ariz. 260. The latter highway leads northwest through the Verde Valley for 12 miles to Cottonwood.

VISITOR INFORMATION   Contact the **Verde Valley Tourism Council,** 1010 S. Main St., Cottonwood (✆ **928/634-7593;** http://tourism.verdevalley.com).

FESTIVALS   Avid birders may want to plan their visit to coincide with the annual **Verde Valley Birding & Nature Festival** (✆ **928/634-8437;** www.birdyverde.org), which is held the last weekend in April.

A RAILWAY EXCURSION

Verde Canyon Railroad   When the town of Jerome was busily mining copper, a railway was built to link the booming town with the territorial capital at nearby Prescott. Because of the rugged mountains between Jerome and Prescott, the railroad was forced to take a longer but less difficult route north along the Verde River before turning south toward Prescott. Today, you can ride these same tracks aboard the Verde Canyon Railroad. The route through the canyon traverses both the remains of a copper smelter and unspoiled desert that is inaccessible by car and is part of the Prescott National Forest. The views of the rocky canyon walls and green waters of the Verde River are quite dramatic, and if you look closely along the way, you'll see ancient Sinagua cliff dwellings. In late winter and early spring, nesting bald eagles can also be spotted. Of the two excursion train rides in Arizona, this is by far the more scenic (although the Grand Canyon Railway certainly has a more impressive destination). Live music and a very informative narration make the ride entertaining as well.

300 N. Broadway, Clarkdale. ✆ **800/293-7245** or 928/639-0010. www.verdecanyonrr.com. Tickets $40 adults, $36 seniors, $25 children 2–12; first-class tickets $60. Call or visit the website for schedule and reservations.

NATIONAL MONUMENTS & STATE PARKS

Dead Horse Ranch State Park   You'll find this state park on the outskirts of Cottonwood, not far from Tuzigoot National Monument. Set on the banks of the Verde River, the park offers picnicking, fishing, swimming, hiking, mountain biking, and camping. Trails wind through the riparian forests along the banks of the river and visit marshes that offer good bird-watching; they also lead into the adjacent national forest, so you can get in many miles of scenic hiking and mountain biking. The ranch was named in the 1940s, when the children of a family looking to buy it told their parents they wanted to buy the ranch with the dead horse by the side of the road.

675 Dead Horse Ranch Rd., Cottonwood. ✆ **928/634-5283.** Admission $5 per car. Daily 8am–8pm. From Main St. on the east side of Cottonwood, drive north on N. 10th St.

Fort Verde State Historic Park   Just south of Montezuma Castle and Montezuma Well, in the town of Camp Verde, you'll find Fort Verde State Historic Park. Established in 1871, Fort Verde was the third military post in the Verde Valley and was occupied until 1891, by which time tensions with the Indian population had subsided and made the fort unnecessary. The military had first come to the Verde Valley in 1865 at the request of settlers who wanted protection from the local Tonto Apache and Yavapai. The tribes, traditionally hunters and gatherers, had been forced to raid the settlers' fields for food after their normal economy was disrupted by the sudden influx of whites and Mexicans into the area. Between 1873 and 1875, most of the Indians in the area were rounded up and forced to live on various reservations. An uprising in 1882 led to the last clash between local tribes and Fort Verde's soldiers.

The state park, which covers 10 acres, preserves three officers' quarters, an administration building, and some ruins. The buildings that have been fully restored house exhibits on the history of the fort and what life was like here in the 19th century. With their white lattices and picket fences, gables, and shake-shingle roofs, the buildings of Fort Verde suggest that life at this remote post was not so bad, at least for officers. Costumed military reenactments are held here on the third Saturday in May, the second Saturday in October, in November (Veteran's Day), and from mid-December to early January.

125 Holloman St., Camp Verde. ✆ **928/567-3275.** Admission $3 adults, $1 children 7–13. Daily 8am–5pm. Closed Christmas.

Montezuma Castle National Monument ✦   Despite the name, the ruins within this monument are neither castle nor Aztec dwelling—as the reference to Aztec ruler Montezuma implies. This Sinagua ruin is, however, one of the best preserved cliff dwellings in Arizona. The site consists of two impressive stone pueblos that were, for some unknown reason, abandoned by the Sinagua people when they disappeared without a trace in the early 14th century.

The more intriguing of the two ruins is set in a shallow cave 100 feet up a cliff overlooking Beaver Creek. Construction on this five-story, 20-room village began sometime in the early 12th century. Because Montezuma Castle has been protected from the elements by the overhanging roof of the cave in which it was built, the original adobe mud that was used to plaster over the stone walls of the dwelling is still intact. Another structure, containing 45 rooms on a total of six levels, stands at the base of the cliff. This latter dwelling, which has been subjected to rains and floods over the years, is not nearly as well preserved as the cliff dwelling. In the visitor center, you'll see artifacts that have been unearthed from the two ruins.

Montezuma Well, located 11 miles north of Montezuma Castle (although still part of the national monument), is a water-filled sinkhole that was a true oasis in the desert for native peoples. This sunken pond was formed when a cavern in the area's porous limestone bedrock collapsed. Underground springs quickly filled the sinkhole, which today contains a pond measuring 368 feet across and 65 feet deep. Over the centuries, the presence of year-round water attracted first the Hohokam and later the Sinagua peoples, who built irrigation canals to use the water for growing crops. Some of these channels can still be seen. An excavated Hohokam pit house, built around 1100, and Sinagua structures are clustered around the sinkhole.

Exit 289 off I-17. © 928/567-3322. www.nps.gov/moca. Admission $3 adults, free for children 16 and under; no charge to see Montezuma Well. Memorial Day weekend to Labor Day weekend daily 8am–6pm; other months daily 8am–5pm.

Tuzigoot National Monument   Perched atop a hill overlooking the Verde River, this small, stone-walled pueblo was built by the Sinagua people and was inhabited between 1125 and 1400. The Sinagua, whose name is Spanish for "without water," were traditionally dry-land farmers relying entirely on rainfall to water their crops. When the Hohokam, who had been living in the Verde Valley since A.D. 600, moved on to more fertile land around 1100, the Sinagua moved into this valley. Their buildings progressed from individual homes called pit houses to the type of communal pueblo seen here at Tuzigoot.

An interpretive trail leads through the Tuzigoot ruins, explaining different aspects of Sinaguan life, and inside the visitor center is a small museum displaying many of the artifacts unearthed here. Desert plants, many of which were used by the Sinagua, are identified along the trail.

Just outside Clarkdale off Ariz. 89A. © 928/634-5564. www.nps.gov/tuzi. Admission $3 adults, free for children 16 and under. Memorial Day weekend to Labor Day weekend daily 8am–7pm; other months daily 8am–5pm. Closed Christmas.

OTHER VERDE VALLEY ATTRACTIONS & ACTIVITIES
IN & AROUND CAMP VERDE

If you have an interest in 19th-century reenactments or antique cowboy and military gear, stop in at **Kicking Mule Outfitters,** 545 S. Main St. (© 928/567-2501), which specializes in reproduction leather holsters, gun belts, saddles, and the like. It also sells Western antiques and rents equipment to movie companies. Out on the edge of town, you'll find Camp Verde's top attraction—**Cliff Castle Casino,** 555 Middle Verde Rd. (© 800/381-SLOT), at Exit 289 off I-17.

You can get a Native American perspective on local history on the van tours offered by **Native Visions** (© 928/567-0205; www.nativevisionstours.com), which operates from adjacent to the Cliff Castle Casino. Tours visit Montezuma

Castle ($20) or Montezuma Well ($25); also available are combination tours ($40–$70) and horseback rides ($35 for 1½ hr. to $85 for 4 hr.).

If you want to do some wine tasting, visit the **San Dominique Winery** (© **480/945-8583**), 11 miles south of Camp Verde. To get here, take Exit 278 off I-17 (the Cherry Rd. exit), go east, and then before the road turns to gravel, turn right on the dirt road that leads to the winery. You might have to look hard to see the winery's small sign. There are always plenty of wines available for tasting. Sandwiches and light meals are available; the winery also sells lots of garlic-flavored foods and different types of pickles. The winery is usually open daily from 10am to 5pm.

IN & AROUND COTTONWOOD & CLARKDALE

Cottonwood, 6 miles from Jerome, isn't nearly as atmospheric as the old copper-mining town up on the hill, but there are a few blocks of historic buildings filled with interesting shops that seem to be spillovers from the old hippie days in Jerome. Old-town Cottonwood's **Main Street,** with its shops, galleries, cafes, and covered sidewalk on one side of the street, is a pleasant place for a stroll. From here, you can also walk the **Jail Trail,** which begins beside the old town jail and leads 1 mile through the cottonwood-willow forests along the banks of the Verde River. At its far end, the trail connects to Dead Horse Ranch State Park, which has many more miles of trails. There's good bird-watching along the Jail Trail, so bring your binoculars. This trail is part of the 6-mile Verde River Greenway, which protects the riparian forests along the river banks. Also in town, though not right downtown, you'll find the **Clemenceau Heritage Museum,** 1 N. Willard St. (© **928/634-2868**), housed in an old school building. The most interesting display is a model railroad layout of the region's old system of mining railroads. It's open Wednesday from 9am to noon, Friday through Sunday from 11am to 3pm. Admission is by donation.

If you'd like to learn more about the historic Cottonwood, take a walking tour of town with Nancy Elkins, better known as **The Tour Lady** (© **928/274-2272;** www.tourlady.com). Tours are offered by reservation and cost $10 per person. Ms. Elkins also offers customized personal tours of the rest of the Verde Valley and nearby Sedona.

WHERE TO STAY

Hacienda de la Mariposa ★★ *Finds*   This modern Santa Fe–style inn is set on the banks of Beaver Creek and is just up the road from Montezuma Castle National Monument. Guest rooms contain rustic Mexican furnishings, gas bee-hive-style fireplaces, small private patios, and lots of character. Bathrooms feature skylights and whirlpool tubs. With a patio overlooking the creek, the Mariposa Creekside room is my favorite. The little Casita de Milagros, a sort of cottage/massage room that serves as a gathering spot for guests, has a huge amethyst geode set into the ceiling. In a walled garden out back, you'll find a swimming pool only steps from the river.

3875 Stagecoach Rd. (P.O. Box 1224), Camp Verde, AZ 86322. © **888/520-9095** or 928/567-1490. Fax 928/567-1436. www.lamariposa-az.com. 5 units. $185–$205 double. AE, DISC, MC, V. No children. **Amenities:** Outdoor pool; massage. *In room:* A/C, TV/VCR, hair dryer, free local calls.

The Lodge at Cliff Castle   Although most people staying at this motel are here to do a little gambling in the adjacent Cliff Castle Casino, it also makes a good base for exploring the Verde Valley, the Sedona area, and even the area north to the Grand Canyon. Rooms are standard motel issue, but between the lodge and the casino, there are nine eating and drinking establishments, including one designed to look like a cave. There's even a bowling alley.

333 Middle Verde Rd. (just off I-17 at Exit 289), Camp Verde, AZ 86322. ℂ **800/524-6343** or 928/567-6611. www.cliffcastle.com. 82 units. $67–$89 double. AE, DC, DISC, MC, V. Pets accepted ($10 fee). **Amenities:** 5 restaurants (American, steakhouse); 4 lounges; outdoor pool (summer only); Jacuzzi; game room; babysitting; casino. *In room:* A/C, TV, coffeemaker, hair dryer.

WHERE TO DINE

Blazin' M Ranch Chuckwagon Suppers *Kids* AMERICAN   Located adjacent to Dead Horse State Park, the Blazin' M Ranch is classic Arizona-style family entertainment—steaks and beans accompanied by cowboy music and comedy. This place is geared primarily toward the young 'uns, with pony rides, farm animals, and a little cow town for the kids to explore. If you're young at heart, you might enjoy the Blazin' M, but it's definitely more fun if you bring the whole family. One of the highlights is the gallery of animated wood carvings, which features humorous Western scenes.

Off 10th St., Cottonwood. ℂ **800/937-8643** or 928/634-0334. www.blazinm.com. Reservations recommended. Dinner $22 adults, $12 children ages 4–12. AE, DISC, MC, V. Wed–Sat gates open at 5pm, dinner at 6:30pm, show at 7:30pm. Closed Jan and Aug.

Murphy's Grill ✦ AMERICAN   With a cheerful and lively atmosphere reminiscent of other Murphy's properties in Prescott, the main focus here is on decently prepared salads, sandwiches, pastas, pizzas, and rotisserie chicken. Service is speedy, and there's a full bar.

747 S. Main St., Cottonwood. ℂ **928/634-7272.** Main courses $6.50–$17. AE, DISC, MC, V. Daily 11am–10pm.

Old Town Café *Finds* CAFE   The almond croissants at this European-style cafe in downtown Cottonwood are the best we've ever had. If that isn't recommendation enough for you, there are also good salads and sandwiches, such as a grilled panini of smoked turkey, spinach, and tomatoes.

1025 "A" N. Main St., Cottonwood. ℂ **928/634-5980.** Sandwiches $7.50. No credit cards. Tues–Sat 8am–3pm.

Piñon Bistro ✦✦ NEW AMERICAN   Tucked into a small, nondescript office plaza next door to a budget motel, this restaurant is the most upscale and sophisticated place in Cottonwood. Piñon's style and menu, which change every week, both draw heavily on the bistros of southern France for inspiration. Not only can you savor the likes of filet mignon with Roquefort butter or duck breast a l'orange with Grand Marnier, but there's also often opera on the stereo and lots of good wine to accompany your meal.

1075 Hwy. 260, Cottonwood. ℂ **928/649-0234.** Reservations recommended. Main courses $15–$22. No credit cards. Thurs–Sun 5–8 or 9pm.

5 Sedona & Oak Creek Canyon ✦✦

56 miles NE of Prescott; 116 miles N of Phoenix; 106 miles S of the Grand Canyon

There is not a town anywhere in the Southwest, perhaps anywhere in the country, with a more beautiful setting than Sedona. On the outskirts of town, red-rock buttes, eroded canyon walls, and mesas rise into blue skies. Off in the distance, the Mogollon Rim looms, its forests of juniper and ponderosa pine dark against the rocks. With a wide band of rosy sandstone predominating in this area, Sedona has come to be known as red-rock country, and each evening

Sedona & Vicinity

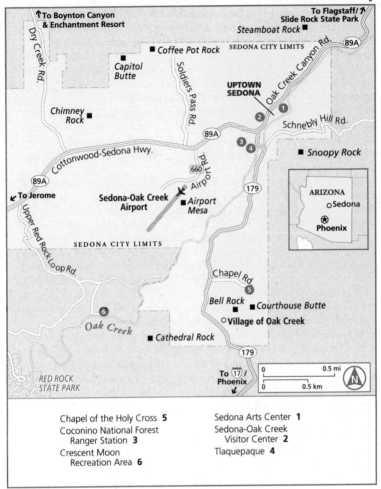

To Boynton Canyon & Enchantment Resort

To Flagstaff/ Slide Rock State Park

Dry Creek Rd.

Steamboat Rock

Coffee Pot Rock

SEDONA CITY LIMITS

Oak Creek Canyon Rd.

89A

Capitol Butte

Soldiers Pass Rd.

UPTOWN SEDONA

Chimney Rock

2 1

Schnebly Hill Rd.

89A

3

4

Cottonwood-Sedona Hwy.

89A

660

Airport Rd.

Snoopy Rock

To Jerome

Sedona-Oak Creek Airport

Airport Mesa

179

Upper Red Rock Loop Rd.

SEDONA CITY LIMITS

ARIZONA

Sedona

Phoenix

Chapel Rd

5

Bell Rock

Courthouse Butte

6

Oak Creek

Village of Oak Creek

Cathedral Rock

179

RED ROCK STATE PARK

To 17 / Phoenix

0   0.5 mi
0   0.5 km

N

Chapel of the Holy Cross **5**
Coconino National Forest
  Ranger Station **3**
Crescent Moon
  Recreation Area **6**

Sedona Arts Center **1**
Sedona-Oak Creek
  Visitor Center **2**
Tlaquepaque **4**

at sunset, the rocks put on an unforgettable light show that is reason enough for a visit.

All this may sound perfectly idyllic, but if you lower your eyes from the red rocks, you'll see the flip side of Sedona—a sprawl of housing developments, highways lined with unattractive strip malls, bumper-to-bumper traffic. Consequently, I have a love-hate relationship with Sedona. I love the setting and the views, I hate the crass commercialism and tourist-trap character that has taken over (wanna buy a time share?). However, not even the proliferation of time-share sales offices disguised as "visitor information centers" can mar the beauty of the backdrop.

With national forest surrounding the city (and even fingers of forest extending into what would otherwise be the city limits), Sedona also has some of the best outdoor access of any city in the Southwest. All around town, alongside highways and down side streets in suburban neighborhoods, there are trail heads. Trek down any one of these trails and you leave the city behind and enter the world of the red rocks. Just don't be surprised if you come around a bend in the trail and find yourself in the middle of a wedding ceremony or a group of 30 people practicing tai chi.

Located at the mouth of Oak Creek Canyon, Sedona was first settled by pioneers in 1877 and named for the first postmaster's wife. Word of Sedona's beauty did not begin to spread until Hollywood filmmakers began using the region's red rock as backdrop to their Western films. Next came artists, lured by the landscapes and desert light (it was here in Sedona that the Cowboy Artists of America organization was formed). Although still much touted as an artists' community, Sedona's art scene these days is geared more toward tourists than toward collectors of fine art.

More recently, the spectacular views and mild climate were discovered by retirees. Sedona's hills are now alive with the sound of construction as ostentatious retirement mansions and celebrity trophy homes sprout from the dust like desert toads after an August rainstorm. Sedona is also a magnet for New Age believers, who come to experience Sedona's unseen cosmic energy fields that are known as vortexes. The vortexes are such a powerful attraction that many New Age proponents have stayed in the area and have turned Sedona into a hotbed of alternative therapies. You can hardly throw a smudge stick around these parts without hitting a psychic (shouldn't they have seen it coming?). Most recently, mountain bikers have begun to ride the red rock, and word is spreading that the biking here is almost as good as up north in Moab, Utah.

The waters of Oak Creek were what first attracted settlers and native peoples to this area, and today this stream still lures visitors to Sedona—especially in summer, when the cool shade and even cooler creek waters are a glorious respite from the heat of the desert. Two of Arizona's finest swimming holes are located on Oak Creek only a few miles from Sedona, and one of these, Slide Rock, has been made into a state park.

With its drop-dead gorgeous scenery, dozens of motels and resorts, and plethora of good restaurants, Sedona makes an excellent base for exploring central Arizona. Several ancient Indian ruins (including an impressive cliff dwelling), the "ghost town" of Jerome, and the scenic Verde Canyon Railroad are all within easy driving distance, and even the Grand Canyon is but a long day trip away.

ESSENTIALS

GETTING THERE   Sedona is on Ariz. 179 at the mouth of Oak Creek Canyon. From Phoenix, take I-17 to Ariz. 179 north. From Flagstaff, head south on I-17 until you see the turnoff for Ariz. 89A and Sedona. Ariz. 89A also connects Sedona with Prescott.

Sedona Phoenix Shuttle (© **800/448-7988** in Arizona, or 928/282-2066; www.sedona-phoenix-shuttle.com) operates several trips daily between Phoenix's Sky Harbor Airport and Sedona. The fare is $40 one-way, $65 round-trip.

VISITOR INFORMATION   The **Sedona–Oak Creek Canyon Chamber of Commerce Visitor Center,** 331 Forest Rd. (© **800/288-7336** or 928/282-7722; www.sedonachamber.com) operates a visitor center at the corner of Ariz. 89A and Forest Road near uptown Sedona.

You can also get information, as well as a Red Rock Pass for parking at area trail heads, at several other visitor centers: **South Gateway Visitor Center,** Tequa Plaza, Ariz. 179 in the Village of Oak Creek (© **928/284-5323**); **North**

Gateway Visitor Center, Oak Creek Vista Overlook, Ariz. 89A (no phone); and **Oak Creek Visitor Center,** in Oak Creek Canyon at Indian Gardens, Ariz. 89A (© **928/203-0624**).

GETTING AROUND   Whether traveling by car or on foot, you'll need to cultivate patience when trying to cross major roads in Sedona. Traffic here, especially on weekends, is some of the worst in the state. Also be prepared for slow traffic on roads that have good views; drivers are often distracted by the red rocks. You may hear or see references to the **"Y,"** which refers to the intersection of Ariz. 179 and Ariz. 89A between the Tlaquepaque shopping plaza and uptown Sedona.

Rental cars are available through **Enterprise** (© **800/736-8222** or 928/282-2052) and **Practical Rent-a-Car** (© **877/467-8578** or 928/282-0554). You can also rent a Jeep from **Farrabee Jeep Rentals of Sedona** (© **800/ 806-5337** or 928/282-8700; www.farabeeadventuresinc.com), which charges $125 to $165 a day. If a Jeep isn't rugged enough for you, you can rent a Harley from **Red Rock Motorcycles,** 1350 W. Hwy. 89A (© **888/200-4647** or 928/204-0795; www.redrockharleyrentals.com). Bikes go for between $170 and $190 per day, with 6-hour rentals available as well.

SPECIAL EVENTS   The **Sedona International Film Festival** (© **928/282-1177;** www.sedonafilmfestival.com), held the first weekend in March, always books plenty of interesting films.

In late September, **Sedona Jazz on the Rocks** (© **928/282-1985;** www.sedonajazz.com) brings world-class jazz to Sedona. Tickets range from around $50 to $200.

In early December, Sedona celebrates the **Festival of Lights** (© **928/282-4838;** www.tlaq.com) at Tlaquepaque by lighting thousands of luminarias (paper bags partially filled with sand and containing a single candle). From Thanksgiving eve until early January, more than a million lights illuminate Los Abrigados Resort (© **800/418-6499** or 928/282-1777; www.redrockfantasy.com) in a **Red-Rock Fantasy.**

EXPLORING RED-ROCK COUNTRY

The Grand Canyon may be Arizona's biggest attraction, but there's actually far more to do in Sedona. If you aren't an active type, there's the option of just gazing in awe at the rugged cliffs, needlelike pinnacles, and isolated buttes that rise from the green forest floor at the mouth of Oak Creek Canyon. Want to see more? Head out into the red rocks on a Jeep tour or drift over the red rocks in a hot-air balloon. Want a closer look? Go for a hike, rent a mountain bike, go horseback riding. (See "Organized Tours" and "Outdoor Pursuits," later in this chapter, for details.)

Although in the past it has been possible for passenger cars to drive **Schnebly Hill Road** for superb views of Sedona, the road is no longer regularly maintained. It's a must, however, if you're driving a high-clearance vehicle or SUV. (You can also check at a visitor center to see if Schnebly Hill Road is once again passable in a regular car.) To reach this scenic road, head south out of Sedona on Ariz. 179, turn left after you cross the bridge over Oak Creek, and head up the road, which starts out paved but soon turns to dirt. The road climbs into the hills above town, every turn yielding a new and breathtaking view, and eventually reaches the top of the Mogollon Rim. At the rim is the Schnebly Hill overlook, offering the very best view in the area. If you can't do this drive in your own vehicle, consider booking a Jeep tour that heads up this way.

Vortex Power

For many years now, Sedona has been one of the world's centers for the New Age movement, and large numbers of people make the pilgrimage here to experience the "power vortexes" of the surrounding red-rock country. Around town, you'll see bulletin boards and publications advertising such diverse services as past-life regressions, crystal healing, angelic healing, tarot readings, reiki, axiatonal therapy, electromagnetic field balancing, soul recovery, channeling, aromatherapy, myofacial release, and aura photos and videos.

According to believers, a vortex is a site where the earth's unseen lines of power intersect to form a particularly powerful energy field. Page Bryant, an adherent of New Age beliefs, determined through channeling that there were four vortexes around Sedona. Scientists may scoff, but Sedona's vortexes have become so well-known that the visitor centers have several handouts to explain them and a map to guide you to them. (Many of the most spectacular geological features of the Sedona landscape also happen to be vortexes.)

The four main vortexes include Bell Rock, Cathedral Rock, Airport Mesa, and Boynton Canyon. **Bell Rock** and **Airport Mesa** are both said to contain masculine or electric energy that boosts emotional, spiritual, and physical energy. **Cathedral Rock** is said to contain feminine or magnetic energy, good for facilitating relaxation. The **Boynton Canyon** vortex is considered an electromagnetic energy site, which means it has a balance of both masculine and feminine energy.

If you're not familiar with vortexes and want to learn more about the ones in Sedona, consider a vortex tour. These are offered by several companies, including **Earth Wisdom Jeep Tours** (© 800/482-4714 or 928/282-4714; www.earthwisdomtours.com), **Spirit Steps** (© 800/728-4562 or 928/282-4562; www.spiritsteps.org), and **Vortex Tours** (© 800/943-3266 or 928/282-2733; www.sedonaretreats.com). All three offer tours that combine aspects of Native American and New Age beliefs. Tours last 2½ to 3 hours and cost $55 to $60 per person.

You can also stock up on books, crystals, and other spiritual supplies at stores such as **Crystal Magic**, 2978 W. Hwy. 89A (© 928/282-1622), or **Center for the New Age**, 341 Hwy. 179 (© 928/282-2085; www.sedonanewagecenter.com).

Just south of Sedona, on the east side of Ariz. 179, you'll see the aptly named **Bell Rock.** There's a parking area at the foot of this formation, and trails lead up to the top. Adjacent to Bell Rock is **Courthouse Butte,** and to the west stands **Cathedral Rock,** the most photographed formation in Sedona. From the Chapel of the Holy Cross (see "Attractions & Activities Around Town," below) on Chapel Road, you can see **Eagle Head Rock** (from the front door of the chapel, look three-quarters of the way up the mountain to see the eagle's head), the **Twin Nuns** (two pinnacles standing side by side), and **Mother and Child Rock** (to the left of the Twin Nuns).

If you head west out of Sedona on Ariz. 89A and turn left onto Airport Road, you'll drive up onto **Airport Mesa,** which commands an unobstructed panorama of Sedona and the red rocks. About halfway up the mesa is a small parking area from which trails radiate. The views from here are among the best in the region, and the trails are very easy.

Boynton Canyon, located 8 miles west of the "Y," is a narrow red-rock canyon and is one of the most beautiful spots in the Sedona area. This canyon is also the site of the deluxe Enchantment resort, but hundreds of years before there were luxury casita suites here, there were Sinagua cliff dwellings. Several of these cliff dwellings can still be spotted high on the canyon walls. **Boynton Canyon Trail** leads 3 miles up into this canyon from a trail head parking area just outside the gates of Enchantment. To get to the trail head, drive west out of Sedona on Ariz. 89A, turn right on Dry Creek Road, take a left at the T intersection, and at the next T take a right.

On the way to Boynton Canyon, look north from Ariz. 89A, and you'll see **Coffee Pot Rock,** also known as Rooster Rock, rising 1,800 feet above Sedona. Three pinnacles, known as the **Three Golden Chiefs** by the Yavapai tribe, stand beside Coffee Pot Rock. As you drive up Dry Creek Road, on your right you'll see **Capitol Butte,** which resembles the U.S. Capitol.

To the west of Boynton Canyon, you can visit the well-preserved Sinagua cliff dwellings at **Palatki Ruins.** To reach the ruins, follow the directions to Boynton Canyon, but instead of turning right at the second T intersection, turn left onto unpaved Boynton Pass Road (Forest Rd. 152), which is one of the most scenic roads in the area. Follow this road to another T intersection and go right onto FR 125, then veer right onto FR 795, which dead-ends at the ruins. You can also get here by taking Ariz. 89A west from Sedona to FR 525, a gravel road leading north to FR 795. To visit Palatki, you'll need a Red Rock Pass (see "The High Cost of Red-Rock Views," below); ruins are usually open daily from 9:30am to 3:30pm. The dirt roads around here become impassable to regular cars when they're wet, so don't try coming out here if the roads are at all muddy.

South of Ariz. 89A and a bit west of the turnoff for Boynton Canyon is Upper Red Rock Loop Road, which leads to **Crescent Moon Recreation Area,** a National Forest Service recreation area that has become a must-see for visitors to Sedona. Its popularity stems from a beautiful photograph of Oak Creek with **Cathedral Rock** in the background—an image that has been reproduced countless times in Sedona promotional literature and on postcards. Hiking trails lead up to Cathedral Rock. Admission is $7 per vehicle May through October and $5 November through April (unless you have previously purchased a Red Rock Grand Pass; see "The High Cost of Red-Rock Views," below). For more information, contact the Red Rock Ranger Station (see below).

If you continue on Upper Red Rock Loop Road, it becomes gravel for a while before becoming Lower Red Rock Loop Road and reaching **Red Rock State**

Fun Fact **The Name Game**

If you're having a hard time remembering which rock is which here in Sedona, you aren't alone. Cathedral Rock was originally named Courthouse Rock, but many years ago it was incorrectly marked on a map and the change stuck.

Park (© **928/282-6907**), which flanks Oak Creek. The views here take in many of the rocks listed above, and you have the additional bonus of being right on the creek (though swimming and wading are prohibited). Park admission is $6 per car. The park offers lots of guided walks and interpretive programs.

South of Sedona, near the junction of I-17 and Ariz. 179, you can visit an ancient petroglyph site at the **V Bar V Ranch.** To get here, head east several miles on the marked dirt road that leads to the Beaver Creek Campground. The entrance to the petroglyph site is just past the campground. From the parking area, it's about a half-mile walk to the petroglyphs, which are open Friday through Monday from 9:30am to 3:30pm. To visit this site, you'll need to purchase a Red Rock Pass for $5.

OAK CREEK CANYON

The **Mogollon Rim** (pronounced "*mug*-ee-un" by the locals) is a 2,000-foot escarpment cutting diagonally across central Arizona and on into New Mexico. At the top of the Mogollon Rim are the ponderosa pine forests of the high mountains, while at the bottom the lowland deserts begin. Of the many canyons cutting down from the rim, Oak Creek Canyon is the most beautiful (and one of the few that has a paved road down through it). Ariz. 89A runs through the canyon from Flagstaff to Sedona, winding its way down from the rim and paralleling Oak Creek. Along the way are overlooks, parks, picnic areas, campgrounds, cabin resorts, and small inns.

If you have a choice of how first to view Oak Creek Canyon, approach it from the north. Your first stop after traveling south from Flagstaff will be the **Oak Creek Canyon Vista,** which provides a view far down the valley to Sedona and beyond. The overlook is at the edge of the Mogollon Rim, and the road suddenly drops in tight switchbacks just south of here. You may notice that one rim of the canyon is lower than the other. This is because Oak Creek Canyon is on a geologic fault line; one side of the canyon is moving in a different direction from the other.

Although the top of the Mogollon Rim is a ponderosa pine forest and the bottom a desert, Oak Creek Canyon supports a forest of sycamores and other deciduous trees. There is no better time to drive scenic Ariz. 89A than between late September and mid-October, when the canyon is ablaze with red and yellow leaves.

In the desert, swimming holes are powerful magnets during the hot summer months, and consequently **Slide Rock State Park** (© **928/282-3034**), located 7 miles north of Sedona on the site of an old homestead, is the most popular spot in all of Oak Creek Canyon. What pulls in the crowds of families and teenagers is the park's natural water slide and great little swimming hole. On hot days, the park is jammed with people splashing in the water and sliding over the algae-covered sandstone bottom of Oak Creek. Sunbathing and fishing are other popular pastimes. The park is open daily; admission is $8 per vehicle. There's another popular swimming area at **Grasshopper Point,** several miles closer to Sedona. Admission is $7 per vehicle, unless you have previously purchased a Red Rock Grand Pass (see "The High Cost of Red-Rock Views," below, for details).

Within Oak Creek Canyon, several hikes of different lengths are possible. By far the most spectacular and popular is the 6-mile round-trip up the **West Fork of Oak Creek.** This is a classic canyon-country hike with steep canyon walls rising up from the creek. At some points, the canyon is no more than 20 feet wide with walls rising up more than 200 feet. You can also extend the hike many more miles up the canyon for an overnight backpacking trip. The trail head for the

The High Cost of Red-Rock Views

A quick perusal of any Sedona real-estate magazine will convince you that property values around these parts are as high as the Mogollon Rim. However, red-rock realty is also expensive for those who want only a glimpse of the rocks. With the land around Sedona split up into several types of National Forest Service day-use sites, state parks, and national monuments, visitors find themselves pulling out their wallets just about every time they turn around to look at another rock. Here's the lowdown on what it's going to cost you to do the red rocks right.

A **Red Rock Pass** will allow you to visit Palatki Ruins and the V Bar V petroglyph site and park at any national forest trail-head parking areas. The cost is $5 for a 1-day pass, $15 for a 7-day pass, and $20 for a 12-month pass. Passes are good for everyone in your vehicle. If you plan to be in the area for more than a week and also want to visit Grasshopper Point (a swimming hole), Banjo Bill (a picnic area), Call of the Canyon (the West Fork Oak Creek trail head), and Crescent Moon (Sedona's top photo-op site), you'll want to buy a **Red Rock Grand Pass,** for $40. These sites each charge $5 to $7 admission per vehicle, so if you aren't planning on going to all of them or you don't expect to be around for more than a week, the Red Rock Grand Pass is not a good deal.

There are also two state parks in the area—Slide Rock ($8 per car) and Red Rock ($6 per car). Admission to the Montezuma Castle or Tuzigoot national monuments will cost you $3 per adult. If there are two or more of you traveling together and you're planning on visiting the Grand Canyon and three or four other national parks or monuments, you might want to consider getting a **National Parks Pass** ($50) or a **Golden Eagle Pass** ($65). These passes are good for a year and will get you into any national park or national monument in the country. If you're 62 or older, definitely get a Golden Age Pass—it's only $10 and is good for the rest of your life. A Golden Age Pass will also get you a Red Rock Grand Pass for half-price.

For more information on the Red Rock passes, visit www.redrock country.org.

West Fork of Oak Creek hike is 9.5 miles up Oak Creek Canyon from Sedona at the Call of the Canyon Recreation Area, which charges a $7 day-use fee per vehicle unless you have already purchased a Red Rock Grand Pass.

Stop by the Sedona–Oak Creek Chamber of Commerce to pick up a free map listing hikes in the area. The **Coconino National Forest's Red Rock Ranger Station,** 250 Brewer Road (© **928/282-4119;** www.fs.fed.us/r3/coconino), just west of the "Y," is also a good source of hiking information.

If you get thirsty while driving through the canyon, hold out for **Garlands Indian Gardens Market,** 3951 N. Hwy. 89A (© **928/282-7702**), about 4 miles north of Sedona. Here, in the fall, you can get delicious organic apple juice made from apples grown in the canyon. For one last view down the canyon, stop at **Midgely Bridge** (watch for the parked cars and small parking area at the north end of the bridge).

ATTRACTIONS & ACTIVITIES AROUND TOWN

Sedona's most notable architectural landmark is the **Chapel of the Holy Cross** (© **928/282-4069**), a small church built right into the red rock on the south side of town. If you're driving up from Phoenix, you can't miss it—the chapel sits high above the road just off Ariz. 179. With its contemporary styling, it is one of the most architecturally important modern churches in the country. Marguerite Brunswig Staude, a devout Catholic painter, sculptor, and designer, had the inspiration for the chapel in 1932, but it wasn't until 1957 that her dream was finally realized. The chapel's design is dominated by a simple cross forming the wall that faces the street. The cross and the starkly beautiful chapel seem to grow directly from the rock, allowing the natural beauty of the red rock to speak for itself. It's open Monday through Saturday from 9am to 5pm and Sunday from 10am to 5pm.

The **Sedona Arts Center,** 15 Art Barn Rd. at Ariz. 89A (© **888/954-4442** or 928/282-3809; www.sedonaartscenter.com), near the north end of uptown Sedona, serves both as a gallery for work by local and regional artists and as a theater for plays and music performances.

To learn a bit about the local history, stop by the **Sedona Heritage Museum,** 735 Jordan Rd. (© **928/282-7038;** www.sedonamuseum.org), in Jordan Historical Park. The museum, which is housed in a historic home, is furnished with antiques and contains exhibits on the many movies that have been filmed in the area. The farm was once an apple orchard, and there's still apple-processing equipment in the barn. Hours are daily from 11am to 4pm (last tour at 3pm); admission is $3.

While Sedona isn't yet a resort destination on par with Phoenix or Tucson, it does have a few spas that might add just the right bit of pampering to your vacation. **Therapy on the Rocks,** 676 N. Hwy. 89A (© **928/282-3002**), with its creekside setting, is a longtime local favorite that offers myofacial release and great views of the red rocks. For personal attention, try the little **Red Rock Spa & Healing Center,** Creekside Plaza, 251 Hwy. 179 (© **928/203-9933;** www.redrockhealing.com), which is just up the hill from Tlaquepaque shopping plaza and offers a variety of massages, wraps, scrubs, and facials. In the Village of Oak Creek, there's the **Hilton Spa,** at the Hilton Sedona Resort, 10 Ridge View Dr. (© **928/284-6975;** www.hiltonsedonaspa.com), offering a variety of treatments (try the Sedona clay wrap) along with a pool, tennis and racquetball courts, and aerobics rooms. Prices for a 60-minute treatment range from $95 to $135.

ORGANIZED TOURS

For an overview of Sedona, take a tour on the **Sedona Trolley,** 270 Hwy. 89A (© **928/282-4211;** www.sedonatrolley.com), which leaves several times daily on two separate tours. One tour visits Tlaquepaque shopping plaza, the Chapel of the Holy Cross, and several art galleries, while the other goes out through west Sedona to Boynton Canyon and Enchantment Resort. Tours are $9 for adults ($16 for both tours) and $5 for children 12 and under ($8 for both tours).

The red-rock country surrounding Sedona is the city's greatest natural attraction, and there's no better way to explore it than by four-wheel-drive vehicle. Although you may end up feeling like every other tourist in town, you quite simply should not leave Sedona without going on a Jeep tour. These tours will get you out onto rugged roads and 4X4 trails with spectacular views. The unchallenged leader in Sedona Jeep tours is **Pink Jeep Tours,** 204 N. Hwy. 89A (© **800/873-3662** or 928/282-5000; www.pinkjeeptours.com), which has been

heading deep into the Coconino National Forest since 1958. It offers tours ranging in length from 1½ to 4 hours, however, the 2-hour "Broken Arrow" tour
($65) is the most adventurous and is the tour I recommend.

For a completely different type of Jeep tour, contact **Adventure Company
Jeep Tours** (© 877/281-6622 or 928/204-1973; www.sedonajeeptours.com),
which offers what it calls "Tag Along Tours." These tours let you drive the Jeep
while a guide in a Jeep ahead leads the way. These tours cost $95 to $125 per
person for the first two people. This company even has Jeep driving school.

If a Jeep just isn't manly enough for you, how about a Hummer? **Hummer
Affair,** 273 N. Hwy. 89A, Suite C (© 928/282-6656; www.hummeraffair.com)
will take you out in the red rocks in the ultimate off-road vehicle. One-hour tours
run $40 to $45, but it's the 2-hour
"Gambler Tour" for $89 that's the
most fun.

How about a chance to play cowboy? **A Day in the West,** 252 N. Hwy.
89A (© 800/973-3662 or 928/282-
4320; www.adayinthewest.com), has
its own private ranch for some of its
Jeep tours and horseback rides. There
are cowboy cookouts, too. Prices range
from $28 to $130.

If you'd like to have a very knowledgeable local tour guide show you

---

> **Tips   Need More Help?**
>
> If you need more help planning
> your visit to Sedona, get in
> touch with Debra Lynn Moss at
> **Concierges of Sedona** (© 888/
> 516-2207 or 928/282-5678). Debra
> can steer you in the direction of
> the things you want to find here
> in Sedona.

---

around at your pace and to places you're interested in seeing, I recommend getting in touch with Steve "Benny" Benedict at **Touch the Earth Adventures**
(© 928/203-9132; www.earthtours.com). Benny likes to take clients to places
that even many locals don't know about. And, if you want to go on a good vortex tour or an off-the-beaten-path guided hike, get in touch with Dennis Andres
of **Meta Adventures** (© 928/204-2201; www.metaadventures.com). Plan to
pay around $500 per couple for a full day of touring with either of these excel-
lent guides. Shorter outings are also available.

For a tour of the Sedona area from a Native American perspective, contact
Chief Kills in the Fog of **Way of the Ancients** (© 866/204-9243 or 928/204-
9243; www.wayoftheancients.com). These 5-hour tours cost $75. There are also
excursions to the Hopi mesas ($125).

As spectacular as Sedona is from the ground, it is even more so from the air.
Arizona Helicopter Adventures (© 800/282-5141 or 928/282-0904; www.
azheli.com) offers short flights to different parts of this colorful region. Prices
start at around $58 per person for a 12-minute flight. **Sky Safari Air Tours**
(© 888/TOO-RIDE or 928/204-5939; www.sedonaairtours.com) offer a variety of flights in small planes. A 15-minute air tour will run you $39 per person,
while a 30-minute tour will cost $59. Flights as far afield as the Grand Canyon
and Canyon de Chelly can also be arranged.

My favorite Sedona air tours are those offered by **Red Rock Biplane Tours**
(© 888/TOO-RIDE or 928/204-5939; www.sedonaairtours.com), which
operates modern Waco open-cockpit biplanes. With the wind in your hair, you'll
feel as though you've entered the world of *The English Patient.* Tours lasting 15
to 30 minutes are offered; a 20-minute tour costs $79 per person.

If something a bit slower is more your speed, how about drifting over the
sculpted red buttes of Sedona in a hot-air balloon? **Northern Light Balloon**

Expeditions (© **800/230-6222** or 928/282-2274; www.northernlightballoon. com) charges $170 per person; **Red Rock Balloon Adventures** (© **800/258-3754;** www.redrockballoons.com) charges $175 per person, while the affiliated **Sky High Balloon Adventures** (© **800/551-7597;** www.skyhighballoons.com), which floats over the Verde Valley and includes a "splash-and-dash" descent to the river, charges $160 per person.

OUTDOOR PURSUITS

Hiking is by far the most popular outdoor activity in the Sedona area, with dozens of trails leading off into the red rocks. The big problem is that nearly everyone who comes to Sedona wants to go hiking, so finding a little solitude along the trail can be difficult. Not surprisingly, the most convenient trail heads also have the most crowded trails. If you want to ditch the crowds, pick a trail head that is *not* on Ariz. 179 or Ariz. 89A. That means that if you stop at any of the trail heads in Oak Creek Canyon or between the Village of Oak Creek and Sedona, you'll likely encounter lots of other people along the trail. You'll enjoy the hiking here much more if you start from a trail head down a side road. Among my personal favorites are the trails that originate at the end of Jordan Road in uptown Sedona, the Cathedral Rock Trail, which starts in a housing development between Sedona and the Village of Oak Creek, and the trails off Boynton Pass Road. And *don't* forget to get your Red Rock Pass before heading out to go for a hike.

This said, the most convenient place to get some red dust on your boots is along the **Bell Rock Pathway,** which begins alongside Ariz. 179 just north of the Village of Oak Creek. This trail winds around the base of Bell Rock and accesses many other trails that lead up to the slopes of Bell Rock. It's about 5 miles to go all the way around Bell Rock. Unfortunately, this is one of the most popular hiking trails in the area and is always crowded.

You'll see fewer tourists if you head to the three-quarter-mile **Cathedral Rock Trail,** which is also located between the Village of Oak Creek and uptown Sedona. The trail follows cairns (piles of rocks) up the slickrock slopes on the north side of Cathedral Rock. (To reach this trail, turn off Ariz. 179 at the sign for the Back o' Beyond housing development and watch for the trail head at the end of the paved road.) For convenience and solitude, you can't beat the **Mystic Trail,** which begins at an unmarked roadside pull-off on Chapel Road halfway between Ariz. 179 and the Chapel of the Holy Cross. This is an easy out-and-back trail that runs between a couple of housing developments, but once you're on the trail, you'll feel all alone.

Among the most popular trails in the Sedona area are those that lead into **Boynton Canyon** (site of Enchantment Resort). Here you'll glimpse ancient Native American ruins built into the red-rock cliffs. Although the scenery is indeed stupendous, the great numbers of other hikers on the trail detract considerably from the experience, and the parking lot usually fills up early in the day. The 1.5-mile **Vultee Arch Trail,** which leads to an impressive sandstone arch, is another great hike. The turnoff for the trail head is 2 miles up Dry Creek Road and then another 3.4 miles on a very rough dirt road. The **Devil's Bridge Trail,** which starts on the same dirt road, is a little easier to get to and leads to an equally impressive sandstone arch. This one is a 1.8-mile round-trip hike.

For the hands-down best views in Sedona, hike all or part of the **Airport Mesa Trail,** a 3.5-mile loop that circles Airport Mesa. With virtually no elevation gain, this is an easy hike. You'll find the trail head about halfway to the top of Airport Mesa on Airport Road. Try this one as early in the day as possible; by midday, the parking lot is usually full and stays that way right through sunset.

For more information on hiking in Oak Creek Canyon (site of the famous West Fork of Oak Creek Trail), see "Oak Creek Canyon," above. For more information on all these hikes, contact the **Coconino National Forest's Red Rock Ranger Station,** 250 Brewer Rd. (© **928/282-4119**), which is located just west of Ariz. 89A and Ariz. 179.

Sedona is rapidly becoming one of the Southwest's meccas for mountain biking. The red rock here is every bit as challenging and scenic as the famed slickrock country of Moab, Utah, and much less crowded. Using Sedona as a base, mountain bikers can ride year-round by heading up to Flagstaff in summer and down to the desert lowlands in winter. One of my favorite places to ride is around the base of Bell Rock. Starting at the trail-head parking area just north of the Village of Oak Creek, you'll find not only the easy Bell Rock Path but also numerous more challenging trails.

Another great ride starts above uptown Sedona, where you can take the Jim Thompson Trail to Midgely Bridge or the network of trails that head toward Soldier Pass. The riding here is moderate and the views are superb. To reach these trails, take Jordan Road to a left onto Park Ridge Road, and follow this road to where it ends at a dirt trail-head parking area. You can rent bikes from **Sedona Sports,** Creekside Plaza (below the "Y"), 251 N. Hwy. 179 (© **928/ 282-1317**), or **Mountain Bike Heaven,** 1695 W. Hwy. 89A (© **928/282-1312;** www.mountainbikeheaven.com). Rates are around $25 to $45 per day. **Sedona Bike & Bean,** 6020 Hwy. 179, Village of Oak Creek (© **928/284-0210;** www.bike-bean.com), across the street from the popular Bell Rock Pathway and its adjacent mountain-bike trails, rents bikes (and serves coffee). Bikes go for $30 to $40 for a full day. Any of these stores can sell you the *Epic Sedona* map or Cosmic Ray's *Fat Tire Tales and Trails* guidebook to the best rides in Arizona.

Trail Horse Adventures (© **800/723-3538** or 928/282-7252; www.trail horseadventures.com) offers guided horseback trail rides. A 2-hour ride (that includes creek crossings) will cost you $60. There are also breakfast, lunch, and sunset rides. **Sedona Red Rock Jeep Tours,** 270 N. Hwy. 89A (© **800/848-7728** or 928/282-6826; www.redrockjeep.com), offers horseback rides ($75 for 2 hr.) that include transportation by Jeep to the ranch where the rides are held.

Oak Creek is well-known in Arizona as an excellent trout stream, and fly-fishing is quite popular here. The creek is stocked with trout during the summer. For supplies and local advice, drop by **On the Creek Sedona Outfitters,** 274 Apple Ave., Suite C (© **928/203-9973**). This shop also offers a guide service. If you want to take the family fishing, try the **Rainbow Trout Farm,** 3500 N. Ariz. 89A (© **928/282-5799;** www.sportsaz.com), 4 miles north of Sedona.

Surprisingly, Sedona has not yet been ringed with golf courses. However, what few courses there are offer superb views to distract you from your game. The **Oakcreek Country Club,** 690 Bell Rock Blvd. (© **928/284-1660;** www. oakcreekcountryclub.com), south of town off Ariz. 179, has stunning views from the course. Greens fees are $55 to $85. The **Sedona Golf Resort** ✦✦, 35 Ridge Trail Dr. (© **877/733-9885** or 928/284-9355; www.sedonagolfresort.com), south of town on Ariz. 179, offers similarly excellent views of the red rocks. Greens fees are $59 to $109. For a leisurely 9 holes of golf, try the **Canyon Mesa Country Club,** 500 Jacks Canyon Rd. (© **928/284-0036**), in the Village of Oak Creek. This course charges only $16 for 9 holes. Carts are $11 additional.

Fun Fact The Red Rocks Return

Every year, the Sedona Chamber of Commerce receives boxes of rocks sent by visitors who took home a few "souvenirs" from their Sedona vacation and then later felt pangs of guilt over having absconded with pieces of this beautiful landscape.

SHOPPING

Ever since the Cowboy Artists of America organization was founded in Sedona back in 1965 (at what is now the Cowboy Club restaurant), this town has had a reputation as an artists' community. Today, with dozens of galleries around town, it's obvious that art is one of the driving forces behind the local economy. Most of Sedona's galleries specialize in traditional Western, contemporary Southwestern, and Native American art, and in some galleries, you'll see works by members of the Cowboy Artists of America. You'll find the greatest concentration of galleries and shops in the uptown area of Sedona (along Ariz. 89A just north of the "Y") and at Tlaquepaque.

With more than 40 stores and restaurants, **Tlaquepaque** (© 928/282-4838; www.tlaq.com), on Ariz. 179 at the bridge over Oak Creek on the south side of Sedona, bills itself as Sedona's arts-and-crafts village and is designed to resemble a Mexican village. (It was named after a famous arts-and-crafts neighborhood in the suburbs of Guadalajara.) The maze of narrow alleys, courtyards, fountains, and even a chapel and a bell tower are worth a visit even if you aren't in a buying mood. Most of the shops here sell high-end art. I wish all shopping centers were such fascinating places.

Unfortunately, many of Sedona's shops now specialize in cheap Southwestern gifts that have little to do with art, and weeding through the tackiness to find the real galleries can be difficult. One place to start is at **Hozho,** with a couple of Sedona's better galleries, on Ariz. 179 just before you cross the Oak Creek bridge in Sedona.

Avant Garden   If you have an eclectic garden aesthetic, then be sure to check out the unusual garden art in this little shop on the outskirts of town. The shop is set on a hillside below the road and overlooks a small apple orchard. 1100 Hwy. 179. © 928/203-4590. www.sedonagardenart.com.

Compass Rose Gallery   Oddly out of place, but certainly welcome on the souvenir-oriented Sedona shopping scene, this store sells old maps (costing as much as $3,000), old prints, and Edward S. Curtis sepia-toned photos. At Hillside Courtyard, 671 Ariz. 179. © 877/653-6277 or 928/282-7904. www.compassrosegallery.com.

Cowboy Corral   If you want to adopt the Wyatt Earp or Annie Oakley look, this shop can outfit you. Definitely not your standard urban cowboy shop, Cowboy Corral goes for the vintage look. There are even classic firearms to accessorize your ensemble. 219 N. Hwy. 89A. © 800/457-2279 or 928/282-2040. www.cowboycorral.com.

El Prado   Located in the Tlaquepaque shopping center, this gallery features the unusual stone furniture of artist Richard Albin and the fascinating copper wind sculptures of Lyman Whittaker. These aren't the sorts of things you can pack in your suitcase for the flight home, but if you've got a new retirement home here in Arizona, these pieces sure would look good in the garden. At Tlaquepaque, Ariz. 179 downhill from the "Y." © 800/498-3300 or 928/282-7390.

Exposures International Gallery of Fine Art   If you've got a big house and need some big art, this is the place to shop for it. Exposures is the biggest gallery in the state and usually has lots of monumental-size sculptures out front. 561 Hwy. 179. ℂ **877/ART-SITE** or 928/282-1125. www.exposuresfineart.com.

Garland's Indian Jewelry   A great location in the shade of scenic Oak Creek Canyon and a phenomenal collection of concho belts, squash-blossom neck-laces, and bracelets make this a worthwhile stop. There are also lots of kachinas for sale. At Indian Gardens, 3953 W. Hwy. 89A (4 miles north of Sedona). ℂ **928/282-6632.** www.garlandsjewelry.com.

Garland's Navajo Rugs   With a large collection of both contemporary and antique Navajo rugs, Garland's is the premier Navajo rug shop in Sedona. It also carries Native American baskets and pottery, Hopi kachina dolls, and Navajo sand paintings. 411 Hwy. 179. ℂ **928/282-4070.** www.garlandsrugs.com.

Geoffrey Roth Ltd   If you're in the market for some unique jewelry, check out this shop in the Tlaquepaque shopping center. At Tlaquepaque, Ariz. 179 downhill from the "Y." ℂ **928/282-7756.** www.geoffreyrothltd.com.

George Kelly Fine Jewelers   This is another great place to shop for beauti-ful jewelry. The designs are highly creative and incorporate a wide range of stones. At Hyatt Shops at Piñon Pointe, 101 N. Hwy. 89A ℂ **928/282-8884.**

Hillside Sedona   This shopping center just south of Tlaquepaque is dedi-cated to art galleries and upscale retail shops, along with a couple of good restau-rants. The hillside location means there are some good views to be had while you shop. 671 Hwy. 179. ℂ **928/282-4500.** www.hillsidesedona.com.

Hoel's Indian Shop   Located 10 miles north of Sedona in a private residence in Oak Creek Canyon (just past Hoel's Cabins), this Native American arts-and-crafts gallery is one of the finest in the region and sells pieces of the highest quality. Most customers are serious collectors. It's a good idea to call before coming out to make sure the store will be open. 9589 N. Hwy. 89A. ℂ **928/282-3925.** www.hoelsindianshop.com.

Hummingbird House   Looking for an unusual gift to take home to someone? Tired of the crowds of tourists at Tlaquepaque and in Uptown? Check out this hidden gift shop in an attractively restored old home set behind a picket fence. You'll find the shop on a back street behind the Burger King that's at the junc-tion of Ariz. 89A and Ariz. 179. 100 Brewer Rd. ℂ **928/282-0705.**

Scherer Gallery   Although this gallery has a wide range of artworks, what makes it truly unique is its collection of kaleidoscopes, which may be the largest in the country. More than 100 kaleidoscope artists from around the world create these colorful concoctions. You'll also find art glass and tasteful contemporary paintings. At Hillside Sedona, 671 Hwy. 179. ℂ **800/957-2673** or 928/203-9000. www.scherergallery.com.

Sedona Arts Center Gallery Shop   Located at the north end of uptown Sedona, this shop is the best place in town to see the work of area artists—every-thing from jewelry and fiber arts to photography and ceramics. Because it's a nonprofit shop, you won't pay any tax here. 15 Art Barn Rd. ℂ **928/282-3865.** www.sedonaartscenter.com.

Son Silver West   For those who love everything Southwestern, this shop is a treasure trove of all kinds of interesting stuff, including Native American and Hispanic art and crafts, antique *santo* (saint) carvings, antique rifles, imported pots, dried-chile garlands *(ristras),* and garden art. 1476 Hwy. 179 (on the south side of town). ℂ **928/282-3580.** www.sonsilverwest.com.

Victorian Cowgirl   This is not your usual urban cowgirl attire. No, this is the sort of place you shop if you need an $800 Victorian lace-and-velvet dress for an upcoming soiree. Shop owner Candace Walters has designed dresses for Crystal Gayle, Diana Ross, Morgan Fairchild, and Jaclyn Smith among others. Oh, and there are less expensive outfits as well. 2445 W. Hwy. 89A. ② **928/282-7992.** www. victoriancowgirl.com.

WHERE TO STAY

Sedona is one of the most popular destinations in the Southwest, with dozens of moderately priced motels around town. However, accommodations here tend to be relatively expensive for what you get. (Blame it on the incomparable views.) My advice is to save money elsewhere on your trip and make Sedona the place where you splurge on a room with a view. Below are some of my favorites of the many lodging options in the area.

VERY EXPENSIVE

El Portal Sedona ★★   You just can't help but fall in love with this amazing inn. Everything is done right and the overall experience makes it one of the very best lodgings in the entire state. Located adjacent to the Tlaquepaque shopping center and built of hand-formed adobe blocks, El Portal, with its pleasant central courtyard, is designed to resemble a 200-year-old Santa Fe–style hacienda and is a monument to fine craftsmanship. Everywhere you look in this inn, there is such attention to detail. Steve Segner, owner and innkeeper along with his wife, Connie, even made many of the interior Arts and Crafts–style doors himself. The inn is filled with antiques, including not only the furniture, but also the door knobs, hinges, and even air-conditioning vents. In the living room, there are huge ceiling beams salvaged from a railroad bridge over the Great Salt Lake. The lodge even has its own fictional history that includes rooms that would have been the original small, rustic home. Consequently, each of the large guest rooms has its own distinctive character, from Arts and Crafts to cowboy chic (rustic log furniture). All but one room have whirlpool tubs, and many rooms have private balconies with red-rock views. Exquisite dinners are served on weekends.

95 Portal Lane, Sedona, AZ 86336. ② **800/313-0017.** Fax 928/203-9401. www.innsedona.com. 12 units. $225–$450 double. Rates include full breakfast and afternoon hors d'oeuvres. 2-night minimum on weekends, 3-night minimum on holidays. AE, DISC, MC, V. Pets accepted ($35 fee). No children under 10. **Amenities:** Restaurant (New American); access to nearby health club and adjacent resort pool; bikes; concierge; massage; laundry service; guided hikes. *In room:* A/C, TV/DVD, dataport, high-speed Internet access, fridge, hair dryer, iron, free local calls, wi-fi.

Enchantment Resort ★★★   Located at the mouth of Boynton Canyon, this resort more than lives up to its name. The setting is breathtaking, the pueblo-style architecture blends in with the landscape, and the affiliated Mii amo spa is one of the finest in the state. The individual casitas can be booked as two-bedroom suites, one-bedroom suites, or single rooms, but it's worth reserving a suite (ask for one of the newer units) just so you can enjoy the casita living rooms, which feature high beamed ceilings and beehive fireplaces. All the rooms, however, have patios with dramatic views. Both the Yavapai Restaurant (p. 201) and a less formal bar and grill offer tables outdoors; lunch on the terrace should not be missed.

The Mii amo spa is actually a separate entity within the resort and has its own restaurant, guest rooms, and rates (see separate review, below). Enchantment Resort guests have access to the spa facilities and can avail themselves of treatments.

525 Boynton Canyon Rd., Sedona, AZ 86336. ② **800/826-4180** or 928/282-2900. Fax 928/282-9249. www. enchantmentresort.com. 220 units. $295–$395 double; $395–$495 junior suite; $555–$755 1-bedroom suite;

$825–$1,025 2-bedroom suite. AE, DC, DISC, MC, V. **Amenities:** 3 restaurants (New American, regional Southwestern, spa cuisine); lounge; 6 pools; 6-hole pitch-and-putt golf course; putting green; 7 tennis courts; croquet court; full-service spa; Jacuzzi; bike rentals; children's programs; concierge; business center; room service; massage; babysitting; guest laundry; laundry service; dry cleaning. *In room:* A/C, TV, dataport, minibar, coffeemaker, hair dryer, iron, safe.

Mii amo, a destination spa at Enchantment ★★★   This full-service health spa inside the gates of the exclusive Enchantment Resort may not be the largest spa in the state, but it easily claims the best location. Designed to resemble a modern Santa Fe–style pueblo from the outside, the spa backs up against red-rock cliffs and is shaded by cottonwood trees. Though small, Mii amo is well designed, with indoor and outdoor pools and outdoor massage cabanas at the foot of the cliffs. Guest rooms, which open onto a courtyard, have a bold, contemporary styling (mixed with African art and artifacts) that makes them some of the finest accommodations in the state. All units have private patios and gas fireplaces. Mii amo is a world unto itself in this hidden canyon, and no other spa in Arizona has a more Southwestern feel.

525 Boynton Canyon Rd., Sedona, AZ 86336. ✆ **888/749-2137** or 928/203-8500. Fax 928/203-8599. www. enchantmentresort.com. 16 units. 3-night packages: Apr–May and Sept–Oct $1,890–$2,790 per person; Nov–Feb $1,590–$2,490 per person; Mar and June–Aug $1,770–$2,670 per person. Rates include all meals and 5 spa treatments. AE, DC, DISC, MC, V. **Amenities:** Restaurant (New American/spa cuisine); 2 pools (indoor and outdoor); exercise room; full-service spa with 24 treatment rooms and wide variety of body treatments; 2 Jacuzzis; bike rentals; concierge; room service; laundry service; dry cleaning. *In room:* A/C, TV, dataport, coffeemaker, hair dryer, iron, safe.

EXPENSIVE

Adobe Village Graham Inn ★★   A garden full of bronze statues of children greets you when you pull up to this luxurious inn in the Village of Oak Creek, 6 miles south of uptown Sedona. The inn lies almost at the foot of Bell Rock and features a variety of themed accommodations. The villas, the Sundance room, and the Sedona suite are the most impressive rooms here; my favorite is the Purple Lizard villa, which opts for a colorful Taos-style interior and an amazing rustic canopy bed. The Wilderness villa is like a log cabin, with a fireplace that can be seen from both the living room and the double whirlpool tub. The Lonesome Dove villa is a sort of upscale cowboy cabin with a fireplace, potbelly stove, and round hot tub in a "barrel." Can you say *romantic?* While the views here aren't as good as at the nearby Canyon Villa, the accommodations are more distinctive. This inn also operates the Adobe Grand Villas in West Sedona.

150 Canyon Circle Dr., Sedona, AZ 86351. ✆ **800/228-1425** or 928/284-1425. Fax 928/284-0767. www.sedonas finest.com. 11 units. $189–$319 double; $329–$558 suite; $359–$449 casita. Rates include full breakfast. AE, DISC, MC, V. **Amenities:** Outdoor pool; Jacuzzi; bikes; concierge; massage. *In room:* A/C, TV, dataport, coffeemaker, hair dryer, iron, safe.

Amara Creekside Resort ★★   With both views of the red rocks and frontage on an Oak Creek swimming hole, this stylish new boutique hotel offers the best of both worlds here in Sedona. As the first and only hip hotel in Sedona, Amara may seem at first like an odd fit for a town that has long boasted its cowboy heritage, but in my opinion, the minimalist decor and Zen-inspired style are a very welcome addition to the Sedona hotel scene. Set downhill from the busy uptown shopping district, the hotel is conveniently located yet feels secluded. From the outside, the hotel fits right in with the red-rock surroundings, while inside, bold splashes of color contrast with black-and-white photos. Guest rooms all have balconies or patios, wonderful pillow-top beds, and furnishings in black and red that make a bold statement about this brash new resort. The resort's dining room, which doubles as an art gallery, draws on interesting flavor influences from around the globe and is one of the best reasons to stay here. Try to arrange for a sunset dinner while you're here.

310 N. Hwy. 89A, Sedona, AZ 86336. © 866/455-6610 or 928/282-4828. Fax 928/282-4825. www.amara resort.com. 100 units. $179–$339 double; $389–$429 suite. Children 18 and under stay free in parent's room. AE, DC, DISC, MC, V. **Amenities:** Restaurant (New American); lounge; outdoor salt-water pool; Jacuzzi; exercise room; concierge; room service; massages and spa treatments; laundry service; dry cleaning. *In room:* A/C, TV/DVD, dataport, high-speed Internet access, fridge, minibar, coffeemaker, hair dryer, iron, wi-fi.

Briar Patch Inn ★★ (Value) If you're searching for tranquillity or a romantic retreat amid the cool shade of Oak Creek Canyon, this is the place. Located 3 miles north of Sedona on the banks of Oak Creek (there are even swimming holes here), this inn's cottages are surrounded by beautiful grounds where birdsong and the babbling creek set the mood. The cottages date from the 1940s, but have been attractively updated (some with flagstone floors), and a Western style now predominates. Most units have fireplaces and kitchenettes. Breakfast is often served on a terrace above the creek, and there's a stone gazebo for creekside massages. All in all, the Briar Patch offers a delightful combination of solitude and sophistication. The only drawback is the lack of red-rock views from the tree-shaded location.

3190 N. Hwy. 89A, Sedona, AZ 86336. © 888/809-3030 or 928/282-2342. Fax 928/282-2399. www.briar patchinn.com. 18 units. $175–$335 double. Rates include full breakfast. Children under 4 stay free in parent's room. AE, MC, V. **Amenities:** Access to nearby health club; concierge; massage; babysitting. *In room:* A/C, TV/VCR, fridge, coffeemaker, hair dryer, iron.

Canyon Villa ★★ Located in the Village of Oak Creek, 6 miles south of Sedona, this bed-and-breakfast offers luxurious accommodations and spectacular views of the red rocks. All rooms but one have views, as do the pool area, living room, and dining room, so if you want to just hole up at the inn, you won't be missing the best of the area—it's right outside your window. Guest rooms are varied in style—Victorian, Santa Fe, country, rustic, Americana, wicker—but no matter what the decor, the furnishings are impeccable, accompanied by such amenities as robes, whirlpool tubs, and double sinks. All rooms have balconies or patios, and several have fireplaces. Breakfast is a lavish affair meant to be lingered over, and in the afternoon there's an elaborate spread of appetizers.

125 Canyon Circle Dr., Sedona, AZ 86351. © 800/453-1166 or 928/284-1226. Fax 928/284-2114. www. canyonvilla.com. 11 units. $189–$304 double. Rates include full breakfast. AE, DC, DISC, MC, V. No children under 11. **Amenities:** Small outdoor pool; concierge. *In room:* A/C, TV, hair dryer, iron, free local calls.

Garland's Oak Creek Lodge ★ (Finds) Located 8 miles north of Sedona in the heart of Oak Creek Canyon, this may be the hardest place in the area to book a room. People have been coming here for so many years and like it so much that they reserve a year in advance (last-minute cancellations do occur, so don't despair). What makes the lodge so special? Maybe it's that you have to drive *through* Oak Creek to get to your log cabin (don't worry—the water's shallow, and the creek bottom is paved). Maybe it's the beautiful gardens overlooking the creek. Or maybe it's the slow, relaxing atmosphere of an old-time summer getaway. The well-maintained cabins, most of which have air-conditioning, are rustic but comfortable; the larger ones have their own fireplaces. Meals include organic fruits and vegetables grown on the property.

P.O. Box 152, Sedona, AZ 86339. © 928/282-3343. www.garlandslodge.com. 16 units. $200–$235 double (plus 15% service charge). Rates include breakfast and dinner. 2-night minimum. Children under 2 stay free in parent's room. MC, V. Closed mid-Nov to Mar and Sun year-round. **Amenities:** Dining room; lounge; tennis court; access to nearby health club; concierge; massage; babysitting. *In room:* No phone.

Hilton Sedona Resort & Spa ★★   This resort boasts not only one of the most breathtaking golf courses in the state, but also the best pool area north of Phoenix. While golf is the driving force behind most stays here, anyone looking for an active vacation will find plenty to keep themselves busy. Guest rooms are suites of varying sizes, with fireplaces and balconies or patios. The resort's restaurant plays up its views of the golf course and red rocks. About the only drawback to this place is that it's quite a ways outside of uptown Sedona itself (actually south of the Village of Oak Creek), so it's a bit of a drive to Sedona's restaurants and Oak Creek Canyon.

90 Ridge Trail Dr., Sedona, AZ 86351. ✆ 800/HILTONS or 928/284-4040. Fax 928/284-6940. www.hilton sedona.com. 219 units. Mar–June $159–$209 double; July–Sept $139–$199 double; Oct to mid-Nov $159–$199 double; late Nov to Feb $119–$189 double. Children under 18 stay free in parent's room. AE, DC, DISC, MC, V. Pets accepted ($50 nonrefundable deposit). **Amenities:** Restaurant (Southwestern/American); lounge; 3 pools; 18-hole golf course; 3 tennis courts; full-service spa; 3 Jacuzzis; sauna; children's programs; concierge; business center; salon; room service; massage; babysitting; guest laundry; laundry service; dry cleaning. *In room:* A/C, TV, dataport, high-speed Internet access, minibar, coffeemaker, hair dryer, iron, safe.

The Inn on Oak Creek ★★   Located right on Oak Creek and just around the corner from the Tlaquepaque shopping plaza, this luxurious modern inn offers the best of both worlds. A shady creekside setting lends it the air of a forest retreat, yet much of Sedona's shopping and many of its best restaurants are within walking distance. There's even a private little park on the bank of the creek. Guest rooms vary considerably in size, but all have gas fireplaces, whirlpool tubs, and interesting theme decors. My favorites are the Garden Gate (with a picket-fence headboard), Hollywood Out West (with old movie posters), the Rose Arbor (with creek views from both the tub and the bed), and the Angler's Retreat (with bentwood furniture, fly-fishing decor, and a fabulous view). Because the inn is built over the creek, you can look straight down into the water from your balcony.

556 Hwy. 179, Sedona, AZ 86336. ✆ 800/499-7896 or 928/282-7896. Fax 928/282-0696. www.sedona-inn.com. 11 units. $190–$285 double. Rates include full breakfast. AE, DISC, MC, V. No children under 10. **Amenities:** Concierge; massage; guest laundry. *In room:* A/C, TV/VCR, dataport, hair dryer, iron.

Junipine Resort ★ *Kids*   If you're with the kids and are looking for a place in the cool depths of Oak Creek Canyon (rather than amid the red-rock views in Sedona proper), this condominium resort is a good bet. All of the condos have loads of space (some with lofts), skylights, decks, stone fireplaces, decorative quilts on the walls, full kitchens, and contemporary styling; some have hot tubs as well. Best of all, the creek is right outside the door of most units. The dining room serves surprisingly sophisticated fare at reasonable prices, so there's no need to drive all the way to uptown Sedona for a good meal.

8351 N. Hwy. 89A, Sedona, AZ 86336. ✆ 800/742-7463 or 928/282-3375. Fax 928/282-7402. www. junipine.com. 50 units. Early Mar to mid-Nov $170–$280 1-bedroom, $240–$345 2-bedroom; mid-Nov to early Mar $125–$245 1-bedroom, $170–$295 2-bedroom. Children under 13 stay free in parent's room. AE, DC, DISC, MC, V. **Amenities:** Restaurant (Southwestern); concierge; room service; massage; babysitting; coin-op laundry. *In room:* TV, kitchen, fridge, coffeemaker, hair dryer, iron.

L'Auberge de Sedona ★★   If you had to forgo your vacation in France this year, consider a stay at this luxurious boutique resort on the banks of Oak Creek. Shaded by towering sycamore trees and filled with colorful flower gardens surrounding its many cottages, the resort is a sort of French country retreat in the middle of the Arizona desert. L'Auberge's cottages, which look like rustic log cabins from the outside, were all completely redone a couple of years ago with a classic styling truly worthy of a luxury French country inn (leather couches, gorgeous beds, plush towels, wood-burning fireplaces). Although there are rooms in the main lodge, the much larger cottages are definitely worth the extra cost. The restaurant, which carries on the French theme in both its decor and menu, has a creekside terrace during the summer.

301 L'Auberge Lane (P.O. Box B), Sedona, AZ 86339. © **800/272-6777** or 928/282-1661. Fax 928/282-2885. www.lauberge.com. 58 units. $169–375 double; $225–$459 cottage; $345–$595 2-bedroom cottage. Children under 12 stay free in parent's room. AE, DC, DISC, MC, V. Pets accepted ($75 fee). **Amenities:** Restaurant (French); small outdoor pool; access to nearby health club; Jacuzzi; concierge; room service; babysitting; laundry service; dry cleaning. *In room:* A/C, TV, dataport, minibar, coffeemaker, hair dryer, iron, safe.

The Lodge at Sedona ⭐   Set amid pine trees that lend an air of seclusion, yet located barely a block off Ariz. 89A in west Sedona, this large bed-and-breakfast inn is decorated in the Arts and Crafts style, which makes it one of the more tasteful and distinctive inns in Sedona. The best rooms are those on the ground floor. These tend to be large, and in fact, several are suites. Second floor rooms are the inn's most economical accommodations and tend to be fairly small. Half the accommodations here are suites, and since these are only slightly more expensive than the inn's deluxe rooms, the suites get the nod for best choices here. However, if you want views, book one of the small upstairs rooms. Breakfasts are five-course affairs that will often tide you over until dinner.

125 Kallof Place, Sedona, AZ 86336. © **800/619-4467** or 928/204-1942. Fax 928/204-2128. www.lodge atsedona.com. 14 units. $160–$300 double. Rates include full breakfast. 2-night minimum on weekends. DISC, MC, V. Pets accepted ($200 deposit plus $35 per night). **Amenities:** Access to nearby health club; concierge; business center; massage; dry cleaning. *In room:* A/C, hair dryer, iron, no phone.

Saddle Rock Ranch ⭐   The stunning views alone would make this one of Sedona's top lodging choices, but in addition to the views, you get classic Western ranch styling (the house was built in 1926) in a home that once belonged to Barry Goldwater. Walls of stone and adobe, huge exposed beams, and plenty of windows to take in the scenery are enough to enchant guests even before they reach their rooms. And the rooms don't disappoint, either. In one you'll find Victorian elegance, in another an English canopy bed and stone fireplace. Dressing areas and private gardens add to the charm. The third room is actually a separate little cottage with a lodgepole-pine bed, flagstone floors, and a beamed ceiling. The pool and whirlpool are surrounded by a flagstone terrace and enjoy one of the best red-rock views in town. A trail out back leads up to Airport Mesa.

255 Rock Ridge Dr., Sedona, AZ 86336. © **866/282-7640** or 928/282-7640. Fax 928/282-6829. www. saddlerockranch.com. 3 units. $159–$209 double. Rates include full breakfast. 2- to 3-night minimum stay. MC, V. No children under 14. **Amenities:** Small outdoor pool; access to nearby health club; Jacuzzi; concierge; laundry service. *In room:* A/C, TV/VCR, hair dryer.

MODERATE

Best Western Inn of Sedona ⭐   Located about midway between uptown and west Sedona, this hotel has great views of the red rocks from its wide terraces and outdoor pool. Unfortunately, although the guest rooms are comfortable enough, not all of them have views. However, the modern Southwestern decor and the setting, surrounded by native landscaping and located beyond the tourist mainstream, make this an appealing choice.

1200 W. Hwy. 89A, Sedona, AZ 86336. © **800/292-6344** or 928/282-3072. Fax 928/282-7218. www.innof sedona.com. 110 units. $134–$179 double. Rates include continental breakfast. Children 12 and under stay free in parent's room. AE, DC, DISC, MC, V. Pets accepted ($10 fee). **Amenities:** Small outdoor pool; exercise room; Jacuzzi; concierge; massage; dry cleaning. *In room:* A/C, TV, dataport, fridge, coffeemaker, hair dryer, iron.

Forest Houses ☆ *Finds*   Set at the upper end of Oak Creek Canyon and built right on the banks of the creek, these rustic houses and apartments date back to the 1940s. Built by a stone sculptor, they feature artistic touches that set them apart from your average cabins. About half of the houses are built right on the creek, and some seem to grow straight from the rocks in the streambed. Terraces let you fully enjoy the setting. One of my favorite units is the two-bedroom Cloud House, with stone floors, peeled-log woodwork, and a loft. This property is certainly not for everyone (no phones, no TVs, and you have to drive through the creek to get here), but those who discover the Forest Houses often come back year after year.

9275 N. Hwy. 89A, Sedona, AZ 86336. ℂ **928/282-2999.** www.foresthousesresort.com. 15 units. $80–$135 double. 2- to 4-night minimum stay. AE, MC, V. Pets accepted ($20 deposit). Closed Jan to mid-Mar. *In room:* Kitchen, no phone.

The Orchards Inn of Sedona ☆☆   Located in the heart of uptown Sedona and affiliated with the L'Auberge de Sedona, the adjacent French country inn/resort (see review, above), this hotel, claims an enviable location on a hillside above Oak Creek. The views from the hillside setting are spectacular and are some of the best in Sedona. Despite the name, this is much more of a hotel than an inn, but the rooms have all been fairly recently redone in a very tasteful and comfortable classic style. Don't be discouraged when you drive up to the front door; though the hotel is located amid the uptown tourist crowds, it seems miles away once you check into your room and gaze out at the red rocks.

254 Hwy. 89A, Sedona, AZ 86336. ℂ **800/272-6777** or 928/282-1661. Fax 928/282-7818. www.orchards inn.com. 41 units. Jan–Feb and late Nov to mid-Dec $125 double, $165 suite; Mar to late Nov and late Dec $145 double, $195 suite. Children under 12 stay free in parent's room. AE, DC, DISC, MC, V. **Amenities:** Restaurant (Regional American); small outdoor pool; access to nearby health club; Jacuzzi; concierge; room service; babysitting; laundry service; dry cleaning. *In room:* A/C, TV, fridge, coffeemaker, hair dryer, iron.

Radisson Poco Diablo Resort ☆   Although not as lavish as Phoenix golf resorts, this aging property on the southern outskirts of Sedona, is one of the few places in town that can claim to be a golf resort. So, if you're here with your clubs, this is an economical option to the more expensive Hilton. The views here are not as good as those at other properties around town, but the staff is courteous and helpful. The Poco Diablo benefited from a complete renovation a few years back, and in spite of the makeover rates are still surprisingly reasonable. Oak Creek runs through the 22-acre grounds, and the fairways of the 9-hole golf course provide a striking contrast to the red rocks and blue skies. Ask for one of the guest rooms with a view of the golf course or the red rocks; these units have whirlpool tubs and fireplaces and are done in a modern rustic style. Upper-end rooms tend to be a bit overpriced.

1752 S. Hwy. 179, Sedona, AZ 86336. ℂ **800/333-3333** or 928/282-7333. Fax 928/282-9712. www.radisson sedona.com. 138 units. $119–$209 double. AE, DC, DISC, MC, V. **Amenities:** Restaurant (New American); lounge; outdoor pool; 9-hole golf course; 4 tennis courts; 2 racquetball courts; exercise room; 2 Jacuzzis; game room; concierge; room service; massage; laundry service; dry cleaning. *In room:* A/C, TV, fridge, coffeemaker, hair dryer.

Rose Tree Inn *Finds*   This little inn, only a block from Sedona's uptown shopping district, is tucked amid pretty gardens (yes, there are lots of roses) on a quiet street. The property consists of an eclectic cluster of older buildings that have all been renovated. Each unit is furnished differently—one Victorian, one Southwestern, two with gas fireplaces. Four guest rooms have kitchenettes, which makes them good choices for families or for longer stays.

376 Cedar St., Sedona, AZ 86336. ℂ **888/282-2065** or 928/282-2065. Fax 928/282-0083. www.rosetree inn.com. 5 units. $89–$135 double. AE, MC, V. **Amenities:** Jacuzzi; concierge; guest laundry. *In room:* A/C, TV/VCR, coffeemaker, hair dryer, iron, free local calls.

INEXPENSIVE

Cedars Resort on Oak Creek   Located right at the "Y" (where it is often difficult to get out of the parking lot) and within walking distance of uptown Sedona, this motel has fabulous views across Oak Creek to the towering red rocks. Guest rooms are large and have been recently refurbished. For the best views, ask for a king-size room. A long stairway leads down to the creek.

20 W. Hwy. 89A (P.O. Box 292), Sedona, AZ 86339. ℂ **800/874-2072** or 928/282-7010. Fax 928/282-5372. www.sedonacedarsresort.com. 38 units. $89–$129 double. Rates include continental breakfast. Children 12 and under stay free in parent's room. AE, DISC, MC, V. **Amenities:** Small outdoor pool; access to nearby health club; Jacuzzi; concierge; massage; coin-op laundry. *In room:* A/C, TV, dataport, fridge, coffeemaker, hair dryer, iron, free local calls.

Matterhorn Lodge   Located in the heart of the uptown shopping district, this choice is convenient to restaurants and shops, and all guest rooms have excellent views of the red-rock canyon walls. Although the Matterhorn also overlooks busy Ariz. 89A, if you lie in bed and keep your eyes on the rocks, you'll never notice the traffic below. This place may not have a lot of character, but it's a great value for Sedona.

230 Apple Ave., Sedona, AZ 86336. ℂ **800/372-8207** or 928/282-7176. www.matterhornlodge.com. 23 units. Mid-Feb to Nov $79–$129 double; Dec to early Feb $69–$119 double. Children under 5 stay free in parent's room. AE, MC, V. Pets accepted. **Amenities:** Small outdoor pool; access to nearby health club; Jacuzzi. *In room:* A/C, TV, dataport, fridge, coffeemaker, hair dryer, iron, free local calls.

Oak Creek Terrace Resort   Wedged between the highway and Oak Creek about 5 miles north of Sedona, this is a sort of budget romantic getaway. For as little as $89, you can get a room with a fireplace and Jacuzzi. Accommodations range from cramped to spacious, most with a modern woodsy feel (with a bit of Southwest styling thrown in). To get closer to the creek and farther from the highway, ask for a unit in back. You can stretch out in the shade in one of the hammocks beside the creek, then save money on your dining budget by taking advantage of the picnic area with barbecue grills.

4548 N. Hwy. 89A, Sedona, AZ 86336. ℂ **800/224-2229** or 928/282-3562. Fax 928/282-6061. www.oakcreek terrace.com. 17 units. $82–$105 double; $120–$225 suite or bungalow. AE, DC, DISC, MC, V. Small dogs accepted ($35 fee). *In room:* A/C, TV, free local calls.

Sky Ranch Lodge   This motel is located atop Airport Mesa and has the most stupendous vista in town. From here you can see the entire red-rock country, with Sedona filling the valley below. Although the rooms are fairly standard motel issue, some have such features as gas fireplaces, barn-wood walls, and balconies. Only the non-view units fall into the inexpensive category, but those great views are just steps away. The more expensive rooms with views aren't really worth the price.

Airport Rd. (P.O. Box 2579), Sedona, AZ 86339. ℂ **888/708-6400** or 928/282-6400. Fax 928/282-7682. www.skyranchlodge.com. 94 units. $75–$189 double. AE, MC, V. Pets accepted ($10 per night). **Amenities:** Small outdoor pool; Jacuzzi; coin-op laundry. *In room:* A/C, TV, dataport.

CAMPGROUNDS

Within the reaches of Oak Creek Canyon along Ariz. 89A, there are five National Forest Service campgrounds. **Manzanita,** 6 miles north of town, is both the largest and the most pleasant (and the only one open in winter). Other

Oak Creek Canyon campgrounds include **Bootlegger,** 9 miles north of town; **Cave Springs,** 12 miles north of town; and **Pine Flat,** 13 miles north of town. All of these campgrounds charge $16 per night. The **Beaver Creek Campground,** 3 miles east of I-17 on FR 618, which is an extension of Ariz. 179 (take Exit 298 off I-17), is a pleasant spot near the V Bar V petroglyph site. Campsites here are $12 per night. For more information on area campgrounds, stop by the **Coconino National Forest's Red Rock Ranger Station,** 250 Brewer Rd. (© **928/282-4119;** www.fs.fed.us/r3/coconino), on Brewer Road just west of the intersection of Ariz. 89A and Ariz. 179. Reservations can be made for Pine Flat and Cave Spring Creek campgrounds by contacting the **National Recreation Reservation Center** (© **877/444-6777;** www.reserveusa.com).

WHERE TO DINE
VERY EXPENSIVE
René at Tlaquepaque ✦ CONTINENTAL/AMERICAN   Although a formal dining experience and traditional French fare may seem out of place in a town that celebrates its cowboy heritage, René's makes fine dining seem as natural as mesquite-grilled steak and cowboy beans. Located in Tlaquepaque, the city's upscale south-of-the-border-themed shopping center, this restaurant is a great place for a special meal. You might start off with escargots or the salad of spinach and wild mushroom, followed by the house specialty, rack of lamb. More adventurous diners may want to try the excellent tenderloin of venison with whiskey–juniper berry sauce. Finish with a flambéed dessert and selections from the after-dinner drink cart.

At Tlaquepaque, 336 Ariz. 179, Suite 118. © **928/282-9225.** www.rene-sedona.com. Reservations recommended. Main courses $8–$16 lunch, $20–$35 dinner. AE, MC, V. Sun–Thurs 11:30am to 2 or 3pm and 5:30–8:30pm; Fri–Sat 11:30am to 2 or 3pm and 5:30–9pm.

Yavapai Restaurant ✦ SOUTHWESTERN   The Yavapai Restaurant, at the exclusive Enchantment Resort, has the best views and most memorable setting of any restaurant in the Sedona area. It is also one of the town's most formal restaurants, which doesn't quite fit with the rugged setting, but is in keep with Enchantment's exclusive character. The menu changes regularly to take advantage of seasonal ingredients, but keep an eye out for veal chops with morel mushrooms and the sesame-crusted ahi tuna. There's just something about the setting that makes these dishes seem just that much better. Because the scenery is every bit as important as the food here, make sure you make dinner reservations to take in the sunset on the red rocks. You can also soak up the views at breakfast and lunch and save quite a bit of money.

At Enchantment Resort, 525 Boynton Canyon Rd. © **928/204-6000.** Reservations required. Main courses $14–$20 lunch, $23–$40 dinner; Sun brunch $35. AE, DISC, MC, V. Daily 6:30–11:15am, 11:30am–2:30pm, and 5:30–9:30pm; Sun 10:30am–2:15pm.

EXPENSIVE
Cowboy Club Grille & Spirits ✦ SOUTHWESTERN   With its big booths, huge steer horns over the bar, and cowboy gear adorning the walls, the restaurant looks like a glorified cowboy steakhouse—but when you see the menu, you'll know it's more than your average meat-and-potatoes joint. This is big flavor country, and the menu isn't the sort any real cowboy would likely have anything to do with. Start out with fried cactus strips with black-bean gravy or perhaps a rattlesnake brochette. For an entree, be sure to try the buffalo sirloin, which is served with some sort of flavorful sauce. At lunch, burgers and sandwiches are

mainstays, but you can also order a buffalo burger or a chopped buffalo sandwich. Service is relaxed and friendly. It was in this building that the Cowboy Artists of America organization was formed back in 1965.

The adjacent Silver Saddle Room is a more upscale spin on the same concept. It offers suede-covered booths, Western paintings, and a similar menu with prices equivalent to those of the Cowboy Club at dinner. The restaurant also operates the adjacent Redstone Cabin, which does specialty and prix-fixe menu dinners.

241 N. Hwy. 89A. ℂ 928/282-4200. www.cowboyclub.com. Reservations recommended. Main courses $8–$18 lunch, $10–$33 dinner. AE, DISC, MC, V. Daily 11am–4pm and 5–10pm.

El Portal Sedona ⋆⋆ NEW AMERICAN/SOUTHWESTERN   Although El Portal is primarily a deluxe bed-and-breakfast inn, it also serves superb dinners on Friday and Saturday nights. While many of the diners are guests at the inn, the meals are open to the public by reservation. These dinners provide anyone who is not staying at this inn a chance to lounge around in the courtyard and living room/dining room and get a sense for what it is like to stay here. The menu is short and usually includes about a half-dozen entrees and an equal number of appetizers and salads. If the baked brie with roasted garlic and raspberry chipotle sauce is on the menu, don't even think of resisting. This dish is heavenly! The salad with organic basil, buffalo mozzarella, tomatoes, pine nuts and an aged balsamic reduction is another big winner. Pine-nut-crusted halibut with smoked jalapeño-and-papaya salsa and lamb tenderloin with a pine-nut-and-mint pesto are just two examples of the sorts of entrees you can expect. Be sure to accompany your dinner with a bottle of wine from Sedona's own Echo Canyon Winery.

95 Portal Lane ℂ 928/203-4942. www.innsedona.com. Reservations required. Main dishes $15–$26. AE, DISC, MC, V. Fri–Sat 5:30–8pm.

The Heartline Cafe ⋆⋆ SOUTHWESTERN/INTERNATIONAL   The heart line, from Zuni mythology, is a symbol of health and longevity; it is also a symbol for the healthful, creative food served here. Attention to detail and imaginative flavor combinations are the order of the day. To start with, don't miss the tea-smoked chicken dumplings with spicy peanut sauce or the Gorgonzola torte with caramelized pear. Memorable entrees include pecan-crusted local trout with Dijon cream sauce. Those searching out variety in vegetarian choices will find it here. The beautiful courtyard and traditionally elegant interior are good places to savor a meal accompanied by a selection from the reasonably priced wine list.

1610 W. Hwy. 89A. ℂ 928/282-0785. www.heartlinecafe.com. Reservations recommended. Main courses $7.50–$15 lunch, $15–$26 dinner. AE, DISC, MC, V. Fri–Mon 11am–3pm and 5–9pm; Tues–Thurs 5–9pm.

Robert's Creekside Café and Grill ⋆ SOUTHWESTERN   Tucked into a nondescript shopping plaza between Uptown and Tlaquepaque, this lively little restaurant has great food and great views, and best of all, it's convenient yet out of the tourist mainstream. If the sun is shining, you should try to get a seat on the patio (be sure to make a reservation). At lunch, I like the panini (Italian sandwiches), especially the aubergine, which has eggplant, goat cheese, and roasted red peppers. At dinner, the seafoods are usually well prepared and the New York steak with a cognac-and-shiitake-mushroom glaze is a good bet. Don't forget to top it all off with Robert's justifiably famous peach cobbler.

Creekside Plaza, 251 Hwy. 179. ℂ 928/282-3671. Reservations recommended. Main courses $7–$11 lunch, $16–$23 dinner. AE, DISC, MC, V. Daily 11am–4pm and 5–9pm.

Shugrue's Hillside Grill ★★ NEW AMERICAN/CONTINENTAL   Located at the back of the Hillside Sedona shopping plaza, this is the most upscale outpost in a small chain of popular Arizona restaurants. Although the prices are high at dinner, if you come before the sun sets, you'll be treated to unforgettable views out the walls of glass. The extensive menu includes influences from around the world. For a starter, try the blackened shrimp saganaki. There are lots of steak and shrimp entrees, but I like the ancho-pepper-marinated pork tenderloin. For dessert, don't miss the bread pudding if it happens to be on the menu that evening.

671 Hwy. 179. © 928/282-5300. www.shugrues.com. Reservations highly recommended. Main courses $8–$18 lunch, $11–$30 dinner. AE, DC, MC, V. Sun–Thurs 11:30am–3pm and 5–9pm; Fri–Sat 11:30am–3pm and 5–10pm.

MODERATE

Cucina Rústica ★★ MEDITERRANEAN/SOUTHWESTERN   Finally there's a restaurant worth recommending in the Village of Oak Creek. With its various distinctly different dining rooms and numerous antique doors, this new venture from the owner's of west Sedona's wonderful Dahl & DiLuca restaurant (see review, below), feels like a luxurious villa. My personal favorite dining room has a central dome that is lit by what appear to be thousands of stars, and for a genuine starlit dinner, ask for a seat on the patio. If you're into guilty pleasures, try the cheese-filled fried olives, otherwise, go for the *bruschetta pomodoro,* a tomato-and-basil appetizer that tastes like a bite of summer. When it comes time to order an entree, just ask for the *gamberi del capitano.* These grilled prawns, wrapped in radicchio and prosciutto, are among the best prawns I've ever had— positively ambrosial.

7000 Hwy. 179, Village of Oak Creek. © 928/284-3010. Reservations recommended. Main courses $12–$26. AE, DC, DISC, MC, V. Daily 5–9 or 10pm.

Dahl & DiLuca ★★ ROMAN ITALIAN   A faux Tuscan villa interior, complete with a bar in a grotto, makes this the most romantic restaurant in Sedona, and the excellent Italian food makes it that much more unforgettable. Be sure to start with some of the *pane romano,* which, as far as we're concerned, is the best garlic bread west of New York's Little Italy. Pasta predominates here, and portions are big. I like the linguine with calamari and mushrooms. The kitchen also serves up a panoply of deftly prepared veal, seafood, chicken, and vegetarian dishes. The eggplant Parmesan and portobello *alla griglia* are real standouts. Genial and efficient service, reasonably priced wines, and nightly live music make this place even more enjoyable. An amaretto crème brûlée or a deceptively light chocolate espresso mousse torte—that's the sort of difficult decision you'll have to make when it comes time for dessert.

2321 W. Hwy. 89A (in west Sedona diagonally across from the Safeway Plaza). © 928/282-5219. www. dahl-diluca.com. Reservations recommended. Main courses $11–$27. AE, DC, DISC, MC, V. Daily 5–9 or 10pm.

Fournos Restaurant ★ (Finds) MEDITERRANEAN   In contrast to the glitz and modern Southwest decor of so many of Sedona's restaurants, Fournos is a refreshingly casual place run by the husband-and-wife team of Shirley and Demetrios Fournos. Step through the front door and you almost have to walk through the kitchen to get to the handful of tables in the dining room. In the kitchen, chef Demetrios cooks up a storm, preparing such dishes as shrimp flambéed in ouzo and baked with feta; lamb Cephalonian with herbs and potatoes; and poached fish Mykonos with a sauce of yogurt, onions, mayonnaise, and butter. Other specialties are rack of lamb and lamb Wellington. For dessert, try the delicious flourless semolina-honey sponge cake with ice cream and fruit.

3000 W. Hwy. 89A. ⓒ **928/282-3331**. Reservations highly recommended. Main courses $16–$20. No credit cards. Thurs–Sat seatings at 6 and 8pm.

INEXPENSIVE

Dining in Sedona tends to be expensive, so your best bets for economical meals are sandwich shops or ethnic restaurants. For breakfast, locals swear by the **Coffee Pot Restaurant,** 2050 W. Hwy. 89A (ⓒ **928/282-6626**). For filling sandwiches, try **Sedona Memories,** 321 Jordan Rd. (ⓒ **928/282-0032**), 1 block off Ariz. 89A in the uptown shopping area. My personal favorite lunch spot is the **Wine Basket at Hillside,** 671 Hwy. 179 E. (ⓒ **928/203-9411**; www.winebasket athillside.com), which does a few sandwiches, a soup of the day and a couple of appetizer platters. Accompany any of these with a glass of wine for a wonderful little lunch. Having a picnic? Stock up at **New Frontiers Natural Foods,** 1420 W. Hwy. 89A (ⓒ **928/282-6311**). When you need good espresso, perhaps for that long drive to the Grand Canyon, stop by **Ravenheart of Sedona,** at the Old Marketplace shopping center, 1370 W. Hwy. 89A (ⓒ **928/282-5777**) or their uptown location at 206 N. Hwy. 89A (ⓒ **928/282-1070**).

The Hideaway Restaurant ITALIAN/DELI   Hidden away at the back of a shopping plaza near the "Y," this casual family restaurant is as popular with locals as it is with visitors. Basic pizzas, subs, sandwiches, salads, and pastas are the choices here, and both the salad dressings and sausages are made on the premises. However, most people come for the knockout views. From the shady porch, you can see the creek below and the red rocks rising across the canyon. Lunch or an early sunset dinner are your best bets. The *paisano* lunch and antipasto salad are both good choices. Keep an eye out for hummingbirds and great blue herons.

Country Sq., Ariz. 179. ⓒ **928/282-4204**. Reservations accepted only for parties of 10 or more. Main courses $6–$15. AE, DISC, MC, V. Daily 11am–9pm.

Javelina Cantina MEXICAN   Although Javelina Cantina is part of a chain of Arizona restaurants, the formula works, and few diners leave disappointed. Sure, the restaurant is touristy, but what it has going for it is good Mexican food, a lively atmosphere, decent views, and a convenient location in the Hillside shops. The grilled fish tacos are tasty, as is the pork adobo sandwich. Other dishes worth trying include the salmon tostadas and the enchiladas made with potatoes, spinach, and cheese. There are also plenty of different margaritas and tequilas to accompany your meal. Expect a wait.

At Hillside Sedona shopping plaza, 671 Hwy. 179. ⓒ **928/203-9514**. Reservations recommended. Main courses $7.25–$18. AE, DC, MC, V. Daily 11:30am–9:30pm.

Pizza Picazzo ★ PIZZA   For down-home pizza in an upscale setting, nothing in Sedona can compare with this artistic pizza place. Throw in an attractive walled patio dining area and a view of Coffee Pot Rock, and you have one of the best values in town. There are good by-the-slice lunch specials, and during happy hour, there are free appetizers. Try the Southwestern pizza, which is made with salsa, spicy chicken or beef, pepper jack cheese, and black beans. Or how about a bacon cheeseburger pizza? Great setting, great view, great pizza, and best of all, by eating here you can avoid the crowds in uptown Sedona.

1855 W. Hwy. 89A. ⓒ **928/282-4140**. Call ahead to get your name on the wait list. Pizzas $11–$21. AE, DC, MC, V. Daily 11:30am–10pm.

Red Planet Diner ⭑ *Kids* INTERNATIONAL   With its flying saucer fountain out front and its totally cosmic decor, this casual diner is a UFO-spotters dream come true. Sip a mothership margarita or Martian martini while you chow down on lunar linguine, moon loaf, teleportation tacos, or any of the other out-of-this-world dishes. The walls are plastered with photos of UFOs. Unfortunately, you may sometimes feel as if aliens have kidnapped your wait person.

1655 W. Hwy. 89A. ℭ **928/282-6070.** Main courses $6–$15. AE, DISC, MC, V. Daily 11am–11pm.

SEDONA AFTER DARK

If you'd like to catch some live theater while you're in town, check out what's on stage at the **Canyon Moon Theatre Company,** 1370 W. Hwy. 89A (ℭ **928/ 282-6212;** www.canyonmoontheatre.org), which has its theater at the back of the Old Marketplace shopping center in west Sedona. Tickets are $8 to $17. Also check the schedule of **Chamber Music Sedona** (ℭ **928/204-2415;** www. chambermusicsedona.org).

If you're searching for good microbrewed beer, head to the **Oak Creek Brewing Co.,** 2050 Yavapai Dr. (ℭ **928/204-1300**), north of Ariz. 89A off Coffee Pot Drive. There's also the affiliated **Oak Creek Brewery and Grill** (ℭ **928/ 282-3882**) in the Tlaquepaque shopping center.

6

The Grand Canyon & Northern Arizona

The Grand Canyon—the name is at once both entirely apt and entirely inadequate. How can words sum up the grandeur of two billion years of the earth's history sliced open by the power of a single river? Once an impassable and forbidding barrier to explorers and settlers, the Grand Canyon is today a magnet that each year attracts millions of visitors from all over the world. The pastel layers of rock weaving through the canyon's rugged ramparts, the interplay of shadows and light, the wind in the pines, and the croaking of ravens on the rim—these are the sights and sounds that never fail to transfix the hordes of visitors who gaze awestruck into the canyon's seemingly infinite depths.

While the Grand Canyon is undeniably the most amazing natural attraction anywhere in the state, northern Arizona contains other worthwhile, and less crowded, natural attractions. Only 60 miles south of the great yawning chasm stand the San Francisco Peaks, the tallest of which, Humphreys Peak, rises to 12,643 feet. These peaks, sacred to the Hopi and Navajo, are ancient volcanoes that today are popular with skiers, hikers, and mountain bikers. Volcanic eruptions 900 to 1,000 years ago helped turn the land northeast of Flagstaff into fertile farmland that allowed the Sinagua people to thrive in this otherwise inhospitable environment. Within a few hundred years, however, the Sinagua disappeared. Today the ruins of their ancient villages are all that remain of their culture.

Amid northern Arizona's miles of windswept plains and ponderosa pine forests stands the city of Flagstaff, which at 7,000 feet in elevation is one of the highest cities in the United States. Flagstaff is home to Northern Arizona University, whose students ensure that this is a lively, liberal town. Born of the railroads and named for a flagpole, Flagstaff is now the main jumping-off point for trips to the Grand Canyon. However, the city has preserved its Western heritage in its restored downtown historic district, and is well worth a visit on its own.

While it's the Grand Canyon that brings many people to northern Arizona, most visitors spend only a day or so in Grand Canyon National Park. So, you may want to take a look at what else there is to do in this part of the state. If, on the other hand, you want only to visit the canyon, there are many different ways to accomplish this goal. You can do so in a group or alone, on foot or by raft, from a mule, a train, or a helicopter. Regardless of what you decide, you'll find that the Grand Canyon more than lives up to its name.

1 Flagstaff ★ ★

150 miles N of Phoenix; 32 miles E of Williams; 80 miles S of Grand Canyon Village

With its wide variety of accommodations and restaurants, the great outdoors at the edge of town, three national monuments nearby, one of the state's finest museums, and a university that supports a lively cultural community, Flagstaff makes an ideal base for exploring much of northern Arizona.

The San Francisco Peaks, just north of the city, are the site of the Arizona Snowbowl ski area, one of the state's main winter playgrounds. In summer, miles of trails through these same mountains attract hikers and mountain bikers, and it's even possible to ride the chairlift for a panoramic vista that stretches 70 miles north to the Grand Canyon. Of the area's national monuments, two preserve ancient Indian ruins and one preserves an otherworldly landscape of volcanic cinder cones.

It was as a railroad town that Flagstaff made its fortunes, and after several years of renovations, the historic downtown offers a glimpse of the days when the city's fortunes rode the rails. The railroad still runs right through the middle of Flagstaff, much to the dismay of many visitors, who find that most of the city's inexpensive motels (and even some of the more expensive places) are too close to the busy tracks to allow them to get a good night's sleep.

ESSENTIALS

GETTING THERE   Flagstaff is on I-40, one of the main east–west interstates in the United States. I-17 starts here and heads south to Phoenix. Ariz. 89A connects Flagstaff to Sedona by way of Oak Creek Canyon. U.S. 180 connects Flagstaff with the South Rim of the Grand Canyon, and U.S. 89 connects the city with Page.

Pulliam Airport, 3 miles south of Flagstaff off I-17, is served by **America West** (© **800/235-9292**) from Phoenix. **Amtrak** (© **800/872-7245**) offers service to Flagstaff from Chicago and Los Angeles. The train station is at 1 E. Rte. 66.

VISITOR INFORMATION   Contact the **Flagstaff Visitor Center,** 1 E. Rte. 66 (© **800/842-7293** or 928/774-9541; www.flagstaffarizona.org). Memorial Day weekend through Labor Day weekend, the visitor center is open daily from 7am to 7pm; the rest of the year, it's open Monday through Saturday from 8am to 6pm and Sunday from 9am to 4pm.

ORIENTATION   Downtown Flagstaff is just north of I-40. Milton Road, which at its southern end becomes I-17 to Phoenix, leads past Northern Arizona University on its way into downtown and becomes Route 66, which runs parallel to the railroad tracks. San Francisco Street is downtown's main street. Humphreys Street leads north out of town toward the San Francisco Peaks and the South Rim of the Grand Canyon.

GETTING AROUND   Car rentals are available from **Avis** (© 800/230-4898 or 928/774-8421), **Budget** (© 800/527-0700), **Enterprise** (© 800/261-7331 or 928/526-1377), **Hertz** (© 800/654-3131 or 928/774-4452), and **National** (© 800/227-7368 or 928/774-3321).

Call **All Star Taxi** (© 928/213-TAXI) if you need a taxi. **Mountain Line Transit** (© 928/779-6624) provides public bus transit around the city; the fare is $1.

OUTDOOR PURSUITS

Flagstaff is northern Arizona's center for outdoor activities. Chief among them is skiing at **Arizona Snowbowl** (② **928/779-1951;** www.arizonasnowbowl. com), on the slopes of Mount Agassiz, from which you can see all the way to the North Rim of the Grand Canyon. There are four chairlifts, 32 runs, 2,300 vertical feet of slopes, ski rentals, and a children's ski program. With an excellent mix of beginner, intermediate, and advanced slopes, and as the ski area that's most accessible from Phoenix, Snowbowl sees a lot of weekend traffic from the snow-starved denizens of the desert. Snow conditions are, however, very unreliable, and the ski area can be shut down for weeks on end due to lack of snow. All-day lift tickets are $42 for adults, $24 for children 8 to 12, $22 for seniors, and free for children under 8 and seniors over 69. In summer, you can ride a chairlift almost to the summit of Mount Agassiz and enjoy the expansive views across seemingly all of northern Arizona. The round-trip lift-ticket price is $10 for adults, $8 for seniors, and $6 for children 8 to 12. To get here, take U.S. 180 north from Flagstaff for 7 miles and turn right onto Snow Bowl Road.

Snowbowl also operates the **Flagstaff Nordic Center,** 16 miles north of Flagstaff (② **928/779-1951,** ext. 195), which has 25 miles of groomed track and 9 miles of snowshoe trails. Equipment rentals and ski lessons are available. Trail passes are $10 ($5 for a snowshoe pass).

When there's no snow on the ground, there are plenty of trails for hiking throughout the San Francisco Peaks, and many national forest trails are open to mountain bikes. Late September, when the aspens have turned a brilliant golden yellow, is one of the best times of year for a hike in Flagstaff's mountains. If you've got the stamina, do the **Humphreys Peak Trail,** which climbs 3,000 feet in 4½ miles. Needless to say, the views from the 12,633-foot summit are stupendous. After all, this is the highest point in Arizona. To reach the trail head, take U.S. 180 north out of Flagstaff for 7 miles, turn right on Snow Bowl Road, and continue to the parking area by the ski lodge. This is my favorite Flagstaff area hike and is nearly as awe inspiring in its own way as hiking down into the Grand Canyon.

If you'd like a short hike with a big pay off, hike to **Red Mountain.** This hike is only about 2.5 miles round-trip, but leads to a fascinating red-walled cinder cone that long ago collapsed to reveal its strange interior walls. To find the trail head, drive north from Flagstaff toward the Grand Canyon on U.S. 180. At milepost 24, watch for a forest road leading west for about a quarter mile to the trail-head parking area.

For information on other hikes in the Coconino National Forest, contact the **Peaks Ranger District,** 5075 N. Hwy. 89, Flagstaff (② **928/526-0866;** www. fs.fed.us/r3/coconino).

If you feel like saddlin' up and hittin' the trail, contact **Flying Heart Ranch** (② **928/526-2788**), located 4½ miles north of I-40 on U.S. 89. This outfitter leads rides up into the foothills of the San Francisco Peaks and out through the juniper and piñon forests of the lower elevations. Prices range from $25 for a 1-hour ride to $100 for an all-day ride.

SEEING THE SIGHTS

Downtown Flagstaff along Route 66, San Francisco Street, Aspen Avenue, and Birch Avenue is the city's **historic district.** These old brick buildings are now filled with shops selling Native American crafts, works by local artists and artisans, Route 66 souvenirs, and various other Arizona mementos such as rocks,

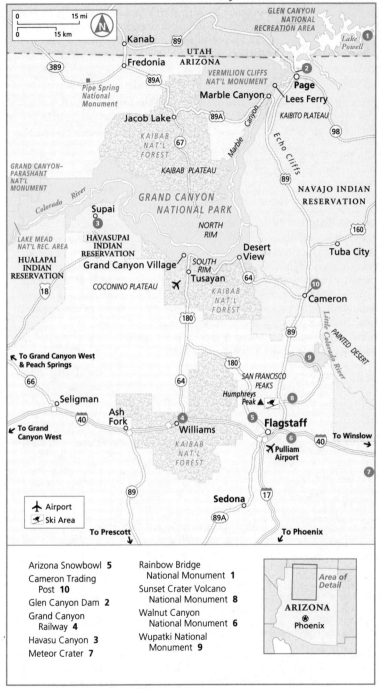

The Grand Canyon & Northern Arizona

0 — 15 mi
0 — 15 km

GLEN CANYON NATIONAL RECREATION AREA

Lake Powell **1**

Kanab 89

UTAH
ARIZONA

Fredonia

389

89A

VERMILION CLIFFS NAT'L MONUMENT

Page **2**

Lees Ferry

Marble Canyon

KAIBITO PLATEAU

Pipe Spring National Monument

Jacob Lake

89A

98

KAIBAB NAT'L FOREST 67

Marble Canyon

Echo Cliffs

KAIBAB PLATEAU

89

NAVAJO INDIAN RESERVATION

GRAND CANYON-PARASHANT NAT'L MONUMENT

Colorado River

GRAND CANYON NATIONAL PARK

Supai **3**

NORTH RIM

160

HAVASUPAI INDIAN RESERVATION

LAKE MEAD NAT'L REC. AREA

Desert View

Tuba City

HUALAPAI INDIAN RESERVATION

Grand Canyon Village

SOUTH RIM

Tusayan 64

18

COCONINO PLATEAU

KAIBAB NAT'L FOREST

Cameron **10**

180

89

Little Colorado River

To Grand Canyon West & Peach Springs

PAINTED DESERT

66

180

SAN FRANCISCO PEAKS

Humphreys Peak ▲

9

8

Seligman

To Grand Canyon West

40

Ash Fork

64

5 Flagstaff

6

✈ Pulliam Airport

40 **To Winslow →**

Williams **4**

KAIBAB NAT'L FOREST

7

✈ Airport
⛷ Ski Area

89

Sedona

17

89A

To Prescott ↓

To Phoenix ↙

Arizona Snowbowl **5**
Cameron Trading Post **10**
Glen Canyon Dam **2**
Grand Canyon Railway **4**
Havasu Canyon **3**
Meteor Crater **7**

Rainbow Bridge National Monument **1**
Sunset Crater Volcano National Monument **8**
Walnut Canyon National Monument **6**
Wupatki National Monument **9**

Area of Detail

ARIZONA
✱ Phoenix

minerals, and crystals. Don't miss **Jonathan Day's Indian Arts,** 20 N. Leroux St. (© **928/779-6099;** www.traditionalhopikachinas.com), a small shop with what just might be the best selection of traditional Hopi kachinas in the state. Also worth a visit is **The Artists Gallery,** 17 N. San Francisco St. (© **928/773-0958;** www.theartistsgallery.com). The historic district is worth a walk-through even if you aren't shopping.

MUSEUMS, PARKS & CULTURAL ACTIVITIES

The Arboretum at Flagstaff   Covering 200 acres, this arboretum, the highest-elevation research garden in the United States, focuses on plants of the high desert, coniferous forests, and alpine tundra, all of which are environments found in the vicinity of Flagstaff. On the grounds are a butterfly garden, an herb garden, a shade garden, and a passive solar greenhouse.

4001 S. Woody Mountain Rd. © 928/774-1442. www.thearb.org. Admission $4 adults, $3 seniors, $1 children 6–12. Daily 9am–5pm. Guided tours at 11am and 1pm. Closed Dec 16–Mar 31.

Arizona Historical Society Pioneer Museum   This small historical museum is housed in a stone building that was constructed in 1908 as a hospital for the indigent (in other words, a poor farm). Today, the old hospital contains a historical collection from northern Arizona's pioneer days. Among the exhibits are pieces of camera equipment used by Emery Kolb at his studio on the South Rim of the Grand Canyon, along with many of Kolb's photos. Barbed wire, livestock brands, dolls, saddles, and trapping and timber displays round out the collection. Don't miss the doctor's office filled with frightening instruments.

2340 N. Fort Valley Rd. © 928/774-6272. Admission $3 adults, $2 seniors and students 12–18. Mon–Sat 9am–5pm. Closed New Year's Day, Thanksgiving, and Christmas.

Lowell Observatory 🔭   This historic observatory is located atop aptly named Mars Hill and is one of the oldest astronomical observatories in the Southwest. Founded in 1894 by Percival Lowell, the observatory has played important roles in contemporary astronomy. Among the work carried out here was Lowell's study of the planet Mars and the calculations that led him to predict the existence of Pluto. It wasn't until 13 years after Lowell's death that Pluto was finally discovered almost exactly where he had predicted it would be. Today, the observatory is still an important research facility, but most astronomical observations are now carried out at Anderson Mesa, 10 miles farther away from the lights of Flagstaff.

The facility consists of several observatories, a visitor center with numerous fun and educational exhibits, and outdoor displays. While it can be interesting to visit during the day, the main attraction is the chance to observe the stars and planets through the observatory's 24-inch telescope. Keep in mind that the telescope domes are not heated, so if you come up to stargaze, be sure to dress appropriately. Also, there are no programs on cloudy nights.

1400 W. Mars Hill Rd. © 928/774-3358. www.lowell.edu. Admission $5 adults, $4 seniors, $2 children 5–17. Mar–Oct daily 9am–5pm (tours at 10am, 1pm, and 3pm); Nov–Feb daily noon–5pm (tours at 1 and 3pm). Telescope viewings: June–Aug Mon–Sat 8pm; Sept–Oct and Mar–May Wed and Fri–Sat 7:30pm; Nov–Feb Fri–Sat 7:30pm. Closed New Year's Day, Easter, Thanksgiving, Christmas Eve, and Christmas.

Museum of Northern Arizona 🔭🔭   This small but surprisingly thorough museum is the ideal first stop on an exploration of northern Arizona. You'll learn, through state-of-the-art exhibits about the archaeology, ethnology, geology, biology, and fine arts of the region. The cornerstone of the museum is an exhibit that explores life on the Colorado Plateau from 15,000 B.C. to the present.

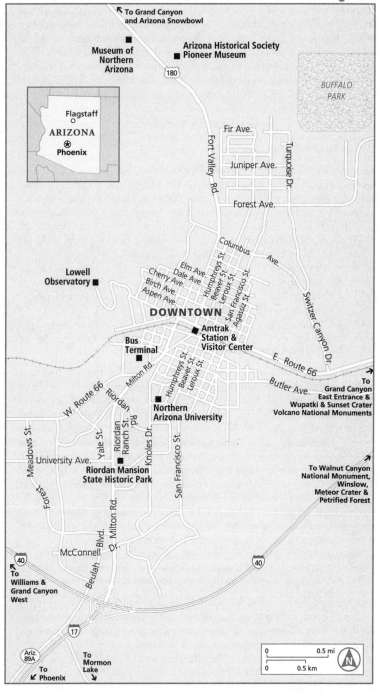

↖ To Grand Canyon
and Arizona Snowbowl

Museum of
Northern
Arizona

Arizona Historical Society
Pioneer Museum

180

BUFFALO
PARK

Flagstaff ○

ARIZONA

✪

● Phoenix

Fort Valley Rd.

Fir Ave.

Juniper Ave.

Forest Ave.

Turquoise Dr.

Columbus Ave.

Elm Ave.
Dale Ave.
Cherry Ave.
Birch Ave.
Aspen Ave.

Lowell
Observatory ■

Humphreys St.
Beaver St.
Leroux St.
San Francisco St.
Agassiz St.

DOWNTOWN

Switzer Canyon Dr.

Bus
Terminal

Amtrak
Station &
Visitor Center

Milton Rd.

E. Route 66

W. Route 66

Riordan Rd.

Humphreys St.
Beaver St.
Leroux St.

Butler Ave.

To
Grand Canyon
East Entrance &
Wupatki & Sunset Crater
Volcano National Monuments

Northern
Arizona University

Yale St.

Riordan
Ranch St.

Knoles Dr.

San Francisco St.

Meadows St.

University Ave.

Riordan Mansion
State Historic Park

To Walnut Canyon
National Monument,
Winslow,
Meteor Crater &
Petrified Forest

Forest

Beulah Blvd.

Milton Rd.

McConnell Dr.

40

40

40
To
Williams &
Grand Canyon
West

17

Ariz.
89A
To
↙ Phoenix

To
Mormon
Lake
↓

0   0.5 mi
0   0.5 km

N

Among the other displays are a life-size kiva ceremonial room and a small but interesting collection of kachinas. The large gift shop is full of contemporary Native American arts and crafts, and throughout the summer there are special exhibits and sales focusing on Hopi, Navajo, and Zuni arts and crafts.

The museum building itself is made of native stone and incorporates a court-yard featuring vegetation from the six life zones of northern Arizona. Outside is a short, self-guided nature trail that leads through a narrow canyon strewn with boulders.

3101 N. Fort Valley Rd. (3 miles north of downtown Flagstaff on U.S. 180). © **928/774-5213.** www. musnaz.org. Admission $5 adults, $4 seniors, $3 students, $2 children 7–17. Daily 9am–5pm. Closed New Year's Day, Thanksgiving, and Christmas.

Riordan Mansion State Historic Park ⭐   Built in 1904 for local timber barons Michael and Timothy Riordan, this 13,000-square-foot mansion—Arizona's finest example of an Arts and Crafts–era building—is actually two houses connected by a large central hall. Each brother and his family occupied half of the house (they had the rooflines constructed differently so that visitors could tell the two sides apart). Although the mansion looks like a log cabin, it's actually only faced with log slabs. Inside, mission-style furnishings and touches of Art Nouveau styling make it clear that this family was keeping up with the times. The west wing of the mansion holds displays on, among other things, Stickley furniture. Guided tours provide a glimpse into the lives of two of Flagstaff's most influential pioneers.

409 E. Riordan Rd. (off Milton Rd./Ariz. 89A, just north of the junction of I-40 and I-17). © **928/779-4395.** www.azstateparks.com. Admission $6 adults, $2.50 children 7–13. May–Oct daily 8:30am–5pm; Nov–Apr daily 10:30am–5pm. Guided tours on the hour. Closed Christmas.

Sunset Crater Volcano National Monument ⭐   Dotting the landscape northeast of Flagstaff are more than 400 volcanic craters, of which Sunset Crater Volcano is the youngest. Taking its name from the sunset colors of the cinders near its summit, Sunset Crater Volcano stands 1,000 feet tall and began form-ing in A.D. 1064. Over a period of 100 years, the volcano erupted repeatedly (creating the red-and-yellow cinder cone we see today), and eventually covered an area of 800 square miles with ash, lava, and cinders. A 1-mile interpretive trail passes through a desolate landscape of lava flows, cinders, and ash as it skirts the base of this volcano. If you want to climb to the top of a cinder cone, take the 1-mile Lenox Crater Trail. In the visitor center (at the west entrance to the national monument), you can learn more about the formation of Sunset Crater and about volcanoes in general. Near the visitor center is the small Bonito Campground, which is open from late May to mid-October.

14 miles north of Flagstaff off U.S. 89. © **928/526-0502.** www.nps.gov/sucr. Admission $5 adults, free for children under 17 (admission also valid for Wupatki National Monument). Daily sunrise to sunset; visitor cen-ter June–Aug daily 8am–6pm, Sept–Nov and Mar–May 8am–5pm, Dec–Feb 9am–5pm. Closed Christmas.

Walnut Canyon National Monument ⭐   The remains of 300 small 13th-century Sinagua cliff dwellings can be seen in the undercut layers of limestone in this 400-foot-deep wooded canyon east of Flagstaff. These cliff dwellings, though not nearly as impressive as those at Montezuma Castle National Monu-ment (50 miles to the south) or Wupatki National Monument (20 miles to the north), are worth a visit for the chance to poke around inside the well-preserved rooms, which were well protected from the elements (and from enemies). The Sinagua were the same people who built and then abandoned the stone pueblos found in Wupatki National Monument. It's theorized that when the land to the

Moments **Join an Archaeological Dig**

Elden Pueblo, located on the north side of Flagstaff on U.S. 89, is a small archaeological site that is open to the public free of charge. Although these Sinagua ruins are not much to look at, you can help out with the excavation of the site, if you're interested. Each summer, the **Elden Pueblo Archaeological Project** (© **928/527-3452**) hosts a field school for members of the Arizona Archaeological Society (AAS). Field schools cost $100 per week (plus $30 to become an AAS member).

north lost its fertility, the Sinagua began migrating southward, settling for 150 years in Walnut Canyon.

A self-guided trail leads from the visitor center on the canyon rim down 185 feet to a section of the canyon wall where 25 cliff dwellings can be viewed up close (some can even be entered). Bring binoculars so you can scan the canyon walls for other cliff dwellings. From Memorial Day to Labor Day on Thursdays, Saturdays, and Sundays, there are guided hikes into the monument's backcountry (reservations required). There's also a picnic area near the visitor center.

7½ miles east of Flagstaff on Walnut Canyon Rd. (take Exit 204 off I-40). © 928/526-3367. www.nps.gov/waca. Admission $5 adults, free for children under 17. June–Aug daily 8am–6pm; Sept–Nov and Mar–May daily 8am–5pm; Dec–Feb daily 9am–5pm; trail closes 1 hr. earlier. Closed Christmas.

Wupatki National Monument ★★   The landscape northeast of Flagstaff is desolate and windswept, a sparsely populated region carpeted with volcanic ash deposited in the 11th century. It comes as quite a surprise, then, to learn that this area contains hundreds of Native American habitation sites. The most impressive ruins are those left by the Sinagua (the name means "without water" in Spanish), who inhabited this area from around A.D. 1100 until shortly after 1200. The Sinagua people built small villages of stone similar to the pueblos on the nearby Hopi Reservation, and today the ruins of these ancient villages can be seen in this national monument.

The largest of the pueblos is Wupatki Ruin, in the southeastern part of the monument. Here the Sinagua built a sprawling three-story pueblo containing nearly 100 rooms. They also constructed what is believed to be a ball court, which, although quite different in design from the courts of the Aztec and Maya, suggests that a similar game may have been played in this region. Another circular stone structure just below the main ruins may have been an amphitheater or dance plaza.

The most unusual feature of Wupatki, however, is a natural phenomenon: a blowhole, which may have been the reason this pueblo was constructed here. A network of small underground tunnels and chambers acts as a giant barometer, blowing air through the blowhole when the underground air is under greater pressure than the outside air. On hot days, cool air rushes out of the blowhole with amazing force.

Several other ruins within the national monument are easily accessible by car. They include Nalakihu, Citadel, and Lomaki, which are the closest to U.S. 89, and Wukoki, near Wupatki. Wukoki Ruin, built atop a huge sandstone boulder, is particularly picturesque. The visitor center is adjacent to the Wupatki ruins and contains interesting exhibits on the Sinagua and Ancestral Puebloan people who once inhabited the region.

36 miles north of Flagstaff off U.S. 89. © **928/679-2365.** www.nps.gov/wupa. Admission $5 adults, free for children under 17. Daily sunrise to sunset. Visitor center June–Aug daily 8am–6pm; Mar–May and Sept–Nov daily 8am–5pm; Dec–Feb daily 9am–5pm. Closed Christmas.

WHERE TO STAY
EXPENSIVE

The Inn at 410 🌟🌟 Situated only 2 blocks from downtown Flagstaff, this restored 1907 Craftsman home is one of the best B&Bs in Arizona, providing convenience, pleasant surroundings, comfortable rooms, and delicious breakfasts. Guests can lounge and enjoy afternoon tea on the front porch, in the comfortable living room and dining room, or out on the pleasant garden patio. Each guest room features a distinctive theme; my favorites are the Dakota Suite and the Southwest Room, which conjure up the inn's Western heritage. All rooms have fireplaces, and three have two-person whirlpool tubs. An adjacent building contains some of the guest rooms, and these rooms are just as nice as those in the main house.

410 N. Leroux St., Flagstaff, AZ 86001. © **800/774-2008** or 928/774-0088. Fax 928/774-6354. www. inn410.com. 9 units. $145–$205 double. Rates include full breakfast. MC, V. No children under 4. **Amenities:** Access to nearby health club; concierge; business center. *In room:* A/C, TV/DVD/VCR, fridge, coffeemaker, hair dryer, iron, no phone, wi-fi.

MODERATE

Arizona Mountain Inn (*Kids*) This family-oriented inn is a quiet mountain retreat set beneath shady pine trees, located just a few minutes south of downtown Flagstaff. Although there are three bed-and-breakfast rooms in the main building, the rest of the accommodations are cabins that sleep 2 to 16 people. Many of the rustic cabins are A-frames or chalets, and each is a little different from the others. The property consists of 13 acres, beyond which are miles of national forest.

4200 Lake Mary Rd., Flagstaff, AZ 86001. © **928/774-8959.** Fax 928/774-8837. www.arizonamountain inn.com. 20 units. $85–$115 double; $85–$400 cabin. Children 2 and under stay free in parent's cabin. AE, DISC, MC, V. Pets accepted in cabins ($10 per night). **Amenities:** Access to nearby health club; volleyball court; coin-op laundry; playground; horseshoe pits. *In room:* Fridge, coffeemaker, no phone.

Arizona Sled Dog Inn 🌟🌟 (*Finds*) Located on the edge of the forest south of the city, the Sled Dog is a contemporary building with lots of wood details (much of the wood was salvaged from buildings that were being torn down). Guest rooms are modern lodge rustic, comfortable and uncluttered. At the end of an active day, the hot tub out back is always welcome, and don't be surprised if you wake up to see elk grazing right outside your window. The inn takes its name from the fact that the owners have a kennel full of Siberian huskies.

10155 Mountainaire Rd., Flagstaff, AZ 86001. © **800/754-0664** or 928/525-6212. Fax 928/525-1855. www.sleddoginn.com. 10 units. $105–$149 double; $175–$185 suite. Rates include full breakfast. AE, DISC, MC, V. No children under 5. **Amenities:** Jacuzzi; sauna; bike rentals. *In room:* A/C, no phone.

Little America Hotel 🌟 (*Value*) Set on 500 acres of pine forest and with a trail that winds for 2 miles through the property, this hotel on the east side of Flagstaff might seem at first to be little more than a giant truck stop. However, on closer inspection you'll find that behind the truck stop stands a surprisingly luxurious and economical hotel set beneath shady pines. The decor is dated but fun, with a sort of French Provincial style predominating. Rooms vary in size, but all have small private balconies. The hotel's formal dining room is one of Flagstaff's better restaurants.

2515 E. Butler Ave., Flagstaff, AZ 86004. ℂ **800/352-4386** or 928/779-7900. Fax 928/779-7983. www. flagstaff.littleamerica.com. 247 units. $79–$119 double; $89–$129 suite. Children 12 and under stay free in parent's room. AE, DC, DISC, MC, V. Take Exit 198 off I-40. **Amenities:** 3 restaurants (American, Continental); lounge; outdoor pool; croquet court; exercise room; access to nearby health club; Jacuzzi; children's playground; concierge; car-rental desk; business center; room service; massage; coin-op laundry; laundry service; dry cleaning. *In room:* A/C, TV, dataport, fridge, coffeemaker, hair dryer, iron.

Radisson Woodlands Hotel Flagstaff ★★

With its elegant marble-floored lobby, the Woodlands Hotel is easily the most upscale lodging in Flagstaff. A white baby grand, crystal chandelier, traditional European furnishings, and contemporary sculpture all add to the unexpected luxury in the public spaces, as do intricately carved pieces of furniture and architectural details from different Asian countries. Guest rooms, most of which have been renovated over the past couple of years, are comfortable, if not overly luxurious. Ask for a renovated one in the north building to be sure of getting a nice room.

1175 W. Rte. 66, Flagstaff, AZ 86001. ℂ **800/333-3333** or 928/773-8888. Fax 928/773-0597. www.radisson. com/flagstaffaz. 183 units. $99–$139 double; $119–$159 suites. AE, DC, DISC, MC, V. **Amenities:** 2 restaurants (Japanese, Continental); lounge; outdoor pool; fitness center; indoor and outdoor Jacuzzis; sauna; steam room; business center; room service; coin-op laundry; dry cleaning. *In room:* A/C, TV, dataport, high-speed Internet access, coffeemaker, hair dryer, iron.

Starlight Pines, A Bed & Breakfast ★★

If you've ever wanted to step back in time and live in the early 20th century, then you might want to stay at this unusual B&B a few miles from downtown. The attention to detail is astounding. There are vintage tubs and sinks, vintage heat grates, vintage light switches, and, of course, plenty of antique furniture. The house was designed as a 1912 Victorian that has been updated to a less cluttered 1920s look. One bedroom has a fireplace, while another has a porch with a view of nearby Mount Elden. Mornings start with coffee in the parlor and then an elaborate Victorian breakfast.

3380 E. Lockett Rd., Flagstaff, AZ 86004. ℂ **800/752-1912** or 928/527-1912. www.starlightpinesbb.com. 4 units. $115–$145 double. Rates include full breakfast. DISC, MC, V. No children. **Amenities:** Access to nearby health club; concierge; massage. *In room:* A/C, dataport, hair dryer, iron, free local calls.

INEXPENSIVE

Historic Hotel Monte Vista

This hotel is definitely not for everyone. Although it is historic, it is also a bit run down and appeals primarily to young travelers who appreciate the low rates and the nightclub just off the lobby. So why stay here? Well, in its day, the Monte Vista hosted the likes of Clark Gable, John Wayne, Carole Lombard, and Gary Cooper. Plus, this place is haunted (ask at the front desk for the list of resident ghosts). Originally opened in 1927, the Monte Vista now has creatively decorated rooms that vary in size and decor. Although the hotel has plenty of old-fashioned flair, don't expect perfection. Check out a room first to see if this is your kind of place.

100 N. San Francisco St., Flagstaff, AZ 86001. ℂ **800/545-3068** or 928/779-6971. Fax 928/779-2904. www.hotelmontevista.com. 50 units, 4 with shared bathrooms. $50–$60 double with shared bathroom; $60–$105 double with private bathroom; $90–$150 suite. AE, DISC, MC, V. Pets accepted ($50 fee plus $10 per night). **Amenities:** Restaurant (Thai); lounge; massage; coin-op laundry. *In room:* TV, hair dryer.

Hotel Weatherford *Value*

As part of an ongoing 20-year restoration, this historic hotel in downtown Flagstaff has been steadily upgrading its rooms. Although only a few of the rooms have yet been renovated, budget-conscious fans of historic hotels will want to check them out. The distinctive stone-walled 1897 building has a wraparound veranda on its second floor, and up on the second floor, you'll also find the beautifully restored Zane Grey Ballroom (now an elegant bar). Downstairs are a casual restaurant and the ever-popular Charly's Pub & Grill, which has been booking live rock, blues, and jazz acts for more than 2 decades. This place isn't fancy, but it has loads of character.

23 N. Leroux St., Flagstaff, AZ 86001. © **928/779-1919.** Fax 928/773-8951. www.weatherfordhotel.com. 8 units, 3 with shared bathrooms. $60–$65 double. AE, MC, V. **Amenities:** Restaurant (American/Southwestern); 2 lounges; access to nearby health club. *In room:* No phone.

WHERE TO DINE

If you're headed north to the Grand Canyon and need a good espresso to get you there, stop at **Late for the Train Espresso,** 1800 N. Fort Valley Rd. (© **928/ 773-0308**), on U.S. 180 as you drive north out of town. Just watch for the old gas station. There's another location at 107 N. San Francisco St. (© **928/ 779-5975**).

EXPENSIVE

Cottage Place Restaurant ★★ CONTINENTAL/NEW AMERICAN Located on the south side of the railroad tracks in a neighborhood mostly frequented by college students, Cottage Place is just what its name implies—an unpretentious little cottage. But despite the casual appearance, dining here is a formal affair. The menu, which tends toward the rich side, is primarily Continental, with Southwestern and Middle Eastern influences as well. The house specialties are chateaubriand and rack of lamb (both served for two); there are always several choices for vegetarians as well. The appetizer sampler, with herb-stuffed mushrooms, charbroiled shrimp, and *tiropitas* (cheese-stuffed phyllo pastries), is a winner. There's a long, award-winning wine list.

126 W. Cottage Ave. © **928/774-8431.** www.cottageplace.com. Reservations recommended. 3-course meals $20–$30. AE, MC, V. Tues–Sun 5–9:30pm.

MODERATE

Black Bart's Steakhouse ★ *(Kids)* STEAKS If your family vacation to the Grand Canyon includes a night or two in Flagstaff, you owe it to the kids (and yourself) to spend an evening at Black Bart's. It's not that the steaks at this kitschy place are so good, it's the entertainment. Singing waiters and waitresses frequently burst into song, and every evening there's a full-blown musical revue for the main event. Then there's the player piano. Sure it's hokey, but it all adds up to loads of fun. By the way, the restaurant is named for the infamous gentleman-poet stagecoach robber of the 1870s and 1880s. The restaurant is right across the street from the Little America Hotel (see the review, above).

2760 E. Butler Ave. © **928/779-3142.** Reservations recommended. Main dishes $11–$26. AE, DC, DISC, MC, V. Daily 5–9pm. Take the Butler Avenue exit (Exit 198) off I-40

Jackson's Grill at the Springs ★★ NEW AMERICAN Set on the outskirts of Flagstaff overlooking a pasture where horses can graze, this modern mountain roadhouse boasts the most attractive setting of any restaurant in town. The food here is also excellent, which makes this place well worth the drive. Start with the spinach salad, which is made with blue cheese, candied pecans, and roasted beets, or the Chinese lettuce wraps filled with spicy chicken. The spit-roasted entrees are among the best bets here. If you are on your way between Flagstaff and Sedona late in the day, this makes a great place for dinner.

7055 S. Hwy. 89A. © **928/213-9332.** Reservations recommended on weekends. Main courses $10–$50. AE, DC, DISC, MC, V. Mon–Thurs 5–9pm; Fri–Sat 5–9:30pm; Sun 11am–2pm and 5–9pm.

Josephine's ★★ REGIONAL AMERICAN Housed in a restored Craftsman bungalow with a beautiful stone fireplace and a wide front porch for summer dining, this restaurant combines historical setting with excellent food that draws on a wide range of influences. The thinly sliced ancho-marinated steak is a real winner. At lunch, try the pecan-crusted fish tacos or the crab-cake po' boy sandwich. There's a good selection of reasonably priced wines also. Be sure to save room for the molten chocolate cake or the unusual half-baked peanut butter–chocolate-chip cookie.

503 N. Humphrey's St. (C) **928/779-3400.** Reservations recommended. Main courses $7.25–$8.75 lunch, $15–$19 dinner. AE, DISC, MC, V. Mon–Sat 11am–2:30pm and 5:30–9pm.

Pasto (★) ITALIAN   Located right in historic downtown Flagstaff, Pasto has a lively urban feel and is frequently a lively boisterous place. The food is some of the best in town and is always reliable. Casual yet sophisticated, Pasto is less formal than The Cottage Place or Josephine's, so if you don't feel like getting dressed up after a day at the canyon, try here. Located in downtown Flagstaff, this place can be boisterous and lively on the weekends, so come prepared for a surprisingly urban scene. As the restaurant's name implies, the menu includes a good assortment of pastas. Try the unusual orange-garlic chicken or the salmon piccata.

19 E. Aspen St. (C) **928/779-1937.** Reservations recommended. Main courses $14–$20. AE, DISC, MC, V. Sun–Thurs 5–9pm; Fri–Sat 5–9:30pm.

INEXPENSIVE
Beaver Street Brewery (Value) BURGERS/PIZZA   This big microbrewery, cafe, and billiards parlor on the south side of the railroad tracks, serves up several good brews, but it also does great pizzas and salads. The Beaver Street pizza, made with roasted-garlic pesto, sun-dried tomatoes, fresh basil, and goat cheese, is particularly tasty. Robust salads include a Mongolian beef version with sesame-ginger dressing. This place stays packed with college students, but a good pint of ale helps any wait pass quickly, especially if you can grab a seat by the woodstove. The brewery also operates the adjacent **Beaver Street Brews and Cues,** 3 S. Beaver St., which has pool tables and a vintage bar.

11 S. Beaver St. (C) **928/779-0079.** www.beaverstreetbrewery.com. Main courses $7.50–$11. AE, DISC, MC, V. Daily 11:30am–10pm (limited bar menu until midnight).

Kokopelli Winery Bistro (★) (Finds) ITALIAN   Located in downtown Flagstaff on Heritage Square, this new wine bar and casual bistro is affiliated with Arizona's own Kokopelli Winery, which produces a wide range of wines. As owner Don Minchella likes to point out, his wines are for the person on the street, not wine snobs. This is primarily a lunch spot and serves excellent soups that are all made with a bit of wine. The French onion soup is one of the best I've ever had. There are also good panini (Italian sandwiches) and salads. At dinner, there's a menu of half a dozen interesting dishes, all of which can be had with that fabulous French onion soup. This is also a great place to grab a light snack (maybe bruschetta with prosciutto and a fig-and-ricotta spread) and a glass of cabernet sauvignon or chianti.

6 E. Aspen St., Suite 110. (C) **928/226-WINE.** Main dishes $6.50–$7.50 lunch, $10–$15 dinner. AE, DISC, MC, V. Mon–Thurs 7am–9pm; Fri–Sat 7am–10pm; Sun noon–5pm.

Macy's European Coffee House & Bakery COFFEEHOUSE/BAKERY
Good espresso and baked goodies draw people in here the first time, but there are also decent vegetarian pasta dishes, soups, salads, and other college-town standbys. This is Flagstaff's counterculture hangout, attracting both students

and professors. For the true Macy's experience, order one of the huge lattes and a scone or other pastry.

14 S. Beaver St. (℃ 928/774-2243. Meals $4.50–$7. No credit cards. Sun–Wed 6am–8pm; Thurs–Sat 6am–10pm.

FLAGSTAFF AFTER DARK

For events taking place during your visit, check *Flagstaff Live*, a free weekly newspaper available at shops and restaurants downtown. The university has many musical and theatrical groups that perform throughout most of the year, and several clubs around town book a variety of live acts.

The **Flagstaff Symphony Orchestra** (℃ **888/520-7214** or 928/523-5661; www.flagstaffsymphony.org) provides the city with a full season of classical music. Most performances are held at Ardrey Auditorium, on Knoles Drive on the campus of Northern Arizona University. Ticket prices range from $22 to $47.

The city's community theater group, **Theatrikos Theatre Company** (℃ **928/774-1662;** www.theatrikos.com), performs at the Flagstaff Playhouse, 11 W. Cherry St. Tickets are $11 to $14. **The Orpheum Theater,** 15 W. Aspen St. (℃ **928/556-1580;** www.orpheumpresents.com), in downtown Flagstaff, gets the best of touring rock, folk, and country acts, so be sure to check the schedule while you're in town.

Flagstaff has three good brewpubs. Our favorite is the **Beaver Street Brewery,** 11 S. Beaver St. (℃ **928/779-0079**), described under "Where to Dine," above. Also try **Flagstaff Brewing Co.,** 16 E. Rte. 66 (℃ **928/773-1442**) or **Mogollon Brewing Co,** 15 N. Agassiz St. (℃ **928/773-8950**). At press time, this latter brewpub had plans to add its own on-site still (the first such operation in Arizona). Climb the stairs to the **Wine Loft,** 17 N. San Francisco St. (℃ **928/773-9463**), a wine bar located above the Artists Gallery in downtown Flagstaff, and, if you're like me, you'll wish you had a place just like this in your town. There's live music by local musicians several nights per week. I wouldn't think of leaving Flagstaff without spending at least one evening hanging out here.

For a livelier scene, check out the **Museum Club,** 3404 E. Rte. 66 (℃ **928/526-9434;** www.museumclub.com), a Flagstaff institution and one of America's classic roadhouses. Built in the early 1900s and often called the Zoo Club, this cavernous log saloon is filled with deer antlers, stuffed animals, and trophy

---

Moments White Buffalo, Watchable Wildlife & a Tiny Chapel

As you drive north to the Grand Canyon on U.S. 180, about 20 miles north of Flagstaff, be sure to watch for Spirit Mountain Ranch (www.sacred whitebuffalo.com), which is home to several white buffalo. These animals are considered sacred by Native Americans, and hundreds of offerings of money, tobacco, and other objects have been tied to fence of the corral that holds them. The buffalo can be visited daily (hours vary with the seasons) and admission is $5.

Across the road from Spirit Mountain Ranch, you can walk the 1.5-mile Kendrick Park Watchable Wildlife Trail. Along this trail, you might spot elk, pronghorn antelope, or mule deer grazing in the meadow. Also in this valley is the rustic little Chapel of the Holy Dove, a roadside chapel with a wall of glass facing the forest.

heads. There's live music on weekends and everything from karaoke (Mon nights) to country dance lessons (Thurs nights).

Other places around town to check for live music include **Charly's Pub & Grill,** 23 N. Leroux St. (© **928/779-1919**), inside the historic Weatherford Hotel. This place has long been a popular student hangout featuring live blues and rock seven nights a week. For a mellower scene, check out what's on the schedule at the **Campus Coffee Bean,** 1800 S. Milton Rd. (© **928/556-0660**).

2 Williams

32 miles W of Flagstaff; 58 miles S of the Grand Canyon; 220 miles E of Las Vegas, Nev.

Although it's almost 60 miles south of the Grand Canyon, Williams is still the closest real town to the national park. Consequently, it has dozens of motels catering to those unable to get a room at or just outside the park. Founded in 1880 as a railroading and logging town, Williams also has a bit of Western history to boast about, which makes it not only a good place to get a room but also an interesting place to explore for a morning or afternoon. Old brick commercial buildings dating from the late 19th century line the main street, while modest Victorian homes sit on the tree-shaded streets that spread south from the railroad tracks. In recent years, mid-20th-century history has taken center stage: Williams was the last town on historic Route 66 to be bypassed by I-40, and the town plays up its Route 66 heritage.

Most important for many visitors, however, is that Williams is where you'll find the Grand Canyon Railway depot. The excursion train that departs from here not only provides a fun ride on the rails but also serves as an alternative to dealing with traffic congestion in Grand Canyon National Park. Of course, there are also the obligatory on-your-way-to-the-Grand-Canyon tourist traps nearby.

Named for famed mountain man Bill Williams, the town sits at the edge of a ponderosa pine forest atop the Mogollon Rim, and surrounding Williams is the Kaibab National Forest. Within the forest and not far out of town are good fishing lakes, hiking and mountain-biking trails, and a small downhill ski area.

ESSENTIALS

GETTING THERE Williams is on I-40 just west of the junction with Ariz. 64, which leads north to the South Rim of the Grand Canyon.

Amtrak (© **800/872-7245**) has service to Williams on its *Southwest Chief* line. There's no station, though—the train stops on the outskirts of town. However, a shuttle van from the Grand Canyon Railway Hotel will pick you up and drive you into town, and since most people coming to Williams by train are continuing on to the Grand Canyon on the Grand Canyon Railway, this arrangement works well.

For information on the **Grand Canyon Railway** excursion trains to Grand Canyon Village, see "Exploring the Area," below.

VISITOR INFORMATION For information on the Williams area, including details on hiking, mountain biking, and fishing, contact the **City of Williams/Forest Service Visitor Center,** 200 W. Railroad Ave. (© **800/863-0546** or 928/635-4707; www.williamschamber.com). The visitor center, which includes some interesting historical displays, is open daily from 8am to 5pm (until 6:30pm in the summer). The shop here carries books on the Grand Canyon and trail maps for the adjacent national forest.

EXPLORING THE AREA: ROUTE 66 & BEYOND

These days, most people coming to Williams are here to board the **Grand Canyon Railway** ★★, Grand Canyon Railway Depot, 233 N. Grand Canyon Blvd. (© **800/843-8724** or 928/773-1976; www.thetrain.com), which operates vintage steam and diesel locomotives and 1920s coaches between Williams and Grand Canyon Village. Round-trip fares (not including tax or the national park entrance fee) range from $58 to $147 for adults and $25 to $114 for children 2 to 16. Although this is primarily a day-excursion train, it's possible to ride up one day and return on a different day—just let the reservations clerk know. If you stay overnight, you'll want to be sure you have a reservation at one of the hotels right in Grand Canyon Village; otherwise, you'll end up having to take a shuttle bus or taxi out of the park to your hotel, which can be inconvenient and add a bit to your daily costs.

Route 66 fans will want to drive Williams's main street, which, not surprisingly, is named Route 66. Along this stretch of the old highway, you can check out the town's vintage buildings, many of which now house shops selling Route 66 souvenirs. There are also a few antiques stores selling collectibles from the heyday of the famous highway.

Both east and west of town, there are other parts of the "Mother Road" that you can drive. However, with the exception of the section of road that begins at Exit 139, these stretches are not very remarkable and are recommended only for die-hard fans of Route 66. East of town, take Exit 167 off I-40 and follow the graveled Old Trails Highway (the predecessor to Rte. 66). A paved section of Route 66 begins at Exit 171 on the north side of the interstate and extends for 7 miles to the site of the Parks General Store. From Parks, you can continue to Brannigan Park on a graveled section of Route 66.

West of Williams, take Exit 157 and go south. If you turn east at the T intersection, you'll be on a gravel section of the old highway; if you turn west, you'll be on a paved section. Another stretch can be accessed at Exit 106. If you continue another 12 miles west and take Exit 139, you'll be on the longest uninterrupted stretch of Route 66 left in the country. It extends from here through the town of Seligman, which has several interesting buildings, and all the way to Kingman.

WHERE TO STAY
MODERATE

Best Western Inn of Williams   Although this modern motel is not within walking distance of historic downtown Williams, the contemporary styling and location in the pines at the west end of town make it a good bet for comfortable, quiet accommodations.

2600 W. Rte. 66 (P.O. Box 275), Williams, AZ 86046. © **800/635-4445** or 928/635-4400. Fax 928/635-4488. www.bestwestern.com. 79 units. Apr to mid-Oct and late Dec $79–$119 double; mid-Oct to Mar $59–$109 double. Rates include full breakfast. AE, DC, DISC, MC, V. **Amenities:** Lounge; outdoor pool; Jacuzzi; coin-op laundry. In room: A/C, TV/VCR, dataport, coffeemaker, hair dryer, iron.

Grand Canyon Railway Hotel ★★   This hotel is operated by the Grand Canyon Railway and combines modern comforts with the style of a classic Western railroad hotel. The high-ceilinged lobby features a large flagstone fireplace and original paintings of the Grand Canyon. The very comfortable guest rooms feature Southwestern styling; ask for a unit in the new wing (which is where you'll find the fitness room, pool, and hot tub). The hotel's elegant lounge, which features a 100-year-old English bar, serves simple meals, and there's a cafeteria-style restaurant adjacent.

233 N. Grand Canyon Blvd., Williams, AZ 86046. © **800/843-8724** or 928/635-4010. Fax 928/773-1610. www.thetrain.com. 298 units. Apr to mid-Oct and holidays $129 double; mid-Oct to Mar $79 double. Railroad/hotel packages available (Apr to mid-Oct and holidays $129 per person; mid-Oct to Mar $99 per person). AE, DISC, MC, V. **Amenities:** Restaurant (American); lounge; indoor pool; exercise room; Jacuzzi; tour desk. *In room:* A/C, TV, dataport, hair dryer, free local calls.

Quality Inn Mountain Ranch ✪   Located 6 miles east of town, this lodging is surrounded by 26 acres of forest and meadow that give it a secluded feeling. (Keep an eye out for elk.) That seclusion and the many recreational opportunities make this a good out-of-town choice in the Williams area. However, the rooms, although large and mostly with views of forest and mountains, are strictly motel issue.

6701 E. Mountain Ranch Rd. (Exit 171 off I-40), Williams, AZ 86046. © **866/687-2624** or 928/635-2693. Fax 928/635-4188. www.mountainranchresort.com. 73 units. $45–$109 double. Rates include continental breakfast. Children under 18 stay free in parent's room. AE, DC, DISC, MC, V. Pets accepted ($25 fee). **Amenities:** Restaurant (American); outdoor pool; 2 tennis courts; volleyball and basketball courts; Jacuzzi; horseback riding. *In room:* A/C, TV, dataport, coffeemaker, hair dryer, iron.

The Sheridan House Inn ✪ *Kids*   Set on a pine-shaded hillside a few blocks from downtown Williams, this is a comfortable, modern B&B with the amenities of a resort (hot tub on the flagstone patio, pool table and bar in the basement, game room for the kids, and plenty of movies to watch on in-room VCRs). Guest rooms are comfortably furnished; our favorite is the Cedar Room. The complimentary buffet dinner is a welcome alternative to the basic burgers-and-steaks menus that predominate in Williams. This inn is child-friendly, making it a good base for families.

460 E. Sheridan Ave., Williams, AZ 86046. © **888/635-9345** or 928/635-9441. www.grandcanyonbedand breakfast.com. 10 units. $150–$220 double (lower rates Jan–Feb). Rates include full breakfast and buffet dinner. AE, DISC, MC, V. **Amenities:** Jacuzzi; game room. *In room:* A/C, TV/VCR, fridge, coffeemaker, hair dryer, no phone.

INEXPENSIVE

In addition to the following choices, there are numerous budget chain motels in Williams, including two Motel 6s, two Super 8s, and an Econo Lodge.

The Canyon Motel ✪ *Finds*   You'll find this updated older motel on the eastern outskirts of Williams, tucked against the trees. While the setting and new rooms in duplex flagstone cottages are nice enough, the real attractions are the railroad cars parked in the front yard. You can stay in a caboose or a Pullman car, which makes this a fun place to overnight if you're planning on taking the excursion train to the Grand Canyon. I prefer the caboose rooms, which have a more authentic feel. A horseshoe pit, swing set, board games, a fire ring, propane barbecues, and a nature trail provide plenty of entertainment for the whole family.

1900 E. Rodeo Rd., Williams, AZ 86046. © **800/482-3955** or 928/635-9371. Fax 928/635-4138. www. thecanyonmotel.com. 22 units. $40–$80 double; $78–$96 caboose; $67–$91 Pullman double. Rates include continental breakfast. DC, DISC, MC, V. Pets accepted. **Amenities:** Small indoor pool. *In room:* TV, fridge, coffeemaker, no phone.

The Red Garter Bed & Bakery ✪ *Finds*   The Wild West lives again at this restored 1897 bordello, but these days the only tarts that come with the rooms are in the bakery downstairs. Located across the street from the Grand Canyon Railway terminal at the top of a steep flight of stairs, this B&B sports high ceilings, new carpets, attractive wood trim, and reproduction period furnishings. A couple of rooms even have graffiti written by bordello visitors in the early 20th century.

137 W. Railroad Ave., Williams, AZ 86046. © **800/328-1484** or 928/635-1484. www.redgarter.com. 4 units. $85–$120 double. Lower rates off season. Rates include continental breakfast. DISC, MC, V. **Amenities:** Bakery. *In room:* TV, no phone.

CAMPGROUNDS

There are several campgrounds near Williams in the Kaibab National Forest. They include **Cataract Lake,** 2 miles northwest of Williams on Cataract Lake Road, with 18 sites; **Dogtown Lake,** 8 miles south of Williams off Fourth Street/County Road 73, with 51 sites; **Kaibab Lake,** 4 miles northeast of Williams off Ariz. 64, with 72 sites; and **Whitehorse Lake,** 19 miles southeast of Williams off Fourth Street/County Road 73, with 105 sites. All campgrounds are first-come, first-served, and charge $10 to $12 per night.

WHERE TO DINE

Cruiser's Café 66 AMERICAN   If you're looking for a taste of old-fashioned Route 66 atmosphere, this is the place. Partly housed in a 1930s gas station, this place is full of Route 66 memorabilia, and just inside the front door is a stuffed bison with a saddle on its back. The menu runs the gamut from steaks and spicy wings to pizza and calzones, but I like to dig into the smoked baby back ribs or the platter of fajitas.

233 W. Rte. 66. © **928/635-2445.** Main courses $6–$18. AE, DISC, MC, V. Daily 4–9:30pm.

Rod's Steak House STEAKHOUSE/SEAFOOD   For a good dinner in Williams, just look for the red neon steer at the east end of town. The menu here may be short, but the food is reliable. Prime rib au jus, the house specialty, comes in three different weights to fit your hunger. If you're not in the mood for steak, opt for barbecued ribs, trout, chicken, or shrimp. There's also a children's menu.

301 E. Rte. 66. © **928/635-2671.** www.rods-steakhouse.com. Reservations recommended. Main courses $9–$29. MC, V. Mar–Sept daily 11:30am–9:30pm; Oct–Feb Mon–Sat 11:30am–9:30pm.

3 The Grand Canyon South Rim ✶✶✶

60 miles N of Williams; 80 miles NE of Flagstaff; 230 miles N of Phoenix; 340 miles N of Tucson

Whether you merely stand on the rim gazing in awe, spend several days hiking deep in the canyon, or ride the roller-coaster rapids of the Colorado River, a trip to the Grand Canyon is an unforgettable experience. A mile deep, 277 miles long, and up to 18 miles wide, the canyon is so large that it is positively overwhelming in its grandeur, truly one of the great wonders of the world. The cartographers who mapped this land were obviously deeply affected by the spiritual beauty of the canyon, and named the landscape features accordingly. Their reverence is reflected in formations named for Solomon, Apollo, Venus, Thor, Zoroaster, Horus, Buddha, Vishnu, Krishna, Shiva, and Confucius. There's also an Angels Gate and a Tabernacle.

Something of this reverence infects nearly every first-time visitor. Nothing in the slowly changing topography of the approach to the Grand Canyon prepares you for what awaits. You hardly notice the elevation gain or the gradual change from windswept scrubland to pine forest. Suddenly, it's there. No preliminaries, no warnings. Stark, quiet, a maze of colors and cathedrals sculpted by nature.

Layers of sandstone, limestone, shale, and schist give the canyon its colors, and the interplay of shadows and light from dawn to dusk creates an ever-changing palette of hues and textures. Written in these bands of stone are more than two billion years of history. Formed by the cutting action of the Colorado River as it flows through the Kaibab Plateau, the Grand Canyon is an open book exposing the secrets of the geologic history of this region. Geologists believe it has taken between three million and six million years for the Colorado River to carve the Grand Canyon, but the canyon's history extends much further back in time.

Millions of years ago, vast seas covered this region. Sediments carried by sea water were deposited and, over millions of years, turned into limestone and sandstone. When the ancient seabed was thrust upward to form the Kaibab Plateau, the Colorado River began its work of cutting through the plateau. Today, 21 sedimentary layers, the oldest of which is more than a billion years old, can be seen in the canyon. Beneath all these layers, at the very bottom, is a stratum of rock so old that it has metamorphosed, under great pressure and heat, from soft shale to a much harder stone. Called Vishnu schist, this layer is the oldest rock in the Grand Canyon and dates from two billion years ago.

In the more recent past, the Grand Canyon has been home to several Native American cultures, including the Ancestral Puebloans (Anasazi), who are best known for their cliff dwellings in the Four Corners region. About 150 years after the Ancestral Puebloans and Coconino peoples abandoned the canyon in the 13th century, another tribe, the Cerbat, moved into the area. Today, the Hualapai and Havasupai tribes, descendants of the Cerbat people, still live in and near the Grand Canyon on the south side of the Colorado River. On the North Rim lived the Southern Paiute, and in the west, the Navajo.

In 1540, Spanish explorer Garcia Lopez de Cárdenas became the first European to set eyes on the Grand Canyon. It would be another 329 years before the first expedition traveled through the entire canyon. John Wesley Powell, a one-armed Civil War veteran, was deemed crazy when he set off to navigate the Colorado River in wooden boats. His small band of men spent 98 days traveling 1,000 miles down the Green and Colorado rivers. So difficult was the endeavor that when some of the expedition's boats were wrecked by powerful rapids, part of the group abandoned the journey and set out on foot, never to be seen again.

How wrong the early explorers were about this supposedly godforsaken landscape. Instead of being abandoned as a worthless wasteland, the Grand Canyon has become one of the most important natural wonders on the planet, a magnet for people from all over the world. By raft, by mule, on foot, and in helicopters and small planes—approximately four million people each year come to the canyon to gaze into this great chasm.

However, there have been those in the recent past who regarded the canyon as mere wasted space, suitable only for filling with water. Upstream of the Grand Canyon stands Glen Canyon Dam, which forms Lake Powell, while downstream lies Lake Mead, created by Hoover Dam. The same thing could have happened to the Grand Canyon, but luckily the forces for preservation prevailed. Today, the Grand Canyon is the last major undammed stretch of the Colorado River.

Named by early Spanish explorers for the pinkish color of its muddy waters, the Colorado River once carried immense loads of silt. Because much of the Colorado's silt load now gets deposited on the bottom of Lake Powell (behind Glen Canyon Dam), the water in the Grand Canyon is much clearer (and colder) than it once was. No longer does the river flow murky and pink from heavy loads of eroding sandstone.

While the waters of the Colorado are now clearer than before, the same cannot be said for the air in the canyon. Yes, you'll find smog here, smog that has been blamed on both Las Vegas and Los Angeles to the west and a coal-fired power plant to the east, near Page. Scrubbers installed on the power plant's smokestacks should help the park's air quality, but there isn't much to be done about smog drifting up from Las Vegas.

But the most visible and frustrating negative impact on the park in recent years has been the traffic congestion at the South Rim during the busy months from spring to fall. With roughly four million people visiting the park each year, traffic during the summer months has become almost as bad at the South Rim as it is during rush hour in any major city, and finding a parking space can be the biggest challenge of a visit to Grand Canyon National Park. This may all change in the next few years if the park goes through with the proposed construction of a new light-rail system connecting the community of Tusayan with the South Rim. The light rail would in turn connect with the alternative-fuel buses that operate along the South Rim. As part of the overall new vision for the park, a multi-use greenway trail is also being built along the South Rim. Unfortunately, as of this writing, the light-rail plan has been put on hold due to falling visitor numbers (and thus, park revenues) and escalating costs.

The first phase of this plan was implemented in late 2000, when the new Canyon View Information Plaza opened. However, this information plaza was designed specifically as part of the light-rail system, which has not yet been built. Consequently, there is no parking near the information plaza, and getting here from the far end of Grand Canyon Village can take 45 minutes or more, which makes the plaza very inconvenient for visitors. Until the light-rail system or some other people-moving system is in place, you can expect continued parking problems, traffic congestion, and the added inconvenience of trying to get to the information plaza. But don't let these inconveniences dissuade you from visiting. Despite the crowds, the Grand Canyon still more than lives up to its name and is one of the most memorable sights on earth.

ESSENTIALS
GETTING THERE
If at all possible, travel to the park by some means other than car. Alternatives include taking the Grand Canyon Railway from Williams, flying into Grand Canyon Airport and then taking a taxi, taking the Open Road Tours bus service from Flagstaff, or coming to the park on a guided tour. There are plenty of scenic overlooks, hiking trails, restaurants, and lodges in the Grand Canyon Village area, and free shuttle buses operate along both the Hermit Road and Desert View Drive.

BY CAR   The South Rim of the Grand Canyon is 60 miles north of Williams and I-40 on Ariz. 64 and U.S. 180. Flagstaff, the nearest city of any size, is 80 miles away. From Flagstaff, it's possible to take U.S. 180 directly to the South Rim or U.S. 89 to Ariz. 64 and the east entrance to the park. This latter route is my preferred way of getting to the canyon since it sees slightly less traffic. Be sure you have plenty of gasoline in your car before setting out for the canyon; there are few service stations in this remote part of the state and what gas stations there are charge exorbitant prices.

Long waits at the entrance gates, parking problems, and traffic congestion have become the norm at the canyon during the popular summer months, and even during the spring and fall there can be backups at the entrance gates and visitors can have a hard time finding a parking space.

BY PLANE   The Grand Canyon Airport is in Tusayan, 6 miles south of Grand Canyon Village. Airlines flying from Las Vegas include **Scenic Airlines** (© **800/ 634-6801;** www.scenic.com), which charges $227 round-trip, and **Air Vegas**

(© **800/255-7474;** www.airvegas.com), which charges $200 round-trip. Alter-
natively, you can fly into Flagstaff and then arrange another mode of transportation the rest of the way to the national park (see "Flagstaff," earlier in this
chapter, for details).

BY TRAIN   The **Grand Canyon Railway** operates excursion trains between
Williams and the South Rim of the Grand Canyon. See "Williams," earlier in
this chapter, for details.

For long-distance connections, **Amtrak** (© **800/872-7245;** www.amtrak.
com) provides service to Flagstaff and Williams. From Flagstaff, it's then possible to take a bus directly to Grand Canyon Village. From Williams, you can take
the Grand Canyon Railway excursion train to Grand Canyon Village. *Note:* the
Amtrak stop in Williams is undeveloped and is on the outskirts of town. If you
plan to take an Amtrak train to Williams, a shuttle from the Grand Canyon
Railway Hotel will pick you up where the Amtrak train drops you off.

BY BUS   Bus service between Phoenix, Flagstaff, and Grand Canyon Village is
provided by **Open Road Tours** (© **800/766-7117** or 602/997-6474; www.
openroadtours.com). Adult fares are $30 one-way or $56 round-trip ($20 and
$39 for children) between Phoenix and Flagstaff and $20 one-way or $40
round-trip ($15 and $30 for children) between Flagstaff and the Grand Canyon.

VISITOR INFORMATION
You can get advance information on the Grand Canyon by contacting **Grand
Canyon National Park,** P.O. Box 129, Grand Canyon, AZ 86023 (© **928/
638-7888;** www.nps.gov/grca).

When you arrive at the park, stop by the **Canyon View Visitor Center,** at
Canyon View Information Plaza, 6 miles north of the south entrance. Here you'll
find exhibits, an information desk, and a shop selling maps, books, and videos.
The center is open daily 8am to 5pm. Unfortunately, the information plaza, which
is well designed for handling large crowds, has no adjacent parking, so you'll have
to park where you can and then walk or take a free shuttle bus. The nearest places
to park are at Mather Point, Market Plaza, park headquarters, and Yavapai Observation Station. If you're parked anywhere in Grand Canyon Village, you'll want to
catch the Village Route bus. If you happen to be parked at Yaki Point, you can take
the Kaibab Trail Route bus. *The Guide,* a small newspaper full of useful information about the park, is available at both South Rim park entrances.

ORIENTATION
Grand Canyon Village is built on the South Rim of the canyon and divided
roughly into two sections. At the east end of the village are the Canyon View
Information Plaza, Yavapai Lodge, Trailer Village, and Mather Campground. At
the west end are El Tovar Hotel and Bright Angel, Kachina, Thunderbird, and
Maswik lodges, as well as several restaurants, the train depot, and the trail head
for the Bright Angel Trail.

GETTING AROUND
As mentioned earlier, the Grand Canyon Village area can be extremely congested, especially in summer. If possible, you may want to use one of the transportation options below to avoid the park's traffic jams and parking problems.
To give you an idea, in summer you can expect at least a 20- to 30-minute wait
at the South Rim entrance gate just to get into the park. You can cut the waiting time here by acquiring either a National Parks Pass, a Golden Eagle Pass,

a Golden Age Pass, or a Golden Access Pass before arriving. With pass in hand, you can use the express lane.

There had been plans to develop a combination light-rail and alternative-fuel bus system for transporting visitors to and around the South Rim and Grand Canyon Village, but the plans have yet to materialize. The idea was to have a light-rail system connect Tusayan, outside the park's south entrance, with the Canyon View Information Plaza, which is the South Rim's main orientation area for visitors. From this transit center, alternative-fuel buses already shuttle visitors to various points along the South Rim. If the light-rail system ever gets built, day visitors will leave their cars outside the park and take light rail to the South Rim, which should alleviate much of the traffic congestion.

BY BUS   March through November, free shuttle buses operate on four routes within the park. The **Village Route** bus circles through Grand Canyon Village throughout the day with frequent stops at the Canyon View Information Plaza, Market Plaza (site of a general store, bank, laundry, and showers), hotels, campgrounds, restaurants, and other facilities. The **Hermit's Rest Route** bus takes visitors to eight canyon overlooks west of Bright Angel Lodge. The **Kaibab Trail Route** bus, which stops at the Canyon View Information Plaza, Pipe Creek Vista, the South Kaibab trail head, and Yaki Point, provides the only access to Yaki Point, the trail head for the South Kaibab Trail to the bottom of the canyon. The **Canyon View/Mather Point Route** is specifically for visitors who need mobility assistance and shuttles between the Mather Point parking lot and the Canyon View Information Center. There's also a Hiker Express bus to Yaki Point. This bus stops at Bright Angel Lodge and the Back Country Information Office. Hikers needing transportation to or from Yaki Point when the bus is not running can use a taxi (© **928/638-2822**).

Trans Canyon (© **928/638-2820**) offers shuttle-bus service between the South Rim and the North Rim. The vans leave the South Rim at 1:30pm and arrive at the North Rim at 6:30pm. The return trip leaves the North Rim at 7am, arriving back at the South Rim at noon. The fare is $65 one-way; reservations are required.

BY CAR   There are service stations outside the south entrance to the park in Tusayan, at Desert View near the east entrance (this station is seasonal), and east of the park at Cameron. Because of the long distances within the park and to towns outside the park, be sure you have plenty of gas before setting out on a drive. Gas at the canyon is very expensive.

BY TAXI   There is taxi service available to and from the airport, trail heads, and other destinations (© **928/638-2822**). The fare from the airport to Grand Canyon Village is $10 for up to two adults ($5 for each additional person). Taxi service is also offered by **Grand Canyon Coaches** (© **866/235-9422** or 928/ 638-0821; www.grandcanyoncoaches.com).

FAST FACTS: **The Grand Canyon**

Accessibility Check *The Guide* for park programs, services, and facilities that are partially or fully accessible. You can also get *The Grand Canyon National Park Accessibility Guide* at park entrances, Canyon View Center, Yavapai Observation Station, Kolb Studio, Tusayan Museum, and Desert

View Information Center. Temporary accessibility permits are available at the park entrances, Canyon View Information Plaza, and Yavapai Observation Station. The national park has wheelchairs available at no charge for temporary use inside the park. You can usually find one of these wheelchairs at the Canyon View Center. Wheelchair-accessible shuttle buses can be arranged a day in advance by calling the national park (© 928/638-0591). Accessible tours can also be arranged by contacting any lodge transportation desk or by calling **Grand Canyon National Park Lodges** (© **928/638-2631**).

Banks & ATMs There's an ATM at the **Bank One** (© **928/638-2437**) at Market Plaza, which is near Yavapai Lodge. The bank is open Monday through Thursday from 9am to 5pm and Friday from 9am to 6pm.

Climate The climate at the Grand Canyon is dramatically different from that of Phoenix, and between the rim and the canyon floor there's also a pronounced difference. The South Rim is at 7,000 feet, and consequently gets very cold in winter. You can expect snow anytime between November and May, and winter temperatures can be below 0°F (–18°C) at night, with daytime highs in the 20s or 30s. Summer temperatures at the rim range from highs in the 80s to lows in the 50s. The North Rim of the canyon, which is slightly higher than the South Rim and stays a bit cooler throughout the year, is open to visitors only from May to October because the access road is not kept cleared of snow.

On the canyon floor, temperatures are considerably higher. In summer, the mercury can reach 120°F (49°C) with lows in the 70s, while in winter, temperatures are quite pleasant with highs in the 50s and lows in the 30s. July, August, and September are the wettest months because of frequent afternoon thunderstorms. April, May, and June are the driest months, but it still might rain or even snow. Down on the canyon floor, there is much less rain year-round.

Fees The entry fee for Grand Canyon National Park is $20 per car (or $10 per person if you happen to be coming in on foot or by bicycle). Your admission ticket, which is good for 7 days, is nothing more than a small paper receipt. Don't lose it, or you'll have to pay again.

Festivals The **Grand Canyon Music Festival** (© **800/997-8285** or 928/ 638-9215; www.grandcanyonmusicfest.org) is held each year in mid-September.

Hospitals/Clinics The **South Rim Walk-In Clinic** (© **928/638-2551**) is on Clinic Drive, off Center Road (the road that runs past the National Park Service ranger office). The clinic is open Monday through Friday from 9am to 6pm (until 7pm in summer) and Saturday from 10am to 2pm (until 4pm in summer). It provides 24-hour emergency service as well.

Laundry A coin-operated laundry is located near Mather Campground in the Camper Services building.

Lost & Found Report lost items or turn in found items at the Canyon View Information Plaza; call © **928/638-7798**. For items lost or found at a hotel, restaurant, or lounge, call © **928/638-2631**.

Parking If you want to avoid parking headaches, try using the lot at the Market Plaza (the general store), which is up a side road near Yavapai

Lodge and the Canyon View Information Plaza. From this large parking area, a paved hiking trail leads to the historic section of the village in less than 1.5 miles, and most of the route is along the rim. Another option is to park at the Maswik Transportation Center parking lot, which is served by the Village Route shuttle bus.

Police In an emergency, dial 𝒸 **911.** Ticketing speeders is one of the main occupations of the park's police force, so obey the posted speed limits.

Post Office The post office is at Market Plaza near Yavapai Lodge.

Radio KSGC, 92.1 FM, provides news, music, the latest weather forecasts, and travel-related information for the Grand Canyon area.

Road Conditions Information on road conditions in the Grand Canyon area is available by calling 𝒸 **888/411-7623** or 928/638-7888.

Safety The most important safety tip to remember is to be careful near the edge of the canyon. Footing can be unstable and may give way. Also, be sure to keep your distance from wild animals, no matter how friendly they may appear. Avoid hiking alone if at all possible and keep in mind that the canyon rim is more than a mile above sea level (it's harder to breathe up here). Do not leave valuables in your car or tent.

DESERT VIEW DRIVE

While the vast majority of visitors to the Grand Canyon enter through the south entrance, head straight for Grand Canyon Village, and proceed to get caught up in traffic jams and parking problems, you can avoid much of this congestion and have a much more enjoyable experience if you enter the park through the east entrance. To reach the east entrance from Flagstaff, take U.S. 89 to Ariz. 64. Following this route, you'll get great views of the canyon sooner after you enter the park and have fewer parking problems. Even before you reach the park, you can stop and take in views of the canyon of Little Colorado River. These viewpoints are on the Navajo Reservation, and at every stop you'll have opportunities to shop for Native American crafts and souvenirs at the numerous vendors' stalls that can be found at virtually every scenic viewpoint on the Navajo Reservation.

Desert View Drive, the park's only scenic road open to cars, extends for 25 miles from Desert View, which is just inside the park's east entrance, to Grand Canyon Village, the site of all the park's hotels and most of its other commercial establishments. Along Desert View Drive, you'll find not only good viewpoints but also several picnic areas. Much of this drive is through forests, and canyon views are limited, but where there are viewpoints, they are among the best in the park.

Desert View, with its trading post, general store, snack bar, service station, information center, bookstore, and historic watchtower, is the first stop on this scenic drive. With its large new parking lot, Desert View seems much better designed for handling large numbers of tourists than does Grand Canyon Village and is a much better introduction to the national park than what visitors encounter when they enter from the south entrance (at Tusayan).

From anywhere at Desert View, the scenery is breathtaking but the very best perspective here is from atop the Desert View Watchtower. Although the watchtower looks as though it was built centuries ago, it actually dates from 1932. Architect Mary Elizabeth Jane Colter, who is responsible for much of the park's

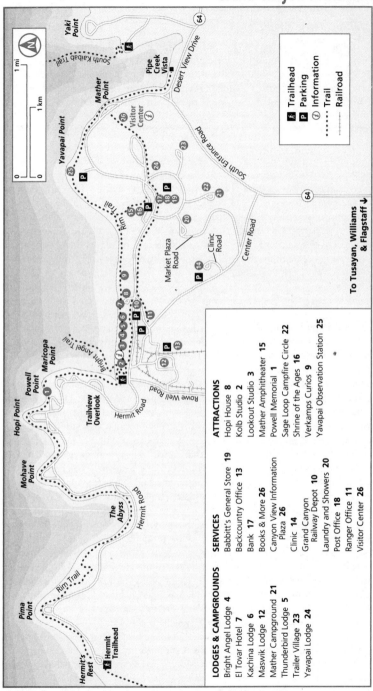

Grand Canyon South Rim

LODGES & CAMPGROUNDS
Bright Angel Lodge **4**
El Tovar Hotel **7**
Kachina Lodge **6**
Maswik Lodge **12**
Mather Campground **21**
Thunderbird Lodge **5**
Trailer Village **23**
Yavapai Lodge **24**

SERVICES
Babbitt's General Store **19**
Backcountry Office **13**
Bank **17**
Books & More **26**
Canyon View Information
Plaza **26**
Clinic **14**
Grand Canyon
Railway Depot **10**
Laundry and Showers **20**
Post Office **18**
Ranger Office **11**
Visitor Center **26**

ATTRACTIONS
Hopi House **8**
Kolb Studio **2**
Lookout Studio **3**
Mather Amphitheater **15**
Powell Memorial **1**
Sage Loop Campfire Circle **22**
Shrine of the Ages **16**
Verkamps Curios **9**
Yavapai Observation Station **25**

(*Tips* **Pack a Lunch**

Lunch options are very limited inside Grand Canyon National Park, and so, if you are driving up from Flagstaff, I suggest packing a picnic lunch. Try stopping in at a grocery store in Flagstaff for supplies. Otherwise you're going to be stuck eating burgers in a cafeteria when you could be sitting on the edge of the canyon gazing out at one of the most awe-inspiring vistas on earth.

---

historic architecture, designed it to resemble the prehistoric towers that dot the Southwestern landscape. Built as an observation tower and rest stop for tourists, the watchtower incorporates Native American designs and art. The curio shop on the ground floor is a replica of a kiva (sacred ceremonial chamber) and has lots of interesting souvenirs, regional crafts, and books. The tower's second floor features work by Hopi artist Fred Kabotie. Covering the walls are pictographs incorporating traditional designs. On the walls and ceiling of the upper two floors are more traditional images by artist Fred Geary, this time reproductions of petroglyphs from throughout the Southwest. From the roof, which, at 7,522 feet above sea level, is the highest point on the South Rim, it's possible to see the Colorado River, the Painted Desert to the northeast, the San Francisco Peaks to the south, and Marble Canyon to the north. Coin-operated binoculars provide close-up views of some of the noteworthy landmarks of this end of the canyon. Several black-mirror "reflectoscopes" provide interesting darkened views of some of the most spectacular sections of the canyon. The gift shop offers a pamphlet describing the watchtower in detail.

At **Navajo Point,** the next stop along the rim, the Colorado River and Escalante Butte are both visible, and there's a good view of the Desert View Watchtower. However, I suggest heading straight to **Lipan Point** ★★, where you get what I think is the South Rim's best views of the Colorado River. You can actually see several stretches of the river, including a couple of major rapids. From here you can also view the Grand Canyon supergroup: several strata of rock tilted at an angle to the other layers of rock in the canyon. Their angle indicates there was a period of geological mountain building before the depositing of layers of sandstone, limestone, and shale. The red, white, and black rocks of the supergroup are composed of sedimentary rock and layers of lava. One of the park's best-kept secrets, a little-known, though very rugged trail, begins here at Lipan Point (see "Hiking the Canyon" below for details).

The **Tusayan Museum** (open daily 9am–5pm) is the next stop along Desert View Drive. This small museum is dedicated to the Hopi tribe and the Ancestral Puebloan people who inhabited the region 800 years ago; inside are artfully displayed exhibits on various aspects of Ancestral Puebloan life. Admission is free. Outside is a short, self-guided trail through the ruins of an Ancestral Puebloan village. Free guided tours are available.

Next along the drive is **Moran Point,** from which you can see a bright-red layer of shale in the canyon walls. This point is named for 19th-century landscape painter Thomas Moran, who is perhaps best known for his paintings of the Grand Canyon.

The next stop, **Grandview Point,** affords a view of Horseshoe Mesa, another interesting feature of the canyon landscape. The mesa was the site of the Last Chance Copper Mine in the early 1890s. Later that same decade, the Grandview

Hotel was built and served canyon visitors until its close in 1908. The steep, unmaintained Grandview Trail leads down to Horseshoe Mesa from here. This trail makes a good less-traveled alternative to the South Kaibab Trail, although it is somewhat steeper.

The last stop along Desert View Drive is **Yaki Point,** which is no longer open to private vehicles. The park service would prefer it if you parked your car in Grand Canyon Village and took the Kaibab Trail Route shuttle bus from the Canyon View Information Plaza to Yaki Point. The reality is that people passing by in cars want to see what this viewpoint is all about and now park their cars alongside the main road and walk up the Yaki Point access road. The spectacular view from here encompasses a wide section of the central canyon. The large, flat-topped butte to the northeast is Wotan's Throne, one of the canyon's most readily recognizable features. Yaki Point is the site of the trail head for the South Kaibab Trail and consequently is frequented by hikers headed down to the bottom of the canyon at Phantom Ranch. The South Kaibab Trail is the preferred hiking route down to Phantom Ranch and is a more scenic route than the Bright Angel Trail. If you're planning a day hike into the canyon, this should be your number-one choice. Be sure to bring plenty of water.

GRAND CANYON VILLAGE & VICINITY

Grand Canyon Village is the first stop for the vast majority of the nearly four million people who visit the Grand Canyon every year (though I recommend coming in from the east entrance and avoiding the crowds). Consequently, it is the most crowded area in the park, but it also has the most overlooks and visitor services. Its many historic buildings, while nowhere near as impressive as the canyon itself, add to the popularity of the village, which, if it weren't so crowded all the time, would have a pleasant atmosphere.

For visitors who have entered the park through the south entrance, that unforgettable initial gasp-inducing glimpse of the canyon comes at **Mather Point.** From this overlook, there's a short paved path to the Canyon View Information Plaza, but because you're allowed to park at Mather Point only for a maximum of 1 hour, you'll have to hurry if you want to take in the views and gather some park information.

Continuing west toward the village proper, you next come to **Yavapai Point,** which has the best view from anywhere in the vicinity of Grand Canyon Village. From here you can see the Bright Angel Trail, Indian Gardens, Phantom Ranch, and even the suspension bridge that hikers and mule riders use to cross the Colorado River near Phantom Ranch. Oh yes, and of course you can also see the Colorado River. This viewpoint is a particularly great spot to take sunrise and sunset photos. Here you'll also find the historic **Yavapai Observation Station,** which houses a small museum and has big walls of glass to take in those extraordinary vistas. A paved pathway extends west from Yavapai Point for more than 3 miles to the west side of Grand Canyon Village. This trail also continues 2 miles east to the Pipe Creek Vista.

Continuing west from Yavapai Point, you'll come to a parking lot at park headquarters and a side road that leads to parking at the Market Plaza, which is one of the closest parking lots to the Canyon View Information Plaza.

West of these parking areas is Grand Canyon Village proper, where a paved pathway leads along the rim providing lots of good (though crowded) spots for taking pictures. The village is also the site of such historic buildings as **El Tovar Hotel** and **Bright Angel Lodge,** both of which are worth brief visits. Adjacent to El Tovar are two historic souvenir and curio shops. **Hopi House Gift Store**

and Art Gallery, the first shop in the park, was built in 1905 to resemble a Hopi pueblo and to serve as a place for Hopi artisans to work and sell their crafts. Today, it's full of Hopi and Navajo arts and crafts, including expensive kachinas, rugs, jewelry, and pottery. The nearby **Verkamps Curios** originally opened in a tent in 1898, but John Verkamp soon went out of business. The store reopened in 1905 and ever since has been the main place to look for souvenirs and crafts. Just inside the door is a 535-pound meteorite. Both shops are open daily; hours vary seasonally.

To the west of Bright Angel Lodge, two buildings cling precariously to the rim of the canyon. These are the Kolb and Lookout studios, both of which are listed on the National Register of Historic Places. **Kolb Studio** is named for Ellsworth and Emory Kolb, two brothers who set up a photographic studio on the rim of the Grand Canyon in 1904. The construction of this studio generated one of the Grand Canyon's first controversies—over whether buildings should be allowed on the canyon rim. Because the Kolbs had friends in high places, their sprawling studio and movie theater remained. Emory Kolb lived here until his death in 1976, by which time the studio had been listed as a historic building. It now serves as a bookstore, while the auditorium houses special exhibits. **Lookout Studio,** built in 1914 from a design by Mary Elizabeth Jane Colter, was the Fred Harvey Company's answer to the Kolb brothers' studio. Photographs and books about the canyon were sold at the studio, which incorporates architectural styles of the Hopi and the Ancestral Puebloans. The use of native limestone and an uneven roofline allow the studio to blend in with the canyon walls and give it the look of an old ruin. It now houses a souvenir store and two lookout points. Both the Kolb and Lookout studios are open daily; hours vary seasonally.

HERMIT ROAD

Hermit Road leads 8 miles west from Grand Canyon Village to Hermit's Rest; mile for mile, it has the greatest concentration of breathtaking viewpoints in the park. Because it is closed to private vehicles March through November, it is also one of the most pleasant places to do a little canyon viewing or easy hiking during the busiest times of year: no traffic jams, no parking problems, and plenty of free shuttle buses operating along the route. Westbound buses stop at eight overlooks (Trailview, Maricopa Point, Powell Point, Hopi Point, Mohave Point, The Abyss, Pima Point, and Hermit's Rest); eastbound buses stop only at Mohave and Hopi points. From December to February, you can drive your own vehicle along this road, but keep in mind that winters usually mean a lot of snow, and the road can sometimes be closed due to hazardous driving conditions.

Because you probably won't want to stop at every viewpoint along this route, here are some tips to help you get the most out of an excursion along Hermit Road. First of all, keep in mind that the earlier you catch a shuttle bus, the more likely you are to avoid the crowds (buses start 1 hr. before sunrise so photographers can get good shots of the canyon in dawn light). Second, remember that the closer you are to Grand Canyon Village, the larger the crowds will be. So, head out early and get a couple of miles between you and the village before getting off the shuttle bus.

The first two stops are **Trailview Overlook** and **Maricopa Point,** both on the paved section of the Rim Trail and within 1½ miles of the village, thus usually pretty crowded. If you just want to do a short, easy walk on pavement, get out at Maricopa Point and walk back to the village. From either overlook, you have a view of the Bright Angel Trail winding down into the canyon from Grand

Canyon Village. The trail, which leads to the bottom of the canyon, crosses the Tonto Plateau about 3,000 feet below the rim. This plateau is the site of Indian Garden, where there's a campground in a grove of cottonwood trees. Because the views from these two overlooks are not significantly different from those in the village, we'd suggest skipping these stops if you've already spent time gazing into the canyon from the village.

Powell Point, the third stop, is the site of a memorial to John Wesley Powell, who, in 1869 with a party of nine men, became the first person to navigate the Colorado River through the Grand Canyon. Visible at Powell Point are the remains of the Orphan Mine, a copper mine that began operation in 1893. The mine went out of business because transporting the copper to a city where it could be sold was too expensive. Uranium was discovered here in 1954, but in 1966 the mine was shut down, and the land became part of Grand Canyon National Park. Again, we recommend continuing on to the more spectacular vistas that lie ahead.

The next stop is **Hopi Point,** which is one of the three best stops along this route. From here you can see a long section of the Colorado River far below you. Because of the great distance, the river seems to be a tiny, quiet stream, but in reality the section you see is more than 100 yards wide and races through Granite Rapids. Because Hopi Point juts out into the canyon, it is one of the best spots in the park for taking sunrise and sunset photos; shuttle buses operate from 1 hour before sunrise to 1 hour after sunset.

The view is even more spectacular at the next stop, **Mohave Point.** Here you can see the river in two directions. Three rapids are visible from this overlook, and on a quiet day, you can sometimes even hear Hermit Rapids. As with almost all rapids in the canyon, these are formed at the mouth of a side canyon where boulders loosened by storms and carried by flooded streams are deposited in the Colorado River. Don't miss this stop; it's got the best view on Hermit Road!

Next you come to **The Abyss,** the appropriately named 3,000-foot drop created by the Great Mojave Wall. This vertiginous view is one of the most awe-inspiring in the park. The walls of The Abyss are red sandstone that's more resistant to erosion than the softer shale in the layer below. Other layers of erosion-resistant sandstone have formed the freestanding pillars that are visible from here. The largest of these pillars is called the Monument. If you're looking for a good hike along this road, get out here and walk westward to either Pima Point (3 miles distant) or Hermit's Rest (4 miles away).

Moments **Leave the Driving to Them**

Now, I'm not a big fan of guided tours, but sometimes, they just make a lot of sense. The Grand Canyon is one of those places, especially if you are usually the designated driver. Why should you have to keep your eyes on the road when there's all that gorgeous scenery right outside the window? Why not let someone else do the driving?

If you're planning on making your visit to the Grand Canyon a day trip from Flagstaff rather than an overnight stay at the park, then you should consider taking a tour with **American Dream Tours** (© **888/203-1212** or 928/527-3369; www.americandreamtours.com). Not only will you get to enjoy the scenery more, but knowledgeable guides will fill you with fascinating information about the canyon. Tours are $80 for adults and $50 for children 10 and under.

The **Pima Point** overlook, because it is set back from the road, is another good place to get off the bus. From here, the Rim Trail leads through the forest near the canyon rim, providing good views undisturbed by traffic on Hermit Road. From this overlook, it's also possible to see the remains of Hermit Camp on the Tonto Plateau. Built by the Santa Fe Railroad, Hermit Camp was a popular tourist destination between 1911 and 1930 and provided cabins and tents. Only foundations remain.

The final stop on Hermit Road is at **Hermit's Rest,** which was named for Louis Boucher, a prospector who came to the canyon in the 1890s and was known as the Hermit. The log-and-stone Hermit's Rest building, designed by Mary Elizabeth Jane Colter and built in 1914, is on the National Register of Historic Places and is one of the most fascinating structures in the park. With its snack bar, it makes a great place to linger while you soak up a bit of park history. The steep Hermit Trail, which leads down into the canyon, begins just past Hermit's Rest.

HIKING THE CANYON

No visit to the canyon is complete without journeying below the rim on one of the park's hiking trails. While the views don't necessarily get any better than they are from the top, they do change considerably. Gazing up at all those thousands of feet of vertical rock walls provides a very different perspective than that from atop the rim. Should you venture far below the rim, you also stand a chance of seeing fossils, old mines, petroglyphs, wildflowers, and wildlife. However, with around four million people visiting the Grand Canyon annually, you can forget about finding any solitude on the park's main hiking trails.

That said, there is no better way to see the canyon than on foot (our apologies to the mules), and a hike down into the canyon will likely be the highlight of your visit. You can get away from *most* of the crowds simply by heading down the Bright Angel or South Kaibab trails for 2 to 3 miles. Keep in mind, though, that these are the two busiest trails below the canyon rim and can see hundreds of hikers per day. If you want to see fewer other hikers and are in good shape, consider heading down the Grandview Trail or the Hermit Trail instead. If you're just looking for an easy walk that doesn't involve hiking back up out of the canyon, the Rim Trail is for you.

The Grand Canyon offers some of the most rugged and strenuous hiking anywhere in the United States, and for this reason anyone attempting even a short walk should be well prepared. Each year, injuries and fatalities are suffered by day hikers who set out without sturdy footgear or without food and adequate amounts of water. Even a 30-minute hike in summer can dehydrate you, and a long hike in the heat can necessitate drinking more than a gallon of water. So, carry and drink at least 2 quarts (2 liters) of water if you go for a day hike during the summer. Don't attempt to hike from the rim to the Colorado River and back in a day. Although there are very fit individuals who have managed the grueling hike to the bottom and back in a day, there are also plenty who have tried this and died. Also remember that mules have the right of way.

DAY HIKES

Hikers tend to gravitate to loop trails, but here on the South Rim, you'll find no such trails. Thus day hikers must reconcile themselves to out-and-back hikes. Still, the vastly different scenery in every direction makes out-and-back hikes here as interesting as any loop trail could be. The only problem is that the majority of the out-and-back trails are the reverse of what you'll find most other places. Instead of starting out by slogging up a steep mountain, you let gravity assist you in hiking down into the canyon. With little negative reinforcement and few natural turnaround destinations, it is easy to hike so far that the return trip back up the trail becomes an arduous death march. Know your limits and turn around before you become tired. On the canyon rim, the only hiking trail is the Rim Trail, while the Bright Angel, South Kaibab, Grandview, and Hermit trails all head down into the canyon.

For an easy, flat hike, your only option is the **Rim Trail,** which stretches from Pipe Creek Vista east of Grand Canyon Village to Hermit's Rest, 8 miles west of the village. Just over 3 miles of this trail are paved, and because this paved portion passes through Grand Canyon Village, it is always the most crowded stretch of trail in the park. To the west of the village, after the pavement ends, the Rim Trail leads another 6.7 miles out to Hermit's Rest. For most of this distance, the trail follows Hermit Road, which means you'll have to deal with traffic noise (mostly from shuttle buses). To get the most enjoyment out of a hike along this stretch, we like to head out as early in the morning as possible (to avoid the crowds) and get off at The Abyss shuttle stop. From here it's a 4-mile hike to Hermit's Rest; for more than half of this distance, the trail isn't as close to the road as it is at the Grand Canyon Village end of the route. Plus, Hermit's Rest makes a great place to rest, and from here you can catch a shuttle bus back to the village. Alternatively, you could start hiking from Grand Canyon Village (it's just over 8 miles from the west end of the village to Hermit's Rest) or any of the seven shuttle-bus stops en route, or take the shuttle all the way to Hermit's Rest and then hike back.

The **Bright Angel Trail,** which starts just west of Bright Angel Lodge in Grand Canyon Village, is the most popular trail into the canyon because it starts right where the greatest number of park visitors tend to congregate (near the ice-cream parlor and the hotels). It is also the route used by mule riders headed down into the canyon. Bear in mind that this trail follows a narrow side canyon for several miles down into the Grand Canyon and thus has somewhat limited views. For these reasons, this trail is worth avoiding if you're on foot. On the other hand, it's the only maintained trail into the canyon that has potable water, and there are four destinations along the trail that make good turnaround points. Both 1½ Mile Resthouse (1,131 ft. below the rim) and 3 Mile Resthouse (2,112 ft. below the rim) have water (except in winter, when the water is turned off). Keep in mind that these rest houses take their names from their distance from the rim; if you hike to 3 Mile Resthouse, you still have a 3-mile hike back up. Destinations for longer day hikes include Indian Garden (9 miles round-trip) and Plateau Point (12 miles round-trip), which are both just over 3,000 feet below the rim. There is year-round water at Indian Garden.

The **South Kaibab Trail** 🎯🎯🎯 begins near Yaki Point east of Grand Canyon Village and is the preferred route down to Phantom Ranch. This trail also offers the best views of any of the day hikes into the canyon, so should you have time for only one day hike, make it this trail. From the trail head, it's 3 miles round-trip to Cedar Ridge or 6 miles round-trip to Skeleton Point. The hike is very strenuous, and there's no water available along the trail.

If you're looking to escape the crowds and are an experienced mountain or desert hiker with good, sturdy boots, consider the unmaintained **Hermit Trail,** which begins at Hermit's Rest, 8 miles west of Grand Canyon Village at the end of Hermit Road. It's a 5-mile round-trip hike to Santa Maria Spring on a trail that loses almost all of its elevation (1,600–1,700 ft.) in the first 1½ miles.

Beyond Santa Maria Spring, the Hermit Trail descends to the Colorado River, but it is a 17-mile hike, one-way, from the trail head. Alternatively, you can do an 8-mile round-trip hike to Dripping Springs. Water from either of these two springs must be treated with a water filter, iodine, or purification tablets, or by boiling for at least 10 minutes, so you're better off just carrying sufficient water for your hike. Hermit Road is closed to private vehicles from March to November, so chances are you'll need to take the free shuttle bus out to the trail head. If you take the first bus of the day, you'll probably have the trail almost all to yourself.

The **Grandview Trail,** which begins at Grandview Point 12 miles east of Grand Canyon Village, is another steep and unmaintained trail that's a good choice for physically fit hikers. The strenuous 6-mile round-trip hike leads down to Horseshoe Mesa, 2,600 feet below the rim-top trail head. There's no water available, so carry at least 2 quarts. Allow at least 7 hours for this rugged hike. Just to give you an idea of how steep this trail is, you'll lose more than 2,000 feet of elevation in the first three-quarters of a mile down to Coconino Saddle!

There's one other trail I have to tell you about, but you have to promise not to tell anyone else. This trail is so secret that the national park service doesn't mark it on any of its maps. It's called the **Tanner Trail** and it starts just downhill from the beginning of the parking lot at Lipan Point near the east end of Desert View Drive. The Tanner Trail started out as a trail used by horse thieves to move stolen horses between Utah and Arizona. This is one of the shortest, steepest, and most challenging trails down into the canyon, and it is probably for good reason that the park service doesn't want you to know about it. They don't want to have to rescue you when you collapse from dehydration hiking back up.

There, now that you are suitably warned, let me tell you about the single best day-hiking experience I've ever had in the Grand Canyon. The Tanner Trail is so unknown that I hiked it twice in two days and only saw one other hiker. He was sitting at the top of the trail dripping with sweat after having hiked all the way to the Colorado River and back (this is an activity that the park service works hard to discourage people from attempting). Therein lies the beauty of this trail—you can have it all to yourself even when the park is packed with tourists! Of course, there is a cost. This trail is not for everyone. You must be in excellent shape with good knees and strong quadriceps. Don't even think of setting foot on this trail unless you are wearing very sturdy boots with excellent ankle support. Take lots of water and drink it. Lastly, remember that it will take you considerably longer to hike back up than it took you to hike down. So how far can you hike on this trail? Well that's up to you. It's 3 miles and a 1,700-foot elevation drop to Escalante Butte, from which you get a good view of Marble Canyon, Hance Rapids, and the bottom of the canyon.

BACKPACKING

Backpacking the Grand Canyon is an unforgettable experience. Although most people are content to simply hike down to Phantom Ranch and back, there are many miles of trails deep in the canyon. Keep in mind, however, that to backpack the canyon, you'll need to do a lot of planning. A **Backcountry Use Permit** is required of all hikers planning to overnight in the canyon, unless you'll be staying at Phantom Ranch in one of the cabins or a dormitory.

Because a limited number of hikers are allowed into the canyon on any given day, it's important to make reservations as soon as it is possible to do so. Reservations are taken in person, by mail, by fax (but not by phone), and online. Contact the **Backcountry Office,** Grand Canyon National Park, P.O. Box 129, Grand Canyon, AZ 86023 (© **928/638-7875** 1–5pm for information; fax

928/638-2125; www.nps.gov/grca). The office begins accepting reservations on the first of every month for the following 5 months. Holiday periods are the most popular—if you want to hike over the Labor Day weekend, be sure you make your reservation on May 1! If you show up without a reservation, go to the Backcountry Information Center (open daily 8am–noon and 1–5pm), adjacent to the Maswik Lodge, and put your name on the waiting list. When applying for a permit, you must specify your exact itinerary, and once in the canyon, you must stick to this itinerary. Backpacking fees include a nonrefundable $10 backcountry permit fee and a $5 per person per night backcountry camping fee. American Express, Diners Club, Discover, MasterCard, and Visa are accepted for permit fees. Keep in mind that you'll still have to pay the park entry fee when you arrive at the Grand Canyon.

There are **campgrounds** at Indian Garden, Bright Angel Campground (near Phantom Ranch), and Cottonwood, but hikers are limited to 2 nights per trip at each of these campgrounds (except Nov 15–Feb 28, when 4 nights are allowed at each campground). Other nights can be spent camping at undesignated sites in certain regions of the park.

The *Backcountry Trip Planner* contains information to help you plan your itinerary. It's available through the Backcountry Office (see contact information, above). Maps are available through the **Grand Canyon Association,** P.O. Box 399, Grand Canyon, AZ 86023 (© **928/638-2481;** www.grandcanyon.org), and at bookstores and gift shops within the national park, including Canyon View Information Plaza, Kolb Studio, Desert View Information Center, Yavapai Observation Station, Tusayan Museum, and, on the North Rim, Grand Canyon Lodge.

The best times of year to backpack are spring and fall. In summer, temperatures at the bottom of the canyon are frequently above 100°F (38°C), while in winter, ice and snow at higher elevations make footing on trails precarious (crampons are recommended). Plan to carry at least 2 quarts, and preferably 1 gallon, of water whenever backpacking in the canyon.

The Grand Canyon is an unforgiving landscape, and as such, many people might feel the need of a professional guide while backpacking through this rugged corner of the Southwest. **Sky Island Treks** (© **520/622-6966;** www.skyislandtreks.com or www.grandcanyonextreme.com) leads trips ranging in length from 3 to 13 days. The easier trips stick to well-traveled trails, while the more challenging treks head off into some of the most remote regions of the park. Prices start at $495 for a 3-day trek.

OTHER WAYS OF SEEING THE CANYON
BUS TOURS
If you'd rather leave the driving to someone else and enjoy more of the scenery, opt for a bus or van tour of one or more sections of the park. **Grand Canyon National Park Lodges** (© **928/638-2631**) offers several tours within the park. These can be booked by calling or stopping at one of the transportation desks, which are at Bright Angel, Maswik, and Yavapai lodges (see "Where to Stay," later in this chapter). Prices range from around $12 for a 1½-hour sunrise tour to around $34 for a combination tour to both Hermit's Rest and Desert View.

MULE RIDES 🅰
Mule rides into the canyon have been popular since the beginning of the 20th century, when the Bright Angel Trail was a toll road. After having a look at the steep drop-offs and narrow path of the Bright Angel Trail, you might decide this isn't exactly the place to trust your life to a mule. Never fear: Wranglers will be

quick to reassure you they haven't lost a rider yet. Trips of various lengths and to different destinations are offered. The 1-day trip descends to Plateau Point, where there's a view of the Colorado River 1,300 feet below. This grueling trip requires riders to spend 6 hours in the saddle. Those who want to spend a night down in the canyon can choose an overnight trip to Phantom Ranch, where cabins and dormitories are available at the only lodge actually in the canyon. From November to March, a 3-day trip to Phantom Ranch is offered; other times of year, you'll ride down one day and back up the next. Mule trips range in price from $133 for a 1-day ride to $361 for an overnight ride. Couples get discounts on overnight rides.

Riders must weigh less than 200 pounds fully dressed, stand at least 4 feet 7 inches tall, and speak fluent English. Pregnant women are not allowed on mule trips.

Because these trail rides are very popular (especially in summer), they often book up 6 months or more in advance (reservations are taken up to 23 months in advance). For more information or to make a reservation, contact **Xanterra Parks & Resorts** (© **888/297-2757** or 303/297-2757; www.grandcanyon lodges.com). If at the last minute (5 days or fewer from the day you want to ride) you decide you want to go on a mule trip, contact **Grand Canyon National Park Lodges** at its Arizona phone number (© **928/638-2631**) for the remote possibility that there may be space available. If you arrive at the canyon without a reservation and decide that you'd like to go on a mule ride, stop by the Bright Angel Transportation Desk to get your name put on the next-day's waiting list.

HORSEBACK RIDES

Trail rides on the rim (but not into the canyon) are available from **Apache Stables** (© **928/638-2891;** www.apachestables.com), located just outside the south entrance to the park. Prices range from $31 for a 1-hour ride to $96 for a 4-hour ride. Evening wagon rides ($13) and evening horseback rides ($41) are also offered. The stables are usually open from March to mid-October (depending on the weather).

THE GRAND CANYON RAILWAY ★★

In the early 20th century, most visitors to the Grand Canyon arrived by train, and it's still possible to travel to the canyon along the steel rails. The **Grand Canyon Railway** (© **800/843-8724** or 928/773-1976; www.thetrain.com), which runs from Williams to Grand Canyon Village, uses early-20th-century steam engines (Memorial Day weekend to Labor Day weekend) and 1950s-vintage diesel engines (during other months) to pull 1920s passenger cars as well as a dome coach car. Trains depart from the Williams Depot, which is housed in the historic 1908 Fray Marcos Hotel, which also contains a railroad museum, gift shop, and cafe. (Grand Canyon Railway also operates the adjacent Grand Canyon Railway Hotel.) At Grand Canyon Village, the trains use the 1910 log railway terminal in front of El Tovar Hotel.

Passengers have the choice of five classes of service: coach, club, first class, deluxe observation class (upstairs in the dome car), and luxury parlor car. Actors posing as cowboys provide entertainment, including music performances, aboard the train. The round-trip takes 8 hours, including 3¼ hours at the canyon. Fares range from $58 to $147 for adults and $25 to $114 for children 16 and under (not including tax or the park entry fee).

Not only is this a fun trip that provides great scenery and a trip back in time, but taking the train also allows you to avoid the traffic congestion and parking problems in Grand Canyon Village. When booking your train trip, you can also book a bus tour in the park, which will help you see more than you would on foot. The railway offers room/train packages as well.

A BIRD'S-EYE VIEW

Despite controversies over noise and safety (there have been a few crashes over the years), airplane and helicopter flights over the Grand Canyon remain one of the most popular ways to see this natural wonder. Personally, we would rather enjoy the canyon on foot or from a saddle. However, the volume of flights over the canyon each day would indicate that quite a few people don't share our opinion. If you want to join the crowds buzzing the canyon, you'll find several companies operating out of Grand Canyon Airport in Tusayan. Air tours last anywhere from 30 minutes to about 2 hours.

Companies offering tours by small plane include **Air Grand Canyon** (© **800/247-4726** or 928/638-2686; www.airgrandcanyon.com) and **Grand Canyon Airlines** (© **866/235-9422** or 928/638-2359; www.grandcanyon airlines.com). Rates for 50-minute flights range from $75 to $89 for adults and $45 to $49 for children.

Helicopter tours are available from **Airstar Helicopters** (© **800/962-3869** or 928/638-2622; www.airstar.com), **Grand Canyon Helicopters** (© **800/541-4537** or 928/638-2764; www.grandcanyonhelicoptersaz.com), and **Papillon Grand Canyon Helicopters** (© **800/528-2418** or 928/638-2419; www.papillon.com). Rates range from $93 to $135 for a 30-minute flight and from $159 to $195 for a 45- to 55-minute flight. Also, check websites for discounts.

INTERPRETIVE PROGRAMS

Numerous interpretive programs are scheduled throughout the year at various South Rim locations. There are ranger-led walks that explore different aspects of the canyon, geology talks, lectures on the cultural and natural resources of the canyon, nature hikes, trips to fossil beds, and stargazing gatherings. At Tusayan Ruin, guided tours are offered. Evening programs are held at Mather Amphitheater or the Shrine of the Ages. Consult your copy of *The Guide* for information on times and meeting points.

THE GRAND CANYON FIELD INSTITUTE

If you're the active type or would like to turn your visit to the Grand Canyon into more of an educational experience, you may want to consider doing a trip with the **Grand Canyon Field Institute** (© **866/471-4435;** www.grandcanyon. org/fieldinstitute). Cosponsored by Grand Canyon National Park and the Grand Canyon Association, the field institute schedules an amazing variety of guided, educational trips, such as challenging backpacking trips through the canyon (some for women only) and programs lasting anywhere from 3 to 11 days. Subjects covered include wilderness studies, geology, natural history, human history, photography, and art.

JEEP TOURS

If you'd like to explore some parts of Grand Canyon National Park that most visitors never see, contact **Grand Canyon Jeep Tours & Safaris** (© **800/320-5337** or 928/638-5337; www.grandcanyonjeeptours.com), which offers three different tours that visit the park as well as the adjacent Kaibab National Forest. One tour stops at a lookout tower that affords an elevated view of the canyon, while another visits an Indian ruin and site of petroglyphs and cave paintings. Prices range from $40 to $94 for adults and $30 to $55 for children 12 and under.

RAFTING THE COLORADO RIVER

Rafting down the Colorado River as it roars and tumbles through the mile-deep gorge of the Grand Canyon is the adventure of a lifetime. Ever since John Wesley Powell ignored everyone who knew better and proved that it was possible to travel by boat down the tumultuous Colorado, running the big river has become a passion and an obsession with adventurers. Today, anyone from grade-schoolers to grandmothers can join the elite group of people who have made the run. Be prepared for some of the most furious white water in the world.

There are numerous companies offering trips through various sections of the canyon. You can spend as little as half a day on the Colorado (downstream from Glen Canyon Dam; see "Lake Powell & Page," in chapter 7) to as many as 19 days. You can go down the river in a huge motorized rubber raft (the quickest way to see the entire canyon), a paddle- or oar-powered raft (more thrills and more energy expended on your part if you have to help paddle), or a wooden dory (the biggest thrill of all). In a motorized raft, you can travel the entire canyon from Lees Ferry to Lake Mead in only 8 days. Should you opt for an oar- or paddle-powered raft or dory, expect to spend 5 to 6 days getting from Lees Ferry to Phantom Ranch or 7 to 9 days getting from Phantom Ranch to Diamond Creek, just above Lake Mead. Aside from the half-day trips near Glen Canyon Dam, any Grand Canyon rafting trip will involve lots of monster rapids. Variables to consider include hiking in or out of Phantom Ranch for a combination rafting-and-hiking adventure.

Most trips start from Lees Ferry near Page and Lake Powell. It's also possible to start (or finish) a trip at Phantom Ranch, hiking in or out from either the North or South Rim. The main rafting season is April through October, but some companies operate year-round. Rafting trips tend to book up more than a year in advance, and most companies begin taking reservations between March and May for the following year's trips. Expect to pay $250 to $350 per day for your whitewater adventure, depending on the length of the trip and the type of boat used.

The following are some of the companies I recommend checking out when you start planning your Grand Canyon rafting adventure:

- **Arizona Raft Adventures,** 4050 E. Huntington Rd., Flagstaff, AZ 86004 (© 800/786-7238; www.azraft.com); 6- to 14-day motor, oar, and paddle trips. Although this is not one of the larger companies operating on the river, it offers lots of different trips, including trips that focus on natural history and geology. They also do trips in paddle rafts that allow you to help navigate and provide the power while shooting the canyon's many rapids. Talk about exciting!

- **Canyoneers,** P.O. Box 2997, Flagstaff, AZ 86003 (© 800/525-0924 or 928/526-0924; www.canyoneers.com); 6-night motorized-raft trips and 4- to 11-night oar-powered trips, plus several short trips. Way back in 1938, this was the first company to take paying customers down the Colorado, and Canyoneers is still considered one of the top companies on the river.

- **Diamond River Adventures,** P.O. Box 1300, Page, AZ 86040 (© 800/343-3121 or 928/645-8866; www.diamondriver.com); 4- to 8-day motorized-raft trips and 5- to 13-day oar trips. This is the only woman-owned and -managed rafting company operating in the Grand Canyon.

- **Grand Canyon Expeditions Company,** P.O. Box O, Kanab, UT 84741 (© 800/544-2691 or 435/644-2691; www.gcex.com); 8-day motorized trips and 14-day dory trips. No question about it: There's no more exciting way to do the canyon than in a dory! If you've got the time, I highly recommend these dory trips as among the most thrilling adventures in the world.

- **Hatch River Expeditions,** P.O. Box 1200, Vernal, UT 84078 (© 800/433-8966; www.hatchriverexpeditions.com); 4- and 7-day motorized trips. The 4-day trips involve either hiking in to the canyon or out of the canyon. On the 7-day trip, a helicopter lifts you out of the canyon at the end of the trip. This company has been in business since 1929 and claims to be the oldest commercial rafting company in the U.S. With so much experience, you can count on Hatch to provide you with a great trip.
- **Outdoors Unlimited,** 6900 Townsend Winona Rd., Flagstaff, AZ 86004 (© 800/637-7238 or 928/526-4511; www.outdoorsunlimited.com); 5- to 13-day oar and paddle trips. This company has been taking people through the canyon for more than 30 years and usually sends people home very happy.
- **Wilderness River Adventures,** P.O. Box 717, Page, AZ 86040 (© 800/992-8022 or 928/645-3296; www.riveradventures.com); 3- to 8-day motorized-raft trips and 6-, 12-, and 14-day oar trips. These 3-day trips involve hiking out from Phantom Ranch. This is one of the bigger companies operating on the canyon and it offers a wide variety of trips, which makes it a good company to check with if you're not sure which type of trip you want to do.

For information on 1-day rafting trips at the west end of the Grand Canyon, see "South Rim Alternatives: Havasu Canyon & Grand Canyon West," later in this chapter. For information on half-day trips near Page, see "Lake Powell & Page," in chapter 7.

ACTIVITIES OUTSIDE THE CANYON

If you aren't completely beat at the end of the day, you might want to take in an evening of **Navajo dancing** at the Grand Hotel (© **928/638-3333**), in Tusayan; call for schedule.

For a virtual Grand Canyon experience, take in a show at the **Grand Canyon IMAX Theater,** Ariz. 64/U.S. 180 (© **928/638-2203;** www.grandcanyonimax theater.com), in Tusayan outside the south entrance to the park. A short IMAX film covering the history and geology of the canyon is shown throughout the day on the theater's seven-story screen. Admission is $10 for adults and $7 for children 3 to 11. There are shows daily between 8:30am and 8:30pm from March to October, daily between 10:30am and 6:30pm from November to February.

Outside the east entrance to the park, the **Cameron Trading Post** (© **800/338-7385** or 928/679-2231; www.camerontradingpost.com), at the crossroads of Cameron where Ariz. 64 branches off U.S. 89, is the best trading post in the state. The original stone trading post, a historic building, now houses a gallery of Indian artifacts, clothing, and jewelry. This gallery offers museum-quality pieces, and even if you don't have $10,000 to drop on a rug or basket, you can still look around. The main trading post is a more modern building and is the largest trading post in northern Arizona. Don't miss the beautiful terraced gardens in back of the original trading post.

WHERE TO STAY

Keep in mind that the Grand Canyon is one of the most popular national parks in the country, and hotel rooms both within and just outside the park are in high demand. Make reservations as far in advance as possible. Don't expect to find a room if you head up here in summer without a reservation. You'll likely wind up driving back to Williams or Flagstaff to find a vacancy. There, is, however, one long-shot option. See "Inside the Park," below, for details. Who knows? You might get lucky.

INSIDE THE PARK

All hotels inside the park are operated by **Xanterra Parks & Resorts.** Reservations are taken up to 23 months in advance, beginning on the first of the month. If you want to stay in one of the historic rim cabins at Bright Angel Lodge, reserve at least a year in advance. However, rooms with shared bathrooms at Bright Angel Lodge are often the last in the park to book up, and although they're small and very basic, they're your best bet if you're trying to get a last-minute reservation.

To make reservations at any of the in-park hotels listed below, contact **Grand Canyon National Park Lodges/Xanterra Parks & Resorts,** 14001 E. Iliff Ave., Suite 600, Aurora, CO 80014 (© **888/297-2757** or 303/297-2757; www. xanterra.com or www.grandcanyonlodges.com). It is sometimes possible, due to cancellations and no-shows, to get a same-day reservation; it's a long shot, but it happens. Same-day reservations can be made by calling © **928/638-2631.** Xanterra accepts American Express, Discover, MasterCard, and Visa. Children under 16 stay for free in their parent's room.

Expensive

El Tovar Hotel ★★   El Tovar Hotel, which first opened its doors in 1905, is the park's premier lodge. Built of local rock and Oregon pine by Hopi craftsmen, it's a rustic yet luxurious mountain lodge that perches on the edge of the canyon (but with views from only a few rooms). The lobby, entered from a veranda set with rustic furniture, has a small fireplace, cathedral ceiling, and log walls on which moose, deer, and antelope heads are displayed. Guest rooms feature modern mission-style furnishings that are somewhat in keeping with the period when the hotel was built. The standard units are rather small, as are the bathrooms. For more legroom, book a deluxe unit. Suites, with private terraces and stunning views, are extremely spacious and done mostly in Southwestern style. The El Tovar Dining Room (see "Where to Dine," below) is the best restaurant in the village. Just off the lobby is a cocktail lounge with a view.

78 units. $123–$176 double; $201–$285 suite. **Amenities:** Restaurant (Continental/Southwestern); lounge; concierge; tour desk; room service. *In room:* TV.

Moderate

Maswik Lodge   Set back ¼ mile or so from the rim, the Maswik Lodge offers spacious rooms and recently renovated cabins that have been comfortably modernized without the loss of their appealing rustic character. If you don't mind roughing it a bit, the 28 old cabins, which are available only in summer, have lots of character and have benefited tremendously from recent upgrades. These cabins now have high ceilings and ceiling fans and are my top choice away from the rim. If you crave modern appointments, opt for one of the Maswik North rooms.

278 units. $77–$119 double (winter discounts sometimes available); $66 cabin. **Amenities:** Cafeteria; lounge; tour desk. *In room:* TV.

Thunderbird & Kachina Lodges   These two side-by-side hotels date from the 1960s and are a far cry from what you might imagine a national park hotel would look like, but they do have one thing going for them. They have the biggest windows of any of the four hotels right on the canyon rim. Better still, there are second-story rooms on the canyon side of the two hotels that are high enough that you don't have to look through crowds of people to see the canyon. If you want a hotel with historic character, stay next door at the El Tovar (see above), but if you want great views, try to get into one of these hotels (but only if you can get a view room!). Sure, the dated "modern" architecture clashes with the traditional design of the adjacent historic lodges, but, after all, you did come here for the views. Kachina Lodge's second-floor canyon-side rooms get the nod for having *the* best views at any hotel in the park. Book early—these two lodges right on the rim are some of the park's most popular accommodations. A recent renovation has given these rooms a fresh new look that makes these two hotels even more recommendable. Thunderbird Lodge registration is handled by Bright Angel Lodge (see below), while Kachina Lodge registration is handled by El Tovar Hotel.

104 units. $123–$133 double. *In room:* TV, dataport, fridge, coffeemaker, hair dryer, iron.

Yavapai Lodge Located in several buildings at the east end of Grand Canyon Village (a 1-mile hike from the main section of the village but convenient to the Canyon View Information Plaza), the Yavapai is the largest lodge in the park and thus is where you'll likely wind up if you wait too long to make a reservation. Unfortunately this is also the least-appealing hotel in the national park and is far from what you might imagine a national park lodge should be like. There are no canyon views here, which is why this place is less expensive than the Thunderbird and Kachina lodges. However, the rooms in the Yavapai East section of the hotel have just undergone extensive renovations that have made these rooms quite a bit more attractive. Set under shady pines, the Yavapai East rooms are now much nicer than the rooms in the Yavapai West section (well worth the price difference). Overall, however, I don't recommend staying here.

358 units. $91–$105 double (winter discounts sometimes available). **Amenities:** Cafeteria; tour desk. *In room:* TV.

Inexpensive

Bright Angel Lodge & Cabins ✸ Bright Angel Lodge, which began operation in 1896 as a collection of tents and cabins on the edge of the canyon, is the most affordable lodge in the park, and, with its flagstone-floor lobby and huge fireplace, it has a genuine, if crowded, mountain-lodge atmosphere. It offers the greatest variety of accommodations in the park and has undergone the most recent renovations. The best and most popular units are the rim cabins; book a year in advance for summer. (The rim cabins with fireplaces aren't worth the extra cost because the fireplaces don't work very well.) Outside the winter months, other rooms should be booked at least 6 months in advance. Most of the rooms and cabins feature rustic furnishings. The Buckey Suite, the oldest structure on the canyon rim, is arguably the best room in the park, with a canyon view, fireplace, and king-size bed. The tour desk, fireplace, museum, and restrooms account for the constant crowds in the lobby.

89 units, 20 with shared bathrooms. $49 double with sink only; $55 double with sink and toilet; $67 double with private bathroom; $84–$240 cabin. **Amenities:** 2 restaurants (American, steakhouse/Southwestern); lounge; ice-cream parlor; tour desk. *In room:* No phone.

Phantom Ranch ✸ Built in 1922, Phantom Ranch is the only lodge at the bottom of the Grand Canyon and has a classic ranch atmosphere. Accommodations are in rustic stone-walled cabins or 10-bed gender-segregated dormitories. Evaporative coolers keep both the cabins and the dorms cool in summer. Make reservations as early as possible, and don't forget to reconfirm. It's also sometimes possible to get a room on the day of departure if there are any last-minute cancellations. To attempt this, you must put your name on the waiting list at the Bright Angel Lodge transportation desk the day before you want to stay at Phantom Ranch.

Family-style meals must be reserved in advance. The menu consists of beef-and-vegetable stew ($21), a vegetarian dinner ($21), and steak ($31). Breakfasts ($18) are hearty, and sack lunches ($10) are available as well. Between meals, the dining hall becomes a canteen selling snacks, drinks, gifts, and necessities. After dinner, it serves as a beer hall. There's a public phone here, and mule-back baggage transfer between Grand Canyon Village and Phantom Ranch can be arranged ($54 each way).

C **928/638-3283** for reconfirmations. 11 cabins, 40 dorm beds. $78 double in cabin; $26 dormitory bed. Mule-trip overnights (with all meals and mule ride included) $361 for 1 person, $642 for 2 people. 2-night trips available Nov–Mar. **Amenities:** Restaurant (American); lounge. *In room:* No phone.

IN TUSAYAN (OUTSIDE THE SOUTH ENTRANCE)

If you can't get a reservation for a room in the park, this is the next closest place to stay. Unfortunately, this area can be very noisy because of the many helicopters and airplanes taking off from the airport. Also, hotels outside the park are very popular with tour groups, which during the busy summer months keep many hotels full. All of the hotels listed here are lined up along U.S. 180/Ariz. 64.

There is one other motel in Tusayan, the **Seven Mile Lodge** (**C** **928/638-2291**), which is usually the least expensive place in town ($68–$78 double). However, this motel does not take reservations and is usually full by 2pm in summer (it starts renting rooms at 9am).

Best Western Grand Canyon Squire Inn ★★ *(Kids)* If you prefer playing tennis to riding a mule, this may be the place for you. Of all the hotels in Tusayan, this one has the most resortlike feel due to its restaurants, lounges, and extensive recreational amenities. With so much to offer, it almost seems as if the hotel were trying to distract guests from the canyon itself. But even if you don't bowl or play tennis, you'll likely appreciate the large guest rooms with comfortable easy chairs and big windows. In the lobby, which is more Las Vegas glitz than mountain rustic, there are cases filled with old cowboy paraphernalia. Down in the basement there's an impressive Western sculpture, waterfall wall, and even a bowling alley.

Ariz. 64 (P.O. Box 130), Grand Canyon, AZ 86023. **C** **800/622-6966** or 928/638-2681. Fax 928/638-2782. www.grandcanyonsquire.com. 250 units. Apr–Oct and Christmas holidays $95–$185 double; Nov–Mar $65–$155 double. Children 12 and under stay free in parent's room. AE, DC, DISC, MC, V. **Amenities:** 2 restaurants (Continental, American); 2 lounges; seasonal outdoor pool; 2 tennis courts; exercise room; Jacuzzi; sauna; game room; concierge; tour desk; coin-op laundry; laundry service. *In room:* A/C, TV, dataport, coffeemaker, hair dryer, iron, free local calls.

Grand Hotel ★★ With its mountain-lodge–style lobby, this modern hotel lives up to its name, and is your best bet outside the park. There's a flagstone fireplace, log-beam ceiling, and fake ponderosa pine tree trunks holding up the roof. Just off the lobby are a dining room (with evening entertainment ranging from Native American dancers to country-music bands) and a small bar that even has a few saddles for bar stools. Guest rooms are spacious, with a few Western touches, and some have small balconies.

Ariz. 64 (P.O. Box 3319), Grand Canyon, AZ 86023. **C** **888/63-GRAND** or 928/638-3333. Fax 928/638-3131. www.visitgrandcanyon.com. 120 units. $89–$149 double. Children 12 and under stay free in parent's room. AE, DC, DISC, MC, V. Pets accepted ($10 per night). **Amenities:** Restaurant (American/Southwestern); lounge; indoor pool; Jacuzzi. *In room:* A/C, TV, dataport, coffeemaker, hair dryer.

Holiday Inn Express–Grand Canyon   This is one of the newest lodgings in the area and has modern, well-designed—if a bit sterile and characterless—guest rooms. The Holiday Inn Express also manages an adjacent 32-suite property whose rooms have a Western theme. Although these suites are fairly pricey, they're among the nicest accommodations inside or outside the park.

Ariz. 64 (P.O. Box 3245), Grand Canyon, AZ 86023. (© 888/473-2269 or 928/638-3000. Fax 928/638-0123. www.gcanyon.com/HI. 194 units. Feb to mid-Oct $129–$199 double, $250–$350 suite; late Oct to Jan $67–$145 double, $175–$195 suite. Rates include continental breakfast. Children under 18 stay free in parent's room. AE, DC, DISC, MC, V. **Amenities:** Indoor pool; Jacuzzi. *In room:* A/C, TV, dataport, high-speed Internet access, hair dryer, iron.

Quality Inn & Suites Canyon Plaza 🦋   This relatively luxurious hotel at the park's south entrance is built around two enclosed skylit courtyards, one of which houses a restaurant and the other a bar and whirlpool. Guest rooms are large and comfortable, with balconies or patios; most also have minibars. The suites contain separate small living rooms, microwaves, and fridges. The hotel is next to the IMAX Theater and is very popular with tour groups.

P.O. Box 520, Grand Canyon, AZ 86023. (© 800/221-2222 or 928/638-2673. Fax 928/638-9537. www.grand canyonqualityinn.com. 232 units. Apr to mid-Oct $128 double, $178 suite; late Oct to Mar $78 double, $128 suite. Children 18 and under stay free in parent's room. AE, DC, DISC, MC, V. **Amenities:** Restaurant (American); lounge; outdoor pool; 2 Jacuzzis. *In room:* A/C, TV, dataport, coffeemaker, hair dryer.

Rodeway Inn Red Feather Lodge (Kids)   With more than 200 units, this motel is often slow to fill up, so it's a good choice for last-minute bookings. Try to get one of the newer rooms, which are a bit more comfortable than the older ones. The pool here makes this place a good bet for families.

Ariz. 64 (P.O. Box 1460), Grand Canyon, AZ 86023. (© 800/538-2345 or 928/638-2414. Fax 928/638-9216. www.redfeatherlodge.com. 236 units. $70–$126 double. Children under 18 stay free in parent's room. AE, DC, DISC, MC, V. Pets accepted ($50 deposit plus $10 per night). **Amenities:** Restaurant (American); seasonal outdoor pool; exercise room; Jacuzzi. *In room:* A/C, TV, dataport, coffeemaker, hair dryer.

OTHER AREA ACCOMMODATIONS

Cameron Trading Post Motel 🌟🌟 (Finds)   Located 54 miles north of Flagstaff on U.S. 89 at the junction with the road to the east entrance of the national park, this motel offers some of the most attractive rooms in the vicinity of the Grand Canyon and is part of one of the best trading posts in the state. The motel, adjacent to the historic Cameron Trading Post, is built around the shady oasis of the old trading post's terraced gardens. The garden terraces are built of sandstone, and there's even a picnic table made from a huge slab of stone. Guest rooms feature Southwestern-style furniture and attractive decor. Most have balconies, and some have views of the Little Colorado River (which, however, rarely has much water in it at this point).

P.O. Box 339, Cameron, AZ 86020. (© 800/338-7385 or 928/679-2231. Fax 928/679-2501. www.cameron tradingpost.com. 62 units. Feb $49–$69 double; Mar–May $69–$99 double; June to mid-Oct $89–$119 double; mid-Oct to Jan $59–$79 double. Suites $99–$159 year-round. AE, DC, DISC, MC, V. Pets accepted. **Amenities:** Restaurant. *In room:* A/C, TV, coffeemaker.

CAMPGROUNDS
Inside the Park

On the South Rim, there are two campgrounds and an RV park. **Mather Campground,** in Grand Canyon Village, has more than 300 campsites. Reservations can be made up to 5 months in advance and are highly recommended for stays between April and November (reservations not accepted for other months). Contact the National Park Reservation Service (© **800/365-2267** or

301/722-1257; reservations.nps.gov). Between late spring and early fall, don't even think of coming up here without a reservation; you'll just be setting yourself up for disappointment. If you don't have a reservation, your next best bet is to arrive in the morning, when sites are being vacated. Campsites are $15 per night.

Desert View Campground, with 50 sites, is 25 miles east of Grand Canyon Village and open from mid-May to mid-October only. No reservations are accepted. Campsites are $10 per night.

The **Trailer Village RV park,** with 80 RV sites, is in Grand Canyon Village and charges $25 per night (for two adults) for full hookup. Reservations can be made up to 23 months in advance by contacting Xanterra Parks & Resorts, 14001 E. Iliff Ave., Suite 600, Aurora, CO 80014 (© **888/297-2757** or 303/297-2757). For same-day reservations, call © **928/638-2631.**

Outside the Park

Getting a campsite inside the park is no easy feat, and if you get shut out, your next best choices lie within a few miles of the south entrance. In Tusayan, you'll find **Grand Canyon Camper Village,** P.O. Box 490, Grand Canyon, AZ 86023-0490 (© **928/638-2887**), open year-round. This is primarily an RV park, but it also has sites for tents. The only drawback is that you're right in town, which is probably not what you were dreaming of when you planned your trip to the Grand Canyon. Rates range from $20 to $46.

Two miles south of Tusayan is the U.S. Forest Service's **Ten-X Campground.** This campground has 70 campsites, is open mid-April through September, and charges $10. This is usually your best bet for finding a site late in the day.

You can also camp just about anywhere within the **Kaibab National Forest,** which borders Grand Canyon National Park, as long as you are more than a quarter mile away from Ariz. 64/U.S. 180. Several dirt roads lead into the forest from the highway, and although you won't find designated campsites or toilets along these roads, you will find spots where others have obviously camped before. This so-called dispersed camping is usually used by campers who have been unable to find sites in campgrounds. Anyone equipped for backpacking could just hike in a bit from any forest road rather than camp right beside the road. One of the most popular roads for this sort of camping is on the west side of the highway between Tusayan and the park's south entrance. For more information, contact the **Tusayan Ranger District,** Kaibab National Forest, P.O. Box 3088, Grand Canyon, AZ 86023-3088 (© **928/638-2443;** www.fs.fed.us/r3/kai).

WHERE TO DINE
INSIDE THE PARK

If you're looking for a quick, inexpensive meal, there are plenty of options. In Grand Canyon Village, choices include **cafeterias** at the Yavapai and Maswik lodges and a **delicatessen** at Canyon Village Marketplace on Market Plaza. The **Bright Angel Fountain,** at the back of the Bright Angel Lodge, serves hot dogs, sandwiches, and ice cream and is always crowded on hot days. My favorite place in the park to grab a quick bite to eat is the **Hermit's Rest Snack Bar,** at the west end of Hermit Road. The stone building that houses this snack bar was designed by Mary Elizabeth Jane Colter, who also designed several other buildings on the South Rim. At Desert View (near the east entrance to the park), there's the **Desert View Trading Snack Bar.** All of these places are open daily for all three meals, and all serve meals for $8 and under.

The Arizona Room SOUTHWESTERN   Because this restaurant has the best view of the three dining establishments right on the South Rim, it is immensely popular. Add to this the fact that the Arizona Room has a menu (chile-crusted pan-seared salmon, baby back ribs with prickly pear or chipotle glaze) almost as creative as that of the El Tovar Dining Room, and you'll understand why there is often a long wait for a table here. To avoid the wait, arrive early, which should assure you of getting a table with a good view out the picture windows. Once the sun goes down, the view is absolutely black, which means you could be dining anywhere—and that would defeat the entire purpose of eating here. In 2004 this restaurant began opening for lunch (simple sandwiches), which provides another great option for dining with a billion-dollar view.

At the Bright Angel Lodge. ✆ **928/638-2631.** Reservations not accepted. Main dishes $8–$11 lunch, $13–$23 dinner. AE, DC, DISC, MC, V. Daily 11am–3pm and 4:30–10pm. Closed Jan to mid-Feb.

Bright Angel Coffee Shop AMERICAN   As the least expensive of the three restaurants right on the rim of the canyon, this casual Southwestern-themed coffeehouse in the historic Bright Angel Lodge stays packed throughout the day. Meals are simple and none too memorable, but if you can get one of the few tables near the windows, at least you get something of a view. The menu includes everything from Southwestern favorites such as tacos and fajitas to spaghetti (foods calculated to comfort tired and hungry hikers), but my favorite offerings are the bread bowls full of chili and stew. Wines are available, and service is generally friendly and efficient.

At the Bright Angel Lodge. ✆ **928/638-2631.** Reservations not accepted. Main courses $6.25–$15. AE, DC, DISC, MC, V. Daily 6:30–10pm.

El Tovar Dining Room ★★ CONTINENTAL/SOUTHWESTERN   If you're staying at El Tovar, you'll want to have dinner in the hotel's rustic yet elegant dining room. But before making reservations at the most expensive restaurant in the park, be aware that meals can be uneven, and few tables have views of the canyon. With this knowledge in hand, decide for yourself whether you want to splurge on a meal that will definitely be the best food available inside the park, but that might not be as good as you would hope after seeing the prices. The menu leans heavily to the spicy flavors of the Southwest (roast duck with sun-dried cranberry–ancho-chile glaze; blue-corn tamales; rainbow trout with hickory-smoked apple–pumpkin-seed salsa). Plenty of milder, more familiar dishes are offered as well. Service is generally quite good.

At the El Tovar Hotel. ✆ **928/638-2631,** ext. 6432. Reservations required for dinner. Main courses $9–$16 lunch, $18–$25 dinner. AE, DC, DISC, MC, V. Daily 6:30–11am, 11:30am–2pm, and 5–10pm.

IN TUSAYAN (OUTSIDE THE SOUTH ENTRANCE)

In addition to the restaurants listed below, you'll also find a steakhouse and a pizza place, as well as familiar chains such as McDonald's, Pizza Hut, and Wendy's.

Canyon Star ★ AMERICAN/MEXICAN   This place aims to compete with the El Tovar and Arizona Room, and serves the most creative Southwestern fare this side of the park boundary, plus you'll have live entertainment while you eat. Try the elk tenderloin with cherry–port wine sauce and wild mushrooms or the barbecued buffalo brisket. Evening shows include performances of Native American songs and dances, as well as traditional cowboy songs or country music. This place is big, so there usually isn't too long a wait for a table, and even if there is, you can head for the saloon and saddle up a bar stool (some of the stools have saddles instead of seats) while you wait. Here in the bar, you can also get a buffalo burger.

At the Grand Hotel, Ariz. 64. © **928/638-3333**. Main courses $14–$25. AE, DISC, MC, V. Daily 7:30–10am and 11am–9pm.

Coronado Room ⭐ CONTINENTAL/SOUTHWESTERN   If you should suddenly be struck with an overpowering desire to have escargot for dinner, don't despair—head for the Best Western Grand Canyon Squire Inn. Now, we're well aware that Best Western and escargot go together about as well as the Eiffel Tower and rattlesnake fritters, but this place really does serve classic Continental fare way out here in the Arizona high country. You'll probably want to stick to the steaks, though (or the wild game such as elk tournedos). You might also want to try a few of the Southwestern appetizers on the menu.

At the Best Western Grand Canyon Squire Inn, Ariz. 64. © **928/638-2681**. Reservations recommended. Main courses $16–$25. AE, DC, DISC, MC, V. Daily 5–10pm.

4 The Grand Canyon North Rim ⭐⭐⭐

42 miles S of Jacob Lake; 216 miles N of Grand Canyon Village (South Rim); 354 miles N of Phoenix; 125 miles W of Page/Lake Powell

Although the North Rim of the Grand Canyon is only 10 miles from the South Rim as the crow flies, it's more than 200 miles by road. Because it is such a long drive from population centers such as Phoenix and Las Vegas, the North Rim is much less crowded than the South Rim. Additionally, due to heavy snowfall, the North Rim is open only from mid-May to late October or early November. There are also far fewer activities or establishments on the North Rim than there are on the South Rim (no helicopter or plane rides, no IMAX theater, no McDonald's). For these reasons, most of the millions of people who annually visit the Grand Canyon never make it to this side—and that is exactly why, in my opinion, the North Rim is a far superior place to visit. If Grand Canyon Village turns out to be more human zoo than the wilderness experience you expected, the North Rim will probably be much more to your liking, although crowds, traffic congestion, and parking problems are not unheard of here, either.

The North Rim is on the Kaibab Plateau, which is more than 8,000 feet high on average and takes its name from the Paiute word for "mountain lying down." The higher elevation of the North Rim means that instead of the junipers and ponderosa pines of the South Rim, you'll see dense forests of ponderosa pines, Douglas firs, and aspens interspersed with large meadows. Consequently, the North Rim has a much more alpine feel than the South Rim. The 8,000-foot elevation—1,000 feet higher than the South Rim—also means that the North Rim gets considerably more snow in winter than the South Rim. The highway south from Jacob Lake is not plowed in winter, when the Grand Canyon Lodge closes down.

ESSENTIALS

GETTING THERE   The North Rim is at the end of Ariz. 67 (the North Rim Pkwy.), reached from U.S. 89A. **Trans Canyon** (© **928/638-2820**) operates a shuttle between the North Rim and the South Rim of the Grand Canyon during the months the North Rim is open. The trip takes 5 hours; the fare is $65 one-way (reservations required).

FEES   The park entry fee is $20 per car and is good for 1 week. Remember not to lose the little paper receipt that serves as your admission pass.

Tips **An Important Note**

Visitor facilities at the North Rim are open only from mid-May to mid-October. From mid-October to November (or until snow closes the road to the North Rim), the park is open for day use only. The campground may be open after mid-October, weather permitting.

VISITOR INFORMATION   For information before leaving home, contact **Grand Canyon National Park,** P.O. Box 129, Grand Canyon, AZ 86023 (© **928/638-7888;** www.nps.gov/grca). At the entrance gate, you'll be given a copy of *The Guide,* a small newspaper with information on park activities. There's also an **information desk** in the lobby of the Grand Canyon Lodge.

EXPLORING THE PARK

While it's hard to beat the view from a rustic rocking chair on the terrace of the Grand Canyon Lodge, the best spots for seeing the canyon are Bright Angel Point, Point Imperial, and Cape Royal. **Bright Angel Point** is at the end of a half-mile trail near the Grand Canyon Lodge, and from here you can see and hear Roaring Springs, which is 3,600 feet below the rim and is the North Rim's only water source. You can also see Grand Canyon Village on the South Rim.

At 8,803 feet, **Point Imperial** is the highest point on the North Rim. A short section of the Colorado River can be seen far below, and off to the east the Painted Desert is visible. The Nankoweap Trail leads north from here along the rim of the canyon, and if you're looking to get away from the crowds, try hiking a few miles out along this trail.

Cape Royal is the most spectacular setting on the North Rim, and along the 23-mile road to this viewpoint you'll find several other scenic overlooks. Across the road from the **Walhalla Overlook** are the ruins of an Ancestral Puebloan structure, and just before reaching Cape Royal, you'll come to the **Angel's Window Overlook,** which gives you a breathtaking view of the natural bridge that forms Angel's Window. Once at Cape Royal, you can follow a trail across this natural bridge to a towering promontory overlooking the canyon.

Once you've had your fill of simply taking in the views, you may want to get out and stretch your legs on a trail or two. Quite a few day hikes of varying lengths and difficulty are possible. The shortest is the half-mile paved trail to Bright Angel Point, along which you'll have plenty of company but also plenty of breathtaking views. If you have time for only one hike while you're here, make it down the **North Kaibab Trail.** This trail is 14 miles long and leads down to Phantom Ranch and the Colorado River. To hike the entire trail, you'll need to have a camping permit and be in very good physical condition (it's almost 6,000 ft. to the canyon floor). For a day hike, most people make Roaring Springs their goal. This hike is 9.5 miles round-trip, involves a descent and ascent of 3,000 feet, and takes 6 to 8 hours. You can shorten this hike considerably by turning around at the Supai Tunnel, which is fewer than 1,500 feet below the rim at the 2-mile point. For a relatively easy hike away from the crowds, try the Widforss Point Trail.

If you want to see the canyon from a saddle, contact **Grand Canyon Trail Rides** (© **435/679-8665;** www.canyonrides.com), which offers mule rides varying in length from 1 hour ($30) to a full day ($105).

EN ROUTE TO OR FROM THE NORTH RIM

Between Page and the North Rim of the Grand Canyon, U.S. 89A crosses the Colorado River at **Lees Ferry** in Marble Canyon. The original **Navajo Bridge** over the river here was replaced in 1995, and the old bridge is now open to pedestrians. From the bridge, which is 470 feet above the Colorado River, there's a beautiful view of Marble Canyon. At the west end of the bridge, you'll find the Navajo Bridge Interpretive Center, which is operated by the National Park Service and is partly housed in a stone building built during the Depression by the Civilian Conservation Corps (CCC). At the east end of the bridge, which is on the Navajo Reservation, there are interpretive signs telling the story of Lees Ferry from the Native American perspective.

Lees Ferry is the starting point for raft trips through the Grand Canyon, and for many years it was the only place to cross the Colorado River for hundreds of miles in either direction. This stretch of the river is legendary among anglers for its trophy trout fishing, and when the North Rim closes and the rafting season comes to an end, about the only folks you'll find up here are anglers and hunters. Lees Ferry has a 30-site campground (© 928/355-2319); campsites are $10 per night and reservations are not accepted.

Lees Ferry Anglers (© 800/962-9755 or 928/355-2261; www.leesferry. com), 11 miles west of the bridge at Lees Ferry, is fishing headquarters for the region. Not only does it sell all manner of fly-fishing tackle and offer advice about good spots to try your luck, but it also operates a guide service and rents waders and boats. A guide and boat costs $280 per day for one person or $350 per day for two people. At Lees Ferry Lodge, there is also a fly shop and you can hire a guide through **Ambassador Guides** (© 800/256-7596; www.ambassador guides.com), which charges $300 per day for one or two anglers if you go out in a boat and also offers a guide service on nearby Lake Powell.

Continuing west, the highway passes under the **Vermilion Cliffs,** so named for their deep-red coloring. At the base of these cliffs are huge boulders balanced on narrow columns of eroded soil. The balanced rocks give the area an otherworldly appearance. Along this unpopulated stretch of road are a couple of very basic lodges.

Seventeen miles west of Marble Canyon, you'll see a sign for **House Rock Ranch.** This wildlife area, managed by the Arizona Game and Fish Department, is best known for its herd of bison (American buffalo). From the turnoff, it's a 22-mile drive on a gravel road to reach the ranch.

One last detour to consider before or after visiting the national park is an area known as the East Rim. This area lies just outside the park in Kaibab National Forest and can be reached by turning east on gravel Forest Road 611 about ¾ mile south of De Motte Park Campground, which is a few miles north of the park entrance. Follow FR 611 for 1.4 miles to FR 610 and turn south. Continue for 3 miles to the East Rim Viewpoint. Another good view can be had from the Marble viewpoint at the end of FR 219, a dead-end spur road off FR 610 about 6 miles from the junction with FR 611. For more information, contact the North Kaibab Ranger Station, 430 S. Main St., Fredonia, AZ 86022 (© 928/ 643-7395; www.fs.fed.us/r3/kai), or the **Kaibab Plateau Visitors Center,** HC 64, Ariz. 67/U.S. 89A, Jacob Lake, AZ 86022 (© 928/643-7298), which is open only during the summer.

NORTH OF THE PARK

To learn more about the pioneer history of this remote and sparsely populated region of the state (known as the Arizona Strip), continue west from Jacob Lake

45 miles on Ariz. 389 to **Pipe Spring National Monument** (📞 **928/643-7105;** www.nps.gov/pisp), which preserves an early Mormon ranch house that was built in the style of a fort for protection from Indians. This "fort" was also known as Winsor Castle and occasionally housed the wives of polygamists hiding out from the law. In summer, there are living-history demonstrations. The monument is open daily (except New Year's Day, Thanksgiving, and Christmas) from 7:30am to 5pm June through September, and from 8am to 5pm the rest of the year. Admission is $4 per adult.

Southwest of Pipe Spring, in an area accessible only via long gravel roads, lies the **Parashant National Monument.** This monument preserves a vast and rugged landscape north of the east end of Grand Canyon National Park. The monument has no facilities and no paved roads. For more information, contact the Arizona Strip Field Office of the **Bureau of Land Management,** 345 E. Riverside Dr., St. George, UT 84790 (📞 **435/688-3200;** www.nps.gov/para).

WHERE TO STAY
INSIDE THE PARK
Grand Canyon Lodge ⭐⭐   Perched right on the canyon rim, this classic mountain lodge is listed on the National Register of Historic Places and is as impressive a lodge as you'll find in any national park. The stone-and-log main building has a soaring ceiling and a viewing room set up with chairs facing a wall of glass, and on either side of this room are flagstone terraces furnished with rustic chairs. Accommodations vary from standard motel units to rustic mountain cabins to comfortable modern cabins. Our favorites are still the little cabins, which, although cramped and paneled with dark wood, capture the feeling of a mountain retreat better than any of the other options. A few units have views of the canyon, but most are tucked back away from the rim. The dining hall has two walls of glass to take in the awesome canyon views.

Xanterra Parks & Resorts, 14001 E. Iliff Ave., Suite 600, Aurora, CO 80014. 📞 **888/297-2757** or 303/ 297-2757, or 928/638-2611 for same-day reservations. Fax 303/297-3175. www.grandcanyonnorthrim.com. 201 units. $91–$116 double. Children 16 and under stay free in parent's room. AE, DISC, MC, V. Closed Oct 15–May 15. **Amenities:** 2 restaurants (American); lounge; tour desk; coin-op laundry.

OUTSIDE THE PARK
North of the national park the next closest lodgings are the Kaibab Lodge and the Jacob Lake Inn. However, I have received complaints about both of these establishments and no longer recommend either of them. Your best bet is to head north to Jacob Lake and then continue 37 miles west to Kanab, Utah, where you'll find numerous budget motels.

EN ROUTE TO THE PARK
If you don't have a reservation at the North Rim's Grand Canyon Lodge, you should call the places recommended below to see if you can get a reservation. If so, you can continue on to the North Rim the next morning. Lodges near the canyon fill up early in the day if they aren't already fully booked with reservations made months in advance.

Cliff Dwellers Lodge   There isn't much else out this way but this remote lodge, which tends to stay filled up with trout anglers. The newer, more expensive rooms are standard motel units with combination tub/showers, while the older rooms, in a stone-walled building, have more character but showers only. The lodge is close to some spectacular balanced rocks, and it's about 11 miles east to Lees Ferry. The views here are wonderful.

U.S. 89A milepost 547 (H.C. 67, Box 1), Marble Canyon, AZ 86036. ℂ **800/962-9755** or 928/355-2261. Fax 928/355-2271. www.leesferry.com. 21 units. $60–$80 double. AE, DISC, MC, V. **Amenities:** Restaurant (American). *In room:* A/C, no phone.

Lees Ferry Lodge   Located at the foot of the Vermilion Cliffs, 3½ miles west of the Colorado River, the Lees Ferry Lodge, built in 1929 of native stone and rough-hewn timber beams, is a small place with rustic accommodations. The rafters and anglers who stay here don't seem to care much about the condition of the rooms, and besides, the patio seating area in front of all the rooms has fabulous views. Unfortunately, the highway is only a few yards away, so traffic noises can disturb the tranquillity. Boat rentals and fly-fishing guides can be arranged through the lodge, and there's a fly-fishing shop on the premises.

U.S. 89A (H.C. 67, Box 1), Marble Canyon, AZ 86036. ℂ **800/451-2231** or 928/355-2231. www.leesferry lodge.com. 12 units. $82–$96 double. Children under 5 stay free in parent's room. AE, MC, V. Pets accepted. **Amenities:** Restaurant; game room. *In room:* A/C, coffeemaker, no phone.

Marble Canyon Lodge   The Marble Canyon Lodge, built in the 1920s just 4 miles from Lees Ferry, is popular with both rafters and anglers. Accommodations vary considerably in size and age, with some rustic units in old stone buildings and newer motel-style rooms available as well. You're right at the base of the Vermilion Cliffs here, and the views are great. In addition to the cozy restaurant, there's a general store and fly shop where you can rent a boat or hire a guide.

P.O. Box 6032, Marble Canyon, AZ 86036. ℂ **800/726-1789** or 928/355-2225. Fax 928/355-2227. www. mcg-leesferry.com. 53 units. $64–$70 double; $134 apt. Children under 12 stay free in parent's room. AE, DISC, MC, V. Pets accepted. **Amenities:** Restaurant. *In room:* A/C, TV, no phone.

CAMPGROUNDS

Located just north of Grand Canyon Lodge, the **North Rim Campground,** with 75 sites and no hookups for RVs, is the only campground at the North Rim. It's open mid-May to mid-October. Reservations can be made up to 5 months in advance by calling the National Park Reservation Service (ℂ **800/ 365-2267** or 301/722-1257; http://reservations.nps.gov). Campsites cost $15 to $20 per night.

There are two nearby campgrounds outside the park in the Kaibab National Forest. They are **DeMotte Park Campground,** which is the closest to the park entrance and has 23 sites, and **Jacob Lake Campground,** which is 30 miles north of the park entrance and has 53 sites. Both charge $12 per night and do not take reservations. You can also camp anywhere in the Kaibab National Forest as long as you're more than a quarter mile from a paved road or water source. So if you can't find a site in a campground, simply pull off the highway in the national forest and park your RV or pitch your tent.

The **Kaibab Camper Village** (ℂ **800/525-0924,** 928/643-7804 in summer, or 928/526-0924 in winter) is a privately owned campground in the crossroads of Jacob Lake, 30 miles north of the park entrance. The campground is open from mid-May to mid-October and has around 100 sites. Rates are $12 for tent sites, $22 for RV sites with full hookups. Make reservations well in advance.

WHERE TO DINE
INSIDE THE PARK

Grand Canyon Lodge has a dining room with a splendid view. Because this restaurant is so popular, reservations are required for dinner. More casual choices at the lodge include a cafeteria and a saloon that serves light meals.

OUTSIDE THE PARK

Your only choices for a meal outside the park are the **Kaibab Lodge,** just north of the entrance, and the **Jacob Lake Inn** (℃ **928/643-7232;** www.jacob lake.com), 45 miles north at the junction with U.S. 89A. Although perhaps most noteworthy for its great cookies (stock up before hitting the trail), the restaurant here also does a good jagerschnitzel. Prices are quite reasonable.

5 South Rim Alternatives: Havasu Canyon ⊛⊛ & Grand Canyon West

Havasu Canyon: 200 miles W of Grand Canyon Village; 70 miles N of Ariz. 66; 155 miles NW of Flagstaff; 115 miles NE of Kingman

Grand Canyon West: 240 miles W of Grand Canyon Village; 70 miles N of Kingman; 115 miles E of Las Vegas, Nev.

With roughly four million people each year visiting the South Rim of the Grand Canyon, and traffic congestion and parking problems becoming the most memorable aspects of many people's trips, you might want to consider an alternative to the South Rim. For most travelers, this means driving around to the North Rim; however, the North Rim is open only from mid-May to late October and itself is not immune to parking problems and traffic congestion.

There are a couple of lesser-known alternatives. A visit to Havasu Canyon, on the Havasupai Indian Reservation, entails a 20-mile round-trip hike or horseback ride similar to that from Grand Canyon Village to Phantom Ranch, although with a decidedly different setting at the bottom of the canyon. Visiting Grand Canyon West, on the Hualapai Indian Reservation, is much less strenuous, and is favored by people short on time or who want to fly down into the canyon (something that isn't permitted within Grand Canyon National Park itself). *Note:* The drive to and from Grand Canyon West involves spending some 28 miles on gravel, so expect lots of dust and some rough stretches. Also remember that Grand Canyon West is particularly popular with tour buses from Las Vegas, and the constant helicopter traffic here precludes any sort of tranquil canyon experience.

ESSENTIALS

GETTING THERE   Havasu Canyon   It isn't possible to drive all the way to Supai village or Havasu Canyon. The nearest road ends 8 miles from Supai at Hualapai Hilltop. This is the trail head for the trail into the canyon and is at the end of Indian Route 18, which runs north from Ariz. 66. The turnoff is 7 miles east of Peach Springs and 31 miles west of Seligman.

The easiest and fastest (and by far the most expensive) way to reach Havasu Canyon is by helicopter from Grand Canyon Airport. Flights are operated by **Papillon Grand Canyon Helicopters** (℃ **800/528-2418** or 928/638-2419; www.papillon.com). The round-trip air-and-ground day excursion is $436; it's also possible to arrange to stay overnight.

Grand Canyon West   If you're headed to Grand Canyon West, you've got several options, two of which entail driving nearly 50 miles of gravel roads that aren't even passable if it has rained any time recently. The best route is to head northwest out of Kingman on U.S. 93, and after 27 miles, turn right onto the Pearce Ferry Road (signed for Dolan Springs and Meadview). After 28 miles on this road, turn right onto gravel Diamond Bar Road, which is signed for Grand Canyon West. Another 14 miles down this road brings you to the Hualapai Indian Reservation. A little farther along, you'll come to the Grand Canyon

West Terminal (there's actually an airstrip here), where visitor permits and bus-tour tickets are sold. You can also drive to Grand Canyon West from Peach Springs via Buck and Doe Road, which adds almost 50 more miles of gravel to your trip.

VISITOR INFORMATION   For information on Havasu Canyon, contact the **Havasupai Tourist Enterprises,** P.O. Box 160, Supai, AZ 86435 (✆ **928/ 448-2121;** www.havasupaitribe.com), which handles all campground reservations. For information on Grand Canyon West, contact **Grand Canyon Resort,** P.O. Box 538, Peach Springs, AZ 86434-0538 (✆ **888/255-9550** or 928/769-2230; fax 928/769-2372; www.grandcanyonresort.com).

HAVASU CANYON ✮✮✮

Imagine hiking for hours through a dusty brown landscape of rocks and cacti. The sun overhead is blistering and bright. The air is hot and dry. Rock walls rise higher and higher as you continue your descent through a mazelike canyon. Eventually the narrow canyon opens into a wide plain shaded by cottonwood trees, a sure sign of water, and within a few minutes you hear the sound of a babbling stream. The water, when you finally reach it, is cool and crystal clear, a pleasant surprise. Following the stream, you pass through a dusty (usually cluttered and unkempt, some say dirty and depressing) Indian village of small homes. Not surprisingly in a village 8 miles beyond the last road, every yard seems to be a corral for horses. Passing through the village, you continue along the stream. As the trail descends again, you spot the first waterfall.

The previously crystal-clear water is now a brilliant turquoise blue at the foot of the waterfall. The sandstone walls look redder than before. No, you aren't having a heat-induced hallucination—the water really is turquoise, and it fills terraces of travertine that form deep pools of cool water at the base of three large waterfalls. Together these three waterfalls form what many claim is the most beautiful spot in the entire state. We aren't going to argue with them.

This is Havasu Canyon, the canyon of the Havasupai tribe, whose name means "people of the blue-green waters." For centuries, the Havasupai have called this idyllic desert oasis home.

The waterfalls are the main attraction here, and most people are content to go for a dip in the cool waters, sun themselves on the sand, and gaze for hours at the turquoise waters. There's also a trail that leads all the way down to the Colorado River, but this is an overnight hike.

In Supai village, there's a small museum dedicated to the culture of the Havasupai people. Its exhibits and old photos will give you an idea of how little the lives of these people have changed over the years.

The Havasupai entry fee is $20 per person to visit Havasu Canyon, and everyone entering the canyon is required to register at the tourist office in the village of Supai. Because it's a long walk to the campground, be sure you have a confirmed reservation before setting out from Hualapai Hilltop. It's good to make reservations as far in advance as possible, especially for holiday weekends. Although you can make reservations with a credit card, be sure to bring enough cash for your stay in the canyon; there are no ATMs here.

If you plan to hike down into the canyon, start early to avoid the heat of the day. The hike is beautiful, but it's 10 miles to the campground. The steepest part of the trail is the first mile or so from Hualapai Hilltop. After this section, it's relatively flat.

Through **Havasupai Tourist Enterprises** (© **928/448-2121;** www.havasupai tribe.com), you can hire a horse to carry you or your gear down into the canyon from Hualapai Hilltop. Horses cost $75 each way. Many people who hike in decide that it's worth the money to ride out, or at least have their backpacks carried out. Be sure to confirm your horse reservation a day before driving to Hualapai Hilltop. Sometimes no horses are available, and it's a long drive back to the nearest town.

If you'd like to hike into Havasu Canyon with a guide, contact **Arizona Outback Adventures,** 16447 N. 91st St., Scottsdale, AZ 85260 (© **866/455-1601** or 480/945-2881; www.azoutbackadventures.com), which leads 4- and 5-day hikes into Havasu Canyon and charges $1,195 to $1,360 per person. **Discovery Treks,** 6890 E. Sunrise Dr., Suite 120-108, Tucson, AZ 85750 (© **888/256-8731** or 520/404-1151; www.discoverytreks.com), offers similar 3-day trips and charges $790 to $960 per person.

GRAND CANYON WEST

Located on the Hualapai Indian Reservation on the south side of the Colorado River, **Grand Canyon West** (© **928/699-0269**) overlooks the little visited west end of Grand Canyon National Park. Although the view is not as spectacular as at either the South Rim or the North Rim, Grand Canyon West is noteworthy for one thing: It is one of the only places where you can legally fly down into the canyon. This is possible because the helicopters operate on land that is part of the Hualapai Indian Reservation. At this point, the south side of the Colorado lies within the reservation, while the north side of the river is within Grand Canyon National Park. The tours are operated by **Papillon Helicopters** (© **888/635-7272** or 702/736-7243; www.papillon.com), which charges $149 to $179 per person for a quick trip to the bottom of the canyon and a boat ride on the Colorado River. *Note:* Lower rates may be available on their website.

There are also guided **bus tours** along the rim of the canyon. These include a barbecue lunch and time to do a bit of exploring at a canyon overlook. Tours stop at Eagle Point, where rock formations resemble various animals and people, and at Guano Point, where bat guano was once mined commercially. The tours, which operate daily throughout the year, cost $37 for adults and $27 for children 6 to 13. No reservations are accepted, so it's a good idea to arrive by 8am when Grand Canyon West opens (if you're coming from Kingman, allow at least 1½ hr. to get here). ATV (all-terrain vehicle) tours are also offered, as are van tours down to the bottom of the Grand Canyon on a dirt road that leads through the Hualapai Indian Reservation.

If you'd just like to take in the view from this end of the canyon, head to **Quartermaster Point,** after first purchasing your sightseeing permit ($14 adults, $10 children) at the Grand Canyon West terminal. At Quartermaster Point, you'll find a trail that leads down a few hundred yards to a viewpoint overlooking the Colorado River. However, it's a long way out here, and once you're here there isn't much to do. Also, the views are not nearly as spectacular as those at the North Rim of South Rim.

Because this is about the closest spot to Las Vegas that actually provides a glimpse of the Colorado River and Grand Canyon National Park, the bus tours and helicopter rides are very popular with tour groups from Las Vegas. Busloads of visitors come and go throughout the day, and the air is always filled with the noise of helicopters ferrying people down into the canyon.

While I can recommend a trip out to Grand Canyon West only as a side trip from Las Vegas or for travelers who absolutely must fly down into the canyon, the drive out here is almost as scenic as the destination itself. Along Diamond Bar Road, you'll be driving below the Grand Wash Cliffs, and for much of the way, the route traverses a dense forest of Joshua trees.

OTHER AREA ACTIVITIES

If you long to raft the Grand Canyon but have only a couple of free days in your schedule to realize your dream, then you have only a couple of options. Here at the west end of the canyon, it's possible to do a 1-day rafting trip that begins on the Hualapai Indian Reservation. These trips are operated by **Hualapai River Runners,** 887 Rte. 66, Peach Springs, AZ 86434-0359 (© **888/255-9550** or 928/769-2419; www.grandcanyonresort.com), a tribal rafting company, and run between mid-March and late October. Expect a mix of white water and flat water. Although not as exciting as longer trips in the main section of the canyon, you'll still plow through some pretty big waves. Be ready to get wet. These trips stop at a couple of side canyons where you can get out and do some exploring. One-day trips cost $265 per person.

Also in this area, you can visit **Grand Canyon Caverns** (© **928/422-4565;** www.gccaverns.com), just outside Peach Springs. The caverns, which are accessed via a 210-foot elevator ride, are open from Memorial Day to October 15, daily from 8am to 6pm, and other months, daily from 10am to 5pm. Admission is $13 for adults, $10 for children 4 to 12. There are also flashlight tours ($15 for adults and $10 for children) and explorers tours ($45).

WHERE TO STAY & DINE

Grand Canyon Caverns Inn   If you're planning to hike or ride into Havasu Canyon, you'll need to be at Hualapai Hilltop as early in the morning as possible, and because it's a 3- to 4-hour drive to the trail head from Flagstaff, you might want to consider staying here at one of only two lodgings for miles around. As the name implies, this motel is built on the site of the Grand Canyon Caverns, which are open to the public. On the premises there is also a general store with camping supplies and food. For much of the year, this motel is used by Elderhostel and stays full.

P.O. Box 180, Peach Springs, AZ 86434. © **928/422-3223.** www.gccaverns.com. 48 units. Summer $57 double; winter $47 double. AE, DISC, MC, V. Pets accepted ($50 deposit, $25 fee per night). **Amenities:** Restaurant (American); lounge; outdoor pool; coin-op laundry. *In room:* A/C, TV.

Hualapai Lodge ★ *(Finds)*   Located in the Hualapai community of Peach Springs, this lodge is by far the most luxurious accommodation anywhere in the region. Guest rooms are spacious and modern, with a few bits of regional decor for character. Most people staying here are in the area to visit Grand Canyon West, to go rafting with Hualapai River Runners, or to hike in to Havasu Canyon. The dining room is just about the only place in town to get a meal.

900 Rte. 66, Peach Springs, AZ 86434-0359. © **888/255-9550** or 928/769-2230. Fax 928/769-2372. www.grandcanyonresort.com. 60 units. Apr–Oct $80–$90 double; Nov–Mar $60–$70 double. Children under 15 stay free in parent's room. AE, DC, DISC, MC, V. **Amenities:** Restaurant (Mexican/Native American/ American); tour desk; coin-op laundry. *In room:* A/C, TV, dataport.

IN HAVASU CANYON

Havasu Campground   The campground is 2 miles below Supai village, between Havasu Falls and Mooney Falls, and the campsites are mostly in the shade of cottonwood trees on either side of Havasu Creek. Picnic tables are provided, but no firewood is available. Cutting any trees or shrubs is prohibited, so be sure to bring a camp stove. Spring water is available, and although it's considered safe to drink, we advise treating it first.

Havasupai Tourist Enterprises, P.O. Box 160, Supai, AZ 86435. ℭ **928/448-2120.** 100 sites. $10 per person. MC, V.

Havasupai Lodge   Located in Supai village, this lodge is, aside from the campground, the only accommodation in the canyon. The two-story building features standard motel-style rooms that are lacking only TVs and telephones, neither of which are much in demand at this isolated retreat. The only drawback of this comfortable though basic lodge is that it's 2 miles from Havasu Falls and 3 miles from Mooney Falls. The Havasupai Café, across from the general store, serves breakfast, lunch, and dinner. It's a very casual place, and prices are high for what you get because all ingredients must be packed in by horse.

P.O. Box 160, Supai, AZ 86435. ℭ **928/448-2201** or 928/448-2111. www.havasupaitribe.com. 24 units. $80 double. MC, V. **Amenities:** Restaurant nearby. *In room:* A/C, no phone.

6 Kingman

180 miles SW of Grand Canyon Village; 150 miles W of Flagstaff; 30 miles E of Laughlin, Nev.; 90 miles SE of Las Vegas, Nev.

Although Kingman is the only town of any size between the Grand Canyon and Las Vegas, it is looked upon by most travelers as little more than a place to gas up before heading out across the desert. In fact, Kingman actually has a fairly long history by Arizona standards and contains some interesting downtown historic buildings. The town's other claim to fame is that it is on the longest extant stretch of historic Route 66.

That Kingman today is more way station than destination is not surprising considering its history. In 1857, Lieutenant Edward Fitzgerald Beale passed through this region leading a special corps of camel-mounted soldiers on a road-surveying expedition. Some 60 years later, the road Beale surveyed would become the National Old Trails Highway, the precursor to Route 66. Gold and silver were discovered in the nearby hills in the 1870s, and in the early 1880s, the railroad laid its tracks through what would become the town of Kingman. Kingman flourished briefly around the start of the 20th century as a railroad town, and today, buildings constructed during this railroading heyday (including the historic Brunswick Hotel) give downtown a bit of historic character.

In the nearby hills, such mining towns as Oatman and Chloride sprung up and boomed until the 1920s, when the mines became unprofitable and were abandoned. However, the lure of gold and silver has never quite died in this area, and in nearby Oatman, the Gold Road Mine is still an operational mine, though giving tours now seems to generate more income than the actual mining of gold.

During the 1930s, as tens of thousands of unemployed people followed Route 66 from the Midwest to Los Angeles, Kingman became a stop on the road to the promised land of California. Route 66 has long since been replaced by I-40, but the longest remaining stretch of the old highway runs east from Kingman to Ash Fork. Over the years, Route 66 has taken on legendary qualities, and today people come from all over the world searching for pieces of this highway's historic past.

Remember Andy Devine? No? Well, Kingman is here to tell you all about its squeaky-voiced native-son actor. Devine starred in hundreds of short films and features in the silent-screen era, but he's perhaps best known as cowboy sidekick Jingles on the 1950s TV Western *Wild Bill Hickok*. In the 1950s and 1960s, he hosted *Andy's Gang*, a popular children's TV show, and in the 1960s, he played Captain Hap on *Flipper*. Devine died in 1977, but here in Kingman his memory lives on—in a room in the local museum, on an avenue named after him, and every October when the town celebrates Andy Devine Days.

ESSENTIALS

GETTING THERE Kingman is on I-40 at the junction with U.S. 93 from Las Vegas. One of the last sections of old Route 66 (Ariz. 66) connects Kingman with Ash Fork.

America West (© **800/235-9292**) flies between Phoenix and Kingman Airport. Car rentals are available here through **Enterprise** (© **800/RENT-A-CAR** or 928/692-1919), **Hertz** (© **800/654-3131** or 928/757-9690), and **Thrifty** (© **800/877-4389** or 928/718-1122).

Amtrak (© **800/872-7245**) offers rail service to Kingman from Chicago and Los Angeles. The station is at 315 E. Andy Devine Ave.

VISITOR INFORMATION The **Kingman Area Chamber of Commerce,** 120 W. Andy Devine Ave. (© **866/427-RT66** or 928/753-6106; www.kingman tourism.org), operates an information center in this restored 1907 powerhouse, which also houses the Route 66 Museum, a Route 66 gift shop, a model railroad, and a 1950s-style soda fountain. Open daily from 9am to 6pm (until 5pm between Dec and Feb).

EXPLORING THE AREA

There isn't much to do right in Kingman, but while you're in town, you can learn more about local history at the **Mohave Museum of History and Arts,** 400 W. Beale St. (© **928/753-3195**). There's also plenty of Andy Devine memorabilia on display. Open Monday through Friday from 9am to 5pm, Saturday and Sunday from 1 to 5pm. Admission is $3 for adults, $2 for seniors, 50¢ for children 12 and under. Afterward, take a drive or a stroll around downtown Kingman to view the town's many historic buildings. (You can pick up a map at the museum.)

If you're interested in historic homes, you can tour the **Bonelli House,** 430 E. Spring St., a two-story stone home built in 1915 and furnished much as it may have been at that time. It's open Monday through Friday from 11am to 4pm, but before heading over, check at the Mohave Museum of History and Arts to see if there will be a guide to show you around. Admission is by donation.

The new **Route 66 Museum,** 120 W. Andy Devine Ave. (© **928/753-9889**), has exhibits on the history of not just Route 66, but also the roads, railroads, and trails that preceded it. There's a great collection of old photos taken during the Depression, and even an "Okie" truck on display. You'll also see a Studebaker Champion and mock-ups of a gas station, diner, hotel lobby, and barbershop. Hours are daily from 9am to 6pm (until 5pm Dec–Feb); admission is $3 for adults, $2 for seniors, and free for children 12 and under.

When you're tired of the heat and want to cool off, head southeast of Kingman to **Hualapai Mountain Park,** on Hualapai Mountain Road (© **928/ 757-0915;** www.co.mohave.az.us/pw/hualapai_park.htm), which is at an elevation of 7,000 feet and offers picnicking, hiking, camping, and rustic rental cabins built in the 1930s by the Civilian Conservation Corps.

GHOST TOWNS

Located 30 miles southwest of Kingman on what was once Route 66 is the busy little mining camp of **Oatman,** a classic Wild West ghost-town tourist trap full of shops selling tacky souvenirs. Founded in 1906 when gold was discovered here, Oatman quickly grew into a lively town of 12,000 people and was an important stop on Route 66—even Clark Gable and Carole Lombard stayed here (on their honeymoon, no less). In 1942, when the U.S. government closed down many of Arizona's gold-mining operations because gold was not essential to the war effort, Oatman's population plummeted. Today, there are fewer than 250 inhabitants, and the once-abandoned old buildings have been preserved as a ghost town. The historic look of Oatman has attracted numerous filmmakers over the years; *How the West Was Won* is just one of the movies that was shot here.

One of Oatman's biggest attractions is its population of almost-wild burros. These animals, which roam the streets of town begging for handouts, are descendants of burros used by gold miners. Be careful—they bite!

Daily staged shootouts in the streets and dancing to country music on weekend evenings are the other two big draws, but you can also tour an inactive gold mine while you're here. The **Gold Road Mine Tour** (© **928/768-1600;** www.gold roadmine.com) takes you underground and also shows you all the topside workings of a modern gold mine. Tours, which are offered daily, last 1 hour; the cost is $12 for adults and $6 for children 12 and under. An extended tour ($24) is also available. The mine is on historic Route 66 about 2½ miles east of Oatman.

Between October 15 and April 15, other activities at the Gold Road Mine include stagecoach rides and horseback riding. **Bartel's Stage Coach Tours** offers 1-hour stagecoach rides for $30 per person ($15 for children ages 3–12). **Gold Road Livery** offers 1-hour horseback rides for $25 per person and 2-hour rides for $40.

Annual events staged here are among the strangest in the state. There are the bed races in January, a Fourth of July high-noon sidewalk egg fry, a Labor Day burro biscuit toss, and in December a Christmas bush festival (bushes along the highway are decorated with tinsel and ornaments). Saloons, restaurants, and a very basic hotel (where you can view the room Clark and Carole rented on their wedding night) provide food and lodging if you decide you'd like to soak up the Oatman atmosphere for a while. For more information, contact the **Oatman Chamber of Commerce** (© **928/768-6222;** www.oatmangoldroad.com).

Chloride, yet another quasi ghost town, is about 20 miles northwest of Kingman. The town was founded in 1862 when silver was discovered in the nearby Cerbat Mountains, and is named for a type of silver ore that was mined here. By the 1920s, there were 75 mines and 2,000 people in Chloride. When the mines shut down in 1944, the town lost most of its population. Today, there are about 300 residents. For more information, contact the **Chloride Chamber of Commerce,** P.O. Box 268, Chloride, AZ 86431 (www.chloridearizona.com).

Much of the center of the town has been preserved as a historic district that includes, among other less-than-remarkable buildings, the oldest continuously operating post office in Arizona.

Every second and fourth Saturday of the month, Chloride comes alive with staged gunfights in the streets (at high noon, of course) at Cyanide Springs, a replica of an old Western town. Some of the town's gunfight shows are staged by the Wild Roses of Chloride, an all-women gunfighters' group.

Chloride's biggest attractions are the **Chloride murals,** painted by artist Roy Purcell in 1966. The murals, sort of colorful hippie images, are painted on the rocks on a hillside about a mile outside town. To find them, drive through town on Tennessee Avenue and continue after the road turns to dirt. You can also see old petroglyphs created by the Hualapai tribe on the hillside opposite the murals.

Get Your Kicks on Route 66

It was the Mother Road, the Main Street of America, and for thousands of Midwesterners devastated by the dust bowl days of the 1930s, Route 66 was the road to a better life. However, on the last leg of its journey from Chicago to California, Route 66 meandered across the vast empty landscape of northern Arizona.

Officially dedicated in 1926, Route 66 was the first highway in America to be uniformly signed from one state to the next. Less than half of the highway's 2,200-mile route was paved, and in those days, the stretch between Winslow and Ash Fork was so muddy in winter that drivers had their cars shipped by railroad between the two points. By the 1930s, however, the entire length of Route 66 had been paved, and the westward migration that characterized the Great Depression was underway.

The years following World War II saw Americans take to Route 66 in unprecedented numbers, but this time for a different reason. Steady jobs, a new prosperity, and reliable cars made travel a pleasure, and Americans set out to discover the West—many on the newly affordable family vacation. Motor courts, cafes, and tourist traps sprang up along the highway's length, and these businesses turned to increasingly more eye-catching signs and billboards to lure passing motorists. Neon lights abounded, looming out of the dark Western nights on lonely stretches of highway.

By the 1950s, Route 66 just couldn't handle the amount of traffic it was seeing. After President Eisenhower initiated the National Interstate Highway System, Route 66 was slowly replaced by a four-lane divided highway. Many of the towns along the old highway were bypassed, and motorists stopped frequenting such roadside establishments as Pope's General Store and the Oatman Hotel. Many closed, while others were replaced by their more modern equivalents. Some, however, managed to survive, and they appear along the road like strange time capsules from another era, vestiges of Route 66's legendary past.

The **Wigwam Motel** (p. 279) is one of the most distinctive Route 66 landmarks. The wigwams in question (actually tepees) were built out of concrete around 1940 and still contain many of their original furnishings. Also in Holbrook are several rock shops with giant signs—and life-size concrete dinosaurs—that date from Route 66 days. Nighttime here comes alive with vintage neon.

Continuing west, between Winslow and Flagstaff, you'll find a landmark that made it into the movie *Forrest Gump*. The **Twin Arrows** truck stop, now little more than an abandoned cafe, has as its symbol two giant arrows constructed from telephone poles.

Flagstaff, the largest town along the Arizona stretch of Route 66, became a major layover spot. Motor courts flourished on the road leading into town from the east. Today, this road has been officially renamed Route 66 by the city of Flagstaff, and many of the old motor courts remain. Although you probably wouldn't want to stay in most of these old motels, their neon signs were once beacons in the night for tired drivers. Downtown Flagstaff has quite a few shops where you can pick up Route 66 memorabilia.

About 65 miles west of Flagstaff begins the longest remaining stretch of old Route 66. Extending for 160 miles from Ash Fork to Topock, this lonely blacktop passes through some of the most remote country in Arizona (and also goes right through the town of Kingman). In the community of Seligman, at the east end of this stretch of the highway, you'll find the **Snow Cap Drive-In** (✆ **928/422-3291**), where owner Juan Delgadillo serves up fast food and quick wit amid outrageous decor. You can't miss it. Next door at **Angel & Vilma Delgadillo's Route 66 Gift Shop & Visitor's Center,** 217 E. Rte. 66 (✆ **928/422-3352**; www.route66gift shop.com), owned by Juan's brother Angel, you'll be entertained by one of Route 66's most famous residents and an avid fan of the old highway. The walls of Angel's old one-chair barbershop are covered with photos and business cards of happy customers. Today, Angel's place is a Route 66 information center and souvenir shop, and Angel is president emeritus of the Route 66 Association of Arizona.

After leaving Seligman, the highway passes through such waysides as Peach Springs, Truxton, Valentine, and Hackberry. Before reaching Peach Springs, you'll come to **Grand Canyon Caverns,** once a near-mandatory stop for families traveling Route 66. At Valle Vista, near Kingman, the highway goes into a curve that continues for 7 miles. Some people claim it's the longest continuous curve on a U.S. highway.

After driving through the wilderness west of Seligman, Kingman feels like a veritable metropolis, and its bold neon signs once brought a sigh of relief to the tired and the hungry. Today, there are dozens of modern motels in Kingman and it is still primarily a resting spot for the road weary. **Mr. D'z Route 66 Diner,** a modern rendition of a 1950s diner (housed in an old gas station/cafe), serves burgers and blue-plate specials and usually has a few classic cars parked out front or next door. Across the street is a restored powerhouse that dates from 1907 and is home to the **Historic Route 66 Association of Arizona** (✆ 928/753-5001; www.azrt66.com), the **Route 66 Museum** (✆ 928/753-9889), the Kingman Area Chamber of Commerce Visitor Center, a 1950s-style malt shop, and a gallery of photos by a local photographer. Each year in late April or early May, Kingman is the site of the **Route 66 Fun Run Weekend,** which consists of a drive along 150 miles of old Route 66 between Topock and Seligman.

The last stretch of Route 66 in Arizona heads southwest out of Kingman through the rugged Sacramento Mountains. It passes through **Oatman,** which almost became a ghost town after the local gold-mining industry collapsed and the new interstate pulled money out of town. Today, mock gunfights and nosy wild burros entice motorists to stop, and shops playing up Route 66's heritage line the wooden sidewalks.

After dropping down out of the mountains, the road once crossed the Colorado River on a narrow metal bridge. Although the bridge is still there, it now carries a pipeline instead of traffic; cars must now return to the bland I-40 to continue their journey into the promised land of California.

WHERE TO STAY

In addition to the accommodations listed below, most of the budget motel chains have branches in Kingman, and rates are among the lowest you'll find anywhere in the state.

Hotel Brunswick 🐾 *Finds*   Built in 1909, the Brunswick Hotel is Kingman's only restored historic lodging, and inside you'll find rooms furnished with antiques and vintage character from those days. Guest rooms vary considerably in size. The suites are extremely spacious and comfortable, while most of those with shared bathrooms have only single beds. Back when the hotel's imposing tufa-stone building was constructed, the railroad was the lifeblood of this town, and although the railroad tracks are still right across the street, triple-paned windows keep things pretty quiet. The restaurant, Hubb's Bistro, serves excellent Continental fare (see "Where to Dine," below).

315 E. Andy Devine Ave., Kingman, AZ 86401. ℂ **888/559-1800** or 928/718-1800. Fax 928/718-1801. www.hotel-brunswick.com. 24 units, 9 with shared bathrooms. $30 single with shared bathroom; $60 double with private bathroom; $88–$115 suite. Rates include deluxe continental breakfast. Children under 12 stay free in parent's room. AE, DC, DISC, MC, V. Pets accepted ($10 per night). **Amenities:** Restaurant (Continental); bar; access to nearby health club; room service; laundry service; dry cleaning. *In room:* A/C, TV, dataport, high-sped Internet access.

WHERE TO DINE

DamBar & Steak House STEAKHOUSE   This steakhouse has long been Kingman's favorite place for dinner out. It's hard to miss—just watch for the steer on the roof of a rustic wooden building. Inside, the atmosphere is very casual, with wooden booths and sawdust on the floor. Mesquite-broiled steaks are the name of the game here, but there are plenty of other hearty dishes as well.

1960 E. Andy Devine Ave. ℂ **928/753-3523.** Reservations recommended on weekends and in summer. Main courses $6–$25. AE, DISC, MC, V. Daily 11am–10pm.

Hubb's Bistro 🐾 CONTINENTAL/FRENCH   Hubb's, a downtown restaurant located in an authentically restored 1909 hotel, offers dishes you might not expect to find in a small town like Kingman. So, if you aren't in the mood for a burger or a steak, check this place out. Where else in the area are you going to get French onion soup or escargot? You can also get a few Asian-inspired dishes, including Indonesian chicken curry and tiger prawns in spicy coconut-milk sauce.

At the Hotel Brunswick, 315 E. Andy Devine Ave. ℂ **928/718-1800.** www.hotel-brunswick.com. Reservations not necessary. Main courses $10–$37. AE, DC, DISC, MC, V. Mon–Sat 5–9pm.

Mr. D'z Route 66 Diner AMERICAN   This 1990s version of a vintage roadside diner is housed in an old gas station now painted an eye-catching turquoise and pink. The retro color scheme continues inside where you can snuggle into a booth or grab a stool at the counter. This place is a big hit with car buffs and people doing Route 66 (Tues night is cruising night, which usually means plenty of vintage cars and hot rods). Punch in a few 1950s tunes on the jukebox, and order up a Route 66 bacon cheeseburger and a root-beer float.

105 E. Andy Devine Ave. ℂ **928/718-0066.** Main courses $4.25–$13. AE, MC, V. Daily 7am–9pm.

The Four Corners Region:
Land of the Hopi & Navajo

Ready for a little trivia quiz? Where in the United States can you stand in four states at the same time? Give up? The answer is way up in the northeastern corner of Arizona where this state meets New Mexico, Colorado, and Utah. This novelty of the United State's westward expansion has long captured the imagination of vacationing families looking for some way of entertaining the kids in the middle of the desert. "Hey, kids, wanna play Twister in four states at the same time?"

Known as Four Corners, this spot is the site of a Navajo Tribal Park. Pay your admission, and you, too, can experience the Four Corners state of mind. However, Four Corners is much more than just a surveyor's gimmick. The term also refers to this entire region, most of which is Navajo and Hopi reservation land. The Four Corners region happens to have some of the most spectacular countryside in the state, with majestic mesas, rainbow-hued deserts, towering buttes, multicolored cliffs, deep canyons, a huge cliff-rimmed reservoir, and even a meteorite crater. Among the most dramatic landscape features are the 1,000-foot buttes of Monument Valley, which for years have symbolized the Wild West of John Wayne movies and car commercials.

The Four Corners region is also home to Arizona's most scenic reservoir—Lake Powell—which is a flooded version of the Grand Canyon. With its miles of blue water mirroring red-rock canyon walls hundreds of feet high, Lake Powell is one of northern Arizona's curious contrasts—a vast artificial reservoir in the middle of barren desert canyons. Although 40 years ago there was a bitter fight over damming Glen Canyon to form Lake Powell, today the lake is among the most popular attractions in the Southwest.

Be forewarned, however: The Four Corners claims some of the most desolate, wind-swept, and monotonous landscapes in the state, so be sure to fill up on both gas and coffee before heading out on the highway for another 100-mile drive to the next destination.

While this region certainly offers plenty of scenery, it also provides one of the nation's most fascinating cultural experiences. This is Indian country, the homeland of both the Navajo and the Hopi, tribes that have lived on these lands for hundreds of years and have adapted different means of surviving in this arid region. The Navajo, with their traditional log homes (called hogans) scattered across the countryside, were herders of sheep, goats, and cattle. The Hopi, on the other hand, congregated in villages atop mesas and built houses of stone. Today, the Hopi still grow corn and other crops at the foot of their mesas in much the same way the indigenous peoples of the Southwest have done for centuries.

These two tribes are only the most recent Native Americans to inhabit what many consider to be a desolate, barren wilderness. The Ancestral Puebloans (formerly called Anasazis) left their mark throughout the canyons of the Four Corners region. Their cliff dwellings date back 700 years or more, and here in Arizona, the most spectacular ruins are in Canyon de Chelly and Navajo national monuments. No one is sure why the Ancestral Puebloans moved up into the cliff walls, but there is speculation that unfavorable growing conditions brought on by drought may have forced them to use every possible inch of arable land. Likewise, no one is certain why the Ancestral Puebloans abandoned their cliff dwellings in the 13th century. With no written record, their disappearance may forever remain a mystery.

The Hopi, who claim the Ancestral Puebloans as their ancestors, have for centuries had their villages on the tops of mesas in northeastern Arizona. They claim that Oraibi, on Third Mesa, is the oldest continuously inhabited community in the United States. Whether or not this is true, several of the Hopi villages are quite old, and for this reason have become tourist attractions. Most of the villages are built on three mesas, known simply as First, Second, and Third, which are numbered from east to west. These villages have always maintained a great deal of autonomy, which over the years has sometimes led to fighting between villages. The appearance of missionaries and the policies of the Bureau of Indian Affairs have also created conflicts among and within villages. Today, the Hopi Reservation is completely surrounded by the much larger Navajo Reservation.

The Navajo Reservation covers an area of 25,000 square miles (roughly the size of West Virginia) in northeastern Arizona and parts of New Mexico, and Utah. It's the largest Native American reservation in the United States and is home to nearly 200,000 Navajos. Although the reservation today has modern towns with supermarkets, malls, and hotels, many Navajo still follow a pastoral lifestyle as herders of

goats and sheep. As you travel the roads of the reservation, you'll frequently encounter flocks of goats and sheep and herds of cattle and horses. These animals have free range of the reservation and often graze beside the highways.

Unlike the pueblo tribes such as the Hopi and Zuni, the Navajo are relative newcomers to the Southwest. Their Athabascan language is most closely related to the languages spoken by Native Americans in the Pacific Northwest, Canada, and Alaska. It's believed that the Navajo migrated southward from northern Canada beginning around A.D. 1000, arriving in the Southwest sometime after 1400. At this time, they were still hunters and gatherers, but contact with the pueblo tribes, which had long before adopted an agricultural lifestyle, began to change the Navajo into farmers. When the Spanish arrived in the Southwest in the early 17th century, the Navajo began raiding Spanish settlements for horses, sheep, and goats and adopted a pastoral way of life, grazing their herds on the high plains and the canyon bottoms.

The continued raids, made even more successful with the acquisition of horses, put the Navajo in conflict with the Spanish settlers who were beginning to encroach on Navajo land. In 1805, the Spanish sent a military expedition into the Navajo's chief stronghold, Canyon de Chelly, and killed 115 people, who, by some accounts, may have been all women, children, and old men. This massacre, however, did not stop the conflicts between the Navajo and Spanish settlers.

In 1846, when this region became part of the United States, American settlers encountered the same problems that the Spanish had. Military outposts were established to protect the new settlers, and numerous unsuccessful attempts were made to establish peace. In 1863, after continued attacks, a military expedition led by Colonel Kit Carson burned crops and homes late in

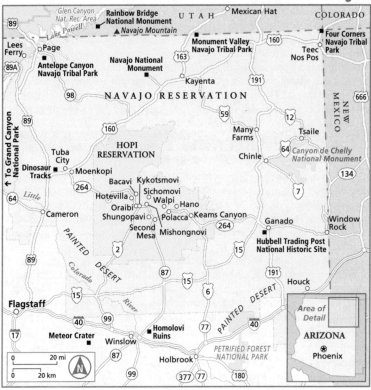

the summer, effectively obliterating the Navajo's winter supplies. Thus defeated, the Navajo were rounded up and herded 400 miles to an inhospitable region of New Mexico near Fort Sumner. This march became known as the Long Walk. Living conditions at Fort Sumner were deplorable, and the land was unsuitable for farming. In 1868, however, the Navajo were allowed to return to their homeland.

Upon returning home, and after continued clashes with white settlers, the Navajo eventually settled into a lifestyle of herding. But today, the Navajo have had to turn to many different livelihoods. Although weaving and silver work have become lucrative businesses, the amount of money these trades garner for the tribe as a whole is not significant. Many Navajo now take jobs as migrant workers. Gas

and oil leases on the reservation provide additional income.

Although the reservation covers an immense area, much of it is of little value other than as scenery. Fortunately, the Navajo have recognized the income potential of their spectacular land. Monument Valley is operated as a tribal park, as is the Four Corners park. Numerous Navajo-owned tour companies also operate on the reservation.

As you travel the reservation, you may notice small hexagonal buildings with rounded roofs. These are hogans, the traditional homes of the Navajo, and are usually made of wood and earth with the doorway facing east to greet the new day. At the Canyon de Chelly and Navajo national monument visitor centers, you can look inside hogans that are part of the parks' exhibits. If you take a tour at Canyon de Chelly or Monument Valley, you may have an opportunity to visit a privately owned hogan. Although most Navajo now live in modest houses or mobile homes, a family will usually also have a hogan for religious ceremonies.

The Navajo and Hopi reservations cover a vast area and are laced with a network of good paved roads, as well as many unpaved roads that are not always passable to cars that don't have four-wheel drive. Keep your gas tank filled because distances are great, and keep an eye out for livestock on the road, especially at night.

1 Winslow

55 miles E of Flagstaff; 70 miles S of Second Mesa; 33 miles W of Holbrook

It's hard to imagine a town that could build its entire tourist fortunes on a mention in a pop song, but that is exactly what Winslow has done ever since the Eagles sang about "standin' on a corner in Winslow, Arizona," in their hit song "Take It Easy." On the corner of Second Street and Kinsley Avenue, the town even has an official Standin' on the Corner Park (complete with a mural of a girl in a flatbed Ford).

Popular songs aside, Winslow can claim a couple of more significant attractions. Right in town is one of the Southwest's historic railroad hotels, La Posada, which is undergoing ongoing renovations that have returned it to its original glory. Twenty miles west of town is mile-wide Meteor Crater. And east of town is Homolovi Ruins State Park, which has ancient ruins as well as extensive petroglyphs. If you happen to be a rock climber, you'll find great climbing routes in Chevelon Canyon south of town.

ESSENTIALS

GETTING THERE   Winslow is on I-40 at the junction with Ariz. 87, which leads north to the Hopi mesas and south to Payson. **Amtrak** (© **800/872-7245**) trains stop in Winslow on East Second Street (at La Posada).

VISITOR INFORMATION   Contact the **Winslow Chamber of Commerce,** 300 N. Park Rd. (© **928/289-2434;** www.winslowarizona.org).

ONE BIG HOLE IN THE GROUND

Meteor Crater ★★   Northern Arizona has more than its fair share of natural attractions, and while most of the region's big holes in the ground were created by the slow process of erosion, there is one hole that has far more dramatic origins. At 550 feet deep and 2½ miles in circumference, Meteor Crater is the best-preserved meteorite impact crater on earth. The meteorite, which estimates put at roughly 150 feet in diameter, was traveling at 40,000 mph when it slammed into the earth 50,000 years ago. Within seconds, more than 175 million tons of rock had been displaced, leaving a gaping crater and a devastated landscape. Today, you can stand on the rim of the crater (there are observation decks and a short trail) and marvel at the power, equivalent to 20 million tons of TNT, that created this otherworldly setting. In fact, so closely does this crater resemble craters on the surface of the moon that in the 1960s, NASA came here to train Apollo astronauts.

On the rim of the crater, there's a small museum that features exhibits on astrogeology and space exploration, as well as a film on meteorites. On display are a 1,400-pound meteorite and an Apollo space capsule. Throughout the day, there are 1-hour hiking tours along the rim of the crater.

20 miles west of Winslow at Exit 233 off I-40. (✆ **800/289-5898**. www.meteorcrater.com. Admission $12 adults, $11 seniors, $6 children 6–17. Memorial Day to Labor Day daily 7am–7pm; Labor Day to Memorial Day daily 8am–5pm.

OTHER AREA ATTRACTIONS

In downtown Winslow, near that famous corner, you'll find the little **Old Trails Museum,** 212 N. Kinsley Ave., at Second Street (✆ **928/289-5861**), which is something of a community attic and has exhibits on Route 66 and the Harvey Girls (who once worked in the nearby La Posada hotel). From April to October, it's open Tuesday through Saturday from 1 to 5pm, and from November to March, it's open Tuesday, Thursday, and Saturday from 1 to 5pm. Admission is free.

Even if you aren't planning on staying the night at the restored **La Posada,** 303 E. Second St. (✆ **928/289-4366**), be sure to stop by just to see this historic railway hotel. Self-guided tours are available for a $2 donation, and guided tours are arranged through Winslow's Harvey Girls association ($5 suggested donation).

On the windswept plains north of Winslow, 1¼ miles north of I-40 at Exit 257, is **Homolovi Ruins State Park** (✆ **928/289-4106**), which preserves more than 300 Ancestral Puebloan archaeological sites, several of which have been partially excavated. Although these ruins are not nearly as impressive as those at Wupatki or Walnut Canyon, a visit here will give you a better understanding of the interrelationship of the many ancient pueblos of this region. Also in the park are numerous petroglyphs; ask for directions at the visitor center. Admission is $5 per vehicle. The ruins are open daily during daylight hours, but the visitor center is open only from 8am to 5pm. Monday through Friday in June and July, you can see archaeologists at work here in the park. There's also a campground, charging $12 to $22 per site.

Continuing north from the state park, you'll find the little known and little visited **Little Painted Desert** 😊, a 660-acre county park. To reach the park and its viewpoint overlooking the painted hills of this stark yet colorful landscape, continue north on Ariz. 87 from Homolovi Ruins State Park for another 12 miles. Although the trail down into the desert itself is closed, unofficially, the parks department doesn't mind if you hike down. For information, contact Navajo County Parks (✆ **928/524-4251**).

If you're in the market for some Route 66 memorabilia, drop by **Roadworks Gifts & Souvenirs,** 101 W. Second St. (✆ **928/289-5423**). If you're more interested in Native American crafts, check out the **Arizona Indian Arts Cooperative,** 523 W. Second St. (✆ **928/289-3986**), which is housed in the historic Lorenzo Hubbell Co. trading post.

WHERE TO STAY

In addition to the following historic hotel, you'll find lots of budget chain motels in Winslow.

La Posada ★★ *Finds* Wow! What an unexpected beauty this place is! Designed by Mary Elizabeth Jane Colter, architect of many of the buildings on the South Rim of the Grand Canyon, this railroad hotel first opened in 1930. Colter gave La Posada the feel of an old Spanish hacienda, and even created a fictitious history surrounding the building. In the lobby are numerous pieces of original furniture as well as reproductions of pieces once found in the hotel. The nicest rooms are the large units named for famous guests—Albert Einstein, Howard Hughes, Harry Truman, Charles Lindbergh, the Marx brothers. The management's artistic flair comes across in these rooms, one of which (the Howard Hughes Room) has wide plank floors, murals, a fireplace, a rustic bed and armoire, Art Deco chairs, and a kilim rug. The bathroom is a classic of black-and-white tile and original fixtures. There are also rooms with whirlpool tubs. The hotel's Turquoise Room (see "Where to Dine," below) is by far the best restaurant in the entire Four Corners region. La Posada is in the slow process of being completely restored and is reason enough to overnight in Winslow.

303 E. Second St. (Rte. 66), Winslow, AZ 86047. (C) **928/289-4366.** Fax 928/289-3873. www.laposada.org. 40 units. $89–$129 double. AE, DC, DISC, MC, V. Pets accepted ($10 fee). **Amenities:** Restaurant (New American/Southwestern); lounge; access to nearby health club; game room; concierge. *In room:* A/C, TV, no phone.

WHERE TO DINE

Need some good coffee? Stop in at the **Seattle Grind Coffeehouse and Art Gallery,** 106 E. Second St. ((C) **928/289-2859**), which doubles as a contemporary art gallery that could hold its own in any major metropolitan area. Right here in Winslow—no foolin'! It's also got another art gallery across the street.

The Turquoise Room 🏵🏵 *Value* NEW AMERICAN/SOUTHWESTERN
When Fred Harvey began his railroad hospitality career, his objective was to provide decent meals to the traveling public. (See "Fred Harvey & His Girls," on p. 285.) Here, in La Posada's reincarnated dining room, you'll get not just decent meals, but superb meals the likes of which you won't find anywhere else in northern Arizona. In summer, herbs and vegetables often come from the hotel's own gardens, and wild game is a specialty. Be sure to start your meal with the sweet corn and black bean soups, which are served side by side in the same bowl to create a sort of yin-yang symbol. On top of all this, you can watch the trains rolling by just outside the window. You can also get a box lunch to go when you head out for a day of exploring the area.

At La Posada, 305 E. Second St. (C) **928/289-2888.** www.laposada.org. Main courses $4–$9 breakfast, $7–$12 lunch, $13–$24 dinner. MC, V. Tues–Sun 7–10am, 11:30am–2pm, and 5–9pm. Closed Mon.

2 The Hopi Reservation

67 miles N of Winslow; 250 miles NE of Phoenix; 100 miles SW of Canyon de Chelly; 140 miles SE of Page/Lake Powell

The Hopi Reservation, often referred to as Hopiland or just Hopi, is completely encircled by the Navajo Reservation, and has at its center a grouping of mesas upon which the Hopi have lived for nearly 1,000 years. This remote region, with its flat-topped mesas and barren landscape, is the center of the universe for the Hopi people. Here the Hopi follow their ancient customs, and many aspects of pueblo culture remain intact. However, much of the culture is hidden from the view of visitors, and although the Hopi perform elaborate religious and social dances throughout the year, many of these dances are not open to outsiders.

The mesas are home to two of the oldest continuously inhabited villages in North America—Walpi and Old Oraibi. Although these two communities show their age and serve as a direct tie to the pueblos of the Ancestral Puebloan culture, most of the villages on the reservation are scattered collections of modern homes. These villages are not destinations unto themselves, but along Ariz. 264 there are numerous crafts shops and studios selling kachinas, baskets, pottery, and silver jewelry. The chance to buy crafts directly from the Hopi is the main reason for a visit to this area, although you can also go on a guided tour of Walpi village.

Important note: When visiting the Hopi pueblos, remember that you are a guest and your privileges can be revoked at any time. Respect all posted signs at village entrances, and remember that *photographing, sketching, and recording are*

prohibited in the villages and at ceremonies. Also, kivas (ceremonial rooms) and ruins are off-limits.

ESSENTIALS

GETTING THERE   This is one of the state's most remote regions. Distances are great, but highways are generally in good condition. Ariz. 87 leads from Winslow to Second Mesa, and Ariz. 264 runs from Tuba City in the west to the New Mexico state line in the east.

VISITOR INFORMATION   For advance information, contact the **Hopi Office of Public Information,** P.O. Box 123, Kykotsmovi, AZ 86039 (© **928/ 734-3283;** www.hopi.nsn.us), or the **Hopi Cultural Preservation Office** (© **928/734-3610;** www.nau.edu/~hcpo-p).

Because each of the Hopi villages is relatively independent, you might want to contact the **community development office** of a particular village for specific information: **Bacavi** (© 928/734-9360), **Sichomovi** (© 928/737-2670), **Hotevilla** (© 928/734-2420), **Kykotsmovi** (© 928/734-2472), **Mishongnovi** (© 928/737-2520), **Upper Moenkopi** (© 928/283-8054), **Lower Moenkopi** (© 928/283-5212), **Shipaulovi** (© 928/737-2570), **Shungopavi** (© 928/734-7135), and **Walpi** (© 928/737-5435). These offices are generally open Monday through Friday from 8am to 5pm.

THE VILLAGES

With the exception of Upper and Lower Moenkopi, which are located near the Navajo town of Tuba City, the Hopi villages are scattered along roughly 20 miles of Ariz. 264. Although Old Oraibi is the oldest, there are no tours of this village, and visitors are not likely to feel very welcome here. Consequently, Walpi, the only village with organized tours, is the best place for visitors to learn more about life in the Hopi villages. I mention all of the Hopi villages below to provide a bit of history and perspective on this area, but for the most part, these villages (with the exception of Walpi and Old Oraibi) are not at all picturesque. However, most do have quite a few crafts galleries and stores selling silver jewelry.

FIRST MESA   At the top of First Mesa is the village of **Walpi,** which was located lower on the slopes of the mesa until the Pueblo Revolt of 1680 brought on fear of reprisal from the Spanish. The villagers moved Walpi to the very top of the mesa so they could better defend themselves in the event of a Spanish attack. Walpi looks much like the Ancestral Puebloan villages of the Arizona canyons. Small stone houses seem to grow directly from the rock of the mesa top, and ladders jut from the roofs of kivas. The view from here stretches for hundreds of miles around.

Immediately adjacent to Walpi are the two villages of **Sichomovi,** which was founded in 1750 as a colony of Walpi, and **Hano,** which was founded by Tewa peoples who were most likely seeking refuge from the Spanish after the Pueblo Revolt. Neither of these villages has the ancient character of Walpi. At the foot of First Mesa is **Polacca,** a settlement founded in the late 1800s by Walpi villagers who wanted to be closer to the trading post and school.

SECOND MESA   Second Mesa is today the center of tourism in Hopiland, and this is where you'll find the Hopi Cultural Center. Villages on Second Mesa include **Shungopavi,** which was moved to its present site after Old Shungopavi was abandoned in 1680 following the Pueblo Revolt. Old Shungopavi is said to be the first Hopi village. Shungopavi is notable for its silver jewelry and its coiled plaques (flat baskets).

Mishongnovi, which means "place of the black man," is named for the leader of a clan that came here from the San Francisco Peaks around A.D. 1200. The original Mishongnovi village, located at the base of the mesa, was abandoned in the early 1700s and the village was reestablished at the current site atop the mesa. The Snake Dance is held here during odd-numbered years and in nearby Gray Spring in even-numbered years. It is doubtful that these dances will be open to non-Hopis, although you could try calling Mishongnovi's Community Development Office (see "Visitor Information," above) to check.

Shipaulovi, which is located on the eastern edge of the mesa, was founded after the Pueblo Revolt of 1680.

THIRD MESA   Oraibi, which the Hopi claim is the oldest continuously occupied town in the United States, is located on Third Mesa. The village dates from 1150 and, according to legend, was founded by people from Old Shungopavi. A Spanish mission was established in Oraibi in 1629, and the ruins are still visible north of the village. Today, Oraibi is a mix of old stone houses and modern ones, usually of cinder block. With permission, you can wander around in Oraibi, where you'll likely be approached by village women and children offering to sell you various local crafts and the traditional blue-corn piki bread. You might also be invited into someone's home to see the crafts they have to offer. For this reason, Old Oraibi is the most interesting village in which to shop for local crafts.

For centuries, Oraibi was the largest of the Hopi villages, but in 1906, a schism occurred over Bureau of Indian Affairs policies and many of the villagers left to form **Hotevilla.** This is considered the most conservative of the Hopi villages and has had frequent confrontations with the federal government. **Kykotsmovi,** also known as Lower Oraibi or New Oraibi, was founded in 1890 by villagers from Oraibi who wanted to be closer to the school and trading post. This village is the seat of the Hopi Tribal Government. **Bacavi** was founded in 1907 by villagers who had helped found Hotevilla but who later decided that they wanted to return to Oraibi. The people of Oraibi would not let them return, and rather than go back to Hotevilla, they founded a new village.

MOENKOPI   One last Hopi community, **Moenkopi,** is located 40 miles to the west. Founded in 1870 by people from Oraibi, Moenkopi sits in the center of a wide green valley where plentiful water makes farming more reliable. Moenkopi is only a few miles from Tuba City off U.S. 160 and is divided into the villages of Upper Moenkopi and Lower Moenkopi.

EXPLORING THE WORLD OF THE HOPI

Start your visit to the Hopi pueblos at the **Hopi Cultural Center,** on Ariz. 264 in Second Mesa (© **928/734-6650**). This combination museum, motel, and restaurant is the tourism headquarters for the area. The museum is open Monday through Friday from 8am to 5pm; in summer, it's also open Saturday and Sunday from 9am to 3pm. Admission is $3 for adults and $1 for children.

Although it's possible to get permission to visit most Hopi villages, the easiest to see is **Walpi** ⓐ, on First Mesa. Guided tours of this tiny village are offered daily between 9:30am and 4pm. Admission is $8 for adults and $5 for youths 6 to 17. To sign up for a tour, drive to the top of First Mesa (in Polacca, take the road that says FIRST MESA VILLAGE) and continue through the village to **Punsi Hall Visitor Center** (© **928/737-2262**), where you'll see signs for the tours. The tours, which last 1 hour, are led by Hopis who will tell you the history of the village and explain a bit about the local culture. On the third or last weekend in September, a harvest festival features 2 days of dancing.

CULTURAL TOURS

One of the best ways to see the Hopi mesas is on a guided small-group tour. With a guide, you will likely learn much more about this rather insular culture than you ever could on your own. Tour companies frequently use local guides and stop at the homes of working artisans. This all adds up to a more in-depth and educational visit to one of the oldest cultures on the continent.

Gary Tso is one local guide who gives tours through his **Left-Handed Hunter Tour Co.** (© **928/734-2567;** lhhunter58@hotmail.com). Gary will take you to Walpi, Old Oraibi, a petroglyph site, and the studios of a kachina carver, a potter, and a silver- and goldsmith. All-day tours (including lunch, transportation, and entry fees) cost $195 for one person, $265 for two, $295 for three, and $345 for four. There are also half-day tours to Old Oraibi for $150 for up to four people.

Bertram Tsavadawa at **Ancient Pathways** (© **928/306-7849**) specializes in tours to Hopi petroglyph sites. These are sites that are not open to the public unless you are with a Hopi guide. Tours also visit Old Oraibi. The cost is $20 per hour per person.

Crossing Worlds Journeys & Retreats, P.O. Box 623, Sedona, AZ 86339 (© **800/350-2693** or 928/203-0024; www.crossingworlds.com), offers 1-day tours from Sedona for $175 per person. There are also 2- to 4-day cultural-seminar trips to the Hopi mesas and Canyon de Chelly.

DANCES & CEREMONIES

The Hopi have developed the most complex religious ceremonies of any of the Southwest tribes. Masked kachina dances, for which they are most famous, are held from January to July. However, most kachina dances are closed to the non-Hopi public. Social dances (usually open to the public) are held August through February, and Snake Dances (usually closed to the non-Hopi public) are held August through December.

Kachinas, whether in the form of dolls or as masked dancers, are representative of the spirits of everything from plants and animals to ancestors and sacred places. More than 300 kachinas appear on a regular basis in Hopi ceremonies, and another 200 appear occasionally. The kachina spirits are said to live in the San Francisco Peaks to the southwest and at Spring of the Shadows in the east. According to legend, the kachinas lived with the Hopi long ago, but the Hopi people made the kachinas angry, causing them to leave. Before departing, though, the kachinas taught the Hopi how to perform their ceremonies.

Today, the kachina ceremonies, performed by men wearing elaborate costumes and masks, serve several purposes. Most important, they bring clouds and rain to water the all-important corn crop, but they also ensure health, happiness, long life, and harmony in the universe. As part of the kachina ceremonies, dancers often bring carved wooden kachina dolls to village children to introduce them to the various spirits.

The kachina season lasts from the winter solstice until shortly after the summer solstice. The actual dates for dances are determined by the position of the sun and usually are announced only shortly before the ceremonies are to be held. Preparations for the dances take place inside kivas (circular ceremonial rooms) that are entered from the roof by means of a ladder; the dances themselves are usually held in a village square or street.

With ludicrous and sometimes lewd mimicry, clowns known as *koyemsi, koshares,* and *tsukus* entertain spectators between the dances, bringing a lighthearted counterpoint to the very serious nature of the kachina dances. Be aware that non-Hopis at kachina dances often become the focus of attention for these clowns.

Despite the importance of the kachina dances, it is the **Snake Dance** that has captured the attention of many non-Hopis. The Snake Dance is held every other year in Mishongnovi and Gray Spring and involves the handling of both poisonous and nonpoisonous snakes. The ceremony takes place over 16 days, with the first 4 days dedicated to collecting snakes from the four cardinal directions. Later, footraces are held from the bottom of the mesa to the top. On the last day of the ceremony, the actual Snake Dance is performed. Men of the Snake Society form pairs of dancers—one to carry the snake in his mouth and the other to distract the snake with an eagle feather. When all the snakes have been danced around the plaza, they are rushed down to their homes at the bottom of the mesa to carry the Hopi prayers for rain to the spirits of the underworld.

Due to the disrespectful attitude of some visitors in the past, many ceremonies and dances are now closed to non-Hopis. However, several Hopi villages do allow visitors to attend some of their dances. The best way to find out about attending dances is to contact the **community development office** of the individual villages (see phone numbers under "Visitor Information," above).

SHOPPING

Most visitors come to the reservation to shop for Hopi crafts. Across the reservation, there are dozens of small shops selling crafts and jewelry of different quality, and some homes have signs indicating that they sell crafts. Shops often sell the work of only a few individuals, so you should stop at several to get an idea of the variety of work available. Also, if you tour Walpi or wander around in Oraibi, you will likely be approached by villagers selling various crafts, including kachinas. The quality is not usually as high as that in shops, but then, neither are the prices.

One of the best places to get a quick education in Hopi art and crafts is **Tsakurshovi** (© 928/734-2478), a tiny shop 1½ miles east of the Hopi Cultural Center on Second Mesa. This shop has an amazing selection of crafts, old-style kachina dolls, native herbs, and coil and wicker plaque baskets. The owners are very friendly and are happy to share their expertise with visitors.

If you're in the market for Hopi silver jewelry, stop in at **Honani Crafts Gallery** (© 928/737-2238), at the intersection of Ariz. 264 and the road up to Second Mesa. Nearby, at the junction with Ariz. 87, you'll also find **Hopi Fine Arts** (© 928/737-2222), another good place to shop for silver jewelry and kachinas. Between First and Second mesas, watch for the blue signs for the **Hopi Market** (© 928/737-9434; www.hopimarket.com). This shop has a wide variety of crafts from area artisans and a great website in case you decide after you get home that you want to buy something.

If you're interested in kachina dolls, be sure to visit Oraibi's **Monongya Gallery** (© 928/734-2344), a big building right on Ariz. 264 outside of Oraibi. It usually has one of the largest selections of kachina dolls in the area.

Also in Oraibi is **Hamana So-o's Arts & Crafts** (© 928/734-9375), which is located in an old stone house and sells artwork and crafts based on kachina images. At Keams Canyon, almost 30 miles east of the cultural center, is **McGee's Indian Art** (© 928/738-2295; www.hopiart.com), another great place to shop for high-quality kachina dolls. This shop is adjacent to a grocery store and has been a trading post for more than 100 years.

WHERE TO STAY & DINE

If you've brought your food along, you'll find picnic tables just east of Oraibi on top of the mesa. These tables have an amazing view!

Hopi Cultural Center Restaurant & Inn   Although it isn't much, this simple motel makes the best base for anyone planning to spend a couple of days shopping for crafts in the area. Because this is the only lodging for miles around, be sure you have a reservation before heading up for an overnight visit. All guest rooms have been remodeled fairly recently and are comfortable enough, though the grounds are quite desolate. The restaurant has a good salad bar and serves American and traditional Hopi meals, including piki bread (a paper-thin bread made from blue corn) and Hopi stew with hominy, lamb, and green chile. Prices are very reasonable, considering the remoteness of the location. There's also a museum and a very basic campground.

P.O. Box 67, Second Mesa, AZ 86043. © **928/734-2401.** Fax 928/734-6651. www.hopiculturalcenter.com. 33 units. Mar 15–Oct 15 $95 double; Oct 16–Mar 14 $65–$70 double. Children 12 and under stay free in parent's room. AE, DC, DISC, MC, V. **Amenities:** Restaurant (American/Hopi); shopping arcade. *In room:* A/C, TV, coffeemaker.

EN ROUTE TO OR FROM THE HOPI MESAS

On the west side of the reservation, in Tuba City, is the **Tuba City Trading Post,** Main Street and Moenave Avenue. (© **928/283-5441**). This octagonal trading post was built in 1906 of local stone and is designed to resemble a Navajo hogan (there's also a real hogan on the grounds). The trading post sells Native American crafts, with an emphasis on books, music, and jewelry.

On the western outskirts of Tuba City, on U.S. 160, you'll find **Van's Trading Co.** (© **928/283-5343**), in the corner of a large grocery store. Van's has a dead-pawn auction on the 15th of each month at 3pm (any pawned item not reclaimed by the owner by a specified date is considered "dead pawn"). The auction provides opportunities to buy older pieces of Navajo silver-and-turquoise jewelry.

In mid-October, Tuba City is the site of the **Western Navajo Fair,** which provides another opportunity for buying Native American crafts.

West of Tuba City and just off U.S. 160, you can see **dinosaur footprints** ☆ preserved in the stone surface of the desert. There are usually a few people waiting at the site to guide visitors to the best footprints (these guides will expect a tip). The scenery out your car window is some of the strangest in the region— red-rock sandstone formations that resemble petrified sand dunes.

The **Cameron Trading Post** ☆ (© **928/679-2231**), 16 miles south of the junction of U.S. 160 and U.S. 89, is well worth a visit. The main trading post is filled with souvenirs, but has large selections of rugs and jewelry as well. In the adjacent stone-walled gallery are museum-quality Native American artifacts (with prices to match). The trading post also includes a motel (p 245).

WHERE TO STAY

Quality Inn Navajo Nation   Located in the bustling Navajo community of Tuba City (where you'll find gas stations, fast-food restaurants, and grocery stores), this modern motel is adjacent to the historic Tuba City Trading Post and is actually a more attractive place to stay in this region than the Hopi Cultural Center. So, if you can, arrange your visit to the Hopi mesas so that you end up in Tuba City at the end of the day. The hotel offers comfortable rooms of average size, but the green lawns, shade trees, and old trading post are what really set

A Native American Crafts Primer

The Four Corners region is taken up almost entirely by the Navajo and Hopi reservations, so Native American crafts are ubiquitous. You'll see jewelry for sale by the side of desolate roads, Navajo rugs in tiny trading posts, and Hopi kachinas being sold out of village homes. The information below will help you make an informed purchase.

Hopi Kachinas   These elaborately decorated wooden dolls are representations of spirits of plants, animals, ancestors, and sacred places. Traditionally, they were given to children to initiate them into the pantheon of kachina spirits. These spirits play important roles in ensuring rain and harmony in the universe. Kachinas have long been popular with collectors, and Hopi carvers have changed their style over the years to cater to the collectors' market. Older kachinas were carved from a single piece of cottonwood, sometimes with arms simply painted on. This older style is much simpler and stiffer than the currently popular style that emphasizes action poses and realistic proportions. A great deal of carving and painting goes into each kachina, and prices today are in the hundreds of dollars for even the simplest. Currently very popular with tourists and collectors are the *tsuku,* or clown kachinas, which are usually painted with bold horizontal black and white stripes and are often depicted in humorous situations or carrying slices of watermelon. In the past few years, young carvers have been returning to the traditional style of kachina, so you now are finding more of these simpler images for sale.

Navajo Silver Work   While the Hopi create overlay silver work from sheets of silver and the Zuni use silver work simply as a base for their skilled lapidary or stone-cutting work, the Navajo silversmiths highlight the silver itself. Silversmithing did not catch on with the Navajo until the 1880s, when Lorenzo Hubbell, who had established a trading post in the area, decided to hire Mexican silversmiths as teachers. The earliest pieces of Navajo jewelry were replicas of Spanish ornaments, but as the Navajo silversmiths became more proficient, they began to develop their own designs. Sand-casting, stamp work, repoussé, and file-and-chisel work give Navajo jewelry its unique look. The squash-blossom necklace, with its horseshoe-shaped pendant, is perhaps the most distinctive Navajo design.

Hopi Overlay Silver Work   Most Hopi silver work is done in the overlay style, which was introduced to Hopi artisans after World War II, when the G.I. Bill provided funds for Hopi soldiers to study silversmithing at a

this place apart. Also, the lobby has a great collection of historic photos on display. There's also an RV park here. Be sure to try the Navajo tacos in the adjacent restaurant.

Main St. and Moenave Ave. (P.O. Box 247), Tuba City, AZ 86045. ℂ **800/644-8383** or 928/283-4545. Fax 928/283-4144. www.qualityinnnavajonation.com. 80 units. Apr–Oct $105–$140 double; Nov–Mar $85–$115 double. Children 18 and under stay free in parent's room. AE, DC, DISC, MC, V. Pets accepted ($20 deposit). **Amenities:** Restaurant (American/Mexican/Navajo); coin-op laundry. *In room:* A/C, TV, coffeemaker, free local calls.

school founded by Hopi artist Fred Kabotie. The overlay process basically uses two sheets of silver, one with a design cut from it. Heat fuses the two sheets, forming a raised image. Designs used in overlay jewelry are often borrowed from other Hopi crafts such as basketry and pottery, as well as from ancient Ancestral Puebloan pottery. Belt buckles, earrings, bolo ties, and bracelets are all popular.

Hopi Baskets   Although the Tohono O'odham of central and southern Arizona are the state's best-known basket makers, the Hopi also produce beautiful work. On Third Mesa, wicker plaques and baskets are made from rabbit brush and sumac and colored with bright aniline dyes. On Second Mesa, coiled plaques and baskets are created from dyed yucca fibers. Throughout the reservation, yucca-fiber sifters are made by plaiting over a willow ring.

Hopi Pottery   With the exception of undecorated utilitarian pottery that's made in Hotevilla on Third Mesa, most Hopi pottery is produced on First Mesa. Contemporary Hopi pottery comes in a variety of styles, including a yellow-orange ware decorated with black-and-white designs. White pottery with red-and-black designs is also popular. Hopi pottery designs tend toward geometric patterns.

Navajo Rugs   After they acquired sheep and goats from the Spanish, the Navajo learned weaving from the pueblo tribes, and by the early 1800s, their weavings were widely recognized as being the finest in the Southwest. The Navajo women primarily wove blankets, but by the end of the 19th century, the craft began to die out when it became more economical to purchase a ready-made blanket. When Lorenzo Hubbell set up his trading post, he immediately recognized a potential market in the East for the woven blankets—if they could be made heavy enough to be used as rugs. Although today the cost of Navajo rugs, which take hundreds of hours to make, has become almost prohibitively expensive, there are still enough women practicing the craft to keep it alive and provide plenty of rugs for shops and trading posts all over Arizona.

The best rugs are those made with homespun yarn and natural vegetal dyes. (Commercially manufactured yarns and dyes are increasingly used to keep costs down.) There are more than 15 regional styles of rugs and quite a bit of overlapping and borrowing. Bigger and bolder patterns are likely to cost quite a bit less than very complex and highly detailed patterns.

3 The Petrified Forest & Painted Desert ⓧ

25 miles E of Holbrook; 90 miles E of Flagstaff; 118 miles S of Canyon de Chelly; 180 miles N of Phoenix

Petrified wood has long fascinated people, and although it can be found in almost every state, the "forest" of downed logs in northeastern Arizona is by far the most extensive. But don't head out this way expecting to see standing trees of stone, leaves and branches intact. Though there is enough petrified timber scattered across this landscape to fill a forest, it is, in fact, in the form of logs and not standing trees. Many a visitor has shown up expecting to find some sort of national forest of stone trees. The reality is much less impressive than the petrified forest of the imagination.

However, this area is still unique. When, in the 1850s, this vast treasure trove of petrified wood was discovered scattered like kindling across the landscape, enterprising people began exporting it wholesale to the East. Within 50 years, so much had been removed that in 1906 several areas were set aside as the Petrified Forest National Monument, which, in 1962, became a national park. A 27-mile scenic drive winds through the petrified forest (and a small corner of the Painted Desert), providing a fascinating high-desert experience.

It may be hard to believe when you drive across this arid landscape, but at one time this area was a vast steamy swamp. That was 225 million years ago, when dinosaurs and huge amphibians ruled the earth and giant now-extinct trees grew on the high ground around the swamp. Fallen trees were washed downstream, gathered in piles in still backwaters, and eventually covered over with silt, mud, and volcanic ash. As water seeped through this soil, it dissolved the silica in the volcanic ash and redeposited this silica inside the cells of the logs. Eventually the silica recrystallized into stone to form petrified wood, with minerals such as iron, manganese, and carbon contributing the distinctive colors.

This region was later inundated with water, and thick deposits of sediment buried the logs ever deeper. Eventually the land was transformed yet again as a geologic upheaval thrust the lake bottom up above sea level. This upthrust of the land cracked the logs into the segments we see today. Wind and water gradually eroded the landscape to create the Painted Desert and northern Arizona's many other spectacular features, and the petrified logs were once again exposed on the surface of the land.

ESSENTIALS

GETTING THERE   The north entrance to Petrified Forest National Park is 25 miles east of Holbrook on I-40. The south entrance is 20 miles east of Holbrook on U.S. 180. **Amtrak** (© **800/872-7245**) has passenger rail service to Winslow, 33 miles west of Holbrook.

FEES   The entry fee is $10 per car. The park is open daily from 8am to 5pm, with longer hours in summer.

VISITOR INFORMATION   For further information on the Petrified Forest or the Painted Desert, contact **Petrified Forest National Park** (© **928/524-6228;** www.nps.gov/pefo). For information on Holbrook and the surrounding region, contact the **Holbrook Chamber of Commerce,** 100 E. Arizona St. (© **800/524-2459** or 928/524-6558; www.ci.holbrook.az.us/holbrookvisitor.htm).

EXPLORING A UNIQUE LANDSCAPE

Although Petrified Forest National Park has both a north and a south entrance, it's probably better to start at the southern entrance and work your way north along the park's 27-mile scenic road, which has more than 20 overlooks. This way, you'll see the most impressive displays of petrified logs early in your visit and save the Painted Desert vistas for last.

The **Rainbow Forest Museum** (© **928/524-6228**), located just inside the south entrance to the park, is the best place to begin your tour. Here you can learn about petrified wood and get oriented. Exhibits chronicle the area's geologic and human history. There are also displays on the reptiles and dinosaurs that once inhabited this region. The museum sells maps and books and also issues free backpacking permits. It's open daily from 8am to 5pm. Adjacent to the museum is a snack bar.

The **Giant Logs self-guided trail** starts behind the museum. The trail winds across a hillside strewn with 4- to 5-foot diameter logs that certainly live up to the name. Almost directly across the parking lot from the museum is the entrance to the **Long Logs** and **Agate House** areas. On the half-mile Long Logs trail, you can see more big trees, while at Agate House, a 1.5-mile round-trip hike will lead you to the ruins of a pueblo built from colorful petrified wood.

Heading north, you'll pass by the unusual formations known as **The Flattops.** These structures were caused by the erosion of softer mineral deposits from beneath a harder and more erosion-resistant layer of sandstone. The Flattops is one of the park's wilderness areas. The **Crystal Forest** is the next stop to the north, named for the beautiful amethyst and quartz crystals once found in the cracks of petrified logs. Concern over the removal of these crystals was what led to the protection of the petrified forest. A three-quarter-mile loop trail winds past the logs that once held the crystals.

At the **Jasper Forest Overlook,** you can see logs that include petrified roots, and a little bit farther north, at the **Agate Bridge** stop, you can see a petrified log that forms a natural agate bridge. Continuing north, you'll reach **Blue Mesa,** where pieces of petrified wood form capstones over easily eroded clay soils. As wind and water wear away at the clay beneath a piece of stone, the balance of the stone becomes more and more precarious until it eventually comes toppling down. A 1-mile loop trail here leads into the park's badlands.

Erosion has played a major role in the formation of the Painted Desert, and to the north of Blue Mesa you'll see some of the most interesting erosional features of the area. It's quite evident why these hills of sandstone and clay are known as **The Teepees.** The layers of different color are due to manganese, iron, and other minerals in the soil.

By this point, you've probably seen as much petrified wood as you'd ever care to see, so be sure to stop at **Newspaper Rock,** where instead of staring at more ancient logs, you can see a dense concentration of petroglyphs left by generations of Native Americans. At nearby **Puerco Pueblo,** the park's largest archaeological site, you can view the remains of homes built by the people who created the park's petroglyphs. This pueblo was probably built sometime around 1400. Don't miss the petroglyphs on its back side.

North of Puerco Pueblo, the road crosses I-40. From here to the Painted Desert Visitor Center, there are eight overlooks onto the southernmost edge of the **Painted Desert.** Named for the vivid colors of the soil and stone that cover the land here, the Painted Desert is a dreamscape of pastels washed across a barren expanse of eroded hills. The colors are created by minerals dissolved in sandstone and clay soils that were deposited during different geologic periods. There's a picnic area at Chinde Point overlook. At Kachina Point, you'll find the **Painted Desert Inn** (© **928/524-6228**), a historic building that's open daily from 9am to 4pm. From here, there's access to the park's other wilderness area. The inn, which was built in 1924 and expanded by the Civilian Conservation Corps, is noteworthy for both its architecture and the Fred Kabotie murals on the interior walls. Ranger-guided tours start here, and you'll usually see Native American craftspeople giving demonstrations. Between Kachina Point and Tawa Point, you can do an easy 1-mile round-trip hike along the rim of the Painted

Desert. An even more interesting route leads down into the Painted Desert from behind the Painted Desert Inn.

Just inside the northern entrance to the park is the **Painted Desert Visitor Center** (© 928/524-6228), open daily 8am to 5pm, where you can watch a short film that explains the process by which wood becomes fossilized. Adjacent to the visitor center are a cafeteria, a book shop, and a gas station.

OTHER REASONS TO LINGER IN HOLBROOK

Although the Petrified Forest National Park is the main reason for visiting this area, you might want to stop by downtown Holbrook's **Old West Museum,** 100 E. Arizona St. (© **928/524-6558**), which also houses the Holbrook Chamber of Commerce visitor center. This old and dusty museum has exhibits on local history, but is most interesting for its old jail cells. It's open Monday through Friday from 8am to 5pm and Saturday and Sunday from 9am to 4pm; admission is free. On weekday evenings in June and July, the Holbrook Chamber sponsors Native American dances on the lawn in front.

Although it is against the law to collect petrified wood inside Petrified Forest National Park, there are several rock shops in Holbrook where you can buy pieces of petrified wood in all shapes and sizes. You'll find them lined up along the main street through town and out on U.S. 180, the highway leading to the south entrance of Petrified Forest National Park. The biggest and best of these rock shops is **Jim Gray's Petrified Wood Co.,** 147 Hwy. 180 (© **928/524-1842**), which has everything from raw rocks to $24,000 petrified-wood coffee tables. This store also has a fascinating display of minerals and fossils. This shop is open daily from 7:30am to 7pm and is well worth a stop.

Three miles west of town is the **International Petrified Forest/Museum of the Americas/Dinosaur Park** (© **888/830-6682** or 928/524-9178), at Exit 292 off I-40. Although this place may seem at first like just another tourist trap, it actually contains the largest collection of pre-Columbian artifacts in the Southwest, with an emphasis on Mayan and Aztec objects, along with plenty of Ancestral Puebloan and Hohokam pieces. There's also a "rock yard" full of petrified wood, dinosaur fossils, geodes, and other interesting rocks, and a 3-mile drive takes you past Triassic dig sites and more petrified wood. Oh yes, and then there are the bison and the "sand boxes" where kids can dig for fossils and artifacts. The museum is open from 8am to 6 or 7pm in summer (9am–5pm the rest of the year); admission is $5 per car. There's also a warehouse-size rock shop.

In town on the north side of I-40 is **McGee's Gallery,** 2114 N. Navajo Blvd. (© **928/524-1977**), a Native American crafts gallery with a wide selection of typical crafts at reasonable prices. There's a particularly good collection of kachina dolls here.

Fun Fact **Rock Talk**

Gift shops throughout this region sell petrified wood in all sizes and colors, natural and polished. This petrified wood does not come from the national park, but is collected on private land in the area. No piece of petrified wood, no matter how small, may be removed from Petrified Forest National Park.

If you're interested in petroglyphs, you may want to schedule a visit to the **Rock Art Ranch** ✦ (© **928/288-3260**), southwest of Holbrook on part of the old Hashknife Ranch, which was the largest ranch in the country during the late 19th century. Within the bounds of this ranch, pecked into the rock walls of Chevelon Canyon, are hundreds of Ancestral Puebloan petroglyphs. The setting, a narrow canyon that is almost invisible until you are right beside it, is enchanting, making this the finest place in the state to view petroglyphs. Tours (reservations required) are available Monday through Saturday year-round (call to get rate information and directions to the ranch).

WHERE TO STAY

Holbrook, the town nearest to Petrified Forest National Park, offers lots of budget chain motels charging very reasonable rates.

Wigwam Motel *(Finds)*   If you're willing to sleep on a saggy mattress for the sake of reliving a bit of Route 66 history, don't miss this collection of concrete wigwams (tepees, actually). This unique motel was built in the 1940s, when unusual architecture was springing up all along famous Route 66. The motel has been owned by the same family since it was built and still has the original rustic furniture. Old cars are kept in the parking lot for an added dose of Route 66 character.

811 W. Hopi Dr., Holbrook, AZ 86025. © **928/524-3048.** Fax 928/524-9335. www.galerie-kokopelli.com/wigwam. 15 units. $42–$48 double. MC, V. Pets accepted. *In room:* A/C, TV.

WHERE TO DINE

Butterfield Stage Co. STEAKHOUSE/SEAFOOD   It's natural to assume that finding a decent meal in an out-of-the-way town might be nearly impossible, so the Butterfield Stage Co. comes as a pleasant surprise. Meals here are pretty good, with a soup-and-salad bar that's usually fresh. Tables have historical panels with amusing information to read while you wait for your pepper steak or filet mignon. The restaurant is named for the famous overland stagecoach line that carried the mail from St. Louis to San Francisco in the mid–19th century.

609 W. Hopi Dr. © **928/524-3447.** Reservations not necessary. Main courses $9–$19. AE, DISC, MC, V. Daily 4–10pm.

4 The Window Rock & Ganado Areas

74 miles NE of Petrified Forest National Park; 91 miles E of Second Mesa; 190 miles E of Flagstaff; 68 miles SE of Canyon de Chelly National Monument

Window Rock, the capital of the Navajo nation, is less than a mile from the New Mexico state line and is named for a huge natural opening in a sandstone cliff just outside town. Today, that landmark is preserved as the **Window Rock Tribal Park,** located 2 miles north of Ariz. 264. As the Navajo nation's capital, Window Rock is the site of government offices, a museum and cultural center, and a zoo. A few miles to the west is the St. Michaels Historical Museum, in the community of St. Michaels. About a half-hour's drive west of St. Michaels is the Hubbell Trading Post, in the community of Ganado.

ESSENTIALS

GETTING THERE   To reach Window Rock from Flagstaff, take I-40 east to Lupton and go north on Indian Route 12.

VISITOR INFORMATION   For advance information, contact **Navajo Tourism,** P.O. Box 663, Window Rock, AZ 86515 (© **928/871-6436;** www.discovernavajo.com).

> **Tips** **What Time Is It?**
>
> The Navajo nation observes daylight saving time, contrary to the rest of the state, so if you're coming from elsewhere in Arizona, the time here will be 1 hour later in months when daylight saving is in effect. The Hopi Reservation, however, does not observe daylight saving time, even though it is completely surrounded by the Navajo Reservation.

SPECIAL EVENTS   Unlike the village ceremonies of the pueblo-dwelling Hopi, Navajo religious ceremonies tend to be held in the privacy of family hogans. However, the public is welcome to attend the numerous fairs, pow-wows, and rodeos held throughout the year. The biggest of these is the **Navajo Nation Fair** (ⓒ **928/871-6478;** www.navajonationfair.com), held in Window Rock in early September. It features traditional dances, a rodeo, a powwow, a parade, a Miss Navajo Pageant, and arts-and-crafts exhibits and sales.

EXPLORING THE AREA

Hubbell Trading Post National Historic Site   Located just outside the town of Ganado, 26 miles west of Window Rock, the Hubbell Trading Post was established in 1876 by Lorenzo Hubbell and is the oldest continuously operating trading post on the Navajo Reservation. Hubbell did more to popularize the arts-and-crafts of the Navajo people than any other person and was in large part responsible for the revival of Navajo weaving in the late 19th century.

Much more than just a place to trade crafts for imported goods, trading posts were for many years the main gathering spot for meeting people from other parts of the reservation and served as a sort of gossip fence and newsroom. Hubbell Trading Post is still in use today, and in the trading post's general store, you'll see basic foodstuffs (not much variety here) and bolts of the cloth Navajo women use for sewing their traditional skirts and blouses. However, today the trading post is more a living museum. Visitors can explore the grounds on their own or take a guided tour, and can often watch Navajo weavers in the slow process of creating a rug.

The rug room is filled with a variety of traditional and contemporary Navajo pieces. And although it's possible to buy a small 12-by-18-inch rug for around $100, most cost thousands of dollars. In another room are baskets, kachinas, and jewelry by Navajo, Hopi, and Zuni artisans. Twice a year, in May and August, there are auctions of Native American crafts here at the trading post.

Ariz. 264, Ganado. ⓒ **928/755-3475.** www.nps.gov/hutr. Free admission. May–Sept daily 8am–6pm; Oct–Apr daily 8am–5pm. Closed New Year's Day, Thanksgiving, and Christmas.

The Navajo Nation Museum   This museum and cultural center is housed in a large modern building patterned after a traditional hogan. Inside, you'll see temporary exhibits of contemporary crafts and art, as well as exhibits on contemporary Navajo culture. Library and gift shops are also on-site.

Ariz. 264 at Post Office Loop Rd. (across from the Navajo Nation Inn), Window Rock. ⓒ **928/871-7941.** Free admission. Mon 8am–5pm; Tues–Fri 8am–8pm; Sat 9am–5pm.

Navajo Nation Zoo & Botanical Park *Kids*   Located in back of the Navajo Nation Inn, this zoo and botanical garden features animals and plants that are significant in Navajo history and culture. Bears, cougars, and wolves are among the animals you'll see. Although small, this zoo is participating in the Mexican wolf

recovery program that is reintroducing Mexican wolves into the wild. The setting, which includes several sandstone "haystack" rocks, is very dramatic, and some of the animal enclosures are quite large and incorporate natural rock outcroppings. Also exhibited are examples of different styles of hogans. Well worth a stop.

Ariz. 264, Window Rock. (C) 928/871-6574. Free admission. Daily 8am–5pm. Closed New Year's Day and Christmas.

St. Michaels Historical Museum   Located in the town of St. Michaels, 4 miles west of Window Rock, this museum chronicles the lives and influence of Franciscan friars who started a mission in this area in the 1670s. The museum is in a small building adjacent to the impressive stone mission church. Back in the early years of the 20th century, a friar here photographed the Navajo of the area, and the chance to see some of these historic photos is one of the best reasons to stop here.

St. Michaels, just south of Ariz. 264. (C) 928/871-4171. Free admission. Memorial Day to Labor Day daily 9am–5pm. Closed the rest of the year.

SHOPPING

The **Hubbell Trading Post,** although a National Historic Site, is still an active trading post and has an outstanding selection of rugs, as well as lots of jewelry (see "Exploring the Area," above). In Window Rock, be sure to visit the **Navajo Arts and Crafts Enterprise** ((C) 928/871-4095), which is next to the Navajo Nation Inn and has been operating since 1941. Here you'll find silver-and-turquoise jewelry, Navajo rugs, baskets, pottery, and Native American clothing.

WHERE TO STAY

Navajoland Days Inn   This modern hotel is situated 2 miles west of Window Rock near the historic St. Michaels Mission and is centrally located for exploring west to the Hopi mesas, north to Canyon de Chelly, and south to Petrified Forest National Park. With its indoor pool and exercise room, this is your best bet in the area. There's a Denny's out front, which is about as good as it gets in this corner of the state.

392 W. Hwy. 264, St. Michaels, AZ 86511. (C) 800/329-7466 or 928/871-5690. Fax 928/871-5699. www.daysinn.com. 73 units. $60–$90 double; $90–$150 suite. Children 12 and under stay free in parent's room. AE, DC, DISC, MC, V. **Amenities:** Restaurant (American); indoor pool; exercise room; Jacuzzi; sauna; room service; coin-op laundry; laundry service. *In room:* A/C, TV, dataport, coffeemaker, hair dryer, iron, free local calls.

Navajo Nation Inn   This older motel is located on the edge of Window Rock, the administrative center of the Navajo Reservation. The rooms, which were all redone in 2003, feature rustic southwestern-style furnishings and are the best rooms you'll find on the reservation. The restaurant and coffee shop serve American and traditional Navajo dishes.

Tips Buying Crafts

All over the Navajo Reservation, you'll see roadside stalls selling jewelry and crafts. While you can sometimes get quality merchandise and bargain prices at these stalls, you'll usually find better items at trading posts, museum and park gift shops, and established shops where you receive some guarantee of quality.

48 W. Ariz. 264 (P.O. Box 2340), Window Rock, AZ 86515. © **800/662-6189** or 928/871-4108. Fax 928/871-5466. www.navajonationinn.com. 56 units. $67–$84 double. Rates include continental breakfast. AE, DC, DISC, MC, V. Pets accepted ($50 deposit). **Amenities:** Restaurant (American/Navajo); business center. *In room:* A/C, TV, dataport.

WHERE TO DINE

In Window Rock, your best bet is the **Navajo Nation Inn** (see "Where to Stay," above), which serves moderately priced American, Mexican, and Navajo food. Try the Navajo tacos or mutton stew. The restaurant is open Monday through Friday from 6am to 9pm and on Saturday and Sunday from 7am to 6pm.

5 Canyon de Chelly National Monument ★★★

68 miles NW of Window Rock; 222 miles NE of Flagstaff; 110 miles SE of Navajo National Monument; 110 miles SE of Monument Valley Navajo Tribal Park

It's hard to imagine narrow canyons less than 1,000 feet deep being more spectacular than the Grand Canyon, but in some ways Canyon de Chelly National Monument is just that. Gaze down from the rim at an ancient Ancestral Puebloan cliff dwelling as the whinnying of horses and clanging of goat bells drift up from far below, and you'll be struck by the continuity of human existence. For nearly 5,000 years, people have called these canyons home, and today there are not only the summer homes of Navajo farmers and sheepherders but also more than 100 prehistoric dwelling sites.

Canyon de Chelly National Monument consists of two major canyons—Canyon de Chelly (which is pronounced "canyon duh shay" and is derived from the Navajo word *tséyi,* meaning "rock canyon") and Canyon del Muerto (Spanish for "Canyon of the Dead")—and several smaller canyons. The canyons extend for more than 100 miles through the rugged slickrock landscape of northeastern Arizona, draining the seasonal snowmelt runoff from the Chuska Mountains.

In summer, Canyon de Chelly's smooth sandstone walls of rich reds and yellows contrast sharply with the deep greens of corn, pastures, and cottonwoods on the canyon floor. Vast stone amphitheaters form the caves in which the Ancestral Puebloans built their homes, and as you watch shadows and light paint an ever-changing canyon panorama, it's easy to see why the Navajo consider this sacred ground. With mysteriously abandoned cliff dwellings and breathtaking natural beauty, Canyon de Chelly is certainly as worthy of a visit as the Grand Canyon.

ESSENTIALS

GETTING THERE   From Flagstaff, the easiest route to Canyon de Chelly is I-40 to U.S. 191 to Ganado. At Ganado, drive west on Ariz. 264 and pick up U.S. 191 north to Chinle. If you're coming down from Monument Valley or Navajo National Monument, Indian Route 59, which connects U.S. 160 and U.S. 191, is an excellent road with plenty of beautiful scenery.

FEES   Monument admission is free.

VISITOR INFORMATION   Before leaving home, you can contact **Canyon de Chelly National Monument** (© **928/674-5500;** www.nps.gov/cach) for information. The visitor center is open daily, May through September from 8am to 6pm (MST) and October through April from 8am to 5pm. The monument itself is open daily from sunrise to sunset.

SPECIAL EVENTS   The annual **Central Navajo Fair** is held in Chinle in August.

> **Tips   Taking Photos on the Reservations**
>
> Before taking a photograph of a Navajo, always ask permission. If it's granted, a tip of $1 or more is expected. Photography is not allowed at all in Hopi villages.

EXPLORING THE CANYON

Your first stop should be the **visitor center,** in front of which is an example of a traditional crib-style hogan, a hexagonal structure of logs and earth that Navajos use as both a home and a ceremonial center. Inside the visitor center, a small museum explores the history of Canyon de Chelly, and there's often a silversmith demonstrating Navajo jewelry-making techniques. Interpretive programs are offered at the monument Memorial Day to Labor Day. Check at the visitor center for daily activities, such as campfire programs and natural-history programs, that might be scheduled.

From the visitor center, most people tour the canyon by car. Very different views of the canyon are provided by the 15-mile North Rim and 16-mile South Rim drives. The North Rim Drive overlooks Canyon del Muerto, while the South Rim Drive overlooks Canyon de Chelly. With stops, either rim drive can easily take 2 to 3 hours. If you have time for only one, make it the South Rim Drive, which provides both a dramatic view of Spider Rock and the chance to hike down into the canyon on the only trail you can explore without hiring a guide. If, on the other hand, you're more interested in the history and prehistory of this area, opt for the North Rim Drive, which overlooks several historically significant sites within the canyon.

THE NORTH RIM DRIVE

The first stop on the North Rim is the **Ledge Ruin Overlook.** On the opposite wall, about 100 feet up from the canyon floor, you can see the Ledge Ruin. This site was occupied by the Ancestral Puebloans between A.D. 1050 and 1275. Nearby, at the Dekaa Kiva Viewpoint, you can see a lone kiva (circular ceremonial building). This structure was reached by means of toeholds cut into the soft sandstone cliff wall.

The second stop is the **Antelope House Overlook.** The Antelope House ruin takes its name from the paintings of antelopes on a nearby cliff wall, believed to date back to the 1830s. Beneath the ruins of Antelope House, archaeologists have found the remains of an earlier pit house dating from A.D. 693. Although most of the Ancestral Puebloan cliff dwellings were abandoned sometime after a drought began in 1276, Antelope House had already been abandoned by 1260, possibly because of damage caused by flooding. Across the wash from Antelope House, an ancient tomb, known as the Tomb of the Weaver, was discovered by archaeologists in the 1920s. The tomb contained the well-preserved body of an old man wrapped in a blanket of golden eagle feathers and accompanied by cornmeal, shelled and husked corn, pine nuts, beans, salt, and thick skeins of cotton. Also visible from this overlook is Navajo Fortress, a red-sandstone butte that the Navajo once used as a refuge from attackers. A steep trail leads to the top of Navajo Fortress, and by using log ladders that could be pulled up into the refuge, the Navajo were able to escape their attackers.

The third stop is **Mummy Cave Overlook,** named for two mummies found in burial urns below the ruins. Archaeological evidence indicates that this giant amphitheater consisting of two caves was occupied for 1,000 years, from A.D. 300 to 1300. In the two caves and on the shelf between are 80 rooms, including three kivas. The central structure between the two caves includes an interesting three-story building characteristic of the architecture in Mesa Verde in New Mexico. Archaeologists speculate that a group of Ancestral Puebloans migrated here from New Mexico. Much of the original plasterwork is still intact and indicates that the buildings were colorfully decorated.

The fourth and last stop on the North Rim is the **Massacre Cave Overlook,** which got its name after an 1805 Spanish military expedition killed more than 115 Navajo at this site. The Navajo at the time had been raiding Spanish settlements that were encroaching on their territory. Accounts of the battle at Massacre Cave differ. One version claims there were only women, children, and old men taking shelter in the cave, but the official Spanish records claim 90 warriors and 25 women and children were killed. Also visible from this overlook is Yucca Cave, which was occupied about 1,000 years ago.

THE SOUTH RIM DRIVE

The South Rim Drive climbs slowly but steadily, and at each stop you're a little bit higher above the canyon floor. Near the mouth of the canyon is the **Tunnel Overlook,** where a short narrow canyon feeds into Chinle Wash, which is formed by streams cutting through the canyons of the national monument. *Tsegi* is a Navajo word meaning "rock canyon," and at the nearby **Tsegi Overlook,** that's just what you'll see when you gaze down from the viewpoint.

The next stop is the **Junction Overlook,** so named because it overlooks the junction of Canyon del Muerto and Canyon de Chelly. Here you can see the Junction Ruin, which has 10 rooms and a kiva. Ancestral Puebloans occupied this ruin during the great pueblo period, which lasted from around 1100 until shortly before 1300. First Ruin, which is perched precariously on a long narrow ledge, is also visible. In this ruin are 22 rooms and two kivas.

The third stop is **White House Overlook,** from which you can see the 80-room White House Ruins, which are among the largest ruins in the canyon. These buildings were inhabited between 1040 and 1275. From this overlook, you have your only opportunity to descend into Canyon de Chelly without a guide or ranger. The **White House Ruins Trail** ★★ descends 600 feet to the canyon floor, crosses Chinle Wash, and approaches the White House Ruins. The buildings of this ruin were constructed both on the canyon floor and 50 feet up the cliff wall in a small cave. Although you cannot enter the ruins, you can get close enough to get a good look. Do not wander off this trail, and please respect the privacy of those Navajo living here. The 2.5-mile round-trip hike takes about 2 hours. Be sure to carry water.

Notice the black streaks on the sandstone walls above the White House Ruins. These streaks, known as desert varnish, are formed by seeping water, which reacts with iron in the sandstone (iron is what gives the walls their reddish hue). To create the canyon's many petroglyphs, Ancestral Puebloan artists would chip away at the desert varnish. Later, the Navajo used paints to create pictographs of animals and historic events, such as the Spanish military expedition that killed 115 Navajo at Massacre Cave. Many of these petroglyphs and pictographs can be seen if you take one of the guided tours into the canyon.

The fifth stop is **Sliding House Overlook.** These ruins were built on a narrow shelf and appear to be sliding down into the canyon. Inhabited from about 900 until 1200, Sliding House contained between 30 and 50 rooms. This overlook is already more than 700 feet above the canyon floor, with sheer walls

Fred Harvey & His Girls

Unless you grew up in the Southwest and can remember back to pre–World War II days, you may have never heard of Fred Harvey and the Harvey Girls. But if you spend much time in northern Arizona, you're likely to run into quite a few references to the Harvey Girls and their boss.

Fred Harvey was the Southwest's most famous mogul of railroad hospitality and an early promoter of tourism in the Grand Canyon State. Harvey, who was working for a railroad in the years shortly after the Civil War, had developed a distaste for the food served at railroad stations. He decided he could do a better job, and in 1876 opened his first Harvey House railway-station restaurant for the Santa Fe Railroad. By the time of his death in 1901, Harvey operated 47 restaurants, 30 diners, and 15 hotels across the West.

The women who worked as waitresses in the Harvey House restaurants came to be known as Harvey Girls. Known for their distinctive black dresses, white aprons, and black bow ties, Harvey Girls had to adhere to very strict behavior codes and were the prim and proper women of the late-19th- and early-20th-century American West. In fact, in the late 19th century, they were considered the only real "ladies" in the West, aside from schoolteachers. So celebrated were they in their day that in the 1940s, Judy Garland starred in a Technicolor MGM musical called *The Harvey Girls*. Garland played a Harvey Girl who battles the evil town dance-hall queen (played by Angela Lansbury) for the soul of the local saloonkeeper.

giving the narrow canyon a very foreboding appearance. The **Face Rock Overlook** provides yet another dizzying glimpse of the ever-deepening canyon. Here you gaze 1,000 feet down to the bottom.

The last stop on the South Rim is one of the most spectacular: **Spider Rock Overlook.** This viewpoint overlooks the junction of Canyon de Chelly and Monument Canyon. The monolithic pinnacle called Spider Rock rises 800 feet from the canyon floor, its two freestanding towers forming a natural monument. Across the canyon from Spider Rock stands the similarly striking **Speaking Rock,** which is connected to the far canyon wall.

ALTERNATIVE WAYS OF SEEING THE CANYON

Access to the floor of Canyon de Chelly is restricted; unless you're on the White House Ruins Trail (see "The South Rim Drive," above), you must be accompanied by an authorized guide in order to enter the canyon. **Navajo guides** charge $15 per hour with a 3-hour minimum and will lead you into the canyon on foot or in your own four-wheel-drive vehicle. **De Chelly Tours** (© **928/674-3772;** dechellytours.com) charges $20 per hour, with a 3-hour minimum, to go out in your four-wheel-drive vehicle; if it supplies the vehicle, the cost goes up to $125 for three people for 3 hours. Similar tours are offered by **Canyon de Chelly Tours** (© **928/674-5433;** www.canyondechellytours.com), which will take you into the canyon in a Unimog truck or a Jeep. Unimog tours are $45 to $47 for

---

> **Tips** **Forget About Having Wine with Dinner**
>
> *Alcohol is prohibited on both Navajo and Hopi reservations.* Unfortu-
> nately, however, despite this prohibition, drunk drivers are a problem on
> the reservations, so stay alert.

---

adults and $30 to $32 for children 12 and under. Tours depart from the Holiday Inn parking lot. Jeep tours are also available. Reservations are recommended. The monument visitor center also maintains a list of guides.

Another way to see Canyon de Chelly and Canyon del Muerto is on what
locals call **shake-and-bake tours** 👣, via six-wheel-drive truck. In summer, these
excursions really live up to the name. (In winter, the truck is enclosed to keep
out the elements.) The trucks operate out of **Thunderbird Lodge** (✆ **800/679-
2473** or 928/674-5841; www.tbirdlodge.com) and are equipped with seats in
the bed. Tours make frequent stops for photographs and to visit ruins, Navajo
farms, and rock art. Half-day trips cost around $40 per person ($31 for children
12 and under), while full-day tours cost around $65 for all ages. Full-day tours,
offered in spring through fall, leave at 9am and return at 5pm.

If you'd rather use a more traditional means of transportation, you can go on
a guided horseback ride. Stables offering horseback tours into the canyon
include **Justin's Horse Rental** (✆ **928/674-5678**), which charges $10 per hour
per person for a horse and $15 per hour per group for a guide, with a 2-hour
minimum. However, I much prefer to leave the crowds behind and drive east
along South Rim Drive to **Tsotsonii Ranch** 👣 (✆ **928/755-6209**), which is 1¼
miles past where the pavement ends. Rides from here visit a more remote part
of the canyon (including the Spider Rock area) and cost the same as at Justin's.

SHOPPING

The **Thunderbird Lodge Gift Shop,** in Chinle (✆ **928/674-5841**), is well
worth a stop while you're in the area. It has a huge collection of rugs, as well as
good selections of pottery and plenty of souvenirs. In the canyon wherever visitors gather (at ruins and petroglyph sites), you're likely to encounter craftspeople selling jewelry and other types of handiwork. These craftspeople, most of
whom live in the canyon, accept cash, personal checks, and traveler's checks and
sometimes credit cards.

WHERE TO STAY & DINE

Holiday Inn–Canyon de Chelly ★★   Located between the town of Chinle
and the national monument entrance, this modern hotel is on the site of the old
Garcia Trading Post, which has been incorporated into the restaurant and gift-
shop building (although the building no longer has any historic character). All
guest rooms have patios or balconies, and most face the cottonwood-shaded
pool courtyard. Because there are Canyon de Chelly truck tours that leave from
the parking lot here and because the restaurant serves the best food in town, this
should be your top choice for a room in Chinle.

Indian Rte. 7, Chinle, AZ 86503. ✆ **800/HOLIDAY** or 928/674-5000. Fax 928/674-8264. www.sixcontinents
hotels.com/holiday-inn/?_franchisee=CHNAZ. 108 units. $80–$114 double. Children under 19 stay free in
parent's room. AE, DC, DISC, MC, V. **Amenities:** Restaurant (American/Navajo); outdoor pool; exercise room;
concierge; room service; coin-op laundry. *In room:* A/C, TV, dataport, fridge, coffeemaker, hair dryer, iron.

Thunderbird Lodge   Built on the site of an early trading post right at the mouth of Canyon de Chelly, the Thunderbird Lodge is the closest hotel to the national monument. The red-adobe construction of the lodge itself is reminiscent of ancient pueblos, and the presence on the property of an old stone-walled trading post gives this place more character than any of the other choices in the area. Guest rooms have both ceiling fans and air-conditioning. The old trading post now serves as a cafeteria (not recommended), but there is a gift shop with a rug room on-site.

P.O. Box 548, Chinle, AZ 86503. ✆ **800/679-2473** or 928/674-5841. Fax 928/674-5844. www.tbirdlodge. com. 73 units. Apr to mid-Nov $101–$106 double; $145 suite; mid-Nov to Mar $65 double, $91 suite. Children 2 and under stay free in parent's room. AE, DC, DISC, MC, V. Pets accepted. **Amenities:** Restaurant (American/Navajo); tour desk. *In room:* A/C, TV, hair dryer, iron, free local calls.

CAMPGROUNDS

Adjacent to the Thunderbird Lodge is the free **Cottonwood Campground,** which has around 100 sites but does not take reservations. The campground has water and restrooms in summer. In winter you must bring your own water, and only portable toilets are available. On South Rim Drive 10 miles east of the Canyon de Chelly visitor center is another option, the private **Spider Rock Campground** (✆ **877/910-CAMP** or 928/674-8261; http://home.earthlink. net/~spiderrock), which charges $10 to $15 per night. This campground also has a couple of hogans for rent for $25 per night. The next nearest campgrounds are at **Tsaile Lake** and **Wheatfields Lake,** both south of the town of Tsaile on Indian Route 12. Tsaile is at the east end of the North Rim Drive.

6 Navajo National Monument ⍟

110 miles NW of Canyon de Chelly; 140 miles NE of Flagstaff; 60 miles SW of Monument Valley; 90 miles E of Page

Navajo National Monument, located 30 miles west of Kayenta and 60 miles northeast of Tuba City, encompasses three of the largest and best-preserved Ancestral Puebloan cliff dwellings in the region—Betatakin, Keet Seel, and Inscription House. It's possible to visit both Betatakin and Keet Seel, but, due to its fragility, Inscription House is closed to the public. The name Navajo National Monument is a bit misleading. Although the Navajo do inhabit the area now, the cliff dwellings were built by Ancestral Puebloans. The Navajo did not arrive in this area until centuries after the cliff dwelling had been abandoned by the Ancestral Puebloans.

The inhabitants of Tsegi Canyon were ancestral Hopi and Pueblo peoples known as the Kayenta Ancestral Puebloans. For reasons unknown, the Ancestral Puebloans began abandoning their well-constructed homes around the middle of the 13th century. Tree rings suggest that a drought in the latter part of the 13th century prevented the Ancestral Puebloans from growing sufficient crops. In Tsegi Canyon, however, there's another theory for the abandonment. The canyon floors were usually flooded each year by spring and summer snowmelt, which made farming quite productive, but in the mid-1200s, weather patterns changed and streams running through the canyons began cutting deep into the soil, forming narrow little canyons called arroyos, which lowered the water table and made farming much more difficult.

ESSENTIALS

GETTING THERE   Navajo National Monument can be reached by taking U.S. 89 north to U.S. 160 to Ariz. 564 north.

FEES Monument admission is free.

VISITOR INFORMATION For information, contact **Navajo National Monument** (✆ **928/672-2700;** www.nps.gov/nava). The visitor center is open daily from 8am to 5pm (except New Year's Day, Thanksgiving, and Christmas). The monument is open daily from sunrise to sunset.

EXPLORING THE MONUMENT

A visit to Navajo National Monument is definitely not a point-and-shoot experience. You're going to have to expend some energy if you want to see what this monument is all about. The shortest distance you'll have to walk is 1 mile, which is the round-trip from the visitor center to the Betatakin overlook. However, if you want to actually get close to these ruins, you're looking at strenuous day or overnight hikes.

Your first stop should be the **visitor center,** which has informative displays on the ancestral Pueblo and Navajo cultures, including numerous artifacts from Tsegi Canyon. You can also watch a couple of short films or a slide show.

The only one of the monument's three ruins that can be seen easily is **Betatakin** ⋆, which means "ledge house" in Navajo. Built in a huge amphitheater-like alcove in the canyon wall, Betatakin was occupied only from 1250 to 1300, and at its height of occupation may have housed 125 people. A 1-mile round-trip paved trail from the visitor center leads to overlooks of Betatakin. The strenuous 5-mile round-trip hike to Betatakin itself is led by a ranger, takes about 5 hours, and involves descending more than 700 feet to the floor of Tsegi Canyon and later returning to the rim. These guided hikes are offered once a day between Memorial Day and Labor Day and leave the visitor center at 8:15am (MST). All participants should carry 1 to 2 quarts of water. Because of the danger of falling rock at the ruin site, tours no longer go inside Betatakin. This very popular hike is limited to 25 people per tour, and it is advisable to line up at the visitor center an hour or more before it opens if you want to be sure of getting a spot. This is a fascinating hike, and because the number of hikers is limited, you won't feel like you're shoulder to shoulder with a herd of tourists. It's well worth planning your schedule around being here early enough to sign up for this hike. Good luck, and don't forget to change your watch (the monument is *not* on Navajo Reservation time).

Keet Seel ⋆, which means "broken pieces of pottery" in Navajo, has a much longer history than Betatakin, with occupation beginning as early as A.D. 950 and continuing until 1300. At one point, Keet Seel may have housed 150 people. The 17-mile round-trip hike or horseback ride is quite strenuous; hikers may stay overnight at a primitive campground near the ruins. You must carry enough water for your trip—2 gallons—because none is available along the trail. Only 20 people a day are given permits to visit Keet Seel, and the trail is open only Memorial Day to Labor Day. You can apply for a permit up to 2 months in advance of your visit by calling the monument (✆ **928/672-2366**).

WHERE TO STAY

There is no lodge at the national monument, but there is a free campground that has 31 campsites and is open year-round. In summer, it's usually full by dark, but there is an overflow camping area.

The nearest reliable motels are 30 miles away in Kayenta. See the section on Monument Valley, below, for details.

7 Monument Valley Navajo Tribal Park (★(★(★

60 miles NE of Navajo National Monument; 110 miles NW of Canyon de Chelly; 200 miles NE of Flagstaff; 150 miles E of Page

In its role as sculptor, nature has, in the north central part of the Navajo Reservation, created a garden of monoliths and spires unequaled anywhere on earth. Whether you've ever been here or not, you've almost certainly seen Monument Valley before. This otherworldly landscape has been an object of fascination for years, and since Hollywood director John Ford first came here in the 1930s, it has served as backdrop for countless movies, TV shows, and commercials.

Located 30 miles north of Kayenta and straddling the Arizona–Utah state line (you actually go into Utah to get to the park entrance), Monument Valley is a vast flat plain punctuated by natural sandstone cathedrals. These huge monoliths rise up from the sagebrush with sheer walls that capture the light of the rising and setting sun and transform it into fiery hues. Evocative names reflect the shapes the sandstone has taken under the erosive forces of nature: The Mittens, Three Sisters, Camel Butte, Elephant Butte, the Thumb, and Totem Pole are some of the most awe-inspiring natural monuments.

The Navajo have been living in the valley for generations, herding their sheep through the sagebrush scrublands, and some families continue to reside here today. However, human habitation in Monument Valley dates back much further. Within the park are more than 100 ancient Ancestral Puebloan archaeological sites, ruins, and petroglyphs dating from before A.D. 1300.

ESSENTIALS

GETTING THERE   Monument Valley Navajo Tribal Park is 200 miles northeast of Flagstaff. Take U.S. 89 north to U.S. 160 to Kayenta, which is 23 miles south of Monument Valley and 29 miles east of Navajo National Monument. Then drive north on U.S. 163.

FEES   Admission to the park is $5 per person (free for children 9 and under). *Note:* Because this is a tribal park and not a federal park, neither the National Park Service's National Park Pass nor its Golden Eagle Pass is valid here.

VISITOR INFORMATION   For information, contact **Monument Valley Navajo Tribal Park** (© 435/727-5870). The park is open May through September, daily from 7am to 7pm; and October through April, daily from 8am to 5pm.

EXPLORING THE PARK

This is big country, and, like the Grand Canyon, is primarily a point-and-shoot experience for most visitors. Because this is reservation land and people still live in Monument Valley, backcountry and off-road travel are prohibited unless you're with a licensed guide. So basically the only ways to see the park are from the overlook at the visitor center, by driving the park's scenic (but very rough) 17-mile dirt loop road, or by taking a guided hiking, horseback, or four-wheel-drive tour. At the park's valley overlook parking area, you'll find a small museum, gift shop, restaurant, snack bar, campground, and tour desk for companies operating Jeep and hiking excursions through the park.

For four-wheel-drive adventures, try **Sacred Monument Tours** (© 928/380-4527; www.monumentvalley.net), which charges from $30 for a 1-hour Jeep tour to $75 for a 4-hour tour. **Totem Pole Tours** (© 800/345-8687 or 435/727-3313; www.moab-utah.com/totempole) offers similar options.

Moments **Monumental Sunsets**

Be sure to save some film on your camera (or storage space in your digital camera) for sunset at Monument Valley. Sure these rocks are impressive at noon, but as the sun sets and the shadows lengthen, they are positively enchanting—one of the most spectacular sites in America.

Because the Jeep tours are such a big business here, there's a steady stream of the 4X4s on the scenic drive throughout the day. To get away from the rumble of engines, I recommend arranging to go out on a guided hike with **Sacred Monument Tours** (© 928/380-4527; www.monumentvalley.net), which charges from $25 per person for a 2-hour hike to $100 per person for an all-day hike. Overnight hikes ($125) can be arranged. **Kéyah Hózhóní Tours** (© 928/309-7440; www.monumentvalley.com) also offers hiking tours and overnight camping trips. Keep in mind that summers can be very hot here.

If nothing but the cowboy thing will do for you in this quintessential Wild West landscape, try **Sacred Monument Tours** (© 435/380-4527; www.monumentvalley.net), which charges from $40 for a 1-hour ride to $140 for an all-day ride. Overnight rides are $150.

If you happen to be staying at Goulding's Lodge, then your best bet is to go out with **Goulding's Tours** (© 435/727-3231; www.gouldings.com), which has its office right at the lodge (see "Where to Stay & Dine," below), just a few miles from the park entrance. Goulding's offers 3½-hour tours ($33 for adults, $21 for children under 8) and full-day tours ($63 for adults, $48 for children).

ACTIVITIES OUTSIDE THE PARK

Before leaving the area, you might want to visit **Goulding's Museum and Trading Post,** at Goulding's Lodge (see "Where to Stay & Dine," below). This old trading post was the home of the Gouldings for many years and is set up as they had it back in the 1920s and 1930s. There are also displays about the many movies that have been shot here. The trading post hours vary with the seasons; admission is by donation.

Also in the area is the **Oljato Trading Post & Museum** (© 435/727-3210), 11 miles west of Monument Valley on the scenic stretch of road that leads past Goulding's. Although this trading post, which dates from 1921, is in Utah, it was originally located in Arizona. The old building, which is open daily from 8am to 8pm, still has a classic trading-post feel—and few tourists venture out this way. Horseback rides are available for $25 for 1 hour, up to $100 for a full day. I like riding from Oljato because you get to escape the crowds within the tribal park.

If you're interested in learning about Navajo culture, stop at Kayenta's **Navajo Cultural Center,** U.S. 160 (© 928/697-3170), located between the Burger King and the Hampton Inn. The center is basically just a display of hogans and other traditional structures, but the explanatory signs are very informative. In summer, you might encounter Navajo artisans giving demonstrations. Inside the adjacent Burger King, there's an interesting exhibit on the Navajo code talkers of World War II. The code talkers were Navajo soldiers who used their own language to transmit military messages, primarily in the South Pacific.

WHERE TO STAY & DINE

In addition to the lodgings listed here, you'll find several budget motels north of Monument Valley in the towns of Mexican Hat and Bluff, both of which are in Utah.

Best Western Wetherill Inn   Located in Kayenta a mile north of the junction of U.S. 160 and U.S. 163 and 20 miles south of Monument Valley, the Wetherill Inn offers neither the convenience of Goulding's Lodge nor the amenities of the nearby Holiday Inn Hampton Inn. The rooms, however, are comfortable enough. A cafe next door serves Navajo and American food.

1000 Main St. (P.O. Box 175), Kayenta, AZ 86033. ℂ 800/937-8376 or 928/697-3231. Fax 928/697-3233. www.bestwestern.com/wetherillinn. 54 units. May 1–Oct 15 $98–$108 double; Oct 16–Nov 15 and Apr $63–$70 double; Nov 16–Mar 31 $50–$55 double. Children 12 and under stay free in parent's room. Rates include continental breakfast. AE, DC, DISC, MC, V. **Amenities:** Indoor pool; tour desk. *In room:* A/C, TV, dataport, coffeemaker, hair dryer, iron, free local calls.

Goulding's Lodge   This is the only lodge actually located in Monument Valley, and should be your first choice of hotel in the area. Just be sure to make your reservation well in advance. Goulding's offers superb views from the private balconies of the large guest rooms, which feature Southwestern decor. The restaurant serves Navajo and American dishes, and its views are enough to make any meal an event. Unfortunately, although the setting is memorable, the service can be somewhat lacking. Also on the grounds are a museum, a video library of films shot in Monument Valley, and a gas station.

P.O. Box 360001, Monument Valley, UT 84536. ℂ 435/727-3231. Fax 435/727-3344. www.gouldings.com. 62 units. Mar 15–Nov 15 $108–$160 double; Nov 16–Mar 14 $68–$78 double. Children 6 and under stay free in parent's room. AE, DC, DISC, MC, V. Pets accepted. **Amenities:** Restaurant (American/Navajo); indoor pool; exercise room; tour desk; coin-op laundry. *In room:* A/C, TV/VCR, dataport, fridge, coffeemaker, hair dryer, iron.

Hampton Inn–Navajo Nation   Located in the center of Kayenta, this is the newest lodging in the area and as such should be your second choice after Goulding's. The hotel is built in a modern Santa Fe style and has spacious, comfortable guest rooms. It's adjacent to the Navajo Cultural Center and a Burger King that has an interesting display on the Navajo code talkers of World War II.

U.S. 160 (P.O. Box 1217), Kayenta, AZ 86033. ℂ 800/HAMPTON or 928/697-3170. Fax 928/697-3189. www.hampton-inn.com. 73 units. $74–$144 double. Rates include continental breakfast. Children under 18 stay free in parent's room. AE, DC, DISC, MC, V. Pets accepted (free to $20 nonrefundable deposit). **Amenities:** Restaurant (American/Navajo); small outdoor pool; room service. *In room:* A/C, TV, dataport, coffeemaker, iron.

Holiday Inn–Kayenta   This Holiday Inn, right in the center of Kayenta, is very popular with tour groups and is almost always crowded. Although the grounds are dusty and a bit run-down, the rooms are spacious and clean. I like the poolside units best. Part of the on-site restaurant is designed to look like an Ancestral Puebloans ruin, and the menu offers both American and Navajo cuisine.

U.S. 160 and U.S. 163 (P.O. Box 307), Kayenta, AZ 86033. ℂ 800/HOLIDAY or 928/697-3221. Fax 928/697-3349. www.sixcontinentshotels.com. 162 units. Apr–Oct $80–$149 double; Nov–Mar $55–$139 double. Children under 19 stay free in parent's room. AE, DC, DISC, MC, V. **Amenities:** Restaurant (American/Navajo); small outdoor pool; exercise room; room service; coin-op laundry. *In room:* A/C, TV, dataport, coffeemaker, iron.

CAMPGROUNDS

If you're headed to Monument Valley Navajo Tribal Park, you can camp in the park at the **Mitten View Campground** (ℂ 435/727-5870), which has 99 sites and charges $10 per night from April to September ($5 per night the rest of the

---

> (*Fun Fact* **More Big Rocks**
>
> Monument Valley isn't the only place in this region with impressive rocks. Just north of Kayenta, on the road to Monument Valley, you'll pass by El Capitan, a huge plug of volcanic rock that rises from the desert floor. Of course, when you pull over to take a picture, you can also shop for cheap jewelry at Navajo vendors' stalls. East of Kayenta on U.S. 160, watch for the red sandstone cliffs known as Baby Rocks. East of Tuba City, also on U.S. 160, watch for the two sandstone towers known as Elephant Feet.

---

year, when there are no facilities and you must be self-contained). Another option, just outside the park, is **Goulding's Campground** (© 435/727-3231; www.gouldings.com), which charges $16 to $26 per night. This campground is open year-round (limited services Nov to mid-Mar) and has an indoor pool, hot showers, a playground, and a coin-op laundry.

DRIVING ON TO COLORADO OR NEW MEXICO: THE FOUR CORNERS MEET

It seems like a supremely silly reason to drive miles out of your way, but lots of people feel they just have to visit the **Four Corners Monument Navajo Tribal Park** (© 928/871-6647). Why? So they can stand in four states—Arizona, Colorado, Utah, and New Mexico—at once and get their photo taken. Located north of Teec Nos Pos in the very northeast corner of the state, this park is the only place in the United States where the corners of four states come together. The scenery is not exactly the most dramatic in the region, and the exact point is just a cement pad surrounded by flags and vendors stalls. The park also has a few picnic tables and a snack bar serving, among other things, Navajo fry bread. The park is open daily from 7am to 7pm between May and mid-August and from 8am to 5pm between late August and April. The park is closed on New Year's Day, Thanksgiving, and Christmas. Admission is $3 for adults, free for children 6 and under.

Also in the area, in the community of Teec Nos Pos, are **Teec Nos Pos Arts and Crafts** (© 928/656-3228) and the **Teec Nos Pos Trading Post** (© 928/656-3224), both of which have good selections of rugs and other crafts.

8 Lake Powell ★★ & Page

272 miles N of Phoenix; 130 miles E of Grand Canyon North Rim; 130 miles NE of Grand Canyon South Rim

Had the early Spanish explorers of Arizona suddenly come upon Lake Powell after traipsing for months across desolate desert, they would have either taken it for a mirage or fallen to their knees and rejoiced. Imagine the Grand Canyon filled with water instead of air, and you have a pretty good picture of Lake Powell. Surrounded by hundreds of miles of parched desert land, this reservoir, created by the damming of the Colorado River at Glen Canyon, seems unreal when first glimpsed. Yet real it is, and, like a magnet, it draws everyone in the region toward its promise of relief from the heat.

Construction of the Glen Canyon Dam came about despite the angry outcry of many who felt that this canyon was even more beautiful than the Grand Canyon and should be preserved in its natural state. Preservationists lost the battle, and construction of the dam began in 1960, with completion in 1963. It took another 17 years for Lake Powell to fill to capacity. Today, the lake is a watery powerboat playground, and houseboats and water-skiers cruise where birds and waterfalls once filled the canyon with their songs and sounds. These days most people seem to agree that Lake Powell is as amazing a sight as the Grand Canyon, and it draws almost as many visitors each year as its downriver neighbor. In the past few years, however, Lake Powell has lost some of its luster as a prolonged drought in the Southwest has caused the lake's water level to drop nearly 100 feet. Although this has left a bathtub-ring effect on the shores of the lake, it has exposed wide expanses of beach in the Wahweap area.

While Lake Powell is something of a man-made wonder of the world, one of the natural wonders of the world—Rainbow Bridge—can be found on the shores of the lake. Called *nonnozhoshi,* or "the rainbow turned to stone," by the Navajo, this is the largest natural bridge on earth and stretches 275 feet across a side canyon of Lake Powell.

The town of Page, a work camp constructed to house the workers who built the dam, has now become much more than a construction camp. With its many motels and restaurants, it's the main base for visitors who come to explore Lake Powell.

ESSENTIALS

GETTING THERE   Page is connected to Flagstaff by U.S. 89. Ariz. 98 leads southeast onto the Navajo Indian Reservation and connects with U.S. 160 to Kayenta and Four Corners. The Page Airport is served by **Great Lakes Airlines** (© 800/554-5111; www.greatlakesav.com), which flies from Phoenix.

FEES   Admission to Glen Canyon National Recreation Area is $10 per car (good for 1 week). There is also a $10-per-week boat fee if you bring your own boat.

VISITOR INFORMATION   For further information on the Lake Powell area, contact the **Glen Canyon National Recreation Area** (© 928/608-6404; www.nps.gov/glca); the **Page/Lake Powell Chamber of Commerce & Visitors Bureau,** 644 N. Navajo Dr., Page (© 888/261-7243 or 928/645-2741; www.pagelakepowellchamber.org); or the **John Wesley Powell Memorial Museum,** 6 N. Lake Powell Blvd., Page (© 888/597-6873 or 928/645-9496; www.powell museum.org). You can also go to www.powellguide.com.

GETTING AROUND   Rental cars are available at the Page Airport from **Avis** (© 800/331-1212 or 928/645-2024) and **Enterprise Rent-a-Car** (© 800/736-8222 or 928/645-1449).

GLEN CANYON NATIONAL RECREATION AREA

Until the flooding of Glen Canyon formed Lake Powell, this area was one of the most remote regions in the contiguous 48 states. However, since the construction of Glen Canyon Dam at a spot where the Colorado River was less than a third of a mile wide, this remote and rugged landscape has become one of the country's most popular national recreation areas. Today, the lake and much of the surrounding land is designated the Glen Canyon National Recreation Area and attracts around two million visitors each year. The otherworldly setting (imagine the Grand Canyon, only flooded) amid the slickrock canyons of northern Arizona and southern Utah is a tapestry of colors, the blues and greens of the lake contrasting with the reds and oranges of the surrounding sandstone cliffs. This interplay of colors and vast desert landscapes easily makes Lake Powell the most beautiful of Arizona's many reservoirs.

Tips **Dam Closures**

For security reasons, Glen Canyon Dam tours do not operate when the country is on Code Orange alert level.

Built to provide water for the desert communities of the Southwest and West, **Glen Canyon Dam** stands 710 feet above the bedrock and contains almost five million cubic yards of concrete. The dam also provides hydroelectric power, and deep within its massive wall of concrete are huge power turbines. However, most visitors are more interested in water-skiing and powerboating than they are in drinking water and power production, but since there would be no lake without the dam, any visit to this area ought to start at the **Carl Hayden Visitor Center** (© 928/608-6404), which is located beside the dam on U.S. 89 just north of Page. Here you can tour the dam and learn about its construction. Visitor center hours are daily from 7am to 7pm between Memorial Day weekend and Labor Day weekend, and from 8am to 5pm other months.

More than 500 feet deep in some places, and bounded by nearly 2,000 miles of shoreline, **Lake Powell** is a maze of convoluted canyons where rock walls often rise hundreds of feet straight out of the water. In places, the long, winding canyons are so narrow there isn't even room to turn a motorboat around. The only way to truly appreciate this lake is from a boat, whether a houseboat, a runabout, or a sea kayak. Water-skiing, riding personal watercraft, and fishing have long been the most popular on-water activities, and consequently, you'll be hard-pressed to find a quiet corner of the lake if you happen to be a solitude-seeking sea kayaker. However, with so many miles of shoreline, you're bound to find someplace where you can get away from it all. Your best bet for solitude is to head up-lake from Wahweap Marina. This will get you away from the crowds and into some of the narrower reaches of the lake.

In addition to the Carl Hayden Visitor Center mentioned above, there's the **Bullfrog Visitor Center,** in Bullfrog, Utah (© 435/684-7400). It's open April through October, daily from 8am to 5pm (closed Nov–Feb; open intermittently in Mar).

BOAT & AIR TOURS

There are few roads penetrating the Glen Canyon National Recreation Area, so the best way to appreciate this rugged region is by boat. If you don't have your own boat, you can at least see a small part of the lake on a boat tour. A variety of tours depart from **Wahweap Marina** (© 800/528-6154 or 928/645-2433; www.lakepowell.com). The paddle wheeler *Canyon King* does a 1-hour tour ($12 for adults, $9 for children) that unfortunately doesn't really show you much more of the lake than you can see from shore. The *Canyon King* also offers sunset dinner cruises ($65). A better choice for those with limited time or finances would be the **Antelope Canyon Cruise** ($30 for adults, $23 for children). To see more of the lake, opt for the full-day tour to Rainbow Bridge (see below for details).

The Glen Canyon National Recreation Area covers an immense area, much of it only partially accessible by boat. If you'd like to see more of the area than is visible from car or boat, consider taking an air tour with **Westwind-Lake Powell Air Tours** (© 800/245-8668; www.westwindairtours.com), which offers several tours of northern Arizona and southern Utah, including flights over Rainbow Bridge, the Escalante River, the Grand Canyon, Canyonlands, Bryce Canyon, Monument Valley, and the Navajo nation. Sample rates are $94 for a 40-minute flight over Rainbow Bridge and $162 to $200 for a 90-minute flight over Monument Valley (the more expensive tour actually lands at Monument Valley and includes a 1½-hour Jeep tour).

RAINBOW BRIDGE NATIONAL MONUMENT

Roughly 40 miles up Lake Powell from Wahweap Marina and Glen Canyon Dam, in a narrow side canyon of the lake, rises **Rainbow Bridge** 𝕬𝕬𝕬, the world's largest natural bridge and one of the most spectacular sights in the Southwest. Preserved in Rainbow Bridge National Monument, this natural arch of sandstone stands 290 feet high and spans 275 feet. Carved by wind and water over the ages, Rainbow Bridge is an awesome reminder of the powers of erosion that have sculpted this entire region into the spectacle it is today.

Rainbow Bridge is accessible only by boat or on foot (a hike of 13 miles minimum); going by boat is by far the more popular method. **Lake Powell Resorts and Marinas** (𝄐 **800/528-6154** or 928/645-2433; www.lakepowell.com) offers full-day tours ($106 for adults, $85 for children) that not only get you to Rainbow Bridge in comfort, but also cruise through some of the most spectacular scenery on earth. Tours include a box lunch and a bit more exploring after visiting Rainbow Bridge. Currently, because the lake's water level is so low from years of drought, the boat must stop about 1¼ mile from Rainbow Bridge, so if you aren't able to walk this distance, you won't even be able to see the sandstone arch.

Rainbow Bridge National Monument (𝄐 **928/608-6404**; www.nps.gov/rabr) is administered by Glen Canyon National Recreation Area. For information on hiking to Rainbow Bridge, contact the **Navajo Parks and Recreation Department,** P.O. Box 2520, Window Rock, AZ 86515 (𝄐 **928/871-6647;** www.navajonationparks.org). The hike into Rainbow Bridge is about a 25-mile round-trip hike, and a Navajo Nation permit is required to make the backpacking trip. Permits are available through the Navajo Parks and Recreation Department and at the **Cameron Visitor Center** (𝄐 **928/679-2303**), in the community of Cameron near the turnoff for the Grand Canyon and at the **LeChee Office** (𝄐 **928/698-2808**), 7 miles south of Page on Navajo Route 20.

ANTELOPE CANYON

If you've spent any time in Arizona, chances are you've noticed photos of a narrow sandstone canyon only a few feet wide. The walls of the canyon seem to glow with an inner light, and beams of sunlight slice the darkness of the deep slot canyon. Sound familiar? If you've seen such a photo, you were probably looking at Antelope Canyon (sometimes called Corkscrew Canyon). Located 2½ miles outside Page off Ariz. 98 (at milepost 299), this photogenic canyon comprises the **Antelope Canyon Navajo Tribal Park** 𝕬𝕬𝕬 (𝄐 **928/698-2808**), which is on the Navajo Indian Reservation and is divided into upper and lower canyons. The entry fee is $6 for adults, free for children 7 and under. From May through October, the upper canyon section of the park is open daily from 8am to 5pm and the lower canyon section is open 8am to 4pm; from November through April, hours vary.

There are currently two options for visiting Antelope Canyon. The most convenient and reliable way is to take a 1½-hour tour with **Antelope Canyon Adventures** (𝄐 **866/645-5501** or 928/645-5501; www.jeeptour.com), or **Roger Ekis' Antelope Canyon Tours** (𝄐 **928/645-9102** or 435/675-9109;

www.antelopecanyon.com), both of which charge $20 (plus Navajo permit fee) per adult for a basic tour. Photographic tours cost between $45 and $62. If you don't want to deal with crowds of tourists ogling the rocks and snapping pictures with their point-and-shoots, I recommend heading out with **Overland Canyon Tours** (© 928/608-4072 or 928.608-4072; www.overlandcanyontours.com) to nearby Canyon X, which is much less visited than Antelope Canyon and is a good choice for serious photographers who want to avoid the crowds.

Alternatively, at both the upper and lower canyons, you'll find Navajo guides collecting park entry fees and fees for guide services. These guides charge $13 to $15 ($6 for children ages 7–12 at the lower section of the canyon). If you want to stay longer than an hour in the canyon, expect to pay $5 more per hour. At Upper Antelope Canyon, the guide will drive you from the highway to the canyon and then pick you up again after your hike. At Lower Antelope Canyon, the guide will likely just show you the entrance to the slot canyon. You'll get more out of your experience if you go on one of the guided tours mentioned above, but you'll save a little money by visiting the canyon on your own. For more information, contact **Antelope Canyon Navajo Tours** (© 928/698-3384 or 928/698-3285; www.navajotours.com).

Just remember that if there is even the slightest chance of rain anywhere in the region, you should not venture into this canyon, which is subject to flash floods. In the past, people who have ignored bad weather have been killed by such floods.

WATERSPORTS

While simply exploring the lake's maze of canyons on a narrated tour is satisfying enough for many visitors, the most popular activities are still houseboating, water-skiing, riding personal watercraft, and fishing. Five marinas (only Wahweap is in Arizona) help boaters explore the lake. At the **Wahweap Marina** (© 800/528-6154 or 928/645-2433; www.lakepowell.com), you can rent various types of boats, along with personal watercraft and water skis. Rates in summer range from about $75 to $310 per day depending on the type of boat. Weekly rates are also available. Small boats and personal watercraft can also be rented from **Lake Powell Water World,** 908 Hemlock St. (© 928/645-8845), and **Doo Powell,** 130 Sixth Ave. (© 800/350-1230 or 928/645-1230; www. doopowell.com). For information on renting houseboats, see "Where to Stay," below.

Fun Fact **So, What's with the Bathtub Ring?**

You'll notice that the red-rock cliff walls above the waters of Lake Powell are no longer red but are instead coated with what looks like a layer of white soap scum. Those are calcium carbonate deposits left on the rock over the past few years as an ongoing drought has caused the lake level to drop nearly 120 feet. The bathtub ring is the least of Lake Powell's worries. The reservoir currently is at less than half its capacity and hasn't been this low in more than 30 years. Some experts believe that if the drought continues, the lake could go completely dry by 2007. Because Arizona, Nevada, and California all rely on the water from Lake Powell, a continued drought could have serious consequences for Phoenix, Tucson, Las Vegas, and Los Angeles.

If roaring engines aren't your speed, you might want to consider exploring Lake Powell by sea kayak. While afternoon winds can sometimes make paddling difficult, mornings are often quiet. With a narrow sea kayak, you can even explore canyons too small for powerboats. Rentals are available at **Lake Powell Kayak Tours,** 811 Vista Ave. (© **928/645-3114;** www.lakepowellkayaktours. com). Sea kayaks rent for $45 to $55 per day, and sit-on-top kayaks for $35 to $45. All-day tours are $95 to $105. Guided kayak tours are also available through **Lake Powell Kayak Adventures** (© **888/854-7862;** www.kayaklake powell.com), which charges $85 for a half-day, $125 for a full day, and $200 for an overnight (longer tours can also be arranged). Rentals go for $25 to $45 per day. **Hidden Canyon Kayak** (© **800/343-3121** or 928/645-8866; www. diamondriver.com/kayak) also does kayak tours, charging $600 to $800 for 4- to 6-day trips.

While most of Glen Canyon National Recreation Area consists of the impounded waters of Lake Powell, the recreation area also contains a short stretch of the Colorado River that still flows swift and free. If you'd like to see this stretch of river, try a float trip from Glen Canyon Dam to Lees Ferry, operated by **Wilderness River Adventures** (© **800/528-6154** or 928/645-3279; www.lakepowell.com), between March and mid-September. Half-day trips cost $59 for adults and $49 for children 12 and under. Try to reserve at least 2 weeks in advance.

If you have a boat (your own or a rental), avail yourself of some excellent year-round fishing. Smallmouth, largemouth, and striped bass, as well as walleye, catfish, crappie, and carp, are all plentiful. Because the lake lies within both Arizona and Utah, you'll need to know which state's waters you're fishing in whenever you cast your line out, and you'll need the appropriate license. (Be sure to pick up a copy of the Arizona and Utah state fishing regulations, or ask about applicable regulations at any of the marinas.) You can arrange licenses to fish the entire lake at **Lake Powell Resorts and Marinas** (© **928/645-2433**), which also sells bait and tackle and can provide you with advice on fishing this massive reservoir. Other marinas on the lake also sell licenses, bait, and tackle. The best season is March through November, but walleye are most often caught during the cooler months. If you'd rather try your hand at catching enormous rainbow trout, try downstream of the Glen Canyon Dam, where cold waters provide ideal conditions for trophy trout. Unfortunately, there isn't much access to this stretch of river. You'll need a trout stamp to fish for the rainbows. If you want a guide to take you where the fish are biting, contact Bill McBurney at **Ambassador Guide Service** (© **800/256-7596;** www.ambassador.com).

If you're just looking for a good place for a swim near Lake Powell Resort, take the Coves Loop just west of the marina. Of the three coves, the third one, which has a sandy beach, is the best. The Chains area, another good place to jump off the rocks and otherwise lounge by the lake, is outside Page down a rough dirt road just before you reach Glen Canyon Dam. The view underwater at Lake Powell is as scenic as the view above it; to explore the underwater regions of the canyon, contact **Twin Finn Diving Center,** 811 Vista Ave. (© **928/645-3114;** www.twinfinn.com), which charges $45 a day for scuba gear and also rents snorkeling equipment.

OTHER OUTDOOR PURSUITS

If you're looking for a quick, easy hike with great views, head north on North Navajo Drive from downtown Page. At the end of this street is the main trail

---

⟨Finds   **Acrophobes, Beware!**

If you have a fear of heights, there are a couple of places in the Page area that you should never visit. On the other hand, if you want some great views, then don't miss the following two scenic vistas.

At the base of Lake Powell Boulevard (the road toward Glen Canyon Dam from Page), go straight through the intersection instead of turning right toward the dam. Here you'll find a parking area and a short path to a viewing platform perched on the edge of sheer cliff walls. Below lie the clear green waters of the Colorado River, while upstream looms Glen Canyon Dam.

If you're up for a short hike, grab the camera and head to the **Horseshoe Bend** ⟨★ viewpoint. Horseshoe Bend is a huge loop of the Colorado River, and the viewpoint is hundreds of feet above the water on the edge of a cliff. It's about a half-mile to the viewpoint from the trail head, which is 5 miles south of the Carl Hayden Visitor Center on U.S. 89 just south of milepost 545.

---

head for Page's **Rimview Trail.** This trail runs along the edge of Manson Mesa, upon which Page is built, and has views of Lake Powell and the entire red-rock country. The entire loop trail is 8 miles long, but if you want to do a shorter hike, I recommend the stretch of trail heading east (clockwise) from the trail head. If you happen to have your mountain bike with you, the trail is a great ride.

At Lees Ferry, a 39-mile drive from Page at the southern tip of the national recreation area, you'll find three short trails (Cathedral Wash, River, and Spencer). The 2-mile **Cathedral Wash Trail** is the most interesting of the three day hikes and follows a dry wash through a narrow canyon with unusual rock formations. The trail head is at the second turnout after turning off U.S. 89A. Be aware that this wash is subject to flash floods. The **Spencer Trail,** which begins along the River Trail, leads up to the top of a 1,500-foot cliff. Lees Ferry is also the southern trail head for the famed **Paria Canyon** ⟨★, a favorite of canyoneering backpackers. This trail is 37 miles long and follows the meandering route of a narrow slot canyon for much of its length. Most hikers start from the northern trail head, which is in Utah on U.S. 89.

In the same area, you'll find the **Coyote Buttes** ⟨★★★, which are among the most unusual rock formations in Arizona. Basically, these striated conical sandstone hills are petrified sand dunes, which should give you a good idea of why one area of the Coyote Buttes is called The Wave. The buttes are a favorite of photographers. There's no actual trail to the buttes, but from the trail head, you can see your destination. You must have a permit ($5 per person) to visit this area, and only 20 people are allowed to visit each day (with a maximum group size of six people). Reservations must be made 7 months in advance on the first of the month at exactly noon. With the exception of reservations for July and August, all available permits are reserved within a few minutes after noon.

For more information on hiking in Paria Canyon or to the Coyote Buttes, contact **Arizona Strip Interpretive Association,** 345 E. Riverside Dr., St. George, UT 84770 (© **435/688-3246;** www.az.blm.gov/asfo/asia.htm).

The 27-hole **Lake Powell National Golf Course** ⟨★, 400 Clubhouse Dr. (© **928/645-2023;** www.lakepowellgolf.com), is one of the most spectacular in the state. The fairways wrap around the base of the red-sandstone bluff atop which sits the town of Page. In places, eroded sandstone walls come right down to the greens. The views stretch on forever. Greens fees are $45.

OTHER AREA ATTRACTIONS

In addition to visiting the museum listed below, you can learn about Navajo culture at **Navajo Village Heritage Center** (℃ **928/660-0304;** www.navajo village.net), a museum and living-history center located on the south side of Page off Haul Road. Programs here include demonstrations by weavers, silver-smiths, and other artisans. Prices range from $30 ($24 for children) for a 2-hour tour to $50 ($35 for children) for a 3-hour evening tour that includes dinner and traditional dances. If you opt for the 2-hour tour, you can also get dinner for an additional $5. Between 9am and 3pm, it is sometimes possible to visit and see Navajo artisans at work ($10 for adults, $5 for children). Although this is definitely a tourist attraction, you will come away with a better sense of Navajo culture. Reservations can be made at the Lake Powell Chamber of Commerce office (see above) and the John Wesley Powell Memorial Museum (see below).

John Wesley Powell Memorial Museum   In 1869, one-armed Civil War veteran John Wesley Powell, and a small band of men spent more than 3 months fighting the rapids of the Green and Colorado rivers to become the first people to travel the length of the Grand Canyon. It is for this intrepid—some said crazy—adventurer that Lake Powell is named and to whom this small museum is dedicated. Besides documenting the Powell expedition with photographs, etchings, artifacts, and dioramas, the museum displays Native American artifacts ranging from Ancestral Puebloan pottery to contemporary Navajo and Hopi crafts. The museum also acts as an information center for Page, Lake Powell, and the surrounding region.

6 N. Lake Powell Blvd. ℃ **888/597-6873** or 928/645-9496. www.powellmuseum.org. Admission $2 adults, $1 children 5–12, free for children 4 and under. Feb–Nov Mon–Fri 9am–5pm. Closed Dec–Jan.

WHERE TO STAY
HOUSEBOATS

Lake Powell Resorts and Marinas *Kids*   Although there are plenty of hotels and motels in and near Page, the most popular accommodations here are not waterfront hotel rooms but houseboats, which function as floating vacation homes. With a houseboat, which is as easy to operate as a car, you can explore Lake Powell's beautiful red-rock country, far from any roads. No special license or prior experience is necessary, and plenty of hands-on instruction is given before you leave the marina. Because Lake Powell houseboating is extremely popular with visitors from all over the world, it's important to make reservations as far in advance as possible, especially if you plan to visit in summer.

Houseboats range in size from 46 to 75 feet, sleep anywhere from 8 to 12 peo-ple, and come complete with hot shower, heating system (more expensive house-boats also have heat pumps or evaporative coolers), and fully equipped kitchen with fridge, stove, oven, and gas grill. The only things you really need to bring are bedding and towels. I recommend going for the largest boat you can afford (you'll appreciate the space), and if you're coming in the heat of summer, splurge on a boat with some sort of cooling system.

100 Lakeshore Dr. (P.O. Box 1597), Page, AZ 86040. ℃ **800/528-6154** or 928/645-2433. Fax 928/645-1031. www.visitlakepowell.com. May to mid-Oct $2,685–$8,897 per week; lower rates late Oct to Apr. 3-, 4-, 5-, and 6-night rates also available. AE, DISC, MC, V. *In room:* Kitchen, fridge, no phone.

HOTELS & MOTELS

Best Western Arizonainn Perched right at the edge of the mesa on which Page is built, this modern motel has a fine view across miles of desert, as do half of the guest rooms. The hotel's pool has a 100-mile view.

716 Rimview Dr. (P.O. Box 250), Page, AZ 86040. 🕐 **800/826-2718** or 928/645-2466. Fax 928/645-2053. www.bestwestern.com. 103 units. Apr–June $49–$74 double; July to mid-Oct $79–$99 double; mid-Oct to Mar $44–$54 double. Rates include continental breakfast. AE, DC, DISC, MC, V. Pets accepted ($10 fee). **Amenities:** Small outdoor pool; exercise room; Jacuzzi; coin-op laundry. *In room:* A/C, TV, dataport, coffeemaker, hair dryer, iron.

Courtyard by Marriott ★ Located at the foot of the mesa on which Page is built and adjacent to the Lake Powell National Golf Course, this is the top in-town choice. It's also the closest you'll come to a golf resort in this corner of the state, though you'll pay a premium for views of the golf course or lake. Guest rooms are larger than those at most area lodgings. Moderately priced meals are served in a casual restaurant that has a terrace overlooking the distant lake. The 18-hole golf course has great views of the surrounding landscape.

600 Clubhouse Dr. (P.O. Box 4150), Page, AZ 86040. 🕐 **800/851-3855** or 928/645-5000. Fax 928/645-5004. www.courtyard.com. 153 units. $59–$129 double. Children under 18 stay free in parent's room. AE, DC, DISC, MC, V. **Amenities:** Restaurant (American); lounge; outdoor pool; 18-hole golf course; exercise room; Jacuzzi; concierge; room service; laundry service; dry cleaning. *In room:* A/C, TV, dataport, coffeemaker, hair dryer, iron.

Lake Powell Resort ★ Simply because it is right on the lake, this hotel at the sprawling Wahweap Marina 5 miles north of Page should be your first lodging choice in the area. As the biggest and busiest hotel in the area, the Lake Powell Resort features many of the amenities and activities of a resort, but it is often overwhelmed by busloads of tour groups. Consequently, don't expect very good service. Guest rooms are arranged in several long two-story wings, and every unit has either a balcony or a patio. Half of the rooms have lake views; those in the west wing have the better vantage point, as the east wing overlooks a coal-fired power plant. The Rainbow Room (see "Where to Dine," below) offers fine dining with a sweeping panorama of the lake and desert, but be prepared for a long wait for a table. Because of all the tour groups that stay here, getting a reservation can be difficult.

100 Lakeshore Dr. (P.O. Box 1597), Page AZ 86040. 🕐 **800/528-6154** or 928/645-2433. Fax 928/645-1031. www.visitlakepowell.com. 350 units. Apr–Oct $129–$149 double, $189–$199 suite; Nov–Mar $89–$99 double, $189 suite. Children under 18 stay free in parent's room. AE, DISC, MC, V. Pets accepted. **Amenities:** 2 restaurants (American/Southwestern; pizza); snack bar; lounge; 2 outdoor pools; Jacuzzi; watersports; boat rentals; tour desk; room service; coin-op laundry. *In room:* A/C, TV, fridge, coffeemaker, hair dryer.

CAMPGROUNDS

There are campgrounds at **Wahweap** (🕐 **928/645-2433**) and **Lees Ferry** (🕐 **928/355-2319**) in Arizona, and at Bullfrog, Hite, and Halls Crossing in Utah. Some scrubby trees provide a bit of shade at the Wahweap site, but the wind and sun make this a rather bleak spot in summer. Nevertheless, because of the lake's popularity, these campgrounds stay packed for much of the year. Wahweap charges $18 per night and Lees Ferry charges $10; reservations are not accepted.

WHERE TO DINE

If you're dying for a latte or cappuccino, head to **Bean's Gourmet Coffee House,** 644-F N. Navajo Dr. (🕐 **928/645-6858**), next to the Page Visitors Bureau.

The Dam Bar & Grille AMERICAN   Page's first and only theme restaurant is a warehouse-size space designed to conjure up images of the Glen Canyon Dam. Big industrial doors are the first hint this is more than your usual small-town dining establishment. Inside, cement walls, hard hats, and a big trans-former that sends out bolts of neon "electricity" will put you in a dam good mood. Sandwiches, pastas, and steaks dominate the menu, with a smattering of seafood. The lounge area is a popular local hangout, and next door is the affili-ated Gunsmoke Saloon, a combination barbecue joint and nightclub.

644 N. Navajo Dr. ⓒ **928/645-2161**. www.damplaza.com. Reservations recommended in summer. Main courses $10–$23. AE, MC, V. May–Oct daily 11:30am–10pm; Nov–May Mon–Sat 5–9pm.

Rainbow Room AMERICAN/SOUTHWESTERN   With sweeping vistas of Lake Powell out the walls of glass, the Rainbow Room is Page's premier restau-rant. As such, be prepared for a wait; this place regularly feeds busloads of tourists. The menu is short (due to the necessity of feeding crowds of people) but usually includes a few dishes with southwestern flavor. Try the pine-nut-crusted rainbow trout or the grilled chicken breast with Anaheim peppers. If you're heading out on the water for the day, the kitchen will fix you a box lunch.

At Lake Powell Resort, Lakeshore Dr. ⓒ **928/645-1162**. Reservations recommended. Main courses $6–$10 lunch, $15–$19 dinner. AE, DC, DISC, MC, V. Daily 6am–2:30pm and 5–9pm.

Zapata's MEXICAN   For casual, inexpensive Mexican food and good mar-garitas, I like this little place in the same shopping complex as The Dam Bar. If it's warm out, try to get a table on the patio. Try the spicy chili verde burrito or chicken enchiladas.

614 N. Navajo Dr. ⓒ **928/645-9006**. Reservations recommended. Main courses $8–$20. MC, V. Daily 11am–10pm.

8

Eastern Arizona's High Country

Cactus and desert landscapes are what come to mind when most people think of Arizona. But that's only part of the picture. Arizona actually has more mountainous country than Switzerland and more forest than Minnesota, and most of these mountains and forests are here in the highlands of eastern Arizona.

In this sparsely populated region, towns with such apt names as Alpine, Lakeside, and Pinetop have become summer retreats for the people who live in the state's low-lying, sun-baked deserts. Folks from Phoenix and its surrounding cities discovered long ago how close the cool mountain forests are. In only a few hours, you can drive up from the cacti and creosote bushes to the meadows and pine forests of the White Mountains.

Dividing the arid lowlands from the cool pine forests of the highlands is the Mogollon Rim (pronounced *Mug-ee-un* by the locals), a 2,000-foot escarpment that stretches for 200 miles from central Arizona into New Mexico. Along this impressive wall, the climatic and vegetative change is dramatic. Imagine sunshine at the base and snow squalls at the top, and you have an idea of the Mogollon Rim's variety. This area was made

famous by Western author Zane Grey, who lived in a cabin near Payson and set many of his novels in this scenic yet oft-overlooked part of Arizona. Fans of Zane Grey's novels can follow in the author's footsteps and visit a small museum with an exhibit dedicated to Grey.

Trout fishing, hiking, horseback riding, and hunting are the main warm-weather pastimes of eastern Arizona, and when winter weather reports from up north have Phoenicians dreaming about snow (it's true, they really do), many head to the White Mountains for a bit of skiing. Sunrise Park Resort, operated by the White Mountain Apache Tribe, is the state's biggest and busiest downhill ski area. There are also plenty of cross-country ski trails in the area.

Much of eastern Arizona is Apache Reservation land. Recreational activities abound on this land, but remember that the Apache tribe requires visitors to have reservation fishing permits and outdoor recreation permits. Fishing is particularly popular on the reservation, which isn't surprising considering there are 400 miles of trout streams and 25 lakes stocked with rainbow and brown trout.

1 Payson & the Mogollon Rim Country

94 miles NE of Phoenix; 90 miles SE of Flagstaff; 90 miles SW of Winslow; 100 miles W of Pinetop-Lakeside

Payson, 94 miles from Phoenix and 5,000 feet above sea level, is one of the closest places for Phoenicians to find relief from the summer heat, and though it is not quite high enough to be considered the mountains, it certainly isn't the

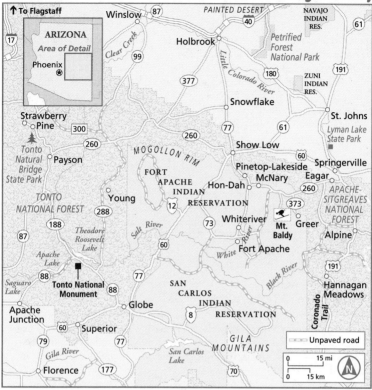

Map labels: To Flagstaff · Winslow · 87 · PAINTED DESERT · 40 · NAVAJO INDIAN RES. · 61 · 17 · ARIZONA Area of Detail · Phoenix · Holbrook · Petrified Forest National Park · Clear Creek · 99 · Little Colorado River · 180 · ZUNI INDIAN RES. · 191 · 377 · Snowflake · Strawberry · Pine · 300 · St. Johns · Lyman Lake State Park · 260 · 77 · 61 · Tonto Natural Bridge State Park · Payson · MOGOLLON RIM · 260 · Show Low · 60 · Springerville · FORT APACHE INDIAN RESERVATION · Pinetop-Lakeside · Eagar · McNary · Hon-Dah · 260 · APACHE-SITGREAVES NATIONAL FOREST · TONTO NATIONAL FOREST · Young · 288 · 12 · 373 · Whiteriver · 73 · Mt. Baldy · Greer · 188 · Theodore Roosevelt Lake · Salt River · 60 · White River · Fort Apache · Alpine · 87 · Apache Lake · 88 · Tonto National Monument · 88 · 77 · SAN CARLOS INDIAN RESERVATION · Black River · 191 · Hannagan Meadows · Saguaro Lake · Globe · Coronado Trail · Apache Junction · 60 · Superior · 8 · 79 · 77 · GILA MOUNTAINS · Unpaved road · Gila River · San Carlos Lake · 0 15 mi · 0 15 km · Florence · 177 · 70

desert (summer temperatures are 20° cooler than in the Valley of the Sun). The 2,000-foot-high, 200-mile-long Mogollon Rim is only 22 miles north of town, and the surrounding Tonto National Forest provides opportunities for hiking, swimming, fishing, and hunting. The nearly perfect climate of Payson has also made the town a popular retirement spot. Summer highs are usually in the 80s or 90s, while winter highs are usually in the 50s and 60s.

ESSENTIALS

GETTING THERE Ariz. 87, the Beeline Highway, connects Payson to Phoenix and Winslow. Ariz. 260 runs east from Payson, climbing the Mogollon Rim and continuing into the White Mountains.

VISITOR INFORMATION Contact the **Rim Country Regional Chamber of Commerce,** 100 W. Main St., Payson (© **800/672-9766** or 928/474-4515; www.rimcountrychamber.com).

SPECIAL EVENTS The **World's Oldest Continuous Rodeo** takes place on the third weekend in August.

OUTDOOR PURSUITS

The area's most popular attraction is **Tonto Natural Bridge State Park,** 10 miles northwest of Payson on Ariz. 87 (© **928/476-4202**), which preserves the largest natural travertine bridge in the world. In 1877, gold prospector David Gowan, while being chased by Apaches, became the first white man to see this natural bridge, which stands 183 feet high and 150 feet across at its widest point. Although it sounds very impressive, this natural bridge looks nothing like the sandstone arches in southern Utah, and seems more like a tunnel than a free-standing arch. This state park also preserves a historic lodge built by Gowan's nephew and the nephew's sons. The lodge has been restored to the way it looked in 1927, but is not open for overnight accommodations. Admission to the park is $6 per car. It's open daily from 9am to 5pm in winter, from 8am to 6pm in spring and fall, and from 8am to 7pm Memorial Day to Labor Day.

If you'd like to go horseback riding try **Kohl's Ranch Stables,** on Highway 260 17 miles north of Payson (© **928/478-0030**). Rates range from $25 for a 1-hour ride to $100 for a half-day ride.

The **Highline Trail** is a 50-mile hike along the lower slope of the Mogollon Rim. You can find out more about this and other area trails, as well as which trails are open to mountain bikes, at the **Payson Ranger Station,** 1009 E. Hwy. 260 (© **928/474-7900**), at the east end of town.

You can also hike this area in the company of llamas that will carry your gear for you. **Fossil Creek Llamas** (© **928/476-5178;** www.fossilcreekllamas.com) offers both two-hour llama hikes ($40 per person) and all-day llama hikes ($65 per person). A tepee "bed-and-breakfast," wellness courses, and retreats are also offered.

OTHER AREA ATTRACTIONS

About 5 miles north of town, off Ariz. 87 on Houston Mesa Road, you can visit the ruins of **Shoofly Village,** in the Tonto National Forest. This village was first occupied nearly 1,000 years ago by peoples related to the Hohokam and Salado. It once contained 87 rooms, though today only rock foundations remain. An interpretive trail helps bring the site to life.

To learn more about the history of the area, stop by the **Rim Country Museum,** 700 Green Valley Pkwy. (© **928/474-3483**), which has displays on the region as well as a special Zane Grey exhibit. The museum, located in Green Valley Park, is housed in the oldest forest ranger station and residence still standing in the Southwest. The museum is open Wednesday through Sunday from noon to 4pm. Admission is $3 for adults, $2.50 for seniors, and $2 for children 12 to 17. Nearby, you'll also find the affiliated **Museum of Rim Country Archaeology,** 510 W. Main St. (© **928/468-1128**), which has interesting displays on the Native American cultures that once inhabited this area. Admission is $3 for adults, $2.50 for seniors, and $2 for students ages 12 to 18. This museum is open the same hours as the Rim Country Museum.

If you're feeling lucky, spend some time and money at the **Mazatzal Casino** (© **800/777-PLAY;** www.777play.com), half a mile south on Ariz. 87. The casino is run by the Tonto Apaches.

SCENIC DRIVES

Scenic drives through this region are among the favorite pastimes of visitors. One of the most popular drives is along the top of the Mogollon Rim on 45-mile-long **Forest Road 300.** On the road, which clings to the edge of the rim, there are numerous views of the forest far below and plenty of places to stop, including lakes, picnic areas, trail heads, and campgrounds. This is a good gravel road in summer and can be negotiated in a standard passenger car. In winter, however, the road is not maintained. From Payson, to access the rim road, head east on Ariz. 260 or north on Ariz. 87 for 30 miles and watch for signs.

About 15 miles north of Payson on Ariz. 87 is the village of **Pine,** and another 3 miles beyond this, the village of **Strawberry.** Here, in a quiet setting in the forest, you'll find a few shops selling antiques and crafts and, in Pine, a small museum that chronicles the history of this area. In Strawberry, on the road that leads west from the center of the village, is the old Strawberry schoolhouse, a restored log building dating from 1885.

Another interesting drive starts west of the old Strawberry schoolhouse. If you continue west on this road, you'll be on the gravel **Fossil Creek Road** 🐾🐾, which leads 10 miles down a deep and spectacular canyon. It's a bit hair-raising, but if you like views, it's well worth the white knuckles and dust. At the bottom, **Fossil Creek** offers some of the most idyllic little swimming holes you could ever hope to find. If you make it down here on a weekday, you just might have a swimming hole all to yourself.

WHERE TO STAY

Majestic Mountain Inn   Although it's located in town, this motel was built in an attractive, modern mountain-lodge style that makes it the most appealing place to stay right in Payson. There's a large stone chimney and fireplace in the lobby, and all of the deluxe and luxury rooms have fireplaces of their own. The luxury units also have tile floors and a double whirlpool tub facing the fireplace. The standard rooms aren't as spacious or luxurious, but are still quite comfortable. There's a steakhouse right next door to the hotel.

602 E. Ariz. 260, Payson, AZ 85541. ℂ **800/408-2442** or 928/474-0185. Fax 928/472-6097. www.majestic mountaininn.com. 50 units. $62–$150 double. Children under 18 stay free in parent's room. AE, DC, DISC, MC, V. Pets accepted ($10 per night). **Amenities:** Outdoor pool; access to nearby health club. *In room:* A/C, TV, dataport, fridge, coffeemaker, hair dryer, iron, free local calls.

CAMPGROUNDS

East of Payson on Ariz. 260 are several national forest campgrounds. These include (from west to east) **Lower Tonto Creek** and **Upper Tonto Creek** (neither of which take reservations) and **Christopher Creek** campgrounds. Information is available from the **Payson Ranger Station** (ℂ **928/474-7900**), on Ariz. 260 at the east end of town.

WHERE TO DINE

Cucina Paradiso 🐾 ITALIAN   Although it's nothing fancy, this casual Italian restaurant on the north side of Payson is the best restaurant in town. Calamari is a specialty of the house, and the calamari Caesar salad is a tasty spin on a classic. There's also a good calamari *fra diavolo* made with a spicy white wine–tomato sauce. The Florentine ravioli in creamy red sauce is another good bet.

512 N. Beeline Hwy. ℂ **928/468-6500.** Main courses $6.50–$10 lunch, $10–$19 dinner. AE, DC, DISC, MC, V. Tues–Thurs 11am–2pm and 4–8:30pm; Fri–Sat 11am–2pm and 4–9pm; Sun 4–8:30pm.

2 Pinetop-Lakeside

90 miles NE of Payson; 185 miles NE of Phoenix; 50 miles S of Holbrook; 140 miles SE of Flagstaff

With dozens of motels and cabin resorts strung along Ariz. 260 as it passes through town, Pinetop-Lakeside, actually two towns that grew together over the years, is the busiest town in the White Mountains. At first glance, it's easy to dismiss the town as too commercial, what with all the strip malls and budget motels, but Pinetop-Lakeside has spent many years entertaining families during the summer months, and it still has plenty of diversions to keep visitors busy.

You just have to look a little harder than you might in other White Mountains communities.

With Apache-Sitgreaves National Forests on one side and the unspoiled lands of the White Mountain Apache Indian Reservation on the other, Pinetop-Lakeside is well situated for anyone who enjoys the outdoors. Nearby are several lakes with good fishing; nearly 200 miles of hiking, mountain-biking, and cross-country ski trails; horseback riding; and downhill skiing. Although summer is the busy season, Pinetop-Lakeside becomes a ski resort in winter. The Sunrise Park ski area is only 30 miles away, and on weekends the town is packed with skiers.

Pinetop-Lakeside is definitely the family destination of the White Mountains, so if you're looking for a romantic weekend or solitude, continue farther into the White Mountains to Greer or Alpine.

ESSENTIALS

GETTING THERE   Pinetop and Lakeside are both located on Ariz. 260.

VISITOR INFORMATION   For information on this area, contact the **Pinetop-Lakeside Chamber of Commerce,** 102C W. White Mountain Blvd., Lakeside (© **800/573-4031** or 928/367-4290; www.pinetoplakesidechamber.com).

OUTDOOR PURSUITS

Old forts and casinos aside, it's the outdoors (and the cool weather) that really draws people here. Fishing, hiking, mountain biking, and horseback riding are among the most popular activities. If you want to saddle up, call **Porter Mountain Stable,** 4048 Porter Mountain Rd. (© **928/368-5306** or 928/368-5800), which charges $22 for a 1-hour ride. At the end of your ride, you can even have a meal at the stable's affiliated steak house.

Meandering through the forests surrounding Pinetop-Lakeside are the 180 miles of trails of the **White Mountain Trail system.** Many of these trails are easily accessible (in fact, some are right in town) and are open to both hikers and mountain bikers. The trails at Pinetop's **Woodland Lake Park** are among our favorites. The park is just off Ariz. 260 near the east end of Pinetop and has 6 miles of trails, including a paved path around the lake. For a panoramic vista of the Mogollon Rim, hike the short **Mogollon Rim Nature Walk** off Ariz. 260 on the west side of Lakeside. For another short but pleasant stroll, check out the **Big Springs Environmental Study Area,** on Woodland Road in Lakeside. This quiet little preserve encompasses a small meadow through which flows a spring-fed stream. There is often good bird-watching here. You can spot more birds at Woodland Lake Park, mentioned above, and at **Jacques Marsh,** 2 miles north of Lakeside on Porter Mountain Road. For more information on area trails, contact the **Lakeside Ranger Station,** 2022 W. White Mountain Blvd., Lakeside (© **928/368-5111**), on Ariz. 260 in Lakeside, or the **Pinetop-Lakeside Chamber of Commerce** (see "Visitor Information," above).

If you're up here to catch the big one, you've got plenty of options. Area lakes hold native Apache trout, as well as stocked rainbows, browns, and brookies. This is also the southernmost spot in the United States where you can fish for Arctic graylings. Right in the Pinetop-Lakeside area, try **Rainbow Lake,** which is a block south of Ariz. 260 in Lakeside and has boat rentals available; **Woodland Lake,** in Woodland Lake Park, toward the east end of Pinetop and just south of Ariz. 260; or **Show Low Lake,** east of Lakeside and north of Ariz. 260. On the nearby White Mountain Apache Indian Reservation, there's good fishing in **Hawley Lake** and **Horseshoe Lake,** both of which are east of Pinetop-Lakeside and south of Ariz. 260. If you plan to fish at either of these latter two

The Rodeo-Chediski Fire

Arizona had been suffering from years of drought, when, in the summer of 2002, two fires began raging through the tinder-dry forests of eastern Arizona. Whipped by hot winds, the fires quickly merged into one massive conflagration that was called the Rodeo-Chediski fire. By the time the fire was contained, it had blackened 470,000 acres of forest and destroyed hundreds of homes and businesses. Although the forests immediately surrounding Pinetop-Lakeside were spared, anyone driving Ariz. 260 between Payson and Show Low will pass through forests that were blackened by the Rodeo-Chediski fire.

lakes, be sure to get a reservation fishing license ($6 per day). It's available at the **Hon-Dah Service Station,** at Ariz. 260 and Ariz. 73 (© **928/369-4311**), **Hon-Dah Ski & Outdoor Sport,** also at Ariz. 260 and Ariz. 73 (© **928/369-7669**), and **Hawley Lake Store,** south of Ariz. 260 between Hon-Dah and Sunrise (© **928/335-7511**).

Several area golf courses are open to the public, including **Pinetop Lakes Golf & Country Club,** Buck Springs Road, Pinetop-Lakeside (© **928/369-4531**), considered one of the best executive courses in the state (play this one if you have time for only one round while you're in the area); **Silver Creek Golf Club,** White Mountain Lake Road, Show Low (© **928/537-2744**); and the **Show Low Golf Club,** 860 N. 36th Dr., Show Low (© **928/537-4564**).

About 50 miles south of Show Low, U.S. 60 crosses a bridge over the narrow, scenic canyon of the Salt River. This stretch of the river is a favorite of whitewater rafters, and several companies offer rafting trips of varying lengths. Try **Wilderness Aware Rafting** (© **800/231-7238;** www.inaraft.com), **Canyon Rio Rafting** (© **800/272-3353;** www.canyonrio.com), or **Mild to Wild Rafting** (© **800/567-6745;** www.mild2wildrafting.com). Prices are between $90 and $115 for a day trip.

OTHER AREA ATTRACTIONS

If you're curious to learn more about the Apaches, drive south from Pinetop-Lakeside to **Apache Cultural Center & Museum** (© **928/338-4625;** wmat.us/wmaculture.shtml), in the town of Fort Apache, which, along with the White Mountain Apache Reservation, was established in 1870 by the U.S. government. The cultural center, approximately 22 miles south of Pinetop on Ariz. 73, includes a museum with small but informative exhibits on Apache culture. Outside the cultural center and down a short trail, there is a reconstructed Apache village. The cultural center is open Monday through Friday (plus Sat in summer) from 8am to 5pm. Admission is $3 for adults, $2 for seniors and students, and free for children under 10. June through August, you'll get much more out of your visit if you take a 1½-hour guided tour, which costs $8 for adults and $7 for seniors and students, and, for an additional $4 for adults and $3 for seniors and students, you can arrange to have the guide take you to the nearby Kinishba ruins. The cultural center is on the grounds of a former Indian school that is now called the Fort Apache Historic Park and includes more than 20 historic buildings, but don't expect to see a Hollywood-style fort. These old buildings are for the most part dreary and in need of restoration.

Tips   A Pleasant Valley Detour

For a bit of back-roads adventure, head south from the Mogollon Rim to the remote community of Young, which sits in the middle of the aptly named Pleasant Valley. The town can be reached only via well-graded gravel roads—24 miles of gravel if you come from the north, 32 miles from the south—which is why a trip to Young is an adventure.

Why visit Young? Most people come just to see the land that spawned the worst range war and family feud in the West. Known as the Pleasant Valley War or Graham-Tewksbury Feud, it likely erupted over conflicts about sheep grazing in the valley and eventually the feud took dozens of lives. Zane Grey memorialized the 1880s range war in his novel *To the Last Man.*

You'll find Young on Ariz. 288, which heads south from Ariz. 260 about midway between Payson and Heber and connects to Ariz. 88 north of Globe (near Theodore Roosevelt Lake).

Also in this area is **Kinishba Ruins,** up a gravel road 2 miles west of Fort Apache on Ariz. 73 and then 3 miles down a rough gravel road. This 200-room pueblo ruin is more than 1,000 years old and was visited by Coronado when he passed through in search of the Seven Cities of Cíbola. Get directions to the ruins at the Cultural Center. The best way to visit is as an add-on to the guided tours offered at Fort Apache Historic Park.

For more information on visiting the White Mountain Apache Reservation, contact the **White Mountain Apache Tribe Office of Tourism** (✆ 877/ **338-9628;** www.wmat.nsn.us), also located in Fort Apache Historic Park.

If you're looking for something to do after dark, head out to the **Hon-Dah Casino** (✆ **800/WAY-UP-HI** or 928/369-0299), owned and operated by the White Mountain Apache Tribe. It's open daily around the clock and is at the junction of Ariz. 73 and Ariz. 260, about 4 miles east of Pinetop-Lakeside.

WHERE TO STAY

Hogan's Lake of the Woods *Kids*   Set on its own private lake right on Ariz. 260, Lake of the Woods is a rustic mountain resort that caters primarily to families. Cabins and houses range from tiny to huge, with rustic and modern side by side. The smallest sleep two or three, while the largest can take up to 20; several have kitchens and fireplaces. Some are on the edge of the lake, while others are tucked away under the pines; be sure to request a location away from the busy highway and ask for a newer cabin, as the accommodations vary considerably in quality. Kids in particular love this place: They can fish in the lake, row a boat, or play in the snow.

2244 W. White Mountain Blvd., Lakeside, AZ 85929. ✆ **928/368-5353.** www.privatelake.com. 31 units. $56–$186 cabin for 2 people; $320–$406 cabin for 20 people. 3- to 5-night minimum stay in summer and on some holidays. DISC, MC, V. Pets accepted. **Amenities:** Exercise room; Jacuzzi; sauna; boat rentals; game room; coin-op laundry; horseshoes; playground. *In room:* TV, kitchen, fridge, coffeemaker, no phone.

Hon-Dah Resort Casino & Conference Center ✿   This hotel, adjacent to the Hon-Dah Casino a few miles east of Pinetop-Lakeside, is the largest and most luxurious lodging in the White Mountains. As with most casino hotels, it was designed to impress. The portico is big enough to hold a basketball court, and inside the front door is an artificial rock wall upon which are mounted stuffed animals, including a cougar, bobcat, bear, ducks, and even a bugling elk. Guest rooms are for the most part very spacious.

777 Ariz. 260 (at junction with Ariz. 73), Pinetop, AZ 85935. © 800/929-8744 or 928/369-0299. www.hon-dah.com. 128 units. $79–$99 double; $150–$180 suite. AE, DC, DISC, MC, V. **Amenities:** Restaurant (American); 2 lounges; year-round outdoor pool; access to nearby health club; Jacuzzi; sauna; video arcade; room service; coin-op laundry; casino. In room: A/C, TV, dataport, fridge, coffeemaker, hair dryer, iron.

Sierra Springs Ranch ⭐   Located east of Pinetop, the Sierra Springs Ranch is the most upscale property around and is as idyllic a mountain retreat as you'll find in Arizona. The cabins are set in a wide clearing in the forest, and each is distinctively furnished. All are spacious and comfortable (the largest cabin sleeps 13). Our favorite is the honeymoon cottage, which is built of logs and has a stone fireplace. All units have full kitchens, which makes up for the lack of a restaurant on the premises. The ranch also has its own meadows and trout pond (fishing gear is available). Keep an eye out for elk in the early morning.

101 Sky High Rd., Pinetop, AZ 85935. © 800/492-4059 or 928/369-3900. Fax 928/369-0741. www.sierra springsranch.com. 8 units. $195 cabin for 2 people. 2-night minimum stay (longer on holidays and in sum-mer). AE, MC, V. **Amenities:** Exercise room; sauna; bikes; game room; horseshoes. In room: TV, kitchen, fridge, coffeemaker, washer/dryer, free local calls.

CAMPGROUNDS

There are four campgrounds in the immediate Pinetop-Lakeside area, including Show Low Lake, Fool Hollow, Lewis Canyon, and Lakeside. Of these, **Show Low Lake County Park** (© **928/537-4126**) and **Fool Hollow Lake Recreation Area** (© **928/537-3680**) are the nicest. There are also numerous camp-grounds nearby on the White River Apache Indian Reservation. For information about these campgrounds, contact the **White Mountain Apache Tribe Wildlife and Outdoor Recreation Division** (© **928/338-4385**) or the **White Moun-tain Apache Tribe Office of Tourism** (© **877/338-9628;** www.wmat.nsn.us).

WHERE TO DINE

Charlie Clark's Steak House STEAKHOUSE/SEAFOOD   Charlie Clark's, the oldest steakhouse in the White Mountains, has been serving up thick, juicy steaks since 1938 (before that, during Prohibition, the building was used as a sort of backwoods speakeasy). Mesquite-broiled steaks and chicken, as well as seafood and prime rib, fill the menu. To find the place, just look for the build-ing with a fake horse on the roof.

1701 E. White Mountain Blvd., Pinetop. © 888/333-0259 or 928/367-4900. www.charlieclarks.com. Reser-vations only for parties of 5 or more. Main courses $6–$21 lunch, $12–$36 dinner. AE, DC, DISC, MC, V. Sun–Thurs 11am–9:30pm; Fri–Sat 11am–10pm.

The Christmas Tree Restaurant AMERICAN/CONTINENTAL   Located in a quiet setting off the main drag, this country restaurant serves good old-fash-ioned American food as well as a few standard Continental offerings. Although you can get the likes of chicken curry, honey duck, and sole almandine, the chicken and dumplings are the specialty of the house, and it is these that you should order. Meals are filling, accompanied by everything from delicious pick-led beets to Boston clam chowder. As the name implies, a Christmas theme pre-vails year-round, and there's also a country gift store.

455 Woodland Rd., Lakeside. © 928/367-3107. Reservations recommended on Sat. Main courses $12–$30. DISC, MC, V. Wed–Sun 5–9pm.

3 Greer & Sunrise Park ⊛

51 miles SE of Show Low; 98 miles SE of Holbrook; 222 miles NE of Phoenix

The tiny community of Greer, set in the lush meadows on either side of the Little Colorado River and surrounded by forests, is by far the most picturesque mountain community in Arizona. The elevation of 8,525 feet usually ensures plenty of snow in winter and pleasantly cool temperatures in summer, and together these two factors have turned Greer into something of an upscale mountain getaway that's popular among lowlanders with an eye for aesthetics. Modern log homes are springing up all over the valley, but Greer is still free of the sort of strip-mall developments that have forever changed the character of Payson and Pinetop-Lakeside.

The Little Colorado River, which flows through the middle of Greer on its way to the Grand Canyon, is little more than a babbling brook up here. Still, it's known for trout fishing, one of the main draws in these parts. In winter, cross-country skiing, ice-skating, ice fishing, and sleigh rides are popular. Greer also happens to be the closest community to the Sunrise Park ski area, which is what gives the village its ski-resort atmosphere.

ESSENTIALS

GETTING THERE From Phoenix, take U.S. 87 north to Payson and then go east on Ariz. 260, or take U.S. 60 east from Phoenix through Globe and Show Low to Ariz. 260 east. Greer is just a few miles south of Ariz. 260 on Ariz. 373.

VISITOR INFORMATION Online, contact the **Greer Business Association** (www.greerarizona.com).

OUTDOOR PURSUITS

Winter is one of the busiest seasons in Greer because the town is so close to the **Sunrise Park Resort** ski area (© 800/772-7669 or 928/735-7669; www.sunriseskipark.com). Located just off Ariz. 260 on Ariz. 273, this ski area, the largest and most popular in Arizona, is operated by the White Mountain Apache Tribe. It usually opens in November, but thaws and long stretches without snow can make winters a bit unreliable (snow-making machines enhance the natural snowfall). Although there are some good advanced runs, beginner and intermediate skiers will be in heaven. We've rarely seen so many green runs starting from the uppermost lifts of a ski area, all of which translates into a very family-oriented place. At the top of 11,000-foot Apache Peak there is a day lodge that provides meals and a view that goes on forever. A ski school offers a variety of lessons. Lift tickets cost $39 for adults and $23 for children. Ski rentals are available here and at numerous shops in Pinetop-Lakeside.

More than 13 miles of groomed cross-country ski trails wind their way through forests of ponderosa pines and across high snow-covered meadows. These trails begin at the **Sunrise General Store** (© 800/772-SNOW), located at the turnoff for the downhill area. All-day trail passes are $6. There are also good opportunities for cross-country skiing in Greer, which has 35 miles of developed trails. At 8,500 feet, the alpine scenery is quiet and serene. Looking for something a bit more old-fashioned? Try a 45-minute sleigh ride with **Blue Sky Stables** (© 928/735-7454) at a cost of $25 per person.

Come summer, the cross-country ski trails become **mountain-biking trails,** and when combined with the nearby **Pole Knoll trail system,** provide mountain bikers with 35 miles of trails of varying degrees of difficulty. Sunrise Park

Resort also opens up its slopes to mountain bikers. Bikes can be rented for $15 for 2 hours; a lift ticket for the day will run you another $15.

This area offers some of the finest mountain hiking in Arizona, and my favorite area trail is the hike up 11,590-foot **Mount Baldy** , the second-highest peak in Arizona. This peak lies on the edge of the White Mountain Apache Indian Reservation and is sacred to the Apaches. Consequently, the summit is off-limits to non-Apaches. There are two trail heads for the hike up Mount Baldy. The most popular and scenic route begins 6 miles south of Sunrise Park ski area (off the gravel extension of Ariz. 273) and follows the West Fork of the Little Colorado River. This trail climbs roughly 2,000 feet and is moderately strenuous, and the high elevation often leaves lowland hikers gasping for breath.

For an easier hike, check out the **Butler Canyon Trail,** a 1-mile-long nature trail along Butler Canyon Stream north of Greer. To reach the trail head, take the East Fork Road, which is 4 miles south of Ariz. 260. From the south end of Greer, you can head out on the **East Fork Trail,** which eventually leads to Mount Baldy. This trail starts with a steep 600-foot climb, but then becomes a much easier ascent. Another good choice for a day hike is the **West Fork Trail,** which begins north of Greer on Osborne Road and meanders through forests and meadows. The turnoff for the trail head is 4.3 miles south of Ariz. 260.

Hikers can also catch a lift up Apache Peak at Sunrise Park Resort, which keeps its lifts running in summer for hikers and anyone else interested in the view from on high. A single-ride lift ticket is $10 for adults and $5 for children.

To explore the Greer area from the back of a horse, contact **Blue Sky Stables,** located between Greer and Ariz. 260 (© **928/735-7454**), which offers rides of varying lengths. Prices start at $25 for a 1-hour ride.

The three Greer Lakes on the outskirts of town—Bunch, River, and Tunnel reservoirs—are popular fishing spots. All three hold brown and rainbow trout. On **River Reservoir,** try the shallows at the south end. On **Tunnel Reservoir,** you can often do well from shore, especially if fly-fishing, though there is a boat launch. However, it's **Big Lake,** south of Greer, that has the biggest fishing reputation around these parts. Fishing is also good on **Sunrise Lake,** but be sure to get a White Mountain Apache Indian Reservation fishing license (available at the Sunrise General Store). If you'd like a guide to take you out for a day of fishing the Arizona high country, contact **The Speckled Trout,** 103 Main St., Greer (© **928/735-7222;** www.cybertrails.com/~cltrout), which charges $225 per day for one angler or $275 for two ($135 or $165 for a half-day).

Sunrise Lake, near the Sunrise Park ski area, is a popular spot in the summer. Boat rentals are available at the **Sunrise Lake Marina** (© **928/735-7669,** ext. 2155). A fishing boat with an outboard motor rents for $60 per day.

(Finds A Cocoon of Creativity

The **Butterfly Lodge Museum** (© **928/735-7514;** www.wmonline.com/ butterflylodge.htm) is a restored historic cabin built in 1914. Owned by James Willard Schultz (a writer) and his son Hart Merriam Schultz (a painter), the museum is a memorial to these two unusual and creative individuals who once called Greer home. It's just off Ariz. 373 between Ariz. 260 and Greer. Memorial Day to Labor Day, it's open Friday through Sunday (and holidays) from 10am to 5pm. Admission is $2 for adults and $1 for youths 12 to 17.

WHERE TO STAY
IN GREER

Cattle Kate's Bed & Breakfast ★   Consisting of several modern log buildings with a classic mountain feel, Cattle Kate's seems to have patterned itself after the nearby Greer Lodge, but it's much more comfortable than its more rustic neighbor. The rooms are furnished in classic Western style, have high ceilings, and look out on small trout ponds and the meadows along the Little Colorado River. In the large dining room, an elk head is mounted over the fireplace, while an antler chandelier hangs from the ceiling. The only drawback is that you're right on the main road through Greer, though this road is rarely very busy.

80 N. Main St. (P.O. Box 21), Greer, AZ 85927. ℂ 928/735-7744. Fax 928/735-7386. www.wmonline.com/cattlekates. 10 units. $75–$85 double; $125 suite; $175 cabin. Rates include full breakfast. AE, DISC, MC, V. **Amenities:** Restaurant (American); lounge; trout ponds, fly-fishing lessons. *In room:* No phone.

Greer Lodge   Fresh from a $1.2-million makeover, this classic mountain lodge is once again looking and feeling like the great mountain getaway it once was. Located only 20 minutes from the Sunrise Park ski area and boasting its own trout ponds and a short stretch of the Little Colorado River, this lodge is a good choice for both skiers and anglers. Rooms in the main building have nice views of the mountains or river and have all been extensively remodeled. For more privacy, book one of the lodge's two cabins. The lodge's restaurant has walls of glass that look out over a river, meadows, and a trout pond, and in winter, there's a cozy fireplace.

44 Main St. (P.O. Box 244), Greer, AZ 85927. ℂ 866/826-8262 or 928/735-7216. Fax 928/735-7720. www.greerlodgeaz.com. 11 units. $185 double; $185–$345 cabin. Lower rates Nov to mid-May. 2-night minimum. AE, DC, DISC, MC, V. No children under 16 in main lodge rooms. **Amenities:** Restaurant; lounge; day spa; fishing ponds; fly-fishing classes. *In room:* Coffeemaker, hair dryer, no phone.

Red Setter Inn & Cottage ★★   If you're headed up to the mountains for a romantic weekend getaway, this three-story log lodge, the most luxurious in Greer, should be your first choice. The inn is built on the banks of the Little Colorado River, which is only steps away from the decks of some guest rooms. Several units have fireplaces and whirlpool tubs, while others have vaulted ceilings and skylights. Cases full of antique toys and a game room with old arcade games make this inn fun as well as romantic. There are also three housekeeping "cottages," one of which has four bedrooms, three bathrooms, and three fireplaces. If you stay 2 nights or longer, the inn will pack sack lunches for you, and on Saturday nights, dinner is available for $25 per person.

8 Main St. (P.O. Box 133), Greer, AZ 85927. ℂ 888/994-7337 or 928/735-7441. www.redsetterinn.com. 14 units. $145–$210 double; from $235 cottage (8-person maximum). 2-night minimum on weekends; 3-night minimum on holidays. Rates include full breakfast. AE, DISC, MC, V. No children under 16. **Amenities:** Game room; river fishing. *In room:* Hair dryer, no phone.

Snowy Mountain Inn *Kids*   Set back from the main road down a gravel driveway and shaded by tall pines, the Snowy Mountain Inn has a remote yet comfortable feel about it. The modern cabins, although a bit cramped inside, are great for family vacations; they come equipped with gas fireplaces, porches, and sleeping lofts, and some have private hot tubs as well. Surrounding the log cabins and main lodge are 100 acres of private forest, so guests have plenty of room to roam. The 1½-acre trout pond is one of the largest in the area. The lodge's restaurant doubles as a sports bar.

38721 Rte. 373, Greer, AZ 85927. ℂ 888/766-9971 or 928/735-7576. Fax 928/735-7705. www.snowymountaininn.com. 10 units. $150–$180 cabin; $275–$350 house. AE, DISC, MC, V. Pets accepted ($15 per day). **Amenities:** Restaurant; lounge; children's playroom; coin-op laundry; fishing ponds. *In room:* TV/VCR, kitchen, fridge, coffeemaker, no phone in cabins.

White Mountain Lodge Bed & Breakfast and Cabins   Situated on the road into Greer with a view across an open, marshy stretch of the valley, this lodge was built in 1892 and is the oldest building in Greer (but you'd never know it to look at it). Knotty pine throughout gives the lodge a classic cabin feel, but the many large windows prevent the rooms from feeling too dark. Guest rooms are done up in a Southwestern or country theme; our favorite has a king-size bed and a view up the valley. The cabins, which are perfect for families or two couples to share, are even more comfortable. There are also a couple of suites with in-room Jacuzzis and fireplaces.

140 Main St. (P.O. Box 143), Greer, AZ 85927. (C) **888/493-7568** or 928/735-7568. Fax 928/735-7498. www.wmlodge.com. 12 units. $85–$145 double; $85–$225 cabin for 2 people. Lodge room rates include full breakfast. 2-night minimum stay on weekends, 3- to 4-night minimum stay on holidays. AE, DISC, MC, V. **Amenities:** Jacuzzi; guest laundry. *In room:* Hair dryer, no phone.

IN MCNARY

Sunrise Park Lodge   Located 20 miles outside Greer in McNary, this is the closest lodge to the Sunrise Park ski area and thus a favorite of downhill skiers. About half of the rooms overlook Sunrise Lake—these are worth requesting. The two on-site restaurants are about your only dinner options in the vicinity; there's also a cozy lounge for après-ski drinks.

Hwy. 273, near intersection of Hwy. 260 (P.O. Box 117), Greer, AZ 85927. (C) **800/772-7669** or 928/735-7669. www.sunriseskipark.com. 100 units. $68–$144 double; $142–$295 suite. AE, DC, DISC, MC, V. **Amenities:** 2 restaurants (American); lounge; small indoor pool; exercise room; 2 Jacuzzis; sauna; bike rentals; courtesy ski-area shuttle. *In room:* A/C, TV.

CAMPGROUNDS

In the immediate vicinity of Greer, there are three campgrounds in Apache-Sitgreaves National Forests. Reservations can be made for the **Benny Creek** ($18 per night), 2½ miles north of Greer, **Rolfe C. Hoyer Campground** ($14 per night), 1 mile north of Greer on Ariz. 373, and the **Winn Campground** ($12 per night), 12 miles southwest of Greer on Ariz. 273 (the road past Sunrise Park Resort), by contacting the National Recreation Reservation Service ((C) **877/444-6777;** www.reserveusa.com). Because of its proximity to Greer and the Greer Lakes, Rolfe C. Hoyer is your best choice in the area. There are also several campgrounds nearby on the White Mountain Apache Indian Reservation (no reservations accepted).

WHERE TO DINE

Your best bets in Greer are the dining rooms at the **Greer Lodge** and **Cattle Kate's,** both of which serve reasonably priced meals. Both feature a bit of Southwestern fare plus familiar American standards. Hours vary considerably with the seasons and the snowfall. See "Where to Stay," above, for details.

4 Springerville & Eagar

56 miles E of Show Low; 82 miles SE of Holbrook; 227 miles NE of Phoenix

Together the adjacent towns of Springerville and Eagar constitute the northeastern gateway to the White Mountains. Although the towns themselves are at the foot of the mountains, the vistas from around Springerville and Eagar take in all the area's peaks. The two towns also like to play up their Wild West backgrounds—in fact, John Wayne liked the area so much that he had a ranch along the Little Colorado River just west of Eagar. Today, large ranches still run their cattle on the windswept plains north of Springerville and Eagar.

Volcanic activity between 300,000 and 700,000 years ago gave the land north of Springerville and Eagar its distinctive character. This area, known as the Springerville Volcanic Field, is the third-largest volcanic field of its kind in the continental United States (the San Francisco Field near Flagstaff and the Medicine Lake Field in California are both larger). The Springerville Volcanic Field covers an area bigger than the state of Rhode Island and contains 405 extinct volcanic vents. It's many cinder cones dotting the landscape give this region such a unique appearance. For a brochure outlining a tour of the volcanic field, contact the Springerville-Eagar Regional Chamber of Commerce (see "Visitor Information," below).

ESSENTIALS

GETTING THERE   Springerville and Eagar are in the northeast corner of the White Mountains at the junction of U.S. 60, U.S. 180/191, and Ariz. 260. From Phoenix, there are two routes: Ariz. 87 north to Payson and then Ariz. 260 east, or U.S. 60 east to Globe and then north to Show Low and on to Springerville (or you can take Ariz. 260 from Show Low to Springerville). From Holbrook, take U.S. 180 southeast to St. Johns and U.S. 180/191 south to Springerville. From southern Arizona, U.S. 191 is slow but very scenic.

VISITOR INFORMATION   For information on the Springerville and Eagar areas, contact the **Springerville-Eagar Regional Chamber of Commerce** (© **928/333-2123;** www.springerville-eagar.com).

INDIAN RUINS

Casa Malpais Archaeological Park & Museum ★ *Finds*   The Casa Malpais ruins are unique in that the pueblo, which dates from A.D. 1250 and was occupied until about 1400, was built to take advantage of existing caves. Many of these caves form a system of catacomb-like rooms under the pueblo. The only way to visit the ruin is on guided tours that leave from the Casa Malpais museum, which is located in downtown Springerville. At the museum, you'll find exhibits on both the Mogollon people and on dinosaurs that once roamed this region.

318 E. Main St., Springerville. © **928/333-5375.** Guided tours $5 adults, $4 students and seniors, $3 children under 12. Museum: daily 8am–4pm. Tours: daily 9 and 11am and 4pm (weather permitting). Closed Thanksgiving, Christmas.

Lyman Lake State Park   Within this state park are the early Ancestral Puebloan ruins of Rattlesnake Point Pueblo, as well as petroglyphs that date back thousands of years. Some of the petroglyphs are accessible only by boat, and during the summer months you can see them on guided tours. There are also summer tours to the ruins.

18 miles north of Springerville. © **928/337-4441.** www.pr.state.az.us. Admission $5 per car. Park daily daylight hours, visitor center daily 8am–5pm; tours May–Sept Sat–Sun.

MUSEUMS

A couple of small museums are worth a look if you have the time. The **Reneé Cushman Art Collection** is housed in the L.D.S. (Mormon) Church in Springerville. It consists of one woman's personal collection of European art and antiques. Among the works are an etching attributed to Rembrandt and three pen-and-ink drawings by Tiepolo. The antique furniture dates back to the Renaissance. The museum is open by appointment only. Contact the **Springerville-Eagar Regional Chamber of Commerce** (© **928/333-2123;** www.springerville-eagar.com) for information on whom to call to arrange a visit.

Local history and old automated musical instruments are the focus of the **Little House Museum** (© 928/333-2286), 7 miles west of Eagar on South Fork Road, off Ariz. 260. Tales of colorful Wild West characters as told by the guide are as much a part of the museum as the displays themselves. Museum visits are by reservation only and cost $7 for adults and $4 for children under 12.

OUTDOOR PURSUITS

If you're interested in fishing, contact **The Speckled Trout,** 224 E. Main St., Springerville (© **928/333-0852;** www.cybertrails.com/~cltrout), a fly shop that also offers a guide service charging $250 per day for one or two anglers ($150 for a half-day). **Lyman Lake State Park** (© **928/337-4441**), 18 miles north of Springerville, is popular for lake fishing. And if it's high summer and you feel like swimming, this is the place for a dip or a day of water-skiing or sailing.

Alternatively, you can head out to the **X Diamond Ranch** (© **928/333-2286**), off Ariz. 260 between Eagar and Greer (take County Rd. 4124). The ranch maintains a section of the Little Colorado River as a fishing habitat. The half-day fishing rate is $30, while a full day costs $40. Horseback rides are also available, with options ranging from 1 hour ($25) to a full day ($125–$150).

For a chance to see pronghorn antelope, elk, and mule deer, head south of Eagar to the **Sipe White Mountain Wildlife Area.** This grassy valley at the foot of the White Mountains was once a cattle ranch, and today the old ranch house serves as a visitor center that's open during the summer months. Several miles of hiking trails wind through forest and pasture and past lakes and ponds. There's good bird-watching here, too. Sipe is 5 miles down a gravel road that begins 2 miles south of Eagar off Ariz. 180/191. For more information, contact the Arizona Game & Fish Department, Pinetop Regional Office, 2878 E. White Mountain Blvd., Pinetop (© **928/367-4281;** www.gf.state.az.us).

WHERE TO STAY

Paisley Corner Bed & Breakfast ★ *Finds* This lovingly restored 1910-vintage colonial revival house is one of the most authentically decorated B&Bs we've visited, and as such is one of our favorites in the state. Victorian antiques and dark color schemes predominate throughout. In contrast to all this authenticity, there's one room done up to resemble an old soda fountain, complete with vintage jukeboxes and telephone booth. The inn's kitchen features a 1910 gas stove and looks as though it came straight out of a 1920s Sears & Roebuck catalog. Guest rooms on the second floor have antique beds; two units have bathrooms with claw-foot tubs and old pull-chain toilets.

287 N. Main St., Eagar (Mailing address: P.O. Box 458, Springerville, AZ 85938). © **928/333-4665.** www.paisleycorner.com. 4 units. $75–$95 double. Rates include full breakfast. MC, V. Children discouraged. **Amenities:** Jacuzzi. *In room:* A/C, hair dryer, no phone.

X Diamond Ranch Long known for its Little House Museum and trout fishing on the Little Colorado River, this ranch also rents a variety of cabins, ranging from an updated old log cabin to a couple of new ones. Activities include fishing, horseback riding, and touring the ranch's archaeological site ($10 for a tour). There's no restaurant on the premises, but cabins have full kitchens.

P.O. Box 113, Greer, AZ 85927. © **928/333-2286.** www.xdiamondranch.com. 6 units. Apr–Oct $105–$175 double; Nov–Mar $84–$180 double. Children under 2 stay free in parents' room. AE, DISC, MC, V. Off Ariz. 260 between Eagar and Greer (take County Rd. 4124). **Amenities:** Horseback riding. *In room:* Kitchen, fridge, coffeemaker, no phone in some units.

CAMPGROUNDS

Lyman Lake State Park (© 928/337-4441), 18 miles north of Springerville on U.S. 180/191, has a campground with sites going for $12 to $22 per night. It's very popular with water-skiers, so don't expect much peace and quiet.

WHERE TO DINE

Vintage Hideaway Restaurant *Finds* AMERICAN   Set in an old house beneath big shade trees, this casual Victorian-inspired restaurant may be most popular with the ladies' lunch crowd of the Springerville-Eagar area, but it also happens to be the best restaurant in town. At lunch, there's a good selection of sandwiches on homemade bread, as well as soups and salads. Dinners focus on steaks and simple seafood dishes. There's a Friday night fish fry, and Saturday nights, there's prime rib.

389 N. Eagar St. (behind the Community First Bank). © 928/333-4398. Main courses $5–$23. MC, V. Tues–Sat 10:30am–9pm.

5 The Coronado Trail ⊛

Alpine: 28 miles S of Springerville; 75 miles E of Pinetop-Lakeside; 95 miles N of Clifton

Winding southward from the Springerville-Eagar area to Clifton and Morenci, the Coronado Trail (U.S. 191) is one of the most remote and little-traveled paved roads in the state. Because this road is so narrow and winding, it's slow going—meant for people who aren't in a hurry to get anywhere anytime soon. If you are *not* prone to carsickness, you may want to take a leisurely drive down this scenic stretch of asphalt.

The Coronado Trail is named for the Spanish explorer Francisco Vásquez de Coronado, who came to Arizona in search of gold in the early 1540s. Although he never found it, his party did make it as far north as the Hopi pueblos and would have traveled through this region on their march northward from Mexico. Centuries later, the discovery of huge copper reserves would make the fortunes of the towns of Clifton and Morenci, at the southern end of the Coronado Trail.

Alpine, at the northern end of the Coronado Trail, is the main base for today's explorers, who tend to be outdoor types in search of uncrowded trails and trout streams where the fish are still biting. Located not far from the New Mexico state line, Alpine offers a few basic lodges and restaurants, plus easy access to the region's many trails.

This area is known as the Alps of Arizona, and Alpine's picturesque setting in the middle of a wide grassy valley at 8,030 feet certainly lives up to this image. Alpine is surrounded by the Apache-Sitgreaves National Forests, which together have miles of trails and several campgrounds. In spring, wildflowers abound and the trout fishing is excellent. In summer, there's hiking on forest trails. In autumn, the aspens in the Golden Bowl on the mountainside above Alpine turn a brilliant yellow, and in winter, visitors come for the cross-country skiing and ice fishing.

ESSENTIALS

GETTING THERE   Alpine is 28 miles south of Springerville and Eagar at the junction of U.S. 191, which continues south to Clifton and Morenci, and U.S. 180, which leads east into New Mexico.

VISITOR INFORMATION   For more information on the region, contact the **Alpine Area Chamber of Commerce,** P.O. Box 410, Alpine, AZ 85920 (© **928/339-4330;** www.alpinearizona.com). For outdoor information, contact the Apache-Sitgreaves National Forests' **Alpine Ranger District,** P.O. Box 469, Alpine, AZ 85920 (© **928/339-4384;** www.fs.fed.us/r3/asnf).

OUTDOOR PURSUITS

Fall, when the aspens turn the mountainside gold, is one of the most popular times of year in this area—there are only a few places in Arizona where fall color is worth a drive, and this is one of them.

Not far outside Alpine, there's cross-country skiing at the **Williams Valley Winter Recreation Area,** which doubles as a mountain-biking trail system in summer.

Visitors can play a round of golf at the **Alpine Country Club** (© **928/339-4944**), 3 miles east of town off U.S. 180. At 8,500 feet in elevation, this is one of the highest golf courses in the country. Greens fees are $15 to $20 for 18 holes (without a cart) or $30 to $45 with a cart.

If you're looking for fish to catch, try **Luna Lake,** east of Alpine off U.S. 180. Here at the lake, you'll also find some easy to moderate mountain-bike trails that usually offer good wildlife-viewing opportunities.

The best hike in the area is the trail up **Escudilla Mountain,** just outside Alpine, where you'll see some of the best displays of aspens in the fall.

Summer or winter, **Hannagan Meadows,** 23 miles south of Alpine, is the place to be. Here you'll find excellent hiking, mountain biking, and cross-country ski trails. Hannagan Meadows also provides access to the **Blue Range Primitive Area,** which is popular with hikers. The Eagle Trail, which starts 5 miles south of Hannagan Meadows off Eagle Creek Road, is a good place to spot wildlife. It is in the remote wilderness areas near here that a Mexican gray wolf recovery project has been underway for several years. The reintroduction has so far met with mixed success, as wolves have been killed by cars, people, disease, and even mountain lions. Some wolves have had to be recaptured because they strayed out of the area set aside for them or because they'd had encounters with humans.

WHERE TO STAY & DINE

Between Springerville-Eagar and Clifton-Morenci, there are nearly a dozen National Forest Service campgrounds. If fishing and boating interest you, head to **Luna Lake Campground,** just east of Alpine on U.S. 180, where the daily campsite fee is $8. Reserve a Luna Lake campsite through the National Recreation Reservation Service (© **877/444-6777;** www.reserveusa.com). For a more tranquil forest setting, try **Hannagan Meadows Campground** (reservations not accepted), which makes a good base for exploring the Coronado Trail. For information on these campgrounds, contact the **Alpine Ranger District** (© **928/339-4384**).

If you're looking for someplace to eat, you'll find a couple of basic restaurants in Alpine.

Hannagan Meadow Lodge   Located 22 miles south of Alpine at an elevation of 9,100 feet, this rustic lodge dates back to 1926 and is set amid cool forests on the winding route of the Coronado Trail. With both rustic cabins and bed-and-breakfast lodge rooms, this place offers plenty of variety and is a good spot for a quiet getaway or a family vacation. In summer, the lodge is a base for exploring the hundreds of miles of hiking trails in the area, while in winter, the lodge rents cross-country skis to its guests.

HC 61, P.O. Box 335, Alpine, AZ 85920. © **928/428-2225** or 928/339-4370. www.hannaganmeadow.com. 18 units. $55–$175 double. MC, V. Lodge room rates include full breakfast. Pets accepted in cabins spring through fall. **Amenities:** Restaurant (American); general store; bike rentals. *In room:* No phone.

Tal-Wi-Wi Lodge Located 3 miles north of Alpine on U.S. 191, Tal-Wi-Wi Lodge is nothing fancy—just a rustic lodge popular with anglers and hunters—but it's the best choice in the area. The deluxe rooms come with a hot tub or woodstove (one unit has both), heat sources that are well appreciated on cold winter nights (Alpine is often the coldest town in Arizona). The furnishings are rustic yet comfortable, and the wood-paneled walls and large front porches give the lodge a classic country flavor. The dining room serves country breakfasts and dinners.

U.S. 191 (P.O. Box 169), Alpine, AZ 85920. © **800/476-2695** or 928/339-4319. Fax 928/339-1962. www. talwiwilodge.com. 20 units. $69–$99 double. 2-night minimum stay on holidays. MC, V. Dogs accepted ($10 per day). **Amenities:** Restaurant (American); lounge. *In room:* Coffeemaker, no phone.

Tucson

Encircled by mountain ranges and bookended by the two units of Saguaro National Park, Tucson is Arizona's second-largest city, and for the vacationer it has everything that Phoenix has to offer, plus a bit more. There are world-class golf resorts, excellent restaurants, art museums and galleries, an active cultural life, and, of course, plenty of great weather. Tucson also has a long history that melds Native American, Hispanic, and Anglo roots. And with a national park, a national forest, and other natural areas just beyond the city limits, Tucson is a city that celebrates its Sonoran Desert setting.

At Saguaro National Park, you can marvel at the massive saguaro cacti that have come to symbolize the desert Southwest, while at the Arizona–Sonora Desert Museum (actually a zoo), you can acquaint yourself with the myriad flora and fauna of this region. Take a hike or a horseback ride up one of the trails that leads into the wilderness from the edge of the city, and you might even meet up with a few desert denizens on their own turf. Look beyond the saguaros and prickly pears, and you'll find a desert oasis, complete with waterfalls and swimming holes, and, a short drive from the city, a pine forest that's home to the southernmost ski area in the United States.

Founded by the Spanish in 1775, Tucson was built on the site of a much older Native American village, and the city's name comes from the Pima Indian word *chukeson,* which means "spring at the base of black mountain," a reference to the peak now known

simply as "A Mountain." From 1867 to 1877, Tucson was the territorial capital of Arizona, but eventually the capital was moved to Phoenix. Consequently, Tucson did not develop as quickly as Phoenix and still holds fast to its Hispanic and Western heritage.

Tucson has a history of valuing quality of life over development, which sets it apart from the Phoenix area. Back in the days of urban renewal, its citizens turned back the bulldozers and managed to preserve at least some of the city's old Mexican character. Likewise, today, in the face of the sort of sprawl that has given Phoenix the feel of a landlocked Los Angeles, advocates for controlled growth are fighting hard to preserve both Tucson's desert environment and the city's unique character.

The struggle to retain an identity distinct from other Southwestern cities is ongoing, and despite long, drawn-out attempts to breathe life into the city's core, known as the Tucson Downtown Arts District, the past few years have seen the loss of downtown's vibrancy as shops, galleries, and restaurants have moved out to the suburbs. However, downtown Tucson still has its art museum, convention center, and historic neighborhoods, and there is still a belief that this part of the city will one day find its stride.

Despite this minor shortcoming, Tucson remains Arizona's most beautiful and most livable city. With the Santa Catalina Mountains for a backdrop, Tucson boasts one of the most dramatic settings in the Southwest, and whether you're taking in the mountain vistas from the tee box of the 12th hole, the saddle of a palomino, or a table for two, we're sure you'll agree that Tucson makes a superb winter vacation destination.

1 Orientation

Not nearly as large and spread out as Phoenix and the Valley of the Sun, Tucson is small enough to be convenient, yet large enough to be sophisticated. The mountains ringing Tucson are bigger and closer to town than those in the Phoenix and Scottsdale area, which gives Tucson a more dramatic skyline. The desert is also closer and more easily accessed here than in Phoenix.

ARRIVING

BY PLANE   Located 6 miles south of downtown, **Tucson International Airport** (✆ 520/573-8000; www.tucsonairport.org) is served by the following major airlines: **Alaska/Horizon** (✆ 800/426-0333; http://horizonair.alaskaair. com), **America West** (✆ 800/235-9292; www.americawest.com), **American** (✆ 800/433-7300; www.aa.com), **Continental** (✆ 800/525-0280; www. continental.com), **Delta** (✆ 800/221-1212; www.delta.com), **Frontier** (✆ 800/ 432-1359; www.flyfrontier.com), **Northwest/KLM** (✆ 800/225-2525; www. nwa.com), **Southwest** (✆ 800/435-9792; www.southwest.com), and **United** (✆ 800/241-6522; www.ual.com).

Visitor centers in both baggage-claim areas can give you brochures and reserve a hotel room if you haven't done so already.

Many resorts and hotels in Tucson provide free or competitively priced airport shuttle service. **Arizona Stagecoach** (✆ **520/889-1000;** www.arizonastagecoach. com) operates 24-hour van service to downtown Tucson and the foothills resorts. Fares to downtown are around $17 one-way and $29 round-trip ($20 and $35 for a couple), and to the foothills resorts around $30 one-way and $48 round-trip ($38 and $64 for a couple). It takes between 45 minutes and 1 hour to reach the foothills resorts. To return to the airport, it's best to call at least a day before your scheduled departure.

You'll also find taxis waiting outside baggage claim, or you can call **Yellow Cab** (✆ 520/623-7308) or **Allstate Cab** (✆ **520/881-2227**). The flag-drop rate at the airport is $4.50 and then $1.50 per mile. A taxi to downtown costs around $19, to the foothills resorts about $25 to $40.

Sun Tran (✆ **520/792-9222;** www.suntran.com), the local public transit system, operates bus service to and from the airport. The fare is $1. Route no. 6, to downtown, runs Monday through Friday from about 4:50am to 7:20pm, Saturday from about 7:20am to 6:20pm, and Sunday from about 6:20am to 5:20pm. Departures are every 30 minutes on weekdays and every hour on weekends. It takes 40 to 50 minutes to reach downtown. Route no. 11 operates on a similar schedule and travels along Alvernon Road to the midtown area.

BY CAR   I-10, the main east–west interstate across the southern United States, passes through Tucson as it swings north to Phoenix. **I-19** connects Tucson with the Mexican border at Nogales. **Ariz. 86** heads southwest into the Papago Indian Reservation, and **Ariz. 79** leads north toward Florence and eventually connects with **U.S. 60** into Phoenix.

If you're headed downtown, take the Congress Street exit off I-10. If you're going to one of the foothills resorts north of downtown, you'll probably want to take the Ina Road exit off I-10.

BY TRAIN   Tucson is served by **Amtrak** (© **800/872-7245;** www.amtrak.
com) passenger rail service. The *Sunset Limited,* which runs between Orlando
and Los Angeles, stops in Tucson. The **train station** is at 400 E. Toole Ave.
(© **520/623-4442**), in the heart of downtown and within walking distance of
the Tucson Convention Center, El Presidio Historic District, and a few hotels.
You'll see taxis waiting to meet the train.

BY BUS   **Greyhound** (© **800/229-9424** or 520/792-3475; www.greyhound.
com) connects Tucson to the rest of the United States through its extensive system. The bus station is downtown at 2 S. Fourth Ave., across the street from the
Hotel Congress.

VISITOR INFORMATION
The **Metropolitan Tucson Convention and Visitors Bureau (MTCVB),** 100
S. Church Ave. (at Broadway), Suite 7199 (© **800/638-8350** or 520/624-1817;
www.visitTucson.org), is an excellent source of information on Tucson and
environs. The visitor center is open Monday through Friday from 8am to 5pm,
Saturday and Sunday from 9am to 4pm.

CITY LAYOUT
MAIN ARTERIES & STREETS   Tucson is laid out on a grid that's fairly regular in the downtown areas, but becomes less orderly the farther you go from the
city center. In the flatlands, major thoroughfares are spaced at 1-mile intervals,
with smaller streets filling in the squares created by the major roads. In the
foothills, where Tucson's most recent growth has occurred, the grid system
breaks down completely because of the hilly terrain.

The main **east–west roads** are (from south to north) 22nd Street, Broadway
Boulevard, Speedway Boulevard, Grant Road (with Tanque Verde Rd. as an
extension), and Ina Road/Skyline Drive/Sunrise Road. The main **north–south
roads** are (from west to east) Miracle Mile/Oracle Road, Stone/Sixth Avenue,
Campbell Avenue, Country Club Road, Alvernon Road, and Swan Road. **I-10**
cuts diagonally across the Tucson metropolitan area from northwest to southeast.

In **downtown Tucson,** Congress Street and Broadway Boulevard are the main
east–west streets; Stone Avenue, Sixth Avenue, and Fourth Avenue are the main
north–south streets.

FINDING AN ADDRESS   Because Tucson is laid out on a grid, finding an
address is relatively easy. The zero (or starting) point for all Tucson addresses is
the corner of Stone Avenue, which runs north and south, and Congress Street,
which runs east and west. From this point, streets are designated either north,
south, east, or west. Addresses usually, but not always, increase by 100 with each
block, so that an address of 4321 E. Broadway Blvd. should be 43 blocks east of
Stone Avenue. In the downtown area, many of the streets and avenues are numbered, with numbered streets running east and west and numbered avenues running north and south.

STREET MAPS   The best way to find your way around Tucson is to pick up
a map at the visitor center at the airport or at the MTCVB (see "Visitor Information," above) for $2. The MTCVB also offers a free map in the *Tucson Offi-
cial Visitors Guide.* The maps handed out by car-rental agencies are not very
detailed, but will do for some purposes. Local gas stations also sell detailed maps.

Tucson at a Glance

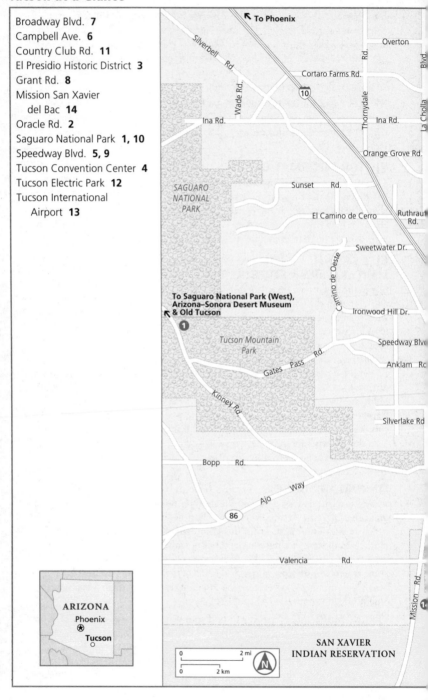

↖ To Phoenix

Silverbell Rd.

Overton Rd.

Blvd.

Cortaro Farms Rd.

Wade Rd.

10

Thornydale

La Cholla

Ina Rd.

Ina Rd.

Orange Grove Rd.

SAGUARO
NATIONAL
PARK

Sunset Rd.

El Camino de Cerro

Ruthrauf Rd.

Sweetwater Dr.

Camino de Oeste

**To Saguaro National Park (West),
Arizona–Sonora Desert Museum
↖ & Old Tucson**

Ironwood Hill Dr.

①

Tucson Mountain
Park

Speedway Blvd

Gates Pass Rd.

Anklam Rd

Kinney Rd.

Silverlake Rd

Bopp Rd.

Ajo Way

86

Mission Rd.

Valencia Rd.

ARIZONA
Phoenix
✪
Tucson
○

0   2 mi
0   2 km

N

SAN XAVIER
INDIAN RESERVATION

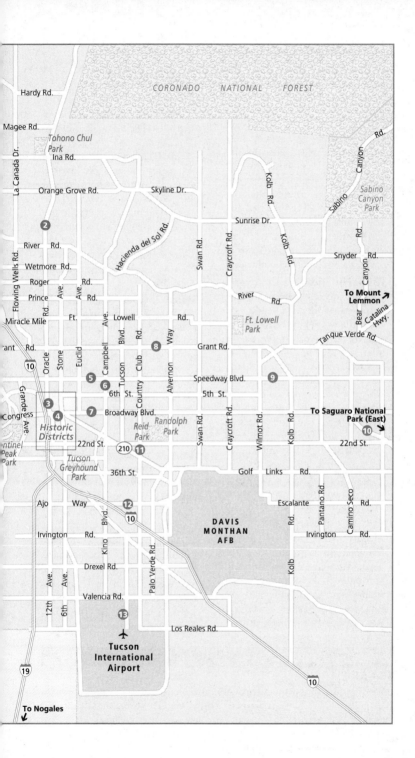

CORONADO NATIONAL FOREST

Hardy Rd.

Magee Rd.

Tohono Chul
Park

Ina Rd.

La Canada Dr.

Orange Grove Rd.

Skyline Dr.

Sunrise Dr.

Kolb Rd.

Kolb Rd.

Sabino Canyon Rd.

Sabino
Canyon
Park

2

Flowing Wells Rd.

River Rd.

Wetmore Rd.

Roger Rd.

Prince Rd.

Miracle Mile

Hacienda del Sol Rd.

Swan Rd.

Craycroft Rd.

Snyder Rd.

To Mount
Lemmon

Bear Canyon Rd.

Catalina Hwy.

River Rd.

Tanque Verde Rd.

Oracle Rd.

Stone Ave.

Euclid Ave.

Campbell Ave.

Ft.

Tucson Blvd.

Country Club Rd.

Lowell

Alvernon Way

Rd.

Ft. Lowell
Park

ant Rd.

10

5

6

Grant Rd.

8

Speedway Blvd.

9

6th St.

5th St.

To Saguaro National
Park (East)

Grandes Ave.

Congress

3

4

7

Broadway Blvd.

Reid
Park

Randolph
Park

Swan Rd.

Craycroft Rd.

Wilmot Rd.

Kolb Rd.

10

ntinel
eak
ark

Historic
Districts

22nd St.

210

11

22nd St.

Tucson
Greyhound
Park

36th St.

Golf Links Rd.

Ajo Way

12

10

Escalante Rd.

Pantano Rd.

Camino Seco Rd.

Irvington Rd.

Kino Blvd.

DAVIS
MONTHAN
AFB

Irvington Rd.

Drexel Rd.

12th Ave.

6th Ave.

Palo Verde Rd.

Kolb

Valencia Rd.

13

19

Tucson
International
Airport

Los Reales Rd.

10

To Nogales

NEIGHBORHOODS IN BRIEF

El Presidio Historic District Named for the Spanish military garrison that once stood on this site, the neighborhood is bounded by Alameda Street on the south, Main Avenue on the west, Franklin Street on the north, and Church Avenue on the east. El Presidio was the city's most affluent neighborhood in the 1880s, and many large homes from that period have been restored and now house restaurants, arts-and-crafts galleries, and a bed-and-breakfast inn. The Tucson Museum of Art anchors the neighborhood.

Barrio Histórico District Another 19th-century neighborhood, the Barrio Histórico is bounded on the north by Cushing Street, on the west by the railroad tracks, on the south by 18th Street, and on the east by Stone Avenue. The Barrio Histórico is characterized by Sonoran-style adobe row houses that directly abut the street with no yards, a style typical in Mexican towns. Although a few restaurants and galleries dot the neighborhood, most restored buildings serve as offices. This is still a borderline neighborhood where restoration is a slow, ongoing process, so try to avoid it late at night.

Armory Park Historic District Bounded by 12th Street on the north, Stone Avenue on the west, 19th Street on the south, and Second Avenue and Third Avenue on the east, the Armory Park neighborhood was Tucson's first historic district. Today, this area is in the midst of an ongoing renaissance.

Downtown Arts District This neighborhood encompasses a bit of the Armory District, a bit of El Presidio District, and the stretch of Congress Street and Broadway Boulevard west of Toole Avenue. Although the area is home to several galleries, nightclubs, and hip cafes, it continues to struggle to survive as an arts district. It is mostly frequented by the young and the homeless. Many young travelers make the Hotel Congress their base while in Tucson.

Fourth Avenue Running from University Boulevard in the north to Ninth Street in the south, Fourth Avenue is the favored shopping district of cash-strapped college students. Shops specialize primarily in ethnic and used/vintage clothing as well as handcrafted items from around the world. Twice a year, in spring and late fall, the street is closed to traffic for a street fair. Plenty of restaurants, bars, and clubs make this the city's favorite college nightlife district as well.

The Foothills Encompassing a huge area of northern Tucson, the foothills contain the city's most affluent neighborhoods. Elegant shopping plazas, modern malls, world-class resorts, golf courses, and expensive residential neighborhoods are surrounded by hilly desert at the foot of the Santa Catalina Mountains.

2 Getting Around

BY CAR

Unless you plan to stay by the pool or on the golf course, you'll probably want to rent a car. Luckily, rates are fairly economical. At press time, Alamo was charging $137 per week ($176 with taxes and surcharges included) for a compact car with unlimited mileage in Tucson. See "Getting Around" in chapter 2 for general tips on car rentals in Arizona.

The following agencies have offices at Tucson International Airport as well as other locations in the area. Because taxes and surcharges add up to about 28% on car rentals at the airport, you might want to consider renting at some other location, where you can avoid paying some of these fees. Among the Tucson car-rental agencies are **Alamo** (© 800/327-9633 or 520/807-0446), **Avis** (© 800/331-1212 or 520/294-1494), **Budget** (© 800/527-0700 or 520/573-8475), **Dollar** (© 800/800-4000 or 520/573-8486), **Enterprise** (© 800/736-8222 or 520/573-5336), **Hertz** (© 800/654-3131 or 520/573-5201), and **National** (© 800/227-7368 or 520/806-4255).

Downtown Tucson is still a relatively easy place to find a parking space, and parking fees are low. There are two huge parking lots at the south side of the Tucson Convention Center, a couple of small lots on either side of the Tucson Museum of Art (one at Main Ave. and Paseo Redondo, south of El Presidio Historic District, and one at the corner of Council St. and Court Ave.), and parking garages beneath the main library (101 N. Stone Ave.) and El Presidio Park (on Alameda St.). You'll find plenty of metered parking on the smaller downtown streets. Almost all Tucson hotels and resorts provide free parking.

Lanes on several major avenues in Tucson change direction at rush hour to facilitate traffic flow, so pay attention to signs. These tell you the time and direction of traffic in the lanes.

BY PUBLIC TRANSPORTATION

BY BUS   Covering much of the Tucson metropolitan area, **Sun Tran** (© **520/792-9222;** www.suntran.com) public buses are $1 for adults and students, 40¢ for seniors, and free for children 5 and under. Day passes are available on buses for $2.

The **Downtown-Ronstadt Transit Center,** at Congress Street and Sixth Avenue, is served by about 30 regular and express bus routes to all parts of Tucson. The bus system does not extend to such tourist attractions as the Arizona–Sonora Desert Museum, Old Tucson, Saguaro National Park, or the foothills resorts, and thus is of limited use to visitors. However, Sun Tran does provide a shuttle for sports games and special events. Call the above phone number for information.

BY TROLLEY   Although they don't go very far, the restored electric streetcars of **Old Pueblo Trolley** (© **520/792-1802;** oldpueblotrolley.org) are a fun way to get from the Fourth Avenue shopping district to the University of Arizona. The trolleys operate on Friday from 6 to 10pm, Saturday from noon to midnight, and Sunday from noon to 6pm. The fare is $1 for adults and 50¢ for children 6 to 12. The fare on Sunday is only 25¢ for all riders. Friday and Saturday all-day passes are $2.50 for adults and $1.25 for children.

T.I.C.E.T., or Tucson Inner City Express Transit (© **520/791-5071**), operates three free downtown-area shuttles. For visitors, the only route that is of much use is the Blue Route, which has stops near the visitor center, the Tucson Convention Center, the Tucson Children's Museum, Old Town Artisans, and the Tucson Museum of Art. Blue Route buses operate Monday through Friday and run every 10 to 20 minutes between 7am and 5:30pm.

BY TAXI

If you need a taxi, you'll have to phone for one. **AAA Yellow Cab** (© **520/624-6611**) and **Allstate Cab** (© **520/881-2227**) provide service throughout the city. The flag-drop rate is between $1.90 and $2.25, and after that it's $1.50

per mile. Although distances in Tucson are not as great as those in Phoenix, it's still a good 10 or more miles from the foothills resorts to downtown Tucson, so expect to pay at least $10 for any taxi ride. Most resorts have shuttle vans or can arrange taxi service to major tourist attractions.

ON FOOT

Downtown Tucson is compact and easily explored on foot, and many old streets in the downtown historic neighborhoods are narrow and much easier to appreciate if you leave your car in a parking lot. Also, although several major attractions—including the Arizona–Sonora Desert Museum, Old Tucson Studios, Saguaro National Park, and Sabino Canyon—can only be reached by car, they require quite a bit of walking once you arrive. These attractions often have uneven footing, so be sure to bring a good pair of walking shoes.

FAST FACTS: Tucson

Babysitters Most hotels can arrange a sitter for you, and many resorts feature special programs for children on weekends and throughout the summer. If your hotel can't help, call **A-1 Messner Sitter Service** (© 520/881-1578), which will send a sitter to your hotel.

Car Rentals See "Getting Around," above.

Dentist Call the Arizona Dental Association (© **800/866-2732**) or Dental Referral Service (© **800/669-4435**) for a referral.

Doctor For a doctor referral, ask at your hotel or call University Health Connection (© **520/694-8888**).

Emergencies For fire, police, or medical emergency, phone © **911.**

Eyeglass Repair **Alvernon Optical** has several stores around town where you can have your glasses repaired or replaced. Locations include 440 N. Alvernon Way (© **520/327-6211**), 7043 N. Oracle Rd. (© **520/297-2501**), and 7123 E. Tanque Verde Rd. (© **520/296-4157**).

Hospitals The **Tucson Medical Center** is at 5301 E. Grant Rd. (© **520/327-5461**). The **University Medical Center** is at 1501 N. Campbell Ave. (© **520/694-0111**).

Information See "Visitor Information" in "Orientation," above.

Internet Access Internet access is free at the main public **library,** in downtown Tucson at 101 N. Stone Ave. (© **520/791-4393**).

Lost Property If you lose something at the airport, call © **520/573-8156**; if you lose something on a Sun Tran bus, call © **520/792-9222.**

Newspapers & Magazines The *Arizona Daily Star* is Tucson's morning daily, while the *Tucson Citizen* is the afternoon daily. The *Tucson Weekly* is the city's news-and-arts journal, published on Thursdays.

Pharmacies Call © **800/WALGREENS** for the Walgreens pharmacy that's nearest you; some are open 24 hours a day.

Police In case of an emergency, phone © **911.**

Post Office There's a post office in downtown Tucson at 141 S. Sixth Ave. (© **800/275-8777** or 520/903-1958; www.usps.com), open Monday through Friday from 8:30am to 5pm.

Radio **KXCI** (91.3 FM) has an alternative mix of programming and is a favorite with local Tucsonans, while **KUAT** (90.5 FM) has all-classical programming and is a good station for news. **KUAZ** (89.1 FM) is the National Public Radio station.

Safety Tucson is surprisingly safe for a city of its size. However, the Downtown Arts District isn't all that lively after dark, and attracts a lot of street people and panhandlers. Be particularly alert if you're down here for a performance of some sort. Just to the south of downtown lies a poorer section of the city that's best avoided after dark unless you are certain of where you're going. Otherwise, take the same precautions you would in any other city.

When driving, be aware that many streets in the Tucson area are subject to flooding when it rains. Heed warnings about possible flooded areas and don't try to cross a low area that has become flooded. Find an alternate route instead.

Taxes In addition to the 5.6% sales tax levied by the state, Tucson levies a 2% city sales tax. Car-rental taxes, surcharges, and fees add up to around 28%. The hotel tax in the Tucson area is usually 10.5% to 11.5%.

Taxis See "Getting Around," above.

Weather For the local weather forecast, call the **National Weather Service** (© **520/881-3333**).

3 Where to Stay

Although Phoenix still holds the title of Resort Capital of Arizona, Tucson is not far behind, and this city's resorts boast much more spectacular settings than most comparable properties in Phoenix and Scottsdale. As far as nonresort accommodations go, Tucson has a wider variety than Phoenix—partly because several historic neighborhoods have become home to bed-and-breakfast inns. The presence of several guest ranches within a 20-minute drive of Tucson also adds to the city's diversity of accommodations. Business and budget travelers are well served with all-suite and conference hotels, as well as plenty of budget chain motels.

At the more expensive hotels and resorts, summer rates, usually in effect from May to September or October, are often less than half what they are in winter. Surprisingly, temperatures usually aren't unbearable in May or September, which makes these good times to visit if you're looking to save money. When making late spring or early fall reservations, always be sure to ask when rates are scheduled to go up or down. If you aren't coming to Tucson specifically for the winter gem and mineral shows, then you'll save quite a bit if you avoid the last week in January and the first 2 weeks in February, when hotels around town generally charge exorbitant rates.

Most hotels offer special packages, weekend rates, various discounts (such as for AARP or AAA members), and free accommodations for children, so it helps to ask about these when you reserve. Nearly all hotels have smoke-free and wheelchair-accessible rooms.

BED & BREAKFASTS   If you're looking to stay in a B&B, several agencies can help. The **Arizona Association of Bed and Breakfast Inns** (© **800/284-2589;**

Tucson Accommodations

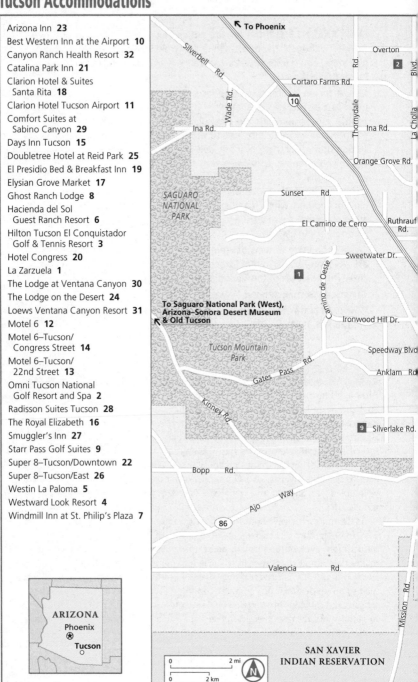

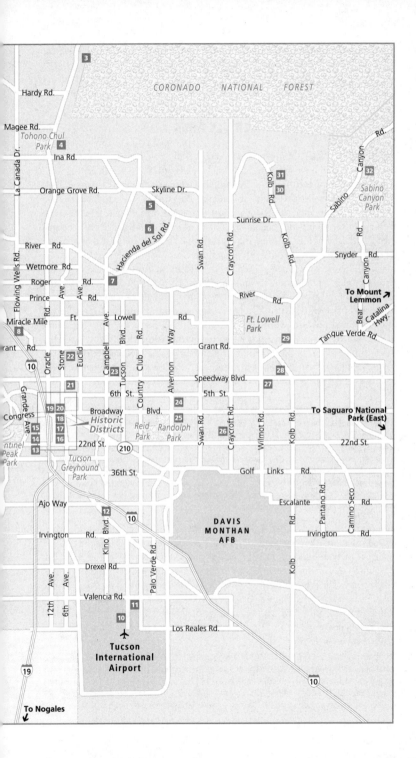

CORONADO   NATIONAL   FOREST

Hardy Rd.

Magee Rd.

Tohono Chul
Park

Ina Rd.

Orange Grove Rd.

Skyline Dr.

La Canada Dr.

Flowing Wells Rd.

River   Rd.

Wetmore Rd.

Roger   Rd.

Prince   Rd.

Miracle Mile

Grant   Rd.

Hacienda del Sol Rd.

Swan Rd.

Craycroft Rd.

Sunrise Dr.

Kolb Rd.

Kolb Rd.

Sabino   Canyon   Rd.

Snyder   Rd.

Sabino
Canyon
Park

To Mount
Lemmon

Bear   Canyon Rd.

Catalina Hwy.

River   Rd.

Ft. Lowell
Park

Tanque Verde Rd.

Ft.

Lowell

Rd.

Grant Rd.

Campbell   Ave.

Stone   Ave.

Oracle Rd.

Euclid   Ave.

Ft.   Blvd.

Country   Club   Rd.

Way

Alvernon   Way

To Saguaro National
Park (East)

10

Speedway Blvd.

6th St.

5th St.

Grande Ave.

Congress

Broadway

Historic
Districts

22nd St.

Reid
Park

Blvd.

Randolph
Park

Swan Rd.

Craycroft Rd.

Wilmot Rd.

Kolb Rd.

22nd St.

ntinel
Peak
Park

Tucson
Greyhound
Park

210

36th St.

Golf   Links   Rd.

Ajo Way

Irvington   Rd.

Kino Blvd.

Palo Verde Rd.

10

Drexel Rd.

DAVIS
MONTHAN
AFB

Escalante   Rd.

Pantano Rd.

Camino Seco   Rd.

Irvington   Rd.

Kolb   Rd.

12th Ave.

6th Ave.

Valencia Rd.

Los Reales Rd.

19

Tucson
International
Airport

10

To Nogales

www.arizona-bed-breakfast.com) has several members in Tucson. **Mi Casa Su Casa** (© **800/456-0682** or 480/990-0682; www.azres.com) will book you into one of its many homestays (informal B&Bs) in the Tucson area or elsewhere in the state, as will **Arizona Trails Reservation Service** (© **888/799-4284** or 480/837-4284; www.arizonatrails.com), which also books tour and hotel reservations.

DOWNTOWN & THE UNIVERSITY AREA
EXPENSIVE

Arizona Inn 🐥🐥🐥   With its pink-stucco buildings and immaculately tended flower gardens, the Arizona Inn is a 14-acre oasis of tranquillity in central Tucson. Originally opened in 1930 by Isabella Greenway, Arizona's first congresswoman, the inn is still family owned and operated, and is imbued with a gracious character and Old Arizona charm you won't find elsewhere in the state. Sipping coffee on a patio, playing a game of croquet, taking high tea (complimentary) in the library, or lounging by the pool, I always feel as if this were my second home. It's easy to imagine that slower-paced time when guests would spend the entire winter here. Guest rooms all vary in size and decor, but most have a mix of reproduction antiques and original pieces custom made for the inn's opening by World War I veterans with disabilities. Guest rooms also have such modern amenities as DVD players (and access to a library of films featuring actors and actresses who were once inn guests). Some units have gas fireplaces, and most suites have private patios or enclosed sun porches. The inn's main dining room (p. 343) is a casually elegant space, and the newly restored bar has a nightly pianist. The pool, although small by today's standards, is surrounded by fragrant flowering trees and vines. Gracious, welcoming, and comfortable, the Arizona Inn is an unforgettable place to spend a vacation.

2200 E. Elm St., Tucson, AZ 85719. © 800/933-1093 or 520/325-1541. Fax 520/320-2182. www.arizona inn.com. 86 units. Mid-Jan to mid-Apr from $259 double, from $319 suite; mid-Apr to May $199 double, from $259 suite; June to mid-Sept from $154 double, from $249 suite; mid-Sept to mid-Dec $169 double, from $249 suite; mid-Dec to mid-Jan $199 double, from $279 suite. Summer rates include full breakfast and complimentary evening ice-cream fountain. Children 2 and under stay free in parent's room (10 and under during summer). AE, DC, MC, V. **Amenities:** 3 restaurants (French/American, International); 2 lounges; heated outdoor pool; 2 Har-Tru clay tennis courts; croquet; well-equipped exercise room; access to nearby health club; saunas; bikes; concierge; business center; room service; massage; babysitting; laundry service; dry cleaning. *In room:* A/C, TV/DVD, fridge, dataport, hair dryer, iron.

The Lodge on the Desert 🐥🐥   Dating from 1936 and set amid neatly manicured lawns and flower gardens, the Lodge on the Desert is a classic old Arizona resort. It offers a lush and relaxing retreat that looks a lot like the Arizona Inn (though certainly not as deluxe and without the emphasis on superb service). Guest rooms are in hacienda-style adobe buildings tucked amid cacti and orange trees. Inside the rooms, you'll find a mix of contemporary and Southwestern furnishings; many units have beamed ceilings or fireplaces, and some are carpeted while others have tile floors. Although the pool is very small, it has a good view of the Catalinas.

306 N. Alvernon Way, Tucson, AZ 85711. © 800/456-5634 or 520/325-3366. www.lodgeonthedesert.com. 35 units. Early Jan to mid-Apr $189–$269 double; mid-Apr to mid-May and mid-Oct to mid-Jan $129–$149 double; mid-May to mid-Oct $99–$119 double. Rates include full breakfast. Children under 15 stay free in parent's room. AE, DC, DISC, MC, V. Pets accepted ($15 per night). **Amenities:** Restaurant (Southwestern); lounge; small outdoor pool; concierge; room service; dry cleaning. *In room:* A/C, TV, coffeemaker, hair dryer, iron.

MODERATE

Catalina Park Inn 🐥🐥   Located close to downtown and overlooking a shady park, this 1927 home has been lovingly restored by owners Mark Hall and Paul

Richard. From the outside, the inn has the look of a Mediterranean villa, while many interesting and playful touches enliven the classic interior. The huge Catalina Room in the basement is one of our favorites. Not only does it conjure up the inside of an adobe, but it also has a whirlpool tub in a former cedar closet and a separate toilet room with a display of colorful Fiesta Ware. Two upstairs rooms have balconies, while two units in a separate cottage across the garden offer more contemporary styling than the rooms in the main house.

309 E. First St., Tucson, AZ 85705. ℂ **800/792-4885** or 520/792-4541. www.catalinaparkinn.com. 6 units. $136–$166 double (lower rates in late spring and fall). Rates include full breakfast. AE, DISC, MC, V. No children under 11. **Amenities:** Concierge. *In room:* A/C, TV, dataport, hair dryer, iron, free local calls.

Doubletree Hotel at Reid Park ★★ I've always liked this in-town high-rise hotel for its location across the street from the Randolph Park municipal golf course and for its pleasant orange-tree-shaded pool area. After the hotel's recent renovation, I like it even more. Not only do the guest rooms boast bright new colors, but there's also a big new exercise room by the pool. The only sad thing is that the citrus trees are getting so old that some have to be taken out. The Doubletree is midway between the airport and downtown Tucson and is something of an in-town budget golf resort. Although the hotel does a lot of convention business and sometimes feels crowded, the gardens, with their citrus trees (feel free to pick the fruit) and lawns, are almost always tranquil. Guest rooms are divided between a nine-story building that offers views of the valley (even-numbered rooms face the pool, odd-numbered rooms face the mountains) and a two-story building with patio rooms overlooking the garden and pool area. The recent renovation has given the guest rooms not only bright colors but a bold contemporary design.

445 S. Alvernon Way, Tucson, AZ 85711. ℂ **800/222-TREE** or 520/881-4200. Fax 520/323-5225. www.dtreidpark.com. 295 units. Mid-Sept to mid-May $119–$289 double, from $194 suite; late May to early Sept $69–$129 double, from $140 suite. Children under 18 stay free in parent's room. AE, DC, DISC, MC, V. Pets accepted ($25 fee). **Amenities:** 3 restaurants (Southwestern, American); 2 lounges; outdoor pool; 3 tennis courts; Jacuzzi; large exercise room; business center; room service; massage; laundry service; dry cleaning. *In room:* A/C, TV, dataport, high-speed Internet access, coffeemaker, hair dryer, iron, wi-fi.

El Presidio Bed & Breakfast Inn ★★ Built in 1886 and lovingly restored by innkeeper Patti Toci, El Presidio is a mix of Victorian and adobe architectural styles and is located in Tucson's most attractive historic district. Located only steps from the Tucson Museum of Art (p. 363), Old Town Artisans (p. 369), and El Charro Café (p. 343), this is the quintessential Tucson territorial home. There are two high-ceilinged suites in the main house, while the other two units, both with kitchenettes, are arranged around a shady courtyard at the center of which is a Mexican fountain. All are decorated with antiques and original art. In addition to the filling breakfast served in the sunroom, complimentary drinks, fruit, and treats are offered in the afternoon and evening.

297 N. Main Ave., Tucson, AZ 85701. ℂ **800/349-6151** or 520/623-6151. Fax 520/623-3860. 4 units. $105–$135 double. Rates include full breakfast. 2-night minimum stay Oct–May. No credit cards. Children 5 and over are welcome. **Amenities:** Access to nearby health club; guest laundry. *In room:* A/C, TV, coffeemaker, hair dryer, iron.

Elysian Grove Market ★ *(Finds)* Located in the Barrio Histórico just a block away from El Tiradito shrine, this former general store (the building still has the old store name painted on the front wall) is now an unusual little inn filled with rustic Mexican antiques and Hispanic folk art. The two suites contain high-ceilinged living rooms that incorporate all manner of salvaged architectural details, colorful textiles, and original grocery-store fixtures (including an old walk-in meat locker that has been turned into a kitchen). Each unit has a bedroom on the ground level and a second bedroom (rather dark but cool) down a flight of steps. Although this funky barrio B&B isn't for everyone, I love the old Mexican atmosphere and abundance of Hispanic art. Travelers searching for the unusual and real sense of place just may appreciate this inn as well.

400 W. Simpson St., Tucson, AZ 85701. © 520/628-1522. www.elysiangrove.com. 2 units. $85 double. Rates include continental/Mexican breakfast. No credit cards. **Amenities:** Access to nearby health club; massage. *In room:* No phone.

The Royal Elizabeth ★★ Just a block away from the Temple of Music and Art in downtown Tucson, the Royal Elizabeth is an 1878 Victorian adobe home in many ways quite similar to the nearby El Presidio B&B. This home's odd combination of architectural styles makes for a uniquely Southwestern-style inn. In classic 19th-century Tucson fashion, the old home looks thoroughly unpretentious from the outside, but inside you'll find beautiful woodwork and gorgeous Victorian-era antique furnishings. Guest rooms open off a large, high-ceilinged central hall, which was a style commonplace in the old adobe homes of this area. The immediate neighborhood isn't as attractive as the El Presidio neighborhood surrounding the Tucson Museum of Art, but the museum, and several good restaurants, are within walking distance.

204 S. Scott Ave., Tucson, AZ 85701. © 877/670-9022 or 520/670-9022. Fax 520/629-9710. www.royal elizabeth.com. 6 units. Sept–May $130–$180 double; June–Aug $90–$130 double. Rates include full breakfast. AE, DISC, MC, V. **Amenities:** Outdoor pool; access to nearby health club; Jacuzzi; business center; massage. *In room:* A/C, TV/VCR, dataport, fridge, hair dryer, iron, safe, free local calls.

INEXPENSIVE

In addition to the choices listed below, you'll find dozens of budget chain motels along I-10 as it passes through downtown. Among the better ones are **Days Inn Tucson,** 222 S. Freeway, Exit 258 (© **520/791-7511**), charging $45 to $69 double; **Motel 6–Tucson/Congress Street,** 960 S. Freeway, Exit 258 (© **520/628-1339**), charging $46 to $56, and **Motel 6–Tucson/22nd Street,** 1222 S. Freeway, Exit 259 (© **520/624-2516**), charging $44 to $54; and **Super 8–Tucson/Downtown,** 1248 N. Stone St., Exit 257 (© **520/622-6446**), with rates of $59 to $120.

Clarion Hotel & Suites Santa Rita ★ *Value* This hotel, only a block from the convention center and close to El Presidio Historic District, isn't exactly luxurious, and you'd never know that the building is nearly 100 years old. However, the hotel does make a decent, economical downtown hotel choice. Although the place stays busy with conventioneers, it can also be a good choice for vacationers. Some of the guest rooms have balconies, and those on the higher floors have views. If you need lots of space, consider the two-story loft rooms. However, as far as I'm concerned, the best reason to stay here is that the hotel is home to Café Poca Cosa (p. 342), one of Tucson's most innovative Mexican restaurants and a personal favorite of mine.

88 E. Broadway Blvd., Tucson, AZ 85701. © 800/CLARION or 520/622-4000. Fax 520/620-0376. www.clarion hotel.com. 161 units. $79–$129 double; $104–$154 suite. Rates include full breakfast. Children under 18 stay free in parent's room. AE, DC, DISC, MC, V. Pets accepted ($25 per night). **Amenities:** Restaurant (Mexican); small outdoor pool; exercise room; Jacuzzi; sauna; business center; coin-op laundry; dry cleaning. *In room:* A/C, TV, dataport, fridge, coffeemaker, hair dryer, iron, free local calls.

Ghost Ranch Lodge ★ Finds   Although Miracle Mile was once Tucson's main drag, today it looks pretty shabby. Ghost Ranch Lodge, which opened in 1941, is one exception. If you're looking for affordable Old Tucson, this is it. Situated on 8 acres, the lodge has a fascinating cactus garden, plus orange trees and extensive lawns that together create an oasis atmosphere. Guest rooms have a bit of Western flavor, with beamed ceilings, painted brick walls, and patios covered by red-tile roofs. The lodge's dining room has a poolside patio and a view of the Santa Catalina Mountains.

801 W. Miracle Mile, Tucson, AZ 85705. © **800/456-7565** or 520/791-7565. Fax 520/791-3898. www.ghost ranchlodge.com. 83 units. Late Dec to Mar $86–$130 double; Apr–May and Oct to mid-Dec $56–$90 double; June–Sept $46–$75 double. Rates include continental breakfast. Children under 12 stay free in parent's room. AE, DC, DISC, MC, V. Pets accepted. **Amenities:** Restaurant (American); small outdoor pool; Jacuzzi; coin-op laundry; dry cleaning. *In room:* A/C, TV, dataport.

Hotel Congress Finds   Located in the heart of downtown Tucson conveniently near the Greyhound and Amtrak stations, the Hotel Congress, built in 1919 to serve railroad passengers, once played host to John Dillinger. Today, it operates as a budget hotel and youth hostel catering primarily to backpacking European travelers. Although the place is far from luxurious, the lobby has been restored to its original Southwestern elegance (straight out of a film-noir set). With antique telephones and old radios that really work, guest rooms remain true to their historical character, so don't expect anything fancy (like TVs). Some bathrooms have tubs only, while others have showers only. There's a classic little diner/cafe off the lobby (think Edward Hopper meets Gen X), as well as a tiny though very genuine Western bar. At night, the Club Congress (p. 387) is a popular (and loud) dance club (hotel guests can pick up free earplugs at the front desk).

311 E. Congress St., Tucson, AZ 85701. © **800/722-8848** or 520/622-8848. Fax 520/792-6366. www.hotel congress.com. 40 units. $49–$99 double; $20–$24 per person in shared hostel rooms. AE, DC, DISC, MC, V. Pets accepted ($10 per day). **Amenities:** Restaurant; saloon; nightclub.

Kids Family-Friendly Hotels

Loews Ventana Canyon Resort (p. 335)   With a playground, kids' club, croquet court, table tennis, and its own waterfall, this resort has plenty to keep the kids busy. There's also a hiking trail that starts from the edge of the property, and Sabino Canyon Recreation Area is nearby.

Smuggler's Inn (p. 334)   Built around a large central courtyard with a very tropical feel, this hotel is a good choice for families on a budget. In addition to a pool and whirlpool, there are lawns for the kids to play on and a meandering pond that's home to fish and ducks.

Westin La Paloma (p. 336)   Kids get their own lounge and game room here. In the summer and during holiday periods, special children's programs give parents a little free time. To top it all off, there's a great water slide in the pool area.

White Stallion Ranch (p. 341)   The Tucson area has several guest ranches, but this is the most family oriented of them. Kids can play cowboy to their hearts' content, ride the range, sing songs by the campfire, go for hayrides, and play with the critters in the petting zoo.

EAST TUCSON
MODERATE

Comfort Suites at Sabino Canyon ⭐   Although it looks rather stark from the outside and is located adjacent to a modern shopping center, this Comfort Suites is surprisingly pleasant inside. Built around four tranquil and lushly planted garden courtyards, the hotel has (for the most part) large rooms, some of which have kitchenettes. There's no restaurant on the premises, but there are plenty of good dining options nearby along Tanque Verde Road. This is a good economical choice close to Sabino Canyon, the Mount Lemmon Highway, and Saguaro National Park's east unit.

7007 E. Tanque Verde Rd., Tucson, AZ 85715. (© 800/424-6423 or 520/298-2300. Fax 520/298-6756. www.choicehotels.com. 90 units. Jan–Apr $89–$169; May–June and Oct–Dec $59–$109 double; July–Sept $49–$79 double. Rates include full breakfast and evening cocktails. Children 18 and under stay free in parent's room. AE, DC, DISC, MC, V. Pets accepted ($25 fee). **Amenities:** Small outdoor pool; access to nearby health club; Jacuzzi; coin-op laundry; dry cleaning. *In room:* A/C, TV, dataport, coffeemaker, hair dryer, iron.

Radisson Suites Tucson ⭐⭐ *Value*   Recently renovated and with large and very attractive rooms, this all-suite hotel is a good choice for both those who need plenty of space and those who want to be in the east-side business corridor. The five-story brick building is arranged around two long garden courtyards, one of which has a large pool and whirlpool. In fact, the pool and gardens are among the nicest at any non-resort hotel in Tucson and are the best reasons for vacationers to stay here.

6555 E. Speedway Blvd., Tucson, AZ 85710. (© 800/333-3333 or 520/721-7100. Fax 520/721-1991. www.radisson.com. 299 suites. Feb–Apr $219–$239 double; May and Oct–Jan $89–$159 double; June–Sept $69–$99 double. Children under 18 stay free in parent's room. AE, DC, DISC, MC, V. Pets accepted ($50 fee). **Amenities:** Restaurant (International); large outdoor pool; exercise room; access to nearby health club; Jacuzzi; concierge; business center; room service; coin-op laundry; dry cleaning. *In room:* A/C, TV, dataport, high-speed Internet access, fridge, coffeemaker, hair dryer, iron, wi-fi.

Smuggler's Inn ⭐ *Value* *Kids*   There's nothing about this comfortable, economical hotel to remind you that you're in the middle of the desert—in fact, the neatly trimmed lawns and tall palm trees give the gardens a tropical look—but the grounds are much nicer than those at most comparably priced hotels in the area. Amid these surroundings are a pool and a whirlpool that lend the place the feel of a budget tropical resort. If you bring the family, the kids will have plenty of space in which to run around, and will enjoy feeding the ducks that frequent the hotel's pond. Guest rooms are spacious, though a nothing fancy.

6350 E. Speedway Blvd. (at Wilmot), Tucson, AZ 85710. (© 800/525-8852 or 520/296-3292. Fax 520/722-3713. www.smugglersinn.com. 149 units. Feb–May $142 double; $162 suite; June–Aug $98 double, $118 suite; Sept–Jan $119–$129 double, $139–$149 suite. Rates include continental breakfast. Children under 18 stay free in parent's room. AE, DISC, MC, V. Pets accepted ($50 fee). **Amenities:** Restaurant; lounge; outdoor pool; putting green; access to nearby health club; Jacuzzi; room service; coin-op laundry; laundry service. *In room:* A/C, TV, dataport, coffeemaker, hair dryer, iron.

THE FOOTHILLS
VERY EXPENSIVE

Hilton Tucson El Conquistador Golf & Tennis Resort ⭐⭐⭐   Although this large resort is a bit out of the way, the view of the Santa Catalina Mountains rising up behind the property makes this northern foothills resort one of my favorites in Tucson. Sunsets are truly spectacular! Most guest rooms are built around a central courtyard with manicured lawns and a large pool that has a long water slide. The pool is popular with families, and anyone seeking a little more peace and quiet may want to opt for a room in the separate casitas area, which has its own pool. For the full Tucson experience, ask for a mountain-view room. All accommodations feature Southwestern-influenced contemporary furniture, spacious marble bathrooms, and balconies or patios. While golf on the resort's three courses is the favorite pastime, nongolfers have plenty of options, too.

10000 N. Oracle Rd., Tucson, AZ 85737. © 800/325-7832 or 520/544-5000. Fax 520/544-1224. www.hilton elconquistador.com. 428 units. Jan to late May $259–$490 double, from $339 suite; late May to early Sept $119–$290 double, from $179 suite; early Sept to Dec $219–$420 double, from $299 suite. Rates do not include $10 daily service fee. AE, DC, DISC, MC, V. Valet parking $11. Pets accepted ($75 deposit). **Amenities:** 5 restaurants (Southwestern, steakhouse, Mexican, American); 2 lounges; 4 pools; 1 9-hole golf and 2 18-hole golf courses; 31 tennis courts; 7 racquetball courts; basketball court; volleyball court; 2 exercise rooms; spa; 5 Jacuzzis; saunas; bike rentals; horseback riding; children's programs; concierge; tour desk; car-rental desk; courtesy shopping shuttle; business center; shopping arcade; salon; room service; massage; babysitting; laundry service; dry cleaning. *In room:* A/C, TV, dataport, minibar, coffeemaker, hair dryer, iron, safe.

The Lodge at Ventana Canyon ★★★ Golf is the name of the game at this boutique resort set within a gated country-club community at the base of the Santa Catalina Mountains. The lodge shares its two highly acclaimed Tom Fazio–designed courses with the nearby Loews Ventana Canyon Resort, and the third hole of the resort's Mountain Course plays across a deep ravine. This just might be the most photographed hole in Tucson. While both resorts are luxurious, this one features an added air of exclusivity. Stay here and you'll feel as though you are a member of an exclusive country club. Though small, the lodge manages to offer plenty of big-resort amenities and places an emphasis on personal service. The accommodations are in spacious suites, most of which have walls of windows facing the Catalinas, modern mission-style furnishings, small kitchens, and large bathrooms with oversize tubs (some are even the old-fashioned footed variety). A few units have balconies, cathedral ceilings, and spiral stairs that lead to sleeping lofts.

6200 N. Clubhouse Lane, Tucson, AZ 85750. © 800/828-5701 or 520/577-1400. Fax 520/577-4065. www.thelodgeatventanacanyon.com. 50 units. Jan to early Apr $279–$519 1-bedroom suite, $449–$719 2-bedroom suite; early Apr to mid-May $189–$419 1-bedroom suite, $359–$619 2-bedroom suite; mid-May to early Sept $99–$175 1-bedroom suite, $189–$275 2-bedroom suite; early Sept to Dec $179–$399 1-bedroom suite, $349–$599 2-bedroom suite. Rates do not include $16 nightly service charge. Children under 18 stay free in parent's room. AE, MC, V. Pets accepted ($50 fee). **Amenities:** Restaurant (New American); lounge; snack bar; outdoor pool; 2 acclaimed 18-hole golf courses; 12 tennis courts; playground; exercise room; Jacuzzi; saunas; bike rentals; concierge; car-rental desk; room service; massage and spa treatments; laundry service; dry cleaning. *In room:* A/C, TV, dataport, high-speed Internet access, kitchen, fridge, minibar, coffeemaker, hair dryer, iron, safe, wi-fi.

Loews Ventana Canyon Resort ★★★ *Kids* For breathtaking scenery, fascinating architecture, and superb resort facilities (including two Tom Fazio golf courses, a full-service spa, and lots of options for kids), no other Tucson resort can compare. The Santa Catalina Mountains rise behind the property, and despite its many amenities, the resort is firmly planted in the desert. Flagstone floors in the lobby give the public rooms a rugged but luxurious appeal. Guest rooms have plush beds with drapes hung from the headboards. Balconies overlook city lights or mountains, and some rooms have fireplaces. Bathrooms include tubs built for two. The Ventana Room (p. 351) is one of Tucson's finest restaurants, while the Flying V (p. 388) has good food and good views. The lobby lounge serves afternoon tea before becoming an evening piano bar. In addition to numerous other amenities, there are jogging and nature trails and a playground on the property.

7000 N. Resort Dr., Tucson, AZ 85750. © 800/234-5117 or 520/299-2020. Fax 520/299-6832. www.loews hotels.com. 398 units. Early Jan to late May $365 double, from $750 suite; late May to early Sept $150 double, from $295 suite; early Sept to early Jan $325 double, from $700 suite. Children under 18 stay free in parent's room. AE, DC, DISC, MC, V. **Amenities:** 5 restaurants (New American, Southwestern, American); 2 lounges; 2 outdoor pools; 2 acclaimed 18-hole golf courses; 8 tennis courts; croquet court; exercise room; full-service spa; 2 Jacuzzis; saunas; bike rentals; children's programs; concierge; tour desk; courtesy shuttle; business center; salon; 24-hr. room service; massage; babysitting; laundry service; dry cleaning. *In room:* A/C, TV, dataport, high-speed Internet access, minibar, hair dryer, iron.

Omni Tucson National Golf Resort and Spa ★★★

As the name implies, golf is the driving force behind most stays at this boutique resort, which is the site of the annual Tucson Open PGA golf tournament—so if you don't have your own clubs, you might feel a bit out of place. Then again, you could just avail yourself of the full-service health spa, which is one of the best in the state. Most of the spacious guest rooms cling to the edges of the golf course and have their own patios or balconies; hand-carved doors and Mexican tile counters in the bathrooms contribute a Spanish colonial feel, while the furniture has a classically modern Mediterranean style. Aside from the least expensive rooms, the accommodations here are the best and most luxurious in Tucson.

2727 W. Club Dr. (off Magee Rd.), Tucson, AZ 85742. © 800/528-4856 or 520/297-2271. Fax 520/297-7544. www.omnitucsonnational.com. 167 units. Jan to early Apr $239–$319 double, $249–$379 suite; mid-Apr to mid-May $159–$219 double, $169–$319 suite; late May to early Sept $84–$139 double, $94–$199 suite; mid-Sept to Dec $159–$219 double, $169–$279 suite. Rates do not include $10 nightly service charge. Children under 18 stay free in parent's room. AE, DC, DISC, MC, V. Pets accepted ($75 nonrefundable deposit). **Amenities:** 3 restaurants (American, Southwestern); 2 lounges; 2 large pools; PGA championship 27-hole golf course; 4 tennis courts; basketball court; volleyball court; health club; full-service spa; 2 Jacuzzis; concierge; salon; room service; massage; babysitting; laundry service; dry cleaning; concierge-level rooms. *In room:* A/C, TV, dataport, minibar, coffeemaker, hair dryer, iron, safe.

Westin La Paloma ★★★ (Kids)

If grand scale is what you're looking for in a resort, this is the place. Everything about La Paloma is big—big portico, big lobby, big lounge, big pool area—and from the resort's sunset-pink Mission Revival buildings, set in the middle of Tucson's prestigious foothills, there are also very big views. While adults will appreciate the resort's tennis courts, exercise facilities, and abundant poolside lounge chairs, kids will love the 177-foot water slide. Guest rooms are situated in 27 low-rise buildings surrounded by desert landscaping. Couples should opt for the king rooms (ask for a mountain or golf-course view if you don't mind spending a bit more). French-inspired Southwestern cuisine is the specialty at Janos (p. 350), which is one of Tucson's finest restaurants. There are also a couple of other great restaurants nearby, which makes this a great choice for foodies.

3800 E. Sunrise Dr., Tucson, AZ 85718. © 800/WESTIN-1 or 520/742-6000. Fax 520/577-5878. www.westin lapalomaresort.com. 487 units. Jan to late May $249–$319 double, from $445 suite; late May to mid-Sept $99–$129 double, from $245 suite; mid-Sept to Dec $209–$279 double, from $375 suite. Rates do not include $11 daily service fee. AE, DC, DISC, MC, V. Valet parking $12. **Amenities:** 4 restaurants (Southwestern, American); 2 lounges, 3 snack bars (including a swim-up bar); 5 pools (1 for adults only); 27-hole golf course; 10 tennis courts; racquetball court; volleyball court; croquet court; health club; full-service Elizabeth Arden Red Door spa; 3 Jacuzzis; children's programs; concierge; car-rental desk; business center; shopping arcade; pro shops; salon; 24-hr. room service; massage; babysitting; laundry service; dry cleaning. *In room:* A/C, TV, dataport, high-speed Internet access, minibar, coffeemaker, hair dryer, iron, safe.

EXPENSIVE

Hacienda del Sol Guest Ranch Resort ★★ (Finds)

With its colorful Southwest styling, historic character, mature desert gardens, and ridgetop setting, Hacienda del Sol is one of the most distinctive hotels in Tucson. The small resort, once a guest ranch, exudes the sort of Old Tucson atmosphere available at only a couple of other lodgings in the city. The lodge's basic rooms are evocative of

Spanish posadas and old Mexican inns and have rustic and colorful Mexican character, with a decidedly artistic flair. These units are in the resort's oldest buildings, set around flower-filled courtyards. If you prefer more modern, spacious accommodations, ask for a suite; if you want loads of space and the chance to stay where Katharine Hepburn and Spencer Tracy may have once stayed, ask for a casita. With large terraces for alfresco dining, The Grill (p. 350) is one of Tucson's best restaurants.

5601 N. Hacienda del Sol Rd., Tucson, AZ 85718. (C) 800/728-6514 or 520/299-1501. www.haciendadel sol.com. 30 units. Early Jan to May $155–$245 double, $325–$335 suite, $375–$460 casita; June–Sept $79–$119 double, $145–$165 suite, $165–$250 casita; Oct to early Jan $135–$215 double, $300–$310 suite, $340–$440 casita. 2-night minimum stay weekends and holidays. Rates include continental breakfast. Children under 5 stay free in parent's room. AE, MC, V. **Amenities:** Restaurant (regional American); small outdoor pool; Jacuzzi; horseback riding; massage. *In room:* A/C, TV, high-speed Internet access.

Westward Look Resort ★★ *Value*   Too often Arizona resorts are far too isolated from the desert. Not so this resort in the Santa Catalina foothills. With natural desert coming right up to the patios of some rooms, this fairly small and reasonably priced resort is a favorite of mine. Take an early morning walk or horseback ride on the resort's nature trail and you'll see all kinds of birds and other desert critters. Built in 1912 as a private estate, Westward Look is the oldest resort in Tucson and although it doesn't have its own golf course, it does have an excellent health spa, riding stables, and plenty of tennis courts. The large guest rooms, all of which were renovated a few years ago, have a Southwestern flavor and private patios or balconies with great views of the city. For the ultimate in Southwest luxury, opt for one of the stargazer spa suites, which have private outdoor hot tubs. The Gold Room restaurant (p. 349) serves excellent Continental and Southwestern cuisine and utilizes herbs and vegetables grown on site in the chef's garden. If you aren't a golfer but do enjoy resort amenities, this is one of your best Tucson choices.

245 E. Ina Rd., Tucson, AZ 85704. (C) 800/722-2500 or 520/297-1151. Fax 520/297-9023. www.westward look.com. 244 units. Jan–Apr $179–$349 double; May $139–$189 double; June–Sept $89–$189 double; Oct–Dec $159–$209 double. Rates do not include $12 daily resort fee. Children under 18 stay free in parent's room. AE, DC, DISC, MC, V. Pets accepted ($50 fee). **Amenities:** 2 restaurants (Continental/Southwestern, American); lounge; 3 pools; 8 tennis courts; exercise room; full-service spa; 3 Jacuzzis; bike rentals; horseback riding; concierge; tour desk; car-rental desk; business center; room service; massage; laundry service; dry cleaning; executive-level rooms. *In room:* A/C, TV, dataport, high-speed Internet access, minibar, coffeemaker, hair dryer, iron, wi-fi.

MODERATE

Windmill Inn at St. Philip's Plaza ★ *Value*   Located on the edge of the foothills in the St. Philip's Plaza shopping center, this hotel offers both a good location and good value. There are several great restaurants and an array of upscale shops right across the parking lot. Out the hotel's back door is a paved pathway along the Rillito River (which is dry for most of the year), and bikes are available to guests. Accommodations are spacious, and every unit contains a work desk, double vanity, wet bar, three phones (one in the bathroom), and two TVs—basically everything to make the business traveler or vacationer comfortable for a long stay.

4250 N. Campbell Ave., Tucson, AZ 85718. (C) 800/547-4747 or 520/577-0007. Fax 520/577-0045. www.windmillinns.com. 122 units. Feb–Mar $139–$159 double; Apr–May $119–$129 double; June–Sept $79–$89 double; Oct–Dec $99–$119 double. Rates include continental breakfast. Children under 18 stay free in parent's room. AE, DC, DISC, MC, V. Pets accepted. **Amenities:** Outdoor pool; access to nearby health club; Jacuzzi; bikes; business center; coin-op laundry; laundry service; dry cleaning. *In room:* A/C, TV, fridge, microwave, hair dryer, iron, free local calls.

WEST OF DOWNTOWN
EXPENSIVE

La Zarzuela ★★   When I come to the desert, I want to be *in* the desert, not in the middle of the city. That's why I love this modern B&B on the west side of Tucson. It sits high on a hill surrounded by saguaros and is just down a dirt road from the Tucson Mountain Park, a natural area every bit as beautiful as Saguaro National Park. La Zarzuela has four colorfully decorated guest rooms spread out around this sprawling modern Santa Fe–style building. The pool and hot tub are built right on the edge of the natural desert, while courtyards and patios have splashes of colorful flowers in their landscaping. It's all very Southwestern, the perfect place to stay if you want to explore the desert. For all this seclusion, the inn is surprisingly close to downtown Tucson, which gives it the edge over Casa Tierra (see below), which is much farther out of the city.

P.O. Box 86030, Tucson, AZ 85754. © 888/848-8225. www.zarzuela-az.com. 5 units. $195–$250 double. Rates include full breakfast and evening wine and hors d'oeuvres. DISC, MC, V. No children under 18. **Amenities:** Outdoor pool; Jacuzzi; concierge. *In room:* A/C, fridge, coffeemaker, hair dryer.

Starr Pass Golf Suites ★★   Located 3 miles west of I-10, Starr Pass is both the closest golf resort to downtown and the most economically priced golf resort in the city. It's a condominium resort, however, which means you won't find the sort of service you get at Tucson's other resorts (but neither will you pay as much). Accommodations are in privately owned Santa Fe–style casitas rented as two-bedroom units or broken down into a master suite and a standard hotel-style room. The master suites are more comfortable, with fireplaces, full kitchens, balconies, and a Southwestern style throughout. The smaller hotel-style rooms are a bit cramped and much less lavishly appointed. The desert-style 18-hole golf course is one of the best courses in the city. There are also hiking/biking trails on the property. Note that the restaurant is open only for breakfast and lunch.

3645 W. Starr Pass Blvd., Tucson, AZ 85745. © 800/503-2898 or 520/670-0500. Fax 520/670-0427. www.starrpasstucson.com. 80 units. Mid-Jan to mid-May $179 double, $309 suite, $429 casita; mid-May to Sept $89 double, $139 suite, $199 casita; Oct to mid-Jan $119 double, $179 suite, $249 casita. Children under 18 stay free in parent's room. AE, DC, DISC, MC, V. **Amenities:** Restaurant (Continental/Southwestern); lounge; outdoor pool; 18-hole golf course; 2 tennis courts; exercise room; Jacuzzi; pro shop. *In room:* A/C, TV, kitchen, fridge, coffeemaker, hair dryer.

MODERATE

Casa Tierra Adobe Bed & Breakfast Inn ★   If you've come to Tucson to be in the desert and you really want to be a *part* of the desert, then this secluded B&B is well worth considering. Built to look as if it has been here since Spanish colonial days, the modern adobe home is surrounded by 5 acres of cactus and palo verde trees on the west side of Saguaro National Park. There are great views, across a landscape full of saguaros, of the mountains to the north, and sunsets are enough to take your breath away. Guest rooms open onto a landscaped central courtyard, which is surrounded by a covered seating area. The two outdoor whirlpool spas make perfect stargazing spots, and there are also a couple of telescopes on the property.

11155 W. Calle Pima, Tucson, AZ 85743. © 866/254-0006 or 520/578-3058. www.casatierratucson.com. 4 units. Aug 15–June 15 $135–$195 double, $200–$325 suite. Rates include full breakfast. 2-night minimum stay. AE, DISC, MC, V. Closed June 16–Aug 14. **Amenities:** Well-equipped exercise room; Jacuzzi; concierge; massage. *In room:* A/C, fridge, hair dryer, iron.

NEAR THE AIRPORT
MODERATE

Best Western Inn at the Airport   If you're the type who likes to get as much sleep as possible before rising to catch a plane, this motel right outside the airport entrance will do it for you—there's no place closer.

7060 S. Tucson Blvd., Tucson, AZ 85706. © **800/772-3847** or 520/746-0271. Fax 520/889-7391. 149 units. Jan–Mar $69–$129 double; Apr–May and Sept–Oct $69–$99 double; June–Aug and Nov–Dec $59–$89 double. Rates include continental breakfast. AE, DC, DISC, MC, V. **Amenities:** Restaurant (American); lounge; small outdoor pool; tennis court; Jacuzzi; business center; coin-op laundry; dry cleaning. *In room:* A/C, TV, dataport, fridge, coffeemaker, hair dryer, iron.

Clarion Hotel Tucson Airport   Located just outside the airport exit, this hotel provides convenience and some great amenities, including a complimentary nightly cocktail reception and midnight snacks. Accommodations are generally quite large; the king rooms are particularly comfortable. The poolside units are convenient for swimming and lounging.

6801 S. Tucson Blvd., Tucson, AZ 85706. © **800/424-6423** or 520/746-3932. Fax 520/889-9934. www.clarion hotel.com. 188 units. Jan–Mar $99–$139 double; Apr–May and Sept–Dec $69–$119 double; June–Aug $59–$79 double. Rates include full breakfast and cocktail hour. Children 18 and under stay free in parent's room. AE, DC, DISC, MC, V. **Amenities:** Restaurant (American); lounge; outdoor pool; exercise room; Jacuzzi; courtesy airport shuttle; business center; room service; coin-op laundry; laundry service; dry cleaning. *In room:* A/C, TV, dataport, high-speed Internet access, fridge, coffeemaker, hair dryer, iron.

INEXPENSIVE

There are numerous budget motels near the Tucson Airport. These include **Motel 6,** 1031 E. Benson Hwy., Exit 262 off I-10 (© **520/628-1264**), which charges $39 to $53 double, and **Super 8–Tucson/East,** 1990 S. Craycroft Rd., Exit 265 off I-10 (© **520/790-6021**), which charges $50 to $90 double.

OUTLYING AREAS
NORTH OF TUCSON

Across the Creek at Aravaipa Farms ★★ *Finds*   Located 60 miles north of Tucson on one of the only year-round streams in southern Arizona, this B&B is a romantic getaway near one of the state's most spectacular desert wilderness areas. Because the inn is 3 miles up a gravel road and then across a stream (high-clearance vehicles recommended), it's a long way to a restaurant. Consequently, innkeeper Carol Steele provides all meals. Guests entertain themselves hiking in the nearby Aravaipa Canyon Wilderness, bird-watching, and cooling off in Aravaipa Creek. The casitas, which are eclectically decorated with a mix of folk art and rustic Mexican furniture, feature tile floors, stone-walled showers, and shady verandas. For either a romantic weekend or a vigorous vacation exploring the desert, this inn makes an ideal base. There is also a three-bedroom house available for groups of six.

89395 Aravaipa Rd., Winkelman, AZ 85292. © **520/357-6901.** www.aravaipafarms.com. 5 units. $285 double. Rates include all meals. 2-night minimum stay weekends and holidays. No credit cards. Children not accepted. **Amenities:** Dining room. *In room:* Coffeemaker, no phone.

C.O.D. Ranch ★ *Finds*   Located 25 minutes north of the Tucson city limits, this place is primarily used by groups and family reunions. However, the rustic ranch setting (that includes two restored 1880s adobe houses) and remote location overlooking the San Pedro Valley, make this lovingly restored ranch an ideal spot for a tranquil getaway between the desert and the mountains. The decor is a mix of rustic Mexican furnishings and contemporary works by regional artists.

Several of the casitas have full kitchens, two have fireplaces, and some have air-conditioning. The ranch borders Oracle State Park, and a section of the Arizona Trail is within a few miles. Horseback rides, roping lessons, and guided nature walks can be arranged.

P.O. Box 241, Oracle, AZ 85623. (C) **800/868-5617** or 520/615-3211. Fax 520/896-2271. www.codranch.com. 12 units, 2 with shared bathroom. $95–$175 double. Rates include full breakfast. Children 10 and under stay free in parent's room. MC, V. Pets accepted. **Amenities:** Small outdoor pool; Jacuzzi; horseback riding; massage; guest laundry. *In room:* No phone.

SOUTH OF TUCSON

Santa Rita Lodge   This lodge in the shady depths of Madera Canyon (p. 374) is used almost exclusively by bird-watchers, and getting a room in late spring, when the birds are out in force, can be difficult. The rooms and cabins are large and comfortable. Perhaps best of all, the lodge offers guided bird walks ($15 per person or $20 with a meal included) from March through August. There are also other natural-history programs offered. Note that the nearest restaurants are 13 miles away, so you should bring food for your stay.

1218 S. Madera Canyon Rd., Madera Canyon, AZ 85614. (C) **520/625-8746.** Fax 520/648-1186. www.santa ritalodge.com. 12 units. $83–$98 double (discounts available Oct–Jan). AE, MC, V. *In room:* A/C, TV, kitchen.

SPAS

Canyon Ranch Health Resort ★★★   Canyon Ranch, one of America's premier health spas, offers the sort of complete spa experience that's available at only a handful of places around the country. On staff are doctors; nurses; psychotherapists and counselors; fitness instructors; massage therapists; and tennis, golf, and racquetball pros. Services offered include health and fitness assessments; health, nutrition, exercise, and stress-management consultations, seminars, presentations, and evaluations; fitness classes and activities (including Pilates and a golf school); massage therapy; therapeutic body treatments; facials, manicures, pedicures, haircuts, and styling; private sports lessons; makeup consultations; cooking demonstrations; and art classes. Guests stay in a variety of spacious and very comfortable accommodations. Three gourmet, low-calorie meals are served daily with options for total daily caloric intake (don't worry, you won't go hungry).

8600 E. Rockcliff Rd., Tucson, AZ 85750. (C) **800/742-9000** or 520/749-9000. Fax 520/749-7755. www.canyonranch.com. 185 units. Late Sept to early June 4-night packages from $5,560 double; early June to late Sept 4-night packages from $4,160 double. Rates include all meals and a variety of spa services and programs. Rates do not include 18% service charge. AE, DC, DISC, MC, V. Pets accepted. No children under 12 (with exception of infants in the care of personal nannies). **Amenities:** Restaurant; aquatic center and 3 outdoor pools; 7 tennis courts; racquetball and squash courts; 7 exercise rooms; 62,000-sq.-ft. spa complex; 8 Jacuzzis; saunas; steam rooms; bikes; concierge; tour desk; courtesy airport shuttle; salon; room service; massage; guest laundry; laundry service; dry cleaning. *In room:* A/C, TV/DVD, dataport, high-speed Internet access, hair dryer, iron, safe, free local calls.

Miraval Life in Balance ★★★   Focusing on what it calls "life balancing," Miraval, one of the country's most exclusive health spas, emphasizes stress management, self-discovery, and relaxation rather than facials and mud baths. To this end, activities at the all-inclusive resort include meditation, tai chi, Pilates, and yoga; more active types can go hiking, mountain biking, and rock climbing (on an outdoor climbing wall). Of course, such desert classics as horseback riding, tennis, and swimming are also available. However, staying busy isn't really the objective here; learning a new way of life is the ultimate goal. Miraval offers lifestyle-management workshops, fitness/nutrition consultations, cooking demonstrations, exercise classes, an "equine experience" program, massage, and skin care and facials. Of the three swimming pools, one is a three-tiered leisure pool surrounded by waterfalls and desert landscaping. Guest rooms, many of which have views of the Santa Catalina Mountains, are done in a Southwestern style. While very large, most of the bathrooms have showers but no tubs.

5000 E. Via Estancia Miraval, Catalina, AZ 85739. © 800/232-3969 or 520/825-4000. Fax 520/825-5163. www.miravalresort.com. 106 units. Oct to mid-May $990–$1,090 double, $1,390–$1,890 suite; mid-May to Sept $770–$830 double, $1,070–$1,570 suite. Rates do not include 17.5% service charge. Rates include all meals, classes, and a $95 per-person per-day spa credit. AE, DC, DISC, MC, V. No children. **Amenities:** 2 restaurants; lounge; 2 snack areas; 4 pools; 2 tennis courts; croquet court; superbly equipped exercise room; spa; 4 Jacuzzis; saunas; steam rooms; horseback riding; concierge; car-rental desk; room service; massage; laundry service; dry cleaning. *In room:* A/C, TV/VCR, dataport, fridge, coffeemaker, hair dryer, iron, safe, wi-fi.

GUEST RANCHES

Lazy K Bar Ranch ⭐   In operation as a guest ranch since 1936, the Lazy K Bar Ranch covers more than 200 acres and is adjacent to Saguaro National Park's west unit. There are plenty of nearby hiking and riding trails, and if you have a hankering for city life, downtown Tucson is only 20 minutes away. Ranch activities include trail rides, guest rodeos, cookouts, and hay rides as well as nature talks, guided hikes, rappelling, and stargazing. Guest rooms vary in size and comfort level (some have whirlpool tubs); try for one of the newest units, which are absolutely gorgeous. Family-style meals consist of hearty American ranch food, with cookouts offered twice a week.

8401 N. Scenic Dr., Tucson, AZ 85743. © 800/321-7018 or 520/744-3050. Fax 520/744-7628. www.lazyk bar.com. 24 units. Oct to mid-Dec $320–$365 double; mid-Dec to Apr $340–$385 double; May–June and Sept $240–$275 double. Rates include all meals and horseback riding. 3-night minimum stay. AE, DISC, MC, V. Closed July–Aug. Children under 2 stay free in parent's room. **Amenities:** Dining room; lounge; small outdoor pool; access to nearby health club; Jacuzzi; game room; horseback riding; courtesy airport shuttle; massage; coin-op laundry. *In room:* A/C, no phone.

Tanque Verde Ranch ⭐⭐   Want to spend long days in the saddle but don't want to give up resort luxuries? Then Tanque Verde Ranch, which was founded in the 1880s and still has some of its original buildings, is for you. This is far and away the most luxurious guest ranch in Tucson. The ranch borders Saguaro National Park and the Coronado National Forest, so there's plenty of room for horseback riding. There are also nature trails and a nature center. At the end of the day, the new spa provides ample opportunities to recover from too many hours in the saddle. Guest rooms are spacious and comfortable, with fireplaces and patios in many units. The newest casitas are absolutely huge and among the most luxurious accommodations in the state. The dining room, which overlooks the Rincon Mountains, sets impressive buffets. There are also breakfast horseback rides and cookout rides.

The Tanque Verde Ranch also operates the Bellota Ranch, which is located far out of town at the end of a rough dirt road. This ranch has a much more authentic feel (more cattle ranch than resort with horses) and is geared toward more experienced riders.

14301 E. Speedway Blvd., Tucson, AZ 85748. © 800/234-DUDE or 520/296-6275. Fax 520/721-9426. www.tanqueverderanch.com. 74 units. Mid-Dec to Apr $360–$480 double; May–Sept $290–$375 double; Oct to early Dec $305–$390 double. Rates include all meals and ranch activities. Children 3 and under $15 extra. AE, DC, DISC, MC, V. **Amenities:** Dining room; lounge; indoor and outdoor pools; 5 tennis courts; exercise room; small full-service spa; Jacuzzi; saunas; horseback riding; bike rentals; children's programs; children's playground; concierge; courtesy airport shuttle with 4-night stay; tennis pro shop; massage; babysitting; coin-op laundry; laundry service; dry cleaning. *In room:* A/C, dataport, fridge.

White Stallion Ranch ⭐ *Kids*   Set on 3,000 acres of desert just over the hill from Tucson, the White Stallion Ranch is perfect for those who crave wide-open spaces. Operated since 1965 by the True family, this spread has a more authentic feel than any other guest ranch in the area. A variety of horseback rides are offered daily Monday through Saturday, and a petting zoo keeps kids entertained. There are also nature trails, guided nature walks and hikes, hayrides, weekly rodeos, and team cattle penning. Guest rooms vary considerably in size and comfort, from tiny, spartan single units to deluxe two-bedroom suites. About a quarter of the rooms were renovated a few years ago and are worth requesting.

9251 W. Twin Peaks Rd., Tucson, AZ 85743. ℂ 888/977-2624 or 520/297-0252. Fax 520/744-2786. www.wsranch.com. 41 units. Sept to early Oct $218–$254 double, $270–$310 suite; early Oct to mid-Dec and May $262–$304 double, $324–$370 suite; mid-Dec to Apr $288–$348 double, $368–$422 suite. Rates do not include 15% service charge. Rates include all meals. 4- to 6-night minimum stay in winter. Children under 3 stay free in parent's room. No credit cards. Closed June–Aug. **Amenities:** Dining room; lounge; small outdoor pool; access to nearby health club; 2 tennis courts; basketball court; volleyball court; Jacuzzi; horseback riding; bikes; concierge; tour desk; courtesy airport shuttle; business center; massage; coin-op laundry. *In room:* A/C, hair dryer, no phone.

4 Where to Dine

Variety, they say, is the spice of life, and Tucson certainly dishes up plenty of variety (and spice) when it comes to eating out. Tucson is a city that lives for spice, and in the realm of fiery foods, Mexican reigns supreme. There's historic Mexican at El Charro Café and El Minuto, *nuevo* Mexican at Café Poca Cosa and J Bar, Mexico City Mexican at La Parilla Suiza, and family-style Mexican at Casa Molina. So if you like Mexican food, you'll find plenty of places in Tucson to get all fired up.

On the other hand, if Mexican leaves you cold, don't despair—there are plenty of other restaurants serving everything from the finest French cuisine to innovative American, Italian, and Southwestern food. This latter fare is almost as abundant in Tucson as Mexican food, and you should be sure to dine at a Southwestern restaurant early in your visit. This cuisine can be brilliantly creative, and after trying it you may want *all* your meals to be Southwestern.

Foodies fond of the latest culinary trends will find plenty of spots to satisfy their cravings. Concentrations of creative restaurants can be found along East Tanque Verde Road and at foothills resorts and shopping plazas. On the other hand, if you're on a tight dining budget, you might want to look for early-bird dinners, which are particularly popular with retirees.

DOWNTOWN
MODERATE

Barrio 🦌 SOUTHWESTERN   Located at the edge of the Barrio Histórico, this neighborhood restaurant is packed throughout the day with both downtown professionals and the art crowd. The food, on the whole, is pleasantly spicy and served with zippy Southwestern accents. If you're not too hungry, one of the little plates will do—try the tasty Anaheim chile stuffed with black beans, garlic, and goat cheese in a red-pepper cream sauce. The jalapeño burger is thick, juicy, and just spicy enough, while the pork tenderloin with a mango-currant-ginger chutney offers an interesting mélange of flavors.

135 S. Sixth Ave. ℂ 520/629-0191. Reservations recommended for dinner. Main courses $8.50–$22. AE, DC, MC, V. Tues–Thurs 11am–2:30pm and 5–10pm; Fri 11am–2:30pm and 5pm–midnight; Sat 5pm–midnight; Sun 5–9pm.

Café Poca Cosa 🦌🦌 *⟨Value⟩* NUEVO MEXICAN   Created by owner/chef Suzana Davila, the food here is not just *any* Mexican food; it's imaginative and different, and the flamboyant atmosphere of red and purple walls and Mexican and Southwestern artwork is equally unusual. The cuisine—which has been compared to the dishes dreamed up in *Like Water for Chocolate*—consists of creations such as grilled beef with a jalapeño chile and tomatillo sauce, and chicken with a dark mole sauce made with Kahlúa, chocolate, almonds, and chiles. The staff is courteous and friendly and will recite the menu for you in both Spanish and English. This lively restaurant is an excellent value, especially at lunch (which is served until 4pm).

At Clarion Hotel & Suites Santa Rita, 88 E. Broadway Blvd. ℂ 520/622-6400. Reservations highly recommended. Main courses $9–$11 lunch, $15–$19 dinner. DC, MC, V. Mon–Thurs 11am–9pm; Fri–Sat 11am–10pm.

El Charro Café ⭐ SONORAN MEXICAN   El Charro, housed in an old stone building in El Presidio Historic District, lays claim to being Tucson's oldest family-operated Mexican restaurant and is legendary around these parts for its unusual *carne seca,* a traditional air-dried beef that is a bit like shredded beef jerky. To see how they make carne seca, just glance up at the restaurant's roof as you approach. The large metal cage up there is filled with beef drying in the desert sun. You'll rarely find carne seca on a Mexican menu outside of Tucson, so indulge in it while you're here—and although other area restaurants serve it, El Charro's is the best. *Warning:* The cafe can be packed at lunch, so arrive early or late.

The adjacent ¡Toma! (p. 387), a colorful bar/cantina, is under the same ownership. There's another El Charro at 6310 E. Broadway (ℂ **520/745-1922**).

311 N. Court Ave. ℂ **520/622-1922**. www.elcharrorestaurant.com. Reservations recommended for dinner. Main courses $6–$17. AE, DC, DISC, MC, V. Daily 11am–9pm.

INEXPENSIVE

Café à la C'Art SALADS/SANDWICHES   Located in the courtyard on the grounds of the Tucson Museum of Art, this cafe serves up tasty sandwiches and makes a good lunch spot if you're downtown wandering the Presidio neighborhood or touring the museum. Try the apricot-almond chicken-salad sandwich or the Cuban sandwich, which is made with roasted pork and ham. Wash it all down with some fresh lemonade and be sure to save room for dessert.

150 N. Main Ave. ℂ 520/628-8533. Sandwiches and salads $5.50–$7.50. MC, V. Mon–Fri 11am–3pm.

El Minuto Cafe MEXICAN   El Minuto, located downtown at the edge of the Barrio Histórico next to El Tiradito shrine, is a meeting ground for both Anglos and Latinos who come for the lively atmosphere and Mexican home cooking. In business since 1936, this establishment is a neighborhood landmark and a prototype that other Mexican restaurants often try to emulate. Cheese crisps (Mexican pizza) are a specialty, and enchiladas, especially *carne seca* (air-dried beef), are tasty. This is a fun place for people-watching—you'll find all types, from kids to businessmen in suits.

354 S. Main Ave. ℂ 520/882-4145. Main courses $4.50–$13. AE, DC, DISC, MC, V. Sun–Thurs 11am–10pm; Fri–Sat 11am–11pm.

CENTRAL TUCSON & THE UNIVERSITY AREA
EXPENSIVE

Arizona Inn ⭐⭐ FRENCH/AMERICAN   The dining room at the Arizona Inn, one of the state's first resorts, is consistently excellent. The pink-stucco pueblo-style buildings are surrounded by neatly manicured gardens that have matured gracefully, and it's romantic to dine in the courtyard or on the bar patio overlooking the colorful gardens. The menu changes regularly, but dishes are

Tucson Dining

Downtown Tucson

University Blvd.

N. 6th Ave.

N. Stone Ave.

N. Court Ave.

N. Main St.

N. 4th Ave.

N. Euclid Ave.

Blvd.

La Cholla

Granada Ave.

6th St

10

Toole

Ave.

E. 9th St.

Alameda St.

Scott Ave.

E. Congress St.

E. Broadway Blvd.

Sunset   Rd.

El Camino de Cerro   Ruthrauf
Rd.

SAGUARO
NATIONAL
PARK

Sweetwater Dr.

Camino de Oeste

**To Saguaro National Park (West),
Arizona–Sonora Desert Museum
& Old Tucson**

Ironwood Hill Dr.

Tucson Mountain
Park

Speedway Blvd

Anklam   Ro

Gates   Pass   Rd.

Kinney Rd.

Silverlake Rd.

Bopp   Rd.

Way

Ajo

86

Valencia   Rd.

ARIZONA

Mission   Rd.

Phoenix
✪

Tucson
○

0   2 mi

0   2 km

N

SAN XAVIER
INDIAN RESERVATION

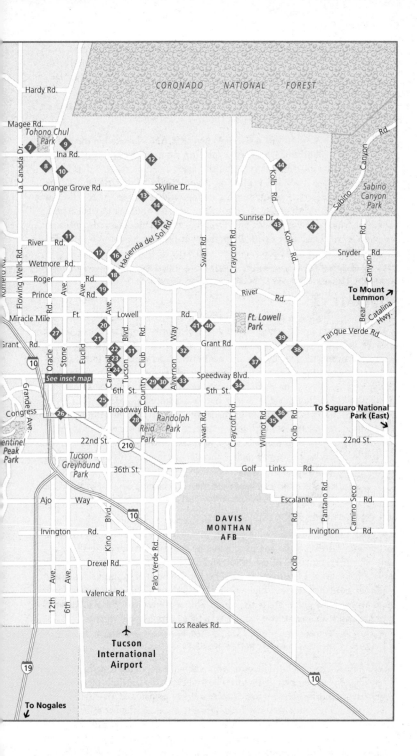

always well prepared. Flavors lean heavily toward classics such as foie gras, oysters Rockefeller, vichyssoise, and bouillabaisse. Presentation is artistic, and fresh ingredients are emphasized more than sauces. The homemade ice creams are fabulous. On weekends, you might catch some live music.

2200 E. Elm St. ✆ 520/325-1541. Reservations recommended. Main courses $7–$15 lunch, $20–$34 dinner; tasting menu $38. AE, DC, MC, V. Daily 7–10am, 11:30am–2pm, and 6–10pm.

The Dish Bistro & Wine Bar ★★ NEW AMERICAN   Located in the rear of the Rumrunner Wine and Cheese Co., this tiny, minimalist restaurant is brimming with urban chic. On a busy night, the space could be construed as either cozy or crowded, so if you like it more on the quiet side, come early or late. The chef has a well-deserved reputation for daring, and turns out such dishes as poblano chile soup with grilled shrimp and an unusual ahi tuna Provençal with a lemon thyme–vin blanc sauce and green-olive tapenade. Naturally, because this place is associated with a wine shop, the wine list is great; the well-informed servers will be happy to help you choose a bottle.

3200 E. Speedway Blvd. (at the Rumrunner). ✆ 520/326-1714. www.dishbistro.com. Reservations highly recommended. Main courses $17–$35. AE, DC, MC, V. Tues–Thurs 5–9pm; Fri–Sat 5–10pm.

MODERATE

Cuvée World Bistro ★★ *Value* INTERNATIONAL   This stylish restaurant in a small, old shopping center effects a sort of Moroccan-palace decor, and if you take a seat in the lounge, you can sprawl on a banquette covered with plush pillows for a thoroughly laid-back and hedonistic experience. The menu travels all over the globe for inspiration and then blends flavors and textures in deliciously creative ways. The menu changes regularly, but if you see something (perhaps wild-mushroom cakes) served over avocado pesto, order it. This pesto is so creamy and rich, it ought to be made into a spa treatment! Almost everything on the menu here sounds utterly tempting, and with prices so reasonable, you just might want to come back a few times and work your way through the menu. On Friday and Saturday nights, there is live music. This place is a good bet for a romantic dinner.

3352 E. Speedway Blvd. ✆ 520/881-7577. www.cuveebistro.com. Reservations recommended. Main dishes $7.50–$13 lunch, $8–$19 dinner. AE, DC, DISC, MC, V. Mon–Thurs 11am–10pm; Fri–Sat 11am–midnight.

Elle ★★ MEDITERRANEAN   Located in the historic Broadway Village shopping plaza, Elle bills itself as a wine-country restaurant. Okay, so Tucson isn't Napa, but the menu does include dozens of wines by the glass. French posters lend the high-ceilinged room a feel of the 1880s, and the dining experience is comfortable without being noisy. I like to start a meal here with a bowl of steamed mussels and a spinach salad with apples, blue cheese, and walnuts. The chile-rubbed lamb chops with potato gratin are outstanding. This is a great spot for a moderately priced romantic dinner, or you can just stop by to sample some wines.

At Broadway Village, 3048 E. Broadway. ✆ 520/327-0500. Reservations recommended. Main courses $8.50–$22. MC, V. Mon–Thurs 11am–9pm; Fri 11am–10pm; Sat 4:30–10pm.

Kingfisher ★ SEAFOOD   If you're serious about seafood, the Kingfisher is definitely one of your best bets in Tucson. The freshest seafood, artfully blended with bright flavors and imaginative ingredients, is deftly prepared as appetizers, sandwiches, and main dishes. You may have difficulty deciding whether to begin with Umpqua Bay oysters, house-smoked trout, or scallop seviche—so why not tackle them all and call it a meal? Both meat eaters and vegetarians will also find items on the menu, and the warm cabbage salad is an absolute must. The atmosphere is upscale and lively, and the bar and late-night menu are a hit with night owls. There's also live jazz and blues on Monday and Saturday nights.

2564 E. Grant Rd. © **520/323-7739**. www.kingfisherbarandgrill.com. Reservations recommended on weekends. Main courses $8–$10 lunch, $14–$22 dinner. AE, DC, DISC, MC, V. Mon–Fri 11am–midnight; Sat–Sun 5pm–midnight.

Nonie New Orleans Bistro ⭐ CAJUN   It's a long way from Tucson to the bayou, but this lively spot goes a long way toward bringing the spirit of New Orleans to the desert. Chef/owner Christopher Leonard, the son of prolific crime-fiction author Elmore Leonard, serves all the Cajun classics, including decent blackened catfish and crawfish étoufée at dinner, and oyster po' boys at lunch. However, you may find yourself filling up on the strangely addictive fried pickles. Wash it all down with a Sazerac cocktail, and you'll think you're in the French Quarter.

2526 E. Grant Rd. © **520/319-1965**. Reservations recommended. Main courses $5.50–$12 lunch, $9–$17 dinner. AE, DC, DISC, MC, V. Tues–Fri 11am–2:30pm and 5–10pm; Sat 5–10pm; Sun 5–9pm.

Pastiche Modern Eatery ⭐⭐ NEW AMERICAN   Located in a shopping plaza that has lots of Tucson character, this high-energy bistro has for several years now been one of *the* hip places to dine in Tucson. The colorful artwork and vibrant contemporary food fairly shout out *trendy*, but the restaurant manages to appeal to a broad spectrum of the population. From mushroom soufflé to spicy jerked chicken to fried jalapeño ravioli, there's enough here to keep everyone at the table happy. Light eaters can get half orders of entrees and desserts. The crowded bar is a popular watering hole that turns out some tasty margaritas.

3025 N. Campbell Ave. © **520/325-3333**. www.pasticheme.com. Reservations recommended. Main courses $8–$24. AE, DC, DISC, MC, V. Mon–Fri 11:30am–midnight; Sat–Sun 4:30pm–midnight.

INEXPENSIVE

Beyond Bread ⭐ AMERICAN/BAKERY   Although ostensibly a bakery, this place is more a bustling sandwich shop that also sells great breads and pastries. You can even get hot breakfasts here, but I much prefer a latte and a selection from the pastry case. The sandwich list is long, with both hot and cold varieties, and they all come on the great bread that's baked here on the premises. Most of the sandwiches are so big that you could split them between two people if you weren't too hungry.

There's a second Beyond Bread over on the east side of town at Monterey Village, 6260 E. Speedway Blvd. (© **520/747-7477**).

3026 N. Campbell Ave. © **520/322-9965**. www.beyondbread.com. No reservations. Main dishes $4.75–$7. AE, DISC, MC, V. Mon–Fri 6:30am–8pm; Sat 7am–8pm; Sun 7am–6pm.

El Cubanito Restaurant ⭐ CUBAN   Located right across the street from the University of Arizona, this place is popular with students. During spring training season (Mar), the restaurant is also popular with Cuban baseball players, and consequently, there are lots of signed baseballs and bats on the walls. What draws everyone back to this nondescript place are the reasonably priced Cuban specialties, including various stews and a Cuban sandwich (a meat- and cheese-filled baguette pressed and warmed on the grill). The fried plantains are also worth trying, and the fruity shakes made with mango, banana, papaya, or other tropical fruits are delicious. Latino soap operas are usually playing on the TV over the bar, which gives this place a very authentic feel.

1150 E. Sixth St. © **520/623-8020**. Main courses $5–$9. MC, V. Mon–Sat 11am–7pm.

Feast ★ *Finds* INTERNATIONAL   This hole-in-the-wall takeout place, with a handful of tables for people who might want to eat on the premises, offers excellent food—gourmet to go—and is the perfect place to pick up food for a sunset picnic dinner at Sabino Canyon Recreation Area or Saguaro National Park. The menu changes regularly, but you might find a sandwich made with rib-eye steak, crumbled blue cheese, and caramelized onions. Other possibilities include duck confit, a leek and goat cheese tart, or Moroccan b'stilla (ground chicken and almonds in phyllo pastry). For dessert, you'd better hope the place is serving the beignets with pistachio-chocolate centers.

4122 E. Speedway Blvd. ℂ **520/326-9363** or 520/326-6500. www.eatatfeast.com. Main dishes $6.50–$13. AE, DC, DISC, MC, V. Tues–Sun 11am–9pm.

Ghini's French Café ★ *Finds* FRENCH   A French cafe and breakfast spot in the middle of Tucson? *Mais oui!* This casual little spot is a real gem. The owner is from Marseille, and here reproduces plenty of favorites from the home country. At breakfast, there are flaky croissants and a Marseille-style omelet made with anchovies. Lunchtime brings interesting salads, sandwiches made from baguettes, and a good range of simple pastas. Everything is available to go.

1803 E. Prince Rd. ℂ **520/326-9095.** Sandwiches and pastas $5–$8.50. AE, DC, DISC, MC, V. Tues–Sat 6:30am–3pm; Sun 8am–2pm.

Yoshimatsu Healthy Japanese Food & Café ★ JAPANESE   I found out about this unusual place from a friend who had recently been to Japan and raved about this restaurant's authenticity. However, that's only part of the story. Not only is there a long menu of health-conscious Japanese dishes, but the decor in this ultra-casual place is truly outrageous, with little glass cases displaying all manner of Japanese toys and action figures. The *okonomiyaki,* sort of a Japanese pizza, is one of our favorite dishes here. For a truly bizarre treat, try the green tea milk shake!

2660 N. Campbell Ave. ℂ **520/320-1574.** Main dishes $4.50–$9.50. MC, V. Sun–Thurs 11:30am–2:45pm and 5–8:45pm; Fri–Sat 11:30am–2:45pm and 5–9:45pm.

EAST TUCSON
MODERATE

Fuego ★ NEW AMERICAN/SOUTHWESTERN   In Spanish, *Fuego* means "fire," and this place takes its name seriously. Not only are there spicy dishes, but there are also actual flambéed dishes on the menu. The atmosphere is slightly formal but unpretentious. Waiters bustle about serving such flavorful dishes as the signature Field of Greens salad, with blue cheese, chile-roasted walnuts, and dried cranberries, or prickly-pear pork tenderloin that is so tender you can cut it with a fork. Lively yet intimate, Fuego appeals to couples, families, and retirees alike, and casual to dressy attire fits in just fine. Sundays are Sinatra night, with live music.

At Santa Fe Sq., 6958 E. Tanque Verde Rd. ℂ **520/886-1745.** www.fuegorestaurant.com. Reservations recommended. Main courses $8.50–$22. AE, DC, DISC, MC, V. Mon–Thurs 4:30–9:30pm; Fri 4:30–10pm; Sat 5–10pm; Sun 5:30–9:30pm.

INEXPENSIVE

Casa Molina MEXICAN   Casa Molina, which sports a festive atmosphere, has been Tucson's favorite family-run Mexican restaurant for many years and is usually abuzz with families, groups, and couples. The margaritas are inexpensive yet tasty, and the *carne seca* (sun-dried beef) shouldn't be missed. Lighter eaters will enjoy a layered *topopo* salad made with tortillas, refried beans, chicken, lettuce, celery, avocado, tomato, and jalapeños. The food is good, and the service efficient.

Other locations include 3001 N. Campbell Ave. (© **520/795-7593**) and 4240 E. Grant Rd. (© **520/326-6663**).

6225 E. Speedway Blvd. (near Wilmot Rd.). © **520/886-5468**. Reservations recommended. Dinners $8–$18; a la carte $2–$14. AE, DC, DISC, MC, V. Daily 11am–10pm.

La Parrilla Suiza MEXICO CITY MEXICAN   Most Mexican food served in the United States is limited to Sonoran style, originating just south of the border. However, the cuisine of Mexico is far more varied than you might suspect from the typical restaurant menu. The meals served at La Parrilla Suiza are based on the style popular in Mexico City, where most of this chain's restaurants are located. Many menu items are sandwiched between two tortillas, much like a quesadilla, and the charcoal broiling of meats and cheeses lends the sandwiches special status. For an appetizer, we like the grilled scallions with lime.

Other locations can be found at 2720 N. Oracle Rd. (© **520/624-4300**) and 4250 W. Ina Rd. (© **520/572-7200**).

5602 E. Speedway Blvd. © **520/748-7124**. Main courses $5.25–$13. AE, DC, DISC, MC, V. Sun–Thurs 11am–10pm; Fri–Sat 11am–11pm.

Little Anthony's Diner (Kids) AMERICAN   This place is primarily for kids, although lots of big kids (including us) enjoy the 1950s music and decor. The menu includes such offerings as a Jailhouse Rock burger and Chubby Checker triple-decker club sandwich. Daily specials and bottomless soft drinks make feeding the family fairly inexpensive. A video-game room will keep your kids entertained while you finish your meal. If you want to make a night of it (and you make a reservation far enough in advance, you can take in an old-fashioned melodrama next door at the Gaslight Theatre. Together, these two places make for a fun night out with the family.

7010 E. Broadway Blvd. (in back of the Gaslight Plaza). © **520/296-0456**. Burgers and sandwiches $4.50–$8.50. MC, V. Mon–Thurs 11am–10pm; Fri 11am–11pm; Sat 10:30am–11pm; Sun 10:30am–10pm.

THE FOOTHILLS
EXPENSIVE
Anthony's in the Catalinas (★★) NEW AMERICAN/CONTINENTAL

From the moment you drive up and let the valet park your car, Anthony's, housed in a modern Italianate building overlooking the city, exudes Southwestern elegance. The waiters are smartly attired in tuxedos, and guests (the cigar-and-single-malt foothills set) are nearly as well dressed. In such a rarefied atmosphere, you'd expect only the finest meal and service, and that's exactly what you get. The duck mousse and black truffle terrine is a fitting beginning, followed by the likes of chateaubriand with a béarnaise and red-wine sauce. Wine is not just an accompaniment but also a reason for dining out at Anthony's; at more than 100 pages, the wine list may be the most extensive in the city. Don't miss out on the next best part of a meal here (after the wine): the day's soufflé (order early).

6440 N. Campbell Ave. © **520/299-1771**. Reservations highly recommended. Main courses $10–$16 lunch, $24–$41 dinner. AE, DC, DISC, MC, V. Mon–Fri 11:30am–2:30pm and 5:30–10pm; Sat–Sun 5:30–10pm.

The Gold Room (★★) SOUTHWESTERN/CONTINENTAL   With its recently updated contemporary Southwestern decor, superb views of the city far below, and expansive terrace for alfresco dining, the Gold Room is one of the best places in Tucson for a truly memorable Southwestern dining experience. The menu, which is equally divided between classic dishes (filet mignon and roast rack of lamb) and regional specialties, aims to satisfy a wide variety of

tastes. We favor the regional cuisine—tender mesquite-grilled buffalo with purple Peruvian mashed potatoes or veal piccata with a charred tomato, chipotle peppers, and lime beurre blanc—which emphasizes flavor over fire. The length of the wine list is staggering, and there's a welcome range of prices. Desserts are delectably rich and amusingly presented—the chocolate bombe is an event in itself. Although you can eat here on the cheap at lunch, the restaurant is most remarkable at night, when the cityscape of Tucson twinkles in the distance.

At the Westward Look Resort, 245 E. Ina Rd. ℂ **520/297-1151**. Reservations recommended. Main courses $11–$18 lunch, $21–$33 dinner; Sun brunch $30. AE, DC, DISC, MC, V. Mon–Sat 7am–11am, 11:30am–2pm, and 5:30–10pm; Sun 10am–1:30pm and 5:30–10pm.

The Grill ★★ REGIONAL AMERICAN   Great food, historic Southwest character, views, live jazz—this place has it all, so don't visit Tucson without having a meal here. Located in a 1920s hacienda-style building at a former foothills dude ranch, the Grill is one of Tucson's best restaurants, and is known not only for its well-prepared meats and vegetables, but also for its classic Southwestern styling and great views of the city. For openers, try the delicious smoked-corn lobster chowder, which comes with truffled croutons. The dry-aged New York strip steak is deservedly the most popular entree on the menu and is big enough for two people to share. If you're looking for greater creativity, opt for the roast duck breast with a lavender-honey-jalapeño glaze. Sunday brunch here is a real treat. The main patio overlooks the Catalinas and the fairways of the Westin La Paloma's golf course. Thursday through Sunday, there is live music.

At the Hacienda del Sol Guest Ranch Resort, 5601 N. Hacienda del Sol Rd. ℂ **520/529-3500**. www.hacienda delsol.com. Reservations recommended. Main courses $25–$42; Sun brunch $30. AE, DC, DISC, MC, V. Mon–Sat 5:30–10pm; Sun 10am–2pm and 5:30–10pm.

Janos ★★★ SOUTHWESTERN/REGIONAL AMERICAN   Janos Wilder, Tucson's most celebrated chef, is not only a world-class chef; he's a real sweetheart, too. Should you happen to bump into him while dining here, he'll make you feel as though you've been a regular at his restaurant for years. It is this conviviality, which spills over into all aspects of a meal here, that makes this restaurant one of my absolute favorites in the entire state. Consequently, the luxuriously appointed restaurant, which is located just outside the front door of the Westin La Paloma, is my top choice for a special-occasion dinner while in Tucson. His menu changes both daily and seasonally, with such complex offerings as the not-to-be-missed lobster with papaya in champagne sauce; New York strip steak with chili hollandaise; and lamb loin with a complex spicy Southwestern rub. This is about as formal a restaurant as you'll find in this otherwise very casual city. If you can't afford the high prices here, try Janos's adjacent J Bar.

At the Westin La Paloma, 3770 E. Sunrise Dr. ℂ **520/615-6100**. www.janos.com. Reservations highly recommended. Main courses $24–$45; 5-course tasting menu $75 ($110 with wines). AE, DC, MC, V. Mon–Thurs 5:30–9pm; Fri–Sat 5:30–9:30pm.

⟮Moments Market Timing

Sunday mornings are a great time to stop by St. Philip's Plaza. No, this isn't a church, it's a shopping center, and on Sunday mornings, there is a wonderful little farmers' market. You can pick up organic bread, prickly-pear cactus juice and jelly, homemade tamales, Mexican cheeses, and plenty of produce. Stock up here and then head to Sabino Canyon Recreation Area for a picnic.

McMahon's Prime Steakhouse ★★ STEAKHOUSE/SEAFOOD   If a perfectly done steak is what you're craving, then McMahon's is the place. This place serves the best steaks in Tucson, and with a decidedly modern opulence that's a far cry from steakhouses of yore, McMahon's boasts an atmosphere that's calculated to impress. A large glass-walled wine room dominates the main dining room, which is ringed with plush booths. You can drop a bundle on dinner here, but no more than you'd spend at such high-end restaurants as Janos or the Ventana Room. The main difference is that your choices at McMahon's are simpler: steak, seafood, or steak and seafood. You'd be wasting a night out, though, if you didn't order a steak (the aged prime beef is superb). There's a separate piano lounge and cigar bar.

2959 N. Swan Rd. ✆ **520/327-7463**. www.metrorestaurants.com. Reservations recommended. Main courses $7–$16 lunch, $20–$40 dinner. AE, DC, DISC, MC, V. Mon–Fri 11:30am–10pm; Sat–Sun 5–10pm.

Ventana Room ★★★ NEW AMERICAN   Fresh from a thorough renovation, the Ventana Room is looking even more posh than it did before (think wall of wine bottles as you enter), though with hints of Southwestern chic. *Ventana* means "window" in Spanish, and the views through the windows of this restaurant are every bit as memorable as the food that comes from the kitchen. Make an early dinner reservation so you can catch the sunset, and request a table on the city-view side of the dining room. Whether you're seated overlooking the resort's waterfall or the lights of Tucson far below, you'll likely have trouble concentrating on your food, but do try; you wouldn't want to miss any of the subtle nuances of such dishes as the velvety Dover sole, which is here done to absolute perfection. Neither should you allow the dessert cart to pass you by. In the restaurant's rarefied atmosphere, you'll be pampered by a bevy of waiters providing professional and unobtrusive service. If you're in the mood for a big splurge and prefer classic presentations instead of the sort of Southwestern flavors you'd find at Janos, then this is the place.

At Loews Ventana Canyon Resort, 7000 N. Resort Dr. ✆ **520/615-5494**. www.ventanaroom.com. Reservations highly recommended. Jackets recommended for men. Prix-fixe menus $75–$105. AE, DC, DISC, MC, V. Tues–Thurs 6–9pm; Fri–Sat 6–10pm.

Yama ★★ JAPANESE   There are plenty of high-end restaurants in the Tucson foothills, but none that serve food like this. With artful sushi rolls and Kobe-style beef (at astronomical prices), this place seems totally out of place in Tucson. It would seem right at home in Los Angeles, San Francisco, or New York, but not the middle of the desert. Still, I'm glad it's here because the sushi here is the best I've ever had. Be sure to try the red dragon sushi roll; it's a little work of art. In fact, the restaurant is boldly contemporary in style and is itself a work of art. So, if you've had enough mesquite-grilled steak, search out this hidden jewel and be prepared to be impressed.

5425 N. Kolb Rd., #115. ✆ **520/615-1031**. Reservations recommended. Main dishes $13–$69. AE, DC, DISC, MC, V. Daily 11am–11pm.

MODERATE
Bistro Zin ★★ REGIONAL AMERICAN   Sophisticated and urbane, Bistro Zin, Tucson's premier wine bar/restaurant, effects an urban feel with its wine-colored walls decorated with black-and-white photos of jazz greats. It's all very classy and cool, and with more than 20 different wine flights available on any given day, this is the perfect place to sample wines from around the world. There's also plenty of good food to accompany the many wines. Try the grilled shrimp or the duck with cherry sauce.

At Joesler Village, 1865 E. River Rd., Suite 101. ✆ **520/299-7799**. www.tasteofbistrozin.com. Reservations recommended. Main courses $8–$12 lunch, $14–$27 dinner. AE, DC, DISC, MC, V. Mon–Sat 11:30am–3pm and 5–11pm; Sun 5–11pm.

Café Terra Cotta ★★ SOUTHWESTERN Café Terra Cotta is Arizona's original Southwestern restaurant, and is one of my favorite Tucson restaurants. The combination of reasonably priced creative Southwestern cooking, a casual atmosphere with loads of contemporary Southwestern appeal, and lots of local artwork make Café Terra Cotta truly distinctive and an Arizona classic. I always start my meals here with the rich-and-creamy garlic custard, which is served with a warm salsa vinaigrette and herbed hazelnuts. The poblano chile rellenos stuffed with either rock shrimp and herbed rice or pork and sweet potato is served on a red-pepper chipotle sauce and is another of my must-have dishes. A large brick oven turns out creative pizzas, while salads, sandwiches, small plates, and main dishes flesh out the long menu. With so many choices, it's often difficult to decide. The wine list includes the largest collection of zinfandels in the country. *Note:* In the summer of 2004, Café Terra Cotta closed due to a fire, but it should reopen by early 2005.

3500 E. Sunrise Dr. ✆ **520/577-8100**. www.cafeterracotta.com. Reservations recommended. Main courses $8.25–$24. AE, DC, DISC, MC, V. Daily 11:30am–10pm.

Firecracker Bistro ★★ PAN-ASIAN With a menu that knows no boundaries and wild architectural touches that include flames issuing from torches atop the building and faux tree trunks in the bar, Firecracker is one of Tucson's hot spots. Hip decor aside, it's the large portions and reasonable prices that keep people coming back. The spicy-chicken lettuce-cup appetizers (sort of roll-your-own burritos) are a fun finger-food starter. Seafood is definitely the strong suit here, and the wok-charred chunks of salmon covered with cilantro pesto are just about the best thing on the menu. While you wait for your table, you can hang out in the wine bar.

2990 N. Swan Rd. (at Fort Lowell). ✆ **520/318-1118**. www.metrorestaurants.com. Reservations recommended. Main courses $7–$12 lunch, $13–$18 dinner. AE, DISC, MC, V. Sun–Thurs 11am–10pm; Fri–Sat 11am–10:30pm.

J Bar ★★★ SOUTHWESTERN The mouthwatering culinary creations of celebrity chef Janos Wilder at half-price? Sounds impossible, but that's pretty much what you'll find here at J Bar, Janos's casual bar and grill adjacent to his famed foothills restaurant. Ask for a seat out on the heated patio, and with the lights of Tucson twinkling in the distance, dig into the best nachos you'll ever taste—here made with chorizo sausage and chili con queso. No matter what you order, you'll likely find that the ingredients and flavor combinations are most memorable. Who can forget spicy jerked pork with cranberry–habañero chile pepper chutney or Yucatán-style plantain-crusted chicken with green coconut-milk curry? You won't want to miss sampling one of the *postres* (desserts).

At the Westin La Paloma, 3770 E. Sunrise Dr. ✆ **520/615-6100**. www.janos.com. Reservations highly recommended. Main courses $13–$22. AE, DC, MC, V. Sun–Thurs 5–9pm; Fri–Sat 5–9:30pm.

Vivace Restaurant ★★ NORTHERN ITALIAN With a beautiful Tuscan-inspired setting, this restaurant serves reasonably priced, creative dishes. The atmosphere is lively, and the food down-to-earth. For starters, we like to indulge in the luscious antipasto platter for two, containing garlic-flavored spinach, roasted red peppers, marinated artichoke hearts, grilled asparagus, and herbed goat cheese. Pasta dishes, such as penne with sausage and roasted-pepper sauce,

Kids Family-Friendly Restaurants

Hidden Valley Inn (p. 355)   This cavernous restaurant has a false-front cow-town facade in bright colors; inside are stables and a dance hall that serve as the dining rooms. Kids will love the miniature action dioramas of funny Western scenes.

Little Anthony's Diner (p. 349)   As you might guess from the name, this place has a 1950s theme that's fun for both kids and adults. The staff is good with children, and there's a video-game room inside and an old-fashioned melodrama theater next door.

Pinnacle Peak Steakhouse (p. 355)   Dinner here is a Wild West event, and there's an entire Western town outside complete with carousel, train rides, and gold panning. Kids love it.

come nicely presented and in generous portions. But it's the crab-filled chicken breast that is most memorable. The wine list has plenty of selections, many fairly reasonably priced.

At St. Philip's Plaza, 4310 N. Campbell Ave. ℂ 520/795-7221. Reservations recommended. Main courses $8–$12 lunch, $12–$27 dinner. AE, DC, DISC, MC, V. Mon–Thurs 11:30am–9pm; Fri–Sat 11:30am–10pm.

Wildflower ★★ NEW AMERICAN   Stylish comfort foods in large portions are the order of the day at this chic and casually elegant north Tucson bistro. A huge wall of glass creates minimalist drama, and large flower photographs on the walls enhance the bright and airy decor. The heaping plate of fried calamari with mizuna greens is a good bet for a starter, and entrees run the gamut from a comforting meat loaf (with port-wine reduction) to herb-crusted rack of lamb. Pasta and salmon both show up in various reliable guises. With so many tempting, reasonably priced dishes to sample, Wildflower is a foodie's delight.

At Casas Adobes Shopping Plaza, 7037 N. Oracle Rd. (at Ina Rd.). ℂ 520/219-4230. Reservations recommended. Main courses $8–$12 lunch, $13–$24 dinner. AE, DC, DISC, MC, V. Tues–Thurs 11:30am–2:30pm and 5–9pm; Fri–Sat 11:30am–2:30pm and 5–10pm; Sun 5–9pm.

INEXPENSIVE

Charro Grill ★ MEXICAN   El Charro Café (p. 343) in downtown Tucson is the oldest family-owned restaurant in the city and is legendary for its delicious *carne seca* (spicy sun-dried beef). This casual, counter-service place puts a new spin on El Charro, bringing the popular Mexican food to an upscale shopping center in the foothills. Decide whether you want a taco, burrito, enchilada, or chimichanga; then pick your filling and place your order at the counter. Personally, I never order anything but the carne seca burrito. If you happen to be on the Atkins diet, they even have "bajo carb" meals.

1765 E. River Rd. ℂ 520/615-1922. www.charrogrill.com. Reservations not accepted. Main courses $6–$10. AE, DC, DISC, MC, V. Sun–Thurs 11am–11pm; Fri–Sat 11am–1am.

HiFalutin Rapid Fire Western Grill ★ AMERICAN   The first time I walked into this lively Western grill, I was absolutely hooked. The smell of burning juniper filled the restaurant, and I could almost taste the steaks. It wasn't until my second visit that I discovered the aroma was actually incense. Still, this place knows how to set the mood, and they come through with tasty comfort food with a Western twist. Get anything with the marinated flank steak and you won't be disappointed. You can get it tossed with pasta, with shrimp, and sometimes in a salad. Wash it all down with one of the great margaritas they serve and you definitely have a hifalutin kind of meal.

6780 N. Oracle Rd. ✆ 520/297-0518. Call ahead waiting list. Main courses $7.25–$16. AE, DC, DISC, MC, V. Sun–Thurs 11am–9pm; Fri–Sat 11am–10pm. Located between Orange Grove and Ina roads.

Tohono Chul Tea Room REGIONAL AMERICAN   Located in a brick territorial-style building in 37-acre Tohono Chul Park (p. 368), this is one of the most tranquil restaurants in the city, and the garden setting provides a wonderful opportunity to experience the desert. Before or after lunching on grilled raspberry-chipotle chicken or tortilla soup, you can wander through the park's desert landscaping and admire the many species of cacti. The patios, surrounded by natural vegetation and plenty of potted flowers, are frequented by many species of birds. The adjacent gift shop is packed with Mexican folk art, nature-theme toys, household items, T-shirts, and books.

7366 N. Paseo del Norte (1 block west of the corner of Ina and Oracle roads in Tohono Chul Park). ✆ 520/797-1222. www.tohonochulpark.org. Reservations accepted only for parties of 6 or more. Main courses $5–$10. AE, MC, V. Daily 8am–5pm.

Zona 78 ⭐ *Finds* PIZZA   I'm a sucker for good pizza, and the pizza here is the best in Tucson. Maybe it's the big stone oven they use or maybe it's all the locally grown organic produce, but whatever it is, this place does it right. Try the Tuscany, an oval-shaped pizza covered with Italian sausage, mozzarella, black olives, fennel, roasted garlic, caramelized red onions, and mushrooms. This pie is just bursting with flavors. To really get the most out of a visit to Zona 78, you need to bring enough people so that you can order the big antipasto plate or the cheese-and-fruit plate, which has lots of great imported cheeses. If you're not that hungry, at least try the Tuscan bean-and-spinach soup. All you Atkins dieters need not pass this place by; there are several low-carb options on the menu.

78 W. River Rd. ✆ 520/888-7878 or 520/888-7879. Main courses $7–$12. AE, DISC, MC, V. Mon–Wed 11am–11pm; Thurs–Fri 11am–1am; Sun 4–11pm.

WEST TUCSON
MODERATE

Ocotillo Café ⭐ REGIONAL AMERICAN   With a terrace set in a beautiful desert garden and backed by colorful walls, the Ocotillo Café could be a destination in itself. Add the experience of visiting the Arizona–Sonora Desert Museum (see "The Tucson Area's [Mostly] Natural Wonders," below), and you have a superb day's outing. You can watch a hummingbird drink from a penstemon flower while you dine on pork chops cured with black tea and mild spices, blackened fish with Sonoran spices, and other Southwestern dishes. Wash everything down with prickly-pear tea or an icy margarita. In summer, the cafe is open Saturday nights only, which is a good time to view the museum's desert inhabitants in their more active nocturnal state.

At the Arizona–Sonora Desert Museum, 2021 N. Kinney Rd. ✆ 520/883-5705. Reservations recommended (required Sat nights). Main courses $16–$19. AE, MC, V. Jan–Apr daily 11am–3pm; June–Sept Sat 5–9pm.

Teresa's Mosaic Café ⭐ *Finds* MEXICAN   Located a mile or so west of I-10, this casual Mexican restaurant is hidden behind a McDonald's on the corner of Grant and Silverbell roads, but is well worth searching out for breakfast or lunch. With mosaic tile tables, mirror frames, and kitchen counter, this colorful restaurant lives up to its name. Try the chilaquiles or chorizo and eggs for breakfast, and don't pass up the fresh lemonade or horchata (spiced rice milk), both of which are displayed in big jars on the counter. This is an especially good spot for a meal if you're on your way to the Arizona–Sonora Desert Museum, Old Tucson, or Saguaro National Park's west unit.

2455 N. Silverbell Rd. ✆ **520/624-4512**. Main courses $4.25–$13. MC, V. Mon–Sat 7:30am–9pm; Sun 7:30am–2pm.

COWBOY STEAKHOUSES

El Corral Restaurant *(Value* STEAKHOUSE   Owned by the same folks who run Tucson's Pinnacle Peak Steakhouse, El Corral is another inexpensive and atmospheric steakhouse. Good prime rib and cheap prices have made this place hugely popular with retirees and families. The restaurant doesn't accept reservations, so expect long lines or come before or after regular dinner hours. Inside, the hacienda building has a genuine old-timey feeling, with flagstone floors and wood paneling that make it dark and cozy. In keeping with the name, there's a traditional corral fence of mesquite branches around the restaurant parking lot. Prime rib is the house specialty, but there are steaks, chicken, pork ribs, and burgers for the kids.

2201 E. River Rd. ✆ **520/299-6092**. Reservations not accepted. Complete dinner $9–$17. AE, DC, DISC, MC, V. Mon–Thurs 5–10pm; Fri–Sun 4:30–10pm.

Hidden Valley Inn ★ *(Kids* STEAKHOUSE   Kids and adults love this brightly colored, false-fronted tourist cow town as much for the filling and inexpensive meals as for the glass cases containing miniature action dioramas of humorous Western scenes. In the restaurant's very authentic dance hall, there are stage performances by magicians, Elvis impersonators, and the like. A second dining room, done up to look like a stable, is a bit less lively. There's also the Red Garter Saloon, where adults can imbibe. This steakhouse is the kind of place people frequent when relatives are visiting or there's a birthday to be celebrated. In other words, a lively party atmosphere reigns, and diners inevitably leave with large doggie bags. Cowpuncher-size steaks and barbecued ribs are the main attraction, although there are some seafood and chicken choices as well.

4825 N. Sabino Canyon Rd. ✆ **520/299-4941**. www.hiddenvalleyinntuc.com. Reservations not accepted. Main courses $8–$20. AE, DC, DISC, MC, V. Daily 11am–11pm.

Pinnacle Peak Steakhouse ★ *(Kids* STEAKHOUSE   Located in Trail Dust Town (p. 368), a Wild West–themed shopping, dining, and family entertainment center, the Pinnacle Peak Steakhouse specializes in family dining in a fun cowboy atmosphere. Stroll the wooden sidewalks past the opera house and saloon to the grand old dining rooms of the restaurant. Once through the doors, you'll be surprised at the authenticity of the place, which really does resemble a dining room in Old Tombstone or Dodge City. Be prepared for crowds—this place is very popular with tour buses. Oh, and by the way, wear a necktie into this place and it will be cut off! Actually, lots of people wear ties just so they can have them added to the collection tacked to the ceiling.

6541 E. Tanque Verde Rd. ✆ **520/296-0911**. Reservations not accepted. Main courses $7–$17. AE, DC, DISC, MC, V. Mon–Fri 5–10pm; Sat–Sun 4:30–10pm.

LATE-NIGHT NOSHING

If the movie didn't let out until 10pm and the popcorn wasn't enough to fill you up, where do you go to satisfy your hunger? Try **Barrio,** 135 S. Sixth Ave. (✆ **520/629-0191**); **Kingfisher,** 2564 E. Grant Rd. (✆ **520/323-7739**); or

Pastiche Modern Eatery, 3025 N. Campbell Ave. (© **520/325-3333**), all of which stay open on Friday and Saturday until midnight. (See earlier in this chapter for full listings.)

BAKERIES, CAFES & QUICK BITES

For the best espresso in Tucson, head to **Raging Sage Coffee Roasters,** 2458 N. Campbell Ave. (© **520/320-5203**); prices are high, but the espresso here sure is tasty. The **Epic Café,** 745 N. Fourth Ave. (© **520/624-6844**), is a popular neighborhood place with colorful artwork, delicious scones, and other light fare. With comfy couches and a place to plug in your laptop, the **Coffee X Change,** 2443 N. Campbell Ave. (© **520/409-9433**), makes a good stop between down-town and the foothills. In the 5600 block of East Broadway, on the north side of the street, you'll find the **Bristol Espresso Bus,** a 1937 British double-decker bus.

For eight-layer cakes and light food in an edgy atmosphere, I like to buzz on over to the **Cup Cafe,** at Hotel Congress, 311 E. Congress St. (© **520/798-1618**). At **La Baguette Bakery,** 1797 E. Prince Rd. (© **520/322-6297**), which is affiliated with Ghini's French Café (p. 348), you can get all kinds of delicious French pastries.

When I need a quick lunch, I dart over to the nearest **Baggins Gourmet Sandwiches** for a delicious sandwich. Baggins has several locations, three of which are at 7201 Speedway Blvd. (© **520/290-9383**), Campbell Avenue and Fort Lowell Road (© **520/327-1611**), and downtown at Church Avenue and Pennington Street (© **520/792-1344**). Good pizza can be had at **Magpies Gourmet Pizza,** downtown at 605 Fourth Ave. (© **520/628-1661**), 4654 Speedway Blvd. (© **520/795-5977**), 105 Houghton Rd. (© **520/751-9949**), 7157 Tanque Verde Rd. (© **520/546-6526**), and 7315 Oracle Rd. (© **520/297-2712**). **Wild Oats Market** is a good place to get picnic supplies: organic fruit, delicious baked goods, cheese, meats, and wine. Locations are at 3360 E. Speedway Blvd. (© **520/795-9844**), and 7133 N. Oracle Rd. (© **520/297-5394**).

5 Seeing the Sights

While there are plenty of interesting things to see and do all over the Tucson area, anyone interested in the desert Southwest or the cinematic Wild West should go west—to Tucson's western outskirts, that is. Here you'll find not only the west unit of Saguaro National Park (with the biggest and best stands of saguaro cactus) but also the Arizona–Sonora Desert Museum (one of Arizona's most popular attractions) and Old Tucson Studios (film site over the years for hundreds of Westerns). Together, these three attractions constitute Tucson's best and most popular day outing.

THE TUCSON AREA'S (MOSTLY) NATURAL WONDERS

Arizona–Sonora Desert Museum ★★ _Kids_   Don't be fooled by the name. This is a zoo, and it's one of the best in the country. The Sonoran Desert, which encompasses much of central and southern Arizona as well as parts of northern Mexico, contains within its boundaries not only arid lands but also forested mountains, springs, rivers, and streams. To reflect this diversity, exhibits here encompass the full spectrum of Sonoran Desert life—from plants to insects to fish to reptiles to mammals—and all are on display in very natural settings. Coy-otes and javelinas (peccaries) seem very much at home in their compounds, which are surrounded by almost invisible wire-mesh fences that make it seem as though there is nothing between you and the animals. These display areas are along the Desert Loop Trail, which is also where you'll find the museum's newest exhibits. In only slightly less natural surroundings, you'll see black bears and mountain lions, beavers and otters, frogs and fish, tarantulas and scorpions, prairie dogs and desert bighorn sheep. Our favorite exhibit is the walk-in hummingbird aviary. The tiny birds buzz past your ears and often stop only inches in front of your face. A separate aviary contains many other bird species, and a garden is devoted to displays on pollinators (insects, birds, and mammals that pollinate desert flowers).

This zoological park is 14 miles west of downtown near Tucson Mountain Park, Saguaro National Park's west unit, and Old Tucson Studios. The museum has two dining options—the cafeteria-style Ironwood Terraces and the sit-down restaurant Ocotillo Café (p. 354), which both serve good food. The grounds here are extensive, so wear good walking shoes; a sun hat of some sort is also advisable. Don't be surprised if you end up staying here hours longer than you had intended; there's an awful lot to see and do.

2021 N. Kinney Rd. (© 520/883-1380. www.desertmuseum.org. Admission Nov–Apr $12 adults, $4 children 6–12; May–Oct $9 adults, $2 children 6–12. Oct–Feb daily 8:30am–5pm; Mar–Sept daily 7:30am–5pm (June–Aug Sat until 10pm, Sept Sat until 9pm). From downtown Tucson, go west on Speedway Blvd., which becomes Gates Pass Rd., and follow the signs.

Colossal Cave Mountain Park *Kids*   It seems nearly every cave in the Southwest has its legends of bandits and buried loot, and Colossal Cave is no exception. A tour through this cavern, which isn't exactly colossal but is certainly impressive, combines a bit of Western lore with a bit of geology for an experience that both kids and adults will enjoy. Not surprisingly for this desert location, this is a dry cave, which means that the stalactites, stalagmites, and other formations are no longer actively growing. Although there was much damage to the formations here before the cave was protected, the narrow passageways and dramatic lighting keep the 45-minute tours interesting. There are also a couple of tours that will take you into little-visited parts of the cave. The Wild Cave Tour ($55) lets you feel like a real spelunker, while the Ladder Tours ($35 with dinner) involve just a bit more climbing than the regular tours. This private park also encompasses the adjacent La Posta Quemada Ranch, a historic working cattle ranch that has been in operation since the 1870s. On the ranch, you can go

---

Moments Driving the Catalina Highway

Within a span of only 25 miles, the Catalina Highway (also called the Sky Island Scenic Byway) climbs roughly 1 mile in elevation from the lowland desert landscape of cacti and ocotillo bushes to forests of ponderosa pines. Passing through several different life zones, this route is the equivalent of driving from Mexico to Canada. When you look at it this way, the $5 use fee is small compared to what a flight to Canada would cost. Along the way there are numerous overlooks, some of which are nauseatingly vertiginous. Other spots are particularly popular with rock climbers. There are numerous hiking trails, picnic areas, and campgrounds along the route. For more information, contact the **Coronado National Forest Santa Catalina Ranger District,** 5700 N. Sabino Canyon Rd. (© **520/ 749-8700**).

Tucson Attractions

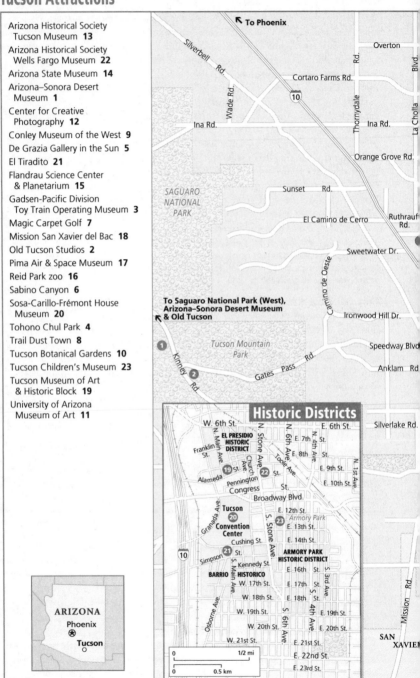

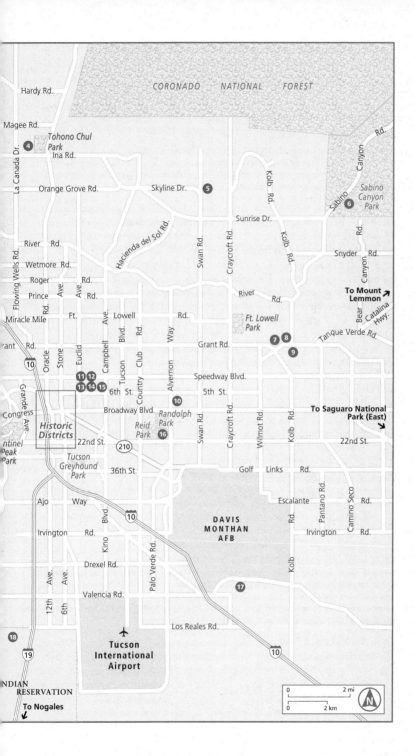

CORONADO NATIONAL FOREST

Hardy Rd.

Magee Rd.

La Canada Dr.

④ Tohono Chul Park
Ina Rd.

Orange Grove Rd.

Skyline Dr.   ⑤

Kolb Rd.

Sabino Canyon Rd.

Sabino Canyon Park   ⑥

Sunrise Dr.

Hacienda del Sol Rd.

Swan Rd.

Craycroft Rd.

Kolb Rd.

Snyder Rd.

Flowing Wells Rd.

River Rd.

Wetmore Rd.

Roger Rd.

Prince Rd.

Miracle Mile

Grant Rd.

⑩ 10

Oracle

Stone

Euclid

Campbell Ave.

Ft. Lowell Rd.

Country Club

Alvernon Way

Grant Rd.

Ft. Lowell Park

River Rd.

Bear Canyon Rd.

Catalina Hwy.

To Mount Lemmon ↗

Tanque Verde Rd.

⑦ ⑧
⑨

Speedway Blvd.

5th St.

⑪ ⑫
⑬ ⑭ ⑮

6th St.

Tucson

Broadway Blvd.

Randolph Park

⑩

Swan Rd.

Craycroft Rd.

Wilmot Rd.

Kolb Rd.

To Saguaro National Park (East) ↘

Grande Ave.

Congress

Sentinel Peak Park

Historic Districts

22nd St.

Reid Park

⑯

22nd St.

Tucson Greyhound Park

(210)

36th St.

Golf   Links   Rd.

Escalante Rd.

Kolb Rd.

Pantano Rd.

Camino Seco Rd.

Ajo   Way

(10)

Irvington   Rd.

Kino Blvd.

DAVIS MONTHAN AFB

Irvington Rd.

Drexel Rd.

Palo Verde Rd.

Valencia Rd.

12th Ave.

6th Ave.

⑰

Los Reales Rd.

✈ Tucson International Airport

(10)

⑱
(19)

INDIAN RESERVATION

To Nogales

0 _____ 2 mi
0 _____ 2 km

N

horseback riding ($27 for a 1-hour ride), visit a small museum with exhibits of artifacts that have been found in Colossal Cave, have a picnic, go for a hike, or attend one of the annual events (including a chili cook-off in Feb). There are also snack bars at both the ranch and the cave. Because this is a private establishment, it seems to see fewer visitors than many of the other major attractions around Tucson, which means you can usually escape the crowds while getting an interesting introduction to the Sonoran Desert.

16721 E. Colossal Cave Rd., Vail. © 520/647-7275. www.colossalcave.com. Cave admission $7.50 adults, $4 children 6–12, in addition to $3 per car for park entry. Mar 16–Sept 15 Mon–Sat 8am–6pm, Sun and holidays 8am–7pm; Sept 16–Mar 15 Mon–Sat 9am–5pm, Sun and holidays 9am–6pm. Take Old Spanish Trail southeast from east Tucson or take I-10 and get off at the Vail exit.

Sabino Canyon Recreation Area ★★ Located in the Santa Catalina Mountains of Coronado National Forest on the northeastern edge of the city, Sabino Canyon is a desert oasis that has attracted people and animals for thousands of years. Today, it's by far the most spectacular and accessible corner of the desert in the Tucson area, containing not only impressive desert scenery but also hiking trails and a stream. The chance to splash in the canyon's waterfalls and swim in natural pools (water conditions permitting) attracts many visitors, but it is equally enjoyable simply to gaze at the beauty of crystal-clear water flowing through a rocky canyon guarded by saguaro cacti. There are numerous picnic tables in the canyon, and many miles of hiking trails wind their way into the Santa Catalinas from here, making it one of the best places in the city for a day hike (the farther you hike, the fewer people you'll see).

A road once allowed automobiles to drive up into the canyon, but cars are now prohibited; instead, a narrated tram shuttles visitors up and down the lower canyon throughout the day. Moonlight tram rides take place three times each month (usually the nights before the full moon) between April and November (but not July or Aug). The Bear Canyon tram is used by hikers heading to the picturesque Seven Falls, which are at the end of a 2.5-mile trail and are our favorite destination within this recreation area. Bring at least 1 quart of water per person if you plan to do any hiking here.

Another good way to experience the park is by bicycling up the paved road during the limited hours when bikes are allowed: Sunday through Tuesday, Thursday, and Friday before 9am and after 5pm. This is a strenuous uphill ride for most of the way, but the scenery is beautiful; if you get an early enough start in the morning, you'll even avoid most of the crowds.

5900 N. Sabino Canyon Rd. © 520/749-8700, 520/749-2861 for shuttle information, or 520/749-2327 for moonlight shuttle reservations. www.fs.fed.us/r3/coronado/scrd/rec/recareas/sabino.htm. Parking $5. Sabino Canyon tram ride $6 adults, $2.50 children 3–12; Bear Canyon tram ride $3 adults, $1.25 children 3–12. Park daily dawn–dusk. Sabino Canyon tram rides daily 9am–4:30pm (until 4pm Mon-Fri July to mid-Dec); Bear Canyon tram rides daily 9am–4pm (both trams more limited in summer). Take Grant Rd. east to Tanque Verde Rd., continuing east; at Sabino Canyon Rd., turn north and watch for the sign.

Saguaro National Park ★★ Saguaro cacti are the quintessential symbol of the American desert and occur naturally only here in the Sonoran Desert. Sensitive to fire and frost and exceedingly slow to mature, these massive, treelike cacti grow in great profusion around Tucson but have long been threatened by both development and plant collectors. In 1933, to protect these desert giants, the federal government set aside two large tracts of land as a saguaro preserve. This preserve eventually became Saguaro National Park. The two units of the park, one on the east side of the city (Rincon Mountain District) and one on the west (Tucson Mountain District), preserve not only dense stands of saguaros,

Moments **Sunset on Signal Hill**

A hike to Signal Hill, located off the Bajada Loop Drive in Saguaro National Park's west unit and only a quarter-mile walk from the parking area, will reward you with not only a grand sunset vista away from the crowds at Gates Pass, but also the sight of dozens of petroglyphs.

but also the many other wild inhabitants of this part of the Sonoran Desert. Both units have loop roads, nature trails, hiking trails, and picnic grounds.

The west unit of the park, because of its proximity to both the Arizona–Sonora Desert Museum and Old Tucson Studios, is the more popular area to visit. This also happens to be where you'll see the most impressive stands of saguaros. Coyotes, foxes, squirrels, and javelinas all eat the sweet fruit of the saguaro, and near the west unit's Red Hills Information Center is a water hole that attracts these and other wild animals, which you're most likely to see at dawn and dusk or during the night. Be sure to take the scenic Bajada Loop Drive, where you'll find good views and several hiking trails (the Hugh Morris Trail involves a long, steep climb, but great views are the reward). To reach the west unit of the park, follow Speedway Boulevard west from downtown Tucson (it becomes Gates Pass Blvd.).

The east section of the park contains an older area of saguaro "forest" at the foot of the Rincon Mountains. This section is popular with hikers because most of it has no roads. It has a visitor center, a loop scenic drive, a picnic area, and a trail open to mountain bikes (the paved loop drive is a great road-bike ride). To reach the east unit of the park, take Speedway Boulevard east, then head south on Freeman Road to Old Spanish Trail.

Rincon Mountain District visitor center: 3693 S. Old Spanish Trail. ✆ 520/733-5153. Tucson Mountain District visitor center: 2700 N. Kinney Rd. ✆ 520/733-5158. www.nps.gov/sagu. Entry fee $6 per car, $3 per hiker or biker (charged in the east section only). Daily 7am–sunset; visitor centers daily 9am–5pm; open to hikers 24 hr. a day. Visitor centers closed New Year's Day, Thanksgiving, and Christmas.

HISTORIC ATTRACTIONS BOTH REAL & REEL

Mission San Xavier del Bac ✵   Called the White Dove of the Desert, Mission San Xavier de Bac, a blindingly white adobe building rising from a sere, brown landscape, is considered the finest example of mission architecture in the Southwest. The beautiful church, which was built between 1783 and 1797, incorporates Moorish, Byzantine, and Mexican Renaissance architectural styles. However, the church was never actually completed, which becomes apparent when the two bell towers are compared. One is topped with a dome, while the other has none.

Although never completed, the mission did undergo an extensive restoration a few years ago, and much of the elaborate interior has taken on a new luster. Restored murals cover the walls, and behind the altar are colorful and elaborate decorations. To the left of the main altar, in a glass sarcophagus, is a statue of St. Francis Xavier, the mission's patron saint, who is believed to answer the prayers of the faithful. A visit to San Xavier's little museum provides a bit of historical perspective and a chance to explore more of the mission. To the east of the church, atop a small hill, you'll find not only an interesting view of the church but also a replica of the famous grotto in Lourdes, France.

Mission San Xavier del Bac is an active Roman Catholic church serving the San Xavier Indian Reservation. Masses are held Monday through Friday at 6:30 and

8:30am, Saturday at 5:30pm, and Sunday at 8am, 11am, and 12:30pm. There are often food stalls selling fry bread in the parking lot in front of the church.

1950 W. San Xavier Rd. (©) **520/294-2624**. www.sanxaviermission.org. Free admission; donations accepted. Daily 7am–5pm. Take I-19 south 9 miles to Exit 92 and turn right.

Old Tucson Studios ★★ *Kids*   Despite the name, this is not the historic location of the old city of Tucson—it's a Western town originally built as the set for the 1939 movie *Arizona*. In the years since, Old Tucson has been used during the filming of John Wayne's *Rio Lobo, Rio Bravo,* and *El Dorado;* Clint Eastwood's *The Outlaw Josey Wales;* Kirk Douglas's *Gunfight at the O.K. Corral;* Paul Newman's *The Life and Times of Judge Roy Bean;* and, more recently, *Tombstone* and *Geronimo.*

Today, Old Tucson is far more than just a movie set. In addition to serving as a site for film, TV, and advertising productions (call ahead to find out if any filming is scheduled), it has become a Wild West theme park with diverse family-oriented activities and entertainment. Throughout the day, there are staged shootouts in the streets, stunt demonstrations, a cancan musical revue, and other performances. Train rides, stagecoach rides, kiddie rides, restaurants, and gift shops round out the experience. Educational shows explain the history of the West, and several multimedia and video presentations complement the live performances.

201 S. Kinney Rd. (©) **520/883-0100**. www.oldtucson.com. Admission $15 adults, $9.45 children 4–11. Daily 10am–6pm. Closed Thanksgiving and Christmas. Take Speedway Blvd. west, continuing in the same direction when it becomes Gates Pass Blvd., and turn left on S. Kinney Rd.

ART MUSEUMS

Center for Creative Photography   Have you ever wished you could see an original Ansel Adams print up close, or perhaps an Edward Weston or a Richard Avedon? You can at the Center for Creative Photography. Originally conceived by Ansel Adams, the center now holds more than 500,000 negatives, 200,000 study prints, and 60,000 master prints by more than 2,000 of the world's best photographers, making it one of the best and largest collections in the world. Although the center mounts excellent exhibits year-round, it's also a research facility that preserves the complete photographic archives of various photographers, including Adams. Prints may be examined in a special room. It's highly recommended that you make an appointment and decide beforehand whose works you'd like to see. You're usually limited to two photographers per visit.

University of Arizona campus, 1030 N. Olive Rd. (east of Park Ave. and Speedway Blvd.). (©) **520/621-7968**. www.creativephotography.org. Admission by donation. Mon–Fri 9am–5pm; Sat–Sun noon–5pm. Bus: 1, 4, 5, 6, 9, 102, or 103.

Moments   **Seeing It All from "A Mountain"**

The best way to get a feel for the geography of the Tucson area is to drive to the top of a mountain—but not just any mountain. "A Mountain" (officially called Sentinel Peak) rises just to the west of downtown Tucson on the far side of I-10. The peak gets its common name from the giant whitewashed letter "A" (for University of Arizona) near the summit. To get here, drive west to the end of Congress Street and turn left on Sentinel Peak Road. The park is open Monday through Saturday from 8am to 8pm and Sunday from 8am to 6pm.

(*Finds* **The Conley Museum of the West**

Little more than a room at the back of the **Mark Sublette Medicine Man Gallery,** 7000 E. Tanque Verde Rd. (© **520/722-7798**), the **Conley Museum of the West** packs a lot into a tiny space. You can see not only 19th- and 20th-century pieces by some of the biggest names in Western art, but also Indian artifacts and art, Spanish colonial antiquities, and historical maps dating back to 1739. This place is a must for fans of Western art. The museum is open Monday through Saturday from 10am to 5pm and, between November and mid-May, Sunday from 1 to 4pm. Admission is free.

De Grazia Gallery in the Sun   Southwestern artist Ettore "Ted" De Grazia was a Tucson favorite son, and his home, a sprawling, funky adobe building in the foothills, is a city landmark and now serves as a museum for this prolific artist. De Grazia is said to be the most reproduced artist in the world because many of his images of big-eyed children were used as greeting cards during the 1950s and 1960s. Today De Grazia's images tend to seem trite and maudlin, but in his day he was a very successful artist. This gallery is packed with original paintings, so it may surprise you to learn that, near the end of his life, De Grazia burned several hundred thousand dollars worth of his paintings in a protest of IRS inheritance taxes. Adjacent to the gallery is a small adobe chapel that De Grazia built in honor of the missionary explorer Father Eusebio Francisco Kino. Although you won't find original paintings for sale here, the gift shop has lots of reproductions and other objects with De Grazia images.

6300 N. Swan Rd. © **800/545-2185** or 520/299-9192. www.degrazia.org. Free admission. Daily 10am–3:45pm.

Tucson Museum of Art & Historic Block 😊   The Tucson Museum of Art is situated in a modern building surrounded by historic adobes and a spacious plaza frequently used to display sculptures. The *Palice Pavilion—Art of the Americas* exhibit is a highlight of the museum and is not to be missed. This exhibit consists of a large collection of pre-Columbian art that represents 3,000 years of life in Mexico and Central and South America. This collection is housed in the historic Stevens/Duffield House, which also contains Spanish colonial artifacts and Latin American folk art. The noteworthy Goodman Pavilion of Western Art comprises an extensive collection that depicts cowboys, horses, and the wide-open spaces of the American West. The museum has also preserved five historic homes on this same block, all open to the public. See "History Museums & Landmark Buildings," below, for details.

140 N. Main Ave. © **520/624-2333.** www.tucsonarts.com. Admission $5 adults, $4 seniors, $2 students, free for children 12 and under; free on Sun. Mon–Sat 10am–4pm; Sun noon–4pm. Closed all national holidays and Mon from Memorial Day to Labor Day. All downtown-bound buses.

The University of Arizona Museum of Art 😊😊   With European and American works from the Renaissance to the 20th century, this collection is even more extensive and diverse than that of the Tucson Museum of Art. Tintoretto, Rembrandt, Picasso, O'Keeffe, Warhol, and Rothko are all represented. Another attraction, the *Retablo of Ciudad Rodrigo,* consists of 26 paintings from 15th-century Spain that were originally placed above a cathedral altar. The museum also has an extensive collection of 20th-century sculpture that includes more than 60 clay and plaster models and sketches by Jacques Lipchitz.

University of Arizona campus, Park Ave. and Speedway Blvd. © **520/621-7567.** http://artmuseum.
arizona.edu. Free admission. Aug 16–May 14 Mon–Fri 9am–5pm, Sat–Sun noon–4pm; May 15–Aug 15
Tues–Fri 10am–3:30pm, Sat–Sun noon–4pm. Closed major holidays. Bus: 1, 4, 5, 6, 9, 102, or 103.

HISTORY MUSEUMS & LANDMARK BUILDINGS

In addition to the attractions listed below, downtown Tucson has a couple of historic neighborhoods that are described in "Walking Tour—Downtown Historic
Districts," below. Among the more interesting buildings are those maintained by
the Tucson Museum of Art and located on the block surrounding the museum.
These restored homes date from 1850 to 1907 and are all built on the former
site of the Tucson presidio. A map and brochures are available at the museum's
front desk, and free (with admission to the museum) guided tours of the historic
block and Corbett House are available.

Arizona Historical Society Tucson Museum   As the state's oldest historical
museum, this repository of all things Arizonan is a treasure trove for the history
buff. If you've never explored a real mine, you can do the next best thing by
exploring the museum's full-scale reproduction of an underground mine tunnel.
You'll see an assayer's office, miner's tent, stamp mill, and blacksmith's shop in
the mining exhibit. A transportation exhibit, displaying stagecoaches and the
horseless carriages that revolutionized life in the Southwest, and temporary
exhibits that cover a wide range of topics, give a pretty good idea of what it was
like back then.

949 E. Second St. © **520/628-5774.** Admission $5 adults, $4 seniors and students ages 12–18, free for children under 12; free for all on the first Sat of each month. Mon–Sat 10am–4pm. Closed major holidays. Bus:
1, 4, 5, 6, 9, 102, or 103.

Arizona Historical Society Wells Fargo Museum   If you want to learn
more about the history of Tucson, this is the museum to visit. Exhibits cover
Spanish presidio days, American army days, merchants, and schools. Through
the use of artifacts and old photos, these exhibits help bring the city's past to life.
One of the most curious exhibits focuses on the gangster John Dillinger, who
was arrested here in Tucson. This museum is fairly new and has been slowly
expanding.

140 N. Stone Ave. © **520/770-1473.** Admission $3 adults, $2 seniors and students ages 12–18, free for children under 12. Mon–Fri 10am–4pm. Closed major holidays. All downtown-bound buses.

Arizona State Museum   This museum, which is the oldest anthropological
museum in the Southwest, houses one of the state's most interesting exhibits on
prehistoric and contemporary Native American cultures of the Southwest, called
Paths of Life: American Indians of the Southwest. It focuses on 10 different tribes
from around the Southwest and northern Mexico, not only displaying a wide
range of artifacts but also exploring the lifestyles and cultural traditions of Indians living in the region today. In addition, the museum showcases a collection
of some 20,000 whole-vessel ceramic pieces. This pottery spans 2,000 years of
life in the desert Southwest.

University of Arizona campus, 1013 E. University Blvd. at Park Ave. © **520/621-6302.** www.statemuseum.
arizona.edu. Admission $3 suggested donation. Mon–Sat 10am–5pm; Sun noon–5pm. Closed major holidays.
Bus: 1, 4, 5, 6, 9, 102, or 103.

Fort Lowell Museum   Located in Fort Lowell Park on the site of a cavalry outpost that was in operation between 1873 and 1891, this museum chronicles the
history of life at the fort. Some of the ruins of the original fort can still be seen.
Before it was a fort, this site was a Hohokam village, and artifacts uncovered from

---

Tips **Passport to Tucson**

The **Tucson Passport** is a great way to save money on admissions to many of the city's top attractions. The passport, available at the downtown Visitors Center (100 S. Church St.; *C* **800/638-8350** or www.visittucson.org), costs $10 and gets you two-for-one admissions to the Arizona–Sonora Desert Museum, Old Tucson Studios, Biosphere 2, the Pima Air & Space Museum, Tohono Chul Park, the Tucson Museum of Art, and many other attractions.

---

archaeological digs are also on display. Renowned medical researcher Walter Reed, who discovered how yellow fever is transmitted, served as base surgeon here in 1876. A display focusing on medical facilities at the fort explains that, despite Hollywood's version of history, injury from Indian attacks was not the biggest medical problem during the wars with the Apaches.

2900 N. Craycroft Rd. *C* **520/885-3832**. Admission $3 adults, $2 seniors and students ages 12–18, free for children under 12. Wed–Sat 10am–4pm. Closed major holidays. Bus: 34.

Sosa-Carillo-Frémont House Museum Located on the shady grounds of the modern Tucson Convention Center, the Sosa-Carillo-Frémont House is a classic example of Sonoran-style adobe architecture. Originally built in 1858 as a small adobe house, the structure was enlarged after 1866. In 1878, it was rented to territorial governor John Charles Frémont, who had led a distinguished military career as an explorer of the West. The building has been restored in the style of this period, with the living room and bedrooms opening off a large central hall known as a *zaguán*. All rooms are decorated with period antiques. The flat roof is made of pine beams called *vigas*, covered with saguaro cactus ribs, and topped by a layer of hard-packed mud. From November to March, this museum offers tours of historic Tucson ($10 for adults, free for children under 12) on Thursday and Saturday mornings at 10am.

151 S. Granada Ave. (in the Tucson Convention Center complex). *C* **520/622-0956**. Admission $3 adults, $2 seniors and students ages 12–18, free for children under 12. Wed–Sat 10am–4pm. Closed major holidays. All downtown-bound buses.

SCIENCE & TECHNOLOGY MUSEUMS

Biosphere 2 *(Overrated* For 2 years, beginning in September 1991, four men and four women were locked inside this airtight, 3-acre greenhouse in the desert 35 miles north of Tucson near the town of Oracle. During their tenure in Biosphere 2 (earth is considered Biosphere 1), they conducted experiments on how the earth, basically a giant greenhouse, manages to support all the planet's life forms. Today there are no longer any people living in Biosphere 2, and the former research facility is operated more as a tourist attraction than as a science center. Tours take visitors inside the giant greenhouse and into the mechanisms that helped keep this sealed environment going for 2 years. The strangest sight is the giant "lung" that allowed for the expansion and contraction of the air within Biosphere 2. Although the building, which sits in the middle of desert hill country, is an impressive sight, the tours are something of a let down.

Ariz. 77, mile marker 96.5. *C* **520/838-6200**. www.bio2.com. Admission $20 ages 13 and older, $13 children 6–12. Daily 9am–4pm. Closed Thanksgiving and Christmas. Take Oracle Rd. north out of Tucson and continue north on Ariz. 77 until you see the sign.

Flandrau Science Center & Planetarium   Located on the campus of the University of Arizona, the Flandrau Planetarium is the most convenient place in Arizona to do a little stargazing through a professional telescope. As such, it should be on the itinerary of anyone coming to Tucson (unless, of course, it's cloudy when you visit). The planetarium theater presents a variety of programs on the stars, and the exhibit halls contain a mineral collection (the largest in the state) and hands-on science exhibits for people of all ages. However, the real reason to visit is a chance to gaze through the planetarium's 16-inch telescope.

University of Arizona campus, 1601 E. University Blvd., at Cherry Ave. (© **520/621-STAR.** www.flandrau.org. Admission to exhibits $3 adults, $2 children 3–13. Telescope viewing free. Planetarium $5.50 adults, $4.50 seniors, $4 children 3–13; children under 3 not admitted. Mon–Wed 9am–5pm; Thurs–Sat 9am–5pm and 7–9pm; Sun 1–5pm. Telescope viewing (weather permitting) Aug 15–May 15 Wed–Sat 6:40–10pm; May 15–Aug 14 Wed–Sat 7:30–10pm. Closed major holidays. Bus: 1, 4, 5, 6, 9, 102, or 103.

The International Wildlife Museum   This castlelike building (modeled after a French Foreign Legion fort), located on the road that leads to the Arizona–Sonora Desert Museum, is a natural-history museum filled with stuffed animals in lifelike poses and surroundings. Animals from all over the world are displayed, and there are exhibits of extinct animals, including the Irish elk and the woolly mammoth. Among the more lifelike displays are the predator-and-prey exhibits. There are also fascinating exhibits of colorful butterflies and other unusual insects. For the kids, there's a crawl-through ferret burrow.

4800 W. Gates Pass Rd. (© **520/629-0100.** www.thewildlifemuseum.org. Admission $7 adults, $5.50 seniors and students, $2.50 children 6–12. Mon–Fri 9am–5pm; Sat–Sun 9am–6pm. Ticket booth closes 45 min. before museum. Closed Thanksgiving and Christmas. Take Speedway Blvd. West, continuing in the same direction when it becomes Gates Pass Blvd. The museum is 5 miles west of I-10.

Pima Air & Space Museum 🐾   Located just south of Davis Monthan Air Force Base, the Pima Air & Space Museum houses one of the largest collections of historic aircraft in the world. On display are more than 250 aircraft, including an X-15 (the world's fastest aircraft), an SR-71 Blackbird, several Russian MiGs, World War II combat gliders, a "Superguppy," a B-17G "Flying Fortress," and numerous experimental aircraft, including a backpack helicopter known as the "Hopicopter." The collection includes a replica of the Wright brothers' 1903 Wright Flyer. Tours are available.

The museum also offers guided tours of Davis Monthan's AMARC (Arizona Maintenance and Regeneration Center) facility, which goes by the name of the Boneyard. Here, thousands of mothballed planes are lined up in neat rows under the Arizona sun. Tours last just under an hour and cost $6 for adults and $3 for children 12 and under. Tour reservations (© **520/618-4800**) should be made about a week in advance.

6000 E. Valencia Rd. (© **520/574-0462.** www.pimaair.org. Admission $9.75 adults, $8.75 seniors and military, $6 children 7–12. Daily 9am–5pm. Closed Thanksgiving and Christmas. Take the Valencia Rd. exit from I-10 and drive east 2 miles to the museum.

Titan Missile Museum 🐾   If you've ever wondered what it would be like to have your finger on the button of a nuclear missile, here's your opportunity to find out. This deactivated intercontinental ballistic missile (ICBM) silo is now a museum—and is the only museum in the country that allows visitors to descend into a former missile silo. The huge Titan missile on display is still a terrifying sight even without its nuclear warhead. The guided tours do a great job of explaining not only the ICBM system but also what life was like for the people who worked here. Operated by the Pima Air & Space Museum, this museum is located 25 miles south of Tucson near the retirement community of Green Valley.

1580 W. Duval Mine Rd., Sahuarita (Exit 69 off I-19). © 520/625-7736. Advance reservations recommended but not necessary. Admission $8.50 adults, $7.50 seniors, $5 children 7–12. May–Oct Wed–Sun 9am–4pm; Nov–Apr daily 9am–4pm. Closed Thanksgiving and Christmas. Take I-19 south to Green Valley; take Exit 69 west a half-mile to main entrance.

PARKS, GARDENS & ZOOS

See "The Tucson Area's (Mostly) Natural Wonders," earlier in this chapter, for details on the Arizona–Sonora Desert Museum, the region's premier zoo.

Reid Park Zoo *Kids* Although small and overshadowed by the Arizona–Sonora Desert Museum, the Reid Park Zoo is an important breeding center for several endangered species. Among the animals in the zoo's breeding programs are giant anteaters, white rhinoceroses, tigers, ruffed lemurs, and zebras. A South American exhibit features a capybara (the largest rodent in the world), piranhas, and black jaguars. Get here early, when the animals are more active and before the crowds hit. If you've got the kids along, there's a good playground in the adjacent park.

1100 S. Randolph Way (at 22nd St. between Country Club Rd. and Alvernon Way). © 520/791-4022. www.tucsonzoo.org. Admission $5 adults, $4 seniors, $2 children 2–14. Daily 9am–4pm. Closed Thanksgiving and Christmas. Bus: 7.

Frommer's Favorite Tucson Experiences

Visiting the Arizona–Sonora Desert Museum. One of the world's finest zoos, the museum focuses exclusively on the animals and plants of the Sonoran Desert of southern Arizona and northern Mexico. See p. 356.

Taking a Full-Moon Desert Hike. There's no better time to explore than at night (when the desert comes alive) under a full moon. Drive to the east section of Saguaro National Park, where the parking lots at the east ends of Speedway and Broadway are open 24 hours. It's also possible to park on Old Spanish Trail outside the main entrance to the east unit of the park. There are also places on the west side where you can park outside the gates and walk into the park. See p. 360.

Making the Drive to Mount Lemmon *★★*. The road up Mount Lemmon is a breathtakingly scenic drive. From the desert, the road twists and turns up into the Santa Catalina Mountains, with cacti and palo verde gradually replaced by pine and juniper. You'll have great views of Tucson along the way. The 25-mile Sky Island Scenic Byway (Catalina Hwy.) begins on the east side of Tucson off Tanque Verde Road. See p. 376.

Spending Time in Sabino Canyon. Biking, hiking, swimming, birding—Sabino Canyon has it all. The canyon, carved by a creek that flows for most of the year, is an oasis in the desert. Although popular with both locals and tourists, it still offers delightful opportunities for escaping the city. See p. 360.

Bird-Watching in Madera Canyon. Located south of the city in the Santa Rita Mountains, this canyon attracts many species of birds, some of which can be seen in only a handful of other spots in the United States. Even if you're not into birding, the canyon offers hiking trails, picnicking, and lots of shade. See p. 374.

Tohono Chul Park ★★ Although this park is fairly small, it provides an excellent introduction to the plant and animal life of the desert. You'll see a forest of cholla cacti as well as a garden of small and complex pincushion cacti. From mid-February to April, the wildflower displays here are gorgeous (if enough rain has fallen in the previous months). The park also includes an ethnobotanical garden; a garden for children that encourages them to touch, listen, and smell; a demonstration garden; natural areas; an exhibit house for art displays; a tearoom (p. 354) that's great for breakfast, lunch, or afternoon tea; and two very good gift shops. Park docents lead guided tours throughout the day, and there are also bird walks and many other special events throughout the cooler months of the year.

7366 N. Paseo del Norte (off Ina Rd. west of the intersection with Oracle Rd.). © 520/742-6455. www. tohonochulpark.org. Admission $5 adults, $4 seniors, $3 students, $2 children ages 5–12; free for all on first Tues of every month. Grounds daily 8am–5pm. Exhibit house daily 9am–5pm. Tearoom daily 8am–5pm. Buildings closed New Year's Day, July 4th, Thanksgiving, and Christmas (free admission to grounds on these days).

Tucson Botanical Gardens Set amid residential neighborhoods in midtown Tucson, these gardens are an oasis of greenery and, though small, are well worth a visit if you're interested in desert plant life, landscaping, or gardening. On the 5½-acre grounds are several small gardens that not only have visual appeal but are also historical and educational. If you live in the desert, you might want to visit just to learn about harvesting rainfall for your desert garden and designing a water-conserving landscape. The sensory garden stimulates all five senses, while in another garden traditional Southwestern crops are grown for research purposes. Also here are a bird garden, a greenhouse with "useful" plants from tropical forests, and a gift shop.

2150 N. Alvernon Way. © 520/326-9686. www.tucsonbotanical.org. Admission $5 adults, $2.50 children 6–11. Daily 8:30am–4:30pm. Closed New Year's Day, July 4th, Thanksgiving, and Christmas. Bus: 11.

ESPECIALLY FOR KIDS

In addition to the museum listed below, two of the greatest places to take kids in the Tucson area are the Arizona–Sonora Desert Museum and Old Tucson Studios. Kids will also get a kick out of the Sabino Canyon tram ride, the Reid Park Zoo, Flandrau Science Center & Planetarium, and the Pima Air & Space Museum. All are described in detail earlier in this chapter.

They'll also enjoy **Trail Dust Town,** 6541 E. Tanque Verde Rd. (© **520/296-4551**), a Wild West–themed shopping and dining center. It has a full-size carousel, a scaled-down train to ride, shootout shows, and miniature golf next door. Basically, it's a sort of scaled-down Old Tucson. If the kids are into miniature golf, they'll probably love **Magic Carpet Golf,** 6125 E. Speedway Blvd. (© **520/885-3691**), as much as I do. Putt balls under and around a sphinx, a skull, a giant Easter Island head, and a huge snake.

Tucson Children's Museum This museum, in the old Carnegie Library in downtown Tucson, is filled with fun and educational hands-on activities. Exhibits change every year or so, but have included a doctor's office, a fire station, and a bubble factory. Expect to find such perennial kid favorites as a firetruck, a police motorcycle, and dinosaur sculptures. Weekends generally feature special performances and programs.

200 S. Sixth Ave. © 520/792-9985. www.tucsonchildrensmuseum.org. Admission $5.50 adults, $4.50 seniors, $3.50 children 2–16; free on 3rd Sun of month (except Oct–Nov). Tues–Sat 10am–5pm; Sun noon–5pm. Closed New Year's Day, Easter, Thanksgiving, and Christmas. All downtown-bound buses.

Kids All Aboard!

If you've got kids who idolize Thomas the Tank Engine, then you better schedule your Tucson visit for the second or fourth Sunday of the month. On those days (with a few exceptions), the **Gadsden-Pacific Division Toy Train Operating Museum**, 3975 N. Miller Ave. (© **520/888-2222**), sends out little engines that think they can. The trains chug around a variety of layouts built in different model railroad gauges. The museum is open from 12:30 to 4:30pm on the two days each month that it is open. Admission is free. In July and August, the museum is closed.

WALKING TOUR   DOWNTOWN HISTORIC DISTRICTS

Start:	Arizona Historical Museum Downtown.
Finish:	Hotel Congress.
Time:	5 hours.
Best Times:	Weekends, when restaurants aren't packed at lunch.
Worst Times:	Summer, when it's just too hot to do any walking.

Tucson has a long and varied cultural history, which is most easily seen on a walking tour of the downtown historic neighborhoods. Start your explorations in El Presidio Historic District, which is named for the Presidio of San Augustín del Tucson (1775), the Spanish garrison built here to protect the San Xavier del Bac Mission from the Apaches. For many years the presidio was the heart of Tucson, and although no original buildings are still standing, there are numerous structures from the mid–19th century.

After finding a parking space at the large public lot at the corner of Court Avenue and Council Street, walk 2 blocks east on Council Street to Stone Avenue. Cross Stone, turn right, and walk a block and a half to the:

❶ Arizona Historical Museum Downtown

This museum, at 140 N. Stone Ave., is housed in the Wells Fargo bank building and is the perfect introduction to the history of Tucson. Spend an hour or so here getting acquainted with the city's past and you'll get much more out of the rest of this walking tour.

From the museum, head west 2 blocks on Alameda Street, turn right on Court Street and continue north for a block to Tucson's premier crafts market:

❷ Old Town Artisans

This adobe building, at 201 N. Court Ave., dates from 1862, and has numerous rooms full of interesting (and occasionally tacky) Southwestern crafts (see "Shopping," later in this chapter, for details). The central courtyard has shady gardens. You could spend hours browsing through the assortment of crafts here, but keep in mind you've still got a long walk ahead of you.

Across Meyer Avenue from this building's southwest corner is:

❸ La Casa Cordova

This building, at 175 N. Meyer Ave., dates from about 1848 and is one of the oldest in Tucson. Although the art museum owns five historic homes on this block, this is the only one that has been restored to look as it might have in the late 1800s. Each year from November to March, this building exhibits a very elaborate *nacimiento*, a Mexican folk-art nativity scene, with images from the Bible and Latin American history all rolled up into one miniature landscape full of angels, greenery, and Christmas lights.

Through a colorful gate just to the south of La Casa Cordova is the entrance to the:

❹ Tucson Museum of Art

This modern building houses collections of pre-Columbian and Western art, as well as exhibits of contemporary works. A visit will not only allow you to see plenty of art, but will also provide a glimpse inside a couple of historic homes that now serve as museum galleries.

After touring the museum, walk back up North Meyer Avenue; at the end of the block, you will find the:

❺ Romero House

This 1868 house may incorporate part of the original presidio wall, but it has been extensively altered over the years. At one time it even served as a gas station. The Romero House now contains the Tucson Museum of Art School.

From the Romero House, turn left onto Washington Street and then left again onto Main Avenue. The first building you'll come to on this side of the art museum's historic block is the:

❻ Corbett House

This restored Mission Revival–style building, at 180 N. Main Ave., was built in 1907. The house, which is set back behind a green lawn, is strikingly different from the older, Sonoran-style adobe homes on this block. On Tuesdays at 11am, the Tucson Museum of Art offers a guided tour of the Corbett House.

Next door to this home is the:

❼ Stevens House

Located at 150 N. Main Ave., this is a Sonoran-style row house completed in 1866. It currently houses the museum's collection of pre-Columbian, Spanish colonial, and Latin American folk art as well as a cafe and is entered through the art museum's courtyard.

Next door is the:

❽ Fish House

This house, at 120 N. Main Ave., was built in 1867 on the site of old Mexican barracks. Named for Edward Nye Fish, a local merchant, it now houses the museum's Western-art collection. Some of the walls of this house are 2 feet thick, and ceilings in some places are made from old packing crates.

From here, head back up Main Avenue; on your right at the far end of the next block, you'll reach the:

❾ Julius Kruttschnidt House

This house, at 297 N. Main Ave., dates from 1886 and now houses El Presidio Bed & Breakfast Inn (p. 331). Victorian trappings, including a long veranda, disguise the adobe origins of this unique and beautifully restored home.

Across Main Avenue from the B&B is the:

❿ Steinfeld House

This house, at 300 N. Main Ave., was built in 1900 in California Mission Revival style and was designed by Henry Trost, Tucson's most noted architect. It served as the original Owl's Club, a gentlemen's club for some of Tucson's most eligible bachelors of the time.

Another block north on Main Avenue stands the:

⓫ Owl's Club Mansion

This impressive mansion, at 378 N. Main Ave., was built in 1902 and designed by Henry Trost in the Mission Revival style, albeit with a great deal of ornamentation. It replaced the Steinfeld House as home to the bachelors of the Owl's Club.

TAKE A BREAK
If you started your tour late in the morning, you're probably hungry by now. Continue north on Main Avenue to Franklin Street and walk east on Franklin to Court Avenue. Turn right onto Court, and you will find **El Charro Café** (p. 343), Tucson's oldest Mexican restaurant. Be sure to order *carne seca,* the house specialty.

Walking Tour: Downtown Historic Districts

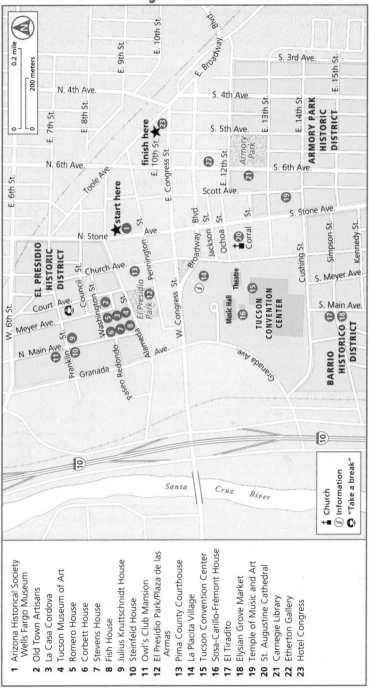

1 Arizona Historical Society
    Wells Fargo Museum
2 Old Town Artisans
3 La Casa Cordova
4 Tucson Museum of Art
5 Romero House
6 Corbett House
7 Stevens House
8 Fish House
9 Julius Kruttschnidt House
10 Steinfeld House
11 Owl's Club Mansion
12 El Presidio Park/Plaza de las
    Armas
13 Pima County Courthouse
14 La Placita Village
15 Tucson Convention Center
16 Sosa-Carillo-Frémont House
17 El Tiradito
18 Elysian Grove Market
19 Temple of Music and Art
20 St. Augustine Cathedral
21 Carnegie Library
22 Etherton Gallery
23 Hotel Congress

From here, continue south on Court Avenue and cross Alameda Street to reach:

⑫ El Presidio Park/Plaza de las Armas

This was once the parade ground for the presidio and is now a shady gathering spot for everyone from downtown office workers to the homeless. Here on the plaza, you'll see a life-size bronze statue of a presidio soldier, as well as a statue commemorating the Mormon Battalion's visit to Tucson in 1846.

Just to the east of the park is the very impressive:

⑬ Pima County Courthouse

Built in 1928, the courthouse, located at 115 N. Church Ave., incorporates Moorish, Spanish, and Southwestern architectural features, including a colorful tiled dome. A portion of the original presidio wall is in a glass case on the second floor.

From the courthouse, continue south 2 blocks (across two pedestrian bridges), to the colorfully painted:

⑭ La Placita Village

This complex of offices and restaurants, at 110 S. Church Ave., was designed to resemble a Mexican village. It houses Tucson's visitor center and also incorporates the Samaniego House, a Sonoran-style row house that dates from the 1880s.

Adjacent to La Placita Village is the:

⑮ Tucson Convention Center

This sprawling complex includes a sports arena, grand ballroom, concert hall, theater, pavilions, meeting halls, and gardens.

Near the fountains in the center of the convention center complex is the historic:

⑯ Sosa-Carillo-Frémont House

This adobe structure, located at 151 S. Granada Ave., was built in the 1850s and later served as the home of territorial governor John C. Frémont. The restored building is open to the public and is furnished in the style of the period.

Continue south through the grounds of the convention center complex, and you will come to Cushing Street, across which lies the Barrio Histórico District. With its 150 adobe row houses, this is the largest collection of 19th-century Sonoran-style adobe buildings in the United States. In the early 1970s, the entire neighborhood was almost razed in the name of urban renewal and highway construction. About half of downtown Tucson, including the neighborhoods that once stood on the site of today's convention center, was razed before the voices for preservation and restoration were finally heard. In fact, if it had not been for the activism of the residents of the Barrio Histórico, I-10 would now run right through much of this area.

Start your exploration of the northern (and more restored) blocks of the Barrio Histórico neighborhood by crossing Cushing Street and then turning down Main Avenue, where you will find, on the west side of the street in the first block:

⑰ El Tiradito

El Tiradito (The Castaway) is the only shrine in the United States dedicated to a sinner buried in unconsecrated soil. People still light candles here in hopes of having their wishes come true.

Continuing south to the corner of West Simpson Street, you will see the:

⑱ Elysian Grove Market

This dilapidated-looking old adobe building, at 400 W. Simpson St., is actually one of the most interesting and artistically decorated bed-and-breakfast inns in the city (p. 331).

Wander a while through the Barrio Histórico District, admiring the Sonoran-style homes that are built right out to the street. Many of these homes sport colorfully painted facades, signs of the ongoing renovation of this neighborhood.

From the corner of Cushing Street and South Meyer Avenue, walk 3 blocks east and turn left on South Scott Avenue, where you'll find the:

⑲ Temple of Music and Art

This building, located at 330 S. Scott Ave., was built in 1927 as a movie and stage theater and is the home of the Arizona Theatre Company (p. 390). Don't miss the little art gallery on the second floor.

From here, walk north on South Scott Avenue, turn left on McCormick Street/13th Street, and then turn right onto South Stone Avenue, which will bring you to:

⑳ St. Augustine Cathedral

The cathedral was built in 1896 and was modeled after the Cathedral of Querétaro, Mexico. Above the door, you'll see a statue of Saint Augustine as well as symbols of the Arizona desert—the horned toad, the saguaro, and the yucca.

From here, walk east on Corral Street, turn left on South Scott Avenue, and then turn right on 12th Street and right again on South Sixth Avenue to reach the front of the old:

㉑ Carnegie Library

The library dates from 1901 and was designed by Henry Trost. The building now houses the Tucson Children's Museum (see "Especially for Kids," above).

Now head north on South Sixth Avenue. In 1 block, you'll pass the:

㉒ Etherton Gallery

This second-floor gallery (p. 381), upstairs from the popular Barrio restaurant (p. 342), has long been one of Tucson's top contemporary art galleries.

Continue 1 more block north and turn right on Congress Street. In 1 block, you will see on the far side of the street the:

㉓ Hotel Congress

This hotel, located at 311 E. Congress St., was built as a railroad hotel in 1919 and once played host to John Dillinger, infamous public enemy number one. Today, the restored budget lodging (p. 333) is popular with European travelers and students, and has a classic Western-style lobby. There's a cafe here, and the lobby is well worth a stroll-through.

6 Organized Tours

Learning Expeditions, a program run by the **Arizona State Museum,** occasionally offers scholar-led archaeological tours. For information, contact the marketing department at the museum (✆ **520/626-8381;** www.statemuseum. arizona.edu).

For a look at a completely different sort of excavation, head south from Tucson 15 miles to the **ASARCO Mineral Discovery Center,** 1421 W. Pima Mine Rd., Sahuarita (✆ **520/625-7513;** www.mineraldiscovery.com), where you can tour a huge open-pit copper mine and learn about copper mining past and present. The center is open Tuesday through Saturday from 9am to 5pm; admission is free. One-hour mine tours, which leave every 20 to 30 minutes, are $6 for adults, $5 for seniors, and $4 for children 5 to 12. To get here, drive south from Tucson on I-19 and take Exit 80. You might want to combine this tour with a visit to the nearby Titan Missile Museum.

Want to taste raw cactus, learn about cholla-extraction devices, and hold a live tarantula or snake? Call **Sunshine Jeep Tours** (✆ **520/742-1943;** www.sunshine jeeptours.com), which charges $48 for adults, $36 for children 11 to 15, and $24 for children 6 to 10. On these tours, you'll head out across a private ranch northwest of Tucson and pass through some of the densest stands of saguaro cacti in the state.

7 Outdoor Pursuits

BICYCLING   Tucson is one of the best bicycling cities in the country, and the dirt roads and trails of the surrounding national forest and desert are perfect for mountain biking. Bikes can be rented for $35 a day at **Bargain Basement Bikes,** 428 N. Fremont Ave., near the university (© **520/628-1015**). This store can also set you up with a bicycling map of the area.

If you'd rather confine your pedaling to paved surfaces, there are some great options around town. The number one choice in town for cyclists in halfway decent shape is the road up **Sabino Canyon** (p. 360). Keep in mind, however, that bicycles are allowed on this road only 5 days a week and then only before 9am and after 5pm (the road is closed to bikes all day Wed and Sat). For a much easier ride, try the **Rillito River Park path,** which currently has a 1-mile paved section between Swan and Craycroft roads and a 6-mile paved section between Campbell Avenue and I-10. The trail parallels River Road and the usually dry bed of the Rillito River, and if you've got knobby tires, you can link the two paved sections or continue west past La Cholla Road after the pavement ends. Another option close to downtown is the 7-mile **Santa Cruz River Park path,** which runs along both sides of the usually dry Santa Cruz River and extends from West Grant Road to Irvington Road.

If mountain biking is more your speed, there are lots of great rides in the Tucson area. For an easy and very scenic dirt-road loop through forests of saguaros, head to the west unit of Saguaro National Park (p. 360) and ride the 6-mile **Bajada Loop Drive.** You can turn this into a 12-mile ride (half on paved road) by starting at the Red Hills Visitor Center.

BIRD-WATCHING   Southern Arizona has some of the best bird-watching in the country, and although the best spots are south of Tucson, there are a few places around the city that birders will enjoy seeking out. Call the **Tucson Audubon Society's Bird Report** (© **520/798-1005**) to find out which birds have been spotted lately.

Roy P. Drachman Agua Caliente Park, 12325 Roger Road (off N. Soldier Trail) in the northeast corner of the city, is just about the best place in Tucson to see birds. The year-round warm springs here are a magnet for dozens of species, including waterfowl, great blue herons, black phoebes, soras, and vermilion flycatchers. To find the park, follow Tanque Verde Road east 6 miles from the intersection with Sabino Canyon Road and turn left onto Soldier Trail. Watch for signs.

Other good places include **Sabino Canyon Recreation Area** (p. 360), the path to the waterfall at **Loews Ventana Canyon Resort** (p. 335), and the **Rillito River path** between Craycroft and Swan roads.

The very best area for bird-watching is **Madera Canyon National Forest Recreation Area** ✦ (© **520/281-2296**), about 40 miles south of the city in the Coronado National Forest. Because of the year-round water to be found here, Madera Canyon attracts a surprising variety of bird life. Avid birders flock to this canyon from around the country in hopes of spotting more than a dozen species of hummingbirds, an equal number of flycatchers, warblers, tanagers, buntings, grosbeaks, and many rare birds not found in any other state. However, before birding became a hot activity, this canyon was popular with families looking for a way to escape the heat down in Tucson, and the shady picnic areas and trails still get a lot of use by those who don't carry binoculars. If you're heading out for the day, arrive early—parking is very limited. To reach Madera Canyon, take the Continental Road/Madera Canyon exit off I-19; from the exit, it's another 12 miles southeast. The canyon is open daily from dawn to dusk for day use; there is a $5 day-use fee. There's also a campground ($10 per night). For information on the canyon's Santa Rita Lodge, see p. 340.

GOLF Although there aren't quite as many golf courses in Tucson as in Phoenix, this is still a golfer's town. For last-minute tee-time reservations, contact **Standby Golf** (© **800/655-5345;** www.discountteetimes.com). No fee is charged for this service.

In addition to the public and municipal links, there are numerous resort courses that allow nonguests to play. Perhaps the most famous of these are the two 18-hole courses at **Ventana Canyon Golf and Racquet Club** ✦, 6200 N. Clubhouse Lane (© **520/577-4015;** www.ventanacanyonclub.com). These Tom Fazio–designed courses offer challenging desert target–style play that is nearly legendary. The 3rd hole on the Mountain Course is one of the most photographed holes in the West. Greens fees are $199 in winter and $89 in summer.

As famous as Ventana Canyon courses are, it's the 27-hole **Omni Tucson National Golf Resort and Spa** ✦, 2727 W. Club Dr. (© **520/575-7540;** www.tucsonnational.com), a traditional course that is perhaps more familiar to golfers as the site of the annual Tucson Open. If you are not staying at the resort, greens fees are $200 in winter, $80 in summer.

El Conquistador Country Club, 10555 N. La Cañada Dr., Oro Valley (© **520/544-1800;** www.elconquistadorcc.com), with two 18-hole courses and a 9-hole course, offers stunning (and very distracting) views of the Santa Catalina Mountains. Greens fees are $115 in winter, $42 in summer.

La Paloma Resort and Country Club, 3660 E. Sunrise Dr. (© **520/742-6100;** www.lapalomacc.com), features 27 holes designed by Jack Nicklaus. Fees are $195 to $215 in winter, $90 in summer. If you aren't staying at the resort, you can book only up to 48 hours in advance.

At **Starr Pass Golf Club,** 3645 W. Starr Pass Blvd. (© **800/503-2898** or 520/670-0300; www.starrpasstucson.com), players are seduced by the deceptively difficult 15th hole that plays right through the narrow Starr Pass, which was once a stagecoach route. Greens fees are $150 in winter, $60 in summer.

There are many public courses around town. The **Arizona National,** 9777 E. Sabino Greens Dr. (© **520/749-3636;** www.arizonanationalgolfclub.com), incorporates stands of cacti and rocky outcroppings into the course layout. Greens fees are $135 to $165 in winter, $55 to $65 in summer. **The Golf Club at Vistoso,** 955 W. Vistoso Highlands Dr. (© **877/548-1110** or 520/797-9900; www.vistosogolf.com), has a championship desert course, with fees of $139 to $159 in winter, $45 to $55 in summer. **Heritage Highlands Golf & Country Club,** 4949 W. Heritage Club Blvd., Marana (© **520/579-7000;** www.heritage highlands.com), is a championship desert course at the foot of the Tortolita Mountains; greens fees are $99 in winter and $30 to $45 in summer.

Tucson Parks and Recreation operates five municipal golf courses, of which the **Randolph North** and **Dell Urich,** 600 S. Alvernon Way (© **520/791-4161**), are the premier courses. The former is the site of the LPGA Open. Greens fees for 18 holes at these two courses are $37 in winter and $16 in summer. Other municipal courses include **El Rio,** 1400 W. Speedway Blvd. (© **520/791-4229**); **Silverbell,** 3600 N. Silverbell Rd. (© **520/791-5235**); and **Fred Enke,** 8251 E. Irvington Rd. (© **520/791-2539**). This latter course is the city's only desert-style golf course. Greens fees for 18 holes at these three courses are $32 in winter and $14 in summer. Golf carts are available for $9. For general information and tee-time reservations for any of the municipal courses, visit **www.tucsoncitygolf.com**.

HIKING Tucson is nearly surrounded by mountains, most of which are protected as city and state parks, national forest, or national park, and within these public areas are hundreds of miles of hiking trails.

Saguaro National Park (© 520/733-5153) flanks Tucson on both the east and west with units accessible off Old Spanish Trail east of Tucson and past the end of Speedway Boulevard west of the city. In these areas, you can observe Sonoran Desert vegetation and wildlife and hike among the huge saguaro cacti for which the park is named. For saguaro-spotting, the west unit is the better choice. See p. 360 for details.

Tucson Mountain Park, at the west end of Speedway Boulevard, is adjacent to Saguaro National Park and preserves a similar landscape. The parking area at Gates Pass, on Speedway, is a favorite sunset spot.

Sabino Canyon (p. 360), off Sabino Canyon Road, is one of Tucson's best hiking areas, but is also the city's most popular recreation area. A cold mountain stream here cascades over waterfalls and forms pools that make great swimming holes. The 5-mile round-trip **Seven Falls Trail,** which follows Bear Canyon deep into the mountains, is the most popular hike in the recreation area. You can take a tram to the trail head or add extra miles by hiking from the main parking lot.

With the city limits pushing right out to the boundary of the Coronado National Forest, there are some very convenient hiking options in Tucson's northern foothills. The **Ventana Canyon Trail** begins at a parking area adjacent to the Loews Ventana Canyon Resort (off Sunrise Dr. west of Sabino Canyon Rd.) and leads into the Ventana Canyon Wilderness. A few miles west, there's the **Finger Rock Trail,** which starts at the top of the section of Alvernon Road accessed from Skyline Drive. There are actually a couple of trails starting here, so you can hike for miles into the desert. Over near the Westward Look Resort is the **Pima Canyon Trail,** which leads into the Ventana Canyon Wilderness and is reached off Ina Road just east of Oracle Road. Both of these trails provide classic desert canyon hikes of whatever length you feel like hiking (a dam at 3 miles on the latter trail makes a good turnaround point). Just south of the Hilton Tucson El Conquistador Golf & Tennis Resort, you'll find the **Linda Vista Trail,** which begins just off Oracle Road on Linda Vista Boulevard. This trail lies at the foot of Pusch Ridge and winds up through dense stands of prickly-pear cactus. Higher up on the trail, there are some large saguaros. Because this trail is shaded by Pusch Ridge in the morning, it's a good choice for a morning hike on a day that's going to be hot.

Catalina State Park, 11570 N. Oracle Rd. (© **520/628-5798**), is set on the rugged northwest face of the Santa Catalina Mountains, between 2,500 and 3,000 feet high. Hiking trails here lead into the Pusch Ridge Wilderness; however, the park's favorite day hike is the 5.5-mile round-trip to **Romero Pools,** where small natural pools of water set amid the rocks are a refreshing destination on a hot day (expect plenty of other people on a weekend). This hike involves about 1,000 feet of elevation gain. Admission to the park is $6 per vehicle. There are horseback-riding stables adjacent to the park, and within the park is an ancient Hohokam ruin.

One of the reasons Tucson is such a livable city is the presence of the cool (and, in winter, snow-covered) pine forests of 8,250-foot Mount Lemmon. Within the **Mount Lemmon Recreation Area,** at the end of the Catalina Highway (also called the Sky Island Scenic Byway), are many miles of trails, and the hearty hiker can even set out from down in the lowland desert and hike up into the alpine forests. For a more leisurely excursion, drive up onto the mountain to start your hike. One of our favorite hikes in the past was the 5-mile Aspen–Marshall Gulch loop, which began beyond the community of Summerhaven at the Marshall Gulch picnic area. However, this area was at the center of the devastating forest fire that swept across Mount Lemmon in June 2003. In the winter, there can be snow atop Mount Lemmon. There is a $5-per-vehicle charge to use any of the sites within this recreation area. Even if you only plan to pull off at a roadside parking spot and ogle the view of the desert far below, you'll need to stop at the roadside ticket kiosk at the base of the mountain and pay your fee. For more information, contact the **Coronado National Forest Santa Catalina Ranger District,** 5700 N. Sabino Canyon Rd. (© 520/749-8700).

HORSEBACK RIDING   If you want to play cowboy or just go for a leisurely ride through the desert, there are plenty of stables around Tucson where you can saddle up. In addition to renting horses and providing guided trail rides, some of the stables below offer sunset rides with cookouts. Although reservations are not always required, they're a good idea. You can also opt to stay at a guest ranch and do as much riding as your muscles can stand.

Pusch Ridge Stables, 13700 N. Oracle Rd. (© 520/825-1664), is adjacent to Catalina State Park and Coronado National Forest. Rates are $25 for 1 hour, $40 for 2 hours, and $30 for a sunset ride.

Over on the east side of Tucson, there's **Spanish Trail Outfitters** (© 520/749-0167), which leads rides into the foothills of the Santa Catalina Mountains off Sabino Canyon Road. Rates are $30 for a 1-hour ride, $50 for a 2-hour ride, and $45 for a sunset ride.

Big Sky Rides (© 520/299-RIDE) offers horseback rides at several locations around the area, including in the Tucson Mountains and Saguaro National Park (west unit) and at Hacienda del Sol Guest Ranch Resort (p. 336). Rates range from $25 for 1 hour to $95 for a full day with lunch. Reservations are requested.

HOT-AIR BALLOONING   **Balloon America** (© 520/299-7744; www. balloonridesusa.com) offers flights over the desert ($150–$185) or a more adventurous trip over the foothills of the Santa Catalina Mountains ($350). The ballooning season runs October through June. **Fleur de Tucson Balloon Tours** (© 520/529-1025; www.fleurdetucson.net) offers rides over the Tucson Mountains, Saguaro National Park, and the Avra Valley. Rates are $135 to $175 per person, including brunch or hors d'oeuvres and a champagne toast.

SKIING   Located 35 miles from Tucson (a 1-hr. drive), **Mount Lemmon Ski Valley** (© 520/576-1321, or 520/576-1400 for snow report) is the southernmost ski area in the United States and offers 15 runs for experienced downhill skiers as well as beginners. The season here isn't very reliable, so be sure to call first to make sure it's open. Locals recommend not using your own skis or snowboard (too many exposed rocks). The ski area often opens only after a new dump of snow (at which time the Catalina/Mount Lemmon Hwy. is usually closed), so be sure to call the road-condition information line (© 520/547-7510) before driving up. In a good year, the season runs from December to April. Full-day lift tickets are $35 for adults.

TENNIS   The **Randolph Tennis Center,** 50 S. Alvernon Way (© 520/791-4896), convenient to downtown, offers 25 lighted courts. During the day, court time is $2.50 per person; at night, it's $10 per court. Many of the city's hotels and resorts provide courts for guest use.

WILDFLOWER-VIEWING   Bloom time varies from year to year, but April and May are good times to view native wildflowers in the Tucson area. While the crowns of white blossoms worn by saguaro cacti are among the most visible blooms in the area, other cacti are far more colorful. **Saguaro National Park** (p. 360) and **Sabino Canyon** (p. 360) are among the best local spots to see saguaros, other cactus species, and various wildflowers in bloom. If you feel like heading further afield, the wildflower displays at **Picacho Peak State Park** (p. 156), between Tucson and Casa Grande, are the most impressive in the state.

8 Spectator Sports

BASEBALL   The **Colorado Rockies** (© 520/327-9467) pitch spring-training camp in March at Hi Corbett Field, 3400 E. Camino Campestre, in Reid Park (at South Country Club Rd. and E. 22nd St.). Tickets are $2 to $11. Both the **Chicago White Sox** and the **Arizona Diamondbacks** have their spring-training camps and exhibition games at Tucson Electric Park, 2500 E. Ajo Way (© 866/672-1343), on the south side of the city near the airport. Tickets range from $3 to $16.

Tucson Electric Park is also where you can watch the **Tucson Sidewinders** (© 520/434-1021; www.tucsonsidewinders.com), the AAA affiliate team of the Arizona Diamondbacks. The season runs April through August; tickets are $5 to $8.

FOOTBALL   The **University of Arizona Wildcats** (© 800/452-2287 or 520/621-2287; www.arizcats.com), a Pac-10 team, play at UA's Arizona Stadium.

GOLF TOURNAMENTS   The **Chrysler Classic of Tucson** (© 800/882-7660; www.tucsonopen.pgatour.com), Tucson's main PGA tournament, is held in mid-February at the Omni Tucson National Golf Resort and Spa. Daily tickets are $15. In mid-March, women golfers compete for big prizes at the **Welch's/Fry's LPGA Championship** (© 520/791-5742; www.tucsonlpga. com), which is held at the Randolph Golf Course Complex. Daily tickets are about $10.

HORSE/GREYHOUND RACING   **Rillito Park Race Track,** 4502 N. First Ave. (© 520/293-5011), was the birthplace of both the photo finish and organized quarter-horse and Arabian racing. It has now been restored for quarter-horse and thoroughbred racing. The ponies run on weekends from early February to early March, and admission is $2 to $3.

Greyhounds race year-round at **Tucson Greyhound Park,** 2601 S. Third Ave. (© 520/884-7576; www.tucdogtrak.com). Grandstand admission is only $1.25. To reach the track, take Exit 261 off I-10.

9 Day Spas

If you'd prefer a massage over a round on the links, consider spending a few hours at a day spa. While full-service health spas can cost $400 to $500 or more per day, for less than $100 you can avail yourself of a spa treatment or two (massages, facials, seaweed wraps, loofah scrubs, and the like) and maybe even get to spend the day lounging by the pool at some exclusive resort. Spas are also great places to while away an afternoon if you couldn't get a tee time at that golf course you wanted to play or if it happens to be raining. While spas in general still cater primarily to women, most also have special programs for men.

The **Elizabeth Arden Red Door Spa,** at the Westin La Paloma, 3800 E. Sunrise Dr. (© 520/742-7866; http://westinlapalomaresort.com/spa), focuses on skin-care services, but there are plenty of body wraps and massages available as well. With a 1-hour treatment (mostly $90–$125), you can use the spa's facilities for the day. However, unlike other spas in town, the Red Door is more about relaxation than staying fit, so you won't find aerobics classes or a pool here. Spa packages range in price from $180 to $490.

For variety of services and gorgeous location, you just can't beat the Spa & Tennis Center at **Loews Ventana Canyon Resort,** 7000 N. Resort Dr. (© 520/299-2020; www.loewshotels.com), which is wedged between the rugged Catalinas and manicured fairways of one of the most fabled golf courses in the state. Soothed by the scent of aromatherapy, you can treat yourself to herbal wraps, mud treatments, different styles of massage, specialized facials, complete salon services, and much more. Treatments run $85 to $120. With any 50-minute body treatment, you get use of the spa's facilities and pool and can attend any fitness classes being held that day.

The Spa at Omni Tucson National Golf Resort, 2727 W. Club Dr. (© 520/575-7559; www.omnihotels.com/spas/tucson/index.html), off Magee Road in the northwestern foothills, offers an equally luxurious day at the spa. Services and prices are comparable to those at other spas around town, and once again, with any body treatment or massage lasting 50 minutes or longer, you have full use of the spa's facilities. For a full day of pampering, opt for one of the packages, which run from $220 to $375. Desert stone massages are a big hit here; couples massages are also available.

With six locations around the Tucson area, **Gadabout Day Spa** (www.gadabout.com) offers the opportunity to slip a relaxing visit to a spa into a busy schedule. Mud baths, facials, and massages as well as hair and nail services are available, and body treatments and massages range from about $35 for a quick massage to $369 for a full day at the spa. You'll find Gadabout at the following locations: St. Philip's Plaza, 1990 E. River Rd. (© 520/577-2000); 6393 E. Grant Rd. (© 520/885-0000); Rancho Center, 3382 E. Speedway Blvd. (© 520/325-0000); Sunrise-Kolb, 6960 E. Sunrise Dr. (© 520/615-9700); and 8303 N. Oracle Rd. (© 520/742-0000). The sixth location is Gadabout Man, 2951 N. Swan Rd. (© 520/325-3300).

10 Shopping

Although the Tucson shopping scene is overshadowed by that of Scottsdale and Phoenix, Tucson does provide a very respectable diversity of merchants. Tucsonans have a strong sense of their place in the Southwest, and this is reflected in the city's shopping opportunities. Southwestern clothing, food, crafts, furniture, and art abound (and often at reasonable prices), as do shopping centers built in a Southwestern architectural style.

The city's population center has moved steadily northward for some years, so it is in the northern foothills that you'll find most of the city's large enclosed shopping malls as well as the more tasteful small shopping plazas specializing in boutiques and galleries.

On Fourth Avenue, between Congress Street and Speedway Boulevard, more than 50 shops, galleries, and restaurants make up the **Fourth Avenue historic shopping and entertainment district.** The buildings here were constructed in the early 1900s, and the proximity to the University of Arizona has helped to keep this district bustling. Many of the shops cater primarily to student needs and interests. Through the underpass at the south end of Fourth Avenue is Congress Street, the heart of the **Downtown Arts District,** where there are still a few art galleries (most, however, have moved to the foothills in the past few years). Despite the city's best efforts for several years now, neither of these neighborhoods seems to have caught on with Tucson shoppers, and both areas seem to be primarily hangouts for college students.

El Presidio Historic District around the Tucson Museum of Art is the city's center for crafts shops. This area is home to Old Town Artisans and the Tucson Museum of Art museum shop. The city's **"Lost Barrio"** section, on the corner of Southwest Park Avenue and 12th Street (a block off Broadway), is a good place to look for Mexican imports and Southwestern-style home furnishings at good prices. There are also stores selling African and New Guinea imports and antiques from around the world. Both the stores and the items for sale here tend to be big.

ANTIQUES & COLLECTIBLES

In addition to the places listed below, a great concentration of antiques shops can be found along Grant Road between Campbell Avenue and Alvernon Way. You can pick up a map of Tucson antiques stores at the **American Antique Mall** (✆ **520/326-3070**), 3130 E. Grant Rd., at Country Club Road.

American Antique Mall   This antiques mall has 100 dealers and is one of the largest such places in southern Arizona. For sale are all manner of collectibles and a few antiques. 3130 E. Grant Rd. ✆ 520/326-3070.

Eric Firestone Gallery   Collectors of Stickley and other Arts and Crafts furniture will not want to miss this impressive gallery, which is located in one of the historic buildings at Joesler Village shopping plaza. In addition to the furniture, there are period paintings and accessories. At Joesler Village, 4425 N. Campbell Ave. ✆ 520/577-7711. www.ericfirestonegallery.com.

Michael D. Higgins   Located next door to the Eric Firestone Gallery, this little shop specializes in pre-Columbian artifacts, but also carries African, Asian, even ancient Greek and Roman pieces. At Joesler Village, 4429 N. Campbell Ave. ✆ 520/577-8330. www.mhiggins.com.

Morning Star Antiques   In a shop that adjoins Morning Star Traders (see "Native American Art, Crafts & Jewelry," later in this chapter), Morning Star Antiques carries an excellent selection of antique Spanish and Mexican furniture as well as other unusual and rustic pieces. 2000 E. Speedway Blvd. ✆ 520/881-3060. www.morningstartraders.com.

Primitive Arts Gallery   This is the best gallery in Tucson for pre-Columbian art, with an eclectic mix of ancient artifacts focusing on ceramics. You'll also find a smattering of other artifacts, from Greek urns to contemporary Argentinean *mate* gourds. At Broadway Village, 3026 E. Broadway. ✆ 520/326-4852.

ART

Tucson's gallery scene is not as concentrated as that in many other cities. Most Tucson galleries have in the past few years abandoned downtown in favor of the foothills and other more affluent suburbs. The current art hot spot is the corner of Campbell Avenue and Skyline Drive, where you'll find **Sanders Galleries** and **Settlers West** (which specialize in Western art) and **El Cortijo Arts Annex** (which has several contemporary art galleries and an upscale restaurant).

One of the best ways to take in the downtown Tucson art scene is on a docent-led Artwalk tour ($5). These walks are held between October and May on Thursday between 5:30 and 7:30pm. Reservations are required. Contact the **Tucson Arts District Partnership** (📞 **520/624-9977**; www.tucsonartsdistrict. org) for information.

Davis Dominguez Gallery   Located just a couple of blocks off Fourth Avenue in downtown Tucson, this huge gallery features some of the best and most creative contemporary art in the city. 154 E. Sixth St. 📞 **520/629-9759.** www.davisdominguez.com.

Dinnerware Contemporary Art Gallery   *Contemporary* is the key word at this gallery. Artists represented tend to have a very wide range of styles and media, so you never know what you'll find. Regardless, you can be sure it will be at the cutting edge of Tucson art. 210 N. Fourth St. 📞 **520/792-4503.** www.dinnerwarearts.com.

El Presidio Gallery   Long one of Tucson's premier galleries, El Presidio deals primarily in traditional and contemporary paintings of the Southwest, and is located in a large, modern space in El Cortijo Arts Annex. Contemporary works tend toward the large and bright and are favorites for decorating foothills homes. At El Cortijo Arts Annex, 3001 E. Skyline Dr. 📞 **520/299-1414.** Also at Santa Fe Square, 7000 E. Tanque Verde Rd. (📞 **520/733-0388**). www.elpresidiogallery.com.

Etherton Gallery   For more than 20 years, this gallery has been presenting some of the finest new art to be found in Tucson, including contemporary and historic photographs. A favorite of museums and serious collectors, Etherton Gallery isn't afraid to present work with strong themes. 135 S. Sixth Ave. 📞 **520/ 624-7370.** Also a smaller location at the Temple of Music and Art, 330 S. Scott Ave. (📞 **520/ 624-7370**).

Gallery 7000   Located in the same shopping plaza that houses both the Mark Sublette Medicine Man Gallery and a branch of the El Presidio Gallery, this gallery features the large and colorful shaman paintings of Arizona artist Lawrence Lee. At Santa Fe Sq., 7000 E. Tanque Verde Rd. 📞 **520/733-7100.**

Jane Hamilton Fine Art   This gallery used to be in Bisbee, where it was one of the best galleries in that small art community. Here in Tucson, this gallery's boldly colored contemporary art still stands out. Much of the artwork here reflects a desert aesthetic. At Joesler Village, 1825 E. River Rd., Suite 111. 📞 **800/555-3051** or 520/529-4886. www.janehamilton-fineart.com.

Mark Sublette Medicine Man Gallery   This gallery has the finest and most tasteful traditional Western art you'll find just about anywhere in Arizona. Artists represented here include Ed Mell and Howard Post, and most of the gallery's artists have received national attention. There's an excellent selection of Native American crafts as well; see "Native American Art, Crafts & Jewelry," below, for more details. The gallery is also the site of the Conley Museum of the West, a small collection of Western art and old maps. At Santa Fe Sq., 7000 E. Tanque Verde Rd. 📞 **800/422-9382** or 520/722-7798. www.medicinemangallery.com.

Philabaum Contemporary Art Glass   For nearly 25 years, this gallery, which was originally located downtown, has been exposing Tucson to the latest trends in contemporary art glass. The gallery is full of lovely and colorful pieces by Philabaum and more than 100 other artists from around the country. In St. Philip's Plaza, 4280 N. Campbell Ave., Suite 105. 📞 **520/299-1939.** www.philabaumglass.com.

BOOKS

Chain bookstores in the Tucson area include **Barnes & Noble,** 5130 E. Broadway Blvd. (📞 **520/512-1166**), and 7325 N. La Cholla Blvd., in the Foothills

Mall (☎ **520/742-6402**); and **Borders,** 4235 N. Oracle Rd. (☎ **520/292-1331**), and 5870 E. Broadway, at the Park Place Mall (☎ **520/584-0111**).

Audubon Nature Shop Nature enthusiasts can pick up field guides and books on natural history, along with educational and children's books. 300 E. University Blvd. ☎ **520/629-0510**.

Clues Unlimited If you forgot to pack your vacation reading, drop by this fun little store. Not only can you shop for the latest Carl Hiassen, but you can say hi to Sophie, the resident pot-bellied pig. Broadway Village, 123 S. Eastbourne St. ☎ **520/326-8533**. www.cluesunlimited.com.

Readers Oasis A small bookstore, but packed with handpicked titles of local and general interest. It occasionally has readings and book signings (local author Barbara Kingsolver has been known to do readings here). 3400 E. Speedway Blvd., no. 114. ☎ **520/319-7887**. www.readersoasis.com.

CRAFTS

Details & Green Shoelaces If you enjoy highly imaginative and colorful crafts with a sense of humor, you'll get a kick out of this place. Unexpected objets d'art turn up in the form of clocks, ceramics, glass, and other media. At Plaza Palomino, 2990 N. Swan Rd. ☎ **520/323-0222**. www.detailsart.com.

Obsidian Gallery Contemporary crafts by nationally recognized artists fill this gallery. You'll find luminous art glass, unique and daring jewelry, imaginative ceramics, and much more. At St. Philip's Plaza, 4320 N. Campbell Ave. (at River Rd.). ☎ **520/577-3598**. www.obsidian-gallery.com.

Old Town Artisans Housed in a restored 1850s adobe building covering an entire city block of El Presidio Historic District, this unique shopping plaza houses half a dozen different shops brimming with traditional and contemporary Southwestern designs. 201 N. Court St. ☎ **800/782-8072** or 520/623-6024. www.oldtownartisans.com.

Tucson Museum of Art Shop The museum's gift shop offers a colorful and changing selection of Southwestern crafts, mostly by local and regional artists. 140 N. Main Ave. ☎ **520/624-2333**. www.tucsonarts.com.

FASHION

See also the listing for the Beth Friedman Collection under "Jewelry," below. For cowboy and cowgirl attire, see "Western Wear," below.

Maya Palace This shop features ethnic-inspired but very wearable women's clothing in natural fabrics. The friendly staff helps customers of all ages put together a Southwestern chic look, from casual to dressy. A second shop can be found at El Mercado de Boutiques, 6332 E. Broadway Blvd. (☎ **520/748-0817**). At Plaza Palomino, 2960 N. Swan Rd. ☎ **520/325-6411**. www.mayapalacetucson.com.

Rochelle K Fine Women's Apparel With everything from the latest in the little black dress to drapey silks and casual linens, Rochelle K attracts a well-heeled clientele. You'll also find beautiful accessories and jewelry here. At Casas Adobes Plaza, 7039 N. Oracle Rd. ☎ **520/797-2279**.

GIFTS & SOUVENIRS

B&B Cactus Farm This plant nursery is devoted exclusively to cacti and succulents and is worth a visit just to see the amazing variety on display. It's a good

---

Tips Seeing Stars

Amateur astronomers, take note. Because of all the great star-viewing opportunities in southern Arizona, Tucson has a large number of stargazers, and they all shop at **Stellar-Vision & Astronomy Shop,** 1835 S. Alvernon Way (✆ **520/571-0877;** www.theriver.com/stellar_vision). This store is packed with telescopes of all shapes and sizes, books, posters, star charts, and meteorite jewelry. It also rents equipment and offers star tours.

---

place to stop on the way to or from Saguaro National Park East. The store can pack your purchase for traveling or ship it anywhere in the United States. 11550 E. Speedway Blvd. ✆ 520/721-4687.

Discount Agate House   If you can't make it to Tucson for the annual gem and mineral shows, don't despair. At this cluttered shop, you can pick through shelves crammed with all manner of rare minerals and strange stones. There are even meteorites here. 3401 N. Dodge St. ✆ 520/323-0781. www.discountagatehouse.net.

Native Seeds/SEARCH   Gardeners, cooks, and just about anyone in search of an unusual gift will likely be fascinated by this tiny shop, which is operated by a nonprofit organization dedicated to preserving the biodiversity offered by native Southwest seeds. The shelves are full of heirloom beans, corn, chiles, and other seeds from a wide variety of native desert plants. There are also gourds and inexpensive Tarahumara Indian baskets, bottled sauces and salsas made from native plants, and books about native agriculture. 526 N. Fourth Ave. ✆ 520/622-5561. www.nativeseeds.org.

Picánte Designs   There's a plethora of Hispanic-theme icons and accessories here, including *milagros,* Day of the Dead skeletons, Mexican crosses, jewelry, greeting cards, and folk art from around the world. This is a great place to shop for distinctive south-of-the-border kitschy gifts. 2932 E. Broadway. ✆ 520/320-5699.

Tohono Chul Museum Shop   This shop is packed with Mexican folk art, nature-theme toys, household items, T-shirts, and books; it makes a good stop after a visit to the surrounding Tohono Chul Park, which is landscaped with desert plants. Add a meal at the park's tearoom, and you've got a good afternoon's outing. For a description of the park, see p. 368. 7366 N. Paseo del Norte (1 block west of the corner of Ina and Oracle roads in Tohono Chul Park). ✆ 520/742-6455. www. tohonochulpark.org.

JEWELRY

In addition to the stores mentioned below, see the listing for the Obsidian Gallery under "Crafts," above.

Beth Friedman Collection   This shop sells a well-chosen collection of jewelry by Native American craftspeople and international designers. It also carries some extravagant cowgirl get-ups in velvet and lace as well as contemporary women's fashions. At Joesler Village, 1865 E. River Rd., Suite 121. ✆ 520/577-6858. www. bethfriedmancollection.com.

Patania's   This small jewelry shop is a showcase for three generations of the Patania family, a silversmithing family that has been crafting fine silver and turquoise jewelry for more than 70 years. The styles span the decades, and jewelry in gold and platinum is also available. 3000 E. Broadway. ✆ 520/795-0086.

Turquoise Door The contemporary Southwestern jewelry here is among the most stunning in the city, made with opals, diamonds, lapis lazuli, amethysts, and the ubiquitous turquoise. At St. Philip's Plaza, 4330 N. Campbell Ave. (at River Rd.). © 520/299-7787. www.turquoisedoorjewelry.com.

MALLS & SHOPPING CENTERS

Foothills Mall This large factory-outlet mall and discount shopping center has, among many other stores, a Nike Factory Store, Off 5th Saks Fifth Avenue outlet, and Barnes & Noble, as well as a brewpub and a couple of good restaurants. 7401 N. La Cholla Blvd. (at Ina Rd.). © 520/219-0650. www.shopfoothillsmall.com.

Plaza Palomino Built in the style of a Spanish hacienda with a courtyard and fountains, this shopping center is home to some of Tucson's fun little specialty shops, galleries, and restaurants. 2970 N. Swan Rd. (at Fort Lowell Rd.). © 520/296-2511.

St. Philip's Plaza This upscale Southwestern-style shopping center contains a couple of good restaurants, a luxury beauty salon/day spa, and numerous shops and galleries, including Bahti Indian Arts and Turquoise Door jewelry. On Sunday mornings, there is a farmers market. Makes a great one-stop Tucson outing. 4280 N. Campbell Ave. (at River Rd.). © 520/529-2775.

Tucson Mall The foothills of northern Tucson have become shopping-center central, and this is the largest of the malls. You'll find more than 200 retailers in this busy, two-story skylit complex. 4500 N. Oracle Rd. © 520/293-7330. www.shop tucsonmall.com.

MEXICAN & LATIN AMERICAN IMPORTS

In addition to the shops mentioned below, the **"Lost Barrio,"** on the corner of Southwest Park Avenue and 12th Street (a block south of Broadway), is a good place to look for Mexican imports and Southwestern-style home furnishings at good prices.

Antigua de Mexico This warehouselike shop is absolutely packed with crafts from Mexico—oversize ceramics and painted plates, wooden and wrought-iron furniture, and punched-metal frames and framed mirrors. Smaller items include crucifixes and candlesticks. 3235 W. Orange Grove Rd. © 520/742-7114. www.mexican mart.com.

La Buhardilla ("The Attic") Okay, so you just cashed out of your place in California, you bought a big house in Arizona, and now you need some sizable furniture to fill up all that space. Buhardilla has it. The hand-carved Spanish baroque furniture come in *grande, mas grande,* and *gigante.* There are also 10-foot carved wood doors and larger-than-life-size carvings of angels and archangels. 2360 E. Broadway Blvd. © 520/622-5200.

Zócalo Although large pieces, including colonial-style furniture, constitute much of the inventory here, there are also decorator items such as Mexican ceramics, glassware, and Mexican-style paintings. A visit to Zócalo provides an opportunity to wander around Broadway Village, a historic shopping plaza. 3016 E. Broadway Blvd. © 520/320-1236. www.zocalomexicanfurniture.com.

NATIVE AMERICAN ART, CRAFTS & JEWELRY

Bahti Indian Arts Family-owned for more than 50 years, this store sells fine pieces—jewelry, baskets, sculpture, paintings, books, weavings, kachina dolls, Zuni fetishes, and much more. At St. Philip's Plaza, 4300 N. Campbell Ave. © 520/577-0290. www.bahti.com.

Gallery West   Located right below Anthony's in the Catalinas restaurant, this tiny shop specializes in very expensive Native American artifacts (mostly pre-1940s), such as pots, Apache and Pima baskets, 19th-century Plains Indian beadwork, Navajo weavings, and kachinas. There is also plenty of both contemporary and vintage jewelry. 6420 N. Campbell Ave. (at Skyline Dr.). © **520/529-7002.** www.indianartwest.com.

Kaibab Courtyard Shops   In business since 1945, this store offers one of the best selections of Native American art and crafts in Tucson. You can find high-quality jewelry, Mexican pottery and folk arts, home furnishings, glassware, kachinas, and rugs. 2841 N. Campbell Ave. © **520/795-6905.**

Mark Sublette Medicine Man Gallery   This shop has the best and biggest selection of old Navajo rugs in the city, and perhaps even the entire state. There are also Mexican and other Hispanic textiles, Acoma pottery, basketry, and other Indian crafts, as well as artwork by cowboy artists. The gallery is also the site of the Conley Museum of the West. At Santa Fe Sq., 7000 E. Tanque Verde Rd. © **800/ 422-9382** or 520/722-7798. www.medicinemangallery.com.

Morning Star Traders   With hardwood floors and a museumlike atmosphere, this store features museum-quality goods: antique Navajo rugs, kachinas, furniture, and a huge selection of old Native American jewelry. This just may be the best store of its type in the entire state. An adjoining shop, Morning Star Antiques, carries an impressive selection of antiques furniture (see "Antiques & Collectibles," earlier in this section). 2020 E. Speedway Blvd. © **520/881-2112.** www.morningstartraders.com.

Silverbell Trading   Not your usual run-of-the-mill crafts store, Silverbell specializes in regional Native American artwork, such as baskets and pottery, and carries unique pieces that the owner has obviously sought out. Small items such as stone Navajo corn maidens, Zuni fetishes, and figures carved from sandstone should not be overlooked. At Casas Adobes Plaza, 7119 N. Oracle Rd. © **520/797-6852.**

WESTERN WEAR
Arizona Hatters   Arizona Hatters carries the best names in cowboy hats, from Stetson to Bailey to Tilles, and the shop specializes in custom-fitting hats to the customer's head and face. You'll also find bolo ties, belts, and other accessories here. 2790 N. Campbell Ave. © **520/292-1320.**

Western Warehouse   If you want to put together your Western-wear ensemble under one roof, this is the place. It's the largest such store in Tucson and can deck you and your kids out in the latest cowboy fashions, including hats and boots. 3030 E. Speedway Blvd. © **520/327-8005.**

WINE
The Rumrunner   Looking for an Arizona wine or a wine you just haven't been able to locate elsewhere? You might find it here at the Rumrunner, along with imported cheeses and other gourmet goodies to accompany your libation. 3200 E. Speedway Blvd. © **520/326-0121.**

11 Tucson After Dark
Tucson after dark is a much easier landscape to negotiate than the vast cultural sprawl of the Phoenix area. Rather than having numerous performing-arts centers all over the suburbs as in the Valley of the Sun, Tucson has a more concentrated nightlife scene. The **Downtown Arts District** is the center of all the

action, with the Temple of Music and Art, the Tucson Convention Center Music Hall, and several nightclubs. The **University of Arizona campus,** only a mile away, is another hot spot for entertainment.

The free *Tucson Weekly* contains thorough listings of concerts, theater and dance performances, and club offerings. The entertainment section of the *Arizona Daily Star,* "Caliente," comes out each Friday and is another good source.

THE CLUB & MUSIC SCENE
COMEDY
Laffs Comedy Caffè   This stand-up comedy club features local comedians and professional comedians from around the country Tuesday through Saturday nights. A full bar and a limited menu are available. At the Village, 2900 E. Broadway Blvd. © 520/323-8669. Cover $6 Tues–Thurs, $9 Fri–Sat.

COUNTRY
Cactus Moon Café   A 20- to 40-something crowd frequents this large and glitzy nightclub, which features primarily country music, although Sundays are currently Top 40 night. 5470 E. Broadway Blvd. (on the east side of town at Craycroft Rd.). © 520/748-0049. Cover $3–$10.

DANCE CLUBS & DISCOS
El Parador   Tropical decor and an overabundance of potted plants set the mood for lively Latin jazz performances and salsa lessons (Sat nights), complete with a salsa band. Customers range from 20- to 60-somethings, giving new meaning to the term "all ages" club. 2744 E. Broadway. © 520/881-2808. Cover $6 Fri–Sat after 9:30pm.

JAZZ
To find out what's happening on the local jazz scene, call the **Tucson Jazz Society** (© 520/903-1265; www.tucsonjazz.org).

The Grill   No other jazz venue in Tucson has more flavor of the Southwest than this restaurant lounge, perched high on a ridgetop overlooking the city. There's live jazz Thursday through Sunday nights. At Hacienda del Sol Guest Ranch Resort, 5601 N. Hacienda del Sol Rd. © 520/529-3500. www.haciendadelsol.com. No cover.

Old Pueblo Grille   With a beautiful setting in a historic home surrounded by tall palm trees, this isn't exactly your classic jazz club. However, with its outstanding selection of tequilas and live jazz Thursday through Sunday, this is the quintessential Tucson jazz spot. 60 N. Alvernon Way. © 520/326-6000. No cover to $3.

MARIACHI
Tucson is the mariachi capital of the United States, and no one should visit without spending at least one evening listening to some of these strolling minstrels.

La Fuente   La Fuente is the largest Mexican restaurant in Tucson and serves up good food, but what really draws the crowds is the live mariachi music. If you just want to listen and not have dinner, you can hang out in the lounge. The mariachis perform nightly. 1749 N. Oracle Rd. © 520/623-8659.

ROCK, BLUES & REGGAE
Berky's Bar   There's live music wailing most nights of the week in this dark and smoky tavern. Mondays are open-jam nights, so you never know who or what you might hear. 5769 E. Speedway Blvd. © 520/296-1981. No cover to $4.

Boondocks Lounge   Long a popular dive bar, this place north of downtown is now one of the city's best spots to hear live blues and reggae. You can't miss this place—just look for the giant chianti bottle out front. 3306 N. First Ave. ℂ 520/690-0991. No cover to $10.

Chicago Bar   Transplanted Chicagoans love to watch their home teams on the TVs at this neighborhood bar, but there's also live music nightly. Sure, blues gets played a lot, but so do reggae and rock and about everything in between. 5954 E. Speedway Blvd. ℂ 520/748-8169. www.chicagobartucson.com. Cover $4 Wed–Sat.

Club Congress   Just off the lobby of the restored Hotel Congress (now a budget hotel and youth hostel), Club Congress is Tucson's main alternative-music venue. There are usually a couple of nights of live music each week, and over the years such bands as Nirvana, Dick Dale, and the Goo Goo Dolls have played here. 311 E. Congress St. ℂ 520/622-8848. www.hotelcongress.com. Cover $5–$15.

The Rialto Theatre   This renovated 1919 vaudeville theater, although not a nightclub, is now Tucson's main venue for performances by bands that are too big to play across the street at Club Congress (Lucinda Williams, Los Lobos, Arturo Sandoval). 318 E. Congress St. ℂ 520/798-3333. www.rialtotheatre.com. Tickets $10–$35.

THE BAR, LOUNGE & PUB SCENE

Arizona Inn   If you're looking for a quiet, comfortable scene, the piano music in the Audubon Lounge at the Arizona Inn is sure to soothe your soul. The lounge, which was recently restored to its original appearance, has a classic feel, and the resort's gardens are beautiful. 2200 E. Elm St. ℂ 520/325-1541.

Cascade Lounge   This is Tucson's ultimate piano bar. With a view of the Catalinas, the plush lounge is perfect for romance or relaxation at the start or end of a night on the town. Several nights a week, there's live piano music or a jazz band. At Loews Ventana Canyon Resort, 7000 N. Resort Dr. ℂ 520/299-2020.

Gentle Ben's Brewing Co.   Located just off the UA campus, Gentle Ben's, a big, modern place with plenty of outdoor seating, is Tucson's favorite micro-brewery. The crowd is primarily college students. Food and drink specials are offered daily, and there's live music a couple of nights per week. 865 E. University Blvd. ℂ 520/624-4177. www.gentlebens.com.

Nimbus Brewing   Located in the warehouse district on the south side of Tucson, this brewpub is basically the front room of Nimbus's brewing and bottling facility. The beer is good, and there's live rock and jazz several nights a week. Hard to find, and definitely a local scene. 3850 E. 44th St. (2 blocks east of Palo Verde Rd.). ℂ 520/745-9175. www.nimbusbeer.com.

Thunder Canyon Brewery   Affiliated with the Prescott Brewing Co. in Prescott, this brewpub is your best bet in Tucson for handcrafted ales and is the most convenient brewpub for anyone staying at a foothills resort. At Foothills Mall, 7401 N. La Cholla Blvd. ℂ 520/797-2652.

¡Toma!   This bar, set in El Presidio Historic District and owned by the family that operates El Charro Café next door, has a fun and festive atmosphere complete with a Mexican hat fountain/sculpture in the courtyard. Drop by for cheap margaritas during happy hour (Mon–Fri 4–6pm). 311 N. Court Ave. ℂ 520/622-1922.

COCKTAILS WITH A VIEW

Just about all the best views in town are at foothills resorts, but luckily they don't mind sharing with nonguests. In addition to those listed below, the lounge at **Anthony's in the Catalinas** has a great view. See p. 349 for details.

388 CHAPTER 9 · TUCSON

Desert Garden Lounge   If you'd like a close-up view of the Santa Catalina Mountains, drop by the Desert Garden Lounge (at sunset, perhaps). The large lounge has live piano music several nights a week. At the Westin La Paloma, 3800 E. Sunrise Dr. ℂ 520/742-6000.

Flying V Bar & Grill   If you can't afford the lap of luxury, you can at least pull up a chair. Set it next to a waterfall just outside the front door of this popular resort watering hole for one of the best views in the city, looking out over the golf course and Tucson far below. At Loews Ventana Canyon Resort, 7000 N. Resort Dr. ℂ 520/299-2020.

Lookout Bar & Grille   The Westward Look, one of Tucson's oldest resorts, took to the hills long before it became the fashionable place to be. The nighttime view of twinkling city lights and stars is unmatched. On Friday and Saturday nights, there's live rock and blues music. At the Westward Look Resort, 245 E. Ina Rd. ℂ 520/297-1151.

SPORTS BARS

Famous Sam's   With about a dozen branches around the city, Famous Sam's (www.famoussams.net) keeps a lot of Tucson's sports fans happy with its cheap prices and large portions. Other convenient locations include 1830 E. Broadway Blvd. (ℂ 520/884-0119), 7930 E. Speedway Blvd. (ℂ 520/290-9666), and 4801 E. 29th St. (ℂ 520/748-1975). 3620 N. First Ave. ℂ 520/292-0314.

GAY & LESBIAN BARS & CLUBS

To find out about other gay bars around town, keep an eye out for the *Observer,* Tucson's newspaper for the gay, lesbian, and bisexual community. You'll find it at **Antigone Books,** 411 N. Fourth Ave. (ℂ 520/792-3715), as well as at the bars listed here.

Ain't Nobody's Bizness   Located in a small shopping plaza in midtown, this bar has long been *the* lesbian gathering spot in Tucson. There are pool tables, a dance floor, and a quiet, smoke-free room where you can duck out of the noise. 2900 E. Broadway Blvd., Suite 118. ℂ 520/318-4838. www.aintnobodysbizness-az.com.

IBT's   Located on funky Fourth Avenue, IBT's has long been the most popular gay men's dance bar in town. The music ranges from 1980s retro to techno, and regular drag shows add to the fun. There's always an interesting crowd. 616 N. Fourth Ave. ℂ 520/882-3053.

THE PERFORMING ARTS

To a certain extent, Tucson is a clone of Phoenix when it comes to the performing arts. Three of Tucson's major companies—the Arizona Opera Company, Ballet Arizona, and the Arizona Theatre Company—spend half their time in Phoenix. This means that whatever gets staged in Phoenix also gets staged in Tucson. This city does, however, have its own symphony, and manages to sustain a diversified theater scene as well.

Usually, the best way to purchase tickets is directly from the company's box office. Tickets to Tucson Convention Center events (but not the symphony or the opera) and other venues around town may be available by calling the **TCC box office** (ℂ 520/791-4266). **Ticketmaster** (ℂ 520/321-1000; www.ticketmaster.com) sells tickets to some Tucson performances.

PERFORMING-ARTS CENTERS & CONCERT HALLS

Tucson's largest performance venue is the **Tucson Convention Center (TCC) Music Hall,** 260 S. Church Ave. (ℂ 520/791-4266). It's the home of the

Tucson Symphony Orchestra and where the Arizona Opera Company usually performs when it's in town. This hall hosts many touring companies, and Ballet Arizona presents its holiday performance of *The Nutcracker* here. The box office is open Monday through Friday from 10am to 6pm.

The centerpiece of the Tucson theater scene is the **Temple of Music and Art,** 330 S. Scott Ave. (© **520/622-2823**), a restored historic theater dating from 1927. The 605-seat Alice Holsclaw Theatre is the Temple's main stage, but there's also the 90-seat Cabaret Theatre. You'll also find an art gallery and gift shop here. The box office is normally open Monday through Friday from 10am to 6pm, unless there are performances scheduled, in which case the box office opens Monday from 10am to 6pm, Tuesday through Friday from 10am to curtain, Saturday and Sunday from noon to curtain.

University of Arizona Centennial Hall, 1020 E. University Boulevard at Park Avenue (© **520/621-3341;** http://uapresents.arizona.edu), on the UA campus, is Tucson's other main performance hall. It stages performances by touring national musical acts, international companies, and Broadway shows. A big stage and excellent sound system permit large-scale productions. The box office is open Monday through Friday from 10am to 6pm and Saturday from noon to 5pm (closed Sat in summer).

The **Center for the Arts Proscenium Theatre,** Pima Community College (West Campus), 2202 W. Anklam Rd. (© **520/206-6988**), is another good place to check for classical music performances. It offers a wide variety of shows. The box office is open Monday through Friday from 10am to 4pm.

OUTDOOR VENUES & SERIES

Weather permitting, Tucsonans head to Reid Park's **DeMeester Outdoor Performance Center,** at Country Club Road and East 22nd Street (© **520/791-4873**), for performances under the stars. This amphitheater is the site of performances by the Tucson Community Theatre and other companies, as well as frequent musical concerts.

The **Tucson Jazz Society** (© **520/903-1265;** www.tucsonjazz.org), which manages to book a few well-known jazz musicians each year, sponsors different outdoor series at various locations around the city, including the foothills' St. Philip's Plaza. Tickets are usually between $12 and $25.

CLASSICAL MUSIC, OPERA & DANCE

Both the **Tucson Symphony Orchestra** (© **520/882-8585** or 520/792-9155; www.tucsonsymphony.org), which is the oldest continuously performing symphony in the Southwest, and the **Arizona Opera Company** (© **520/293-4336** or 520/321-1000; www.azopera.com), the state's premier opera company, perform at the Tucson Convention Center Music Hall. Symphony tickets run $12 to $51; opera tickets are $25 to $115.

If you want to catch some economical classical music, check out the schedule at the University of Arizona College of Fine Arts School of Music and Dance (© **520/621-1162;** www.music.arizona.edu). Performances are held between September and April and include classical music and opera performances held in Crowder Hall and Holsclaw Hall, both of which are near the intersection of Speedway Boulevard and Park Avenue on the UA campus.

THEATER

Tucson doesn't have a lot of theater companies, but what few it does have stage a surprisingly diverse sampling of both classic and contemporary plays.

Arizona Theatre Company (ATC; ✆ **520/622-2823;** www.aztheatreco.org), which performs at the Temple of Music and Art, splits its time between here and Phoenix and is the state's top professional theater company. Each season sees a mix of comedy, drama, and Broadway-style musical shows; tickets cost $26 to $39.

The **Invisible Theatre,** 1400 N. First Ave. (✆ **520/882-9721**), a tiny theater in a converted laundry building, has been home to Tucson's most experimental theater for more than 30 years (it does off-Broadway shows and musicals). Tickets go for about $16 to $22.

The West just wouldn't be the West without good old-fashioned melodramas, and the **Gaslight Theatre,** 7010 E. Broadway Blvd. (✆ **520/886-9428**), is where evil villains, stalwart heroes, and defenseless heroines pound the boards. You can boo and hiss, cheer and sigh as the predictable stories unfold on stage. It's all great fun for kids and adults. Tickets are $15 for adults, $13 for students and seniors, and $6.95 for children 12 and under. Performances are held Tuesday through Sunday, with two shows nightly on Friday and Saturday plus a Sunday matinee. Tickets sell out a month in advance, so get them as soon as possible.

CASINOS

Casino of the Sun   Located 15 miles southwest of Tucson off I-19 (take the Valencia Rd. exit) and operated by the Pascua Yaqui tribe, this is one of the two largest casinos in southern Arizona. There are plenty of slot machines, plus keno, bingo, and a card room. 7406 S. Camino de Oeste. ✆ 520/879-5400. www.casinosun.com.

Desert Diamond Casino   Operated by the Tohono O'odham tribe and located just off I-19 south of Tucson, this casino offers the same variety of slot and video poker machines found at other casinos in the state. A card room, bingo, and keno round out the options. Exit 80 (Pima Mine Rd.) off I-19. ✆ 866/DDC-WINS or 520/294-7777. www.desertdiamondcasino.com.

Southern Arizona

Although southern Arizona has its share of prickly pears and saguaros, much of this region has more in common with the Texas plains than it does with the Sonoran Desert. In the southeastern corner of the state, the mile-high grasslands, punctuated by forested mountain ranges, have long supported vast ranches where cattle range across wide-open plains. It was also here that much of America's now-legendary Western history took place. Wyatt Earp and the Clantons shot it out at Tombstone's O.K. Corral, Doc Holliday played his cards, and Cochise and Geronimo staged the last Indian rebellions.

Long before even the prospectors and outlaws arrived, this region had gained historical importance as the first part of the Southwest explored by the Spanish. This inaugural Spanish expedition was led by Francisco Vásquez de Coronado in 1540, and today a national monument in the region commemorates Coronado's visit.

Nearly 150 years later, Father Eusebio Francisco Kino founded a string of Jesuit missions across the region the Spanish called the Pimeria Alta, an area that would later become northern Mexico and southern Arizona. Converting the Indians and building mission churches, Father Kino left a long-lasting mark on this region. Two of the missions he founded—San Xavier del Bac (p. 361), 9 miles south of present-day Tucson, and San José de Tumacacori (see the listing for Tumacacori National Historical Park, below), in Tubac—still stand.

More than 450 years after Coronado marched through this region, the valley of the San Pedro River is undergoing something of a population explosion, especially in the town of Sierra Vista, where retirement communities sprawl across the landscape. Nearby, in the once nearly abandoned copper-mining town of Bisbee, urban refugees and artists have taken up residence and opened numerous galleries and B&Bs, making this one of the most interesting small towns in the state.

The combination of low deserts, high plains, and even higher mountains has given this region a fascinating diversity of landscapes. Giant saguaros cover the slopes of the Sonoran Desert throughout much of southern Arizona, and in the western parts of this region, organ pipe cacti reach the northern limit of their range. In the cool mountains, cacti give way to pines, and passing clouds bring snow and rain. Narrow canyons and broad valleys, fed by the rain and snowmelt, provide habitat for hundreds of species of birds and other wildlife. This is the northernmost range for many birds usually found only south of the border. Consequently, southeastern Arizona has become one of the nation's most important bird-watching spots.

The region's mild climate has also given rise to the state's small wine industry. Throughout southeastern Arizona there are a handful of vineyards and wineries, and touring the wine country is a favorite weekend excursion for residents of Tucson and Phoenix.

1 Organ Pipe Cactus National Monument ★ ★

135 miles S of Phoenix; 140 miles W of Tucson; 185 miles SE of Yuma

Located roughly midway between Yuma and Tucson, Organ Pipe Cactus National Monument is a preserve for the rare cactus for which the monument is named. The organ pipe cactus resembles the saguaro cactus in many ways, but instead of forming a single main trunk, organ pipes have many trunks, some 20 feet tall, that resemble—you guessed it—organ pipes.

This is a rugged region with few towns or services. To the west lie the inaccessible Cabeza Prieta National Wildlife Refuge and the Barry M. Goldwater Air Force Range (a bombing range), and to the east is the large Tohono O'odham Indian Reservation. The only motels in the area are in the small town of Ajo. This former company town was built around a now-abandoned copper mine, and the downtown plaza, with its tall palm trees and arched and covered walkways, has the look and feel of a Mexican town square. Be sure to gas up your car before leaving Ajo.

ESSENTIALS

GETTING THERE   From Tucson, take Ariz. 86 west to Why and turn south on Ariz. 85. From Yuma, take I-8 east to Gila Bend and drive south on Ariz. 85.

FEES   The park entry fee is $5 per car.

VISITOR INFORMATION   For information, contact **Organ Pipe Cactus National Monument** (© 520/387-6849; www.nps.gov/orpi). The visitor center is open daily from 8am to 5pm, although the park itself is open 24 hours a day.

EXPLORING THE MONUMENT

Two well-graded gravel roads lead through different sections of this large national monument. The Puerto Blanco Drive, formerly a long loop drive, is currently a 5-mile route leading only to the Red Tanks trail head, while the Ajo Mountain Drive is a 21-mile one-way loop drive. Guides available at the park's visitor center explain natural features of the landscape along both drives. There are also a number of hiking trails along the roads.

WHERE TO STAY

There are two campgrounds within the park (although nonvehicle camping is allowed in the backcountry with a permit). Campsites are $6 in the primitive **Alamo Campground** and $10 in the more developed **Twin Peaks Campground.** The nearest lodgings are in Ajo, where there are several old and very basic motels as well as a B&B. There are also plenty of budget chain motels in the town of Gila Bend, 70 miles north of the monument. They include a **Best Western** (© 800/WESTERN or 928/683-2273) and a **Super 8** (© 800/800-8000 or 928/683-6311).

Guest House Inn Bed & Breakfast   Built in 1925 as a guesthouse for mining executives, this B&B has attractive gardens in the front yard, a mesquite thicket off to one side, and a modern Southwestern feel to its interior decor. Guest rooms are cool and dark, which is often appreciated in the desert heat here in Ajo. There are also sunrooms on both the north and the south sides of the house.

700 Guest House Rd., Ajo, AZ 85321. © 520/387-6133. www.guesthouseinn.biz. 4 units. $89 double. Rates include full breakfast. DC, MC, V. *In room:* A/C, fridge, hair dryer, iron.

Southern Arizona

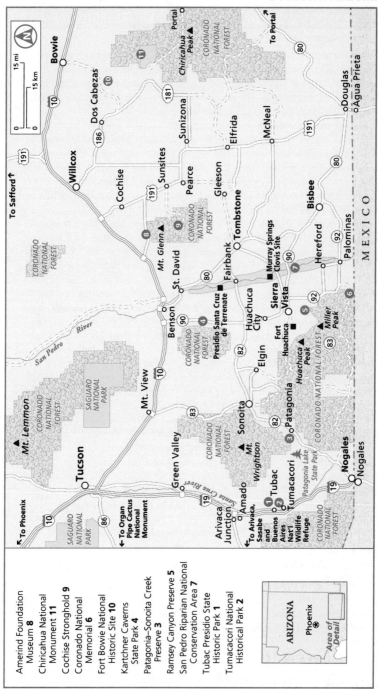

Amerind Foundation
Museum **8**
Chiricahua National
Monument **11**
Cochise Stronghold **9**
Coronado National
Memorial **6**
Fort Bowie National
Historic Site **10**
Kartchner Caverns
State Park **4**
Patagonia–Sonoita Creek
Preserve **3**
Ramsey Canyon Preserve **5**
San Pedro Riparian National
Conservation Area **7**
Tubac Presidio State
Historic Park **1**
Tumacacori National
Historical Park **2**

2 Tubac ★★ & Buenos Aires National Wildlife Refuge ★

45 miles S of Tucson; 21 miles N of Nogales; 84 miles W of Sierra Vista

Located in the fertile valley of the Santa Cruz River 45 miles south of Tucson, Tubac is one of Arizona's largest arts communities. The town's old buildings house more than 80 shops selling fine arts, crafts, unusual gifts, and lots of Southwest souvenirs. This concentration of shops, artist studios, and galleries makes Tubac one of southern Arizona's most popular destinations, and a small retirement community is beginning to develop.

In 1691, Father Eusebio Francisco Kino established Tumacacori as one of the first Spanish missions in what would eventually become Arizona. At that time, Tubac was a Pima Indian village, but by the 1730s, the Spanish had begun settling here in the region they called Pimeria Alta. After a Pima uprising in 1751, Spanish forces were sent into the area to protect the settlers, and in 1752 Tubac became a presidio (fort).

Although the European history of this area is more than 300 years old, the area's human habitation dates far back into prehistory. Archaeologists have found evidence that there have been people living along the Santa Cruz River for nearly 10,000 years. The Hohokam lived in the area from about A.D. 300 until their mysterious disappearance around 1500, and when the Spanish arrived some 200 years later, they found the Pima people inhabiting this region.

Tubac's other claim to fame is as the site from which Juan Bautista de Anza III, the second commander of the presidio, set out in 1775 to find an overland route to California. De Anza led 240 settlers and more than 1,000 head of cattle on this grueling expedition, and when the group finally reached the coast of California, they founded the settlement of San Francisco. A year after de Anza's journey to the Pacific, the garrison was moved from Tubac to Tucson, and, with no protection, Tubac's settlers moved away from the area. Soldiers were once again stationed here beginning in 1787, but lack of funds caused the closure of the presidio again when, in 1821, Mexican independence brought Tubac under a new flag. It was not until this region became U.S. territory that settlers returned, and by 1860, Tubac was the largest town in Arizona.

After visiting Tubac Presidio State Historic Park and Tumacacori National Historical Park to learn about the area's history, you'll probably want to spend some time browsing through the shops. Keep in mind, however, that many of the local artists leave town in summer, prompting many local shops to close on weekdays in the summer, so, if you visit during the summer, it's best to visit on weekends. The shops are open daily during the busy season of October through May.

ESSENTIALS

GETTING THERE   The Santa Cruz Valley towns of Amado, Tubac, and Tumacacori are all due south of Tucson on I-19.

VISITOR INFORMATION   For information on Tubac and Tumacacori, contact the **Tubac Chamber of Commerce** (© 520/398-2704; www.tubacaz.com) or the **Tubac-Santa Cruz Visitor Center,** 4 Plaza Rd. (© 520/398-0007; www.toursantacruz.com).

SPECIAL EVENTS   The **Tubac Festival of the Arts** is held in February. Artists from all over the country participate. On the third weekend in October, the **Anza Days Historic Celebration** commemorates Captain Juan Bautista de Anza's 1775 westward trek that led to the founding of San Francisco.

ART & HISTORY IN THE SANTA CRUZ VALLEY

Tubac Center of the Arts ✿   Tubac is an arts community, and this Spanish colonial building serves as its center for cultural activities. Throughout the season, there are workshops, traveling exhibitions, juried shows, an annual crafts show, and theater and music performances. The quality of the art at these shows is generally better than what's found in most of the surrounding stores. There is also a good little gift shop here.

9 Plaza Rd. 𝄐 520/398-2371. www.tubacarts.org. Suggested donation $2. Tues–Sat 10am–4:30pm; Sun 1–4:30pm. Closed mid-May to Labor Day and major holidays.

Tubac Presidio State Historic Park   Although little but buried foundation walls remains of the old presidio (fort), this little park does a good job of presenting the region's Spanish colonial history. The nearby Tumacacori mission (see below) was founded in 1691, but it was not until 1752 that Tubac Presidio was established in response to a Pima Indian uprising. In 1775, the presidio's military garrison was moved to Tucson, and, with no protection from raiding Apaches, most of Tubac's settlers left the area. A military presence was reestablished in 1787, but after Mexican independence in 1821, insufficient funds led to the presidio's closing. Villagers once again abandoned Tubac because of Apache attacks. After the Gadsden Purchase, Tubac became part of the United States and was again resettled.

Park exhibits focus on the Spanish soldiers, Native Americans, religion, and contemporary Hispanic culture in southern Arizona. Also on the grounds is the old Tubac School, which was built in 1885 and is the oldest schoolhouse in the state. Living-history presentations are staged from January through March on Sundays between 1 and 4pm. Among the characters you'll meet are Spanish soldiers, settlers, and friars. There are also archaeological tours on Wednesdays between mid-February and the end of March. Also in March, there are nature walks on Tuesdays and Sundays at 1:30pm.

Presidio Dr. 𝄐 520/398-2252. Admission $3 adults, $1 children 7–13. Daily 8am–5pm. Closed Christmas.

Tumacacori National Historical Park ✿   Founded in 1691 by Jesuit missionary and explorer Father Eusebio Francisco Kino, the San José de Tumacacori mission was one of the first Anglo settlements in what is today Arizona. Father Kino's mission was to convert the Pima Indians, and for the first 60 years, the mission was successful. However, in 1751, during the Pima Revolt, the mission was destroyed. For the next 70 years, this mission struggled to survive, but during the 1820s, an adobe mission church was constructed. Today, the mission ruins are a silent and haunting reminder of the role that Spanish missionaries played in settling the Southwest. Much of the old adobe mission church still stands, and the Spanish architectural influences can readily be seen. A small museum contains exhibits on mission life and the history of the region. On weekends between September and May, Native American and Mexican craftspeople give demonstrations of indigenous arts. On the third Wednesday of the month, between September and April, there are also special living history tours to two sister missions—San Cayetano de Calabazas and Los Santos Ángeles de Guevavi. These tours are by reservation and cost $18 per person. **La Fiesta de Tumacacori,** a celebration of Indian, Hispanic, and Anglo cultures, is held the first weekend of December.

1891 E. Frontage Rd. 𝄐 520/398-2341. www.nps.gov/tuma. Admission $3 adults, free for children 16 and under. Daily 8am–5pm. Closed Thanksgiving and Christmas. Take I-19 to Exit 29; Tumacacori is 3 miles south of Tubac.

SHOPPING

While tourist brochures like to tout Tubac as an artists' community, the town is more of a Southwest souvenir mecca. There are a few genuine art galleries here, but you have to look hard amid the many tourist shops to find the real gems.

Some of the better fine art in the area is found at the **Karin Newby Gallery,** Mercado de Baca, 19 Tubac Rd. (© **520/398-9662;** www.karinnewbygallery.com). For traditional Western art, some by members of the prestigious Cowboy Artists of America, visit the **Big Horn Galleries,** 37 Tubac Rd. (© **520/398-9209;** www.bighorngalleries.com). For beautiful and evocative landscapes, check out the Michael Gibbons Studio/Gallery, 18 Calle Iglesia (© **520/398-3109;** www. michaelgibbons.net).

If you're in the market for jewelry, be sure to visit **Blackstar,** E. Frontage Road (© **520/398-0451**), in nearby Amado. This small jewelry store specializes in locally mined opal and other exotic gemstones. You'll find this gallery at Exit 48 off I-19.

If you want to take the flavor of the area home, stop in at **The Chile Pepper,** on Tubac Road in downtown Tubac (© **520/398-2921**), for gourmet foods with a Southwestern accent. Down near Tumacacori National Historical Park, you'll find all things hot (chiles, hot sauces, salsas) arranged on the shelves of one of the more genuine Tubac-area institutions, the **Santa Cruz Chile and Spice Company,** 1868 E. Frontage Rd. (© **520/398-2591;** www.santacruzchili.com), a combination store and packing plant. There's an amazing assortment of familiar and obscure spices for sale. In back, you can see various herbs being prepared and packaged. The shop is open Monday through Saturday from 8am to 5pm.

BUENOS AIRES NATIONAL WILDLIFE REFUGE ✯

If you're a bird-watcher, you'll definitely want to make the trip over to **Buenos Aires National Wildlife Refuge,** P.O. Box 109, Sasabe, AZ 85633 (© **520/ 823-4251;** http://southwest.fws.gov/refuges/arizona/buenos.html), about 28 miles from Tubac. To get here, head north from Tubac on I-19 to Arivaca Junction, then drive west on a winding two-lane road. The refuge begins just outside the small community of Arivaca.

Your first stop should be at **Arivaca Cienega,** a quarter of a mile east of Arivaca. *Cienega* is Spanish for "marsh," and that is exactly what you will find here. A boardwalk leads across this marsh, which is fed by seven springs that provide year-round water and consequently attract an amazing variety of bird life. This is one of the few places in the United States where you can see a gray hawk, and vermilion flycatchers are quite common. Other good birding spots within the refuge include **Arivaca Creek,** 2 miles west of Arivaca, and **Aguirre Lake,** a half-mile north of the refuge headquarters and visitor center, which is off Ariz. 286 north of Sasabe.

The **visitor center** is a good place to spot one of the refuge's rarest birds, the masked bobwhite quail. These quail disappeared from Arizona in the late 19th century, but have been reintroduced in the refuge. Other birds you might spot outside the visitor center include Bendire's thrashers, Chihuahuan ravens, canyon towhees, and green-tailed towhees. The visitor center is open daily from 7:30am to 4pm. In the town of Arivaca, the **Arivaca Information Office** is open from 8am to 4pm when volunteers are available to staff it.

Other wildlife in the refuge includes pronghorn antelopes, javelinas, coatimundis, white-tailed deer, mule deer, and coyotes. Guided birding and other tours are offered weekends throughout the year. Call for details; reservations are

---

> ⌒ *Moments*   **The Ruby Road**
>
> If you enjoy scenic drives and don't mind gravel roads, you won't want to pass up the opportunity to drive the Ruby Road from Arivaca through Coronado National Forest to **Peña Blanca Lake** and **Nogales**. This road winds its way through the mountains just north of the Mexican border, passing Arivaca Lake and the privately owned ghost town of **Ruby** (ℂ 520/744-4471; admission $12) before reaching picturesque Peña Blanca Lake, where the pavement resumes. Be sure to call first to make sure the caretaker is available. You can also visit Ruby on tours sponsored by Pima Community College in Tucson (ℂ **520/206-3952**), which charges $69 for an all-day tour. If you want to camp, you'll find a couple of campgrounds at Peña Blanca Lake.

---

required. There is primitive **camping** at more than 100 designated spots along rough gravel roads. Look for the brown campsite signs along the road, and bring your own water.

These roads also offer good mountain biking. If you're looking for a strenuous hike, try the **Mustang Trail,** which has its trail head 2 miles west of Arivaca. The trail climbs up from Arivaca Creek into the surrounding dry hills and makes for a 5-mile round-trip hike.

OTHER OUTDOOR PURSUITS

Linking Tubac with Tumacacori is the 8-mile **de Anza Trail,** which follows the Santa Cruz River for much of its route and passes through forests and grasslands. This trail is part of the **Juan Bautista de Anza National Historic Trail,** which stretches from Nogales to San Francisco and commemorates the overland journey of the Spanish captain who, in 1775 and 1776, led a small band of colonists overland to California. These settlers founded what is now the city of San Francisco. Today, bird-watching is the most popular activity along the trail. History buffs will also get to see an excavation of part of the Spanish colonial settlement of Tubac. The most convenient trail head is beside Tubac Presidio State Historic Park. **Rex Ranch** (ℂ 520/398-2914) offers horseback rides for $25 per hour.

If golf is more your speed, you can play a round at the **Tubac Golf Resort** (ℂ **520/398-2211**), just north of Tubac off East Frontage Road. Greens fees range from $30 to $75.

WHERE TO STAY
IN AMADO

The Inn at Amado Territory Ranch ✿   This modern inn just off I-19 in the crossroads of Amado is built in the territorial style, and succeeds in capturing the feel of an old Arizona ranch house. Guest rooms are outfitted in a mix of Mexican rustic furnishings and reproduction East Coast antiques, much in the style that homes would have been furnished in Arizona 100 years ago. Rooms on the second floor feature balconies with views across the farm fields of the Santa Cruz Valley, while those on the ground floor have patios. The Amado Café is right next door.

3001 E. Frontage Rd. (P.O. Box 81), Amado, AZ 85645. ℂ 888/398-8684 or 520/398-8684. www.amado-territory-inn.com. 9 units. Nov–June $105–$135 double; July–Oct $90–$105 double. Rates include full breakfast. AE, DISC, MC, V. No children under 12. *In room:* A/C, no phone.

The Rex Ranch ⭐ *Finds*   With its classic Southwestern styling and location adjacent to the de Anza Trail, this place is truly a hidden getaway. Just getting to this remote property is something of an adventure, since you have to drive *through* the Santa Cruz River to reach it. When you arrive and see the pink-walled Mission Revival building in the middle of the desert, you'll know you've arrived someplace distinctly different. Although not all of the guest rooms are as attractively decorated as the public areas, the new rooms and the more recently renovated rooms are quite comfortable. Primarily a conference center and economical health spa, the ranch offers a wide variety of spa treatments and massages. The attractive little dining room is one of this area's best restaurants (see Cantina Romantica under "Where to Dine," below).

131 Amado Montosa Rd. (P.O. Box 636), Amado, AZ 85645. ⓒ **888/REX-RANCH** or 520/398-2914. Fax 520/398-8229. www.rexranch.com. 35 units. Sept–May $145–$225 double; June–Aug $135–$205 double. 2-night minimum stay. Rates include continental breakfast. AE, DISC, MC, V. **Amenities:** Restaurant (Southwestern/New American); outdoor pool; spa; Jacuzzi; mountain-bike rentals; concierge; massage; horseback riding. *In room:* A/C, fridge, coffeemaker, no phone.

IN TUBAC

Tubac Golf Resort ⭐⭐ *Value*   This economical golf resort is built on the Otero Ranch, which dates back to 1789 and is the oldest Spanish land-grant ranch in the Southwest. With its green fairways, this resort is a lush oasis of green amid the seared hills of the Santa Cruz Valley. The ranch has recently undergone an extensive renovation aimed at turning it into a modern golf resort capable of competing with resorts in Tucson. They just might be succeeding. Tubac Golf Resort has more a classic Southwestern feel than most of the Tucson golf resorts, and because it is fairly small, it has a low-key feel that I like. The oldest buildings on the ranch/resort are the old stables, which now house an excellent restaurant. The red-tile roofs and brick archways throughout the resort help conjure up the Spanish heritage, while guest rooms are spacious and modern and situated in buildings set amid expansive lawns. Casitas have patios, beamed ceilings, and beehive fireplaces; newer rooms are worth requesting. If you're looking for a secluded gold getaway, this is a great choice. Oh, yes, and watch out for the cows on the golf course; they were added to return a little old-time character to the resort.

1 Otero Rd. (P.O. Box 1297), Tubac, AZ 85646. ⓒ **800/848-7893** or 520/398-2211. Fax 520/398-9261. www.tubacgolfresort.com. 44 units. $95–$195 double; $125–$295 suite. Children under 12 stay free in parent's room. AE, DISC, MC, V. Pets accepted ($50 refundable deposit plus $25 per night). **Amenities:** Restaurant (Continental); lounge; outdoor pool; 18-hole golf course; tennis court; Jacuzzi; room service; coin-op laundry. *In room:* A/C, TV, fridge, coffeemaker, hair dryer, iron.

IN SASABE

Rancho de la Osa ⭐⭐   Steeped in history and sharing a fence line with the Mexican border, this ranch is roughly 200 years old and was one of the last Spanish haciendas built in what later became the United States. It's now owned by Richard and Veronica Schultz, avid art collectors who have brought to the place an aesthetic unknown at other Arizona guest ranches. The adobe buildings are painted in vibrant shades of pink and turquoise, while the guest rooms are furnished with rustic Mexican antiques. Most have fireplaces and porches. Meals are gourmet Southwestern-fusion fare, and there's a 300-year-old cantina in what may be the oldest building in the state. Although horseback riding is the favorite activity, the ranch also attracts a few birders due to its proximity to Buenos Aires National Wildlife Refuge.

P.O. Box 1, Sasabe, AZ 85633. © **800/872-6240** or 520/823-4257. Fax 520/823-4238. www.ranchodelaosa. com. 19 units. $350–$440 double (plus 15% service charge). 3- to 4-night minimum stay. Rates include all meals, hiking, biking, and horseback riding. MC, V. No children under 6. **Amenities:** Dining room (Southwestern); lounge; outdoor pool; Jacuzzi; bikes; massage; laundry service. *In room:* No phone.

WHERE TO DINE

In addition to the restaurants mentioned below, the **Tubac Golf Resort** (see "Where to Stay," above) has a good restaurant.

IN AMADO

Amado Café MEDITERRANEAN/AMERICAN   There aren't a lot of dining options out here, making this restaurant, in a handsome territorial-style building just off I-19, a real asset to the community. The best part of the experience is sitting out back on the rustic flagstone patio, listening to the gurgling fountain, and contemplating the view of the mountains in the distance. The menu includes sandwiches, salads, and more filling fare such as prime rib. The Greek dishes, including a Greek salad and stuffed grape leaves, are good bets.

3001 E. Frontage Rd. (Exit 48 off I-19), Amado. © **520/398-9211.** Main courses $7–$10 lunch, $11–$20 dinner. AE, DISC, MC, V. Tues–Sat 11:30am–2pm and 5–8pm; Sun 11:30am–2pm.

Cantina Romantica ✸✸ SOUTHWESTERN/NEW AMERICAN   Located in a historic adobe hacienda at the Rex Ranch resort (see "Where to Stay," above), 6 miles north of Tubac, Cantina Romantica is a culinary oasis in this neck of the woods. The menu has a metropolitan flair, and includes the likes of pecan-crusted pork and filet mignon with mushroom-cabernet sauce. The setting is rustic and colorful, and the restaurant is reached by driving *through* the Santa Cruz River. Because the route to the restaurant is so unusual and because the Rex Ranch is so colorful, you should be sure to schedule an early dinner so you can enjoy the sights.

131 Amado Montosa Rd., Amado. © **520/398-2914.** Reservations recommended. Main courses $18–$32. AE, DISC, MC, V. Wed–Sun 5:30–9pm. Call ahead during extreme heat in summer; restaurant may be closed.

Kristofer's ✸ *Value* ECLECTIC/INTERNATIONAL   Whether you're just looking for a good cup of coffee, a pastry, a light lunch, or a creative dinner, this pretty little place can fill your needs. Located adjacent to the Inn at Amado Territory Ranch, Kristofer's is casual, with a sort of Mediterranean decor. The lunch menu is pretty straightforward, with salads and sandwiches. Try the crab burger. At dinner, however, chef Charles Deeby gets much more creative. You can either start with the crab cakes as an appetizer, or have them as an entree. (Do you get the idea that someone in your party needs to get the crab cakes?) If you don't like crab, try the Black Angus steak with brandy-soaked porcini-mushroom sauce.

E. Frontage Rd., (Exit 48 off I-19), Amado. © **520/625-0331.** Main courses $6–$9 lunch, $11–$18. MC, V. Mon–Sat 9am–7pm.

IN TUBAC & TUMACACORI

Shelby's Bistro AMERICAN   Tucked into the back of the Mercado de Baca shopping plaza and with only about a dozen tables, this casual place is usually crammed with tourists at lunchtime, when the pizzas and sandwiches really pack 'em in. At dinner, more upscale cuisine—such as Cuban-style braised pork loin—is offered. Prime rib is served on Friday and Saturday nights.

19 Tubac Rd., Tubac. © **520/398-8075.** Reservations recommended for dinner. Main courses $7.25–$12 lunch, $8–$25 dinner. AE, MC, V. Sun–Tues 11am–4pm; Wed–Sat 11am–4pm and 5–9pm.

Starry, Starry Nights

Southern Arizona's clear skies and the absence of lights in the surrounding desert make the night sky here as brilliant as anywhere on earth. This fact has not gone unnoticed by the world's astronomers—southern Arizona has come to be known as the Astronomy Capital of the World.

Many observatories are open to the public; make tour reservations well in advance. In addition to the ones listed below, the **Flandrau Science Center** (p. 366) in Tucson offers public viewings. In Flagstaff, there are public viewing programs at the **Lowell Observatory** (p. 210).

The **Smithsonian Institution Whipple Observatory,** located atop 8,550-foot Mount Hopkins, is the largest observatory operated by the Smithsonian Astrophysical Observatory. Tours last about 6 hours. No food is available here, so be sure to bring a picnic lunch. It's located on Mount Hopkins Road, near Amado (© **520/670-5707**). Tours are offered March through November Monday, Wednesday, and Friday and cost $7 for adults, $2.50 for children 6 to 12; no children under 6 allowed. Reservations are required and should be made 4 to 6 weeks in advance.

Located in the Quinlan Mountains atop 6,875-foot Kitt Peak, **Kitt Peak National Observatory** ✪ is the largest and most famous astronomical observatory in the region. This is the area's only major observatory to offer public nighttime viewing. Day visitors must be content with a visitor center and museum. A box meal is supplied with evening stargazing programs; day visitors should pack a lunch. The observatory is 56 miles southwest of Tucson off Ariz. 86 (© **520/318-8200** or, for stargazing reservations, 520/318-8726; www.noao.edu/kpno). Nighttime stargazing (reservations required; call 4–8 weeks in advance) $36 adults; $31 students, seniors, and children under 18.

Mount Graham International Observatory, one of the nation's newest, stands atop Mount Graham. Tours last 7 hours and include lunch, but do not include actual viewing through the telescopes at the observatory. There are, however, telescopes for public viewings at **Gov Aker Observatory at Safford's Discovery Park.** Both are located near Safford (© **888/837-1841** or 928/428-6260; www.discoverypark.com). Mount Graham International Observatory tours are $40 (reservations required); Discovery Park admission is $5 adults, $3 children 6 to 12.

Situated on the grounds of the privately owned Vega-Bray Observatory, an amateur observatory with six telescopes and a planetarium, **Skywatcher's Inn** ✪ is one of the most unusual lodgings in the state. The inn provides guests with not only a bed for the night, but also a chance to observe the night sky and the sun through the observatory's telescopes. Viewing programs range from $70 to $130 per night. The inn is located 4 miles outside Benson; call for directions (© **520/615-3886**; www.skywatchersinn.com). Rates are $85 to $175 double.

Wisdom's Cafe *(Finds* MEXICAN Located between Tubac and Tumacacori, this roadside diner is a Santa Cruz Valley institution, in business since 1944. With a cement floor and walls hung with old cowboy stuff, this place feels a bit like a cross between a cave and an old barn. A big TV in the corner plays old Westerns, favorites of retirees down from nearby Green Valley. The menu is short but includes some twists on standard Mexican fare, including tostadas, tacos, and enchiladas made with turkey. Don't eat too much, though, or you won't have room for this restaurant's main draw—huge fruit burros that are basically Mexican fruit pies. To find this place, just watch for the giant chicken statues out front.

1931 E. Frontage Rd., Tumacacori. © 520/398-2397. Main dishes $5–$9. AE, DISC, MC, V. Mon–Sat noon–3pm and 5–8pm.

3 Nogales

63 miles S of Tucson; 175 miles S of Phoenix; 65 miles W of Sierra Vista

Situated on the Mexican border, the twin towns of Nogales, Arizona, and Nogales, Sonora, Mexico (known jointly as Ambos Nogales), form a bustling border community. All day long, U.S. citizens cross into Mexico to shop for bargains on Mexican handicrafts, pharmaceuticals, tequila, and Kahlúa, while Mexican citizens cross into the United States to buy products not available in their country.

ESSENTIALS
GETTING THERE Nogales is the last town on I-19 before the Mexican border. Ariz. 82 leads northeast from town toward Sonoita and Sierra Vista.

VISITOR INFORMATION Contact the Nogales–Santa Cruz County Chamber of Commerce, 123 W. Kino Park Way (© 520/287-3685; www. nogaleschamber.com).

EXPLORING NORTH & SOUTH OF THE BORDER
Most people who visit Nogales, Arizona, are here to cross the border to Nogales, Mexico. The favorable exchange rate makes shopping in Mexico very popular with Americans, although many of the items for sale in Mexico can often be found at lower prices in Tucson. Many people now cross the border specifically to purchase prescription drugs, and pharmacies line the streets near the border crossing.

To learn more about the history of this area, stop by the **Pimeria Alta Historical Society,** at Grand Avenue and Crawford Street (© 520/287-4621), near the border crossing in downtown Nogales. The society maintains a small museum, library, and archives on the region of northern Mexico and southern Arizona that was once known as Pimeria Alta. It's open daily from 10:30am to 4:30pm. Admission is by donation.

Just a couple of miles outside Nogales on the road to Patagonia, you'll see signs for the **Arizona Vineyard Winery,** 1830 Patagonia Rd. (© 520/287-7972), open daily from 10am to 6pm. You may not think of Arizona as wine country, but the Spanish began growing grapes and making wine as soon as they arrived in the area several centuries ago.

If you'd like to ride the range while you're in the area, contact **Arizona Trail Tours** (© 800/477-0615 or 520/281-4122; www.aztrailtours.com), which has its stables in Rio Rico, about 10 miles north of Nogales, and offers everything from 2-hour rides ($40) to 6-day pack trips ($1,250).

Nogales, Mexico, is a typical border town filled with tiny shops selling crafts and souvenirs and dozens of restaurants serving simple Mexican food. Some of the better deals are on wool rugs, which cost a fraction of what a Navajo rug costs, but are not nearly as well made. Pottery is another popular buy. Our personal favorites are the ceramic sinks and handblown glasses and pitchers.

Many good shops and restaurants in Nogales, Mexico, are within walking distance of the border, so unless you're planning to continue farther into Mexico, it's not a good idea to take your car. There are numerous pay parking lots and garages on the U.S. side of the border where your vehicle will be secure for the day. If you should take your car into Mexico, be sure to get Mexican auto insurance beforehand—your U.S. auto insurance will not be valid. There are plenty of insurance companies set up along the road leading to the border.

Most businesses in Nogales, Mexico, accept U.S. dollars. You may bring back $400 worth of merchandise duty-free, including 1 liter of liquor (if you are 21 or older). U.S. citizens need only a driver's license to walk across the border. (For those under driving age, birth certificates are recommended, but not required.)

WHERE TO STAY

Rio Rico Resort & Country Club ★★ (Value)   Located just a few miles north of Nogales, Rio Rico is a secluded hilltop golf resort that has just undergone an extensive renovation. The resort is now looking better than ever, and the new rooms, which are done in a very tasteful Spanish colonial decor, have attractive tile work in the bathrooms and are some of the prettiest rooms in southern Arizona. The accommodations and amenities are the equal of many of the resorts in Tucson, and the views across the Santa Cruz Valley are almost as good. If you want to get away from it all, this is a good bet. The only drawback here is that the Robert Trent Jones golf course is a short drive away on the far side of the freeway. The dining room serves excellent food and has very nice views. The resort makes a good base for exploring east to Patagonia and west to Buenos Aires National Wildlife Refuge.

1069 Camino Caralampi, Rio Rico, AZ 85648. (℃ **800/288-4746** or 520/281-1901. Fax 520/281-7132. www. rioricoresort.com. 180 units. $85–$149 double; $169–$375 suite. AE, DC, DISC, MC, V. Pets accepted. **Amenities:** Restaurant (Southwestern/Continental); lounge; Olympic-size outdoor pool; 18-hole golf course; 4 tennis courts; exercise room; Jacuzzi; sauna; business center; massage; laundry service; dry cleaning; horseback riding. *In room:* A/C, TV, fridge, dataport, high-speed Internet access, coffeemaker, hair dryer, iron.

WHERE TO DINE

La Roca Restaurant ★ (Finds) MEXICAN   La Roca is as unexpected a restaurant as you're likely to find in a border town. Built into a cliff and cool as a cave, it conjures up images of colonial Mexico. White-jacketed waiters provide a level of professional service found only in the most expensive establishments north of the border. Folk art and paintings in the spacious rooms seem to make the interior glow, and at night the place is lit with candles ensconced on the stone walls. The Guaymas shrimp and chicken *mole* are our longtime favorites. The shrimp are reliably succulent, and the mole is a brilliantly flavorful balance between chile and chocolate. Don't miss the margaritas. Downstairs from the restaurant, you'll find El Changarro, a shop selling high-end Mexican pottery, furniture, antiques, and handwoven rugs.

Calle Elias 91, Nogales, Mexico. (℃ **011/52/631/312-0760.** Main courses $8.50–$19. MC, V. Daily 11am–midnight. Walk through the border checkpoint, continue 300 ft., cross the railroad tracks on your left, and look for a narrow side street along the base of the cliff you saw as you crossed into Mexico. The restaurant is about 100 ft. down this street. After dark, solo travelers might want to avoid this restaurant if they are on foot.

4 Patagonia ★★ & Sonoita ★

Patagonia: 18 miles NW of Nogales; 60 miles SE of Tucson; 171 miles SE of Phoenix; 50 miles SW of Tombstone

A mild climate, numerous good restaurants, bed-and-breakfast inns, and a handful of wineries have turned the small communities of Patagonia and Sonoita into a favorite weekend getaway for Tucsonans. Sonoita Creek, one of the only perennial streams in southern Arizona, is also a major draw, attracting bird-watchers from all over the country. Because this creek flows year-round, it attracts an amazing variety of bird life.

Patagonia and Sonoita are only about 12 miles apart, but they have decidedly different characters. Patagonia is a sleepy little hamlet with tree-shaded streets, quite a few old adobe buildings, and a big park in the middle of town. The Nature Conservancy preserve on the edge of town makes Patagonia popular with bird-watchers. Sonoita, on the other hand, sits out on the windswept high plains and is really just a highway crossroads, not a real town. The landscape around Sonoita, however, is filled with expensive new homes on small ranches, and not far away are the vineyards of Arizona's wine country.

ESSENTIALS

GETTING THERE   Sonoita is at the junction of Ariz. 83 and Ariz. 82. Patagonia is 12 miles southwest of Sonoita on Ariz. 82.

VISITOR INFORMATION   The **Patagonia Visitor Information Center,** 307 McKeown Ave. (© **888/794-0060** or 520/394-0060; www.patagoniaaz.com), shares a building with Mariposa Bookstore in the center of Patagonia. Open Monday and Wednesday through Saturday from 10am to 5pm, Sunday from 11am to 4pm.

BIRD-WATCHING, WINE TASTING & OTHER AREA ACTIVITIES

Patagonia, 18 miles north of Nogales on Ariz. 82, is a historic old mining and ranching town 4,000 feet up in the Patagonia Mountains. Surrounded by higher mountains, the little town has for years been popular with film and television crews. Among the films that have been shot here over the years are *Oklahoma!, Red River, A Star Is Born,* and *David and Bathsheba.* TV programs filmed here have included *Little House on the Prairie* and *The Young Riders.* Today, however, bird-watching and tranquillity draw most people to this remote town.

The **Patagonia–Sonoita Creek Preserve** (© **520/394-2400;** http://nature. org) is owned by the Nature Conservancy and protects 1½ miles of Sonoita Creek riparian (riverside) habitat, which is important to migratory birds. More than 300 species of birds have been spotted at the preserve, which makes it a popular destination with birders from all over the country. Among the rare birds that can be seen are 22 species of flycatchers, kingbirds, and phoebes, plus the Montezuma quail. A forest of cottonwood trees, some of which are 100 feet tall, lines the creek and is one of the best remaining examples of such a forest in southern Arizona. At one time, these forests grew along all the rivers in the region. To reach the sanctuary, which is just outside Patagonia on a dirt road that parallels Ariz. 82, turn west on Fourth Avenue and then south on Pennsylvania Street, cross the creek and continue about 1 mile. From April to September, hours are Wednesday through Sunday from 6:30am to 4pm; from October to March, hours are Wednesday through Sunday from 7:30am to 4pm. Admission is $5 ($3 for Nature Conservancy members). On Saturdays at 9am, there are naturalist-guided walks through the preserve; reservations aren't required.

On your way to or from the Nature Conservancy Preserve, be sure to drop by **Paton's Birder's Haven,** which is basically the backyard of Marion Paton. Numerous hummingbird feeders and variety of other feeders attract an amazing range of birds to the yard, making this a favorite stop of avid birders who are touring the region. If you're heading out to the Nature Conservancy preserve, just watch for the BIRDER'S HAVEN sign at 477 Pennsylvania Rd. after you cross the creek.

Another required birders' stop in the area is at the **Patagonia Roadside Rest Area** 4.2 miles south of Patagonia on Ariz. 82. This pull-off is a good place to look for rose-throated becards, varied buntings, and Zone-tailed hawks.

Avid birders will also want to visit **Las Cienegas National Conservation Area** (© 520/258-7200; www.az.blm.gov/nca/lascienegas/lascieneg.htm), which has grasslands, wetlands, and oak forests. This is a good place to look for the rarely seen gray hawk. Access is off the east side of Ariz. 83, about 7 miles north of Sonoita.

Patagonia Lake State Park (© 520/287-6965), about 7 miles south of Patagonia off Ariz. 82, is a popular boating and fishing lake formed by damming Sonoita Creek. The lake is 2½ miles long and stocked in winter with rainbow trout. Other times of year, people fish for bass, crappie, bluegill, and catfish. Park facilities include a picnic ground, campground, and swimming beach. There is also good bird-watching here—elegant trogons, which are among the most beautiful of southern Arizona's rare birds, have been spotted. During much of the year, there are boat tours several mornings each week. These tours focus on the birds and history of the area. The park day-use fee is $7. Campsites are $15 to $22. Adjacent to the park, you'll find the **Sonoita Creek State Natural Area** (© 520/287-2791), a 5,000-acre preserve along the banks of Sonoita Creek. Although the natural area is still in the process of building trails, there is a visitor center.

Sonoita proper is little more than a crossroads with a few shops and restaurants. Surrounding the community are miles of rolling grasslands that are primarily cattle ranches. Also out on those high plains, however, are acres and acres of vineyards that have made Sonoita Arizona's own little wine country. Just west of the village of Elgin, about 10 miles east of Sonoita, you'll find **Callaghan Vineyards,** 336 Elgin Rd. (© 520/455-5322; www.callaghanvineyards.com), which is open for tastings Friday through Sunday from 11am to 3pm. This winery produces by far the best wine in the region, and, in fact, the best wine in the state. The two other area wineries don't do nearly as good a job, but you can be the judge yourself. In the ghost town of Elgin, there's the **Village of Elgin Winery** (© 520/455-9309; www.elginwines.com), which is open daily from 10am to 5pm. Three miles south of Elgin, you'll find **Sonoita Vineyards,** on Canelo Road (© 520/455-5893; www.sonoitavineyards.com), which is open daily from 10am to 4pm. The above tasting-room hours are subject to change, so you might want to call ahead.

While in Patagonia, be sure to check out the interesting shops and galleries around town. You'll also find interesting books and gifts at **Mariposa Books,** 436 Naugle Ave. (© 520/394-9186). The **Mesquite Grove Gallery,** 371 McKeown Ave. (© 520/394-2358), has a good selection of works by area artists. At **Global Arts Gallery,** 315 McKeown Ave. (© 520/394-0077), you'll find a wide range of ethnic arts, fine art, jewelry, and women's clothing.

WHERE TO STAY
IN PATAGONIA

Circle Z Ranch ⭐ In business since 1926, this is the oldest continuously operating dude ranch in Arizona. Over the years it has served as a backdrop for numerous movies and TV shows, including *Gunsmoke* and John Wayne's *Red River*. The 6,500-acre ranch on the banks of Sonoita Creek is bordered by the Nature Conservancy's Patagonia–Sonoita Creek Sanctuary, Patagonia State Park, and the Coronado National Forest. Miles of trails ensure everyone gets in plenty of riding in a variety of terrain, from desert hills to grasslands to the riparian forest along the creek. The adobe cabins provide an authentic ranch feel that's appreciated by guests hoping to find a genuine bit of the Old West.

Ariz. 82 (between Nogales and Patagonia), P.O. Box 194, Patagonia, AZ 85624. ℂ **888/854-2525** or 520/394-2525. Fax 520/394-2058. www.circlez.com. 24 units. $400 double. Rates do not include 15% service charge. Lower rates for children 17 and under. Weekly rates available. Rates include all meals and horseback riding. 3-night minimum stay. MC, V. Closed mid-May to Oct. **Amenities:** Dining room; BYOB lounge; small outdoor pool; tennis court; game room; guest laundry; horseback riding. *In room:* No phone.

Duquesne House B&B ⭐ This old adobe building with a shady front porch was built at the turn of the 20th century as a miners' boardinghouse. Today, each unit has its own entrance, sitting room, and bedroom. Our favorite room has an ornate woodstove and claw-foot tub. At the back of the house, an enclosed porch overlooks the garden and fishpond. The owner of the B&B also runs a local gallery, and artists will feel right at home here.

357 Duquesne Ave. (P.O. Box 772), Patagonia, AZ 85624. ℂ **520/394-2732** or 520/604-6162. 4 units. $75 double. Rate includes full breakfast. No credit cards. *In room:* Fridge, coffeemaker, no phone.

Stage Stop Inn Though nothing fancy, this small hotel in the center of town is large enough that it usually has a few rooms available. Furnishings are motel basic, but there's a small pool in the courtyard if you happen to be here in the heat of summer.

303 W. McKeown St. (P.O. Box 273), Patagonia, AZ 85624. ℂ **800/923-2211** or 520/394-2211. Fax 520/394-2212. 43 units. $60–$80 double; $99–$129 suite. Children 5 and under stay free in parent's room. AE, DISC, MC, V. Pets accepted ($25 fee). **Amenities:** Restaurant (Mexican/American); small outdoor pool. *In room:* A/C, TV, fridge.

IN SONOITA

La Hacienda de Sonoita ⭐ Located on the east side of Sonoita and not too far out of town, this hacienda-style B&B has unobstructed views that stretch to the distant mountain ranges that surround these high plains. The inn is built around a central courtyard, which has a bubbling fountain and covered porches. There's also another covered porch that looks out to the eastern views. The decor in the guest rooms ranges from country to colorful Southwestern. My personal favorite is the Grand Canyon Room.

34 Swanson Rd. (P.O. Box 408), Sonoita, AZ 85637. ℂ **520/455-5308.** Fax 520/455-5309. www.hacienda sonoita.com. 4 units. $110–$130 double. AE, DISC, MC, V. *In room:* No phone.

Rancho Milagro ⭐ Located in the grasslands outside the village of Elgin and in the heart of the local wine country, this B&B has just about the biggest skies in the area. There's nothing out here but wide-open country and plenty of tranquillity. The building, although new, is constructed in a pueblo/territorial style, and each unit has dyed cement floors, a woodstove, and a whirlpool tub. All rooms have separate entrances and are built around a courtyard where breakfast is served. Horses are also welcome.

11 E. Camino del Corral (P.O. Box 981), Elgin, AZ 85637. ℂ 520/455-0381. www.ranchomilagrobb.com. 3 units. $125 double. 2-night minimum. Rates include continental breakfast. MC, V. No children. **Amenities:** Exercise room. *In room:* TV/VCR, no phone.

Sonoita Inn Housed in a barnlike building, the Sonoita Inn plays up the area's ranching history. The building was originally constructed by the owner of the famed Triple Crown–winning thoroughbred Secretariat, but in 1999 was converted into an inn. The lobby, with its wooden floors, huge fireplace, and ranch brands for decoration, is cool and dark (a welcome escape on hot summer days). Guest rooms feature Indian rugs and 1950s-inspired bedspreads for a retro cowboy touch. Although it's right on Sonoita's main road, the fascinating decor more than makes up for the less-than-quiet location. A popular steakhouse is adjacent to the inn.

At intersection of Ariz. 82 and Ariz. 83, P.O. Box 99, Sonoita, AZ 85637. ℂ 800/696-1006 or 520/455-5935. Fax 520/455-5069. www.sonoitainn.com. 18 units. $85–$140 double. Rates include deluxe continental breakfast. AE, DISC, MC, V. Pets accepted ($25 per night). *In room:* A/C, TV/VCR.

WHERE TO DINE
IN PATAGONIA

For good coffee and pastries, check out **Gathering Grounds,** 319 McKeown Ave. (ℂ 520/394-2097), which also serves ice cream and has a deli. Looking for a bit of night life? Don't miss **La Mision de San Miguel,** 355 McKeown St. (ℂ 520/394-0123; www.lamisionpatagonia.com), which looks like an old mission church from the front and inside is a Mexican-inspired bar with live music and dancing on Friday and Saturday nights. There are also wine tastings here every other Wednesday.

Santo's Mexican Cafe *Finds* MEXICAN A reader alerted me to this place. It's about as nondescript and basic as a roadside diner can be, but the Mexican food served here is always fresh and flavorful. If the weather is good, sit out front under the canopy that shades the patio.

328 Naugle Ave. ℂ 520/394-2597. Main dishes $4.25–$7. No credit cards. Daily 7am–3pm.

Velvet Elvis Pizza Company ITALIAN This casual hangout sums up the unusual character of Patagonia's residents. Faux-finished walls ooze artiness, while paeans to pop culture include shrines to both the Virgin Mary and Elvis. There's even a genuine velvet Elvis painting on display. The menu features pizzas heaped with veggies, cheeses, and meats. Add an organic salad and accompany it with some fresh juice, microbrew, espresso, or organic wine.

292 Naugle Ave. ℂ 520/394-2102. www.velvetelvispizza.com. Pizzas $6.50–$19. MC, V. Thurs–Sun 11:30am–8:30pm.

IN SONOITA

Grab good breads and pastries, hot breakfasts, and sandwiches at the **Grasslands Bakery/Café,** 3119 Ariz. 83 (ℂ 520/455-4770; www.grasslandsbakery.com), which is an outpost of organic foods. There are even tastings of organic wines and loads of house-made salsas, jams, and other items for sale. The bakery is open Wednesday through Friday from 10am to 3pm, Saturday and Sunday from 8am to 3pm.

Café Sonoita AMERICAN A tiny place with just a handful of tables, this cafe serves the best food in the area and has long been a favorite with locals. The menu, which changes daily and is limited to a handful of dishes that are listed on a blackboard, is surprisingly creative. Ingredients are always fresh, which is why the menu changes all the time, and there are local wines to accompany the meals. Although you can get straightforward traditional fare such as steaks and prime rib, the best reason to eat here is for the more creative dishes, including the duck in cherry sauce (which shows up frequently). This place could hold its own in Tucson or Phoenix; don't miss it.

3280 Ariz. 82 (at the east end of town). © 520/455-5278. Reservations recommended at dinner for parties of 5 or more. Main courses $9–$18. MC, V. Wed–Thurs 5–8pm; Fri–Sat 11am–2:30pm and 5–8pm.

The Steak Out ✯ STEAKHOUSE   This is ranch country, and this big barn of a place is where the ranchers and everyone else for miles around head when they want a good steak. A classic cowboy atmosphere prevails: There's even a mounted buffalo head just inside the front door. The restaurant's name and the scent of a mesquite fire should be all the hints you need about what to order—a grilled steak, preferably the exceedingly tender filet mignon. Wash it down with a margarita and you've got the perfect cowboy dinner.

At intersection of Ariz. 82 and Ariz. 83. © 520/455-5205. Reservations recommended. Main courses $7–$31. AE, DISC, MC, V. Mon–Thurs 5–9pm; Fri 5–10pm; Sat–Sun 11am–10pm.

5 Sierra Vista & the San Pedro Valley ✯

70 miles SE of Tucson; 189 miles SE of Phoenix; 33 miles SW of Tombstone; 33 miles W of Bisbee

Located at an elevation of 4,620 feet above sea level, Sierra Vista is blessed with the perfect climate—never too hot, never too cold. This fact more than anything else has contributed in recent years to Sierra Vista becoming one of the fastest-growing cities in Arizona. Although the city itself is a modern, sprawling community outside the gates of the U.S. Army's Fort Huachuca, it is wedged between the Huachuca Mountains and the valley of the San Pedro River. Consequently, Sierra Vista, with its many inexpensive motels, makes a good base for exploring the region's natural attractions.

Within a few miles' drive of town are the San Pedro Riparian National Conservation Area, Coronado National Memorial, and the Nature Conservancy's Ramsey Canyon Preserve. No other area of the United States attracts more attention from birders, who come in hopes of spotting some of the 300 species that have been sighted in southeastern Arizona. About 25 miles north of town is Kartchner Caverns State Park, the region's biggest attraction, located 9 miles south of Benson.

ESSENTIALS
GETTING THERE   Sierra Vista is at the junction of Ariz. 90 and Ariz. 92 about 35 miles south of I-10.

VISITOR INFORMATION   The **Sierra Vista Convention & Visitors Bureau,** 3020 Tacoma St. (© **800/288-3861** or 520/417-6960; www.visit sierravista.com), can provide information on the area. To find the visitor center, turn onto Carmichael Avenue from Fry Boulevard; the office is 2 blocks off Fry Boulevard on the left.

SPECIAL EVENTS   In February, cowboy poets, singers, and musicians come together at the **Cochise Cowboy Poetry & Music Gathering** (© **800/288-3861** or 520/417-6960; www.cowboypoets.com).

ATTRACTIONS AROUND BENSON

While Kartchner Caverns is the main draw in the Benson area, you might also want to visit the remarkable **Singing Wind Bookshop** (© 520/586-2425), on a ranch down a dirt road north of town. The store is the brainchild of Winifred Bundy, who, with her late husband, began the business more than 25 years ago with only a couple of shelves of books. Now the inventory is well into the thousands, with an emphasis on the Southwest, natural sciences, and children's literature. To get here, take Exit 304 from I-10 in Benson. Drive north 2¼ miles and take a right (east) at the sign that says SINGING WIND ROAD. Drive to the end, opening and closing the gate. The store is open daily from 9am to 5pm.

Tucson may have Old Tucson Studios, but Benson has **Mescal** (© 520/883-0100). This Western town movie set is operated by Old Tucson Studios and has been used for years in the making of Westerns, as well as TV shows and commercials. However, until recently, Mescal was strictly business, and no visitors were allowed. It's now possible to take an hour-long walking tour of Mescal and get a feel for the many movies that have been shot here. While Old Tucson Studios feels like an amusement park, this place seems like an old ghost town. For fans of old Westerns, this is a must. Tours are available Tuesday, Thursday and Saturday between 10am and 2pm and cost $8. Roughly 35 miles east of Tucson, take Exit 297 off I-10, then head north for 3 miles on Mescal Road. When the pavement ends, head west for ½ mile on the dirt road to the town, which is visible on the hill ahead.

Kartchner Caverns State Park ★★   These caverns, which were discovered in 1974 and opened to the public in 1999, are among the largest and most beautiful caverns in the country. Because these are wet caverns, stalactites, stalagmites, soda straws, and other cave formations are still growing. To ensure that these delicate formations continue to grow as they have for thousands of years, air-lock doors have been installed in the caverns.

Within the caverns are two huge rooms, each larger than a football field with ceilings more than 100 feet high. These two rooms can be visited on two separate tours. On the shorter Rotunda/Throne Room Tour, you will see, in the Rotunda Room, thousands of delicate soda straws. In fact, Kartchner Caverns contains the longest soda straw formation in the U.S., at 21 feet 2 inches. The highlight of this tour is the Throne Room, at the center of which is a 58-foot-tall column known as Kubla Khan. The second, and longer tour, visits the Big Room and leads past many strange and rare cave formations. Within the park, there are also several miles of hiking trails through the hills that hide the caverns. A campground charging $22 per night provides a convenient place to stay in the area.

Because the caverns are a popular attraction and tours are limited, try to make a reservation in advance, especially if you want to visit on a weekend. However, it is sometimes possible to get same-day tickets if you happen to be passing by.

Off Ariz. 90, 9 miles south of Benson. © **520/586-4100** for information, or 520/586-CAVE for tour reservations. www.azstateparks.com. Admission $5 per car to enter the park and visit aboveground exhibits; cave

---

⌒Finds Navajo Rugs

If you happen to be in the market for a Navajo rug, get in touch with Steve Getzwiller.at **Spear G Ranch** (© 520/586-2579; www.navajorug.com), which is located outside Benson. Here you'll find one of Arizona's best selections of contemporary and old Navajo rugs.

tours $19–$23 adults, $9.95–$13 children 7–13. Park open daily 7:30am–6pm; cave tours approximately every 20 min. 8am–5pm.

ATTRACTIONS AROUND SIERRA VISTA

Arizona Folklore Preserve   Set beneath the shady cottonwoods and sycamores of Ramsey Canyon, the Arizona Folklore Preserve is the brainchild of Dolan Ellis, Arizona's official state balladeer, and his wife, Rose. Ellis was first appointed state balladeer back in 1966 and has been writing songs about Arizona for more than 30 years. He performs most weekends and often welcomes guests to the stage of his performance hall. In the past, there have been cowboy poets, folk artists, a fiddle maker, saddle makers, and musicians.

44 Ramsey Canyon Rd. (Ariz. 92 south of Sierra Vista). ☎ 520/378-6165. www.arizonafolklore.com. Admission by donation. Showtime Sat–Sun 2pm. Reservations required.

Fort Huachuca Museum   Fort Huachuca, an army base at the mouth of Huachuca Canyon just west of Sierra Vista, was established in 1877. The buildings of the old post have been declared a National Historic Landmark, and one is now a museum dedicated to the many forts that dotted the Southwest in the latter part of the 19th century. Interesting aspects of the exhibits include the quotes by soldiers that give an idea of what it was like to serve back then. The associated **U.S. Army Military Intelligence Museum,** at Hungerford and Cristi streets, has displays on early code machines, surveillance drones, and other pieces of equipment formerly used for intelligence gathering.

At the Fort Huachuca U.S. Army base, Grierson Rd., Sierra Vista. ☎ 520/458-4716. Suggested donation $2. Mon–Fri 9am–4pm; Sat–Sun 1–4pm. Closed New Year's Day, Thanksgiving, and Christmas.

BIRDING HOT SPOTS & OTHER NATURAL AREAS

Bird-watching has become big business over the past few years, with birders' B&Bs, bird refuges, and even birding festivals. Each year in August, the **Southwest Wings Birding Festival** (☎ 520/432-5421; www.swwings.org) is held in Bisbee, about 30 miles east of Sierra Vista.

If you'd like to join a guided bird walk along the San Pedro River or up Carr Canyon in the Huachuca Mountains, an owl-watching night hike, or a hummingbird banding session, contact the **Southeastern Arizona Bird Observatory** (☎ 520/432-1388; www.sabo.org), which also has a public bird-viewing area at its headquarters 2 miles north of the Mule Mountain Tunnel on Ariz. 80 north of Bisbee (watch for Hidden Meadow Lane). Most activities take place between April and September and cost $15 to $60. Workshops and tours are also offered.

Serious birders who want to be sure to add lots of rare birds to their life lists might want to visit this area on a guided tour. Your best bet is **Mark Pretti Nature Tours** (☎ 520/803-6889; www.markprettinaturetours.com), run by the resident naturalist at Ramsey Canyon Preserve. A half-day birding tour costs $100 and a full-day tour costs $150 to $200. Three-day ($450–$550) and 8-day ($1,150) trips are also offered. **High Lonesome Ecotours** (☎ 800/743-2668 or 520/458-9446; www.hilonesome.com), another local tour company, charges about $925 per person for a 4-day birding trip.

In addition to the birding hot spots listed below, there are a few other places that serious birders should not miss. **Garden Canyon,** at Fort Huachuca, has 8 miles of trails, and 350 species of birds have been sighted. There are also Indian pictographs along one of the trails through the canyon. This is a good place to look for elegant trogons and Mexican spotted owls. Get directions at the fort's front gate, and be prepared to show your license, vehicle registration, and proof of vehicle insurance. The canyon is open to the public daily during daylight

---

Moments **Hummingbird Heaven**

If it's summer and you're looking to add as many hummingbirds to your life list as possible, take a drive up Miller Canyon (south of Ramsey Canyon) to **Beatty's Miller Canyon Guest Ranch and Orchard,** 2173 E. Miller Canyon Rd., Hereford (© 520/378-2728; www.beattysguestranch.com), where a public hummingbird-viewing area is set up. Fifteen species of hummers have been sighted here.

---

hours, but is sometimes closed due to military maneuvers, so you must check with the **Range Control Office** (© **520/533-7095**) before heading out.

South of Ramsey Canyon off Ariz. 92, you'll find **Carr Canyon,** which has a road that climbs up through the canyon to some of the higher elevations in the Huachuca Mountains. Keep your eyes open for buff-breasted flycatchers, red crossbills, and red-faced warblers. The one-lane road is narrow and winding (usually navigable by passenger car), and not for the acrophobic. It climbs 5 miles up into the mountains and goes to Reef Townsite, an old mining camp.

The **Sierra Vista Wastewater Wetlands,** 3 miles east of Ariz. 92 on Ariz. 90, is a good place to see yellow-headed blackbirds, ducks, peregrines, and harriers from fall to spring. The area is open daily.

Coronado National Memorial About 20 miles south of Sierra Vista is a 5,000-acre memorial dedicated to Francisco Vásquez de Coronado, the first European to explore this region. In 1540, Coronado, leading more than 700 people, left Compostela, Mexico, in search of the fabled Seven Cities of Cíbola, said to be rich in gold and jewels. Sometime between 1540 and 1542, Coronado led his band of weary men and women up the valley of the San Pedro River, which this monument overlooks. At the visitor center, you can learn about Coronado's fruitless quest for riches and check out the wildlife observation area, where you might see some of the memorial's 140 or more species of birds. Outside the visitor center, a trail leads ¾ mile to 600-foot-long Coronado Cave. (You'll need to bring your own flashlight and get a permit at the visitor center if you want to explore this cave.) After stopping at the visitor center, drive up to 6,575-foot Montezuma Pass, which is in the center of the memorial and provides far-reaching views of Sonora, Mexico, to the south, the San Pedro River to the east, and several mountain ranges and valleys to the west. Along the .8-mile round-trip Coronado Peak Trail, you'll also have good views of the valley and can read quotations from the journals of Coronado's followers. There are also some longer trails where you'll see few other hikers.

4101 E. Montezuma Canyon Rd. © 520/366-5515. www.nps.gov/coro. Free admission. Daily 8am–5pm. Closed Thanksgiving and Christmas.

Ramsey Canyon Preserve ✪ Each year, beginning in late spring, a buzzing fills the air in Ramsey Canyon, but it's not the buzzing of the bees. It's the buzzing of countless hummingbirds. This preserve has become internationally known as home to 14 species of hummingbirds. Wear bright-red clothing when you visit, and you're certain to attract the little avian dive bombers, which will mistake you for the world's largest flower. Situated in a wooded gorge in the Huachuca Mountains, this Nature Conservancy preserve covers only 380 acres. However, because Ramsey Creek, which flows through the canyon, is a year-round stream, it attracts a wide variety of wildlife, including bears, bobcats, and nearly 200 species of birds. A short nature trail leads through the canyon, and a second trail leads higher up the canyon. April and May are the busiest times here, while August and May are the best times to see hummingbirds. Guided walks are offered March through October.

27 Ramsey Canyon Rd., off Ariz. 92, 5 miles south of Sierra Vista. ✆ 520/378-2785. www.nature.org. Admission $5 ($3 for Nature Conservancy members). Mar–Oct daily 8am–5pm; Nov–Feb daily 9am–4pm. Closed New Year's Day, Thanksgiving, and Christmas.

San Pedro Riparian National Conservation Area ✪ Located 8 miles east of Sierra Vista, this conservation area is one of Arizona's rare examples of a natural riverside habitat. Over the past 100 years, the Southwestern landscape has been considerably altered by the human hand. Most deleterious of these changes has been the loss of 90% of the region's free-flowing year-round rivers and streams that once provided water and protection to myriad plants, animals, and even humans. Fossil findings from this area indicate that people were living along this river 11,000 years ago. At that time, this area was a swamp, not a desert, but today, the San Pedro River is all that remains of this ancient wetland. As rivers go, the San Pedro is pretty small. In fact, most people would call it a creek. However, much of the river's water flows underground due to an earthquake a century ago. The conservation area is most popular with birders, who have a chance of spotting more than 300 species here.

Also within the riparian area is the **Murray Springs Clovis Site,** where 16 spear points and the remains of a 10,000-year-old mammoth kill were found in the 1960s. Although there isn't much to see other than some trenches, there are numerous interpretive signs along the short trail through the site. It's just north of Ariz. 90 about 5 miles east of Sierra Vista.

For a glimpse of the region's Spanish history, visit the ruins of the **Presidio Santa Cruz de Terrenate,** about 20 miles northeast of Sierra Vista off Ariz. 82 near the ghost town of Fairbank. This military outpost was established in 1775 or 1776 by Irish mercenary Hugh O'Conor, who also founded Tucson. Only decaying adobe walls remain of this military outpost, which was never completed due to the constant attacks by Apaches. To reach this site, take Ariz. 82 east from U.S. 90 and drive north 1¾ miles on Ironhorse Ranch Road, which is at milepost 60. It's a 1.2-mile hike to the site.

For bird-watching, the best place to visit is the system of trails at the Ariz. 90 crossing of the San Pedro. Here you will find the **San Pedro House** (✆ 520/508-4445), a 1930s ranch that is operated as a visitor center and bookstore. It's open daily from 9:30am to 4:30pm. Throughout the year, there are guided walks and hikes, bird walks, bird-banding sessions, and other scheduled events. Check with the San Pedro House for a calendar.

Ariz. 90. ✆ 520/458-3559. azwww.az.blm.gov/nca/spnca/spnca-info.htm. Free admission. Parking areas open sunrise to sunset.

⟨ *Finds* **A Holy Bird Sanctuary**

In the community of St. David, 5 miles south of Benson on Ariz. 80, you'll find the **Holy Trinity Monastery** (✆ 520/720-4642), which is located near the banks of the San Pedro River and has a 1.3-mile birding trail.

OTHER OUTDOOR PURSUITS

The near-perfect climate of Sierra Vista has made it a great place to golf. You can play a round at the **Pueblo del Sol Country Club,** 2700 St. Andrew's Dr. (© **520/378-6444**), which is off Ariz. 92 on the east side of town and has a great view of the Huachuca Mountains. Greens fees run from $35 to $47.

Horseback riding at Fort Huachuca's **Buffalo Corral** (© **520/533-5220**) is a good deal, at a cost of $19 for a 2-hour trail ride. Special family rates are available. Rides are offered Wednesday through Sunday.

Hikers will find numerous trails in the Huachuca Mountains, which rise to the west of Sierra Vista. There are trails at Garden Canyon near Fort Huachuca, at Ramsey Canyon Preserve, at Carr Canyon in Coronado National Forest, and at Coronado National Memorial. See "Birding Hot Spots & Other Natural Areas," above, for details. For information on hiking in the Coronado National Forest, contact the **Sierra Vista Ranger District,** 5990 S. Hwy. 92 (© **520/ 378-0311**), 8 miles south of Sierra Vista.

WHERE TO STAY

IN BENSON

Holiday Inn Express ⚐ If you're looking for lodging close to Kartchner Caverns, try this off-ramp budget motel in Benson. The motel's lobby is done in Santa Fe style with flagstone floors and rustic Southwestern furniture. Guest rooms are strictly motel modern, but they are roomy.

630 South Village Loop, Benson, AZ 85602. © **888/263-2283** or 520/586-8800. Fax 520/586-1370. www. sixcontinentshotels.com/h/d/hiex/hd/bsnaz. 62 units. $67–$99 double. Rates include deluxe continental breakfast. Children under 18 stay free in parent's room. AE, DC, DISC, MC, V. **Amenities:** Outdoor pool; exercise room; access to nearby health club; business center; coin-op laundry. *In room:* A/C, TV, dataport, fridge, coffeemaker, hair dryer, iron, free local calls.

IN SIERRA VISTA

Windemere Hotel & Conference Center This three-story conference hotel on the south side of town is one of Sierra Vista's best lodgings, as well as one of the closest to Ramsey Canyon. Although it makes a good choice for avid bird-watchers, it is much more popular with conferences. Guest rooms feature contemporary furnishings.

2047 S. Hwy. 92, Sierra Vista, AZ 85635. © **800/825-4656** or 520/459-5900. Fax 520/458-1347. www. windemerehotel.com. 149 units. $85 double; $175–$195 suite. Rates include full breakfast and evening cocktails. Children under 18 stay free in parent's room. AE, DC, DISC, MC, V. Pets accepted ($50 deposit). **Amenities:** Restaurant (American); lounge; outdoor pool; exercise room; access to nearby health club; Jacuzzi; courtesy car; room service; coin-op laundry; laundry service; dry cleaning. *In room:* A/C, TV, dataport, fridge, coffeemaker, hair dryer, iron, free local calls.

IN HEREFORD

Casa de San Pedro ⚐ Built with bird-watching tour groups in mind, this modern inn is set on the west side of the San Pedro River on 10 acres of land. While the setting doesn't have the historic character of the San Pedro River Inn (see below), it is much more up-to-date, with large, comfortable hotel-style guest rooms. Built in the territorial style around a courtyard garden, the inn has a large common room where birders gather to swap tales of the day's sightings. This is by far the most upscale inn in the region and is our favorite place to stay in the area.

8933 S. Yell Lane, Hereford, AZ 85615. © **888/257-2050** or 520/366-1300. Fax 520/366-0701. www. bedandbirds.com. 10 units. $129–$149 double. Rates include full breakfast. AE, DISC, MC, V. No children under 12. **Amenities:** Outdoor pool; Jacuzzi; guest laundry. *In room:* A/C, Internet access, hair dryer.

Ramsey Canyon Inn Bed & Breakfast ☆   Located adjacent to the Nature Conservancy's Ramsey Canyon Preserve, this inn, which was completely renovated in early 2003, is the most convenient choice in the area for avid birders here to see the canyon's famous hummingbirds. The property straddles Ramsey Creek, with guest rooms in the main house and apartments in small cabins reached by a footbridge over the creek. A large country breakfast is served in the morning, and in the afternoon you're likely to find a fresh pie made with fruit from the inn's orchard. Guests have 24-hour access to the preserve—a real plus for serious birders. Book early.

29 Ramsey Canyon Dr., Hereford, AZ 85615. ℂ 520/378-3010. www.ramseycanyoninn.com. 9 units. $130–$150 double; $150–$225 suite. Room rates include full breakfast. MC, V. No children under 16. *In room:* No phone.

San Pedro River Inn   With the character of a small guest ranch, this family-friendly inn is a casual place that will please avid birders who prefer Old Arizona character over spotless modern accommodations. Located on the east side of the San Pedro Riparian National Conservation Area, the four eclectically furnished cottages are set beneath huge old cottonwood trees.

8326 S. Hereford Rd., Hereford, AZ 85615. ℂ/fax 520/366-5532. www.sanpedroriverinn.com. 4 units. $105 double. Rates include continental breakfast. 2-night minimum weekends, holidays, and peak season. No credit cards. **Amenities:** Guest laundry. *In room:* TV/VCR, kitchen, fridge, coffeemaker, free local calls.

CAMPGROUNDS

There are two Coronado National Forest campgrounds—16-site **Reef Townsite** and 8-site **Ramsey Vista**—up the winding Carr Canyon Road south of Sierra Vista off Ariz. 92. Both charge $10 per night. For information, contact the Coronado National Forest Sierra Vista Ranger District, 5990 S. Hwy. 92, Hereford, AZ 85615 (ℂ **520/378-0311;** www.fs.fed.us/r3/coronado/svrd).

WHERE TO DINE

Sierra Vista supports quite a number of good Asian restaurants, with an emphasis on Chinese, Japanese, and Korean cuisine.

The Mesquite Tree ☆ STEAKHOUSE   This casual steakhouse south of town (and not far from the mouth of Ramsey Canyon) has long been a favorite of locals. It's funky and dark, but the prices can't be beat. Although you can get a variety of chicken and fish dishes done in a variety of traditional Continental styles, most people come here for the steaks. Try the Vargas rib-eye, which is smothered with green chiles, jack cheese, and enchilada sauce—a real border-country original. When the weather is warm, try to get a seat on the patio.

S. Ariz. 92 and Carr Canyon Rd. ℂ 520/378-2758. Reservations recommended. Main courses $10–$20. AE, DISC, MC, V. Tues–Sat 5–9pm; Sun 5–8pm.

The Outside Inn STEAKHOUSE/SEAFOOD/ITALIAN   Much more formal than the nearby Mesquite Tree, the Outside Inn has long been Sierra Vista's top special-occasion restaurant. Housed in a cottagelike building south of town and just north of the turnoff for Ramsey Canyon, the Outside Inn may not be in the most picturesque of surroundings, but the food is definitely among the best you'll find in the area. In the main dining room or out on the patio, you can enjoy such fare as chicken with a Gorgonzola–white wine sauce, blackened mahimahi, or crab-stuffed giant Guaymas shrimp.

4907 S. Ariz. 92. ℂ 520/378-4645. Reservations recommended. Main courses $5.50–$9 lunch, $13–$22 dinner. AE, MC, V. Mon–Fri 11am–1:30pm and 5–9pm; Sat 5–9pm.

Tanuki Sushi Bar & Garden JAPANESE Of all the many Asian restaurants in Sierra Vista, this is one of my favorites. Take a glance around at the signed plates on the walls, and you'll see that other visitors, including actor Tom Selleck, like the food here, too. I like to get the sushi, but there are plenty of traditional hot Japanese dishes available as well. At lunch, there are quick, inexpensive specials, while at dinner, there's a fun "love boat" special that includes a variety of sushi and tempura.

1221 E. Fry Blvd. © 520/459-6853. Main courses $6–$19. AE, MC, V. Mon–Thurs 11am–2:30pm and 5–9:30pm; Fri–Sat 11am–2:30pm and 5–10pm.

6 Tombstone ✶

70 miles SE of Tucson; 181 miles SE of Phoenix; 24 miles N of Bisbee

All it took was a brief blaze of gunfire more than a century ago to seal the fate of this former silver-mining boomtown. It was on these very streets, at a livery stable known as the O.K. Corral, that Wyatt Earp, his brothers Virgil and Morgan, and their friend Doc Holliday took on the outlaws Ike Clanton and Frank and Tom McLaury on October 26, 1881. Today, Tombstone, "the town too tough to die," is one of Arizona's most popular attractions, but we'll leave it up to you to decide whether it deserves its reputation (either as a tough town or as a tourist attraction).

Tombstone was named by Ed Schieffelin, a silver prospector who ventured into this region at a time when the resident Apaches were fighting to preserve their homeland. Schieffelin was warned that all he would find here was his own tombstone, so when he discovered silver, he named the strike Tombstone. Within a few years, the town of Tombstone was larger than San Francisco, and between 1880 and 1887, an estimated $37 million worth of silver was mined here. Such wealth created a sturdy little town, and as the Cochise County seat of the time, Tombstone boasted a number of imposing buildings, including the county courthouse, which is now a state park. In 1887, an underground river flooded the silver mines, and despite attempts to pump the water out, the mines were never reopened. With the demise of the mines, the boom came to an end and the population rapidly dwindled.

Today, Tombstone's historic district consists of both original buildings that went up after the town's second fire and newer structures built in keeping with the architectural styles of the late 19th century. Most house souvenir shops and restaurants, which should give you some indication that this place is a classic tourist trap, but kids (and adults raised on Louis L'Amour and John Wayne) love it, especially when the famous shootout is reenacted.

ESSENTIALS

GETTING THERE From Tucson, take I-10 east to Benson, from which Ariz. 80 heads south to Tombstone. From Sierra Vista, take Ariz. 90 north to Ariz. 82 heading east.

VISITOR INFORMATION The **Tombstone Chamber of Commerce** (© 888/457-3929 or 520/457-9317; www.tombstone.org) operates a visitor center at the corner of Allen and Fourth streets.

SPECIAL EVENTS Tombstone's biggest annual celebrations are **Ed Schieffelin Territorial Days,** on the third weekend in March; **Wyatt Earp Days,** in late May; and **Helldorado Days,** on the third weekend in October. The latter celebrates the famous gunfight at the O.K. Corral and includes countless shootouts in the streets, mock hangings, a parade, and contests.

GUNSLINGERS & SALOONS: IN SEARCH OF THE WILD WEST

As portrayed in novels, movies, and TV shows, the shootout has come to epito-mize the Wild West, and nowhere is this great American phenomenon more glo-rified than in Tombstone, where the star attraction is the famous **O.K. Corral,** 308 E. Allen St. (✆ **520/457-3456;** www.ok-corral.com), site of a 30-second gun battle that has taken on mythic proportions over the years. Inside the cor-ral, you'll find not only displays on the shootout, but also an exhibit on local photographer C. S. Fly, who ran the boardinghouse where Doc Holliday was staying at the time of the shootout. Next door is **Tombstone's Historama,** a sort of kitschy multimedia affair that rehashes the well-known history of Tombstone's "bad old days." The O.K. Corral and Tombstone Historama are open daily from 9am to 5pm and admission is $5.50; for $7.50, you can visit both attractions and take in a shootout reenactment almost on the very site of the original gunfight.

If you aren't able to catch one of the staged shootouts at the O.K. Corral (daily at 2pm), don't despair—there are plenty of other shootouts staged in Tombstone. In fact, all over Arizona there are regular reenactments of gunfights, with the sheriff in his white hat always triumphing over the bad guys in black hats. However, nowhere else in the state are there as many modern-day gun-slingers entertaining so many people with their blazing six-guns as in Tomb-stone. Shootouts occur fairly regularly around town between noon and 4pm. Expect to pay $4 for any of these shows. For a little fun and games, try to catch the Tombstone Cowboys shootout at **Helldorado,** Fourth and Toughnut streets (✆ **520/457-9153**). Shows are held Monday through Friday at 12:30 and 3pm and Saturday and Sunday at 11:30am and 1 and 3pm. These shootouts are more hysterical than historical.

When the smoke cleared in 1881, three men lay dead. They were later carted off to the **Boot Hill Graveyard** (✆ **800/457-9344** or 520/457-9344), on the north edge of town. The cemetery is open to the public and is entered through a gift shop on Ariz. 80. The graves of Clanton and the McLaury brothers, as well as those of others who died in gunfights or by hanging, are well marked. Entertaining epitaphs grace the gravestones; among the most famous is that of Lester Moore—"Here lies Lester Moore, 4 slugs from a 44, No Les, no more." The cemetery is open daily from 7:30am to 6pm; admission is free.

When the residents of Tombstone weren't shooting each other in the streets, they were likely to be found in the saloons and bawdy houses that lined Allen Street. Most famous is the **Bird Cage Theatre** (✆ **800/457-3423** or 520/457-3421) so named for the cagelike cribs (what most people would think of as box seats) that are suspended from the ceiling. These velvet-draped cages were used by prostitutes to ply their trade. For old Tombstone atmosphere, this place is hard to beat. Admission is $6 for adults, $5.50 for seniors, and $5 for children 8 to 18; the theater is open daily from 8am to 6pm (Thurs–Sat until 7pm).

If you want to down a cold beer, Tombstone has a couple of very lively saloons. The **Crystal Palace,** at Allen and Fifth streets (✆ **520/457-3611**), was built in 1879 and has been completely restored. This is one of the favorite hang-outs for the town's costumed actors and other would-be cowboys and cowgirls. **Big Nose Kate's,** 417 E. Allen St. (✆ **520/457-3107**), is an equally entertain-ing spot full of Wild West character and characters.

Tombstone has long been a tourist town, and its streets are lined with souvenir shops selling wind chimes, Beanie Babies, and other less-than-wild souvenirs. There are also several small museums scattered around town. At the **Rose Tree**

Inn Museum, at Fourth and Toughnut streets (© 520/457-3326), you can see what may be the world's largest rose bush. Inside are antique furnishings from Tombstone's heyday in the 1880s. It's open daily from 9am to 5pm (closed Thanksgiving and Christmas). Admission is $3 (free for children 14 and under).

Tombstone Courthouse State Park, at 219 Toughnut St. (© 520/457-3311), is the most imposing building in town and provides a much less sensationalized history of this town. Built in 1882, the courthouse is now a state historic park and museum containing artifacts, photos, and newspaper clippings that chronicle Tombstone's lively past. In the courtyard, you can still see the gallows that once ended the lives of outlaws. The courthouse is open daily from 8am to 5pm; the entrance fee is $4 for adults and $1 for children 7 to 13.

At the **Tombstone Epitaph Museum,** Fifth Street between Allen and Fremont streets (© 520/457-2211), you can inspect the office of the town's old newspaper. It's open daily from 9:30am to 5pm; admission is free. To see what life was like for common folk in the old days, pay a visit to the **Pioneer Home Museum,** on Fremont Street (Ariz. 80) between Eighth and Ninth streets (© 520/457-3853; www.tombstone1880.com/phm). It's open daily from 9am to 5pm; a $2 donation is requested.

Don't leave town without visiting the new **Tombstone Western Heritage Museum,** Ariz. 80 and Sixth St. (© 520/457-3800), a privately owned museum that is filled with Tombstone artifacts. Included in this impressive collection are artifacts that once belonged to Wyatt and Virgil Earp, rare photos of the Earps and the outlaws of Tombstone. There are also all kinds of original documents that date to the days of the shootout at the O.K. Corral. The museum is open Monday through Saturday from 9am to 5pm and Sunday from 12:30 to 5pm; admission is $5 for adults and $3 for children 12 to 18.

At several places along Allen Street, you can hop aboard a reproduction stagecoach or covered wagon, and for a few dollars get a narrated tour of town. To gain a broader perspective on Tombstone history, take a ride with **Curly Bill's Jeep Tours,** 210 N. Ninth St. (© 520/457-3858; www.curlybillsbandb.com). These tours head out into the hills surrounding town to visit the sites of some of the old silver mines. Half-day tours are $80 per person; all-day tours are $125 per person.

WHERE TO STAY

Best Western Lookout Lodge   This comfortable motel is a mile north of town overlooking the Dragoon Mountains. Stone walls, porcelain doorknobs, Mexican tiles in the bathrooms, and old-fashioned "gas" lamps give the spacious guest rooms an Old West feel. Ask for a room with a view of the mountains.

Ariz. 80 W. (P.O. Box 787), Tombstone, AZ 85638. © 877/652-6772 or 520/457-2223. Fax 520/457-3870. www.tombstone1880.com/bwlookoutlodge. 40 units. $59–$99 double. Rates include continental breakfast. Children under 12 stay free in parent's room. AE, DC, DISC, MC, V. Pets accepted ($20 per night). **Amenities:** Small outdoor pool. *In room:* A/C, TV, dataport, coffeemaker, hair dryer, iron, free local calls.

Holiday Inn Express ⭐   Located on the northern outskirts of Tombstone, right next door to the older Best Western, this is the newest and most reliable hotel in Tombstone. The decor draws on a bit of Southwestern styling and Spanish colonial styling, but basically this is just a modern motel.

1001 N. Ariz. 80 (P.O. Box 1730), Tombstone, AZ 85638. © 800/465-4329 or 520/457-9507. Fax 520/457-9506. www.holidayinntombstone.com. 60 units. $59–$139 double. Rates include deluxe continental breakfast. Children under 18 stay free in parent's room. AE, DC, DISC, MC, V. Pets accepted ($10 fee). **Amenities:** Outdoor pool; Jacuzzi; concierge; coin-op laundry. *In room:* A/C, TV, dataport, fridge, coffeemaker, hair dryer, iron, free local calls.

Tombstone Boarding House   Housed in two whitewashed 1880s adobe buildings with green trim, this inn is in a quiet residential neighborhood only 2 blocks from busy Allen Street. The main house was originally the home of Tombstone's first bank manager, while the guest rooms are in an old boarding-house. Accommodations are comfortable and clean, with country decor. Hardwood floors and antiques lend a period feel. See "Where to Dine," below, for information on the inn's Lamplight Room restaurant.

108 N. Fourth St. (P.O. Box 906), Tombstone, AZ 85638. ℂ **877/225-1319** or 520/457-3716. www.tombstone boardinghouse.com. 6 units. $69–$89 double. Rates include full breakfast. AE, DISC, MC, V. **Amenities:** Restaurant (Continental). *In room:* No phone.

WHERE TO DINE

If you thought you could only get beer and whiskey in Tombstone, mosey on over to the **Tombstone Coffee & Tea Co.,** 414 E. Allen St. (ℂ **520/457-3045**) and ask the barkeep (barista) for a latte or mocha. Then check out the 1880s stagecoach parked inside the coffeehouse.

Big Nose Kate's Saloon SANDWICHES   Okay, so the food here isn't all that memorable, but the atmosphere sure is. Big Nose Kate's dates back to 1880 and is primarily a saloon. As such, it stays packed with visitors who have come to revel in Tombstone's outlaw past. So, while you sip your beer, why not order a sandwich and call it lunch?

417 E. Allen St. ℂ 520/457-3107. $6.25–$7. MC, V. Daily 11am–5pm.

The Lamplight Room ✦ CONTINENTAL   Located a few blocks off busy Allen Street, this restaurant serves the best food in Tombstone. The restaurant is in the living room of an old 1880s home, which also lends this place more character than that of any of the other restaurants in town. The menu is short, but in addition to such dishes as chicken cordon bleu and roasted pork loin, there's good Mexican food. On Friday and Saturday nights, there is live classical guitar music.

At the Tombstone Boarding House, 108 N. Fourth St. ℂ 520/457-3716. Reservations recommended. Main courses $11–$17. AE, DISC, MC, V. Sun–Thurs 11am–2pm and 5–8pm; Fri–Sat 11am–2pm and 5–9pm.

O.K. Café AMERICAN   Because it's on the main drag in Tombstone, this place is touristy, but we really enjoy the buffalo burgers and homemade soups. Other options include ostrich, emu, veggie, and, of course, beef burgers, as well as bratwurst, BLTs, and chicken. It's also a good place for breakfast.

220 E. Allen St. (at Third St.). ℂ 520/457-3980. Main courses $4.25–$8.50. MC, V. Daily 7am–2pm.

7 Bisbee ✦✦

94 miles SE of Tucson; 205 miles SE of Phoenix; 24 miles NW of Douglas

Arizona has a wealth of ghost towns that boomed on mining profits and then quickly went bust when the mines played out, but none is as impressive as Bisbee, which is built into the steep slopes of Tombstone Canyon on the south side of the Mule Mountains. Between 1880 and 1975, Bisbee's mines produced more than $6 billion worth of metals. When the Phelps Dodge Company shut down its copper mines here, Bisbee nearly went the way of other abandoned mining towns, but because it's the Cochise County seat, it was saved from disappearing into the desert dust.

Bisbee's glory days date from the late 19th and early 20th centuries, and because the town stopped growing in the early part of the 20th century, it is now one of the best-preserved historic towns anywhere in the Southwest. Old brick buildings line narrow winding streets, and miners' shacks sprawl across the hill-sides above downtown. Television and movie producers discovered these well-preserved streets years ago, and since then, Bisbee has doubled as New York, Spain, Greece, Italy, and, of course, the Old West.

The rumor of silver in "them thar hills" is what first attracted prospectors in 1877, and within a few years the diggings attracted the interest of some San Francisco investors, among them Judge DeWitt Bisbee, for whom the town is named. However, it was copper and other less-than-precious metals that would make Bisbee's fortune. With the help of outside financing, large-scale mining operations were begun in 1881 by the Phelps Dodge Company. By 1910, the population had climbed to 25,000, and Bisbee was the largest city between New Orleans and San Francisco. The town boasted that it was the liveliest spot between El Paso and San Francisco—and the presence of nearly 50 saloons and bordellos along Brewery Gulch backed up the boast.

Tucked into a narrow valley surrounded by red hills, Bisbee today has a cosmopolitan air. Many artists call the town home, and urban refugees have been dropping out of the rat race to restore Bisbee's old buildings and open small inns, restaurants, and galleries. Between the rough edges left over from its mining days and this new cosmopolitan atmosphere, Bisbee is one of Arizona's most interesting towns.

ESSENTIALS

GETTING THERE   Bisbee is on Ariz. 80, which begins at I-10 in the town of Benson, 45 miles east of Tucson.

VISITOR INFORMATION   Contact the **Bisbee Chamber of Commerce,** 31 Subway St. (© **866/224-7233** or 520/432-5421; www.bisbeearizona.com).

SPECIAL EVENTS   Bisbee puts on **coaster races** (similar to a soap-box derby) on the Fourth of July; **Brewery Gulch Daze** in September; a **Fiber Arts Festival, Gem and Mineral Show,** and the **Bisbee Stair Climb** in October.

EXPLORING THE TOWN

At the Bisbee Chamber of Commerce visitor center, right in the middle of town, pick up walking-tour brochures that will lead you past the most important buildings and sites. On the second floor of the **Copper Queen Library,** 6 Main St. (© **520/432-4232**), are some great old photographs that give a good idea of what the town looked like in the past century.

Don't miss the **Bisbee Mining and Historical Museum** ★, 5 Copper Queen Plaza (© **520/432-7071;** www.bisbeemuseum.org), housed in the 1897 Copper Queen Consolidated Mining Company office building. This small but comprehensive museum features exhibits on the history of Bisbee. It's open daily from 10am to 4pm; admission is $4 for adults, $3.50 for seniors, and free for children 16 and under.

For another look at early life in Bisbee, visit the **Muheim Heritage House,** 207 Youngblood Hill (© **520/432-7698**), which is reached by walking up Brewery Gulch. The house was built between 1902 and 1915 and has an unusual semicircular porch. The interior is decorated with period furniture. It's open Thursday through Tuesday from 10am to 4pm; admission is $2 for adults.

O.K. Street, which parallels Brewery Gulch but is high on the hill on the southern edge of town, is a good place to walk for views of Bisbee. At the top of O.K. Street, there's a path that takes you up to a hill above town for an even better panorama of Bisbee's jumble of old buildings. Atop this hill are numerous small

Moments **Stepping Back in Time**

A tour of Bisbee with Michael Patrick Lundin is not just a fact-filled stroll around town. Lundin not only brings the highlights of the town's history to life, he dresses the part. With his knee-high leather boots, cane, and 10-gallon hat, he is as dapper as any gentleman who ever walked the narrow winding streets of Bisbee. His tours, which leave every hour on the hour, cost only $5 and begin at the Copper Queen Hotel (see "Where to Stay," below).

colorfully painted shrines built into the rocks and filled with candles, plastic flowers, and pictures of the Virgin Mary. It's a steep climb on a rocky, very uneven path, but the views and the fascinating little shrines make it worth the effort.

Mining made this town what it is, so you should be sure to head underground on a mine tour to find out what it was like to be a miner here in Bisbee. **Queen Mine Tours** ⚐ (© **866/432-2071** or 520/432-2071) takes visitors down into one of the town's old copper mines. Tours are offered daily between 9am and 3:30pm and cost $12 for adults, $5 for children 4 to 15. The ticket office and mine are just south of the Old Bisbee business district at the Ariz. 80 interchange.

For a good overview of Bisbee and its history, hop aboard the **Warren Bisbee Railway** (© **520/940-7212** or 520/432-7020), which is actually a trolley-style bus that loops through the town. Tours operate several times a day and cost $10 for adults and $7 for children. You'll find the trolley bus parked at the Copper Queen Plaza at the bottom of town. For an exploration of some of the steeper and narrower streets of Bisbee, take a 90-minute tour ($33) of old Bisbee with **Lavender Jeep Tours** (© **520/432-5369**). Several other tours are also available.

Bisbee has lots of interesting stores and galleries, and shopping is the main recreational activity here. To get a look at some of the quality jewelry created from minerals mined in the area, stop by **Czar Jewelry,** 5 Howell Ave. (© **520/ 432-3027**), which has a second location at 149 Main St. (© **520/432-2698**). Another good place to shop for jewelry is **Bisbee Blue,** at the Lavender Pit View Point on Ariz. 80 (© **520/432-5511;** www.bisbeeblue.com), an exclusive dealer of the famous Bisbee Blue turquoise. Turquoise is associated with copper mines, and Bisbee's mines produce some of the most famous turquoise in the country.

If it's art you're after, check out some of the great galleries in town. At the **Johnson Gallery,** 28 Main St. (© **520/432-2126**), you'll find an outstanding selection of Native American crafts, including kachinas, pottery, jewelry, and lots of Zuni fetishes. The **Meridian Gallery,** 18 Brewery Ave. (© **520/ 432-4843**), features colorful and whimsical works by local artists. **Bisbee Clay,** 30 Main St. (© **520/432-1916**), has beautiful pottery, both functional and decorative, in unusual designs and colors.

To protect your face from the burning rays of the sun (and make a fashion statement), visit **Optimo Custom Hat Works,** 47 Main St. (© **888/FINE-HAT** or 520/432-4544; www.optimohatworks.com), which sells and custom-fits Panama straw hats as well as felt hats. By the way, Panama hats actually come from Ecuador.

WHERE TO STAY

Bisbee Grand Hotel ⚐⚐   The Bisbee Grand Hotel is the sort of place you'd expect Wyatt Earp and his wife to have patronized. At street level, there's a historic saloon with a pressed-tin ceiling and an 1880s bar, while upstairs there are beautifully decorated guest rooms. The Oriental Suite features an incredibly ornate Chinese wedding bed, claw-foot tub, and skylight, while the Victorian Suite has a red-velvet canopy bed. The Old Western Suite has the most unusual bed—a covered wagon. While all units have private bathrooms, some of them are not in the room itself but across the hall. For 1890s atmosphere, this hotel can't be beat. The hotel also has an annex up the road that includes a "Safari Suite."

61 Main St., Bisbee, AZ 85603. © 800/421-1909 or 520/432-5900. http://bisbeegrandhotel.com. 15 units. $75–$150 double. Rates include breakfast. Mention this book and children stay free in parent's room. AE, DISC, MC, V. **Amenities:** Saloon. *In room:* A/C, no phone.

Canyon Rose Suites ⚹ *(Value)*   Located on the second floor of a commercial building just off Bisbee's main street, this property offers spacious suites with full kitchens, which makes it a good bet for longer stays. All units have hardwood floors and high ceilings, and the works by local artists and the mix of contemporary and rustic furnishings give the place plenty of Bisbee character. Constructed on a steep, narrow street, the building housing this lodging has an unusual covered sidewalk, making it one of the more distinctive commercial buildings in town.

27 Subway at Shearer St. (P.O. Box 1915), Bisbee, AZ 85603-2915. © 866/296-7673 or 520/432-5098. www.canyonrose.com. 7 units. $75–$200 double. Children under 12 stay free in parent's room. DISC, MC, V. **Amenities:** Access to nearby health club; guest laundry. *In room:* TV/VCR, kitchen, fridge, coffeemaker, hair dryer, iron, free local calls.

Copper Queen Hotel   Built in 1902 by the Copper Queen Mining Company and located right at the center of town, this is Bisbee's grande dame hotel. The atmosphere is casual yet quite authentic. Behind the check-in desk, there's an old oak rolltop desk and a safe that has been here for years. Spacious halls lead to guest rooms that are furnished with antiques but that vary considerably in size (the smallest being quite cramped). The hotel has been undergoing renovations for several years; be sure to ask for one of the renovated units, which are up-to-date and attractively furnished. The restaurant serves decent food, and out front is a terrace for alfresco dining. And what would a mining-town hotel be without its saloon?

11 Howell Ave. (P.O. Drawer CQ), Bisbee, AZ 85603. © 800/247-5829 or 520/432-2216. Fax 520/432-4298. www.copperqueen.com. 48 units. $85–$200 double. Children under 10 stay free in parent's room. AE, DC, MC, V. **Amenities:** Restaurant (American); lounge; small outdoor pool. *In room:* A/C, TV.

Harlequin Hotel ⚹   Located at the bottom of Brewery Gulch in a restored historic building, this hotel offers simply furnished rooms, some with decent views over the rooftops of town to the nearby hills. For the best views and great light, ask for a south- or west-facing room. Most units are fairly spacious, and large windows and high ceilings make them feel even more so. The hotel's location on Brewery Gulch, home to several bars, means you can expect a bit of noise on weekend nights.

1 Howell Ave., Bisbee, AZ 85603. © 520/432-1832. www.harlequinhotel.com. 6 units. $69–$79 double. DISC, MC, V. *In room:* A/C, TV, dataport.

Shady Dell RV Park *(Finds)*   Yes, this really is an RV park, but you'll find neither shade nor dell at this roadside location just south of the Lavender Pit mine. What you will find are eight vintage trailers and a 1947 Chris Craft yacht that have been lovingly restored. Although the trailers don't have their own private bathrooms (there's a bathhouse in the middle of the RV park), they do have all kinds of vintage decor and furnishings—even tapes of period music and radio shows. In the trailers that have vintage TVs, there are VCRs and videotapes of old movies. After numerous write-ups in national publications, the Shady Dell has become so famous that reservations need to be made far in advance. **Dot's Diner** (© **520/432-5885**), a 1957 vintage diner, is also located on the premises.

1 Douglas Rd., Bisbee, AZ 85603. © 520/432-3567. www.theshadydell.com. 9 units. $35–$125 per trailer (for 1–2 people). No credit cards. No children under 10. **Amenities:** Restaurant; coin-op laundry. *In room:* Kitchen, fridge, coffeemaker, no phone.

WHERE TO DINE

Big Sky Café, 203 Tombstone Canyon Rd. (© **520/432-5025**), is a hip little cafe and bakery that also serves the best breakfasts in town. It also does good sandwiches. **Café Cornucopia,** 14 Main St. (© **520/432-4820**), offers fresh juices, smoothies, and sandwiches. It's open Thursday through Monday from 10am to 5pm. For good coffee and a mining-theme decor, check out the **Bisbee Coffee Co.,** Copper Queen Plaza, Main Street (© **520/432-7879**). For burgers and homemade Bisbeeberry pie in a vintage diner, drop by **Dot's Diner,** at the Shady Dell RV Park, described above (© **520/432-5885**). This fabulously retro place is open Thursday through Monday from 7am to 3pm.

The Bisbee Grille ✸ REGIONAL AMERICAN Located in the Art Deco Copper Queen Plaza building at the bottom of Main Street, this is one of Bisbee's best casual restaurants. Not only is the food decent, but there are also large photographs of old Bisbee that give the place a lot of historic character. At lunch, the spicy chicken Caesar salad is a good bet. Entrees at dinner include pasta dishes, mesquite-grilled chicken, and Bisbee-style fajitas. Grab a seat by the window for great people-watching.

2 Copper Queen Plaza. © 520/432-6788. Main courses $8–$11 lunch, $11–$19 dinner. AE, DISC, MC, V. Daily 11am–9pm.

Café Roka ✸✸ CONTEMPORARY Wow! The food at Café Roka is so good that it is reason enough for a visit to Bisbee. Casual and hip, this place is a real find in such an out-of-the-way town and offers good value as well as delicious and imaginatively prepared food. All meals here are four-course dinners that include salad, soup, sorbet intermezzo, and entree. The grilled salmon with a Gorgonzola crust and artichoke-and-portobello lasagna are two of our favorites. There's usually a vegetarian dish or two. Flourless chocolate cake with raspberry sauce is an exquisite ending. Local artists display their works, and on some evenings jazz musicians perform.

35 Main St. © 520/432-5153. Reservations highly recommended. Main courses $12–$23. AE, MC, V. Wed–Sat 5–9pm.

BISBEE AFTER DARK

For more than a century, Bisbee's Brewery Gulch has been known for its many bars. Today, although there aren't nearly as many drinking establishments as there were 100 years ago, there are still a few dive bars that are especially popular with the weekend Harley-riding crowd from Tucson. Our favorite nightspot is **Hot Licks Barbecue & Blues Saloon,** 37 O.K. St. (© **520/432-7200**), which overlooks Brewery Gulch from high above town. This bar, in a restored historic building, has live music several nights a week and serves a limited menu of barbecue and the like. The beer of choice here is O.K. Ale, made here in Bisbee. Also be sure to check out the schedule at the **Bisbee Repertory Theatre,** 94 Main St. (© **520/432-3786**).

8 Exploring the Rest of Cochise County (★

Willcox: 81 miles E of Tucson; 192 miles SE of Phoenix; 74 miles N of Douglas

Although the towns of Bisbee, Tombstone, and Sierra Vista all lie within Cochise County, much of the county is taken up by the vast Sulphur Springs Valley, which is bounded by multiple mountain ranges. It is across this wide-open landscape that Apache chiefs Cochise and Geronimo once rode. Gazing out across this country today, it is easy to understand why the Apaches fought so hard to keep white settlers out.

The Apaches first moved into this region of southern Arizona sometime in the early 16th century. They pursued a hunting and gathering lifestyle that was supplemented by raiding neighboring tribes for food and other booty. When the Spanish arrived in the area, the Apaches acquired horses and became even more efficient raiders. They attacked Spanish, Mexican, and eventually American settlers, and despite repeated attempts to convince them to give up their hostile way of life, the Apaches refused to change. Not long after the Gadsden Purchase of 1848 made Arizona U.S. soil, more people than ever began settling in the region. The new settlers immediately became the object of Apache raids, and eventually the U.S. Army was called in to put an end to the attacks; by the mid-1880s, the army was embroiled in a war with Cochise, Geronimo, and the Chiricahua Apaches.

Although the Chiricahua and Dragoon mountains, which flank the Sulphur Springs Valley on the east and west respectively, are relatively unknown outside the region, they offer some of the Southwest's most spectacular scenery. Massive boulders litter the mountainsides, creating fascinating landscapes. The Chiricahua Mountains are also a favorite destination of bird-watchers, for it is here that the colorfully plumed elegant trogon reaches the northern limit of its range.

In the southern part of this region lies the town of Douglas, an important gateway to Mexico. Unless you're heading to Mexico, though, there aren't many reasons to visit. But if you do find yourself passing through, be sure to stop in at the historic Gadsden Hotel (see "Where to Stay," below), and if you don't mind driving on gravel roads, the Slaughter Ranch is worth a visit.

ESSENTIALS

GETTING THERE   Willcox is on I-10, with Ariz. 186 heading southeast toward Chiricahua National Monument.

VISITOR INFORMATION   The **Willcox Chamber of Commerce and Agriculture,** 1500 N. Circle I Rd. ((©) **800/200-2272** or 520/384-2272; www.willcoxchamber.com), can provide information.

SPECIAL EVENTS   **Wings Over Willcox** (www.wingsoverwillcox.com), a festival celebrating the return to the area of more than 30,000 sandhill cranes, takes place in January.

WILLCOX

Railroad Avenue in downtown Willcox is slowly developing into something of a little historic district. Here you'll find the town's two museums, plus the recently restored **Southern Pacific Willcox Train Depot,** 101 S. Railroad Ave., a redwood depot built in 1880. Inside the old depot is a small display of historic Willcox photos. Also worth checking out is the **Willcox Commercial,** 180 S. Railroad Ave. ((©) **520/384-2448**), a general store that has been around since the days of Geronimo.

Rex Allen Museum   If you grew up in the days of singing cowboys, then you're probably familiar with Willcox's favorite hometown star: Rex Allen, who made famous the song "Streets of Laredo." Here at the small museum dedicated to him, you'll find plenty of Allen memorabilia as well as a Cowboy Hall of Fame exhibit. The town celebrates Rex Allen Days every October.

150 N. Railroad Ave. Ⓒ 520/384-4583. Admission $2 per person, $3 per couple, $5 per family. Daily 10am–4pm. Closed New Year's Day, Thanksgiving, and Christmas.

SOUTHWEST OF WILLCOX
SCENIC LANDSCAPES
While Chiricahua National Monument claims the most spectacular scenery in this corner of the state, there are a couple of areas southwest of Willcox in the Dragoon Mountains that are almost as impressive. The first of these, **Texas Canyon,** lies right along I-10 between Benson and Willcox and can be enjoyed from the comfort of a speeding car. Huge boulders are scattered across this rolling desert landscape.

South of the community of Dragoon, which is now known for its many pistachio farms (many of which are open to the public), lies a much less accessible area of the Dragoon Mountains known as **Cochise Stronghold** ⚡ (**www.cochise stronghold.com**). During the Apache uprisings of the late 19th century, the Apache leader Cochise used this rugged section of the Dragoon Mountains as his hideout and managed to elude capture for years. The granite boulders and pine forests made it impossible for the army to track him and his followers. Cochise eventually died and was buried at an unknown spot somewhere within the area now called Cochise Stronghold. This rugged jumble of giant boulders is reached by a rough gravel road, at the end of which you'll find a campground, picnic area, and hiking trails. For a short, easy walk, follow the .4-mile Nature Trail. For a longer and more strenuous hike, head up the Cochise Trail. The Stronghold Divide makes a good destination for a 6-mile round-trip hike. For more information, contact the **Coronado National Forest Douglas Ranger District,** 3081 N. Leslie Canyon Rd., Douglas (Ⓒ **520/364-3468;** www.fs.fed.us/r3/coronado/douglas). There is a $3 day-use fee per vehicle at Cochise Stronghold.

A MEMORABLE MUSEUM IN AN UNLIKELY LOCALE
Amerind Foundation Museum ⚡⚡   It may be out of the way and difficult to find, but this museum is well worth seeking out. Established in 1937, the Amerind Foundation is dedicated to the study, preservation, and interpretation of prehistoric and historic Indian cultures. To that end, the foundation has compiled the nation's finest private collection of archaeological artifacts and contemporary items. There are exhibits on the dances and religious ceremonies of the major Southwestern tribes, including the Navajo, Hopi, and Apache, and archaeological artifacts amassed from the numerous Amerind Foundation excavations over the years. Many of the pieces came from right here in Texas Canyon. Fascinating ethnology exhibits include amazingly intricate beadwork from the Plains tribes, old Zuni fetishes, Pima willow baskets, old kachina dolls, 100 years of Southwestern tribal pottery, and Navajo weavings. The art gallery displays works by 19th- and 20th-century American artists, such as Frederic Remington, whose paintings focused on the West. The small museum store has a surprisingly good selection of books and Native American crafts and jewelry.

Dragoon. Ⓒ 520/586-3666. www.amerind.org. Admission $5 adults, $4 seniors, $3 children 12–18. Oct–May daily 10am–4pm; June–Sept Wed–Sun 10am–4pm. Closed major holidays. Located 64 miles east of Tucson between Benson and Willcox; take the Dragoon Rd. exit (Exit 318) from I-10 and continue 1 mile east.

EAST OF WILLCOX

In the town of Bowie, the **Fort Bowie Vineyard,** 156 N. Jefferson St. (© **888/ 299-5951** in Arizona or 520/847-2593), has a tasting room and sells some very drinkable, inexpensive wines. It also produces an unusual pecan-flavored sparkling wine and sells locally grown pecans, pistachios, walnuts, and peaches. The tasting room is open Monday through Saturday from 8:30am to 4pm and Sunday from 10am to 3pm.

Chiricahua National Monument ★★ Sea Captain, China Boy, Duck on a Rock, Punch and Judy—these may not seem like appropriate names for land-scape features, but this is no ordinary landscape. These gravity-defying rock for-mations—called "the land of the standing-up rocks" by the Apache and the "wonderland of rocks" by the pioneers—are the equal of any of Arizona's many amazing rocky landmarks. Rank upon rank of monolithic giants seem to have been turned to stone as they marched across the forested Chiricahua Mountains. Some of these rocks, including Big Balanced Rock and Pinnacle Balanced Rock, appear ready to come crashing down at any moment. Formed about 25 million years ago by a massive volcanic eruption, these rhyolite badlands were once the stronghold of renegade Apaches. If you look closely at Cochise Head peak, you can even see the famous chief's profile. If you're in good physical condition, don't miss the chance to hike the 7.5-mile round-trip **Heart of Rocks Trail** ★★ , which can be accessed from the visitor center or the Echo Canyon or Massai Point parking areas. This trail leads through the most spectacular scenery in the monument. A shorter loop is also possible. Within the monument are a visitor center, a campground, a picnic area, miles of hiking trails, and a scenic drive with views of many of the most unusual rock formations.

Ariz. 186, 36 miles southeast of Willcox. © **520/824-3560.** www.nps.gov/chir. Admission $5 adults. Visitor center daily 8am–4:30pm. Closed Christmas.

Fort Bowie National Historic Site ★ The Butterfield Stage, which carried mail, passengers, and freight across the Southwest in the mid-1800s, followed a route that climbed up and over Apache Pass, in the heart of the Chiricahua Mountains' Apache territory. Near the mile-high pass, Fort Bowie was estab-lished in 1862 to ensure the passage of the slow-moving stage as it traversed this difficult region. The fort was also used to protect the water source for cavalry going east to fight the Confederate army in New Mexico. Later it was from Fort Bowie that federal troops battled Geronimo until the Apache chief finally sur-rendered in 1886. Today, there's little left of Fort Bowie but some crumbling adobe walls, but the hike along the old stage route to the ruins conjures up the ghosts of Geronimo and the Indian Wars.

Off Ariz. 186. © **520/847-2500.** www.nps.gov/fobo. Free admission. Visitor center daily 8am–4:30pm; grounds daily dawn–dusk. Closed Christmas. From Willcox, drive southeast on Ariz. 186; after about 20 miles, watch for signs; it's another 8 miles up a dirt road to the trail head. Alternatively, drive east from Willcox to Bowie and go 13 miles south on Apache Pass Rd. From the trail head, it's a 1½-mile hike to the fort.

DOUGLAS & ENVIRONS

The town of Douglas abounds in old buildings, and although not many are restored, they hint at the diverse character of this community. Just across the border from Douglas is Agua Prieta, in Sonora, Mexico, where Pancho Villa lost his first battle. In Agua Prieta, whitewashed adobe buildings, old churches, and sunny plazas provide a contrast to Douglas. At the **Douglas Chamber of Commerce Visitor Center,** 1125 Pan American Ave. (© **888/315-9999** or

520/364-2478), pick up a map to the town's historic buildings as well as a rough map of Agua Prieta.

Slaughter Ranch Museum ⭐ *Finds*   Down a dusty gravel road outside the town of Douglas lies a little-known Southwestern landmark: the Slaughter Ranch. If you're old enough, you might remember a Walt Disney TV show about Texas John Slaughter. This was his spread. In 1884, former Texas Ranger John Slaughter bought the San Bernardino Valley and turned it into one of the finest cattle ranches in the West. Slaughter later went on to become the sheriff of Cochise County and helped rid the region of the unsavory characters who had flocked to the many mining towns of this remote part of the state. Today, the ranch is a National Historic Landmark and has been restored to its late-19th-century appearance. Surrounding the ranch buildings are wide lawns and a large pond that together attract a variety of birds, making this one of Arizona's best winter birding spots. For the-way-it-was tranquillity, this old ranch can't be beat.

6153 Geronimo Trail, about 14 miles east of Douglas. © **520/558-2474.** www.slaughterranch.com. Admission $5 adults, free for children under 14. Wed–Sun 10am–3pm. From Douglas, go east on 15th St., which runs into Geronimo Trail; continue east 14 miles.

BIRDING HOT SPOTS

At the **Willcox Chamber of Commerce,** 1500 N. Circle I Rd. (© **800/200-2272** or 520/384-2272; www.willcoxchamber.com), you can pick up several birding maps and checklists for the region.

To the east of Chiricahua National Monument, on the far side of the Chiricahuas, lies **Cave Creek Canyon** ⭐, one of the most important bird-watching spots in the United States. It's here that the colorful elegant trogon reaches the northern limit of its range. Other rare birds that have been spotted here include sulfur-bellied flycatchers and Lucy's, Virginia's, and black-throated gray warblers. Stop by the visitor center for information on the best birding spots in the area. Cave Creek Canyon is just outside the community of Portal; in summer, it can be reached from the national monument by driving over the Chiricahuas on graded gravel roads. In winter, you'll likely have to drive around the mountains, which entails going south to Douglas and then 60 miles north to Portal or north to I-10 and then south 35 miles to Portal.

The **Cochise Lakes** ⭐ (actually the Willcox sewage ponds) are another great bird-watching spot. Birders can see a wide variety of waterfowl and shorebirds, including avocets and ibises. To find the ponds, head south out of Willcox on Ariz. 186, turn right onto Rex Allen Jr. Drive at the sign for the Twin Lakes golf course, and go past the golf course.

Between October and March, as many as 30,000 sandhill cranes gather in the Sulphur Springs Valley south of Willcox, and in January, the town holds the **Wings Over Willcox** festival, a celebration of these majestic birds. There are a couple of good places in the area to see sandhill cranes during the winter. Southwest of Willcox on U.S. 191 near the Apache Station electric generating plant and the community of Cochise, you'll find the **Apache Station Wildlife Viewing Area.** About 60 miles south of Willcox, off U.S. 191 near the town of Elfrida, is the **Whitewater Draw Wildlife Area.** To reach the viewing area, go south from Elfrida on Central Highway, turn right on Davis Road, and in another 2½ miles, turn left on Coffman Road and continue 2 miles. The last 2 miles is on a dirt road that should be avoided after rainfall. The Sulphur Springs Valley is also well known for its large wintering population of raptors, including ferruginous hawks and prairie falcons.

Near Douglas, the **Slaughter Ranch,** which has a large pond, and the adjacent **San Bernardino National Wildlife Refuge** are good birding spots in both summer and winter. (See the description of the Slaughter Ranch Museum, above, for directions.)

North of Willcox, at the end of a 30-mile gravel road, lies the **Muleshoe Ranch Cooperative Management Area** (℗ **520/507-5229** or 520/622-3861; http://muleshoelodging.org), a Nature Conservancy preserve that contains seven perennial streams. These streams support endangered aquatic life as well as riparian zones that attract a large number of bird species. To get here, take Exit 340 off I-10 and go south; turn right on Bisbee Avenue and then right again onto Airport Road. After 15 miles, watch for a fork in the road and take the right fork. If the road is dry, it is usually navigable by passenger car. The headquarters, which includes the visitor center, is open from mid-February to mid-May, daily from 8am to 4pm; mid-May to late May and September to early February, Thursday through Monday from 8am to 5pm; and June through August, Saturday and Sunday from 8am to 5pm. The backcountry is accessible year-round, 24 hours a day. Overnight accommodations in casitas ($95–$155 double) are available by reservation (2-night minimum Sept–May).

WHERE TO STAY
IN & NEAR WILLCOX
Cochise Stronghold B&B ⭐ *(Finds)* Set on 15 acres of private land within the Cochise Stronghold, this unusual B&B is not only a superb base for exploring the area's fascinating rock formations, but also a great place to learn about solar-home design and the preservation of the desert environment. The inn is a straw-bale, passive solar home with two housekeeping suites. For a more rustic experience, there is also a tepee. In-room breakfast options include Southwestern dishes such as mesquite-cornmeal pancakes that are made with flour produced by grinding mesquite-bean pods. By prior arrangement, you can also have other meals prepared for you.

2126 W. Windancer Trail (P.O. Box 232), Pearce, AZ 85625. ℗ **877/426-4141** or 520/826-4141. www.cochisestrongholdbb.com. Oct–Apr $149–$199 double, $75 tepee. Rates include full breakfast. 2-night minimum stay. AE, DISC, MC, V. **Amenities:** Jacuzzi; massage. *In room (but not in tepee):* A/C, TV/VCR, kitchenette, fridge, coffeemaker, hair dryer, free local calls.

IN DOUGLAS
Gadsden Hotel Built in 1907, the Gadsden bills itself as "the last of the grand hotels," and its listing on the National Register of Historic Places backs up that claim. The marble lobby, though dark, is a classic. Vaulted stained-glass skylights run the length of the ceiling, and above the landing of the Italian marble stairway is a genuine Tiffany window. Although the carpets in the halls are well worn and rooms aren't always spotless, many units have been renovated and refurnished. The bathrooms are, however, a bit worse for the wear. The lounge is a popular local hangout, with more than 200 cattle brands painted on the walls.

1046 G Ave., Douglas, AZ 85607. ℗ **520/364-4481.** Fax 520/364-4005. 160 units. $50–$75 double; $90–$100 suite. AE, DISC, MC, V. **Amenities:** Restaurant (American/Mexican); lounge; room service; coin-op laundry; laundry service; dry cleaning. *In room:* A/C, TV.

IN PORTAL
Portal Peak Lodge, Portal Store & Cafe This motel-like lodge, located behind the general store/cafe in the hamlet of Portal, has fairly modern guest rooms that face one another across a wooden deck. Meals are available in the

adjacent cafe. If you're seeking predictable accommodations in a remote location, you'll find them here.

2358 Rock House Rd. (P.O. Box 16282), Portal, AZ 85632. © **520/558-2223**. Fax 520/558-2473. www. portalpeaklodge.com. 16 units. $75 double. AE, DISC, MC, V. **Amenities:** Restaurant (American). *In room:* A/C, TV, coffeemaker.

Southwestern Research Station, The American Museum of Natural History ★ *(Finds* Located far up in Cave Creek Canyon, this is a field research station that takes guests when the accommodations are not filled by scientists doing research. As such, it is the best place in the area for serious bird-watchers, who will find the company of researchers a fascinating addition to a visit. Guests stay in simply furnished cabins scattered around the research center. Spring and fall are the easiest times to get reservations and the best times for bird-watching.

P.O. Box 16553, Portal, AZ 85632. © **520/558-2396**. Fax 520/558-2396. http://research.amnh.org/swrs. 15 units. Mar–Oct $141 double (rate includes all meals); Nov–Feb $80 double (no meals provided). Children under 4 stay free in parent's room. DISC, MC, V. **Amenities:** Dining room; outdoor pool; guest laundry; volleyball court. *In room:* No phone.

AREA GUEST RANCHES

Grapevine Canyon Ranch ★ Located about 35 miles southwest of Willcox in the foothills of the Dragoon Mountains adjacent to Cochise Stronghold, this guest ranch can be either a quiet hideaway where you can enjoy the natural setting or a place to experience traditional ranch life—horseback riding, rounding up cattle, mending fences. The landscape of mesquite and yucca conjures up images of the high chaparral, and a variety of rides are offered, with an emphasis on those for the experienced. If you don't care to go horseback riding, sightseeing excursions can be arranged. The small cabins (with shower-only bathrooms) and larger casitas (with combination shower/tubs) are set under groves of manzanita and oak trees; you can view wildlife and the night sky from the decks. Unfortunately, rooms are a bit short on Western character.

P.O. Box 302, Pearce, AZ 85625. © **800/245-9202** or 520/826-3185. Fax 520/826-3636. www.grapevine canyonranch.com. 12 units. $256–$376 double. Rates include all meals. 3-night minimum stay. Various 1-week packages available. AE, DISC, MC, V. No children under 12. **Amenities:** Dining room; outdoor pool; Jacuzzi; guest laundry; horseback riding. *In room:* A/C, fridge, coffeemaker, hair dryer, no phone.

Sunglow Guest Ranch ★★ *(Value* Located in the western foothills of the Chiricahua Mountains roughly 40 miles southeast of Willcox, this remote ranch is surrounded by Coronado National Forest and is one of the most idyllic spots in the state. I could easily spend an entire vacation right here on the ranch. There's a small lake just downhill from the ranch buildings, and rising behind this lake are the peaks of the Chiricahuas. There's great bird-watching both on the ranch and in the nearby hills, and guests can rent mountain bikes. The guest rooms are quite large and contain hardwood and rustic Mexican furnishings. Most units have woodstoves, and three rooms have been recently renovated. These renovated rooms are worth requesting. This guest ranch is different from others around the state in that it doesn't offer horseback riding, but it does sometimes have telescopes set up for stargazing. There's a beautiful little dining hall/cafe built in classic Western-ranch style that serves some of the best food available in this corner of the state. Sunsets here are among the prettiest anywhere in Arizona.

14066 S. Sunglow Rd., Pearce, AZ 85625. © **866/786-4569** or 520/824-3334. www.sunglowranch.com. 9 units. $202–$299 double. Rates include breakfast, afternoon tea, and dinner. Children 5 and under stay free in parent's room. AE, DISC, MC, V. Pets accepted ($25 per night). **Amenities:** Dining room; bike rentals. *In room:* No phone.

CAMPGROUNDS

There's a 25-site campground charging $12 per night at **Chiricahua National Monument** (described above), on Ariz. 186 (✆ **520/824-3560**), and along the road to Portal not far from the national monument, there are several small national forest campgrounds charging $10 for a site. At **Cochise Stronghold,** which is 35 miles southwest of Willcox off U.S. 191, there is a 10-site campground charging $10 per night. For information on the national forest campgrounds, contact the Coronado National Forest Douglas Ranger District (✆ **520/364-3468;** www.fs.fed.us/r3/coronado/douglas). Reservations are not accepted for any of these campgrounds.

WHERE TO DINE
IN WILLCOX

Right across the parking lot from the Willcox Chamber of Commerce (off I-10 at Exit 340), you'll find **Stout's Cider Mill** ✮, 1510 N. Circle I Rd. (✆ **520/384-3696;** www.cidermill.com), which makes delicious concoctions with apples. You can get cider, cider floats, "cidersicles," apple cake, and the biggest (and contender for the best) apple pie in the world. Open daily from 9am to 5:30pm.

Rodney's *Finds* BARBECUE   Willcox doesn't have much in the way of good restaurants, but if you're a fan of barbecue, you'll want to schedule a stop at Rodney's. This hole in the wall near the Rex Allen Museum is so nondescript that you can easily miss it. Inside, you'll find Rodney Brown, beaming with personality and dishing up lip-smackin' barbecued pork sandwiches and plates of ribs, shrimp, and catfish. If you're really hungry, try the gumbo.

118 N. Railroad Ave. No phone. Main courses $3–$9. No credit cards. Tues–Sun 11am–8pm.

NORTH TOWARD PHOENIX: THE SAFFORD AREA & MOUNT GRAHAM

Roughly 50 miles north of Willcox, off U.S. 191 in a unit of Coronado National Forest, rise the Pinaleño Mountains and 10,717-foot **Mount Graham.** Because its cool heights offer respite from the heat, Mount Graham is a favorite summer vacation spot for desert dwellers. Here you'll find campgrounds, hiking trails, and an astronomical observatory (see "Starry, Starry Nights," p. 400). This observatory, funded partly by the University of Arizona and partly by the Vatican, was built despite concerns that the mountaintop was the last remaining habitat of 400 endangered Mount Graham red squirrels.

To the northwest of Mount Graham, at the end of a 45-mile gravel road, is the **Aravaipa Canyon Wilderness,** through which flows the perennial Aravaipa Creek. This scenic canyon is bordered on both ends by the Nature Conservancy's **Aravaipa Canyon Preserve.** Together these natural areas protect Arizona's healthiest population of native desert fishes, as well as cougars, desert bighorn sheep, bobcats, and 200 species of birds. Permits, which are required for hiking in the canyon, can be requested from the **Bureau of Land Management,** Safford District Office, 711 14th Ave., Safford, AZ 85546 (✆ **928/348-4400;** www.az.blm.gov/sfo/index.htm), 13 weeks in advance of your visit (spring and fall are the most difficult times to get reservations).

Not far from the turnoff for Mount Graham and just south of Safford, you'll find **Roper Lake State Park** (✆ **928/428-6760;** www.pr.state.az.us/Parks/parkhtml/roper.html), which has a hot spring, a campground, and a lake with a swimming beach. The day-use fee is $6 per car; camping costs $12 to $22. There's good bird-watching here and at the nearby Dankworth Ponds (where you'll find a nature trail and an outdoor exhibit on the various Native American cultures that used this site in centuries past). The state park is off U.S. 191, about 6 miles south of Safford; the Dankworth Ponds site is another 2 miles farther south.

In this same area is the **Kachina Mineral Springs Spa** (© 928/428-7212; www.kachinasprings.com), on Cactus Road, 6 miles south of Safford in the shadow of Mount Graham. Visitors can soak in hot mineral waters, enjoy a sweat wrap, and get a massage. A soak costs $7; treatments range from $15 for a 20-minute soak and sweat wrap to $85 for a soak, sweat wrap, foot reflexology, sinus treatment, and 1-hour massage. Just around the corner is **Essence of Tranquility,** 6074 Lebanon Loop (© 877/895-6810 or 928/428-9312), which offers similar services. Use of tubs is $5 per person for 1 hour; 1-hour massages go for $45.

Just south of Safford off U.S. 191, you'll find **Discovery Park,** 1651 Discovery Park Blvd. (© 928/428-6260; www.discoverypark.com), an interesting stop for both kids and adults. This science park includes the Gov Aker Observatory, which provides opportunities for exploring the heavens. The space-flight simulator ride ($6) is one of the park's top attractions. There's also a reproduction of a 19th-century ranch homestead, as well as a narrow-gauge railroad that takes visitors on 2-mile rides ($3) around the park. A marsh offers good birding opportunities. The park is open Friday from 6pm to 10pm and Saturday from 4pm to 10pm; admission is $5 for adults, $3 for children 6 to 12.

Twenty miles northeast of Safford off U.S. 70, you'll come to the **Gila Box Riparian National Conservation Area,** a popular hiking area on BLM land. As at Aravaipa Canyon, this area preserves the landscape around a perennial stream, in this case the upper reaches of the Gila River. There is no fee to hike the area.

For more information on the Safford area, contact the **Graham County Chamber of Commerce,** 1111 W. Thatcher Blvd., Safford (© 888/837-1841 or 928/428-2511; www.graham-chamber.com), or the **Bureau of Land Management,** Safford Field Office, 711 14th Ave., Safford (© 928/348-4400; www.az.blm.gov/sfo/index.htm).

11

Arizona's "West Coast"

Although it is hundreds of miles from the Pacific Ocean, Arizona has a west coast, and it is to the waters of this inland "coast" that boaters, water-skiers, and anglers head throughout the year.

Separating Arizona from California and Nevada are 340 miles of Colorado River waters, most of which are impounded in three huge reservoirs—Lake Mead, Lake Mohave, and Lake Havasu—that provide the water and electricity to such sprawling Southwestern boomtowns as Phoenix and Las Vegas. It is because of all this water that the region has come to be known as Arizona's West Coast.

In some ways, Arizona's West Coast is actually superior to California's Pacific coastline. Although there aren't many waves on this stretch of the Colorado River, both the weather and the water are warmer than California's. Consequently, watersports of all types are extremely popular, and the fishing is some of the best in the country. Due to convolutions in the landscape, Lake Havasu, Lake Mohave, and Lake Mead also offer thousands of miles of shoreline.

While the Colorado River has always been the lifeblood of this rugged region, it was not water that first attracted settlers. A hundred years ago, prospectors ventured into this sun-baked landscape hoping to find gold in the mountains flanking the Colorado River. Some actually hit pay dirt, and mining towns sprang up overnight, only to be abandoned a few

years later when the gold ran out. Today, Oatman (see chapter 6, "The Grand Canyon & Northern Arizona" for details) is the most famous of these mining boomtowns, but it has too many people and wild burros to be called a ghost town.

People are still venturing into this region in hopes of striking it rich, but now they head across the river from Bullhead City, Arizona, to the casinos in Laughlin, Nevada, where a miniature version of Las Vegas has grown up on the banks of the Colorado.

Laughlin, Nevada, and Bullhead City, Arizona, aren't the only towns in this area with an abundance of waterfront accommodations. As with any warm coastline, Arizona's West Coast is lined with lakefront resorts, hotels, RV parks, and campgrounds. For the most part, it's a destination for desert residents, so you won't find any hotels or resorts even remotely as upscale or expensive as those in Phoenix, Tucson, or Sedona. You will, however, see plenty of houseboats for rent. These floating vacation homes are immensely popular with families and groups. With a houseboat, you can get away from the crowds, dropping anchor and kicking back when you find a remote cove, the best fishing, or the most spectacular views. You can even houseboat to London Bridge, which is no longer falling down, but rather bridges a backwater of Lake Havasu and is now one of Arizona's biggest tourist attractions.

1 Lake Mead National Recreation Area

70 miles NW of Kingman; 256 miles NW of Phoenix; 30 miles SE of Las Vegas, Nev.

Lake Mead National Recreation Area straddles the border between Arizona and Nevada, and, with its two reservoirs and scenic, free-flowing stretch of the Colorado River, is a vast watersports playground. Throughout the year, anglers fish for striped bass, rainbow trout, channel catfish, and other sport fish, while during the hot summer months, lakes Mead and Mohave attract tens of thousands of water-skiers and personal watercraft riders. Due to its proximity to Las Vegas and the fact that there are more facilities on the Nevada side of Lake Mead, the recreation area tends to be more popular with Nevadans than with Arizonans.

The larger reservoir, Lake Mead, was created by the Hoover Dam, which was constructed between 1931 and 1935. Hoover Dam was the first major dam on the Colorado River, and by supplying huge amounts of electricity and water to Arizona and California, it set the stage for the phenomenal growth the region experienced in the second half of the 20th century.

ESSENTIALS

GETTING THERE U.S. 93, which runs between Las Vegas and Kingman, crosses over Hoover Dam, and traffic backups at the dam can be horrendous. However, since trucks have been prohibited from crossing the dam, the traffic jams have lessened somewhat. Several small secondary roads lead to various marinas on the lake. There are also many miles of unpaved roads within the recreation area. If you have a high-clearance or four-wheel-drive vehicle, these roads can take you to some of the least visited shores of the two lakes.

VISITOR INFORMATION For information, contact the **Lake Mead National Recreation Area,** 601 Nevada Hwy., Boulder City, NV 89005 (© **702/293-8907;** www.nps.gov/lame), or stop by the **Alan Bible Visitor Center** (© **702/293-8990**), between Hoover Dam and Boulder City.

DAM, LAKE & RIVER TOURS

Standing 726 feet tall, from bedrock to the roadway atop it, and tapering from a thickness of 660 feet at its base to only 45 feet at the top, **Hoover Dam** (© **866/291-TOUR** or 702/294-3517; www.usbr.gov/lc/hooverdam) is the tallest concrete dam in the Western Hemisphere. Behind this massive dam lie the waters of **Lake Mead,** which at 110 miles long and with a shoreline of more than 550 miles is the largest artificial lake in the United States. U.S. 93 runs right across the top of the dam, and a visitor center chronicles the dam's construction. It's open daily from 9am to 5pm (closed Thanksgiving and Christmas). Guided tours last cost $10 for adults, $8 for seniors, and $5 for children 7 to 16. Parking is an additional $5. Including a tour, it takes about 2 hours to visit the dam.

If you'd like to tour the lake and the dam, call **Lake Mead Cruises** (© **702/ 293-6180;** www.lakemeadcruises.com) to book passage on the *Desert Princess* paddle wheeler. These cruises leave from Lake Mead Cruises Landing, off Lakeshore Drive on the Nevada side of Hoover Dam. Day tours, which go to the dam, last 1½ hours and cost $19 for adults and $9 for children 2 to 11. Other options include dinner cruises ($40 for adults, $21 for children), and weekend dinner-and-dancing cruises ($51).

One of the most interesting ways to see remote parts of Lake Mohave is by sea kayak. **Desert River Outfitters,** 2649 U.S. 95, Suite 23 (© **888/KAYAK-33;**

www.desertriveroutfitters.com), will rent you a boat and shuttle you and your gear to and from put-ins and take-outs. The trip through Black Canyon ($55 per person), which starts at the base of Hoover Dam, is the most interesting route. (*Note:* This trip requires advance planning because a permit is necessary.) You can also paddle past the casinos in Laughlin ($25), through the Topock Gorge ($45), or around Lake Mohave ($35). Raft trips through Black Canyon are offered by **Black Canyon/Willow Beach River Adventures** (© 800/455-3490 or 702/294-1414; www.blackcanyonadventures.com). The one-day rafting trips are an easy float through a scenic canyon and cost $106 for adults, $103 for children ages 12 to 15, and $78 for children ages 5 to 11. If you're not a paddler, this is a great way to see this remote stretch of river, definitely a highlight of a visit to this corner of the state. This company also has a marina where it rents a variety of motorboats.

OUTDOOR PURSUITS

As you would expect, swimming, fishing, water-skiing, sailing, windsurfing, and powerboating are the most popular activities in Lake Mead National Recreation Area. On Arizona shores, there are swimming beaches at Lake Mohave's Katherine Landing (outside Bullhead City) and Lake Mead's Temple Bar (north of Kingman off U.S. 93). Picnic areas can be found at these two areas as well as Willow Beach on Lake Mohave and more than half a dozen spots on the Nevada side of Lake Mead.

Fishing for monster striped bass (up to 50 lb.) is one of the most popular activities on Lake Mead, and while Lake Mohave's striped bass may not reach these awesome proportions, fish in the 25-pound range are not uncommon. Largemouth bass and even rainbow trout are plentiful in the national recreation area's waters due to the diversity of habitats. Try for big rainbows in the cold waters that flow out from Hoover Dam through Black Canyon and into Lake Mohave. To fish from shore, you'll need a license from either Arizona or Nevada (depending on which shore you're fishing from). To fish from a boat, you'll need a license from one state and a special-use stamp from the other. Most Lake Mead marinas sell both licenses and stamps.

The season for striped bass starts around the beginning of April, when the water begins to warm up. If you don't have your own boat, try fishing from the shore of Lake Mohave near Davis Dam, where the water is deep. Anchovy pieces work well as bait, but put some shot on your line to get it down to the depths where the fish are feeding. You can get bait, tackle, licenses, and fishing tips at the **Lake Mohave Resort marina** (© 928/754-3245), at Katherine Landing.

In Arizona, marinas can be found at Katherine Landing on Lake Mohave (just outside Bullhead City), near the north end of Lake Mohave at Willow Beach (best access for trout angling), and at Temple Bar on Lake Mead. There's also a boat ramp at South Cove, north of the community of Meadview at the east end of Lake Mead. This latter boat ramp is the closest to the Grand Canyon end of Lake Mead. On the Nevada side of Lake Mohave, there's a marina at Cottonwood Cove, and on the Nevada side of Lake Mead, you'll find marinas at Boulder Beach, Las Vegas Bay, Callville Bay, and Echo Bay. These marinas offer motels, restaurants, general stores, campgrounds, and boat rentals. At both **Temple Bar** (© 800/752-9669 or 928/767-3211) and **Lake Mohave Resort** (© 800/752-9669 or 928/754-3245), you can rent ski boats, fishing boats, and patio boats for between $90 and $260 per day. Personal watercraft are available for $110 for two hours or $285 a day.

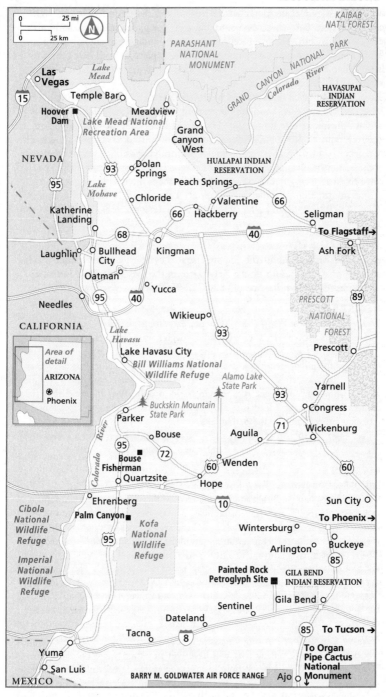

Western Arizona

0 25 mi
0 25 km

N

KAIBAB
NAT'L FOREST

*Lake
Mead*

PARASHANT
NATIONAL
MONUMENT

GRAND CANYON NATIONAL PARK

Colorado River

HAVASUPAI
INDIAN
RESERVATION

**Las
Vegas**

15

Temple Bar

**Hoover
Dam**

Meadview

Grand
Canyon
West

Lake Mead National
Recreation Area

NEVADA

95

93

*Lake
Mohave*

Dolan
Springs

Peach Springs

HUALAPAI INDIAN
RESERVATION

Chloride

Valentine

66

66

Hackberry

Seligman

Katherine
Landing

68

Kingman

40

To Flagstaff →

Ash Fork

Laughlin

Bullhead
City

Oatman

PRESCOTT

95

40

Yucca

89

Needles

Wikieup

NATIONAL

CALIFORNIA

*Lake
Havasu*

93

FOREST

Area of
detail

ARIZONA

Prescott

Phoenix

Lake Havasu City

*Bill Williams National
Wildlife Refuge*

*Alamo Lake
State Park*

Yarnell

93

Congress

*Buckskin Mountain
State Park*

Colorado River

Parker

Wickenburg

Bouse

Aguila

71

60

95

72

Wenden

**Bouse
Fisherman**

60

Quartzsite

Hope

10

Sun City

Ehrenberg

To Phoenix →

*Cibola
National
Wildlife
Refuge*

Palm Canyon

*Kofa
National
Wildlife
Refuge*

95

Wintersburg

Buckeye

*Imperial
National
Wildlife
Refuge*

Arlington

85

**Painted Rock
Petroglyph Site**

GILA BEND
INDIAN RESERVATION

Gila Bend

Sentinel

85

Dateland

To Tucson →

Tacna

8

**To Organ
Pipe Cactus
National
Monument
↓**

Yuma

San Luis

MEXICO

BARRY M. GOLDWATER AIR FORCE RANGE

Ajo

Despite the area's decidedly watery orientation, there's quite a bit of mountainous desert here that's home to bighorn sheep, roadrunners, and other wildlife. This land was also once home to several indigenous tribes, and petroglyphs pecked into rocks are reminders of the people who lived here before the first settlers arrived. The best place to see petroglyphs is at Grapevine Canyon, due west of Laughlin, Nevada, in the southwest corner of the National Recreation Area. To reach Grapevine Canyon, take Nev. 163 west from Laughlin to milepost 13 and turn right on the marked dirt road. From the highway, it's about 1½ miles to the turnoff for the parking area. From here, it's less than a quarter mile to the petroglyph-covered jumble of rocks at the mouth of Grapevine Canyon. Covering the boulders are thousands of cryptic symbols, as well as ancient illustrations of bighorn sheep. To see these petroglyphs, you'll have to do a lot of scrambling, so wear sturdy shoes (preferably hiking boots).

For information on other hikes, contact **Lake Mead National Recreation Area** (© **702/293-8907,** 702/293-8990, or, in Arizona, 928/754-3272; www.nps.gov/lame).

WHERE TO STAY

All three of the options listed below are operated by Seven Crown Resorts, which also runs two other resorts on the Nevada side of the lake. For more information, contact **Seven Crown Resorts** (© **800/752-9669;** www.sevencrown.com).

HOUSEBOATS

Seven Crown Resorts ⭐ *(Kids)*   Why pay extra for a lake-view room when you can rent a houseboat that always has a 360-degree water view? There's no better way to explore Lake Mead than on one of these floating vacation homes. You can cruise for miles, tie up at a deserted cove, and enjoy a wilderness adventure with all the comforts of home. Houseboats come complete with full kitchens, air-conditioning, and space to sleep up to 13 people. Bear in mind that the scenery here on Lake Mead isn't nearly as spectacular as that on Lake Powell, Arizona's other major houseboating lake.

P.O. Box 16247, Irvine, CA 92623-6247. © 800/752-9669. www.sevencrown.com. $1,250–$3,050 per week. DISC, MC, V. Pets accepted. *In room:* A/C, kitchen, fridge, no phone.

MOTELS

Lake Mohave Resort *(Kids)*   Just up Lake Mohave from Davis Dam and only a few minutes outside Bullhead City, the Lake Mohave Resort is an older motel, but the huge rooms are ideal for families. Most have some sort of view of the lake, which is across the road, and some have kitchenettes. Also across the road is the resort's nautical-theme restaurant and lounge, which overlook the marina. The resort also has a convenience store and a bait-and-tackle store.

Katherine Landing, 2690 E. Katherine Landing Spur Rd., Bullhead City, AZ 86429. © 800/752-9669 or 928/754-3245. www.sevencrown.com. 51 units. Mid-Apr to early Sept $85–$115 double, $240 suite; early Sept to mid-Apr $35–$65 double, $240 suite. Children 5 and under stay free in parent's room. DISC, MC, V. Pets accepted ($50 deposit plus $10 per night). **Amenities:** Restaurant; lounge; boat and personal watercraft rentals. *In room:* A/C, TV.

Temple Bar Resort   Although basically just a motel, the Temple Bar has a wonderfully remote setting that will have you thinking you're on vacation in Baja California. With a beach right in front, great fishing nearby, and 40 miles of prime skiing waters extending from the resort, this place makes an excellent getaway. A restaurant and lounge overlook the lake and provide economical meals. The resort offers ski rentals, powerboat rentals, and a convenience store.

Temple Bar, AZ 86443. ✆ **800/752-9669** or 928/767-3211. www.sevencrown.com. 18 units. Apr–Oct $80–$115 double; Nov–Mar $65–$90 double. Children 5 and under stay free in parent's room. DISC, MC, V. Pets accepted ($50 deposit plus $10 per night). **Amenities:** Restaurant; lounge; boat and personal watercraft rentals. *In room:* A/C, TV.

CAMPGROUNDS

In Arizona, there are campgrounds at Katherine Landing on Lake Mohave and at Temple Bar on Lake Mead. Both of these campgrounds have been heavily planted with trees, so they provide some semblance of shade during the hot, but popular, summer months. In Nevada, you'll find campgrounds at Cottonwood Cove on Lake Mohave and at Boulder Beach, Las Vegas Bay, Callville Bay, and Echo Bay on Lake Mead. Campsites at all campgrounds are $10 per night. For more information, contact **Lake Mead National Recreation Area** (✆ **702/ 293-8907,** 702/293-8990, or, in Arizona, 928/754-3272; www.nps.gov/lame).

2 Bullhead City & Laughlin, Nevada

30 miles W of Kingman; 60 miles N of Lake Havasu City; 216 miles NW of Phoenix

You may find it difficult at first to understand why anyone would ever want to live in Bullhead City. This is one of the hottest places in North America, with temperatures regularly topping 120°F (49°C) in summer. However, to understand this town's attraction, you need only gaze across the Colorado River at the gambling mecca of Laughlin, Nevada, where the slot machines are always in action and the gaming tables are nearly as hot as the air outside. Laughlin is the southernmost town in Nevada and, before the advent of Indian casinos, was the closest place to Phoenix to do any gambling. The 10 large casino hotels across the river in Nevada still make Bullhead City one of Arizona's busiest little towns.

Laughlin is a perfect miniature Las Vegas. High-rise hotels loom above the desert like so many glass mesas, miles of neon lights turn night into day, and acres of asphalt are always covered with cars and RVs as hordes of hopeful gamblers go searching for Lady Luck. Cheap rooms and meals lure people into spending on the slot machines what they save on food and a bed. It's a formula that works well. Why else would anyone endure the heat of this remote desert? Actually, a lot of the area's residents only come here in the winter when the weather is just about perfect.

ESSENTIALS

GETTING THERE   From Phoenix, take U.S. 60, which becomes U.S. 93, northwest to I-40. From Kingman, take Ariz. 68 west to Bullhead City.

Currently, you can fly into Bullhead City on **Sun Country Airlines** (✆ **800/FLY-N-SUN;** www.suncountry.com). However, Las Vegas has better airline connections. Shuttle-bus service between Laughlin and the Las Vegas McCarran Airport is operated by **Tri-State Super Shuttle** (✆ **800/801-8687** or 928/704-9000), which charges $37 one-way and $64 round-trip.

VISITOR INFORMATION   For information on Bullhead City and Laughlin, contact the **Bullhead Area Chamber of Commerce,** 1251 Hwy. 95, Bullhead City (✆ **800/987-7457** or 928/754-4121; www.bullheadchamber.com). In Laughlin, stop by the **Laughlin Visitors Bureau,** 1555 S. Casino Dr. (✆ **800/ 452-8445** or 702/298-3321; www.visitlaughlin.com).

GETTING AROUND   For car rentals in the area, contact **Avis** (✆ **800/831- 2847** or 928/754-4686), **Enterprise** (✆ **800/736-8222** or 928/754-2700), or **Hertz** (✆ **800/654-3131** or 928/754-4111). Public bus service within Laughlin is provided by **Citizens Area Transit (CAT)** (© 800/228-3911 or 702/228-7433). The fare is $1.50. There's a shuttle van service that operates between the casinos, plus ferries that shuttle to and from parking lots on the Arizona side of the river and water taxis that go from casino to casino.

CASINOS & OTHER INDOOR PURSUITS

The casinos of Laughlin, Nevada, just across the Colorado River from Bullhead City, Arizona, are known for having liberal slots—that is, the slot machines pay off frequently. Consequently, Laughlin is a very popular weekend destination for Phoenicians and other Arizonans. In addition to the slot machines, there's keno, blackjack, poker, craps, off-track betting, and sports betting. All of the hotels in Laughlin offer live entertainment of some sort, including an occasional headliner, but gambling is still the main event after dark.

If you'd like to learn more about the history of this area, visit the **Colorado River Museum,** 355 Hwy. 95, Bullhead City (© 928/754-3399), a half-mile north of the Laughlin Bridge. It's open Tuesday through Sunday from 10am to 4pm (closed July and Aug). Admission is free, but donations are welcome.

BOAT TOURS

If you'd like to see a bit of the Colorado River, daily paddle-wheeler cruises are available through **Laughlin River Tours** (© 800/228-9825 or 702/298-1047; www.steamboatwedding.com) at the **Flamingo Laughlin** and the **Edgewater Hotel & Casino** (see "Where to Stay," below). These cruises cost $11 for adults and $6 for children 4 to 12; dinner cruises ($30) are also available. At the **Riverside Resort Hotel & Casino** (© 800/227-3849, ext. 5770, 702/298-2535, ext. 5770, or 928/763-7070, ext. 5770), you can take a tour on the 65-foot USS *Riverside* to Davis Dam. These excursions last 80 minutes and cost $10 for adults and $6 for children.

If you'd rather look at natural surroundings instead of casino towers, consider booking a 6-hour jet-boat tour to the London Bridge with **London Bridge Jet Boat Tours** (© 888/505-3545 or 702/298-5498; www.jetboattour.com). On the way, the boat passes through scenic Topock Gorge. These powerful boats cruise at up to 40 mph and make the 58-mile one-way trip in 2 hours. Tours cost $52 for adults, $47 for seniors, and $32 for children ages 3 to 12.

OUTDOOR PURSUITS

Desert River Outfitters, 2649 U.S. 95, Suite 23 (© 888/KAYAK-33; www.desertriveroutfitters.com), will rent you a boat and shuttle you and your gear to and from put-ins and take-outs. Its least expensive trip is down the Colorado River past the casinos in Laughlin ($25 per person).

For information on fishing in nearby Lake Mohave, see the section on Lake Mead National Recreation Area, above. If you'd rather just feed the fish, check out the carp that hang out at the dock behind the Edgewater Hotel & Casino. There are machines dispensing carp chow so you can feed these piscine vacuums.

In Laughlin, golfers can play a round at the scenic and challenging **Emerald River Golf Course,** 1155 S. Casino Dr. (© 702/298-4653), 2 miles south of Harrah's. Greens fees range from $80 to $90 in the cool season. The **Mojave Resort Golf Club,** 9905 Aha Macav Pkwy. (© 702/535-4653; www.mojaveresortgolfclub.com), adjacent to the Avi Resort & Casino, has wide, user-friendly fairways and charges greens fees of $59 to $84. In Bullhead City, try the **Desert Lakes Golf Course,** 5835 Desert Lakes Dr. (© 928/768-1000),

15 miles south of town off Ariz. 95. Greens fees range from $68 to $78 in the cooler months.

Bird-watching is excellent in **Havasu National Wildlife Refuge** (© 760/ **326-3853;** http://southwest.fws.gov/refuges/arizona/havasu/index.html), a wintering area for many species of waterfowl. However, much of this refuge lies within the scenic Topock Gorge and is accessible only by boat. The most accessible birding areas are along the marshes in the vicinity of the communities of Golden Shores and Topock, which are both north of the I-40 bridge over the Colorado. Topock Gorge, one of the most scenic stretches of the lower Colorado River, is a 15-mile stretch of river bordered by multicolored cliffs.

WHERE TO STAY
IN BULLHEAD CITY
Bullhead City has numerous budget chain motels, including a **Super 8,** 1616 U.S. 95 (© **800/800-8000** or 928/763-1002), which charges $32 to $40 double.

IN LAUGHLIN, NEVADA
Laughlin, Nevada, currently has 10 huge hotel-and-casino complexes, 8 of which are right on the west bank of the Colorado River (the 9th is across the street from the river, and the 10th is on the river but several miles south of town). All offer cheap rooms (usually under $30 on weeknights) to lure potential gamblers. In addition to huge casinos with hundreds of slot machines and every sort of gaming table, these hotels have several restaurants (with ridiculously low prices in at least one restaurant, which usually has long lines), bars and lounges (usually with live country or pop music nightly), swimming pools, video arcades, ferry service to parking lots on the Arizona side of the river, valet parking, room service, car-rental desks, airport shuttles, gift shops, and gaming classes. The only real difference between most of these places is the theme each has adopted for its decor.

Should you wish to stay at one of these hotels, here's the information you'll need:

- **Avi Resort & Casino,** 10000 Aha Macav Pkwy., Laughlin, NV 89029 (© 800/430-0721 or 702/535-5555; www.avicasino.com)
- **Colorado Belle Hotel & Casino,** 2100 S. Casino Dr., Laughlin, NV 89029 (© 866/352-3553 or 702/298-4000; www.coloradobelle.com)
- **Edgewater Hotel & Casino,** 2020 S. Casino Dr., Laughlin, NV 89029 (© 800/677-4837 or 702/298-2453; www.edgewater-casino.com)
- **Flamingo Laughlin,** 1900 S. Casino Dr., Laughlin, NV 89029 (© 888/ 662-5825 or 702/298-5111; www.flamingolaughlin.com)
- **Golden Nugget,** 2300 S. Casino Dr., Laughlin, NV 89028 (© 800/955- 7278 or 702/298-7111; www.gnlaughlin.com)
- **Harrah's Laughlin,** 2900 S. Casino Dr., Laughlin, NV 89029 (© 800/ HARRAHS or 702/298-4600; www.harrahs.com)
- **Pioneer Hotel & Gambling Hall,** 2200 S. Casino Dr., Laughlin, NV 89029 (© 800/634-3469 or 702/298-2442; www.pioneerlaughlin.com)
- **Ramada Express,** 2121 S. Casino Dr., Laughlin, NV 89029 (© 800/243- 6846 or 702/298-4200; www.ramadaexpress.com)
- **River Palms Resort & Casino,** 2700 S. Casino Dr., Laughlin, NV 89029 (© 800/835-7904 or 702/298-2242; www.river-palms.com)
- **Riverside Resort Hotel & Casino,** 1650 S. Casino Dr., Laughlin, NV 89029 (© 800/227-3849, 702/298-2535 or 928/763-7070; www. riversideresort.com)

WHERE TO DINE

The dozens of inexpensive casino hotel restaurants are usually the top choice of visitors to Laughlin and Bullhead City. Cheap steaks, prime rib, and all-you-can-eat buffets are the specialties of these places.

3 Lake Havasu & the London Bridge

60 miles S of Bullhead City; 150 miles S of Las Vegas, Nev.; 200 miles NW of Phoenix

London Bridge is falling down, falling down, falling down. Well, not anymore it isn't. There once was a time when the London Bridge really was falling down, but that was before Robert McCulloch, founder of Lake Havasu City, hit upon the brilliant idea of buying the bridge and having it shipped to his under-touristed little planned community in the middle of the Arizona desert. That was more nearly 35 years ago, and today London Bridge is still standing and still attracting tourists by the millions. An unlikely place for a bit of British heritage, true, but the London Bridge has turned Lake Havasu City into one of Arizona's most popular tourist destinations.

Lake Havasu was formed in 1938 by the building of the Parker Dam, but it wasn't until 1963 that McCulloch founded the town of Lake Havasu City. In the town's early years, not too many people were keen on spending time in this remote corner of the desert, where summer temperatures are often over 110°F (43°C). Despite its name, Lake Havasu City at the time was little more than an expanse of desert with a few mobile homes on it. It was then that McCulloch began looking for ways to attract more people to his little "city" on the lake. His solution proved to be a stroke of genius.

Today, Lake Havasu City attracts an odd mix of visitors. In winter, the town is filled with retirees, and you'll rarely see anyone under the age of 60. On weekends, during the summer, and over spring break, however, Lake Havasu City is popular with Arizona college students. In fact, the city has become something of a Fort Lauderdale or Cancun in the desert, and businesses now cater primarily to young partiers. Expect a lot of noise if you're here on a weekend or a holiday. Summers bring out the water-ski and personal-watercraft crowds.

ESSENTIALS

GETTING THERE From Phoenix, take I-10 west to Ariz. 95 north. From Las Vegas, take U.S. 95 south to I-40 east to Ariz. 95 south.

America West (✆ 800/235-9292) has regular flights to Lake Havasu City from Phoenix. The **Havasu/Vegas Express** (✆ 800/459-4884 or 928/453-4884; www.havasushuttle.com) operates a shuttle van between Lake Havasu City and Las Vegas. Fares are $53 one-way and $93 round-trip.

VISITOR INFORMATION For more information on this area, contact the **Lake Havasu Tourism Bureau,** English Village (✆ 800/242-8278 or 928/453-3444; http://golakehavasu.com), which is located at the foot of the London Bridge.

GETTING AROUND Taxi (actually shared-ride) service is available from **City Transit Services** (✆ 928/453-7600). For car rentals, try **Avis** (✆ 800/831-2847 or 928/764-3001), **Enterprise** (✆ 800/736-8222 or 928/453-0033), or **Hertz** (✆ 800/654-3131 or 928/764-3994).

LONDON BRIDGE

Back in the mid-1960s, when London Bridge was indeed falling down—or, more correctly, sinking—into the Thames River due to heavy car and truck traffic, the

British government decided to sell the bridge. Robert McCulloch and his partner paid nearly $2.5 million for the famous bridge; had it shipped 10,000 miles to Long Beach, California; and then trucked it to Lake Havasu City. Reconstruction of the bridge was begun in 1968, and the grand reopening was held in 1971. Oddly enough, the 900-foot-long bridge was not built over water; it just connected desert to more desert on a peninsula jutting into Lake Havasu. It wasn't until after the bridge was rebuilt that a mile-long channel was dredged through the base of the peninsula, thus creating an island offshore from Lake Havasu City.

Although the bridge that now stands in Arizona is not very old by British standards, the London Bridge has a long history. The first bridge over the Thames River in London was probably a pontoon bridge built by the Romans in A.D. 43. The first written record of a London Bridge comes from the mention of a suspected witch being drowned at the bridge in 984. In 1176, the first stone bridge over the Thames was built. They just don't build 'em like that one anymore—it lasted for more than 600 years but was eventually replaced in 1824 by the bridge that now stands in Lake Havasu City.

At the base of the bridge sits **English Village,** which is done up in proper English style and has shops, restaurants, and a waterfront promenade. You'll find several cruise boats and boat-rental docks here, as well as the chamber of commerce's visitor center.

Unfortunately, the London Bridge is not very impressive as bridges go, and the tacky commercialization of its surroundings makes it something of a letdown for many visitors. On top of that, over the years the jolly olde England styling that once predominated around here has been supplanted by a Mexican beach-bar aesthetic designed to appeal to partying college students on spring break.

LAND, LAKE & RIVER TOURS

Several companies offer different types of boat tours on Lake Havasu. **Bluewater Jetboat Tours** (© **888/855-7171** or 928/855-7171; www.coloradoriverjetboat tours.com) runs jet-boat tours that leave from the London Bridge and spend 2½ hours cruising up the Colorado River to the Topock Gorge, a scenic area 25 miles from Lake Havasu City. The cost is $35 for adults, $32 for seniors, and $18 for children 10 to 16.

You can also cruise on the *Dixie Belle* (© **928/453-6776**), a small replica paddle-wheel riverboat. Cruises are $13 for adults and $7 for children 4 to 12.

To explore the desert surrounding Lake Havasu City, arrange a four-wheel-drive tour with **Outback Off-Road Adventures** (© **928/680-6151;** www. outbackadventures.com), which charges $65 for a half-day tour and $130 for a full-day tour.

WATERSPORTS

While the London Bridge is what made Lake Havasu City, these days watersports on 45-mile-long Lake Havasu are the area's real draw. Whether you want to go for a swim, take a leisurely pedal-boat ride, try parasailing, or spend the day water-skiing, there are plenty of places to get wet. Lake Havasu is also known as the Jet Ski Capital of the World, so don't expect much peace and quiet when you're out on the water.

London Bridge Beach is the best in-town beach, located in a county park behind the Island Inn, off West McCulloch Boulevard. This park has a sandy beach, lots of palm trees, and views of both the London Bridge and the distant desert mountains. There are also picnic tables and a snack bar. Just south of the London Bridge on the "mainland" side, you'll find the large **Rotary Community**

Moments **Canoeing the Colorado**

Paddling down a desert river is an unusual and unforgettable experience: rocks and cacti on the banks and cool water beneath your boat. If you're interested in a scenic canoe tour, there are a couple of outfitters in the area. Both provide boats, paddles, life jackets, maps, and shuttles to put-in and take-out points, but usually no guide. **Western Arizona Canoe and Kayak Outfitters** (© 888/881-5038 or 928/855-6414; www.azwacko.com) offers self-guided kayak or canoe trips through the beautiful and rugged Topock Gorge, where you can see ancient petroglyphs and possibly bighorn sheep. Trips take 5 to 6 hours, and the cost is $39 per person, which includes the use of a kayak or canoe, paddles, life jackets, dry bags, and coolers, and, most importantly, the shuttle service to the put-in point and back from the take-out point. **Jerkwater Canoe Company** (© 800/421-7803 or 928/768-7753; www.jerkwater.com) offers a similar Topock Gorge excursion and also arranges other canoe and kayak trips of varying lengths. Jerkwater's Topock Gorge self-guided 5-to 6-hour trip is $35 per person if you opt for a canoe or $45 per person if you opt for a kayak. Another popular trip is through Black Canyon, but advance planning (6 months–1 year) is required to get the necessary permit. It's easier to get a permit for Black Canyon midweek than on a weekend. Some trips include additional overnight campground or bunkhouse bed-and-breakfast fees.

Park, which is connected to the bridge by a paved waterside path. Adjacent to the park is the **Lake Havasu Aquatic Center,** 100 Park Ave. (© 928/453-2687), which has a wave pool, 254-foot water slide, and lots of other facilities. There are more beaches at **Lake Havasu State Park** (© 928/855-2784), 2 miles north of the London Bridge, and **Cattail Cove State Park** (© 928/855-1223), 15 miles south of Lake Havasu City. Lake Havasu State Park also has 20 miles of shoreline to the south of Lake Havasu City, but there are no roads to this shoreline. If you have your own boat, you'll find lots of secluded little beaches. Both state parks charge an $8 day-use fee.

The cheapest way to get out on the water in Lake Havasu also happens to involve the greatest expenditure of energy. At the **Adventure Center,** in English Village (© 928/453-4386), you can rent pedal boats for $16 an hour. In this same area, you can also go for a ride on the **London Bridge Gondola** (© 928/486-1891); the gondolier even sings in Italian as you cruise beneath the London Bridge. A 10-minute ride is only $5. If kayaking or canoeing is more your style, contact **Western Arizona Canoe and Kayak Outfitter** (© 888/881-5038 or 928/855-6414; www.azwacko.com), which charges $25 to $40 per day for canoes and kayaks.

If you didn't bring your own boat, you can rent one at **Blue Water Boat Rentals,** in English Village beside the bridge (© 888/855-7171 or 928/453-9613). Pontoon boats cost $220 per day. Boats are also available at **Fun Time Boat Rentals,** 1633 Industrial Blvd. (© 800/680-1003 or 928/680-1003; www.funtimerentals.com). Ski boats come with water skis or knee boards.

If your main reason for getting out on the water is to catch some fish, you'll likely come away from a visit to Lake Havasu with plenty of fish stories to tell. Striped bass, also known as stripers, are the favorite quarry of anglers here. These fish have been known to reach almost 60 pounds in these waters, so be sure to bring the heavy tackle. Largemouth bass in the 2- to 4-pound range are also fairly common, and giant channel catfish of up to 35 pounds have been caught in Topock Marsh. The best fishing starts in spring, when the water begins to warm up, but there is also good winter fishing.

GOLF

Lake Havasu City has three courses, all of which are open to the public. Panoramic views are to be had from each of the courses here, and there's enough variety to accommodate golfers of any skill level.

London Bridge Golf Club, 2400 Club House Dr. (© **928/855-2719**), with two 18-hole courses, is the area's premier championship course. High-season greens fees (with cart) top out at $42 to $89 on the West Course and $25 to $59 on the East Course. The **Havasu Island Golf Course,** 1040 McCulloch Blvd. (© **928/855-5585**), is a 4,012-yard, par-61 executive course with lots of water hazards. Greens fees are $23 if you walk and $31 if you ride. The 9-hole **Bridgewater Links,** 1477 Queen's Bay Rd. (© **928/855-4777;** www.londonbridge resort.com), at the London Bridge Resort, is the most accessible and easiest of the area courses. Greens fees are $16 if you walk and $21 if you ride.

Golfers also won't want to miss the **Emerald Canyon Golf Course** 🏌️, 72 Emerald Canyon Rd., Parker (© **928/667-3366**), about 30 miles south of Lake Havasu City. This municipal course is the most spectacular in the region and plays through rugged canyons and past red-rock cliffs, from which there are views of the Colorado River. One hole even has you hitting your ball off a cliff to a green 200 feet below! Expect to pay around $50 for greens fees in the cooler months. Also in Parker is the golf course at the **Havasu Springs Resort** (© **928/667-3361**), which some people claim is the hardest little 9-hole, par-3 course in the state. It's atop a rocky outcropping with steep drop-offs all around. If you aren't staying here, greens fees are only $10 for 9 holes and $15 for 18 holes.

WHERE TO STAY

In addition to the accommodations listed here, Lake Havasu City has numerous budget chain motels, including a **Motel 6,** 111 London Bridge Rd. (© **928/855-3200**), charging $58 to $68 double, and a **Super 8,** 305 London Bridge Rd. (© **928/855-8844**), charging $39 to $89 double.

Agave Inn 🏌️🏌️ *Finds*　Located at the foot of the London Bridge, this new boutique hotel is by far the hippest hotel between Scottsdale and Las Vegas. Guest rooms are reminiscent of those at W hotels, although here you get much more room at a much lower price. Rooms are large and have balconies, and most overlook the bridge or the water. Platform beds, stylish lamps, and a sort of Scandinavian modern aesthetic make this the most distinctive hotel on this side of the state. Room no. 305, a corner room, has a great view of the bridge and is my favorite in the hotel.

1420 McCulloch Blvd N., Lake Havasu City, AZ 86403. © 866/854-2833 or 928/854-2833. Fax 928/854-1130. www.agaveinn.com. 17 units. Mar–Oct $159–$359 suite; Nov and Feb $139–$299 suite; Dec–Jan $119–$259 suite. AE, DISC, MC, V. **Amenities:** Restaurant (Mexican); exercise room. *In room:* A/C, TV, dataport, high-speed Internet access, fridge, coffeemaker, hair dryer, iron.

Island Inn Hotel　The Island Inn is across the London Bridge from downtown and has one of the nicest hotel settings in Lake Havasu City. Although it's not right on the water, it is close to one of the area's best public beaches. Guest rooms are large and have seen a lot of wear and tear. Ask for a room with a balcony; units on the upper floors have the better views (and higher prices).

1300 W. McCulloch Blvd., Lake Havasu City, AZ 86403. ℂ 800/243-9955 or 928/680-0606. Fax 928/680-4218. www.havasumotels.com. 117 units. Mar–Oct $58–$229 double; Nov–Feb $49–$85 double. Children under 16 stay free in parent's room. AE, DISC, MC, V. Pets accepted ($10 nonrefundable deposit). **Amenities:** Restaurant; lounge; outdoor pool; Jacuzzi; coin-op laundry. *In room:* A/C, TV, dataport, fridge.

London Bridge Resort ⭐   Merrie Olde England was once the theme here, with Tudor half-timbers jumbled up with turrets, towers, ramparts, and crenellations. However, England has given way to the tropics and the desert as the resort strives to please its young, partying clientele (who tend to make a lot of noise and leave the hotel looking much the worse for wear). Although the bridge is just out the hotel's back door, and a replica of Britain's gold State Coach is inside the lobby, guests are more interested in the three pools and the tropical-theme outdoor nightclub. The one- and two-bedroom units, however, are spacious, comfortable and attractive, and those on the ground floor have double whirlpool tubs. Keep in mind that this is a timeshare condo resort.

1477 Queens Bay, Lake Havasu City, AZ 86403. ℂ 800/624-7939 or 928/855-0888. Fax 928/855-5404. www.londonbridgeresort.com. 122 units. Mar–Aug $159–$209 1-bedroom condo; Sept–Feb $79–$159 1-bedroom condo. AE, DISC, MC, V. **Amenities:** Restaurant (American); 2 lounges; 3 pools; 9-hole executive golf course; tennis court; Jacuzzi; coin-op laundry. *In room:* A/C, TV/VCR, kitchen, fridge, coffeemaker, hair dryer.

CAMPGROUNDS

There are two state park campgrounds in the Lake Havasu City area. **Lake Havasu State Park** (ℂ 928/855-2784) is 2 miles north of the London Bridge on London Bridge Road, while **Cattail Cove State Park** (ℂ 928/855-1223) is 15 miles south of Lake Havasu City off Ariz. 95. The former campground has no hookups and charges $14 to $16 per night per vehicle, while the latter charges $19 to $22 for a full hookup. Reservations are not accepted. In addition to sites in these campgrounds, there are also boat-in campsites within Lake Havasu and Cattail Cove state parks.

WHERE TO DINE

Chico's Tecate Grill *Finds* MEXICAN   This Mexican fast-food place is great for a quick, cheap bite to eat. The carne asada and chicken carbón are excellent, and there's a fresh salsa bar for you to do your own doctoring of your meal.

At the Basha's Center, 1641 McCulloch Blvd. ℂ 928/680-7010. Main courses $2.50–$6.50. DISC, MC, V. Sun–Thurs 8:30am–9pm; Fri–Sat 8:30am–10pm.

Javelina Cantina MEXICAN   Located at the foot of the London Bridge on the island side, this large, modern Mexican restaurant is affiliated with Shugrue's on the other side of the street. As at Shugrue's, there is a great view of the bridge. In this case it is from a large patio area that is kept heated even during the cooler winter months. The bar has an excellent selection of tequilas, and margaritas are a specialty here. Accompany your libations with tortilla soup, fish tacos, or a salad made with blackened scallops, papaya, pecans, blue cheese, and other ingredients.

1420 McCulloch Blvd. ℂ 928/855-8226. Main courses $7–$15. AE, DISC, MC, V. Sun–Thurs 11am–9pm; Fri–Sat 11am–10pm. Open 1 hr. later every night in summer.

London Arms Restaurant, Pub & Playhouse AMERICAN   Combining a fine-dining restaurant with live theater, this restaurant isn't exactly a dinner theater, but it certainly isn't a pub either. However, the location, at the foot of the London Bridge, makes this a very undesertlike spot of luxury. At lunch, the menu does include a bit of pub fare (including a decent shepherd's pie), but at dinner, expect the likes of prime rib, crab cakes, and scallops Rockefeller. Theater performances lean toward musicals, light opera, and comedies. Dinner and a show can be had for $32 to $39.

422 English Village. ℭ 928/855-8782. www.londonarmspub.com. Reservations recommended. Main courses $9–$12 lunch, $15–$35 dinner. AE, DISC, MC, V. Sun and Wed–Thurs 11am–9pm; Fri–Sat 11am–10pm.

Mudshark Brewing Co. ⚲ SOUTHWESTERN/INTERNATIONAL Located a few blocks south of the London Bridge, this place serves some excellent brews. The beers here go especially well with pizzas and pastas, but there are more substantial dishes as well. Try the Arizona Caesar, which comes in a tortilla shell; the cranberry-brandy pork tenderloin; or the grilled salmon with tequila sauce. There's a movie theater right next door, which makes this a good spot for a night out.

210 Swanson Ave. ℭ 928/453-2981. Reservations not necessary. Main courses $7.50–$17. AE, MC, V. Daily 11am–midnight.

Shugrue's 𝘒𝘪𝘥𝘴 STEAKHOUSE/SEAFOOD   Located just across the London Bridge from the English Village shopping complex, Shugrue's seems to be popular as much for its view of the London Bridge as for its food. Offerings include seafood, prime rib, burgers, sandwiches, and a short list of pastas. This place is a favorite of vacationing retirees and families, especially for its inexpensive sunset dinners, which are served Sunday through Thursday from 5 to 6:30pm. There's also a children's menu. The adjacent affiliated Barley Brothers Brewpub has the same good view of the bridge, and serves a menu calculated to appeal to a younger clientele.

At the Island Mall, 1425 McCulloch Blvd. ℭ 928/453-1400. www.shugrueslhc.com. Reservations recommended. Main courses $7–$12 lunch, $13–$25 dinner. AE, DC, DISC, MC, V. Sun–Thurs 11am–9pm; Fri–Sat 11am–10 or 11pm.

EN ROUTE TO YUMA
THE PARKER AREA

About 16 miles south of Lake Havasu City stands the **Parker Dam,** which holds back the waters of Lake Havasu and is said to be the deepest dam in the world because 73% of its 320-foot height is below the riverbed. Beginning just above the dam and stretching south to the town of Parker is one of the most beautiful stretches of the lower Colorado River. Just before you reach the dam, you'll come to the **Bill Williams National Wildlife Refuge** (ℭ 928/667-4144; http:// southwest.fws.gov/refuges/arizona/billwill.html), which preserves the lower reaches of the Bill Williams River. This refuge offers some of the best birdwatching in western Arizona. Keep your eyes open for vermilion flycatchers, Yuma clapper rails, soras, Swainson's hawks, and white-faced ibises.

Continuing south, you'll reach a dam overlook and the Take-Off Point boat launch, where you can do some fishing from shore. Below the dam, the river becomes narrow and red-rock canyon walls close in. Although this narrow gorge is lined with mobile-home parks, the most beautiful sections have been preserved in two units of **Buckskin Mountain State Park** (ℭ 928/667-3231 or 928/667-3386 for River Island; www.pr.state.az.us). Both units—Buckskin Mountain and River Island—have campgrounds ($19 for campsites and $22 for cabanas at Buckskin; $14 to $16 for campsites at River Island) as well as day-use areas that include river beaches and hiking trails leading into the Buckskin Mountains. The day-use fee is $7 per vehicle at either park. Reservations for camping are not accepted. In this area you'll also find the spectacular Emerald Canyon Golf Course (see "Golf," above, for details).

On the north side of town, keep an eye out for **Lemon Tree Nursery,** 500 Riverside Dr. (© **928/669-8002**), which sells fresh local citrus fruit in season.

For more information on the Parker area, contact the **Parker Area Chamber of Commerce,** 1217 California Ave., Parker (© **888/733-7275** or 928/669-6511;www.parkertourism.com).

Where to Stay

Blue Water Resort and Casino 🎯🎯   Located 37 miles south of Lake Havasu City, this riverside casino resort is western Arizona's most impressive hotel. Even if you aren't interested in spending your time at the slot machines, you'll find something here that appeals. There's a big indoor pool complex (with water slide) designed to resemble ancient ruins, a marina, and a mile of riverfront land, plus miniature golf and a theater for live entertainment. Guest rooms are all close to the water, which means nice river views but also traffic noise from the ski boats. Furnishings are standard motel modern.

11300 Resort Dr., Parker, AZ 85344. © **888/243-3360.** www.bluewaterfun.com. 200 units. $45–$125 double; $99–$199 suite. AE, DISC, MC, V. **Amenities:** 2 restaurants; snack bars; 2 lounges; 4 pools; miniature golf; exercise room; Jacuzzi; video arcade; room service; laundry service; casino. *In room:* A/C, TV, dataport, coffeemaker, hair dryer.

THE QUARTZSITE AREA

For much of the year, the community of **Quartzsite** is little more than a few truck stops at an interstate off-ramp. But the population explodes with the annual influx of winter visitors (also known as snowbirds), and from early January to mid-February it's the site of numerous gem-and-mineral shows that attract more than a million rock hounds. Among these shows is the **Quartzsite Pow Wow,** which is held in late January and is one of the largest gem-and-mineral shows in the country. During the winter months, Quartzsite sprouts thousands of vendor stalls, as flea markets and the like are erected along the town's main streets. A variety of interesting food makes it a great place to stop for lunch or dinner. For more information, contact the **Quartzsite Chamber of Commerce** (© **928/927-5600;** www.quartzsitechamber.com).

For information on parking your RV in the desert outside Quartzsite, contact the **Bureau of Land Management,** Yuma Field Office, 2555 East Gila Ridge Rd., Yuma (© **928/317-3200;** www.az.blm.gov/yfo/index.htm). Alternatively, you can get information and camping permits at the Long-Term Visitor Area entrance stations just south of Quartzsite on U.S. 95. The season here runs from September 15 to April 15, with permits going for $140 for the season and $30 for 14 consecutive days.

There are only three places in Arizona where palm trees grow wild, and if you'd like to visit one of these spots, watch for the Palm Canyon turnoff 18 miles south of Quartzsite. Palm Canyon lies within the boundaries of the **Kofa National Wildlife Refuge,** which was formed primarily to protect the desert bighorn sheep that live here in the rugged Kofa Mountains. The palms are 9 miles off U.S. 95 in a narrow canyon a short walk from the end of the well-graded gravel road, and although there are only a couple of dozen trees, the hike to see them provides an opportunity to experience these mountains up close. Keep your eyes peeled for desert bighorn sheep. Incidentally, the Kofa Mountains took their name from the King of Arizona Mine. For maps and more information, contact the Kofa National Wildlife Refuge, 356 W. First St., Yuma (© **928/783-7861;** http://southwest.fws.gov/refuges/arizona/kofa.html).

> **Finds The Bouse Fisherman**
>
> If ancient rock art interests you, be sure to watch for Plomosa Road as you travel between Parker and Quartzsite. Off this road, you'll find a 30-foot intaglio (or geoglyph) known as the **Bouse Fisherman**. This primitive image of a person spearing fish was formed by scratching away the rocky crust of the desert soil. Its origin and age are unknown, but it is believed to have been created centuries ago by native peoples and may depict the god Kumastamo, who created the Colorado River by thrusting a spear into the ground. To find it, drive 8 miles up Plomosa Road, which is approximately 6 miles north of Quartzsite, and watch for a wide parking area on the north side of the road. From here, follow the trail for a quarter of a mile over a small hill.

Back in the 19th century, the mountains of this region were pockmarked with mines. To get an idea of what life was like in the mining boomtowns, make a detour to **Castle Dome City Mines, Museum, and Ghost Town** (ⓒ **928/920-3062**), a reconstructed mining town in the middle of the desert. To find this place, turn east at the Castle Dome turnoff near milepost 55 and continue another 10 miles (only the first mile or so is paved). The museum/ghost town is open Tuesday through Sunday from 10am to 5pm and admission is $4.50. There are guided tours ($5) on Wednesday at 10am.

4 Yuma ⊛

180 miles SW of Phoenix; 240 miles W of Tucson; 180 miles E of San Diego, Calif.

According to the book *Guinness World Records,* Yuma is the sunniest place on earth. Of the possible 4,456 hours of daylight each year, the sun shines in Yuma for roughly 4,050 hours, or about 90% of the time. Combine all that sunshine with the warmest winter weather in the country, and you've got a destination guaranteed to attract sun worshippers and other refugees from colder climes. In fact, each winter, tens of thousands of snowbirds (retired winter visitors) drive their RVs to Yuma from as far away as Canada. However, by late spring, all those RVers head north to escape the steadily rising temperatures, and by high summer, Yuma starts posting furnacelike high temperatures that make this one of the hottest cities in the country.

Long before RVers discovered Yuma, way back in the middle of the 19th century, this was one of the most important towns in the region, known as the Rome of the Southwest because all roads led to Yuma Crossing—the shallow spot along the Colorado River where this town was founded. Despite its location in the middle of the desert, Yuma became a busy port town during the 1850s as shallow-draft steamboats traveled up the Colorado River from the Gulf of California. Later, when the railroad pushed westward into California in the 1870s, it passed through Yuma. Today, it is I-8, which connects San Diego with Tucson and Phoenix, that brings travelers to Yuma and across the Colorado River.

However, despite having more than a dozen golf courses and two important historic sites, Yuma has had to struggle to attract visitors (blame it on the lure of San Diego, which is just a few hours away). In the hopes of luring more travelers off the interstate, Yuma has in the past few years been working hard to restore its downtown historic buildings, expand its historic sites, and preserve its natural setting on the Colorado River. There is even a new visual arts center downtown that rivals any gallery in Scottsdale, and an adjacent historical movie theater has been restored to its former glory and now serves as a performing-arts center.

ESSENTIALS

GETTING THERE　Yuma is on I-8, which runs from San Diego, California, to Casa Grande, Arizona. **Amtrak** (© **800/872-7245**) runs passenger service to Yuma from Los Angeles and New Orleans. The station is on Gila Street.

The Yuma Airport, 2191 32nd St., is served from Phoenix by **American West** (© **800/235-9292**) and from Los Angeles by **United Express** (© **800/241-6522**).

VISITOR INFORMATION　Contact the **Yuma Convention and Visitors Bureau,** 377 S. Main St. (© **800/293-0071** or 928/783-0071; www.visit yuma.com).

GETTING AROUND　Rental cars are available from **Avis** (© **800/831-2847** or 928/726-5737), **Budget** (© **800/527-0700** or 928/344-1822), **Enterprise** (© **800/325-8007** or 928/344-5444), and **Hertz** (© **800/654-3131** or 928/726-5160).

SPECIAL EVENTS　The Yuma area is a major producer of lettuce, and celebrates this during the **Lettuce Festival** in late January. **Yuma River Daze,** in late February, features historical reenactments, tours of historic sites, and train rides. In mid-April, the **Yuma Birding & Nature Festival** offers a chance to spot plenty of the 380 species of birds that frequent the area.

HISTORIC SITES

Arizona Historical Society Sanguinetti House Museum　If you'd like to find out more about pioneer life in Yuma, stop by this territorial-period home, which is full of historic photographs and artifacts and surrounded by lush gardens and aviaries containing exotic birds. Adjacent to the museum is the Garden Cafe, an excellent lunch spot (see "Where to Dine," below).

240 S. Madison Ave. © **928/782-1841.** Admission $3 adults, $2 seniors and students 12–18, free for children under 12. Tues–Sat 10am–4pm.

Yuma Crossing State Historic Park ✪　In 1865, Yuma Crossing, the narrow spot on the Colorado River where the town of Yuma sprang up, became the site of the military's Quartermaster Depot. Yuma was a busy river port during this time, and after supplies shipped from California were unloaded, they went to military posts throughout the region. When the railroad arrived in Yuma in 1877, the Quartermaster Depot began to lose its importance in the regional supply network, and by 1883, the depot was closed. Today, the depot's large wooden buildings have been restored, and although they are now set back from the current channel of the Colorado River, it's easy to imagine being stationed at this hot and dusty outpost in the days before air-conditioning. Exhibits tell the story of those who lived and worked at Yuma Crossing.

201 N. Fourth Ave. (at the Colorado River). © **928/329-0471.** www.pr.state.az.us. Admission $4 adults, $2 children 7–13. Daily 9am–5pm. Closed Christmas.

Yuma Territorial Prison State Historic Park ✪　This prison first housed convicts in 1876, but operated for only 33 years before being replaced by a larger prison. Despite the thick stone walls and iron bars, this was considered a model penal institution in its day. It even had its own electric-generating plant and ventilation system. The prison museum has some interesting displays, including photos of many of the men and women who were incarcerated here.

1 Prison Hill Rd. (✆ 928/783-4771. www.pr.state.az.us. Admission $4 adults, $2 children 7–13. Daily 8am–5pm. Closed Christmas.

DOWNTOWN YUMA

While Yuma may not seem at first like the sort of place to expect to see cutting-edge contemporary art, that's just what you sometimes encounter at the new **Yuma Art Center,** 254 S. Main St. (✆ **928/373-5214**), which is located next door to the Historic Yuma Theatre and is a gorgeous gallery that could hold its own in Scottsdale. The **Yuma Symposium,** held here each year in February, brings in talented artists from all over the country. Don't leave town without stopping by to see what's on view. The center is open Tuesday through Saturday from 10am to 6pm and Sunday from 1 to 5pm.

Historic downtown Yuma isn't exactly a bustling place, and it doesn't abound in historic flavor, but the south-of-the-border atmosphere is worth a visit; the plaza in the center of the shopping district is similar to those found in towns all over Mexico. Funky and inexpensive crafts and antiques shops occupy an occasional storefront, and down a landscaped alleyway off Main Street (at 224 Main St., across from Lutes Casino), there's a potpourri of small tourist-oriented stores. Just off Main Street, you'll also find two pottery studio/galleries: **One Percent Gallery,** 78 W. Second St. (✆ **928/782-1934**), and **Colorado River Pottery,** 67 W. Second St. (✆ **928/343-0413**).

Nearby, in a restored adobe building, you'll find **Picaflor,** 206 S. First Ave. (✆ **928/782-6535**), which sells Mexican decorative items. At the **Gandolfo Art Gallery,** 202 S. First Ave., Suite 204 (✆ **928/343-9105**), you can check out works by local artists.

Within just a couple of blocks of downtown, you can play in the sand or go for a stroll along the Colorado River at **Colorado River Crossing Beach Park.** The park is at the north end of Madison Avenue.

DATES & DESERT TOURING

Date palms, which are among the most ancient of cultivated tree crops, flourish in the heat of the Arizona desert. Here in Yuma, you'll find **Ehrlich's Date Garden,** 868 Ave. B (✆ **928/783-4778**), which sells nearly a dozen varieties of organically grown dates, as well as organic oranges. Prices are incredibly low. The old-fashioned fruit stand is open Monday through Friday from 9am to 5pm (but closed mid-May to Aug).

The Colorado River has been the lifeblood of the Southwestern desert for centuries, and today there's a wealth of history along its banks. **Yuma River Tours** (✆ **928/783-4400;** www.yumarivertours.com), operates narrated jet-boat tours from Yuma to the **Imperial National Wildlife Refuge** (see below) and an extended trip to Draper. Along the way, you'll learn about the homesteaders, boatmen, Native Americans, and miners who once relied on the Colorado River. Tours cost $35 to $75, and lunch and dinner tours are available. This company does more low-key boat tours in a paddle-wheeler. Three-hour tours are $35 ($42 with lunch), and 2-hour sunset dinner cruises are $47.

While the river was the reason for Yuma's existence, it was the railroad that finally forced the town to abandon its connection to the Colorado. Today, during the cooler months, you can ride the rails on the historic **Yuma Valley Railway** (✆ **928/783-3456**), which offers 34-mile excursions along the

Colorado River. You may spot birds and other wildlife on the banks of the river, and you'll get views of Mexico across the river and of rich agricultural lands on this side. Passengers ride in a 1922 Pullman coach. Trains depart Sundays (and sometimes Sat) at 1pm. Fares are $17 for adults, $16 for seniors, and $8 for children ages 4 to 12.

If you're a bird-watcher, an angler, or a canoeist, you'll want to spend some time along the Colorado River north of Yuma. Here you'll find the Imperial and Cibola national wildlife refuges, comprising extensive marshes and shallow lakes alongside the river. Plenty of bird species, good fishing and canoeing, and several campgrounds make it a popular area. For more information, contact the **Imperial National Wildlife Refuge** (© **928/783-3371;** http://southwest.fws. gov/refuges/arizona/imperial.html) or the **Cibola National Wildlife Refuge** (© **928/857-3253;** http://southwest.fws.gov/refuges/arizona/cibola.html).

One of the best ways to explore the Imperial National Wildlife Refuge is by canoe. You can rent one from **Martinez Lake Resort** (© **800/876-7004** or 928/783-9589; www.martinezlake.com) for $18 a day, plus shuttle and delivery charges. Both 1- and 2-day canoe trips are possible along this stretch of the lower Colorado, which features rugged, colorful mountains and quiet backwater areas.

Bird-watchers will want to head out to the **Betty's Kitchen Wildlife and Interpretive Area** ($5 day-use fee per vehicle) and the adjacent **Mittry Lake Wildlife Area.** To get there, take U.S. 95 east out of town, turn north on Avenue 7E, and continue 9 miles, at which point the road turns to gravel. Turn left in a quarter of a mile to reach Betty's Kitchen; continue straight to reach Mittry Lake. Fall and spring migrations are some of the best times of year for birding at these spots; many waterfowl winter in the area as well. For information on Betty's Kitchen and Mittry Lake, contact the **Bureau of Land Management,** Yuma Field Office, 2555 E. Gila Ridge Rd., Yuma (© **928/317-3200;** www.az.blm. gov/yfo/index.htm).

WHERE TO STAY
MODERATE

Best Western Coronado Motor Hotel ⭐ With its red-tile roofs, white-washed walls, and archways, this Mission Revival building on the edge of downtown is the picture of a mid-20th-century motel—but rooms are as up-to-date as you would expect from a major chain. The convenient location puts you within walking distance of several good restaurants, Yuma Crossing State Historic Park, the Arizona Historical Society Sanguinetti House Museum, and the Yuma Valley Railway.

233 Fourth Ave., Yuma, AZ 85364. © 800/234-5567 or 928/783-4453. Fax 928/782-7487. www.bwcoronado. com. 86 units. $69–$135 double. Rates include full breakfast. Children 12 and under stay free in parent's room. AE, DC, DISC, MC, V. Pets accepted. **Amenities:** Restaurant (American); lounge; 2 outdoor pools; Jacuzzi; coin-op laundry. *In room:* A/C, TV, dataport, hair dryer, iron, safe, free local calls.

La Fuente Inn & Suites Conveniently located just off the interstate, this appealing hotel is done in Spanish-colonial style with red-tile roof, pink-stucco walls, and a fountain out front, and the theme continues in the lobby, which has rustic furnishings and a tile floor. French doors open onto the pool terrace and a large courtyard, around which the guest rooms are arranged. Standard units feature modern motel furnishings, while the well-designed suites offer much more space. The Spanish styling and pleasant courtyard pool area set this place apart from other off-ramp hotels in Yuma.

1513 E. 16th St., Yuma, AZ 85365. ✆ **877/202-3353** or 928/329-1814. Fax 928/343-2671. www.lafuenteinn. com. 96 units. $83–$109 double. Rates include continental breakfast and evening happy hour. Children 12 and under stay free in parent's room. AE, DC, DISC, MC, V. **Amenities:** Pool; exercise room; access to nearby health club; Jacuzzi; coin-op laundry. *In room:* A/C, TV/VCR, dataport, fridge, coffeemaker, hair dryer, iron.

INEXPENSIVE

In addition to numerous older budget motels, Yuma has several newer chain motels, including a **Super 8,** 1688 S. Riley Ave. (✆ **800/800-8000** or 928/ 782-2000) and two branches of **Motel 6** (✆ **800/4-MOTEL-6**).

WHERE TO DINE

Java on the Main, 111 Main St. (✆ **928/819-0291**), in Yuma's downtown multiplex movie theater, is a good place to get a latte before making the long drive to Phoenix.

The Garden Cafe ★★ BREAKFAST/SANDWICHES/SALADS   In back of the Arizona Historical Society Sanguinetti House Museum is Yuma's favorite breakfast and lunch spot. Set amid quiet terraced gardens and large aviaries full of singing birds, the Garden Cafe provides a welcome respite from Yuma's heat. On the hottest days, misters spray the air with a gentle fog that keeps the gardens cool. There's also an indoor dining area. The menu consists of various delicious sandwiches, daily special quiches, salads, and rich desserts. Pancakes with lingonberry sauce are a breakfast specialty. On Sunday, there's a brunch buffet. This place is a favorite among retirees.

250 Madison Ave. ✆ **928/783-1491.** Main courses $7–$13. AE, MC, V. Tues–Fri 9am–2:30pm; Sat–Sun 8am–2:30pm. Closed late May to early Oct.

Lutes Casino *Kids* BURGERS/SANDWICHES   Lutes, in business since the 1920s, is a dark and cavernous restaurant known for serving the best hamburgers in town and for having the strangest decor, too. You don't need to see a menu—just walk in and ask for a special, or *especial* (this is a bilingual joint). What you'll get is a cheeseburger/hot dog combo. Then cover your special with Lutes' own secret-recipe hot sauce to make it truly special. You won't find any slot machines or poker tables at Lutes Casino anymore, just a few very serious domino players.

221 S. Main St. ✆ **928/782-2192.** Sandwiches and burgers $2.75–$5.25. No credit cards. Mon–Thurs 9am–8pm; Fri–Sat 9am–9pm; Sun 10am–6pm; sometimes closes earlier.

River City Grill ★★ INTERNATIONAL   With its hip, big-city decor and colorful exterior paint job, this restaurant is definitely a novelty in Yuma, but the lines out the door are testimony to the fact that this town obviously craves just such a dining experience. Seafood dominates the menu. The crab cakes with yellow bell pepper–saffron sauce are a must for a starter, and the tequila snapper is one of my favorite entrees. Flavor combinations range all over the globe: Vietnamese spring rolls, Mediterranean salad, seafood gumbo, jerk chicken. If you're here on a weekend, ask about the sushi.

600 W. Third St. ✆ **928/782-7988.** Reservations highly recommended. Main courses $8–$22. AE, DC, DISC, MC, V. Mon–Thurs 11:30am–2pm and 5–9pm; Fri–Sat 11:30am–2pm and 5–10pm; Sun 5–9pm.

YUMA AFTER DARK

In most small towns across Arizona, you'll find an old downtown movie theater. Most of them are boarded up and abandoned. Not so with Yuma's old theater. Fresh from a total renovation and updating, the **Historic Yuma Theatre,** 254 S. Main St. (✆ **928/373-5214**), is now playing host to live theater productions and touring musical groups. Originally opened in 1912, the theater has been restored to the way it looked in the 1930s when it sported a distinctive Art Deco decor.

Looking for something else to do after dark in Yuma? You can try your luck at the **Paradise Casino Arizona,** 450 Quechan Dr. (℗ 888/777-IWIN; www. paradise-casinos.com), across the Colorado River on the Quechan Indian Reservation, or at the **Cocopah Casino,** U.S. 95 (℗ 800/23-SLOTS; www. wincocopahcasino.com), 15 minutes south of Yuma in Somerton.

EAST TOWARD TUCSON

It's a long stretch of desert from Yuma east to Tucson, and there's not much to break up the monotony of the drive. However, if you're interested in old tractors, watch for Exit 21 (21 miles east of Yuma). Off this exit you'll find the **Dome Valley Museum,** Dome Valley Road (℗ 928/785-9081; www.dome valleymuseum.com), and oh, Deere, does this place have an impressive collection of old tractors! At last count there were 40 green-and-yellow John Deere tractors lined up in the barnlike display building. Many more tractors are parked under the desert sun. In total, there are more than 300 tractors here that date from 1906 to 1960. In addition, there's lots more old stuff to see. The museum is open November to April daily from 10am to 5pm, and admission is $7 for adults ($12 couples), $4 for children ages 12 to 16, and $3 for children 11 and under. You'll find the museum north of the freeway.

Continuing east on I-8, keep an eye out for Exit 67, the Dateland exit. Although **Dateland Palms** (℗ 928/454-2772) is little more than a gift shop and diner, it is well-known for its thick and creamy date shakes (on a hot afternoon, nothing tastes better). You can also now get prickly-pear shakes here.

The next exit to watch for is Exit 102 (Painted Rock Dam Rd.). Getting off at this exit will lead you north to an impressive collection of petroglyphs at the Bureau of Land Management's **Painted Rocks Petroglyph Site.** To find this ancient rock art, drive north on Painted Rock Dam Road for 11 miles to a left turn onto dirt Rocky Point Road. Continue another .6 mile to the parking area. For more information, contact the BLM Phoenix Field Office, 21605 N. 7th Ave. (℗ 623/580-5500).

WEST TOWARD SAN DIEGO

West of Yuma, I-8 heads out across the desert toward San Diego soon passing through barren windswept sand dunes that Hollywood has long used to represent the Sahara. This region may seem like the middle of nowhere to you, but according to Jacques-Andres Istel, it is the **Official Center of the World** (℗ 760/572-0100; www.felicityusa.com). Actually it was a dragon in a fairy tale that claimed that Felicity, California, was the center of the world, and, of course, as everyone knows, fairy tales are always true. The fact that Istel wrote the fairy tale shouldn't matter. Make a pilgrimage to this unusual attraction and you can stand inside a pyramid at the exact center of the world and even get a certificate to prove you were there. As an added bonus, you can admire Istel's monument to the history of French aviation. The Official Center of the World is open for tours from Thanksgiving to Easter daily from 10am to 5pm. You'll find Jacques-Andres, Felicity, and the center of the world 9 miles west of Yuma at the Sidewinder Road exit off I-8.

Appendix:
Arizona in Depth

Despite the searing summer temperatures, the desolate deserts, and the lack of water, people have been lured to Arizona for generations. In the 16th century, the Spanish came looking for gold—but settled for saving souls. In the 19th century, cattle ranchers came (despite frightful tales of spiny cactus forests) and found that a few corners of the state actually had lush grasslands. At the same time, sidetracked forty-niners were scouring the hills for gold (and found more than the Spanish did). However, boomtowns—both cattle and mining—soon went bust. Despite occasional big strikes, mining didn't prove itself until the early 20th century, and even then, the mother lode was not gold or silver, but copper, which Arizona has in such abundance that it is called the Copper State.

In the 1920s and 1930s, Arizona struck a new source of gold. The railroads made travel to the state easy, and word of the mild winter climate spread to colder corners of the nation. Among the first "vacationers" were people suffering from tuberculosis. These "lungers," as they were known, rested and recuperated in the dry desert air. It didn't take long for the perfectly healthy to realize that they, too, could enjoy winter in Arizona, and wintering in the desert soon became fashionable with wealthy Northerners.

Today, it's still the golden sun that lures people to Arizona, and Scottsdale, Phoenix, Tucson, and Sedona are home to some of the most luxurious and expensive resorts in the country. The state has seen a massive influx of retirees, many of whom have found the few pockets of Arizona where the climate is absolutely perfect—not too hot, not too cold, and plenty of sunshine.

Although the Grand Canyon attracts the most visitors to Arizona, the state has plenty of other natural wonders. The largest meteorite crater, the Painted Desert, the spectacular red-rock country of Sedona, the sandstone buttes of Monument Valley, and "forests" of saguaro cacti are just a few examples.

The human hand has also left its mark on Arizona. More than 1,000 years ago, the Ancestral Puebloan (formerly called Anasazi), Sinagua, and Hohokam tribes built villages on mesas, in valleys, and in the steep cliff walls of deep canyons. In more recent years, much larger structures have risen in canyons across the state. The Hoover and Glen Canyon dams on the Colorado River are among the largest dams in the country and have created the nation's largest and most spectacular reservoirs, although at the expense of the rich riparian areas that once thrived in the now flooded desert canyons. Today, these reservoirs are among the state's most popular destinations, especially with Arizonans.

Just as compelling as its sunshine, resorts, and reservoirs are the tall tales of Arizona's fascinating history. This is the Wild West, the land of cowboys and Indians, of prospectors and ghost towns, coyotes and rattlesnakes. Scratch the glossy surface of modern, urbanized Arizona and you'll strike real gold—the story of the American West.

1 The Natural Environment

Although the very mention of Arizona may cause some people to turn the air-conditioning on full blast, this state is much more than a searing landscape of cacti and creosote bushes. From the baking shores of the lower Colorado River to the snowcapped heights of the San Francisco Peaks, Arizona encompasses virtually every North American climatic zone. Cactus flowers bloom in spring, and mountain wildflowers have their turn in summer. In autumn, the aspens color the White Mountains golden, and in winter, snows blanket the higher elevations from the Grand Canyon's North Rim to the Mexican border.

But it's the Sonoran Desert, with its massive saguaro cacti, that most people associate with Arizona, and it is here in the desert that the state's two largest cities—Phoenix and Tucson—are to be found. The Sonoran Desert is among the world's most biologically diverse deserts. This is due in large part to the relatively plentiful rains in the region. In the Arizona desert, rain falls during both the winter and the late summer. This latter rainy season, when clamorous thunderstorms send flash floods surging down arroyos, is known as the monsoon season and is the most dramatic time of year in the desert. The sunsets are unforgettable, but then so, too, are the heat and humidity.

Before the introduction of dams and deep wells, many Arizona rivers and streams flowed year-round and nurtured a surprising variety of plants and animals. Today, however, only a few rivers and creeks still flow unaltered through the desert. They include Sonoita and Aravaipa creeks and the San Pedro, Verde, and Hassayampa rivers. The green riparian areas along these watercourses are characterized by the rare cottonwood-willow forest and serve as magnets for wildlife, harboring rare birds as well as fish species unique to Arizona.

The saguaro cactus, which can stand 40 feet tall and weigh several tons, is the Sonoran Desert's most conspicuous native inhabitant. Massive and many-armed, these are the cacti of comic strips and Hollywood Westerns. This desert is also home to many other lesser-known species of cactus, including organ pipe cactus (closely related to the saguaro), barrel cactus, and various species of prickly pears and chollas. Despite their spiny defenses, cacti are still a source of food and shelter for many species of desert animals. Bats sip the nectar from saguaro flowers, and in the process act as pollinators. Javelinas (collared peccaries), which are similar to wild pigs, chow down on the prickly pear fruit—spines and all. Gila woodpeckers nest in holes in saguaro trunks, while cactus wrens build their nests in the branches of cholla cacti.

Just as cacti have adapted to the desert, so too have the animals that live here. Many desert animals spend sweltering days in burrows and venture out only in the cool of the night. Under cover of darkness, coyotes howl, rattlesnakes and great horned owls hunt kangaroo rats, and javelinas root about for anything edible. Gila monsters, one of only two poisonous lizards found in the world, drag their ungainly bodies through the dust, while tarantulas tiptoe silently in search of unwary insects.

Outside the desert regions, there is great diversity as well. In the southern part of the state, small mountain ranges rise abruptly from the desert floor, creating refuges for plants and animals that require cooler climates. It is these so-called sky islands that harbor the greatest varieties of bird species in the continental United States. Birds from both warm and cold climates find homes in such oases as Ramsey, Madera, and Cave Creek canyons.

Although rugged mountain ranges crisscross the state, only a few rise to such heights that they support actual forests. Among these are the Santa Catalinas outside Tucson, the White Mountains along the state's eastern border, and the San Francisco Peaks north of Flagstaff. However, it's atop the Mogollon Rim and the Kaibab Plateau that the ponderosa pine forests cover the greatest areas. The Mogollon Rim is a 2,000-foot-high escarpment that stretches from central Arizona all the way into New Mexico. The ponderosa pine forest here is the largest in the world, and is dotted with lakes well known for their fishing. The Mogollon Rim area is also home to large herds of elk. At more than 8,000 feet in elevation, the Kaibab Plateau is even higher than the Mogollon Rim; it is through this plateau that the Grand Canyon cuts its mighty chasm.

2 Arizona Today

Combining aspects of Native American, Hispanic, and European cultures, Arizona is one of the most culturally diverse states in the country. Here the Old West and the New West coexist. While the wealthy residents of Scottsdale raise Arabian horses as investments, the Navajos of the Four Corners region ride hard-working horses to herd sheep, which they still raise for sustenance and wool. Vacationers on Lake Powell water-ski through flooded canyons while cowboys in the southeast corner of the state still ride the range.

Although Arizonans are today more likely to drive Mustangs and Thunder-birds than to ride pintos and appaloosas, Western wear is still the preferred fashion of rich and poor alike. Cowboy boots, cowboy hats, blue jeans, and bola ties are acceptable attire at almost any function in the state. Horses are still used on ranches, but most are kept simply for recreational or investment purposes. In Scottsdale, one of the nation's centers of Arabian-horse breeding, horse auctions attract a well-heeled (read lizard-skin-booted) crowd, and horses sell for tens of thousands of dollars. Even the state's dude ranches, which now call themselves "guest ranches," have changed their image, and many are as likely to offer nature hikes and massages as horseback riding.

A long legacy of movies being filmed here has further blurred the line between the real West and the Hollywood West. More city slickers wander the streets of the Old Tucson movie set and videotape shootouts at the O.K. Corral than ever saddle up a palomino or ride herd on a cattle drive. Even dinner has been raised to a cowboy entertainment form at Arizona's many Wild West steakhouses, where families are entertained by cowboy bands, staged gunfights, hayrides, and sing-alongs, all in the name of reliving the glory days of "cowboys and Indians."

For Arizona's Indians, those were days of hardship and misery, and today the state's many tribes continue to strive for the sort of economic well-being enjoyed by the state's nonnative population. Traditional ways are still alive, but tribes struggle to preserve their unique cultures—their languages, religious beliefs, ceremonies, livelihoods, and architecture.

Arizona is home to the largest Indian reservation in the country—the Navajo nation—as well as nearly two dozen smaller reservations. As elsewhere in the United States, poverty and alcoholism are major problems on Arizona reservations. However, several of the state's tribes have, through their arts and crafts, managed to both preserve some of their traditional culture and share it with nonnatives.

Lately, however, many nonnatives have been visiting reservations not out of an interest in learning about another culture, but to gamble. Throughout the state, casinos have opened on reservation land, and despite the controversies surrounding such enterprises, many native peoples are finally seeing some income on their once-impoverished reservations.

Many of the people who visit these new casinos are retirees, who are among the fastest-growing segment of Arizona's population. The state's mild winter climate has attracted tens of thousands of retirees over the past few decades. Many of these winter residents, known as snowbirds, park their RVs outside such warm spots as Yuma and Quartzsite. Others have come to stay, settling in retirement communities such as Sun City and Green Valley.

This graying of the population, combined with strong ranching and mining industries, has made Arizona one of the most conservative of states. Although by today's standards Barry Goldwater could almost be considered a liberal, his conservative politics were so much a part of the Arizona mindset that the state kept him in the Senate for 30 years.

Arizona's environmental politics have been somewhat contentious in recent years. Although many people think of the desert as a wasteland in need of transformation, others see it as a fragile ecosystem that has been endangered by the encroachment of civilization. Saguaro cacti throughout the state are protected by law, but the deserts they grow in are not. In Tucson, environmentalists have for several years been fighting (with limited success) to stop the suburban sprawl that's pushing farther and farther into saguaro country. The balance in this battle tipped in favor of preservation a few years ago when rare ferruginous pygmy owls were found nesting in the Tucson area.

However, in many parts of the metropolitan area, Tucson has built right up to the edge of national forest lands. The consequences of creating such a stark line between wild and developed came to the forefront of the news in early 2004 when mountain lions moved into the popular Sabino Canyon recreation area and were even seen on the grounds of a public school. The presence of the big cats caused the immediate closure of Sabino Canyon and other nearby trails into the national forest.

Way up at the north end of the state, remote Grand Canyon National Park is suffering from its own popularity. With roughly four million visitors a year, the park now sees summer traffic jams and parking problems that have made a visit an exercise in patience. To help alleviate congestion and air pollution, the national park has begun using alternative-fuel buses for transporting visitors around the South Rim and Grand Canyon Village. There is also a plan to build a light-rail system to shuttle visitors into the park from a parking lot outside the park's boundaries. Such a system would solve the parking problems within the park, but questions about the cost have now stalled implementation.

If the current years-long drought continues, one environmental battle may become moot. Many environmentalists have long called for the draining of Lake Powell, but such an idea has been bitterly opposed by watersports enthusiasts who flock to the lake to fish, water-ski, and ride personal watercraft. Nature seems to be stepping in and settling the argument on its own. The lake is currently down close to 120 feet from what is known as full pool. The lake hasn't been this low in 30 years, and by some accounts the lake would take another 20 years to refill if annual precipitation levels were to return to normal.

In his last year in office, President Clinton signed legislation creating five new national monuments in Arizona. The Parashant National Monument, in the northwest corner of the state adjacent to Grand Canyon National Park, preserves one of the most remote and inhospitable regions of the state. To the north of Grand Canyon National Park, near Glen Canyon National Recreation Area, the Vermilion Cliffs National Monument preserves another remote and rugged region. In the Agua Fria National Monument, north of Phoenix, hundreds of archaeological sites are hidden among the cacti and rocks. Sonoran Desert National Monument, 40 to 60 miles southwest of Phoenix, encompasses some of the most pristine areas of the Sonoran Desert, while Ironwoods National Monument, 40 to 50 miles northwest of Tucson, preserves an area of the Sonoran Desert noteworthy for its 800-year-old ironwood trees. At this time, none of these monuments have anything in the way of visitor facilities.

Efforts at preserving the state's environment make it clear that Arizonans value the outdoors, but a ski boat in every driveway doesn't mean the arts are ignored. Although it hasn't been too many years since evening entertainment in Arizona meant dance-hall girls or a harmonica by the campfire, Phoenix and Tucson have become centers for the visual and performing arts. The two cities share an opera company and a ballet company, and the Valley of the Sun is home to a number of symphony orchestras and theater companies.

The arts, though, are often overshadowed by the Phoenix area's obsession with professional sports. Downtown Phoenix has positioned itself as the state's sports and entertainment mecca, with Bank One Ballpark, the America West Arena, numerous sports bars and nightclubs, and even a combination barbecue joint and sports bar operated by former rock star Alice Cooper. However, it isn't just downtown Phoenix that is big on professional sports. The city of Glendale, west of Phoenix, is now home to the Glendale Arena, where the NHL's Phoenix Coyotes play professional hockey. In 2006, the Arizona Cardinals will also be moving to Glendale from their current home in Tempe, where they play at Arizona State University's Sun Devil Stadium.

There are signs that even Phoenicians are tiring of the metro area's incessant sprawl. Inner-city Phoenix neighborhoods are beginning to be rediscovered, and old homes are finally being restored. There are even hip new loft-style condominiums being built near downtown Phoenix and a hip, urban art scene has begun to flourish in long-abandoned commercial and industrial neighborhoods in downtown Phoenix.

This new urban vibe that is taking hold in the Phoenix metro area is most evident in the Old Town Scottsdale area, which this past year saw the opening of the ultra-hip James Hotel. Scottsdale also now has one of the hottest nightlife scenes between New York and Los Angeles. High-style bars and clubs keep attempting to outdo each other with their daring interior decors.

It isn't just in Phoenix that Arizona style is changing. Hip hotels have also opened in Sedona and even Lake Havasu City. Prescott, a classic small-town-America sort of place, now has a great little jazz club and a wine bar that features live folk music. What's a cowboy to do?

Today, the New West and the Old West are coming to grips in Arizona. Hopi still perform their age-old dances atop their mesas, while in Phoenix and Tucson, SUVs and convertible sports cars jockey for parking spaces at glitzy shopping centers. Grizzled wranglers lead tourists on horseback rides across open range, and ranchers find they have something in common with environmentalists—preserving Arizona's ranch lands. All these people share something else: a love of sunshine, which, of course, Arizona has in abundance.

Index

Great Trips Like Great Days Begin with a Plan

FranklinCovey and Frommer's Bring You *Frommer's Favorite Places*® Planner

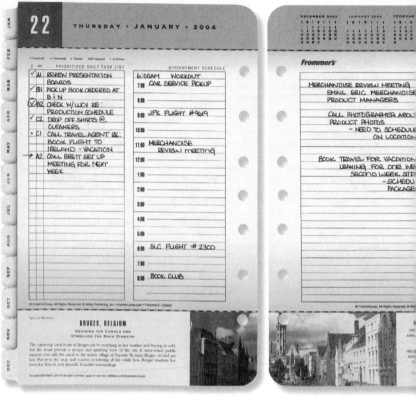

Classic Size Planning Pages $39.

The planning experts at FranklinCovey have teamed up with the travel experts at Frommer's. The result is a full-year travel-themed planner filled with rich images and travel tips covering fifty-two of Frommer's Favorite Places.

- Each week will make you an expert about an intriguing corner of the world
- New facts and tips every day
- Beautiful, full-color photos of some of the most beautiful places on earth
- Proven planning tools from FranklinCovey for keeping track of tasks, appointments, notes, address/phone numbers, and more

Save 15%

when you purchase Frommer's Favori Places travel-themed planner and a binder.

Order today before yo next big trip.

www.franklincovey.com/frommers
Enter promo code 12252 at checkout for discount. Offer expires June 1, 2005.

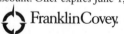 FranklinCovey.

Frommer's is a trademark of Arthur Frommer.

FROMMER'S® NATIONAL PARK GUIDES

Algonquin Provincial Park
Banff & Jasper
Family Vacations in the National
  Parks

Grand Canyon
National Parks of the American
  West
Rocky Mountain

Yellowstone & Grand Teton
Yosemite & Sequoia/Kings
  Canyon
Zion & Bryce Canyon

FROMMER'S® MEMORABLE WALKS

Chicago
London

New York
Paris

San Francisco

FROMMER'S® WITH KIDS GUIDES

Chicago
Las Vegas
New York City

Ottawa
San Francisco
Toronto

Vancouver
Walt Disney World® & Orlando
Washington, D.C.

SUZY GERSHMAN'S BORN TO SHOP GUIDES

Born to Shop: France
Born to Shop: Hong Kong,
  Shanghai & Beijing

Born to Shop: Italy
Born to Shop: London

Born to Shop: New York
Born to Shop: Paris

FROMMER'S® IRREVERENT GUIDES

Amsterdam
Boston
Chicago
Las Vegas
London

Los Angeles
Manhattan
New Orleans
Paris
Rome

San Francisco
Seattle & Portland
Vancouver
Walt Disney World®
Washington, D.C.

FROMMER'S® BEST-LOVED DRIVING TOURS

Austria
Britain
California
France

Germany
Ireland
Italy
New England

Northern Italy
Scotland
Spain
Tuscany & Umbria

THE UNOFFICIAL GUIDES®

Beyond Disney
California with Kids
Central Italy
Chicago
Cruises
Disneyland®
England
Florida
Florida with Kids
Inside Disney

Hawaii
Las Vegas
London
Maui
Mexico's Best Beach Resorts
Mini Las Vegas
Mini Mickey
New Orleans
New York City
Paris

San Francisco
Skiing & Snowboarding in the
  West
South Florida including Miami &
  the Keys
Walt Disney World®
Walt Disney World® for
  Grown-ups
Walt Disney World® with Kids
Washington, D.C.

SPECIAL-INTEREST TITLES

Athens Past & Present
Cities Ranked & Rated
Frommer's Best Day Trips from London
Frommer's Best RV & Tent Campgrounds
  in the U.S.A.
Frommer's Caribbean Hideaways
Frommer's China: The 50 Most Memorable Trips
Frommer's Exploring America by RV
Frommer's Gay & Lesbian Europe
Frommer's NYC Free & Dirt Cheap

Frommer's Road Atlas Europe
Frommer's Road Atlas France
Frommer's Road Atlas Ireland
Frommer's Wonderful Weekends from
  New York City
The New York Times' Guide to Unforgettable
  Weekends
Retirement Places Rated
Rome Past & Present

Travel Tip: He who finds the best hotel deal has more to spend on facials involving knobbly vegetables.

Hello, the Roaming Gnome here. I've been nabbed from the garden and taken round the world. The people who took me are so terribly clever. They find the best offerings on Travelocity. For very little cha-ching. And that means I get to be pampered and exfoliated till I'm pink as a bunny's doodah.

travelocity®

Travel Tip: Make sure there's customer service for any change of plans — involving friendly natives, for example.

One can plan and plan, but if you don't book with the right people you can't seize le moment and canoodle with the poodle named Pansy. I, for one, am all for fraternizing with the locals. Better yet, if I need to extend my stay and my gnome nappers are willing, it can all be arranged through the 800 number at, oh look, how convenient, the lovely company coat of arms.

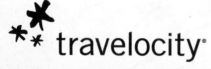

Travel Tip: He who finds the best hotel deal has more to spend on facials involving knobbly vegetables.

Hello, the Roaming Gnome here. I've been nabbed from the garden and taken round the world. The people who took me are so terribly clever. They find the best offerings on Travelocity. For very little cha-ching. And that means I get to be pampered and exfoliated till I'm pink as a bunny's doodah.

* * travelocity

1-888-TRAVELOCITY / travelocity.com / America Online Keyword: Travel